1997 Edition

WHAT'S ON THE WEB®

Internet Media

Publisher & Editor:

ERIC GAGNON

Contributing Reviewers:

JAMES PORTEOUS
EDWINNA VON BAEYER
LEE STRAL
HILARY LANE
NORINE FULLAN
CHRISTINE PAUSTIAN
LIZ TOMPKINS
CARON ELLIS
DR. ROBERT BOGIN, M.D.
JON VAN OAST
RIC BOHANNON
SARA BROWN
TIM WINDSOR

What's on the Web
1997 Edition

Published by Internet Media Corp.

Internet Media Corp.
Phone: (718) 596-5668
FAX: (718) 875-4589
WEB: http://www.jumpcity.com/

Editor: Eric Gagnon, INTERNET: eric@jumpcity.com
Designer: Chris Gagnon
Production/Layout: Chris Gagnon

Distribution
Internet Media books are distributed to the U.S. bookstore trade by Publishers Group West, 4065 Hollis St., Emeryville, CA 94609, phone (800) 788-3123 or (510) 658-1834. For bulk sales outside of the U.S. bookstore trade, contact Internet Media directly at (718) 596-5668.

ISBN 1-884640-21-4

0 9 8 7 6 5 4 3 2

Printed and bound in the United States of America

Contents

WHAT'S ON THE WEB

Preface 1

Chapter 1: Introduction 3

There's a revolution being waged by thousands of ordinary people doing extraordinary things with words, images, and sounds over the Internet.

Using little more than their own talent and a few simple electronic tools, these individuals are creating, day by day, a new media for the 21st Century.

There's a simple name for this revolutionary new media. It's called the Web...

▲ *Roulette on the Web graphic, from* **U Roulette**, *at* Jump **0108** *and* ◀ *vintage 1934 Popular Mechanics cover, from* **The PM Zone**, *at* Jump **2355**.

Chapter 2: Searching & Linking on the Web 28

The Web makes it easier than ever to locate the information you're looking for, and many helpful Web users have created a wide variety of big Web indexes and other Web searching features to help you find what you're looking for. We show you where the best ones are, so you can get to them and be productive on the Web—immediately.

Big Web Hotlists & Indexes 30

Finding Web Sites 34

Internet & Web Resources 36

Chapter 3: Business, Consumer, Health, Investment, & Self-Help 50

Looking for information on expanding your business, or starting a new one? Or, how about putting up your own Web site? The Web is also a gold mine of information for the entrepreneur, with lots more useful information on many consumer, financial, and self-help subjects, too.

Business & Entrepreneurship	**63**
Consumer, Health, & Self-Help	**52**
Help Wanted & Careers	**77**
Investment & Legal	**81**
Virtual Marketplaces	**97**

Chapter 4: Politics & Democracy 112

The leaders of both political parties have not yet noticed that the ground has shifted beneath their shiny black shoes. Now that talk radio, the Internet, and the Web have put tremendous political organizing power into the hands of individual citizens, things will never be the same for the current power structure.

Citizen Political Resources	**114**
Conservative Politics	**120**
Current Controversies	**124**
History, Policy, & War	**129**
Liberal Politics	**132**
President Clinton	**136**

Chapter 5: Social & Support 137

The Web is as much a social phenomenon as it is a technological one. You'll find a vast range of Web sites offering information and resources to meet almost any medical, support, affinity, social, cultural, or religious need.

Affinity & Social Groups	**139**
Caring & Support	**146**
Cultural News & Pages	**164**
Religion & Philosophy	**165**

▲ *Uncle Sam hot air balloon, from* **Cyberspace World Railroad Home Page**, *at* Jump **2119**.

▲ *Teatime on the Web, from* **geekgirl**, *at* Jump **1504**.

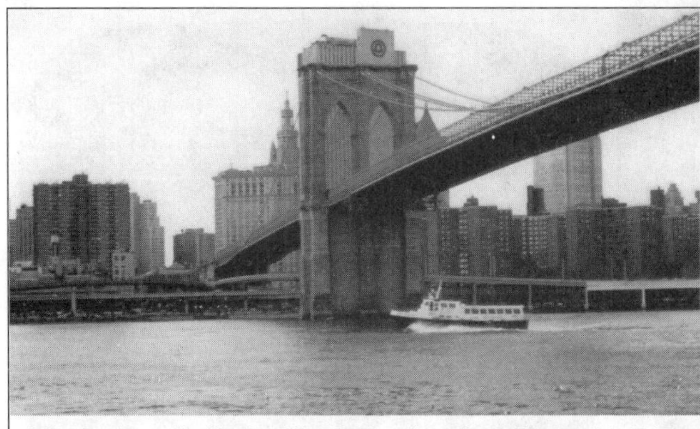

▲ *Boat going under the Brooklyn Bridge, from* **JumpCity** *and* ▲ *Trixie, a Jack Russell pup, from* **http://www.lucy-the-dog.com/index.html**, *and fantastic fashion for the stylish, from* **Geek Chic**, *at* Jump **7477**.

Chapter 6: Hobbies, Special Interests, & Travel 169

There are thousands of sites along the Web with tons of information, advice, and contacts for most any hobby or special interest. The Web is also a vast storehouse of useful, money-saving travel and vacation advice, too.

▲ *A round of coffee, from* **Ragu Presents Mama's Cucina**, *at* Jump **2145** *and* ▲ *portion of Michelangelo's Sistine Ceiling, from* **Index of/Multimedia/Pics/Art/**, *at* Jump **0161**.

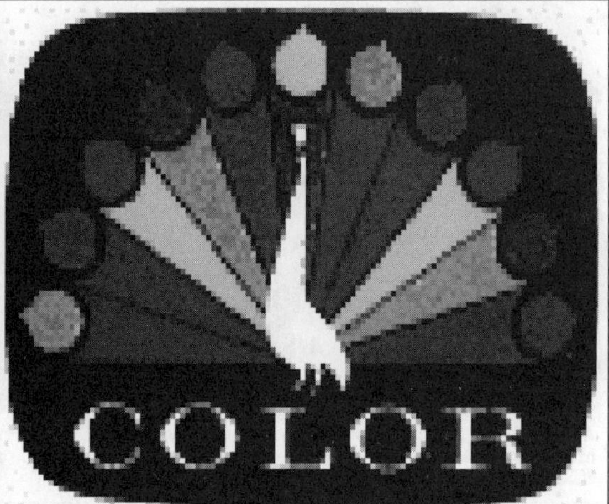

▲ *Monoclonius yearling, from* **Dinosaur Society**, *at* Jump **5878** *and* ▲ *Vintage NBC color television logo from* **Ad Age**, *at* Jump **7311**.

▲ *1958 MZTV Pedestal television, from* **Museum of Television**, *at* Jump **0220**.

Chapter 7: News, Info, & New Web Media **230**

The Web has emerged as a completely new and exciting broadcast media form, giving literally anyone who creates a Web site a forum for publishing and self-expression to an audience of millions. The Web also gives you real-time, anytime access to a wide variety of news and current events information.

News & Information **232**

The New Web Media **253**

Chapter 8: Entertainment & the Media **282**

Whatever your interests in books, music, TV or the movies, there's someone out there who's created a Web site to satisfy the fan in you. What's more, entertainment-related Web sites, because they're created by devoted (maybe even obsessed) people, are sometimes even more entertaining than the Web sites which have been created by the big-media movie studios, networks, publishers and other owners of these forms of entertainment themselves.

Contents

▲ *Dave Brubeck fans buying his latest record, from* **WNUR-FM Jazz Web**, *at* Jump 2371 *and* ▲ *MTV logo, from* **Hype! International**, *at* Jump 2183.

▲ *Bach," from* **J.S. Bach**, *at* Jump 7466 *and* ▲ *Spock and Kirk in"Star Trek, from* **Virtual Image Archive**, *at* Jump 7315.

Chapter 9: Science, Education & Technology 356

Thanks to the Internet's origins in academia and scientific research, the Web features a rich collection of educational resources for all ages, with sites to make science both colorful and accessible to all.

Academia	357
Educational Resources	358
Science & Technology	384
Space Exploration	392

Chapter 10: Personal Computing Resources 399

There have always been tremendous amounts of information, software and other resources available on the Internet for personal computer users. Now the Web makes access to this wealth of productivity-boosting power easy, fast, and, best of all—free.

Computer Help	400
Computer Marketplace	403
Computers: Other	405
Macintosh Resources	407
Multimedia Authoring Resources	410
Net & Web Tech Resources	418
PC & Windows Resources	421
Shareware Archives	425
Web Page Development	429

▲ *A walk in space, via* **Images, Icons and Flags**, *at* Jump **2047** *and* ▲ *T-Rex, from* **Dinosaur Hall**, *at* Jump **2583**.

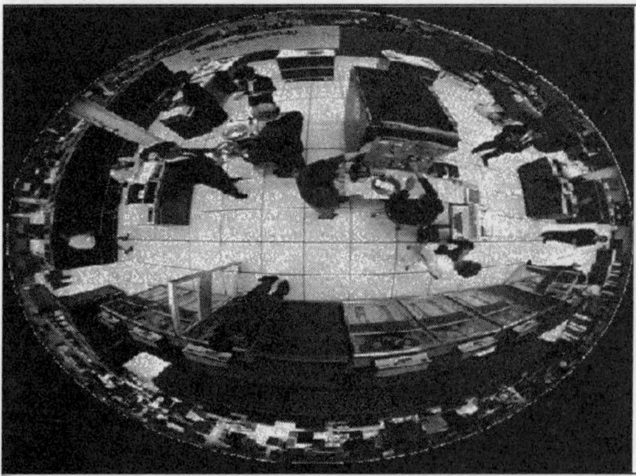

◀ *Sixties era data center, from* **Commercial Computing Museum Homepage**, *at* Jump **3639** *and* ▲ *Scene from the 60s TV show, "The Time Tunnel," from* **Hype! International**, *at* Jump **2183** *and* ▲ *vintage computer photo, from* **Historical Computer Images**, *at* Jump **0179**.

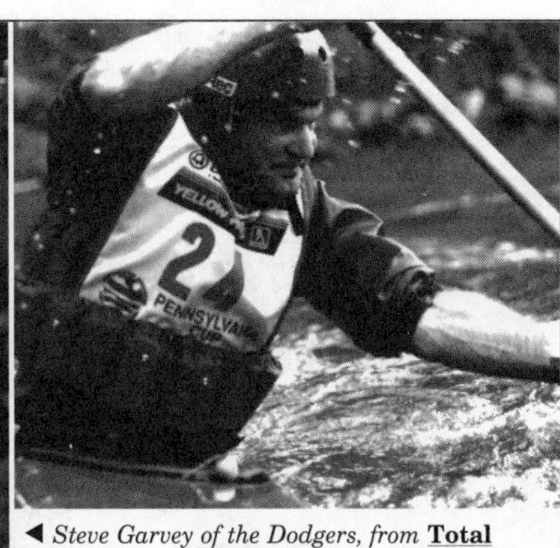

◀ *Steve Garvey of the Dodgers, from* **Total Baseball**, *at* Jump **5840** ◀ *Steve Smith of the Hawks, from* **NBA.COM**, *at* Jump **5706** *and* ▲ *kayaker, via* **Preston's Kayak Page**, *at* Jump **2559**.

Chapter 11: Sports Talk, & Recreation 434

Like you, many Web site authors have active lives beyond the computer screen. On the Web, they share their information, experiences and other resources on a wide variety of outdoor sports and recreational activities. For pro sports fans, the Web is also an instant source for news, scores, and fan talk.

Active Sports & Recreation 435

Spectator Sports 444

Chapter 12: Local & International 452

Although most people think of the Web as a global network, there are many Web sites that focus on specific cities, towns and countries, and can be used as virtual travel and culture guides for many exciting locations around the world.

Metro Area U.S. Sites 453

International Sites 457

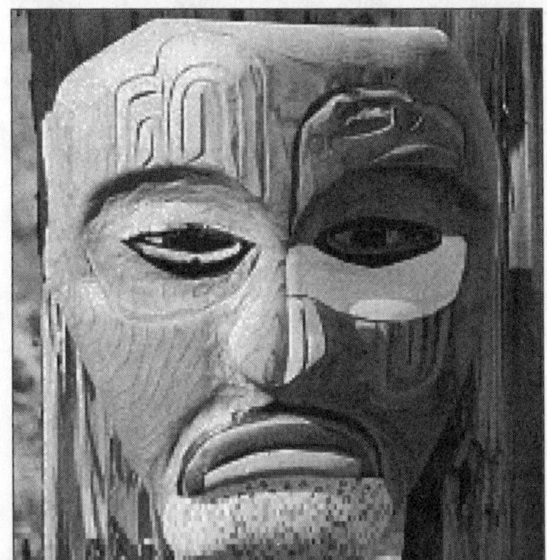

▲ *Northwestern United States Indian mask, from* **NativeWeb**, *at* Jump **7060** *and* ▲ *Japanese elevator girl, via* **Images, Icons and Flags**, *at* Jump **2047**.

▲ *A graphic demonstration of the combustible nature of strawberry Pop Tarts, from* **Strawberry Pop-Tart Blow-Torches**, *at* **Jump 4055** *and* ◀ *beard or no beard, from* **dimFLASH e-zine**, *at* **Jump 2216** *and* ◀ *1950s glimpse into the future of domestic chores, from* **Wall 'O Shame**, *at* **Jump 0111**.

Preface

There are people out there, just like you, doing extraordinary things on the Internet's World Wide Web. Some of these people are technically sophisticated, but most are not. Rather, they are enthusiastic experts in specific subjects, or creative self-publishers turning out world-class writing, graphics, music, and art, or talented entrepreneurs and business owners risking their time, effort, and money to advance their personal visions of successful publishing ventures on the Internet's World Wide Web.

This book is dedicated to these people.

What all these talented individuals have in common is that each of them is helping to shape the new, *truly* interactive communications media of the 21st Century. It's a truly interactive medium, since, as a member of its audience, you can be *both* reader and publisher.

As an audience member in this "New Media," you become much more than a passive channel surfer or page turner. With the Web and a personal computer, you have the simple but powerful tools at hand to access, select, and shape an incredible amount of information on an almost endless spectrum of subjects. The Web has reduced the mechanics of accessing everything on the Internet to the click of your mouse key, making access to all of this available information as easy as it possibly can be.

The Web also puts powerful publishing and broadcasting tools within your reach. Creators of information no longer face the typical barriers to entry of traditional "Old Media:" printing expenses, scarce broadcast airwaves, editorial requirements, elitism, media bias or other economic, technological, or human limits to mass communication.

But while the Web is in many ways a completely new media form, those who use it to publish and broadcast information must still follow the age-old principles of publishing and editorial professionalism. To attract Web audiences, information published on Web sites must be substantive, factual, and informative. Web sites must fill a useful need, or provide worthwhile entertainment interest. A Web site's design, graphics, and multimedia features must also meet the high production values that sophisticated audiences have come to expect from the traditional "Old Media" forms, such as television shows, magazine features, or newspaper spreads.

Now that the Web has mostly solved the mechanics of information access on the Internet, an even greater challenge to you, as a Web audience member, has arisen: that of *selection*, *quality*, and *context*. With over millions of Web pages in existence already, and this number increasing exponentially every few months, the mystery of accessing all this information (now solved by the Web) has given way to a nearly overwhelming sense of confusion concerning all the choices available. What's out there? Is it any good? Where can I find a Web site that meets my particular need? When I get there, what will I find?

That's where ***What's on the Web*** comes in: our reviewers spend countless hours searching the Web—finding, comparing, selecting, and reviewing only those sites which stand out among all the rest as your first, best, and most useful stops along the Web. Throughout the pages of this book, and its extensive Subject Index, you'll find many useful starting points for your Web journeys.

But ***What's on the Web*** is not just a book; it's also a Web site. You can reach all of the Web sites covered in this book through our own Web site, **JumpCity**, simply by entering the four-digit Jump Code (patent pending) we've assigned to every Web site reviewed here. And while you're linked to **JumpCity**, you'll also get free access to our reviews of the Web's hottest new sites, plus other special new enhancements we're adding to make ***What's on the Web*** and **JumpCity** one of your first, best starting points for whatever you need to find on the Internet's World Wide Web.

I hope that this book will open many new and exciting opportunities and connections for you as it has for us. If you have any comments or suggestions for ways we can improve future editions (published twice each year) of ***What's on the Web***, let us know by sending e-mail to me at **eric@jumpcity.com**.

Special thanks to Chris, my wife and partner of 17 years, for working with me, side by side, on the design, layout, and production of this book, and for creating the book's informational graphics. Thanks also all our reviewers: James Porteous, Edwinna von Baeyer, Lee Stral, Liz Tompkins, Hilary Lane, Norine Fullan, Christine Paustian, Jon van Oast (who is also the designer of our Web site, **JumpCity**), Ric Bohannon, Sara Brown, and Tim Windsor. This book would not have been possible without their efforts. Thanks also to Web site authors David Siegel and Tim Windsor, for allowing us to use their Web sites as examples for our book's informational graphics.

See you on the Net!

Eric Gagnon (**eric@jumpcity.com**)

1: Introduction

There's a revolution being waged by thousands of ordinary people doing extraordinary things with words, images, and sounds over the Internet.

Using little more than their own talent and a few simple electronic tools, these individuals are creating, day by day, a new media for the 21st century.

There's a simple name for this revolutionary new media.

It's called the Web...

The Internet is a global network of chatty computers crammed with a galaxy of information—mostly in unappealing text that only the techno-intelligentsia can access, let alone appreciate. But as more people get online, the one stretch of the Internet that is growing faster than all others is the World Wide Web. The Web lets you instantly jump from one Web site to another by clicking on highlighted words and pictures. If you're reading about expressionism on a Web page and see the words "The Starry Night" highlighted, a click of the mouse on the title will transport you to another Web site, perhaps thousands of miles away, that delivers the image of the van Gogh masterwork to your computer.

Michel Marriott with Anne Underwood, "Super Cyber Surfers," ***Newsweek***

The Web: The New Media Challenge to the Old Media

Unlike today's conventional old media—television, newspapers, radio, or magazines—this Web gives each and every one of us the power to be our own broadcaster, with direct, anytime access to an audience of millions.

It's a new media where *you* can be *both* broadcaster and audience, with instant access to a virtually infinite, unfiltered variety of information, whatever your needs or special interests. The Web is the latest and possibly the most revolutionary change in media since the invention of moveable type.

This revolution is taking shape, right now, over the Internet, the global "network of networks" that's taking the personal computer market—and our culture—by storm.

The Web and the Internet

The Web, also known as the **World Wide Web**, is the latest and greatest evolution of **the Internet**, or **the Net**, a worldwide network of more than 100,000 individual computer networks and over 50 million users—an all-encompassing network now consisting of almost every large corporation, university, government, organization, and many businesses both large and small, around the world.

Arguably the niftiest American pop culture spin-off from physics since the transistor, the semiconductor laser and The Bomb, the Web is an exceedingly clever medium for bundling bits. Designed not by hackers or telco entrepreneurs but—can you believe it?! —by European particle physicists looking for new ways to publish their data, the WWW makes it possible to create hypertext multimedia pages that can be viewed by anyone with graphical access to the Internet. You can even add sound and video to your pages.

Michael Schrage, "Web Spinners," *ADWEEK*

Initially, many people find it difficult to grasp the concept of the Internet, and its latest incarnation, the Web. That's partly because the Internet is the ultimate expression of a decentralized ideal: an anarchic collection of individual computer networks, connected by high-speed telephone and satellite data links, all connected by a freely available, public-domain communications software standard. Second, it's also important to understand that there is no central office, management, or editorial structure controlling the Net, no "Internet Corporation," no chrome-and-glass Internet headquarters building, either.

Control of the Net has been thrown to the farthest ends of its structure, where owners and operators of the individual computer networks comprising the Internet (such as operators of computer facilities owned by businesses, colleges or other organizations) each make their own separate decisions on how they connect to the Internet, and to how much of the Internet's features they choose to connect.

The Internet: The Cold War's Nuke-Proof Net

The Internet can trace its origins to the late 1960s when it was established as a U.S. Defense Department computer communications research project for defense contractors and universities. At that time, the purpose of the Internet was to create a military computer network which could still function reliably if any parts of it were destroyed in a nuclear war. To ensure against the inherent unreliability of telephone lines and exposed telephone switching stations, the developers of the Internet created a series of standardized ways, or **communications protocols**, for sending information around a computer network.

For over 25 years, the Internet grew slowly but steadily as a research-oriented computer communications network for universities, defense contractors, governments, and organizations in science and academia. During these years, its proven, freely available communications protocols were also adopted by the computer and telecommunications industries and—key to its growth in the commercial sector—by large corporations, who used the Internet for electronic mail communications between and among their companies.

1992: The Government Steps Aside... and the Net Takes Off

The real explosion in the growth of the Internet occurred only after 1992, when the federal government dramatically slashed its funding, and turned over operation of the Net's high-speed data links to commercial communications networks.

The amazing growth of the Internet was also fueled by, and coincided with, the explosion in the use of personal computers, local area networks (private networks of PCs connected within private companies), bulletin board systems (BBSs), and consumer-oriented online services. Each of these events converged to create a critical mass for the acceptance of the Internet as the standard means for the worldwide connection of individual computer networks of all kinds and sizes, and eventually, every single personal computer user.

Most experts agree the Internet crowd is changing to include more mainstream consumers. A recent report by Forester Research Inc. Cambridge, Mass...predicted that the Web, currently used by about 2 million of the estimated 20 million people tapping into the Internet, will soar to 22 million users by the year 2000.

Cyndee Miller, "Marketers find it's hip to be on the Internet," *Marketing News*

While it's difficult for research firms to agree on an single number, many estimates say the Internet has around 50 million users worldwide, and is growing at a rate of 10% to 20% per month. This explosive growth has occurred primarily due to the widespread acceptance of the Internet as the standard for electronic mail, which is rapidly replacing the FAX machine and (thankfully, as far as many are concerned) the U.S. Postal Service, as the preferred means for sending and receiving business and personal communications.

The Internet is best known for three main features: electronic mail, for rapid text-based communications among one or many individuals; Usenet newsgroups, thousands of online discussion groups covering a wide variety of business, personal and technical subjects and the latest, perhaps greatest, Internet phenomenon, the World Wide Web.

The World Wide Web: It's the Internet "For the Rest of Us"

The World Wide Web, or the Web as it's more commonly known, is the Internet's current, and its highest, form of evolution. The Web is a standardized method of combining the display of graphics, text, video and audio clips, as well as other features, such as secure credit card transactions, into a standardized, graphical, friendly interface that's easy for anyone to use.

These standard protocols work in combination with a **Web browser**, which runs on your personal computer and handles the chores of accessing and displaying graphics and text, and playing back video and audio files found on the Web. In addition to Web access, Web browsers and the Web tie together all of the Internet's other useful features that existed, before the advent of the Web, such as newsgroups, FTP text file access, access to the Net's Gopher sites, and sending or receiving electronic mail.

Your own Web site. The cyberspace equivalent of "Let's do lunch" is "Check out my home page." This means you are directing someone to peruse your personal corner of the World Wide Web. While many Web sites have an obvious purpose —promoting a product—an astounding number of them are amateur and often ingenious show-and-tell exhibitions, a morph of a virtual open house and digital performance art. As it becomes easier to set up these Web sites, of course, the cachet of having one diminishes. True status comes from the popularity of your site. How many "hits" (calls) did you rack up last week? Do other well-known Web sites offer direct links to your location? Was your site mentioned in Yahoo (page 44) or the Net Surf page in WIRED? If the answer is no, better hire a consultant.

Steven Levy, "Virtual Social Climbing," *Newsweek*

Origins of the World Wide Web

Like the Internet, the Web was originally created in the academic community as an open and freely distributed system. The World Wide Web was created by Tim Berners-Lee and a programming team at the European Particle Physics Laboratory in Switzerland, also known as CERN. Originally designed as a standardized method to help physicists organize and access their research data for international distribution online the World Wide Web standards are essentially a text coding, or "markup" method, where selected elements in a text file, such as article headlines, subheads, images, and important words highlighted in the body of a text file can, by the insertion of special, bracketed codes (called **HTML**, or HyperText Markup Language codes), be turned into **hotlinks** that are easily and instantly accessible by anyone with a Web browser.

Like the networking, electronic mail, and newsgroup software and communications protocols for the Internet that came before it, the standard protocols for the World Wide Web were (and still are) freely distributed as an "open system"—which means that they may be used by anyone on the Net to create their own Web sites, free of charge. On the Internet, freely available software has a way of spreading like wildfire (especially if it's really useful) and in a brief period of time, from 1992 to 1993 the Web became an underground phenomenon on the Internet, especially after a group of programmers from the National Center for Supercomputing Applications (NCSA) in Illinois, including lead programmer Mark Andreessen, developed a graphical, window-based interface for accessing Web documents and graphics called **MOSAIC**.

As the first browser for the Web, MOSAIC was also available, free of charge, for downloadable distribution over the Internet—all of which gave an immense boost to the Web's growth. Andreessen and his team of NCSA programmers who helped develop MOSAIC were hired away by Jim Clark, the founder of Unix workstation manufacturer Silicon Graphics, to form Netscape Communications Corporaton, currently the largest provider of Web browsers on the Net, and a hot company in the Net industry.

The Web's open standards, combined with the widespread free distribution of downloadable Web browers like Mosaic and Netscape's Navigator browser, on a try-before-you-buy basis, has fueled the explosive growth of the Web in the past year, sealing the widespread acceptance of the Web and of Web browsers as the Internet's new standard means of access.

Just how fast are the Internet and the Web growing? International Data Group, Inc., a market research firm, estimates that the number of devices connected to the Internet will grow by *1,752%*, and the number of Internet users will increase by *912%* in the next five years! Good estimates on the current size of the Internet are hard to find—and change every week—but recent available figures put the number of individual Web locations, or "domains," at over 200,000, and over 31 million individual Web pages on over 476,000 computers (also known as "servers"). And, given the Web's explosive growth, it's certain these numbers, too, will be out of date by the time you read this.

With the introduction of WebTV and other products that turn television sets into Internet access devices, it's quite possible that number of Internet users could easily rival that of broadcast and cable television in just a few more years. Not bad for something that started life as an obscure scientific research document-reading program just five years ago!

The World Wide Web is the true Information Superhighway, the equivalent of the Interstate Highway System, and "scalable to infinity," in the words of D.C. Denison, editor of the definitive *Global Network Navigator*, a publication available on the Web but nowhere else. The textual Internet is no different than the cow paths that became the impenetrable streets of Boston. The Web, however, is a whole other story, both slick and expandable. Traffic on The Web is doubling every few months. There are said to be some 10,000 servers on the Web alone, with the number expected to keep on doubling for the foreseeable future.

Michael Conniff, "A Tangled Web For Newspapers," *Editor & Publisher Magazine*

The Web: A New Broadcast Medium

But the Web is much more than a set of typographical codes that sit on top of the Internet, or a fancy screen interface. The Web lays the foundation for the use of the Internet as an entirely new broadcast medium. Unlike the current "Old Media"—newspapers, broadcast television/radio, magazines or books,—as "New Media," the Web provides individuals, groups and companies with unprecedented new opportunities for broadcast communication:

- **Ease of Entry:** Learning how to create your own Web site is a fairly easy process even for non-technical personal computer users. By renting space with one of many available Internet services, a Web site can be created in a few hours and made available to millions on the Net for a cost as low as $20 per month.
- **Self-Publishing:** The Web already gives an outlet to thousands of creative individuals, entrepreneurs, and small business owners who use it as a means to self-publish articles, graphics, video clips, and audio files over the Net. Anyone who creates their own Web sites—whether they're writers, musicians, artists, or would-be Web publishing tycoons, can bypass established big-time distribution channels such as TV networks, radio stations, newspapers, and magazine publishers, delivering their creative works, promotional information, and content directly to their end-user audiences on the Net.
- **A Vast, Web-Browsing Audience:** Since any individual Web site can be freely accessed by anyone else with Web access, anyone who creates

Historically, business has stayed on the sidelines of cyberspace. It's been made wary by the Internet's renegade-culture reputation, arduous Unix commands, and very real lack of security. But in the last few months, the emergence of the World Wide Web network and the wildly popular Mosaic graphical browser has significantly reduced the complexity of viewing Internet data.

The immediate reaction: Hundreds of businesses have established a home page; the first screen of a hypertext system; on the Web. They range from small businesses like Alberto's Nightclub in Mountain View, Calif., and the Vermont Teddy Bear Co. to corporate giants such as GE and Lockheed Corp. Regardless of who creates these home pages, all are equally accessible to the same market: Mosaic [Web browser] users.

Clinton Wilder, "The Internet Pioneers—The emergence of the World Wide Web and Mosaic has convinced early corporate adopters of the viability of doing business online," *Information Week*

a Web site has a forum for broadcasting their information, news, announcements, or creative works to an audience of millions. Any member of this audience may also interact with the author of a Web site via Internet electronic mail, giving instant feedback to the site's creator and adding a whole new level of two-way communication to this new broadcast medium.

The Web has become an explosively growing grassroots publishing phenomenon, putting the most powerful media-creation power ever created into the hands of anyone who's willing to expend the modest effort required to set up their own Web site.

Now that there's a Web, empowering any individual with the ability to be his or her own media broadcaster, the much-touted prospect of big media's 500-channel cable TV universe, when compared to the possibilities and the explosive growth of the Web, looks pretty uninspiring indeed.

What's Good About the Web?

The Web provides several key benefits for Internet users; these benefits are what's helping to fuel the Web's explosive growth and, ultimately, the acceptance of the Internet as the world's de facto computer communications medium.

First, using the Web is simplicity itself. Compared to the confusing, Unix-based commands which were required to use the Net just a couple of years ago, using a Web browser provides you with the same friendly, graphical point-and-click access to all of the Internet's features that you've come to expect from any good stand-alone Windows or Macintosh commercial software product. Once you're up and running on the Web, any of the hundreds of thousands of available Web sites and their linked articles, text articles, graphic images, video/audio clips, extensive software libraries, and communications features are easily accessible with a click of your mouse key. Any good Web browser, such as Netscape's Navigator, also opens up the Web's exciting multimedia potential by giving you instant, automatic access to helper applications that automatically video play and sound clips—now one of the Web's big attractions.

All Web browsers also have a **bookmark**, or **hotlist**, feature, which allows you to capture and save the location of any Web site you visit, so you can access that site by clicking on it from your Web browser any time you wish.

Now, Everyone Can Be a Broadcaster

Another strong attraction of the Web is its wide-open access and low barriers to entry, that both *democratizes* and *individualizes* the publishing process. For conventional publishers and other sellers of information, the Web is an excellent, low-cost information delivery channel, providing publishers with a convenient forum for distribution of their information products and the same high production values they've come to expect from print media such as four-color magazines, books, and newspapers. Publishers now have the added attraction of enhancing their information with video and audio multimedia.

For entrepreneurs and small business owners, the Web provides exciting new opportunities to promote products and services. Commercial Web sites, if they are creatively conceived and frequently updated, can be a profitable promotional tool for broadcasting product information or promoting a business, and, perhaps most important, providing a forum for real-time electronic communications, prospects, and customers.

[Interviewer at Investor's Business Daily]: "Could the Internet ever become so popular that demand for bandwidth exceeds the network capacity?" [Netscape's Marc] Andreessen: "Nope, no way. Bandwidth over time is infinite."

[Interview], *Investor's Business Daily*

Web Sites: More like Radio Stations than Printed Pages

However, creating a commercially oriented Web site entails much more than just scanning a few color product photos from your company brochure and posting a couple of press releases to your company's Web site. Unfortunately, most commercially oriented Web sites created by businesses on the Web are little more than static "brochure sites" that, in our view, make insufficient use of the Web's great potential for business communication. There are, however, a number of innovative and successful commercially sponsored sites along the Web, which we've reviewed and which can be found here in ***What's on the Web***.

If you're a business owner or entrepreneur, you should realize that a commercially oriented Web site requires a fair amount of planning, execution and, most important—continuous updating—to be successful. The more successful commercially-sponsored Web sites, such as Reebok's Planet Reebok, Sony, Time Warner's Pathfinder, and ESPN's SportsZone, are all successful in that they provide users with solid and abundant information content, a compelling, ever-changing array of new features, sometimes updated several times each day.

Frequent updating of Web sites is critical, because it's a fact that the more successful commercially sponsored Web sites often share more than a passing resemblance to their bigger, "Old Media" cousins—

"Push Media:" The Internet's Emerging Form

While Net users today must actively search out and link to Web sites of interest, companies like PointCast and Marimba are seeking to convert the Net into a "broadcast" mode, where information is sent automatically to the user's computer at regular intervals.

This new "push" model of the Internet is more attractive to Net advertisers, who can be guaranteed that larger numbers of viewers will see their on-screen ads, as measured against the Internet's current "pull" model—where users must locate and connect to an advertiser's Web site.

Anatomy Of A Web Site

Web sites, also known as Web pages, are where individuals, companies, and other organizations have published their millions of Web users. You can access any Web site by entering its URL (see or, for sites reviewed in this book, by entering its four-digit Jump Code from our

Location: http://www.charm.net/~windsor/todayad.html

▲ URL: Stands for **Uniform Resource Locator**, a confusing string of slashes, subdirectories, and file names which must be typed in exactly (including upper and lower case letters) in order to connect you to the exact location, or address, of a specific Web site on the Internet. **All Web sites reviewed in *What's On The Web*** can be reached by typing the four-digit Jump Code listed for each reviewed Web site, when you access our own Web site, **JumpCity**. So, for all the sites featured in this book, you only have to enter one URL... **http://www.jumpcity.com/**

Compiled by Tim Windsor

Brought to you in part by Charm.net

▲ Links: Links, also known as **hotlinks** or **hypertext links**, are the nuts and bolts that hold the Web together. When seen on a Web page, they're the underlined words and phrases you can click on with your mouse on your PC's Web browser. **Clicking on a Web page's link** will instantly send you to another portion of text, picture or multimedia item related to that link within that Web site—or to a completely different Web site elsewhere on the Web. When used correctly, links can be an efficient and helpful way of getting you quickly to the information you need anywhere else on the Web.

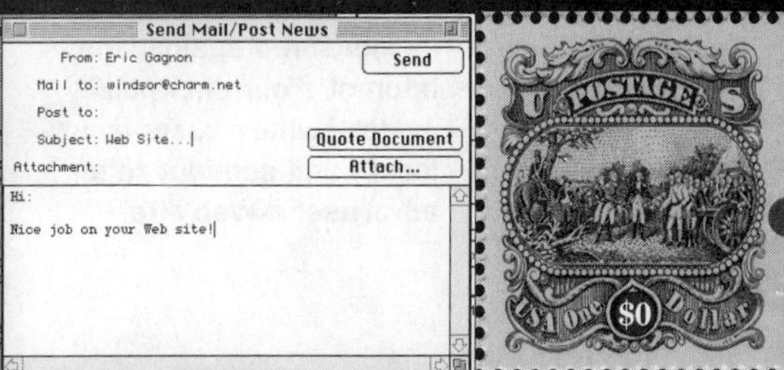

◄ E-mail Contact: Nearly all Web site authors list their **feedback** or comments, telling them how you liked their Web site. e-mail screen so you can send a brief message. Since they are usually sources of additional information, tips, and advice on a wide variety o

virtual places on the Web
information for access by
below) on your Web browser
own Web site, **JumpCity**.

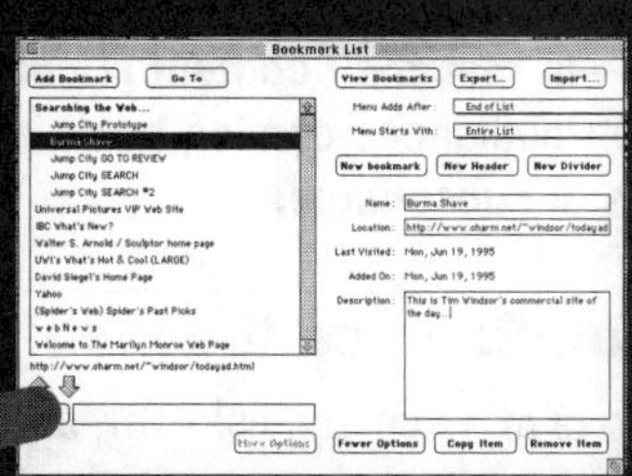

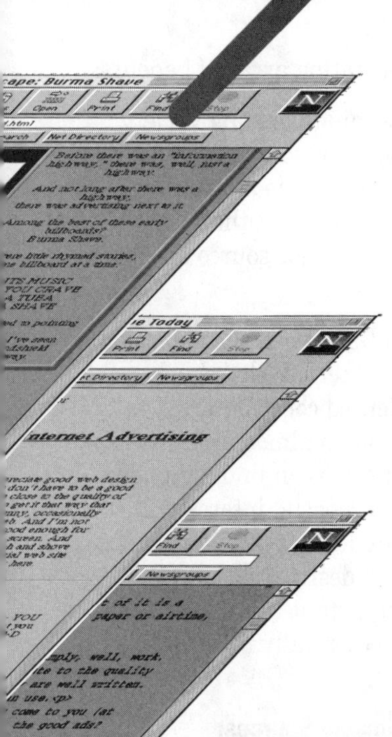

With thousands of Web sites covering an almost infinite spectrum of subjects, the Web offers a rich and varied collection of information, communications, and entertainment—all of it instantly accessible with the click of your mouse key...

own Internet e-mail addresses and encourage you to **contact them with**
Clicking on this e-mail hotlink, on most Web browsers, usually brings up an
quite knowledgeable on their Web site's topic, Web site authors can be good
subjects.

Bookmarks: One of your Web browser's **most valuable features**, a bookmarks file allows you to save the URLs (Web site locations) for the favorite Web sites you've visited. With a simple keyboard command, **you can "bookmark" any site** when you're actually connected to it, so you can come back to it anytime you want. Bookmark windows for many Web browsers also save the Web site's name and allow you to type in some brief comments on a site you've just visited. In this way, **bookmarks preserve your sanity along the Web** by helping you save *only* those Web sites which interest you, so you can reach them, anytime, by just clicking on their names in your Web browser's bookmarks window.

```
<TD WIDTH=30%><IMG SRC="burmacar_copy.gi
<TD ALIGN=CENTER WIDTH=70%><text>Before
And not long after there was a highway,
Among the best of these early billboards
They were little rhymed stories, <br>tol
HALF A POUND<br>
FOR<br>
HALF A DOLLAR<br>
SPREAD ON THIN<br>
ABOVE THE COLLAR<br>
BURMA-SHAVE<p>
This site is dedicated to pointing out <
sped along the I-way. </text></TD>
</TABLE>
```

HTML: Stands for **HyperText Markup Language**, a method of encoding text files, pictures, links, and other Web site elements so that they may be properly displayed and accessed on the Web via your Web browser. HTML is essentially a method of surrounding Web elements in codes which are themselves surrounded by left- and right-hand brackets (<>). The actual HTML-encoded text file for Tim Windsor's Burma Shave site is shown underneath the top page you'd actually see in your Web browser. HTML also controls the fonts, type sizes, and text displayed on a Web page, and is not at all difficult to learn, if you're interested in creating your own Web site.

colorful, weekly tabloid newspapers and popular big city music radio stations—in that their content is changed and enhanced frequently to keep their audiences coming back, and to attract new audience members or subscribers.

The European Laboratory for Particle Physics, which was set up to investigate the Big Bang at the beginning of space and time, set off a significant explosion of its own by inventing the World Wide Web, an intuitive way of using computers that is powering the phenomenal growth of the Internet.

Laboratory officials said traffic on the Internet increased 350,000 percent last year as the cyberworld discovered the ease of using the Web.

If the Internet is the information superhighway, the Web is the equivalent of the trucks that carry the mail. It carries, in fact, the digital equivalent of the entire works of Shakespeare every second. The growth is likely to become even more exponential once users discover that they can use the Web to make phone calls all over the world for the price of a local call.

Barry James, "The Web: Out of the Lab and Spun around the World," *International Herald Tribune*

How You Can Use the Web

The Web is an exciting, colorful, and rapidly expanding world of information, entertainment, and communications features, and can provide you with many hours of fascinating "Web surfing" time in front of your computer screen.

As a Web user, you get instant access to a fascinating array of benefits:

Instant, Easy Information Access: There's a mind-boggling variety of information, entertainment, and interactive resources available now along the Web, and getting to them is as simple as clicking your mouse key (there's so much interesting stuff out there that surfing the Web now rivals TV-watching as a major source of information and entertainment!).

Practical Information on Most Any Subject: Because of the explosion of new Web sites created by thousands of writers, Web publishers, companies, and many other extremely talented contributors, you get access to useful, practical information on an almost infinite variety of subjects. The Web has everything: tips on finding a new job, advice and resources for your hobbies or special interests, resources for improving your computing productivity, or for finding affordable, exciting new travel and vacation destinations, and—most exciting of all—the Web gives you an instant connection to millions of friendly, sociable, or otherwise potentially rewarding connections to other people on the Internet.

Access to Unconventional Media and Multimedia Sources: The Web is technology's ultimate gift to the ideal of free speech. It provides virtually anyone, anywhere in the world, who has information to publish or an axe to grind, their own forum for broadcasting their information to anyone else via the Web. This gives you access to a rich and compelling variety of information, news, and entertainment features that are free from the expense, editorialization, and other barriers to entry found in the traditional "Old Media." Whatever your interests, political beliefs or cultural background, you'll find items of interest on the Web you'd never find anywhere else. Many Web sites also take advantage of the Web's multimedia capabilities, giving you instant access to fascinating collections of graphic files, photographs, video, sound and movie clips, downloadable software programs, and electronic magazines, all of which can be viewed on your own personal computer.

Current Web multimedia sites are a fascinating preview of the future direction of the Web as a broadcast distribution channel and may well obsolete the other "interactive TV" plans now underway by many cable and phone companies. And, as modem communication speeds, or "bandwidth," increases on the Web, you'll see even greater use of video and audio on Web sites—eventually even full-length movies, music albums, and other content-rich features.

Resources for Small Business Owners and Entrepreneurs: There's also plenty of useful, practical, and nowhere-else-to-be-found information and resources for small business owners, marketers, professionals, consultants, and entrepreneurs. From stock quotes and investment advice to specialized business industry information, to networks of independent owners of home-based businesses, entrepreneurs, and business owners of all types, the Web is a vast, rich source for practical advice on selecting, starting, expanding, and promoting your business.

Moreover, the better commercially sponsored Web sites can give you inspiration and ideas for creating your own Web site, so you can use the Web as a low-cost way to provide your customers with information about your business' products or services, news about your company, and goodwill-enhancing tips, advice and customer service to hold on to your existing customers, and to attract new ones as well, via the Web.

Another benefit to using the Web, and one that's not readily apparent when you're a new user, comes from making direct e-mail contact with authors of Web sites. Web site authors are often experts in their fields, and are anxious to hear feedback on their sites, and, because of their enthusiasm for the Web, can often help you with advice, opinions, or referrals.

From a recent survey of online usage, conducted by Jupiter Communications:

- **Projected number of people with access to the Internet by the year 2000: 36 million**
- **Projected percentage of users accessing the Internet via television by 2000: 16%**
- **Percentage of users who have purchased products via the Web: 14%**
- **Percentage of femaie Net users: 37%**

Web Tech: How the Web Works (Mercifully, a Brief Section)

Using a Web browser on the Web takes care of most of the technical stuff you used to need to know to use the Internet a few years ago. This is a good thing, because only a masochist would enjoy having to learn the tedious and confusing array of Unix commands and other

What makes the Web such a powerful cyber-helper is a software technique known as hyperlinking. When composing a Web page, an author can create hyperlinks—words that appear in bold type and indicate a shortcut to some other information. Using a program known as a Web browser on your PC, you can read pages stored on any Web computer. Say you're reading a page that describes recent discoveries about allergies. You see the word "antigen" in bold type. Using your computer mouse, you click on the word and—without any further effort on your part—you are transferred to another Web page that tells you what an antigen is. That page could be in the system where the first page was or in another computer thousands of miles away.

Amy Cortese, "Cyberspace," *Business Week*

esoterica which was required for using the Net, pre-Web.

In fact, most Web browsers are so simple even a chimpanzee could use one, since nearly all you need to know about using the Web consists of knowing, more or less, which arrow to click on your Web browser to get to a Web site's next or previous page, and of clicking on a Web site's underlined links to go somewhere else on the Web.

Web Jargon

Unless you want to design and create your own Web site (also not a terribly difficult job, technically speaking, and well within reach of most personal computer users), the only other technical stuff you need to know about the Web are these commonly used buzzwords:

Web Browser: A graphical,window-based software program you use on your own personal computer to access the Web. Handles all aspects of connecting to the Web, viewing Web site graphics, and multimedia files. The most popular Web browsers are the Netscape Navigator, Netcom's NetCruiser, and the proprietary Web browsers provided by each of the major online services such as CompuServe, America Online, MCI, and Prodigy. Depending on who's providing your Internet service, you may or may not be able to choose which Web browser you use.

Web Site or Web Page: Interchangeable terms used to describe an individual "place" on the Web containing a single Web-published feature. Physically speaking, a **Web site** is little more than a collection of files located under a directory somewhere on someone's computer connected to the Internet.

Think of the relationship between a Web site and the Web as being exactly like that of a book to a (very) large library. However, Web sites can be created by individuals, groups, companies, or other organizations for far less money than it costs to print and publish a book. A Web site may consist of one Web page, or of many Web pages, and usually also includes on-screen graphics, pictures, text—and increasingly—video and audio clips, or an archive of software you can download, store, and use freely on your own personal computer.

Links, Hotlinks, and Hypertext: Links and **hotlinks** are two interchangeable terms used to describe words or groups of words which are highlighted on Web pages. When you click on a link with your mouse, you are then immediately linked to another Web site or location on the current Web site containing the information that's referred to by the link. **Hypertext** is the term coined by information visionary Ted Nelson that describes the concept of being able to access information in ways that are almost totally controlled by the reader. What this means is that if you're reading a Web page on zoo animals, and come across the word "elephant" that's **hotlinked** within the text of the paragraph you're reading, you can click on the word **elephant** and then immediately jump to more detailed information that's specifically related to elephants, which has been hotlinked by the Web site's creator.

Web hotlinks are the Web's most famous, its most used, and abused feature. Any single Web site may contain dozens, hundreds, or even thousands of hotlinks, both to other sections within the same site, or to other Web sites located anywhere else in the world.

Links Page or Jump Site: Web sites consisting almost entirely of links to other Web sites. Many Web page authors have created **links pages** (also known as **hotlists**) consisting of lists of links to many other Web sites. These are often a Web site author's favorite sites, or feature links to Web sites pertaining to a specific subject. Since it's easy to create a Web site, and it's also easy to do nothing more with that site than to slap up lists of links to other Web sites, there are way too many of these kinds of Web sites around. Links pages do serve a purpose, however, when they are well organized and contain well-selected, annotated links. That's because they can help you greatly narrow the choice of Web sites which fit your particular interests. We cover the better links pages on the Web, and organize them by subject category, in this book.

Search Engines and Web Spiders: In an environment as chaotic and rapidly growing as the Web, no one can really say how many new Web sites are added every day, what they're about, or what's in them. If this eruption can't (or shouldn't) be controlled, some helpful Web programmers out there have at least developed software that attempts to seek out and grab what's there. These **search engines** and **Web spiders**, such as **AltaVista** and **Lycos**, are software applications that "travel" all over the Internet collecting new Web site locations, grabbing sample text segments from Web pages, and building lists of keywords. Web sites that feature these search engines, while not perfect, can help you find the sites you're looking for, and are especially good for locating newly created Web sites.

HTML: Stands for **HyperText Markup Language**, a method of inserting special codes within and around text files, graphics, pictures, or multimedia in order to make them accessible on the Web. These are codes within brackets (**< and >**) that tell special software on the Internet what part of a text file, for example,

Hotlinks are a good thing; they're the nuts and bolts that hold the Web together. But sometimes hotlinks can be too much of a good thing. If used on a Web page in a gratuitous fashion, they skim you along the Web without allowing you to read any material of substance. When misused in this way, links are sometimes like the proverbial Chinese restaurant meal, leaving you hungry, informationally speaking, right after you realize that your repeated linking has lead you on an information search to nowhere.

After a few days of cruising the World Wide Web, I realized there was no going back to inexpensive text-based Net access. The Mosaic software is a pleasure to use, and the range of information available on the Web is staggering. I went to the source for business information from the Social Security Administration, Small Business Administration, and the IRS. I read online versions of newspapers and magazines from across the country. I browsed legal advice (and lawyer jokes) from Nolo Press. And I looked up 800 numbers free of charge from AT&T's online directory.

Steve Morgenstern, "Confessions of an Internet Virgin," *Home Office Computing*

should be set as a headline, subhead, or hotlink. **HTML** also tells the computer where pictures should be placed on a Web site, which fonts should be used, and how large the text should appear on your screen.

If you'd like to create your own Web site, learning HTML is a pretty straightforward process, the basics of which can be mastered by most anyone in a couple of hours. If you're interested in creating your own Web pages, we've covered many Web sites that can provide you with excellent tutorials, instructions, downloadable software, and other resources to help you get started;

URL: Stands for **Uniform Resource Locator**, a fancy term which describes a Web site's exact address, or location, on the Web. If you've ever had to work with files located under multiple subdirectories, such as those under a pre-Windows MS-DOS operating system, you'll recognize **URLs** for what they are: a confusing string of subdirectories, files or executable commands, separated by slashes, which only a computer nerd could love, and which must be typed into your Web browser *exactly* as they appear (including the correct use of upper and lower-case letters) in order to go to a Web site. Fortunately, you can avoid having to do this, for the most part when you're using the Web, since clicking on hotlinks will get you to a Web site without having to type in a URL, or copying a URL from a text file (if it's located on your PC), and pasting it into your Web browser on-screen, can also save you from this arduous task. **Bookmarks** or **hotlists** (see below) also let you store lists of URLs for future use; and on ***What's On The Web's*** **Jump City**, this book's own Web site, you can spare yourself the ordeal of typing URLs by simply entering the site's specific four-digit **Jump Code** for every Web site in this book, once you're on our Web site. Unfortunately, you will have to type in at least one URL—ours—to get to our Web site: **http://www.jumpcity.com/**.

Bookmark or Hotlists File: A very handy feature of Web browsers, a **bookmark** or **hotlist** capability allows you to save a Web site's URL to a file in your own personal computer's Web browser with a click of your mouse key. Once a Web site's URL is stored in your bookmarks or hotlists file, you can instantly link to that site anytime just by clicking on its menu option displayed on your personal computer's screen. Many Web browsers also give you the ability to import and export your bookmark file to HTML format, which means your list of favorite Web sites and their locations may be displayed both as Web pages on screen, or sent by e-mail to someone else—a great way to exchange links to great Web sites with a friend, family member, co-worker, or business associate.

SLIP and PPP: Stands for **Serial Line Interface Protocol**, and **Point-to-Point-Protocol**, two ways of providing your personal computer with a direct connection to the Internet. That's all you have to know about these two technical terms, because any Internet access provider worth using will have already supplied you with an easy way to access the Web with a Web browser, without you having to learn the intricacies of this Net access jargon. The chief advantage of a **SLIP** or **PPP** account is that it gives you the option of selecting your own choice of any commercially available, stand-alone Web browser such as the popular Netscape Navigator. However, a few other commercial, nationwide Internet access providers, such as Netcom, are also "open systems," in that they allow you to choose the type of Web browser you prefer for your Web access. Separating the Internet service from the Web browser gives you maximum choice in your selection of a Web browser, and seems to be an emerging trend in the industry.

Helper Applications: These are small, add-on programs, sometimes shareware, used along with your Web browser to allow you to easily view downloadable graphics, play video/audio files, use downloaded software, send and receive electronic mail, and access the Internet's Usenet newsgroups, all from the convenience of your own Web browser. The Netscape Navigator Web browser, for example, does a particularly fine job of using **helper applications**, by taking care of all the picayune functions involved in downloading, accessing, and playing Web multimedia and other applications, automatically.

For example, using Netscape, you simply click on a hotlink for a video clip and Netscape takes care of the rest—downloading it, and then immediately grabbing a helper application such as Sparkle, (a QuickTime video viewer for the Macintosh), launching this application, and then playing the video clip back right away for your movie viewing enjoyment.

If you want to get fancy, you can even set up some Web browsers, including Netscape, to use any particular helper application you like, such as **offline news readers**, that make Internet newsgroup access far easier by letting you download multiple newsgroup messages to your own PC's hard disk, so you can read them without incurring additional online connect time charges.

The Web's Multimedia Future:

Increasingly, audio and video are becoming more important aspects of the Web.

RealAudio, a new Net software product, lets Web users listen to stored radio programs, music, and other Web audio features in real time, over their personal computers.

StreamWorks, from Xing Technologies, promises real-time delivery of Web video and audio over ordinary phone lines.

Java, a new, play-anywhere programming language from Sun Microsystems, could become the "operating system for the Internet," allowing for the rapid transmission of multimedia content, called "applets," which can then be played on any desktop personal computer.

As a freely-available operating system, Java may break Microsoft's current stranglehold on PC operating systems, allowing for pay-per-use pricing of software applications and cheap, on-demand use of full-bore multimedia on inexpensive "Web TVs."

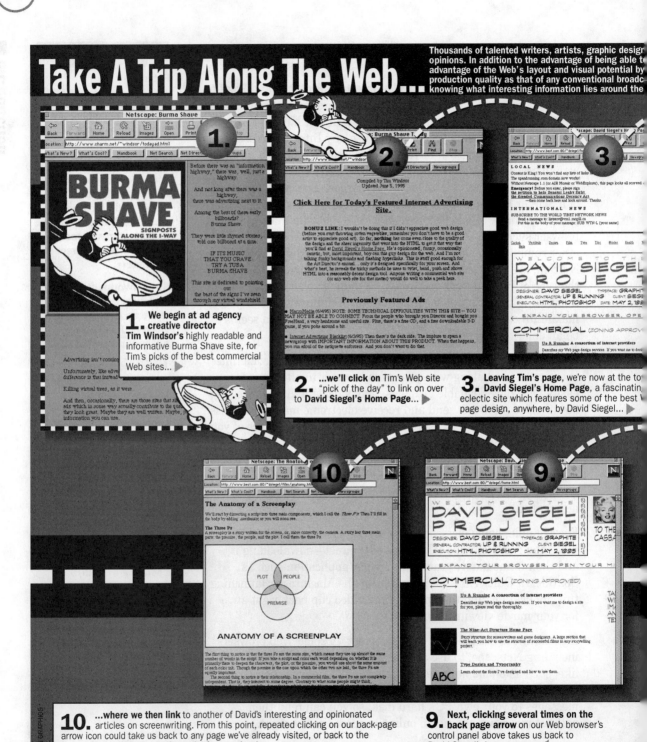

Take A Trip Along The Web...
Thousands of talented writers, artists, graphic desigr
opinions. In addition to the advantage of being able t
advantage of the Web's layout and visual potential by
production quality as that of any conventional broadc
knowing what interesting information lies around the
1. We begin at ad agency creative director Tim Windsor's highly readable and informative Burma Shave site, for Tim's picks of the best commercial Web sites...
2. ...we'll click on Tim's Web site "pick of the day" to link on over to David Siegel's Home Page...
3. Leaving Tim's page, we're now at the to David Siegel's Home Page, a fascinatin eclectic site which features some of the best page design, anywhere, by David Siegel...
10. ...where we then link to another of David's interesting and opinionated articles on screenwriting. From this point, repeated clicking on our back-page arrow icon could take us back to any page we've already visited, or back to the Burma Shave site, the starting point for our trip.
9. Next, clicking several times on the back page arrow on our Web browser's control panel above takes us back to David Siegel's home page...
©GAA GRAPHICS

and business owners use their small corner of the Web to provide you with instant access to all kinds of helpful information and thought-provoking bypass traditional media channels like broadcast networks, newspapers or other print media, many of these talented Web mediameisters take full adding all kinds of compelling, original graphics and Web page layout techniques that, when well executed, give many Web pages the same high print product created by the media mega-giants. Thanks to hypertext links, you can spend many enjoyable hours linking from site to site, never hotlink. Here's an example of an actual Web session that shows the interesting twists and turns any random Web journey can take...

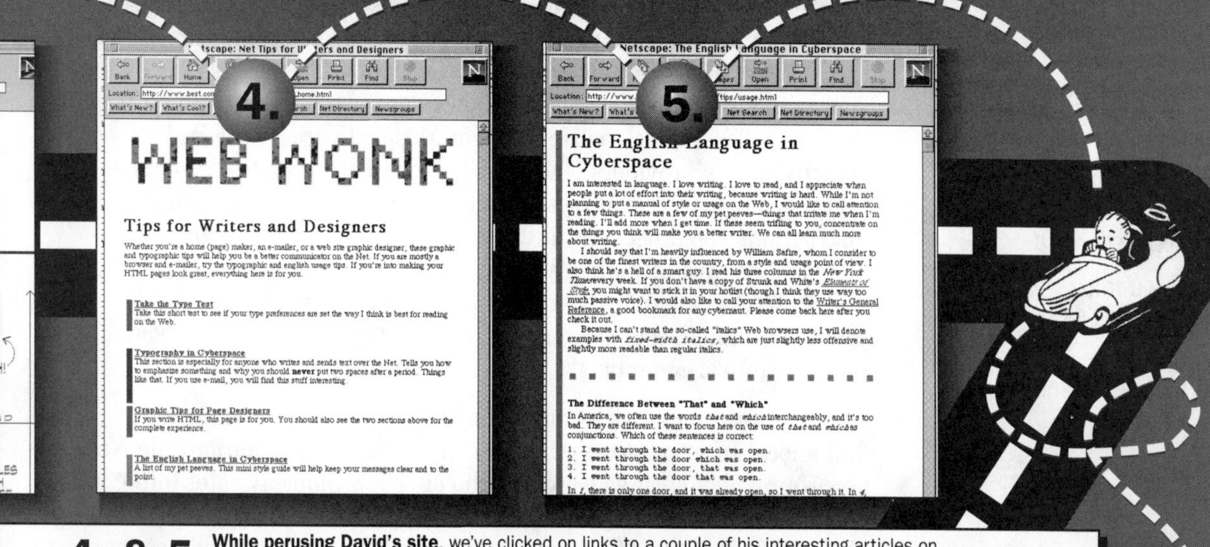

4. & 5. While perusing David's site, we've clicked on links to a couple of his interesting articles on Web page design, layout, and writing style. We also found a link to another site featuring many electronic reference works, all available free over the Internet. Let's go there...

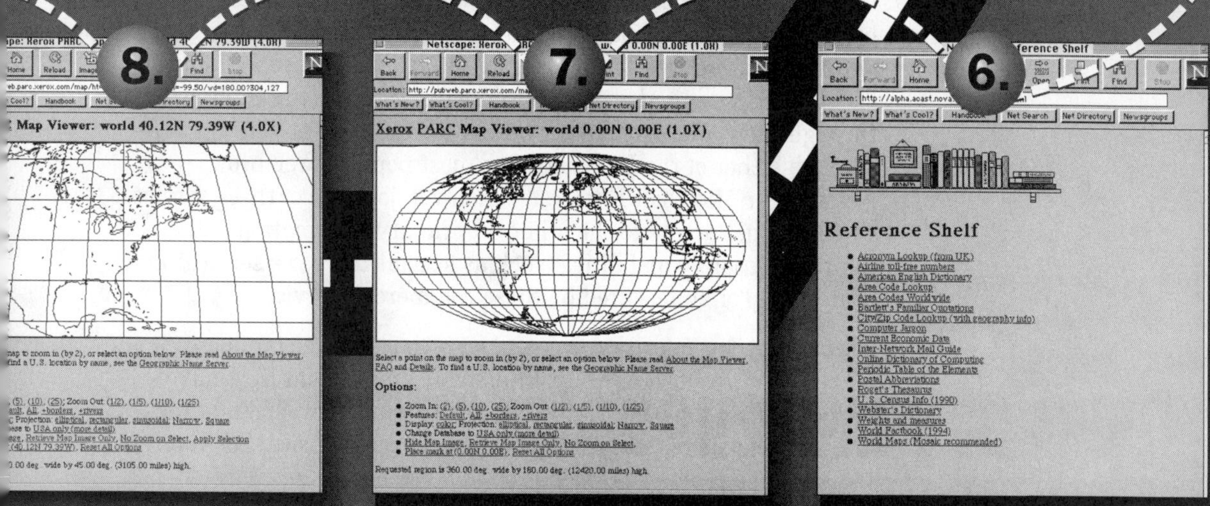

7. & 8. ... the Xerox PARC Map Viewer, a Web site developed by the legendary advanced research center at Xerox, a fun, graphically-oriented Web site featuring a map of the world which can be zoomed in on to reveal increasingly detailed maps for any specific area on earth...

6. Now that we've linked to this site, we're presented with an on-screen menu of a wide variety of handy, Net-accessible reference works. Clicking on the World Maps link above, we're linking to...

Internet and Web Access Providers:

- **America Online:** **1-(800) 827-6364**
- **Compuserve:** **1-(800) 848-8990**
- **AT&T:** **1-(800) 967-5363**
- **Sprint:** **1-(800) 877-4646**
- **InternetMCI:** **1-(800) 444-6245**
- **Netcom:** **1-(800) 353-6600**

Getting Connected to the Web

SLIP/PPP Accounts: The first, and (somewhat) more complicated, way to get access to the Web is to obtain a SLIP or PPP account (also referred to as a **Shell account**), usually from a local Internet access provider. A SLIP account connects your personal computer directly to the Internet and—using various utilities that you must also install on your personal computer—enables you to use popular stand-alone Web browser software such as Netscape or Mosaic to access the Web. Usually, access providers who sell SLIP or PPP accounts also do a pretty good job of providing the necessary additional utilities and instructions you'll need for direct Web access. If you follow their instructions carefully when you set up your SLIP account, this method of Web access is usually trouble-free, but can sometimes be tricky if you're a complete computer novice, or if you're not very good about reading software manuals.

The key advantage to this method of access is that you can usually find a local Internet access provider in your area, or a nationwide Net access provider, such as Netcom, who offer low monthly rates (often $30 or less per month) for unlimited hourly service, through a local phone call. Also, if all you want is access to the Internet, and not the additional information features offered by commercial online services, then you should consider getting a direct Internet connection.

Commercial Services: The second, and easier, way to access the Web is by going with one of the well-known online services, such as America Online, CompuServe, AT&T, Sprint, or Netcom. These well-known online services can also provide you with access to the Internet, through their own proprietary access software, or, at your option—through either of the Internet's two most popular Web browsers, Netscape or Microsoft Explorer. When you join one of these services, you'll also get access to the other proprietary information and communications capabilities (such as specialized news services and chat rooms) often featured by these commercial services.

Internet Set-Top Television Boxes: Major consumer electronics manufacturers, such as Sony, Philips/Magnavox, and RCA have introduced set-top boxes, which attach to your television and turn it into an inexpensive, easy-to-use Internet access device. For Internet access, these products, priced around $300, can give you an inexpensive alternative to purchasing a costlier personal computer (around $2,000), and provide great value for their cost. Many of these products, such as the WebTV unit that's licensed to Sony and Philips, also include Internet access at around $20 per month for unlimited use.

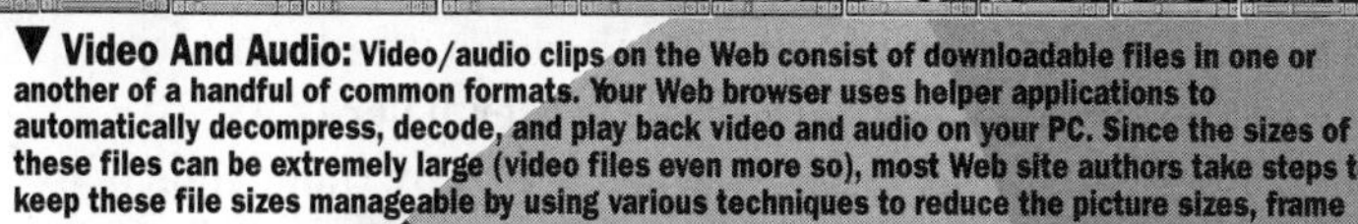

▼ Video And Audio: Video/audio clips on the Web consist of downloadable files in one or another of a handful of common formats. Your Web browser uses helper applications to automatically decompress, decode, and play back video and audio on your PC. Since the sizes of these files can be extremely large (video files even more so), most Web site authors take steps to keep these file sizes manageable by using various techniques to reduce the picture sizes, frame rates, and sound quality of Web multimedia files. For video, this means that video clips may be about the size of a Saltine cracker and appear somewhat grainy and jerky as well; since file sizes are smaller with audio, fewer such compromises are usually made. Even though being a Web pioneer may have its price (we're sure the first television owners of the 1940s could have reported similar problems in their day), Web multimedia, even in its current form, adds a valuable new dimension to many Web sites where it is used, and gives you a sneak preview of the Web's exciting multimedia future.

▲ See the latest fashions, by downloading a video clip of a runway fashion show like the Galliano video clip above, from **Fashion Page**, at Jump 2160.

SoundMachine Progress
barney.au
8.0 kHz ▼
00:00:00

▲ Audio helper applications, like SoundMachine for the Mac, help you download and play CD-quality audio on your PC.

Multimedia

Many Web sites contain full color photo files, video clips, and audio files, all of which can be downloaded, saved, and played on your personal computer. As modem communication speeds increase, and the Web becomes accessible via higher-bandwidth channels such as ISDN phone lines and cable television, Web site developers will, no doubt, expand their use of full-screen video and CD-quality audio content on the Web—solidifying the Web's emergence as an entirely new broadcast medium.

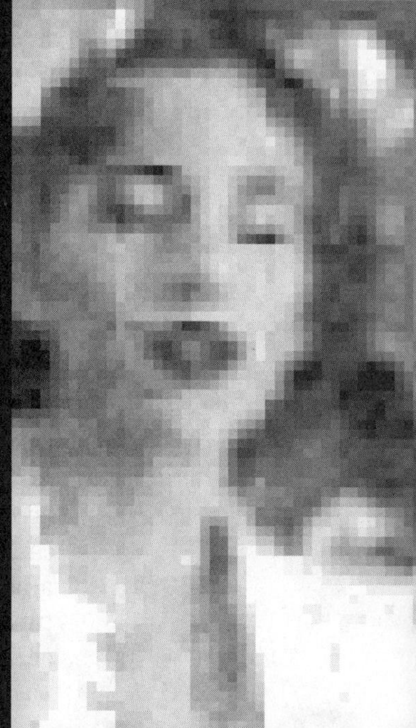

▲ Online electronic magazines, like **Citizen Poke**, at Jump 1507 use Adobe Acrobat to deliver a polished editorial product to the reader via the Web.

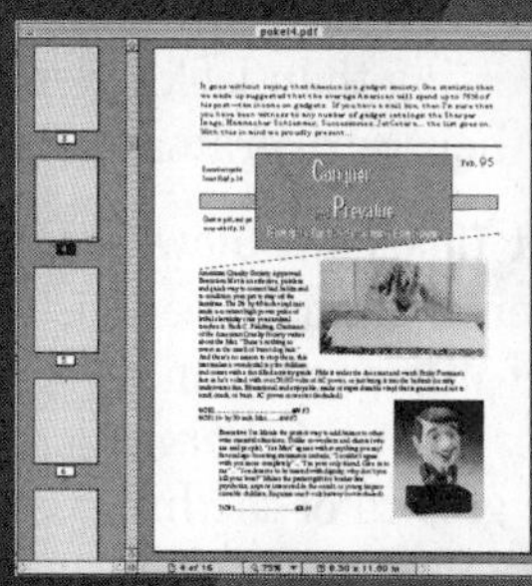

▲ Page 2 of *Citizen Poke*...looks a lot like a magazine you'd receive through the mail!

Adobe Acrobat: ▶ A freely available, widely distributed graphics viewing format created by Adobe, the creators of Postscript, the standard typographical graphics printing language used by desktop publishers and other media content creators. Acrobat frees Web site authors of many of the Web's current design constraints by allowing them to create on-screen pages using any font, color, or graphic they select. This total flexibility brings a higher level of production quality to Web content, and one which more closely resembles that of a four-color magazine than the usual Web page. Text files, electronic magazines, and other publications created in Adobe Acrobat format can be freely downloaded, saved, viewed and printed on your own personal computer, using the Adobe Acrobat viewer, which is made available all over the Web, free of charge, by Adobe. Since Adobe has announced key product development alliances with leading Web browser software developers and other major Internet industry players, you can expect Adobe Acrobat to be even more fully integrated into Web pages, greatly improving the Web's production values and its visual appeal.

To set the stage, the Useless Web Pages home page provides the best pointer to the results of combining people with too much time on their hands with modern technology.

The results can range from people making a list of all their CDs available to the Net community, to those connecting their hot tub controls to the World Wide Web.

To take the inane even further, there are pointers to other pages including a list of games for the Atari 2600, as if anyone sophisticated enough technologically to get on the Net would still own an Atari 2600, and a home page in Gaelic—soon to be available in Bushman and Sumerian.

Arman Danesh, "Cyberspace: The Surreal Frontier," *South China Morning Post*

What's Not So Good about the Web?

The happy anarchy the Web shares with its alter-ego, the Internet, does not come without a price for you as a Web user. There's a downside to the freedom and individuality expressed by thousands of talented amateurs on the Web, which brings with it a number of disadvantages that get in the way of your getting the most from using the Web:

Shallow Content: The fact is, many of the hundreds of thousands of individual Web sites out there really don't offer much in the way of truly useful information or other benefits. Once you get over the novelty of using your Web browser for the first time, you'll realize there's a lot out there on the Web that doesn't provide you with much useful or current information. Since it doesn't really take very much money or time to slap a few pictures and a couple of text files on a Web server, anyone can be a publisher on the Web, and this means that everyone is—even people who apparently don't have any notion of what it takes to provide their fellow Web users with interesting, useful, informative, or entertaining information.

Examples of this waste of Web space (and your time) include some commercial "brochure sites" that are content-thin and consist of little more than a couple of scanned-in color photos from the company's printed brochure, along with a handful of company press releases. There are also a fair number of "personal Web pages," consisting of a color photograph of the Web site's creator and a brief listing of his or her personal interests. While some of these sites are quite useful and creative, a lot of them are actually less interesting than looking at the stuff most families stick to the fronts of their refrigerator doors.

Long Wait Times and Slow Response: It's a sad fact of Internet life: You'll often experience periods of sluggish response and slow loading of Web pages while you use the Internet. As telecom companies and other service providers struggle to keep up with the explosive growth of the Internet, it's likely that periods of slow access will continue until technological developments and added capacity can solve the problem. Whenever you experience slow access on the Internet, you can solve this problem (most of the time) by simply disconnecting, and immediately reconnecting—chances are, you'll get a better connection when you hook up the next time.

Linkomaniacs: Emphasizing the shallowness of many Web sites are those sites which consist of nothing more than lists of links to other Web sites. While in some cases, a links page Web site serves a valuable purpose in that its author has collected and organized many related links on a specific subject (and the better links pages, many of which are covered in this book, feature the Web site author's hand-picked, commented links to other Web sites), most of the creators of these kinds of Web pages mistakenly believe that mere list-making can substitute for content. This problem is compounded by the sheer volume of Web links pages out there, most of which do little more than link you to each other's useless Web links pages. Spending your first few hours on the Web skimming along pages like these can be a frustrating and information-starving experience—like visiting a bookstore where all you could browse were the torn-out indexes from each book.

In general, while the Web certainly makes everything on the Internet easy to find and access, getting to the best that's out there still requires the human element, and that's where we come in. Web sites chosen for inclusion in ***What's on the Web*** represent the Web's very best sites for your business, personal, professional, social, personal productivity, and entertainment use.

Our reviewers are savvy, experienced Web users and editorial experts who know what you're looking for when it comes to content, usefulness, entertainment, and value in the time you spend surfing the Web. While surfing the Web is the Web's biggest sport (and the biggest fun we have!) ***What's on the Web***, combined with our own Web site, **JumpCity**, helps you save time and get the most from your Web experience by letting you get to the best the Web has to offer, whatever your particular needs or interests.

Fighting Web Chaos with *What's on the Web*

While the Web certainly makes access to information easy, free, and fun, and liberates you from the tyranny of having to learn all the nuts and bolts of using the Internet, this newfound ease of use also presents you with a bewildering array of information choices: there are hundreds of thousands of Web sites out there, with several hundred (or more) being added each day, and, given this chaotic expansion, there aren't any editors or gatekeepers, either (and given concerns about censorship of the Internet, there probably shouldn't ever be).

Underlying this happy chaos and compounding the kudzu-like growth of the Web is the power that everyone has to put up their own Web

The Melding of Media: Will the Web Replace Books?

In the next 10 years or so, not likely. But after that, look for laptop and hand-held devices, evolving from those like Apple's Newton, but with super-high resolution, full-color screen displays, and cheap wireless communications.

With low cost (around $200) and screen resolution and contrast values comparable to that for black printed type on white paper (now reportedly seen in laboratory prototype screen displays), books may eventually be distributed via wireless communications to handheld devices.

If, or when, this happens, will books become Web sites? Conversely, could a Web site become a book?

How we select Web sites for review in *What's on the Web* (from our *Reviewer's Guidelines*):

- **Content:** **Does the Web site contain a substantial amount of original information, graphics, or multimedia? Is this information comparable in value and amount to information available from traditional, professionally created media, such as newspapers or magazines? Is the information updated on a reasonably frequent basis?**
- **Usefulness:** **Does the site's information provide advice, news or entertainment value? Does it help the Web reader solve a problem?**
- **Presentation:** **Does the site have good design and production values? Are the graphics interesting, professional-looking and appropriate from the standpoint of Web design?**
- **Authorship:** **Who is the site's author(s)? What are their qualifications? Let's give these individuals credit for their work wherever possible.**

page and "be their own publisher." In a place like the Web, where anyone can be a publisher, there are people who probably shouldn't be. From a quality point of view, many Web sites fall well below the commercially polished editorial products you're used to seeing, such as newspapers, television shows, movies, and magazines. When it comes to publishing quality, the Web can be a very erratic place, where seemingly endless collections of shallow links pages seem to link endlessly to one another, never reaching any material of substance. Large portions of Web space are also occupied by sites with grossly outdated or mediocre content as well.

If you're a new Web user, surfing the Web for hours without really getting anywhere can be fun (you'll still enjoy doing it, even after you've logged many hours on the Web, we can assure you!). But what happens when you really need to find something on the Web? How can you use the Web to solve a business-related problem? What resources exist on the Web to help you improve your way of life? Make better personal investment decisions? Or find information, resources, or support for a family health problem? Locate useful and entertaining information and advice on your personal hobbies or other special interests? Or get the latest news and specialized industry information?

To answer these questions and to solve these problems, the Web holds the potential of being a powerful information and communications resource. But this tremendous problem-solving power is obscured by the immense and confusing volume of Web sites—and the widely varying quality of one Web site relative to another.

Even if you're a novice Web user, you'll soon realize that the ease-of-use your Web browser gives you, by letting you click from site to site, is simply not enough. For example, while it couldn't be easier to type in the keyword "business" on any of the popular Web search sites and receive a list of 500 sites that claim to be business-related, do you really have the time to check out each and every one of those sites when you're looking for specific business news or information?

Out of the hundreds of thousands of Web sites out there, which of these actually have enough information to be worth your time? How many are just
a waste of your time? Of the sites that are worthwhile, what's their content like? What are their features? Who's responsible for the information contained on the site? And, most important, *how can these Web sites help you?* That's where this book comes in!

How to Use *What's on the Web*

What's on the Web provides you with the all-important *human element* to help you save time, solve problems, and get the most from the best Web sites out there. Our reviewers, each one of them a professional writer and editorial expert, are also enthusiastic Web users in their own right. Our reviewers spend many hours a week, surfing the Web far and wide, sorting through thousands of Web sites to select and review only those sites which provide you with the highest information value.

Unlike those thick-as-a-brick "Yellow Pages" guides to the Web, which are 700-page tomes listing hundreds of mediocre, "filler" Web sites, or even duplicate listings, many of which are just a waste of your time (and which are put there to make their books fatter, thereby giving the illusion of value), we spend more time to get you the *best* of what's out there on the Web, and to tell you *why* you should use it.

The 1,800-plus Web sites covered in ***What's on the Web*** don't represent the largest selection of Web sites to be found in any book, but they do give you the largest selection of *the best.* You'll find the best Web sites meeting your needs for information on just about any subject you're looking for, by turning to any one of our 12 subject chapters, and their 75 individual chapter subcategories. You can also use our 7,200-plus word subject index to locate and access Web sites related to a specific subject, when you need to find something even faster on the Web.

You can reach all the Web sites reviewed in *What's on the Web*, and much more: reviews of the latest, hottest Web sites, Web news and views, features, online discussion areas and more, by going to our own Web site, JumpCity.

In your Web browser's URL entry window, type:

http://www.jumpcity.com/

Once you're on JumpCity, reaching any of the sites reviewed here is as simple as entering each review's own Jump Code, the four-digit number following the Jump icon.

Our Own Web Site: *What's On The Web's* JumpCity

What's on the Web is also the first book of any kind to be fully integrated with its own Web site. As a buyer of this book, you're entitled to free, full access to its Web companion, ***JumpCity***.

JumpCity is the on-the-Web counterpart to ***What's on the Web***, featuring instant Web access to each of the reviews in this book, plus much more: the hottest news and reviews of the newest and best Web sites, updated daily, current Web-related news and announcements, electronic tip sheets for getting the most from the Web, plus more new and exciting surprise features, all updated continuously.

What's on the Web is, in fact, specifically designed to be used alongside ***JumpCity***. Not only can you search for, scroll, retrieve, and read detailed reviews of all the Web sites covered in this book on ***JumpCity*** (plus many more new ones which have been added after this book's publication), you can also use the four-digit **Jump Code**

(patent pending) for each site reviewed in this book to link instantly to that site—without having to type in those long, pesky URLs. Go to ***JumpCity*** and you'll also be able to give us your comments on the Web sites you've visited, and vote on your favorite Web sites.

Descriptions of Web Site Reviews in *What's on the Web*

Here's a description of the features of each Web site review in this book:

Title: The title of our Web site review, as defined by us;

Name: The actual name of the Web site, given by its author, as it would appear in the top window of your Web browser, on-screen;

Web Site Type: Each Web site has been organized into one of three types, to provide you with additional detail on the nature of the information a site has to offer:

LINKS **LINKS:** Site reviews with the LINKS icon are Web sites featuring lists of many *links* to other Web sites, usually relating to a specific subject;

CONTENT **CONTENT:** Site reviews with a CONTENT icon comprise the majority of sites reviewed in this book, and consist of *content*: original text, articles, news, editorial features, pictures, graphics, software, or multimedia resources;

COMMERCE **COMMERCE:** Commerce sites have been developed or sponsored by companies both large and small, usually to promote that company's goods and services. We've selected only the best commercial Web sites for inclusion in ***What's on the Web***; only those sites containing useful editorial content or other resources which you may find inherently valuable, as opposed to purely promotional, or commercial sites, have been included;

Jump **Jump Code:** Each site reviewed has its own four-digit number which can be used whenever you're online with our own Web site, ***JumpCity***. Simply enter this four-digit Jump ***Code*** and you can instantly link to any Web site in this book, without having to type those tedious URLs (this feature's probably worth the price of this book all by itself!) To access JumpCity, you do have to type this one URL into your Web browser:

http://www.jumpcity.com/

Review: We tell you all about the Web site—its features, the links it may have to other related Web sites, who developed the site, and, most important—how the site benefits you;

URL ▶ **URL:** If you really must torture yourself and type in the site's URL on your own, we also print it here;

KEY NEWSGROUP **Key Newsgroup:** The subject matter of many Web sites reviewed in ***What's on the Web*** is often related to a Usenet Internet discussion newsgroup, where you can engage in lively online discussions on literally thousands of interesting subjects (we cover all of the best of these Net newsgroups in ***What's on the Internet***, another book we co-publish, along with Peachpit Press, a guide to over 2,200 Net discussion groups). Many Web sites also contain links to relevant Internet newsgroups, adding a new level of interactivity to your Web browsing experience;

Thumbnail Graphics: Where applicable, we've also included a small screen capture of a visually-interesting graphic from the actual Web site, to give you a sampling of the wealth of visual artistry that's been created by many talented Web authors and designers;

Reviewer: The initials of the person who wrote the Web site review are listed at the end of each review. To find out who wrote a review, check our reviewer's bios at the back of this book.

Our Books—and Web Site—Help You Stay on Top of the Best of the Net

Internet Media currently publishes two books on the Internet: ***What's on the Web***, and our companion guide to over 2,200 of the best and most popular Internet discussion groups, ***What's on the Internet***. Our team of reviewers and editorial group differs from other publishers of Net-related books in that we *first* became hooked on the Internet, and then decided to share our enthusiasm for the Net by publishing books to tell others about it. We hope that this enthusiasm for the tremendous potential of the Internet and the Web is contagious; we also hope that, as it has with us, the Web will open many new and exciting worlds for you and your family to explore. We also hope that you'll continue to allow us to be your guides to both "what's on the Internet" and "what's on the Web."

On your bookshelf, on the Web, and on your computer screen, let us be your guides to the best that's on the Internet and the Web...stay with us as we help you stay on top of the best and most up-to-date features for your business, personal, social, technical, and special interests.

We'd Like to Hear from You!

If you have any comments or ideas for editions of *What's on the Web*, send us e-mail at:

eric@jumpcity.com

If you have a Web site you'd like to have reviewed for future editions of *What's on the Web*, go to JumpCity at:

http://www.jumpcity.com/

and fill out the on-screen site submission form.

If you're still wondering what the World Wide Web is good for, ask John Foster. Two weeks ago, Foster sat in his Silicon Valley office thinking about the scuba diving trip he wanted to take the next weekend. But this winter's fickle weather had him worried. Would there be a storm? "So I did a Yahoo," says the software engineer. "I found out the weather was going to be crappy."

A Yahoo? Welcome to one of the most popular destinations on the Web. Like many whimsically named creations of the Internet, Yahoo is an acronym that sounds retrofitted — it stands for "Yet Another Hierarchical Officious Oracle." Whatever that means, Yahoo is basically a catalog of other Web home pages organized by subject, a kind of *Yellow Pages* for the Internet. Click on "Entertainment," and Yahoo will retrieve headings from "Auto-mobiles" to "Comics" to "Paranormal Phenomena." Click again, and the list narrows down one more level. Yahoo's inventory of more than 30,000 entries doesn't winnow the unwidely Web down to a pamphlet—but it's better than searching alone.

Jennifer Tanaka with Dogen Hannah, "A (Free and) Easy Guide to the Web," *Newsweek*

Searching & Linking on the Web

The Web makes it easier than ever to locate the information you're looking for, and many helpful Web users have created a wide variety of big Web indexes and other Web searching features to help you find it on the Web. We show you where the best ones are, so you can get to them and be productive on the Web—immediately.

Big Web Indexes and Web Searching Worms, Spiders, and Other Cyberspace Creatures

Using the Web to find anything on the Web requires the use of one of two different methods:

Web indexes are Web sites containing lists of many links to other Web sites, and are usually organized in some type of logical fashion; for example, with sites organized under menu-oriented subheadings like business, education, entertainment, etc. Some Web indexes feature keyword search capabilities to assist you in narrowing down the list of Web sites you're looking for.

The biggest, and perhaps the best, example of a Web index is Yahoo, the Web's biggest mega-index (which is also keyword-searchable) created by Stanford postgraduate students David Filo and Jerry Wang. Yahoo has become such a promising development for these two that they've put their studies on hold to pursue Yahoo on a full-time basis—with the help of a sizable amount of venture capital funding. There are many other helpful big Web indexes out there to help you, some of which cover certain subject-specific areas, like business- or education-related Web sites, and helpful indexes covering announcements of brand-new Web sites.

The second online method of finding Web sites, **Web search engines**, such as Lycos (named after an aggressive, predatory spider!) and Oliver McBryan's World Wide Web Worm don't just organize the Web site links that authors submit to them, they employ custom-developed Internet software applications which actually comb the Internet at regular intervals to gather information on all currently accessible Web sites, their URLs, plus brief snippets of descriptive text from each Web site to give you an idea of the Web site's *context* and *content*.

Finding Things on the Web

How you search for things on the Web depends entirely on your sense of urgency, and whether or not you're trying to locate Web sites on a specific subject. Searching the big Web indexes, such as Yahoo or AltaVista, will generally get you to a handful of Web sites on just about any given subject. From that point, it's up to you to sample those sites to see if any one of them has the information you're looking for. There are also many Web indexes containing Web links for a large number of Web sites on specific topics, such as business, personal computing, entertainment, education, etc., many of which are covered in this chapter.

Keyword searching is another, somewhat more advanced, method of finding Web sites, and can be the fastest and most exact way to locate Web sites on a specific subject, if you're thoughtful and exact in your choice of keywords. For example, if you're looking for information on marketing tips for a home-based business, using keywords like "home business marketing," or "mailing lists" will get you a smaller, more relevant list of Web sites than using broader search keywords such as "small business," or "entrepreneurship."

Then, of course, if you have time on your hands, you can spend many fascinating hours surfing the Web to find many interesting Web sites. Don't forget to make liberal use of your Web browser's bookmarks capability to save the locations of these Web sites for future visits.

Big Web Hotlists & Indexes

Yahoo's Guide to the World Wide Web

Yahoo - A Guide to WWW Jump 0043

No listing of Web searching resources would be complete without a description of Yahoo!, the Net's best-known monster Web links site. It's a savvy, well-done, and nicely organized site with links to tens of thousands individual Web sites, intelligently sorted by scores of subject categories. Yahoo! does a solid job organizing its huge number of sites into human-accessible categories for hours and hours of Web-linking fun! There's more material here than we could ever describe—links to business sites, music and multimedia pages, Web events, local Web information, society and culture, and much more, all kept current and updated on a daily basis. It also features a handy keyword search capability, and "What's new?," "What's cool?," and "What's popular?" pages with links to many more interesting sites. —(E.G.)

URL▶ http://www.yahoo.com/

Yahoo!'s Web Search Engine for Kids

Yahooligans! LINKS

Jump 5852

Isn't it funny that one of the nicest search engines on the Web is also one that's designed for children? Well, it's no coincidence, perhaps, but many search engines could learn a great deal from Yahooligans!, the kid-oriented section of the well-known Yahoo! Web directory. While it's a perfect example of simplicity at its finest, it still manages to get the job done. Structured like the regular Yahoo!, kids will find the navigation easy to handle and understand, with links to plenty of educational and entertaining sites. Subjects include "Around the World," for culture and politics, "School Bell" for programs and homework answers, as well as sections for computers, sports, science, and much more. —(J.P.)

URL▶ http://www.yahooligans.com/

NET SURF CENTRAL
(the good, the bad, and the utterly useless)

HotWired's Web Reviews

HotWired: Net Surf Central

Jump 5751

If you've got some time to kill and you'd like to spend it surfing the Web, link on over to NetSurf Central, part of HotWired's great daily Web news and comment site. It's a searchable collection of Web site reviews and commentary that have appeared in past online issues; according to HotWired, "the good, the bad, and the utterly useless." The reviews on this site are superbly written and very well-chosen by June Cohen. The searching itself will take some getting used to, as the crew here have opted for a few terms that are somewhat unorthodox in the world of searching. For example, search options include keyword ("pets" is an example), genre (fan pages), adjective (dopey) and date (item first appeared). You'll find a helpful glossary of these terms in the FAQ and other tips on searching the site. And the Graveyard—that's the place they send sites that, although they have not been updated for eons, remain on the Web just the same, like ghosts of Web-days past. —(J.P.)

URL▶ http://www.hotwired.com/surf/

Finding Out WHO is WHERE on the Net . . .

WhoWhere? Jump 5769

Think about it—it would take only about 20 seconds on the Web to answer a stupid TV trivia question, but if you need to find someone's e-mail address, you pretty much have to call them collect. Well, the tide has turned, with new sites like WhoWhere. Just type in the name and (optionally) the city or state, hit the search button, and you can pull up matching names and e-mail addresses from its database. This is lots of fun for locating long-lost friends, old girlfriends, boyfriends, and relatives—even if you don't find a listing for yourself (and why would you be looking for your own e-mail address, anyway?). —(J.P.)

URL▶ http://www.whowhere.com/

Changeable Web Sites Listing

Spider's Web Daily, Weekly, Monthly, and Random Goodies

Jump 2435

Bob Allison, creator of the Spider's Web and its many entertaining and informative pages, has another winner. For the forgetful surfer, the one whose bookmark file has grown out of control, or the just plain lazy, he's searched the Web and created a page of links to sites that change regularly. All you need do to keep current on the Web is stop by every week or so and run through the list. He's got everything here: newspapers, magazines, comics, general entertainment, and the Web's various "cool sites of the day" pages. And, with its random links, you can come by anytime and find something new and interesting. —(L.S.)

URL▶ http://gagme.wwa.com/~boba/dwr.html

▲ *Roulette on the Web graphic, from* U Roulette, *at* Jump 0108.

Marty's Cool Links Page

Marty's Cool Links Page

Jump 0042

Marty (sorry, couldn't find his last name) has an interesting personal Web page with all kinds of neat links to other well-known Web sites, covering a wide variety of Marty-selected subjects. His page also features links to other Websters' personal Web pages, too. —(E.G.)

URL▶ http://garnet.acns.fsu.edu:80/~msalo/index.html

Cool Sites to Visit

Cool Site of the Day **Jump 1537**

Want to find out the best of the Web? Approximately 22,000 of you tune into Glenn Davis' picks each day. He sorts through massive amounts of Web cyberjunk to feature different sites that have outstanding "content, style and presentation, innovation, and graphics." See if you concur, whether it be serious (the Halifax Police Dept.) to frivolous (WWW Dating Game) to wacky (iComiX!). Even the days here have ever-changing names—Moanday for Monday, Frightday for Friday, depending on Davis' whim. If you have a sound card, listen to the Cool Site introduction. Visit the previous Cool Sites, listed by month, and read the FAQs to see if you want to submit yours for consideration. What makes his own site cool? "I don't know," Davis says, "It oftentimes depends on the kind of day I've had." —(H.L.)

URL▶ http://cool.infi.net/

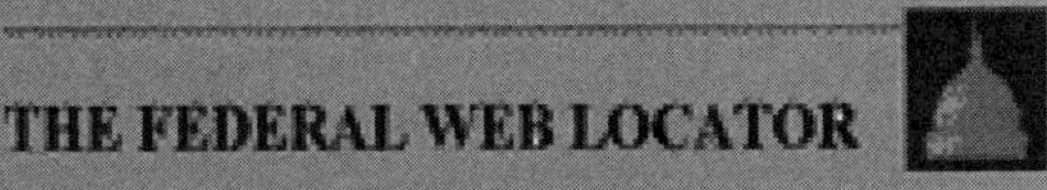

Government on the Web

The Federal Web Locator **Jump 2026**

It seems that nearly every federal agency has a Web presence, and the Villanova Center for Information Law and Policy makes it easy to find the one you want—or just browse through to see your tax dollars at work—with the Federal Web Locator. Major headings include the federal legislature, NASA, Department of Defense, Department of Justice, and Executive Branch. The folks as Villanova want to make this a one-stop Federal links page, and invite people to let them know of sites not listed. Those that help out are listed on the Friends of Villanova CIL page. —(L.S.)

KEY NEWSGROUP bit.listserv.govdoc-l URL▶ http://www.law.vill.edu/fed-agency/fedwebloc.html

Starting Point for Starting Points

Navigation Tools Jump 2449

One of the better, if not the best, pages of starter links to finding things on the Internet, Nikos Markovits's Navigation Tools makes it easy for you to begin general or specific quests. He's found the higher-quality searching and catalog resources, and describes each one to help you decide which are the best ones for your current needs. The page starts off with the best of the What's New pages, then goes on to list sites for general resources, mailing lists, and search engines. This is not one of those Web-notorious "metalists," with very long pages of link after link—this is an easy to manage, easy to navigate page of resources that's especially good for newcomers or anyone who wants to add focus to their Web surfing. —(L.S.)

KEY NEWSGROUP comp.infosystems.www.users URL▸ http://www.algonet.se/~nikos/navigate.html

Customize Your What's New Search

What's New Too! Jump 2460

Most what's new lists on the Web just give you one long set of links to browse. What's New Too! gives you that, but also lets you customize your browsing. Just choose the categories that interest you, and What's New Too! will show you only the new sites that fit. The customized search covers any combination of 12 different categories, and you can search that day's additions, or go as far back as three days. However you configure it, you can save your personal setup as a bookmark in your own Web browser, so you need only make your choices once. —(L.S.)

URL▸ http://newtoo.manifest.com/WhatsNewToo/index.html

Random Web Links Give You the Illusion of Control

Dave's Site Chock Full O'Random Links Jump 2490

Random link sites usually take you where they want, with little consideration for the feeling of helplessness they force upon you. Dave Maher takes the random link concept, and with an eye toward the control freak in all of us, lets you decide which random link to follow. How? The page is full of colored buttons. Choose one based on your mood, a desire to systematically move from color to color, or pretend it's a Ouija board and let your mouse go where it may. If you want, you can even add a link, and pick a button color for it while you're there. —(L.S.)

URL▸ http://www.bucknell.edu/~dmaher/links/

U.S. Government Web Sites Directory

FedWorld Home Page Jump 3515

One of the greatest—and most annoying—things about the Web is its inherent lack of structure. It's totally non-linear, letting you go wherever the mood strikes. But what do you do when you need something specific and you don't have a week-and-a-half to browse from link to link in search of the Holy Grail? Well, if you're looking for specific government information, this Web site is the only place to begin. Every government server is listed here, complete with links, and they're all organized into alphabetical subject areas that begin with Administration and end with Urban Technology. —(C.P.)

URL▸ http://www.fedworld.gov/index.html#usgovt

Carnegie Mellon/Fuzine Big Hotlist

Fuzzie's Most Recent Hotlist Jump 0072

A big, scrollable hotlist compiled by Fuzine, the Carnegie Mellon Web site features links to many other interesting and unusual Web sites. The folks at Carnegie Mellon also developed Lycos, the excellent, popular, and powerful Web searcher. —(E.G.)

URL▸ http://networth.galt.com/www/home/welcome/

The World Wide Web Wanderer

A Ton of Web Sites Jump 0004 

A collection of nearly 5,000 individual Web sites, compiled by Matthew Gray of MIT. Contains links to Web sites, including domains, which are the general Internet classifications for Web Site locations around the world. The highlight of this site is its massive single list of almost 5,000 Web page links, which you can download and save in your own Web browser (such as Netscape) for ready reference. The Wanderer also has a basic, qualitative keyword search capability that produces "best," "good," and "OK" matches for your keyword search. —(E.G.)

URL▶ http://www.mit.edu:8001/afs/sipb/user/mkgray/ht/comprehensive.html

Giant Catalog of Internet Resources

CMC Information Sources Jump 0012 

If you're looking for a useful way to explore all of the Internet (and not just Web sites) this is the place to begin! John December has compiled this comprehensive selection of the best of the Internet to give you a stunningly broad sampling of the vast array of information and communications resources available. John's jump page gives you one-click access to many of the best Internet resources written and developed by many of the Internet's "old hands." These include many informative Internet tutorial files for first-time Net users, an extensive selection of text files, reports, and directories for those of you interested in doing business on the Internet and links to the Internet's oldest and best repositories of text files, graphics, and multimedia resources. We suggest you download John's "Whole list in one file" and save it in your bookmarks file, print it out and use it for ready reference to many of the Internet's best and most useful information resources. —(E.G.)

URL▶ http://www.rpi.edu/Internet/Guides/decemj/icmc/toc2.html

Announcements of New Web Sites

Web News Jump 0025 

A mind-blowing Web resource that should be tops on your list of Web browsing tools, Web News, developed by the Department of Computer and Information Sciences at The University of Alabama at Birmingham, is a one-stop compilation of all announcements of newly created Web sites that have been posted to Internet newsgroups by Web site developers, and cover the entire range of new sites on the Web. This huge, searchable index can provide you with hours of Web browsing fun, since the URLs listed in each message have also been hot-linked to each announced site, so you can jump to them right from here. Web News is at the top of our Web searching hotlist and should be at the top of yours, too. —(E.G.)

KEY NEWSGROUP **news.announce.newgroups** URL▶ http://twinbrook.cis.uab.edu:70/webNews.80

Search Web Sites by Category

Web of Wonder Jump 0038 

Those of us right-brained (creative) people like to skim the Web by jumping from link to link, while those of you left-brained (analytical) folks like to do your Web searching in a more organized, methodical way. For you left brainers, we submit this handy hierarchical Web site featuring links to over 8,000 other Web sites, organized in a menu-based, subject-oriented fashion. Lance Weitzel and WCI have done a nice job organizing all these Web pages in a clean, simple, straightforward menu structure to help you point and shoot to the sites you need by scrolling down a subject menu. Even us right-brainers confess we've put Web of Wonder at the top of our bookmark screen! —(E.G.)

KEY NEWSGROUP **news.newusers.questions** URL▶ http://www.digimark.net/wow/

Something for Everyone

The Eclectics' Homepage Jump 5082 

Something for everyone—especially readers, writers, and anyone with eclectic interests. This page has many good jumping-off points, including general search tools, writing resources, tax help, and plenty of areas that are just for fun. It has more info and links to more great sites than maybe any other that we've seen. It's kind of like the well-known Yahoo Web menu site, but better looking, in this reviewer's opinion —(S.B.)

URL▶ http://ids.net/~rsinclair/home.html

Finding Web Sites

AltaVista: Digital's Super Searcher for the Web

Alta Vista: Main Page Jump 8025

If you need to look something up on the Internet, you'll have to use one of the Internet's "search engines," maintained by a number of companies (such as Lycos, InfoSeek, etc.) to find the information you're looking for. In our opinion, Digital's AltaVista is the Internet's best search engine. Fast, powerful, and accurate, AltaVista is best at letting you search the entire Internet by a key word or phrase, giving you access to over 11 billion words found in nearly 22 million Web pages, along with a full-text index of over 13,000 newsgroups. Created as a showcase for Digital's super-fast Alpha microprocessor computers and software, AltaVista often runs your searches so fast it feels like you're the only one using it—and that's never true, since it's one of the Web's most popular sites. It's easy to use, and the information AltaVista retrieves for you is right on target. —(E.v.B.)

KEY NEWSGROUP comp.infosystems.www.users URL▸ http://www.altavista.digital.com/

ClNet's Top Search Site

SEARCH.COM Jump 5727

Perhaps it's unfair to call this an all-in-one search stop. After all, many so-called "all-in-one search sites" are little more than a collection of a few search engines readily available just about anywhere. But SEARCH.COM is different, in a big way. In fact we would go so far as to say that if you were stuck on a desert island (humor us) with only one Web site (and a laptop computer, a browser, a phone line and a modem, no less!), this would be the site many of us would pick. Not only does SEARCH.COM bring together the best of the search engines, but it throws in a few nice surprises, like letting you search for phone numbers, movies, stock quotes, weather reports, sports results, jobs and even the latest TV listings. And that doesn't even include their remarkable A-Z List, a collection of links to just about everything else in the known Web universe! —(J.P.)

URL▸ http://www.search.com/

HotBot Search Engine

HotBot Jump 5737

HotBot is one of the latest in the battle of the Web search engines. A joint project of HotWired (the online sibling of *Wired* Magazine) and Inktomi ("ink to me"), HotBot claims to be the first search engine to "index and search the entire World Wide Web" in such a way that its technology will expand to match the Web's growth as it doubles and doubles again. Time will tell about the last claim, of course, but in the meantime the results are pretty impressive. The interface is clean and the results are presented in a list of ten, with the highest matches presented at the top. Be sure to check out HotBot's help section to find out how to create and save your own custom search settings. —(J.P.)

URL▸ http://www.hotbot.com/index.html

Infoseek Ultra Search Engine

Infoseek Ultra Jump 6887

What's so different about this search engine? For starters, it produces better search results on the newest sites launched on the Web. No more waiting days to search for the latest sites pertaining to a breaking news story, or those sites you know to be online. Second, it produces very accurate results at some of the fastest speeds we've seen since AltaVista's early days. Most importantly, the results are all live sites. Infoseek Ultra also regularly weeds out millions of dead and duplicate links to save you from going to these "dead links." —(L.T.)

URL▸ http://ultra.infoseek.com/

Lycos Search Engine

The Lycos Home Page: Hunting WWW Information 
Jump 0001

If you need to find something—anything—on the Web, Lycos should be one of your first stops on the Web. This awesome Web site (named after "Lycosidae," a family of large active ground spiders that catch their prey by pursuit, rather than in a web), performs a scan of every one of the almost two million (and counting) Web sites on the Internet. Lycos then indexes and abstracts the results of its searches, allowing you to locate Web sites by typing a subject key word. There are several other Web searchers out there, but Lycos consistently brings the greatest number of hits on any keyword you select; usually double the number of hits of any other Web search utility. Type the subject term you're looking for on the Web, and Lycos will return a list of up to 999 hits, including Web page titles, content summaries, and, of course, URLs, so you can easily jump to the sites that interest you. Our Lycos searches for "Beatles" turned up 266 hits across dozens of Beatles-related Web sites; a search for sites containing the word "investment" turned up 1,132 hits! But what makes Lycos the best Web searcher to date is not just quantity alone—it also presents you with short excerpts of each Web site's content, allowing you to make an intelligent judgment on the appropriateness of a found Web site before you jump to it. And since they're making continuous improvements to Lycos, we expect that Lycos will continue to be one of your best bets for scanning the Web (next to our Web site JumpCity, of course!). A gentle warning: Lycos searching can be addictive and time consuming! We spent many fascinating hours jumping to many different Web sites during our use of Lycos for this book...maybe we should start a "Lycoholics Anonymous" support group! —(E.G.)

URL ▸ http://lycos.com/

Internet Search Gateway

BARD—Bodleian Access to Remote Databases 
Jump 2411

This is a very handy bookmark for the inveterate Web searcher or surfer. Maintained by Bodleian Library in the United Kingdom, it lets you easily link to databases at thousands of sites around the world. It has an excellent gateway to library resources, and also offers general "meta-lists" with gateways and search engines for the Web, Gopher, WAIS databases, Usenet newsgroups, and FTP sites. Basic help for each function is quickly accessible, and there's an extended help page that will tell you everything there is to know about how to reach all that's available through this site. —(L.S.)

URL ▸ http://www.rsl.ox.ac.uk/bardhtml/bardmenu.html

Library Search Page

Library Catalogs with Web Interfaces Jump 2329 

Keeping bookmarks for Web-based online versions of academic, corporate, and public libraries you visit often on the Net is a good idea. But no single library will have everything you'll need, and bookmarking all the virtual libraries is cumbersome. Hunter Monroe makes even thinking about it unnecessary with this page of links to libraries with Web-capable search interfaces. The best for general searching are the ones with the Z39.50 interface, since they search multiple libraries. —(L.S.)

KEY NEWSGROUP bit.listserv.circplus URL ▸ http://www.lib.ncsu.edu/staff/morgan/alcuin/wwwed-catalogs.html

Search the Internet in One Stroke

All-in-One Search Page Jump 3701 CONTENT

How do you find what you're looking for on the Web? We all have our favorite search methods, but doesn't it seem that sometimes we just can't find what we're looking for? Now you can try All-in-One. All-in-One combines the best of the best search engines on the Web, such as Lycos, Infoseek, Jump City (that's us!), Yahoo, and others, and puts them all in one convenient place, with a consistent "look and feel" (which translates into EASY searching and retrieval). And if you're looking for something a little more specialized, try one of the other search routines listed here. You can search under various categories like People, News and Weather, Publications, Documentation.

You can also look for downloadable free software. Search for publications, books, CDs . . . the lists go on and on! You can even link to the Federal Express and UPS sites to track a package you've sent. Never come up empty-handed again! —(N.F.)

URL▶ http://www.albany.net/~wcross/all1srch.html

Oliver McBryan's "World Wide Web Worm"

WWWW - The World Wide Web Worm Jump 0003

A Web searcher developed the University of Colorado's Oliver McBryan, "The Worm" scans the Web, compiling a database of over 300,000 different Web site items. WWWW allows the most flexible key word searching of all Web search sites, letting you search for Web sites by their location, file type, or key word. Using The Worm, for example, you can find all the Web home pages about colleges or universities, home pages from specific countries, or graphics and video files. With all this flexibility, it's no wonder that The Worm is one of the Web's most popular search sites, and should be on your bookmark list, too! —(E.G.)

URL▶ http://www.cs.colorado.edu/home/mcbryan/WWWW.html

Newsgroups: Searchable Archive

Internet Business Directory Jump 2428

The two great things about Usenet newsgroups is the broad range of topics discussed and, flamers and kooks aside, the wealth of information available from other Netters. The downside is the more you take advantage of Usenet, the longer it takes to read through the postings, until it seems you're doing little else. The publishers of the Internet Business Directory offer a solution with this searchable database of the day's newsgroup postings. Just enter your search query and the engine looks through your news server for matches. The return not only indicates exact matches, but also lesser matches coded by how close they are to exact. IBD also gives you a three-day backlog of HTML-ized newsgroup postings that you can browse, although not as many groups are covered. As long as you're at this site, you might want to browse the Internet Business Directory itself, a catalog of business home pages, and an online resume database, too. —(L.S.)

KEY NEWSGROUP **news.misc** URL▶ http://ibd.ar.com/

Find a Web Friend

Who's Who on the Internet Jump 7202

Kirk Bowe likes us all to keep in touch. Accordingly, he has compiled an immense listing of home pages on the Web that you can search. Trying to find an old friend, make a new one, or trying to find the home pages of eminent personalities? This is the place to go. You can also browse, from this page, other directories of "who's who"-style Web sites —(E.v.B.)

KEY NEWSGROUP **alt.culture.internet** URL▶ http://web.city.ac.uk/citylive/pages.html

Internet & Web Resources

Free Electronic Mail!

Juno - Free Internet E-Mail Service Jump 5736

Here's a site that will appeal to anyone who would like a reliable electronic mail address but doesn't want to spend money on all the frills. Juno offers a free e-mail address to anyone. Free as in no cost to you. How do they do it? They rely on revenues derived largely from selectively targeted advertising, interactive online market research, and billable services. In other words, when you sign on to read your mail you'll have to see either a banner ad (graphics or text at the top of the screen) or what they call "showcase advertising" (which appears while your e-mail is being loaded). There is special software available on-site (also free) and instructions on how to set apply for an account. Download the software and you're all set. —(J.P.)

URL▶ http://www.juno.com

Searching the Net, on the Run

All-Internet Shopping Directory: Find It Fast! Page Jump 1549

This site helps you search for all kinds of Net and Web resources: newsgroups, discussion groups, cool Web sites, "all the gopher servers in the world," commercial and computer-related pages, and a virtual library of research information. Site creator Tom Brown outdid himself here by putting together this amazing collection of links to almost everything you'll ever need. Click on Cool Sites, then sit back and relax while taking his Auto-Pilot tour of all the auto dealers with Web pages. If, surprisingly, you can't find what you're looking for here, by all means, activate the search function. You can even add your own business's Web site here. —(H.L.)

URL ▶ http://www.webcom.com/~tbrown/findpage.html

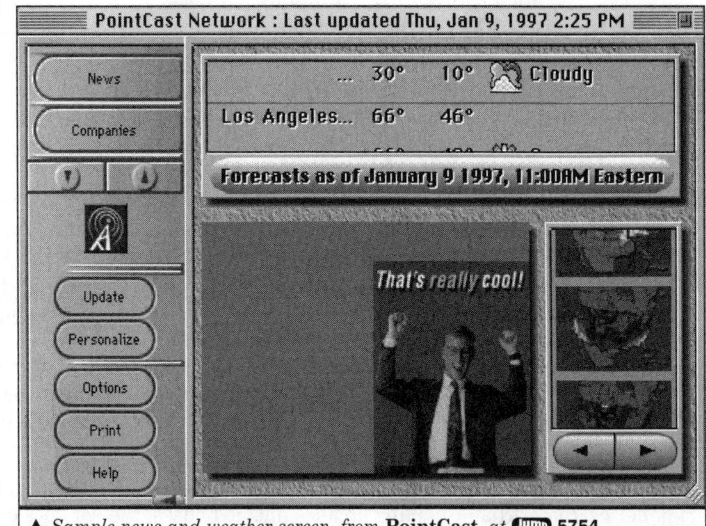

▲ *Sample news and weather screen, from* **PointCast**, *at* Jump 5754.

PointCast

PointCast Jump 5754

Of all the innovations introduced on the Web of late, few have captured the market's attention (and its imagination) as completely as PointCast, the most well-known in a new line of "Web broadcasting" products that deliver Web pages or information directly to your desktop. In order to use PointCast, you have to first download its special software (which is free), but once that's done you can configure it to deliver whatever kind of news and information you want to see, instead of hunting around for it all over the Web. And you do see it; is scrolls across the top of you computer screen—news of the world, sports scores, stock info, pretty much whatever you want. One of the Web's hottest new ideas, and quite possibly an advance view of the future look of the Internet.—(J.P.)

URL ▶ http://pioneer.pointcast.com/index.html#1

internet @ddress.finder

Finding E-Mail Addresses

Internet Address Finder 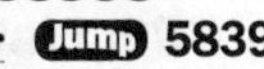 5839

Can over 5 million people be wrong? Perhaps not. The Internet Address Finder, another Web directory service, claims to have 5,507,311 listings available in its online e-mail and address database. Once you register (for free), you can use their search engine to tap into this massive list. And they suggest you add your own information as well. In that way you'll help them create an ever bigger database—and make yourself more accessible to long-lost friends and relatives, too. —(J.P.)

KEY NEWSGROUP comp.mail.misc URL ▶ http://www.iaf.net/

The Web's Monster Phone Directory

Switchboard Jump 6728

Take every telephone directory in the United States, glue them all together, put them all on the Internet and make the whole thing searchable in a heartbeat, and you've found Switchboard, the Web's huge, free directory service. listing over ninety million names, telephone numbers and addresses, Switchboard proves that bigger is indeed better, and practically guarantees you'll find any listed individual in seconds. This handy tool even lets you search through ten million-plus U.S. businesses. —(L.T.)

URL ▶ http://www.switchboard.com/

The Definitive FTP Link for the Net

FTP Interface Jump 2018

Bookmark this page and you'll have a quick interface to virtually every software archive of note on the Internet. It's a nice companion for readers of **comp.archives**, the newsgroup that announces additions to FTP sites. When you see a file you want, just load your Web browser, call this page, find the site, and go for it. It's not an archive browser, so if you want a specific file, you need know it's in an archive, or find which archive has it with Archie. —(L.S.)

KEY NEWSGROUP **comp.archives** URL▶ http://hoohoo.ncsa.uiuc.edu/ftp-interface.html

Virtual Town Helps You Handle the Web

Cybertown Home Page Jump 3726

Links pages take us from the Web site we're currently visiting to another entirely separate site. Sometimes a links page may be jazzed up with cute graphics and colors, but oftentimes they're simply lists of text. Cybertown blows the traditional links page design right out of the water. It's a sprawling, dazzling, colorful map of a town, with a 21st Century flavor. The purpose? A one-stop shop to help us navigate around the Web—a links page, in its own right, but so much more. Click on the Education center, and from there, jump to numerous educational sites. Visit the Reference Library, where you'll find links to Internet tools, dictionaries, over 30 different sites in all. Town Hall links you to tons of government, legal and political stops. Clicking on the Entertainment "building" brings you to art galleries, concert halls, gaming arcades, movie houses, the list goes on. Visit Cyberhood, with its Vox Populi section, where user contributions of music, writing, and art are available. Take up residence in one of the Apartments in the Colonies (the rent's free) and people can visit you by linking to your home page. —(N.F.)

URL▶ http://www.directnet.com/cybertown/

UGC™

Find a Computer User Group

User Group Connection Jump 6509

User groups are people who are bound together for the specific purpose of helping each other use their computers. There are thousands of user groups around the U.S. (and the world) and finding the right one can be a chore, until now. That's what The User Group Connection does, allowing you to search their complete database by locale, zip code, state or computer type, including Macintosh, PC/Windows/DOS, OS/2, and Internet systems, to find the closest computer user group in your area. Keeping in mind that most user groups charge a yearly membership fee of $10-$45, the return on such an investment includes monthly meetings where technical questions are answered, experienced users help novices get started, and new computer products are demonstrated. Most groups also publish newsletters with notices, news, reviews, and advice. If you're seeking computer advice with a human touch, stop on by and find a group waiting to meet you. —(L.T.)

KEY NEWSGROUP **comp.answers** URL▶ http://www.ugconnection.org/

Massive BBS Lists & Links

Everclear's Useful BBS-List Jump 0174

Dan Vishnesky's massive list of Bulletin Board Systems (BBSs) for a mind-boggling variety of special interests. What Dan's list lacks in style, it certainly makes up in substance, and it provides you with hours of interesting Net fun, as you can also link to many of these wild and woolly BBSs over the Net. —(E.G.)

KEY NEWSGROUP **alt.bbs.lists** URL▶ http://www.dsv.su.se/~mats-bjo/bbslist.html

Learn Net Lingo

net lingo - The Internet Language Dictionary Jump 6877

If Webster's were to create a dictionary of Net slang, this is probably what it would look like. Here you can look up the hidden meanings of words you'll undoubtedly see all over the Net, like "smiley," and "bandwidth." This handy dictionary will answer all of your Internet jargon needs. And you're welcome to participate in this site's Net Linguistics online forum, where participants discuss related topics, and help to post and define new terms found online. —(L.T.)

KEY NEWSGROUP **bit.listserv.words-l** URL▶ http://www.netlingo.com/

Cyberspace Dictionary

Cyberspace Dictionary Jump 6785 

Unfortunately, the Internet has more than its share of jargon to confuse and intimidate the new user. Fortunately, once you learn the 20 or 30 buzzwords everyone else uses—like "browser," "SLIP connection," or "hotlink"—you'll start sounding like an old Net hand yourself. Designed mainly for the computer novice, this hypertext dictionary provides easy-to-understand definitions for commonly-used computer-related and Internet terms. Wondering what BRB stands for, or what encryption is? These and many other commonly-used words are defined here. This site also includes relevant links within the definitions for further Web exploration. —(L.T.)

KEY NEWSGROUP **alt.answers** URL▶ http://www.edmweb.com/steve/cyberdict.html

Real-Time Chats on the Internet

Internet Relay Chat Information Jump 0175 

Your best Web link to the fascinating world of Internet Relay Chat (IRC), where you can participate in live keyboard discussions on a wide variety of subjects with other Internet users around the world. This comprehensive Web links page; compiled by "Red Rum," and features solid information for IRC beginners, technical setup information, links to other IRC Web sites, IRC conferences listings, and conferencing tips for this new use of the Net! —(E.G.)

KEY NEWSGROUP **alt.irc** URL▶ http://www2.undernet.org:8080/~cs93jtl/IRC.html

Web Development Services

Yahoo Internet Presence Providers: Web Consultants Jump 2610 

There are other listings of World Wide Web consultants, but none as comprehensive as Yahoo's. Besides, if you want help creating your own Web presence, do you really want to hire someone who doesn't know how to get listed on the Web's most popular links site? Granted, the company descriptions here aren't as full as some other sites, but since no site actually reviews Web development services, anything you read anywhere has been written by the company itself. The descriptions will help you narrow your selections, but you still need to visit the developer's site to see for yourself whether reality matches puffery. —(L.S.)

KEY NEWSGROUP **alt.internet.services**
URL▶ http://www.yahoo.com/Business/Corporations/Internet_Presence_Providers/Consulting/

Guidelines for Children Using the Internet

Child Safety on the Information Superhighway Jump 2647 

The talk of Net-based pornography and child stalking is overblown with misinformation and frightening stories that are, in most cases, more apocryphal than real. But this doesn't mean there aren't potential dangers for children online, or material parents would rather their children not access. There are, and responsible parents looking for hints and tips as to how to guide their children toward safe, responsible use of the Internet and online services should visit this site. Created by computer writer Lawrence Magid, this online brochure offers calm, common-sense information about the nature and benefits of the Internet, putting the issues and risks in perspective. You'll also find straightforward rules and guidelines for parents to follow when introducing their children to the online world. —(L.S.)

KEY NEWSGROUP **misc.kids.computer** URL▶ http://www.4j.lane.edu/InternetResources/Safety/Safety.html

Internet Software to Block Sexual Material

SurfWatch Home Page Jump 2670 

Demo Web site for SurfWatch, commercial software for Windows and Macintosh computers which is claimed to prevent access to sexually explicit material on the Internet, whether it comes from the Web, FTP, newsgroups, Gopher or chat. It uses a database of Internet site addresses that contain forbidden material that can be updated by subscription to their service, and also includes a facility for blocking out sites that contain obscenities in their titles. —(L.S.)

KEY NEWSGROUP **misc.kids** URL▶ http://www.surfwatch.com/surfwatch/demo.html

Helping to Keep the Net Safe for Kids

SafeSurf Home Page Jump 2666

SafeSurf is an organization that promotes self-regulation, rather than censorship, of the Internet, to help make the Net safe for children. Its major effort toward encouraging self-regulation is asking authors to identify pages without adult themes with a special code, while encouraging browser developers to design their software to look for the code. In addition, they offer tips for parents on how they can protect their children from exposure to unsuitable material and a list of links to Web pages devoted to children's education and entertainment. —(L.S.)

KEY NEWSGROUP **misc.kids** URL▸ http://www.safesurf.com/wave/

Internet Monitor for Kids

Net Nanny (Trove Investment Corporation) Jump 2671

Net Nanny is software that will prevent children from accessing material parents don't want them to see. Unlike some similar software, Net Nanny's monitoring is based on a user-defined dictionary, so you can specify specific words and phrases that you want to trigger the blocking. In addition, the developers say the product functions for material sent from your computer as well, so you can include your credit card number, for example, to prevent your children from buying things online. It also works on any file or software, so you can prevent the loading of violent or sexually explicit CD-ROMs, for example, or access to personal files you'd rather your children not see. —(L.S.)

KEY NEWSGROUP **misc.kids** URL▸ http://www.netnanny.com/netnanny/nnfaq.html

Internet Help for Women

Women's Web InfoNet Jump 2677

Although it's geared specifically to women, this is a page for anyone new to the Internet. There are getting-started tutorials and software reviews, and a page where visitors can ask technical questions and receive answers via e-mail. There's also a daily newsletter highlighting women's news, and links to Web sites about and by women. It's hardly comprehensive, but it's not supposed to be. It provides enough information, and a bit more, to get you started without overwhelming you, along with pointers you can follow when you're ready. —(L.S.)

KEY NEWSGROUP **soc.women** URL▸ http://cyber-active.com/wwin/

Internet Content Filter

CYBERSitter Jump 2683

Solid Oak says its CYBERSitter software provides full Internet filtering of objectionable Net material from children, including the Web, newsgroups and even e-mail. It can also be configured to prevent children from transmitting your address and telephone number. The software includes a file that determines what material is to be blocked, and free updates are available by using the built-in FTP client. In addition, parents can create custom definitions for additional filtering and blocking. —(L.S.)

KEY NEWSGROUP **misc.kids** URL▸ http://www.rain.org/~solidoak/cybersit.htm

Net Blocking Software for Children

Cyber Patrol Jump 7346

At this site, Microsystems Software, Inc. offers a demo version of their new software title, Cyber Patrol. Cyber Patrol, an Internet access management utility, helps parents and teachers control children's access to the Internet. Among many features, Cyber Patrol can be used to restrict access to certain times of day, limit the total time spent online per day and per week, and block access to specific Internet resources and sites by content. This site also offers links to related Internet resources of interest to teachers, parents, and children. —(E.v.B.)

KEY NEWSGROUP **comp.infosystems** URL▸ http://www.microsys.com/CYBER/

Blocking Your Child's Access to Adult Material on the Net

WebTrack(tm) from Webster - Controlling and Tracking the Web Jump 7347 

Information on WebTrack, Internet control and monitoring software, is offered at this site. Business owners or parents can use it to block access to certain sites though WebTrack's extensive database of sites and URLs. The software also helps monitor what sites your employees or children log onto, and offers summary statistical reports of Internet access activity, and exports the data to PC-based spreadsheet programs such as Microsoft Excel. You can download a free demo program at this site and see what you think. —(E.v.B.)

KEY NEWSGROUP **alt.answers** URL▶ http://www.webster.com/

Users Helping Users on the Web

Ask Dr. Internet Index Jump 3706 CONTENT

This index was created by a consortium of veteran Internet volunteers who donate their time helping others understand and use the Internet. Structured in a question-and-answer format, each issue of the "Ask Dr. Internet" index is easy to read, and covers a wide variety of Net topics. There's a good list of links to further your understanding, too. If you don't see your particular issue covered, drop them a note by e-mail and they'll respond. Put this one on your Web browser's bookmark list (the Doctor will tell you how!). —(N.F.)

URL▶ http://promo.net/gut/

Hear the Internet with RealAudio

RealAudio Homepage Jump 7273 

RealAudio is a hot new Internet technology that providers of news and entertainment can use to make their sounds available through the Internet, on a real-time basis, without download delays. RealAudio makes it super-easy to download the RealAudio Player and hear for yourself the possibilities of broadcasting over the Internet in real time. The sound quality is somewhat less than that of an AM radio, but the possibilities for the Net are tremendous: radio features, news and commentaries, music samples, audio dialogues, sound clips and more, all available when you want them. You can also download the encoder and create your own audio files with RealAudio. The RealAudio pages also contain some neat files to listen to. Check this site often for news of upgrades and progress on this exciting new Web development. —(E.v.B.)

KEY NEWSGROUP **rec.audio.tech** URL▶ http://www.realaudio.com/

Excellent Net Tutorial Links for New Users

Imajika's Guide For New Users Jump 7288 

Imajika is a good Net citizen. She has collected various Web links to useful sites for newcomers to the Internet. More important, she has organized them according to subject—e-mail, FTP, Usenet, IRC, you name it, she's found it. Tutorials abound. Imajika gently advises Net newbies that: "A little reading now will save you from a lifetime of flames later on!" —(E.v.B.)

KEY NEWSGROUP **alt.answers** URL▶ http://www.sir.com/sir/www/be/

Easy Help for Total Net Novices

FutureNet : .net 1, Dec '94 - Easy Internet - Introduction Jump 7343 

Lost your way on the Info Highway? Maybe it's because you just can't find the right exit ramp. Well, new Net drivers one and all, take heart! Davey Winder extends a helping hand, supported by the British FutureNet magazine. He explains what the Internet is and how it works. More importantly, he patiently explains how you can connect and what you can then use the Net for. Feeling more confident? Then surf on over and read the online editions of FutureNet, before you head out into new territory. A polished, well-written introduction for first-time Net users. —(E.v.B.)

KEY NEWSGROUP **alt.answers** URL▶ http://www.futurenet.co.uk/netmag/Issue1/Easy/index.html

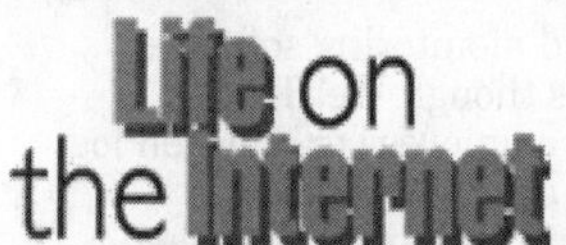

The Complete Internet for Novices

Life on the Internet Jump **7344**

Life on the Internet is designed as the online companion to the television shows shown on the Canadian Discovery cable channel. You can read articles on the hot Net-related program topics of the week, and then surf to links related to the topics. As well, you can participate in the discussion forums, follow links to download Internet software, read helpful guides to navigating the electronic highway, and explore over 200 links to the best sites on the Web. —(E.v.B.)

KEY NEWSGROUP **alt.answers** URL▶ http://www.screen.com/understand/start.nclk

Find an Internet Provider

THE LIST Jump **7460**

Mecklermedia, a publisher of many Internet-related publications and a sponsor of Net and Web trade shows, presents a heck of a site. It lists nearly 1,600 Internet service providers worldwide. You can search for a provider by name, by region, by telephone area code, by country, by state, even by country telephone code. So, no more excuses—you can find a provider near you who will put you on the Net. —(E.v.B.)

KEY NEWSGROUP **alt.internet.services** URL▶ http://www.thelist.com/

Newsgroup Searching Fast & Easy

DejaNews Research Service Jump **2650**

Usenet newsgroups are a great resource, but it can be tedious wading through the hundreds of postings many groups get to find the gems that make the effort worthwhile. DejaNews does it for you, with Web-based forms that make searching for the topics you want quick and easy. The **alt.***, **soc.***, **talk.***, and ***.binaries** groups aren't included, unfortunately, but that doesn't make it any less useful for the thousands of groups that are. And it's a free service, too! —(L.S.)

KEY NEWSGROUP **news.misc** URL▶ http://www.dejanews.com/

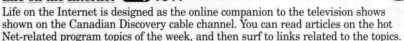

Find Those Net E-Mail Lists Fast

The ListServer Page Jump **2652**

Ever hear about a really interesting e-mail list, but can't remember where you put the subscription info? Or did that great-sounding list turn into a waste of time, and you forgot to save the "unsubscribe" instructions? Your answer is here, thanks to Cleandro Viana. More than 650 lists are registered with this site, and more are added all the time. If you know the name of the list, a few clicks will take you to the information you need. If you don't, you can search the list descriptions, and get all the ones registered that match. From there, well-designed and easy-to-use forms let you subscribe or unsubscribe, as you wish, as well as issue other standard listserv commands. Registering new lists is just as easy, and if you're a list manager looking for new subscribers, this is one place you shouldn't miss. —(L.S.)

KEY NEWSGROUP **bit.listserv.new-list** URL▶ http://www.cuc.edu/cgi-bin/listservform.pl

Mega E-Mail Directory

How to find people's e-mail addresses Jump **7291**

Masha Boitchouk likes to stay in touch! She has compiled an incredibly useful set of information and links to make it easy to track down a long-lost friend, a favorite professor, or an army buddy. As long as they're wired, they probably can be found by following Masha's logically clear instructions, and then by using her comprehensive list of search engines, directories, and other white pages from networks, freenets, and businesses. —(E.v.B.)

KEY NEWSGROUP **comp.mail.misc** URL▶ http://sunsite.oit.unc.edu/~masha/

Where Is That Net Mailing List?

Liszt: Searchable Directory of e-Mail Discussion Groups Jump 7328 CONTENT

Wow! What a great program. Using Liszt's easy-to-navigate search program, you can locate an e-mail discussion group out of its directory of 23,190 Listserv, Listproc, Majordomo, and independently managed mailing lists representing ongoing discussions on a virtually infinite range of topics. All you have to do is type in a keyword descriptive of the group you're searching for, and before you can say "holy cyberspace," Liszt finds a group related to your search term. —(E.v.B.)

KEY NEWSGROUP **news.groups** URL▶ http://www.liszt.com/

SIFT Netnews Server

Newsgroup Information Filtering Service

Stanford Net News Filtering Service Jump 0114 

An experimental service from the Electronic Library project at Stanford University in California, the SIFT Net News server lets you submit a list of search key words (like "travel" or "Hawaii") and then e-mails you its selections of Usenet newsgroup messages where these keywords have been found. It's a wonderful idea and a great timesaver too—like having a research assistant scanning the Internet to filter out and select only the information that's important to you! These kinds of services, called information agents, will one day become everyday tools for using the Net. Here's your chance to sample these powerful information retrieval tools today. —(E.G.)

URL▶ http://woodstock.stanford.edu:2000/

Internet Mailing Lists Web Site

Publically Accessible Mailing Lists Jump 0176 

The Net's best and most comprehensive directory of electronic mailing lists, compiled by dedicated Net list maven, Stephanie da Silva. There are thousands of mailing lists on the Internet covering a wide variety of subjects, featuring electronic mail messages and discussions contributed by their online subscribers. When you join a mailing list, you receive a periodic electronic mail message containing a string of smaller e-mail messages which make up the content of that list for that time period. Mailing lists are usually run and sponsored by "moderators," who select the messages to be included in each mailing list issue. As to content, mailing lists are similar in subject coverage to the Net's Usenet newsgroups and provide you with yet another way to engage in online dialogues on virtually any subject that's of interest to you. Stephanie's Web page is nicely organized by mailing list name and subject and she gives full instructions for "subscribing" to each mailing list. A valuable Net service and fascinating range of Net content for you to explore. Highly recommended! —(E.G.)

KEY NEWSGROUP **news.lists** URL▶ http://www.NeoSoft.com:80/internet/paml/

News, News, News

Newsgroups Available in Oxford Jump 2182 

Not all news servers carry all newsgroups. Particularly in the United States, many servers refuse to handle some newsgroups because of concerns about copyright and pornography. If you're looking for groups not handled by your server, instead of posting a "where can I find" message, Web over to Oxford University's Libraries Automation Service server. Not only will you find most of the groups not carried elsewhere, but you'll get short descriptions of most of them, taking a lot of the hit-and-miss out of newsgroup selection. —(L.S.)

KEY NEWSGROUP **news.groups** URL▶ http://www.lib.ox.ac.uk/internet/news/

Newsgroup Access Via the Web

Forum News Gateway Jump 2235 

The current releases of the more popular Web browsers let you read and post to newsgroups. They're just simple newsreaders, though. They don't let you utilize the features of Hypertext Markup Language as part of the process. This gateway, written by The Geometry Forum, overcomes these limitations. In addition to giving you all the benefits of a standard news server, this software lets you post and read articles as HTML files, so graphics and hypertext links can be included. The gateway here will let you try this new level of newsreading with a few select groups. Unfortunately, if you want to be able to read all newsgroups, you'll have to find another server, or convince your access provider to install it. —(L.S.)

KEY NEWSGROUP news.software.readers URL▶ http://forum.swarthmore.edu/forum.news.gateway.html

Information Files on Thousands of Subjects: FAQs

Directory of\Pub\USENET Jump **0006**

The easy Web link to thousands of useful Frequently Asked Questions (FAQ) files—well-written and informative text files containing information on everything from archery to Asian movies, travel, politics, history, and much more. FAQ files are an outgrowth of the Internet's Usenet newsgroups (the main focus of this book's sister publication, ***What's on the Internet***) and have been written by helpful Net volunteers to address the basic questions asked by novices to that newsgroup's particular subject. FAQ files contain a wealth of useful information and have been written by those who are quite knowledgeable on the FAQ's subject. The Web now makes it a point-and-click operation to get access to all of these invaluable information files, which are stored on this MIT Web site. A great Web informational site and highly recommended as a help to using many subject-specific Internet newsgroups. —(E.G.)

KEY NEWSGROUP news.answers URL▶ ftp://pit-manager.mit.edu/pub/usenet/

Entering the World-Wide Web: A Guide to Cyberspace

A World Wide Web Primer

Guide to Cyberspace 6.1: Contents

Jump **0136**

CONTENT

Web site designer Kevin Hughes' excellent overview of the World Wide Web for first-time Web users. This excellent Web primer document has all the info a first-time Webster needs to know—Web history, growth, how to find things on the Web, how to find Web software utilities, interesting places on the Web, and more. Includes a neat "hypermedia timeline" covering highlights in the development of the concept of hypermedia dating back to Vannevar Bush in 1945, plus a nice index and glossary. Highly recommended as one of your best orientation stops along the Web! —(E.G.)

KEY NEWSGROUP comp.infosystems.www.users URL▶ http://www.eit.com/web/www.guide/

Info For Web Novices

The World Wide Web for Dummies Jump **0140**

Rei's short and sweet intro to the World Wide Web is an excellent introduction for those of you who don't know the difference between a Web site and Jack Webb (he was the serious, crew-cut guy on the 1950s TV show "Dragnet!"). Rei does a nice job explaining the Web to newbies. —(E.G.)

KEY NEWSGROUP comp.infosystems.www.users URL▶ http://www.mit.edu:8001/people/rei/wwwintro.html

Learning the Rules of Civil Behavior for the Net

I'm NOT Miss Manners of the Internet Jump **2190**

The Internet has no real rules, but there are customs and courtesies that many newcomers are not aware of. Newbies can avoid a lot of frustration and hate mail if they take the few minutes it takes to read this short, yet comprehensive guide to Net manners. Arlene Rinaldi covers everything from e-mail to Telnet, and the Web. There are basic instructions, pointers to where to find information on how a specific service or group functions, and guidelines for being a good Net citizen. It should be required reading for anyone online. —(L.S.)

KEY NEWSGROUP alt.culture.internet URL▶ http://www.fau.edu/faahr/netiquette.html

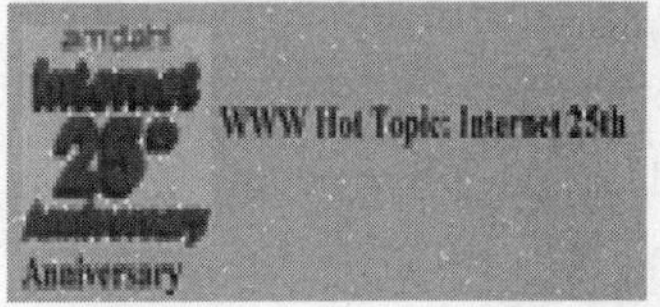

History of the Internet

Hot Topic: Internet 25th Anniversary Jump **2198**

Amdahl created this page in 1994, when the Internet turned 25, and they kindly and wisely keep it available today as a reliable resource of historical information. There's a brief, general article about the beginnings of the Internet, with links to more detailed histories from InterNIC and the Internet Society, and an Internet timeline for a quick overview. You can also learn more about Usenet's (newsgroups) history, the 25th anniversary of the Unix operating system, and the history of information processing in general. It's interesting stuff, and handy to have as a bookmark to settle arguments about ARPANet, the role of the military in the Internet's development, and who really holds all this bandwidth together. —(L.S.)

KEY NEWSGROUP **alt.culture.internet** URL▶ http://www.amdahl.com/internet/events/inet25.html

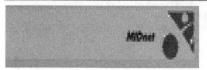

Internet New Features & Announcements

Library of Information Resources Jump **2204**

Keep current with new Internet resources, Webspaces and Gopher servers, general software, newsgroups and mailing lists, and anything else that's new and interesting with this archive maintained by MidNet. It's more than an archive, really—it's a hypertext version of announcement resources that lets you see what's new, and then lets you link directly to it, so you can check it out right now instead of later (that is, if you remember it later!). There are hypertext versions of Gleason Sackman's Net-Happenings announcements, the **comp.infosystems.www.announce** newsgroup, PC and Mac software announcements from **comp.archives** and other lists, and a list of special interest-oriented Net mailing lists. Most of the archives here are also searchable by keywords, so whether you want to learn what's new today, or just need to catch up on a specific area, this is the best place to go. —(L.S.)

KEY NEWSGROUP **comp.infosystems.announce** URL▶ http://www.mid.net:80/MIDNET/resources/

Wish List on the Net

Things I'd Like to See in CyberSpace Jump **2221**

There's plenty to see and do on the Internet, but even the most experienced Net surfers sometimes wipe out. If there's a resource you want, but can't find, add it to John Makulowich's Wish List. As he surfs looking to fulfill his wishes, he'll keep an eye out for yours, too. If he finds it, the link will be posted on this page. All the "reasonable" requests John receives are posted here, too, and if you're looking to challenge your surfing skills, lend a hand in this cyberspatial wish fulfillment service. —(L.S.)

KEY NEWSGROUP **alt.culture.internet** URL▶ http://www.clark.net/pub/journalism/wishes.html

How to Find (Almost) Anyone on the Net

Four11 Home Page Jump **3632**

Ever punch up 411 on your telephone to get Directory Assistance? Well, the Net's own version of Directory Assistance is here in the form of Four11—a free directory service that allows you to search for long-lost friends or other people on the Net by first name, last name, location, and old e-mail address, as well as a number of Group Connection categories, including: current organization, past organization, interests, Net hangouts, consulting services, research topics, etc. You can list yourself in this cool directory and search for other online users—it's free of charge, but you must be listed to be able to search. So if you haven't yet, get thee to Four11 today! —(C.P.)

KEY NEWSGROUP **soc.net-people** URL▶ http://www.four11.com/Sled.html

What's New on the Web: The GNN/NCSA Web Site

NCSA What's New Jump **5006**

NCSA and GNN (Global Network Navigator from O'Reilly & Associates) have joined together to create a list of new Web sites. Ellie Cutler and the GNN staff update this list three times per week. Each entry offers a summary of the Web site and a link to the site's page. You can also view the entries, search the What's New Archives, or submit an entry yourself. —(S.B.)

URL▶ http://www.ncsa.uiuc.edu/SDG/Software/Mosaic/Docs/whats-new.html

MCI's Web Services

welcome.html Jump 7137

NetworkMCI, part of the Internet pioneer MCI Communications Corporation, provides a number of free services to the Netters in addition to its popular commercial offerings of Internet access, software, and electronic mail. You can download free software from video to audio programs, and its directory of services includes comprehensive government lists, newsgroups, links to other online search "engines" such as ClarkNet and Lycos, as well as a beginner's guide to navigating the rapidly growing Internet. —(E.v.B.)

URL▶ http://www.internetMCI.com/welcome.html

PGP: Encrypt Your Net Communications

The World Wide Web Virtual Library: Cryptography Newsgroup Jump 0040

Small Web page with links to important information about Net message encryption, particularly Phil Zimmerman's PGP (Pretty Good Privacy) shareware for Windows, Macs, and UNIX PCs. You might recall that the Net was up in arms not too long ago over attempts by the federal government to make it easier for government agencies to "wiretap" Net communications. With software like PGP, anyone can safely encrypt (i.e., "scramble") their e-mail messages and important business text files they transmit over the Net. At the same time, encrypted messages might just keep your important data away from the snoopy eyes of government bureaucrats, credit bureaus and everyone else—not a bad idea, either. —(E.G.)

KEY NEWSGROUP alt.security.pgp URL▶ http://draco.centerline.com:8080/~franl/crypto.html

Securing E-mail & Data

PGP User's Guide, Volume I: Essential Topics Jump 2068

PGP, or Pretty Good Privacy, is an encryption program for personal computers that protects the e-mail and data you send over the Net. These pages, written by Phil Zimmermann; the author of PGP, can give you more than you need to install and learn to use PGP, and there's a quick overview if you just want the basics. But if you want more, this is one of the best resources for straight information on Internet security in general, and PGP in particular. —(L.S.)

KEY NEWSGROUP alt.security.pgp URL▶ http://www.pegasus.esprit.ec.org/people/arne/pgpdoc1/pgpdoc1.html

Sending E-mail Anonymously

Remailer List Jump 2571

If you ever want to send anonymous e-mail, this is the place to start. Ralph Levien begins the page with a list of available anonymous remailers, including configuration options, special features and uptime statistics for the previous 12 days. It makes a handy resource if you frequently use remailer services. He then offers you André Bacard's anonymous remailer FAQ, an excellent overview of non-technical people, along with FAQs and other information to help you use, or even set up your own, anonymous remailers. —(L.S.)

KEY NEWSGROUP alt.privacy URL▶ http://www.cs.berkeley.edu/~raph/remailer-list.html

Pretty Good Page for Pretty Good Privacy

MIT Distribution Site for PGP Jump 2582

In addition to being a distribution site for Phil Zimmerman's Pretty Good Privacy software, this page will give you everything you need to understand PGP, as well as how to set it up for yourself and begin ensuring the privacy of your e-mail. There are good FAQs, instructions for integrating PGP into mail programs, and links to public keyservers and other sites with more information on PGP and how to use it. —(L.S.)

KEY NEWSGROUP alt.security.pgp URL▶ http://web.mit.edu/network/pgp.html

Your Personal Web Robot

The URL Minder Jump 2768

Once you've been surfing the Web awhile, you'll find your bookmark file has grown to where it can take more time than it's worth just to check each to see if they've changed. With this free service, you can save yourself that time. Just type in the Web addresses you want to track, and when the pages change, you'll get a notice via e-mail. You can even register a search request, such as one you've used with Yahoo or another URL database, and the URL Minder will periodically run that search to see if anything new pops up. And, in addition to Web pages, URL Minder checks anything else accessible with your Web browser, including FTP sites and Gopher servers. —(L.S.)

KEY NEWSGROUP **comp.infosystems.www.misc**

URL ▸ http://www.netmind.com/URL-minder/URL-minder.html

Send Messages Anonymously over the Net

W3 - Based Anonymous Remailer Interface

Jump **5505**

When you send an e-mail message over the Internet, your e-mail address is always associated with the message. This site enables you to send e-mail anonymously. This is easy to do: just enter the name of the recipient, the subject, and the message itself into a form, then select one or more "remailers" from a scrolling list. A "remailer" is an Internet site that strips your address from your message, and then sends the message to the recipient *without* your original address. —(F.R.)

KEY NEWSGROUP **alt.privacy** URL ▸ http://www.c2.org/remail/by-www.html

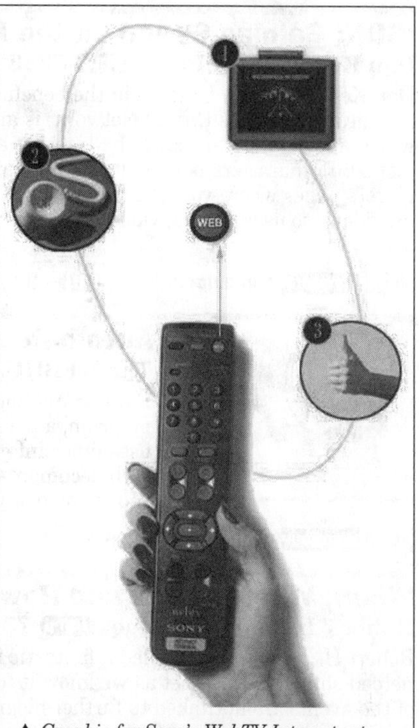

▲ *Graphic for Sony's WebTV Internet set-top box , from* Sony Online, *at* Jump **4027**.

The Best Web Users' Survey

The GVU Center's WWW User Survey Jump 2761

The Graphics, Visualization, & Usability Center of the College of Computers at the Georgia Institute of Technology, working with the Hermes Project at the University of Michigan, have blazed the trail in developing useful data on consumer and business use of the World Wide Web. Stop by and see the results of their most recently completed survey, including graphs and charts, and data on the impact of commercial online services on Web usage, all available at no charge. You can also participate in the current survey while you're here. —(L.S.)

KEY NEWSGROUP **comp.infosystems.www.misc** URL ▸ http://www.cc.gatech.edu/gvu/user_surveys/survey-04-1995/

Interactive Radio Discussions for the Web

WebChat Broadcasting System Jump 3700

Take several hundred interesting Web site topics, newsgroups, and special-interest areas, assign them station names, put them on a dial, allow people to talk to others around the world, and what have you got? WebChat! The WebChat Broadcasting System is a real-time "radio" that allows you to do more than just listen! You'll have the opportunity to chat with others about any of these topics, then spin the dial and talk about something else. You'll find "stations" in such categories as Best of the Web, Arts & Entertainment, Community Support, Science & Technology, and many, many more. Drop by one of the special events programs on the dial. WebChat lets you have a voice on your favorite topic, so stop by—and start talking! —(N.F.)

URL ▸ http://www.IRsociety.com/wbs.html

ISDN: Gaining Speed on the Internet

Dan Kegel's ISDN Page Jump 7255

Dan Kegel certainly believes in the benefits of ISDN connections to the Internet. As he points out, ISDN (Integrated Services Digital Network) is an expanding service, usually offered by your local telephone company, which allows users to access the Internet at lightning speeds up to 128,000 characters per second (compared with just 3,600 characters per second with today's speediest 28.8 kbps modems). Interested? Then, full throttle over to Kegel's pages where you'll find everything you ever wanted to know about this service, from magazines to providers, to user groups, videoconferencing, and relevant databases you can search for further information. —(E.v.B.)

KEY NEWSGROUP **comp.dcom.isdn** URL▶ http://www.alumni.caltech.edu/~dank/isdn/

Automated Web Searching

The WEBHUNTER WWW Interface Jump 7308

Put the Webhound on the scent of new, interesting Web sites. Use the WEBHUNTER program, a personalized Web document filtering system that periodically (or on demand) uses fancy information-processing software to recommend new Web documents based on Web documents that have interested you in the past. It's worth a try, and will relieve you of some of your Web information-gathering burdens. —(E.v.B.)

KEY NEWSGROUP **comp.infosystems.announce** URL▶ http://webhound.www.media.mit.edu/projects/webhound/

When, Where, What and How of the Internet

Hobbes' Internet Timeline Jump 7370

Robert H. Zakon has compiled a fantastic timeline that highlights some of the key events and technologies that helped shape the Internet as we know it today. However, the site isn't just a compilation of dates and names. Most of the events are hotlinked to further biographies of major players or in-depth sites such as research institutions, private providers such as Compuserve, and other important players in the Net industry. As well, Zakon includes some interesting graphs showing the growth of Internet hosts, domains, and users. —(E.v.B.)

KEY NEWSGROUP **alt.answers** URL▶ http://info.isoc.org/guest/zakon/Internet/History/HIT.html

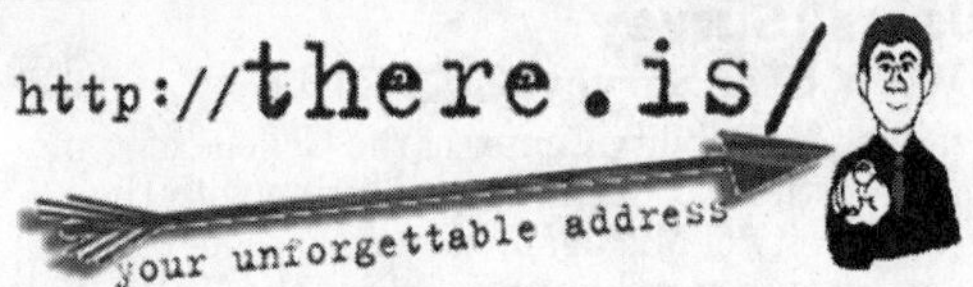

Easy Web Addresses

there.is/home Jump 5911

There was a time not so long ago when people would laugh if you said you were afraid of forgetting your address. Then came the Web, and those oh-so forgettable and long URLs. You forget, and so do they. THERE.IS has a possible solution to this dilemma. The idea is simple enough. You sign on to their fee-based service and your address—no matter what (or where) it is—will be rerouted through WHERE.IS. So you can publish your address as http://there.is.mysite, even though your real address is the usual complex web of dot.coms. Any questions are answered in the FAQ. —(J.P.)

URL▶ http://there.is/

City Yellow Pages on the Web

CitySurf Jump 5912

City Surf is a Web yellow pages directory that is an easy way to find just about any product, service or business in your hometown. You can search by city name, state or zip, or you can browse through a collection of preselected cities. Once a city is selected, you are presented with a terrific list of categories for that city, including home and garden, home services, travel, health, food and dinner, homes, entertainment and more. Did we miss any? Indeed we did. And if you own a business, you can have your company's information added to the database. —(J.P.)

URL▶ http://www.citysurf.com/

IBM's Custom Information Searcher

infoMarket Jump 5880 

There is little doubt that the Internet is filled with vast quantities of information. The trouble thus far has been in finding the right information for your needs, and since much "quality" information is not yet available for free, users are faced with a difficult quandary. IBM addresses both of these problems with their infoMarket search engine. Here you can conduct a search for free—searching over 75 newswires, 300 newspapers, almost 7,000 journals and more—but you only pay for the documents you actually want to see. And, since most of what the search will find is material that's never been available on the Internet, they're confident you'll want to see plenty! —(J.P.)

URL▶ http://www.infomkt.ibm.com/

Free Long Distance Phone Calls on the Internet

VocalTec Jump 5935 

VocalTec pioneered the breakthrough technology that lets people use the Internet to make free long-distance phone calls to anyone, anywhere in the world. Using their software, two people can communicate, by voice, across the Internet, for the price of your basic Internet connection. And, thanks to VocalTec (and others), someday you might well be able to see whoever we are talking to on the Internet as well. If you want to be the first on your block to try out the next wave in this hot new Internet application, you'll want to check out their site. Once there, you'll notice that this is not a new fad, but a technology that this company has been working on for quite some time. You can download some of the software here, as well as read a multitude of press releases, help tips, and other news. A great site for getting the lowdown on this exciting new use of the Internet —(J.P.)

URL▶ http://www.vocaltec.com/

Internet Phone Resources and Commentary

Pulver.com
Jump 5936 

Jeff Pulver has put together an excellent site dedicated to the "voice of telephony on the Internet." Pulver, a well-known Internet telephony consultant and seminar sponsor, is pushing a revolutionary concept that might someday allow full telephone service on the Internet, at a fraction of the high current cost. Much of the groundwork for this new technology has already been established, and you can read about the latest advances here at Jeff's site. You'll see plenty of feature articles here, as well as links to other key sites. Read the Pulver Report for a look at emerging technologies in Internet telephony and check out Jeff's book on the subject, here, too. —(J.P.)

URL▶ http://www.pulver.com/

What works on the Web, and what doesn't? "People come to the Internet for information, so companies that post a lot about their products are going to succeed," says Cliff Kurtzman, president of Tenagra Corp., a Houston consultancy that helps companies establish a Web presence.

Clinton Wilder, "Internet Marketing; an Electronic Bridge to Customers — Buying and Selling on the Internet's World Wide Web Isn't a Dream," *InformationWeek*

Consumer, Business, Health, Investment, & Self-Help

Looking for information on expanding your business, or starting a new one? Or, how about putting up your own Web site?

You'll find it here! The Web is also a gold mine of information for the entrepreneur, with lots more useful information on many consumer, financial, and self-help subjects, too.

Consumer Info, Health, & Legal Advice

The Web can be an excellent place to get all kinds of useful tips and advice before you make any kind of significant consumer product, investment, legal, or personal health care decision. There are all kinds of subject-specific Web sites, created by companies, knowledgeable experts, and advocacy groups that can give you good information you'd find nowhere else. In many cases this information pulls fewer punches than information on similar subjects found in newspapers, magazines, or books. That's because authors of consumer, health, investment, and legal Web sites are passionate about their interests, and there are usually no editors or advertisers on hand to inhibit the viewpoints expressed in their Web-published information.

Be warned, however that anyone can say anything on the Internet. As a result, some of the consumer or health information you read on Web sites may contain untrue or misleading information. So it's a good idea to be a little bit skeptical when you see information on the Net that sounds "too good to be true," or that's been published by sources you're not familiar with.

Information for Entrepreneurs & Small Business Owners

When it comes to information resources for businesses both large and small, the Web can provide you with instant access to a wealth of helpful, problem-solving advice. To be sure, many of the big-name business publications now have Web sites offering fair to very good business news and features, culled from the print versions of their own publications, but the best business and entrepreneurial information you'll find on the Web is generated by a host of independent entrepreneurs and consultants who publish all kinds of street-smart business advice to provide you with useful information on starting a new business, or expanding your existing business into new markets. If you're an entrepreneur, some of these sites are also quite valuable in that they can connect you, via e-mail, to one or many other entrepreneurs, through certain Web sites that serve as virtual "entrepreneur's exchanges."

Help-Wanted Web Sites

If you're looking for a better job or to find good career advice, there are also a large number of Web sites with help-wanted listings for thousands of career positions of all kinds, located all across the U.S., as well as helpful career counseling, resume writing, and other job-getting information.

These days, Grant's Flower gets two to five orders a day from its cybershop on the Internet's World Wide Web hypermedia system. The orders come from all over the world especially on holidays. On Mother's Day, he says, he received 40 orders for bouquets through the Internet, compared with 45 from the international FTD network. Although Internet orders are still a relatively small part of his total sales, their importance is growing steadily.

"His Web Page Delivers," Scholastic, Inc., *Home Office Computing*

Consumer, Health & Self-Help

Practical Guide to Crime Prevention

Practical Guide to Crime Prevention

Jump 6613

CONTENT

It's a rare occurrence on the Net when you can obtain free access to professionally-written guides on crime prevention and safety, without feeling the pressure of having to buy a product that'll do the protecting for you, that is, until the Practical Guide to Crime Prevention came along. Without sales pressure, the Practical Guide to Crime Prevention gives you truly useful tips and ideas on personal and child safety, home and car security, as well as advice on neighborhood watch activities. Other areas covered include security issues for special age groups, such as children and the elderly. Every guide includes a help panel with telephone numbers and addresses. —(L.T.)

KEY NEWSGROUP clari.news.crime.misc URL▶ http://www.crime-prevention.org.uk/home_office/guide/

Learning to Protect and Defend Yourself

Assault Prevention Information Network Home Page Jump 2488

CONTENT

Eternal optimism notwithstanding, it's a dangerous world, and getting more so every day. This page, maintained by Judith Weiss of Personal Power Assault Prevention Training, offers tips, ideas, support, and general information on avoiding or defending yourself and your family against violent assault. You can learn how to develop defense strategies and evaluate a self-defense course, teach your children to defend themselves, and the facts to debunk self-defense myths. You can also link to related sites, including those concerned with martial arts and workplace violence. There's a descriptive bibliography of books for further reading, and an opporunity to contribute your own thoughts and comments on the subjects covered. —(L.S.)

KEY NEWSGROUP alt.support URL▶ http://galaxy.einet.net/galaxy/Community/Safety/Assault-Prevention/apin/APINintro.html

The Art of the Deal: Leasing a New Car

Automobile Leasing Jump 2665

CONTENT

'Twas a time you could actually buy a car. You know, go in, pick a model, haggle with the salesman, write a check, and drive away actually owning it. Then, you needed a loan, and while you felt like you owned the car, you really shared ownership with the bank. These days, most people don't even bother trying to pretend they own the vehicle. They lease instead. But while there are real benefits to leasing over taking out an auto loan, if you're not careful, it can end up costing much more. Al Hearn has leased his cars for more than 10 years, and here he shares his knowledge and experience. He covers the basic concepts of leasing, provides a glossary of terms you'll encounter, helps you decide if leasing is right for you, and offers tips on how to get the best deal in a lease. Check it out before you go car shopping, and you could save yourself some real money. —(L.S.)

KEY NEWSGROUP rec.autos URL▶ http://www.mindspring.com/~ahearn/lease/lease.html

Current Auto Prices

AutoWorld Welcome Page Jump 2672

CONTENT

There's nothing worse than trying to figure out the price you should pay for a car, especially a used car. The Blue Book gives you a starting point, but it doesn't really take into account the wide variety of conditions a used car can be in. This resource does. Using on-screen forms, you select the make, model and year of the car you want the price for, and AutoWorld tells you the prices for various conditions, from excellent to not so good. For new cars, you can get pricing information that also includes prices of options you can add. —(L.S.)

KEY NEWSGROUP rec.autos.marketplace URL▶ http://www.autoworld.com/

Easy Calculators for All Kinds of Financial Decisions

FinanCenter Jump 0226

FinanCenter has come up with a great little Web site, featuring dozens of useful calculators and worksheets for many common personal and family financial decisions. This site will help you with many of the basic money decisions each of us have to make, such as choosing between buying a new or used car, how much to save for a major purchase, how long it takes to pay off your credit card balance, mortgage calculators, growth vs. income stocks, family budget decisions, and more. Keep this link handy, because you'll never know when you'll need to make any of these everyday financial calculations. —(E.G.)

URL▶ http://www.financenter.com/

U.S. Driving Distance Calculator

How Far Is It? Jump 7193

Ever have a burning need to know exactly what the distance between Kansas City and Los Angeles is? Well, the Distance Service is at your command. All you have to do is enter two points (only for locations in the United States) and the service will immediately compute the mileage and then display a map showing the two places you've chosen...couldn't be simpler! —(E.v.B.)

URL▶ http://gs213.sp.cs.cmu.edu/prog/dist

Web Loan Calculator

Loan Inputs Jump 5745

Simplicity is sometimes a good thing. In this case it is a very good thing. Jay Herder has put together a nifty on-screen loan calculator that does just what it says it does! You fill in the data, amount of loan, number of months, monthly payments, and annual interest rate, click the calculate button and it's all done. Except for coming up with the money to pay off the loan. You'll have to figure out that part on your own—Jay is accommodating, but he can't help you there.—(J.P.)

URL▶ http://www2.southwind.net/~jherder/cgi-bin/loan.pl

Protect Yourself from Consumer Fraud

Consumer Fraud Jump 5794

No one is immune to fraud. Those who think so are often the most likely to fall victim to the sort of sly underhanded deceits that are the stock-and-trade of con-men and groups. How can you protect yourself? Well, while there are few foolproof measures, you'll find plenty to stir your imagination here at the Consumer Fraud page, developed by San Jose attorney Richard Alexander. Although laws and regulations vary from state to state, the purpose here really is to open your eyes to the kinds of problems that most often seem to strike. For example, the section on investment lists cons as varied as bank examiner & pigeon drop schemes, credit card scams, get-rich-quick (pyramid) schemes, home equity loans and investment scams. Other sections covered include health, automobiles, entertainment and more. —(J.P.)

KEY NEWSGROUP **alt.consumers.experiences** URL▶ http://consumerlawpage.com/article/fraud/fraud.shtml

Protect Yourself from Con Artists

Consumer Fraud Alert Network Jump 2739

There's no need to fall prey to the scams of con artists, so long as you check this page. Here you can learn about the latest scams, what to look for when you're approached with an offer that looks to good to be true, and how to take action against the perpetrators of these frauds. While this page concentrates on consumer fraud, there's a link to another page maintained by the same people covering home business scams, with alerts and tips on how to avoid being taken by the growing number of unscrupulous people trying to separate you from your wallet. —(L.S.)

KEY NEWSGROUP **alt.consumers.experiences** URL▶ http://www.world-wide.com/homebiz/fraud.htm

Find a Home on the Web

Homebuyer's Fair Jump 4002

The folks at ASK Real Estate Information Services bring the search for a new home to the Web. Accessible real-estate listings, mortgage and home buyer information, prototype housing displays, classified listings and even an apartment search area (including geographic regions covering the entire country) make this site a must if you're searching for the perfect place to hang your hat. Currently only the Washington, D.C., and Philadelphia regions are online, but more is promised, and you can sign up to have a free *New Homes Guide* snail-mailed to you, covering any one of (currently) 23 metropolitan areas. —(R.B.)

KEY NEWSGROUP misc.invest.real-estate URL▶ http://www.homefair.com/homegrap.html

Junk Mail Roulette

Catalog Mart Home Page Jump 2091

If you like getting catalogs in the mail, and you're not very selective about the catalogs you'd like to receive, this is your home page. Catalog Mart is a source for some 10,000 catalogs, organized into 800 categories. Fill in the form with your name and address, choose the categories you want, and Catalog Mart forwards your request to the appropriate merchants. Soon enough, your "snailmailbox" will be overflowing! —(L.S.)

KEY NEWSGROUP misc.consumers URL▶ http://catalog.savvy.com/

Online Mortgage Calculator

Form for Mortgage Payment Query Jump 2022

Hugh Chou makes it easy to figure what that new house will cost. Just key in the principal loan balance, interest rate, length of mortgage, and other pertinent information and—voilà!—you have monthly payments and the option to show the full amortization table. You can run as many calculations as you like and save the results to review and analyze later. While you're here, check out his income tax calculator, too! —(L.S.)

KEY NEWSGROUP misc.consumer.house URL▶ http://ibc.wustl.edu/mort.html

Mortgage Tutorials and Help

HomeOwners Finance Jump 2466

Finding a home you want to buy is difficult enough, but the fun really starts when you try to arrange financing. Even simple, fixed-rate mortgages aren't so simple anymore, and adjustable rate loans, while good deals for many people, are so confusing that it's hard for the average person to tell what the deal really is. HomeOwners Finance, a California-based mortgage broker, offers some help with online tutorials to guide you through the mortgage maze. The tutorial on adjustable rate mortgages is particularly good, offering a basic overview of what they are and how rates are figured. There's also a dictionary of mortgage and real-estate terms, a sample closing-cost estimate that details standard fees, and an online mortgage calculator to help you determine how much you can afford to spend on a home. —(L.S.)

KEY NEWSGROUP misc.invest.real-estate URL▶ http://www.internet-is.com/homeowners/in-yahoo.html

Insurance Answers for Consumers

Welcome to Insurance News Network Jump 2135

CONTENT

Few doubt the value of good insurance, but it seems that fewer really understand their needs, what their policies cover, and the archaic terminology of insurers. The articles here are written by financial journalists, not insurance providers, so you're getting relatively clear, unbiased information on auto, home, and life insurance, presented in a way that helps you analyze your situation and understand the terms. Topics covered include the different types of policies and coverages available, relative costs, and options. There's also a resource for insurance carrier ratings, and information on state insurance regulators if you want specific information on your local regulations. —(L.S.)

KEY NEWSGROUP misc.consumers URL▶ http://www.insure.com/

Paint Estimator

Books that WorkPaint Estimator Jump 7001 

If your idea of a good time is watching paint dry, this site is for you. To calculate exactly how much paint you have to buy to cover a room, simply enter the perimeter of the room, number of doors and windows, and how many coats. Voilà! The paint estimator then displays exactly how much paint—down to the tenth of a percent—you'll need. —(E.v.B.)

KEY NEWSGROUP **misc.consumers.house**

URL▸ http://www.btw.com/applets/paint_calc.html

▲ *Vintage 1934 Popular Mechanics cover, from* **The PM Zone**, *at* Jump 2355.

Popular Mechanics on the Web

The PM Zone

Jump 2355 

For nearly a century, the editors of *Popular Mechanics* magazine has made new technologies understandable and usable for the tinkerer as well as the merely curious. They continue that tradition with their Web pages, beginning with very helpful sections about using the Web and the Net in general. Beyond these, there are daily technology updates, a QuickTime downloadable movie archive with a new addition each week, and a monthly feature taken from the print magazine. For auto buffs who depend on PM for specs, evaluations, pictures, and the latest new car news aren't forgotten either. They'll find all this, plus PM's Owners Report evaluations online, too. —(L.S.)

KEY NEWSGROUP **alt.technology.misc** URL▸ http://popularmechanics.com/

Student Loan Information

Signet Bank Student Loan Home Page Jump 2268 

With college costs increasing steadily, and the cost of everything else likewise rising, figuring out how to pay for a college education is daunting at best. Signet Bank does a big business in student loans, but even if you don't borrow from them, they've created a site that all college-bound students and their families should visit and study. Beginning with the online version of the book, *Don't Miss Out: A Student's Guide to Financial Aid*, these pages are thick with information on loans, grants, and other aid programs, how they work, and how to take advantage of them. There's also a tutorial on government-sponsored student loan programs, a section covering alternative financing options, including private loans and savings and investment programs, and a dictionary of key financial terms and phrases. —(L.S.)

KEY NEWSGROUP **soc.college** URL▸ http://www.infi.net:80/collegemoney/

I'm from the Government, and I'm Here to Help

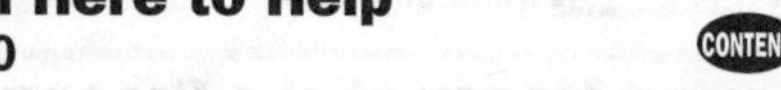

Consumer Information Center Jump 8520

Admit it: Like most of us, you wonder where all your taxes go, and if they go for anything worthwhile. This site is proof that the government can do something really well. The Consumer Information Center is a clearinghouse for government pamphlets covering just about any consumer issue you can imagine. And it also includes a good deal of information about the federal government's own programs. The best part of this site is that you can download any of the pamphlets for free, even though a hard copy may cost as much as several dollars. There are plenty of health pamphlets, too. Nursing homes, exercise, menopause, contraception and quack arthritis cures are just a few of the topics covered here. Check this site out for lots of useful information that, whether you like it or not, you've already paid for. —(R.B.)

URL▸ http://www.pueblo.gsa.gov/

Consumer Education for Teens

Street Cents Online Jump 2062

Teenagers represent a major market for goods and services and this online version of a Canadian television show is geared to helping teens become tough consumers. But even if adolescence is a mere memory to you, there's good information here for any consumer regardless of age. Each week there is a new show, the information is summarized and put online. Topics cover a broad range, including music, stocks and investing, breaking bad habits, clothes, health, and other issues of interest to teens. —(L.S.)

KEY NEWSGROUP misc.consumers URL▶ http://www.screen.com/streetcents.html

Be a Smarter Consumer

NICE Home Page Jump 2470

CONTENT

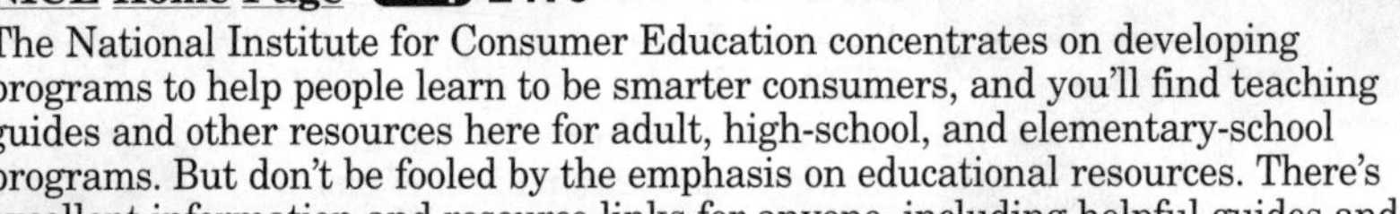

The National Institute for Consumer Education concentrates on developing programs to help people learn to be smarter consumers, and you'll find teaching guides and other resources here for adult, high-school, and elementary-school programs. But don't be fooled by the emphasis on educational resources. There's excellent information and resource links for anyone, including helpful guides and pointers on subjects such as credit, personal finance, home mortgages, cars, video and fraud. —(L.S.)

KEY NEWSGROUP misc.consumer URL▶ http://www.emich.edu/public/coe/nice/nice.html

Penny Pinchers Unite!!!

Frugal Tip of the Week Jump 5746

The subtitle of this site is "Julie's Frugal Tips." We learn here that Julie can squeeze pennies out of rocks, so already we know we're in good hands. The idea here is, quite simply, to provide you with tips on how you can save money on the day-to-day things that tend to wear us down. And the more you read, the more you'll like these suggestions. Buying flowers for someone? Why not take an old vase with you to the flower shop? You'll save a few dollars right there. Check your photos before leaving the store—many film processing outfits will reimburse you for your bad shots. And how about using old newspapers for cleaning glass and windows? It couldn't be cheaper and it doesn't streak. You can send in your own suggestions, and there's even a few dozen other links to sites that might save you even more money. —(J.P.)

URL▶ http://www.brightok.net/~neilmayo/

Pennypincher's Guide to Life

$tarving $hirley's Savings Page Jump 7087

Save, save, save is Shirley's middle name. Shirley tells you how to make money selling clothing to consignment stores, gives you recipes for cheap eats, and explains how to hang on to your food money by the creative use of coupons and rebate offers. Follow Shirley's tips and you might just save enough to buy that supercharged stereo you've had your eye on. —(E.v.B.)

KEY NEWSGROUP misc.consumer URL▶ http://www.mindspring.com/~kmims/ss.html

Saving Money at the Grocery Store

The Coupon Clipper Jump 5098

This service provides you with the opportunity to receive discount coupons, rebates, and special magazine offers from the comfort of your home. It is a useful, money-saving resource and an innovative use of the Web. However, those of you who are sticklers for protecting your privacy should be warned, since the sponsors of this site make the completion of a rather detailed, personal Web-based survey form a prerequisite for access to this site. —(S.B.)

URL▶ http://csii.com/Coupon/form.html

Efficient and Renewable Energy

DOE Energy Efficiency & Renewable Energy Network Jump 3536

Here's where you'll find consumer-friendly information on the latest energy efficiency technologies—energy practices and systems that will save you money, while helping to prevent pollution and other environmental problems. EREN offers a Web-based interface that locates and organizes qualitative information on these topics, providing links to over 70 different Internet sites that contain information on energy. The search engine is easy to use, and there's an online tutorial to use just in case you get stuck. —(C.P.)

KEY NEWSGROUP **bit.listserv.devel-l** URL▶ http://www.eren.doe.gov/

Emergency Planning & Information

Emergency Preparedness Information Center Jump 5132

Here's where you can access important news on the West Coast earthquake threat, get information on how to prepare for a natural disaster, take steps to establish your own family's disaster plan. The Emergency Preparedness Information Center, keeper of this site, provides a checklist here to aid you in your preparation, and offers products to help you prepare. —(S.B.)

URL▶ http://nwlink.com/epicenter/

Emergency Preparedness: Insider's Tips & Advice

How to prepare for an emergency Jump 6011

Do you have a family disaster plan? How prepared are you for an emergency such as an earthquake, tornado, flood, or hurricane? This extensive, content-rich site will help you create such a plan, and will raise issues you've never even thought of. Learn what supplies you should have in your car, at home, even in the office. The creators of this site learned these tips the hard way, by surviving hurricane Iniki in Hawaii in 1992. Do yourself a favor—profit from their experiences—and develop a plan today. —(N.F.)

KEY NEWSGROUP **misc.survivalism** URL▶ http://nwlink.com/epicenter/howto.html

Better Eating

Ask the Nutritionist Jump 2663

It seems that every time you turn around, there's a new diet that claims to be the best for losing weight, or enhancing sports performance, or fighting disease, or curing whatever happens to ail you at the time. But good diet is mostly common sense and based on an understanding of what your body needs and what foods fulfill those needs. Joanne Larsen, a registered dietician, has straightforward, easy-to-understand answers to most of the questions you may have, in this page clearly organized by topic. And if the answer isn't here, e-mail your question to Joanne and she'll add the answer. —(L.S.)

KEY NEWSGROUP **sci.med.nutrition** URL▶ http://www.hoptechno.com/rdindex.htm

Skip the Fries with that Burger!

Food Finder Jump 8523

You're running late. You're hungry. You order a value meal at a nearby fast food restaurant, take your first bite, and wonder, "How many calories am I eating?" Well, wonder no longer. This cute and interactive site will help you figure out just how unhealthy that meal really was. You can use this site two ways. First, you can set up criteria for what you'd allow yourself to eat at any fast food joint, using things like maximum calories or maximum percentage of fat. Or, you can look at many items on one restaurant's menu to see how they compare. Sure, sometimes the truth hurts. But when you see those incredibly high fat values for your favorite dish, next time you might just choose the healthier route—the salad bar! —(R.B.)

URL▶ http://www.olen.com/food/index.html

You Are What You Eat

IFIC Foundation Jump 2041

If you are what you eat, here's the place to learn what you're becoming! The International Food Information Council offers this page of consumer information, including tips on healthy eating for children and adults, food additives, and food allergies. This is one of a series of IFIC pages, and you can find more information, including pages for educators, health professionals, and reporters, and links to other food and nutrition sites, all Web-linkable through these pages. —(L.S.)

KEY NEWSGROUP alt.food URL▶ http://ificinfo.health.org/info-con.htm

Organic Food & Recipes

Don't Panic Eat Organic Jump 1513

If you don't like the idea of eating sprayed fruits and vegetables and are wondering how to grow them without using pesticides, definitely peruse this site. It contains a wealth of information about organic growing, including descriptions of rare fruits and vegetables. For example, do you know what a Cherimoya is? A clue: it was one of Mark Twain's favorite fruits. The pages are filled with facts and reports leaning toward supporting a healthful, ecologically accountable agriculture throughout the country. Mostly designed by members of the California Certified Organic Farmers, or CCOF, and representatives of the organic foods industry, you'll find articles about almost anything related to organic food, along with pictures of insects that can destroy crops. You'll also find descriptions of predators, like the barn owl, that help the organic farmer keep the insects under control. This Web page also has dozens of links to organic, agricultural, and environmental sources, including articles about alternative farming techniques, urban farming, and even *The Old Farmer's Almanac*. —(H.L.)

URL▶ http://www.rain.org/~sals/my.html

Conventional and Alternative Health Care: Ask Dr. Weil

Ask Dr. Weil

Jump 5932

Here's a doctor who is not only always in, but also makes house calls. Part of the Hotwired stable, Dr. Weil is a best-selling author and practicing M.D. who takes up residence here as a medical advisor who advocates the use of both conventional and alternative medical treatments. If you've got a problem, you can "Ask the Doctor," and he might well include your query as the question of the day. Or you can search the database to see if the topic has been covered before. You'll also find links to information on pet health, answers to questions about record confidentiality, and more info from Dr. Weil's newsletter. —(J.P.)

KEY NEWSGROUP sci.med URL▶ http://www.hotwired.com/drweil/

Wellness Web

Wellness Web Home Page Jump 5719

As more and more cutbacks strike the medical field, it is sometimes difficult to find answers to questions that, while important, are not necessarily life-threatening. Increasingly, perhaps, we will be turning to places like the Wellness Web Home Page. The mandate here is to "help you find the best and most appropriate medical information and support available." They want to "help you get and stay well," which they do with useful, timely information on a vast array of subjects. You'll find a smoking section, articles in this site's Heart Center, the Cancer and Senior Center, and much more. "Be Happy and Well" is this site's motto. Sound advice! —(J.P.)

URL▶ http://www.wellweb.com/

Health World: The Web's Major Health Site

Health World Online Jump 8536

This is as big, and as complete, as any health-related site you'll find on the Web. The best part of this site is the "Library of Health and Medicine," containing the Holy Grail of online medical information—free access to Medline, the search tool for the National Library of Medicine. Use MedLine to locate any scientific publication in recent history on any disease or health condition. This site's Health Clinic section also contains information on conventional and alternative medical therapies. Go to this site when you're looking for a piece of specific online health information, and chances are you'll find it. —(R.B.)

URL▶ http://www.healthy.net/

Health Information Online

Online Health Network Jump 6629

A quick search through the Online Health Network will give you instant access to reliable health information. Recent articles have included information on why airbags and infant car safety seats don't mix, news on the latest in gene therapy research, and support information for those who suffer panic attacks. This site also covers the latest developments in the health care field. Have a health-related question? Stop by their online forums, hosted by doctors and other healthcare professionals. You can also sign up here for a free subscription to their monthly e-mail bulletin, Housecall. —(L.T.)

KEY NEWSGROUP **clari.biz.industry.health** URL▶ http://healthnet.ivi.com/

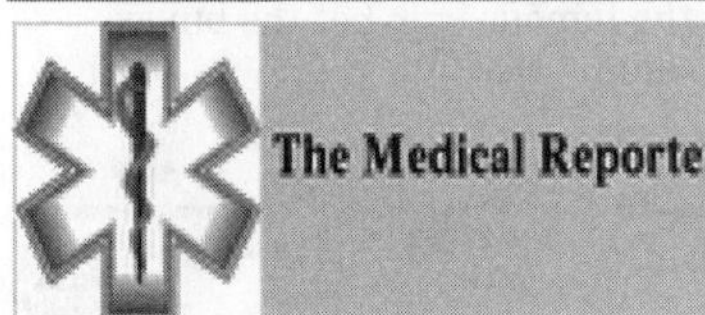

Healthcare Info & Advice

The Medical Reporter Jump 1566

Editor Joel Cooper has put together a comprehensive, easy-to-understand monthly cyber-journal of medicine for enlightened healthcare consumers. The Medical Reporter emphasizes preventive medicine, primary care, patient advocacy, education, and support on all kinds of topics interesting to men, women, and children. Articles written by medical professionals cover topics ranging from endometriosis, vulvodynia, and polycystic kidney disease to pelvic inflammatory disease, fetal alcohol syndrome, eye diseases, E. coli, prostate cancer, health hazards of secondhand smoke, and mental health. Cooper invites you to participate in discussions, such as "Do you think toll-free hotlines, staffed by registered nurses, is a good idea?" It's your chance to speak out about your likes and dislikes of the medical profession. —(H.L.)

URL▶ http://www.dash.com/netro/nwx/tmr/tmr.html

KidsHealth

KidsHealth.org Jump 6606

KidsHealth is a fun, interactive resource which addresses the health care concerns of parents, providing accurate, current information on topics like child behavior, development, and nutrition, safety tips, common childhood illnesses, and immunizations. Kids will also discover an amusing place here, with online games, polls, quizzes, and kid-to-kid online forums. You'll also find a Tip of the Day, which addresses specific issues, such as "Why you shouldn't try to cure everything with antibiotics"—and, if you miss a few days, full archives are also available here to browse. —(L.T.)

KEY NEWSGROUP **misc.kids** URL▶ http://KidsHealth.org

Facts about Alcohol, Tobacco, Caffeine & Other Drugs

Drug Education Page Jump 2476

Recreational drug use isn't limited to marijuana, cocaine, heroin and other illegal or controlled substances. Alcohol and tobacco are legal, but just as potentially dangerous over the long term. Whatever the drug, Jill Lampi has it covered with this informative Web page. Information presented here can be frightening, too, and not because Jill uses any scare tactics. Articles presented here are enough to make even the most dedicated legal drinkers or smokers think about what they are doing to their bodies. And when you delve into the sections on illegal substances, it's even worse. In short, this isn't a page for drug fans, or even antidrug people. It's a page for people who need and want to be informed. —(L.S.)

KEY NEWSGROUP alt.drugs URL▶ http://www.magic.mb.ca/~lampi/new_drugs.html

Health Tips for Kids and the Family

Family Internet Jump 6886

A healthy reference desk for whole family, Family Internet is full of special sections for kids, at-home dads, travel and pets. If you're a new parent, you'll have a field day in the baby section. This site also features a virtual Q&A library of basic childhood medical information, like infant diseases, nutrition, toddler falls, and more. Think of it as having a pediatrician on-call, 24 hours a day, answering your questions about allergic reactions, teething and animal bites.—(L.T.)

KEY NEWSGROUP clari.news.family URL▶ http://www.familyinternet.com/

E-Zine for the Fit (and Those Who Want to Be)

The Body Project Jump 8529

Do you love fitness and healthy eating? Are you the type who aims for a body fat percentage under 10%, loves vitamins, and has a body that's the envy of your friends? You've found your home! This is a fitness e-zine with a wide spectrum of fun and informative articles: Why you should eat more garlic; the benefits of 5 minutes a day of meditation; the importance of taking breaks when using your computer (O.K., not all the articles are cutting edge). It isn't hard science, but most of it is interesting and helpful. The only caveat is the famous one: Let the buyer beware. Some of this site's sponsoring companies offer products of questionable value. —(R.B.)

URL▶ http://www.bodyzine.com/

Welcome to the Medical Tent

For Serious Athletes Only...

The Medical Tent Jump 8521

If twenty six point two miles is just a jog for you, then you'll feel right at home here. This page is really a performance enhancing tool (and it's perfectly legal!) for anyone interested in endurance sports, from running to ultramarathons. The important topics are all covered: stretching (using text and viewable pictures), introductions to physiology topics, hydration, vitamins, and dangers of overtraining. Subjects unique to serious athletes are found here too (why did the blood bank reject my blood, anyway?). And naturally, there's a good selection of infomation on sports-related injuries. —(R.B.)

URL▶ http://riceinfo.rice.edu/~jenkins/medtent.1.html

Physiotherapy Online

CONTENT

American Physical Therapy Association Jump 7195

The American Physical Therapy Association provides something for everyone—from the professional physiotherapist to the general public. The professional will find an online newsletter highlighting who's who in the profession, research news and fellowships, conferences, and funding possibilities. The interested bystander can read up on the history of the profession, descriptions of what's involved in a course of therapy, and can access a referral service. Links are also provided to many other physical therapy resources on the Net. —(E.v.B.)

KEY NEWSGROUP misc.health.alternative URL▶ http://www.edoc.com/apta/

Test Your Own Health...

The Rand 36 Item Health Survey Jump 8542

Are you wondering just how healthy you really are? The best way to know—without being evaluated by a doctor—is at this site. It's an online version of the famous health questionnaire developed by the Rand Corporation, a private research foundation. It asks about many different aspects of your own health, primarily based on symptoms. What makes this questionnaire different is that it's a true scientific approach; a significant change in your score means that your health has changed significantly, too. The authors at this site will let you take the test up to once a month. It's an interesting—and valid—way to check how you're doing. And it's just 36 multiple-choice questions. But don't worry about the time involved; it's not called the "Short Form -36" for nothing! —(R.B.)

URL▶ http://www.mcw.edu/midas/health/

Cool Medical Site Of The Week

Hypochondria Heaven

Cool Medical Site of the Week Jump 2744

End all that tedious searching for the latest and greatest on the malaise front. Quickly add to your list of diseases of the week featured on ER. Amaze your doctors and your friends with a growing array of symptoms and self-diagnostic tips. It's as easy as point and click with the Cool Medical Site of the Week. Actually, these sites, selected by Dr. William C. Donlon, can be very helpful, although some of them are intended more for practioners than patients. But if you're looking for the best sites among the growing number of hospitals and med school departments on the Web, this is the place to go. —(L.S.)

KEY NEWSGROUP sci.med URL▶ http://www.hooked.net/users/wcd/cmsotw.html

PLASTIC SURGERY INFORMATION SERVICE

A New You...for a Price

Plastic Surgery Information Service
Jump 8526

You've probably thought about it. Maybe your nose is a little too droopy; or maybe those bags under your eyes seem to grow larger every day. Actually, plastic surgery includes many non-cosmetic procedures, such as cleft palate repair, and breast reconstruction after mastectomy. This site, sponsored by the American Society of Plastic and Reconstructive Surgeons, gives a good general overview of all of these services. You'll find a FAQ section on specific procedures, and listings of plastic surgeons who are members of this association. But the most helpful part of this site is the information on how to pick your doctor. It gives great advice on what to look for, and how to look for it. There's a checklist at the end to help you decide if you're on the right track. After thinking about it, you might decide cosmetic surgery isn't for you, after all. But if it is, this is a great place to start. —(R.B.)

URL▶ http://www.plasticsurgery.org/

Intro E-Zine for Fitness

The Worldguide Health and Fitness Forum Jump 8522

Here's an interesting health and fitness e-zine which has one of the widest spectrums of information available. In about an hour this site will get you up to speed on a wide range of general exercise topics. Strength training, cardiovascular exercise, nutrition, and fitness topics like body fat and injury care are all covered. It's not a textbook, and it isn't a substitute for your doctor's advice, but all in all it's a good start to a fitness program. And isn't that what you need? —(R.B.)

URL▶ http://www.worldguide.com:80/home/dmg/Fitness/hf.html

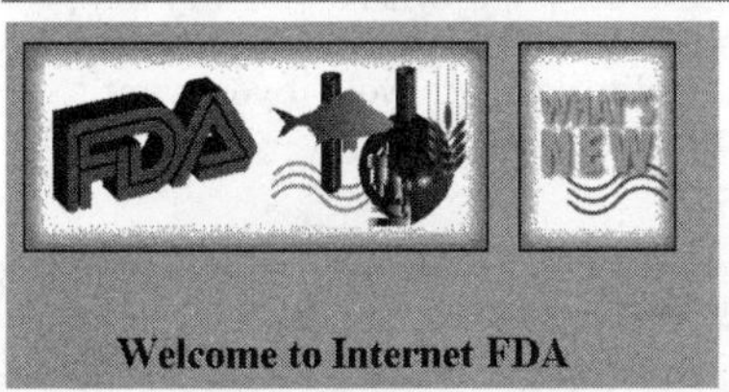

Welcome to Internet FDA

FDA's Web Site for Food & Drugs Safety

Internet FDA Jump 8512

CONTENT

Curious about how the government is protecting you from what goes into your body? The Food and Drug Administration (FDA) has a home page with news and information about their latest investigations and approvals. There's no question this site has a scientific leaning—expect to find many chemical names and medical devices that have that 21st century-sounding names. Even so, there's plenty of information on cosmetics, food labeling and food safety, and downloadable consumer information files. For scientists, physicians, and investors, there's also a listing of recently approved medications and devices. Skip the governmentese, and you'll find lots of interesting information on some of the latest pharmaceutical and medical progress. —(R.B.)

URL▶ http://www.fda.gov/fdahomepage.html

Patient Care Resources

Medscape Jump 2767

Intended for medical professionals, but also offered as a resource for healthcare consumers, Medscape offers regularly updated information and peer-reviewed articles organized by specialty, including infectious diseases, AIDS, immunology, surgery, and managed care. As you would expect of a site intended primarily for doctors, the material is clinical and heavy, but it's as current as anything you'll find on the Web, and possibly in print. Each article is also annotated with links to relevant Internet resources, including research sites and experts. If you're a healthcare professional, it's a definite bookmark. If you're a consumer, and have the inclination to wade through the clinical terminology, it can be an excellent resource to help you become better informed as well. —(L.S.)

KEY NEWSGROUP sci.med URL http://www.medscape.com/

Acupuncture on the Web

Acupuncture.com Jump 2489

Some people swear by acupuncture, saying it has improved conditions that traditional medicine couldn't help, and even medical traditionalists have begun to see the value of this ancient Chinese therapy. This page by Al Stone serves as your basic introduction to acupuncture, with a comparison of Western and Eastern medicines, statistics on the effectiveness of acupuncture in improving various conditions, and an overview of the theory behind the treatment. If you want to try it out, you'll find state-by-state listings of acupuncture practioners and information on state laws governing them. —(L.S.)

KEY NEWSGROUP misc.health.alternative URL http://www.acupuncture.com/acupuncture/

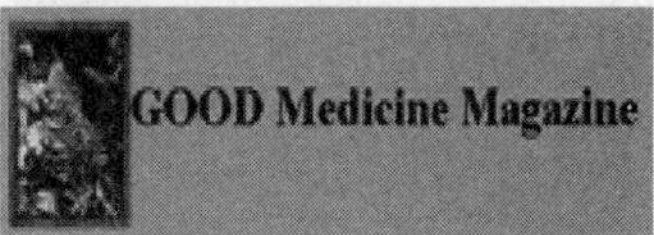

Combining Alternative and Traditional Healthcare

Good Medicine Magazine

Jump 2522

There are those who swear by alternative medicine techniques, and there are traditionalists who frown upon anything that isn't taught in Western medical schools. *Good Medicine Magazine* covers both, and while the emphasis is definitely on the alternative, the quarterly journal writes about them in the context of enhancing traditional medical practice. You can read each issue separately, or you can use the nifty online form to create a personalized edition that scans the last three issues and returns the articles that relate to your areas of interest.—(L.S.)

KEY NEWSGROUP misc.health.alternative URL http://none.coolware.com/health/good_med/ThisIssue.html

The Wide World of Yoga

Yoga Paths Jump 7141

The ways of yoga are many. Rene Muller has done an admirable job of collecting the different paths, from the Hindu karma yoga, to asana yoga, to sahaja yoga. She also lists non-Hindu disciplines taught by various yoga masters. A number of articles on yoga have also been entered, along with a glossary of Sanskrit terms, other online yoga resources, bibliographies, and major texts such as the Bhagavad Gita. You can download lessons from each path you might want to follow to begin your own meditations. As well, if you want to discuss yoga and meditation with others, Muller also lists pertinent IRC channels and newsgroups. —(E.v.B.)

KEY NEWSGROUP alt.yoga URL http://zeta.cs.adfa.oz.au/Spirit/Yoga/Overview.html

Alternative Medicine Web Jump Site

The Alternative Medicine Homepage Jump 2521

This is your best starting point for investigating alternative healthcare options. Charles B. Wessel of the Falk Library of the Health Sciences at the University of Pittsburgh has compiled a comprehensive list of Internet resources with descriptions that will help guide your own Web browsing. In addition, there are links to various studies of alternative therapies, including the National Institutes of Health's study. Together, the links on this page not only give you the starting point for learning about specific therapies, they also will give you the resources to help you evaluate them. —(L.S.)

KEY NEWSGROUP **misc.health.alternative** URL▶ http://www.pitt.edu/~cbw/altm.html

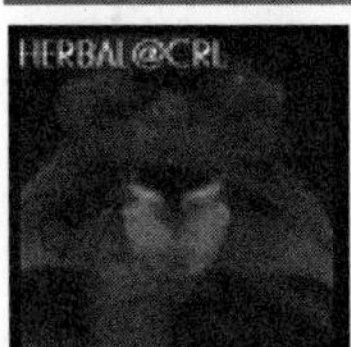

All about Herbal Remedies

Herbal Hall Jump **2524**

If it's about herbs and herbal remedies, the information is either on this Web site, or there's a link to it. Although it's intended primarily for professional herbalists, there's a glossary and a dictionary to help the neophyte understand technical terms—and plenty of general, clearly written information, too. The page starts with the herb article of the month, which describes, among other things, the spotlighted herb's cultivation, processing and uses. There's also a monthly book review, books about herbal remedies available for downloading, an image archive, and links to various Internet resources for news, discussion, and general or specific information about herbs and herbal remedies. —(L.S.)

KEY NEWSGROUP **misc.health.alternative** URL▶ http://www.crl.com/~robbee/herbal.html

Business & Entrepreneurship

The Internet Money Game

iWorld's Guide to Electronic Commerce Jump **5748**

One of the most pressing concerns many people associate with the Internet is how—or when—it will become a money-making proposition. So far, at least, corporations have been willing to invest with no hope of substantial (or otherwise) return on their investment, but may continue doing so indefinitely. Those interested in the progress of this area of commerce will find much of interest at iWorld's Guide to Electronic Commerce. iWorld presents an optimistic view of Net commerce, and the background articles and reports featured here highlight many of the strategies that top corporations have implemented. —(J.P.)

KEY NEWSGROUP **misc.entrepreneurs** URL▶ http://e-comm.iworld.com/

SOHO: Business Advice for Your Small Office/Home Office

Your Small Office Jump **5652**

From the publishers of *Small Business Computing* and *Home Office Computing* comes a site that wonderfully compliments the style and scope of these entrepreneurial publications. The feature articles are smart and timely and the Daily Memos section offers short, concise tips and observations. Add to the mix this site's other features—Tech Expert, Money Miser and Marketing Guru—and you have a year's worth of entrepreneurial information in one Web stop. —(J.P.)

URL▶ http://www.smalloffice.com/

Searching for Businesses on the Net

NetPartners Company Site Locator Jump **8020**

Using the forms on the NetPartners Company Locator page, you can search for either company names or domain names to see which U.S.-based businesses maintain Web sites or other Net-based services. However, their database is restricted only to lists of U.S. companies. The great thing about this site is that once you've located a company, Net Partners provides the link so you can go right to the company's site. —(E.v.B.)

KEY NEWSGROUP **biz.misc** URL▶ http://www.netpart.com/company/search.html

Industry News & Information

Industry.Net - The Ultimate Business Connection Jump **8023**

Industry.Net's mission is to bring corporate buyers and sellers together online in order to streamline the buying and selling process between companies. Information on over 4,000 companies, 250,000 suppliers, and reviews of their products is offered here. Catalog information, brochures, product photos—all can be browsed online. This site's Industry.Net Daily covers the latest news and developments in manufacturing and industry, engineering and industrial automation, computers, and communications—all on a daily basis, with superb regional coverage as well. You can also join online industry-related discussion groups for networking and information sharing. —(E.v.B.)

KEY NEWSGROUP biz.misc URL ▸ http://www.industry.net/

Rugged Individualists in Business and Life

American Individual Magazine & Coffeehouse Jump 8041

The American Individual Magazine shines its spotlight on the individual—the foundation of the American belief system. You can read about topics such as starting your own home-based business. All kinds of subjects of particular interest to the individual like career, personal finance, home schooling, consumer, health, and fitness information, or information on community and political activism, are discussed here. Web links have also been provided to most related topics. This site also features established forums where you can chat with others of similar interests. —(E.v.B.)

KEY NEWSGROUP alt.zines URL ▸ http://www.aimc.com/aimc/

African-American Business Help

The Network Journal Jump 8044

The Network Journal offers African-American professionals and small business owners news and views on management techniques, marketing, legal matters, taxes and office technology. Profiles of successful professionals and small business owners are also published in this monthly e-zine. Past issues are also archived at this site. —(E.v.B.)

KEY NEWSGROUP biz.misc URL ▸ http://www.tnj.com/

Trade Show Database

Trade Show Central Home Page Jump 8050

Trade Show Central helps you find trade shows to help you enter new markets and meet your company's current promotional needs. Use this site's easy interface to its 10,000-record database providing comprehensive information on worldwide trade shows and events. Trade show information can be accessed in either summary or detailed formats. —(E.v.B.)

KEY NEWSGROUP clari.nb.general URL ▸ http://www.tscentral.com/

Successful Trade Shows

Terrific Trade Show Tips Jump 5862

Trade shows are certainly a great selling vehicle for your business, but isn't there a way to learn the tricks of the trade beforehand? There is now! You'll find just about everything you need to know right here at the Terrific Trade Show Tips page, produced by Margit Weisgal of Sextant Communications. You begin on this site with a very important the section entitled: "What to Learn Before the Show." Everything is spelled out, allowing you to easily sail into the other information-packed parts of this site, which cover many other aspects of putting on a successful trade show presence. —(J.P.)

URL ▸ http://www.thevine.com/sextant/contents.htm

Web Marketing Tips and Tools

1st Steps: Cool Marketing Resources and Tools Jump 8076

You're poised to blast your new, super, space-aged-designed product onto the Web. But have you checked out all the information available on how to do this effectively? Stop on by the Web Marketing page and find out the latest information on Web consumers, and how to market to emerging niche markets on the Internet. You'll find marketing tips, the latest Web marketing news, information on Web page design for effective marketing, best places to advertise on the Web, how to monitor your competition, and marketing tools related to the Net. —(E.v.B.)

KEY NEWSGROUP **biz.misc**

URL▶ http://www.interbiznet.com/ibn/nomad.html

Business on the Internet: Overview

Thomas Ho's Favorite Electronic Commerce Sites
Jump **0107**

LINKS

Thomas Ho's huge outline-format Web jump site contains links to a massive array of Net and Web-based business information and Net technical resources. You could spend hours scrolling and linking to the hundreds of useful and informative business information resources here, which include links to businesses on the Net, general Internet information, service and technology providers, industry groups, electronic publishers, emerging services and Internet publications. Thomas Ho is the chair and professor of the Department of Computer Technology at Indiana University and a member of the Internet Society, and his Web site serves as an excellent overview for all business activity on the Net. —(E.G.)

KEY NEWSGROUP **alt.business.misc**

URL▶ http://www.engr.iupui.edu/~ho/interests/commmenu.html

Selling in Cyberspace

by Diana Pohly

November/December 1995

Marketing Tools

You're under pressure to take your company online, or to produce a CD-ROM, but you're not sure how to go about it. All the hype about "multimedia" and the "information superhighway" hasn't told you a thing about what the new media will do for your organization. As you review what solid facts you can find, your mind buzzes with unanswered questions.

"How does interactive fit with my existing marketing program?" "What's the difference between the World Wide Web and commercial online services?" "Does anyone really understand this stuff?" "Does it really work?"

Fortunately, cyber-marketing isn't a radical departure from traditional advertising. It's really about selling--a principal as old as civilization itself. To create a successful campaign, you just have to adapt marketing's conventional wisdom to fit the new media.

Let's consider the first question.How does interactive fit with my existing marketing campaign?Interactive marketing is all about extending the reach, frequency and power of your communications. In your current communications program, you probably integrate public relations, print, direct marketing, and perhaps radio and TV in some combination. Whether you add networked media (commercial online services, the Internet, the World Wide Web) or stand-alone interactive media (CD-ROM, disks or digital kiosks) to this mix, successful interactive projects work the same way as traditional vehicles: in harmony with your wider communications plan.

▲ *Marketing tips for the entrepreneur, from* **Marketing Tools Magazine** *at* Jump **7490**.

The Power of Selling

Selling Power on the We
Jump **5860**

CONTENT

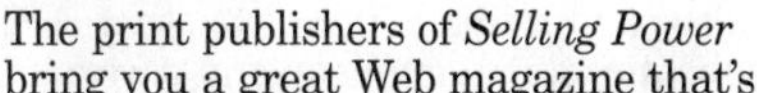

SellingPower ON THE WEB

The print publishers of *Selling Power* bring you a great Web magazine that's neatly divided into three very distinct and useful sections. The first is "New Ideas," all relating, of course, to the power of selling. These are how-to type features, but most are written by executives who have information about selling that they want to share with readers. For example, as was the case with a recent feature on Disney, the piece was actually written by Michael Eisner. There's also a section entitled "Products." Here you'll find books, tapes and other aids to help you build your selling skills. And finally, the "Resources" section, where you can read about the best companies for particular products, a list of guest speakers, a chat area, a job mart, and more. —(J.P.)

KEY NEWSGROUP **alt.business.misc** URL▶ http://www.sellingpower.com/

Guerrilla Marketing Online

GMO - Tactics - The Weekly Guerrilla Archive Jump **8077**

CONTENT

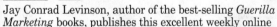

Jay Conrad Levinson, author of the best-selling *Guerilla Marketing* books, publishes this excellent weekly online newsletter bringing you the latest tips on waging marketing war with lots of smarts but little cash. Jay's practical advice is tailored specifically to entrepreneurs and small business owners, and clearly reflects much proven, street-savvy business selling experience. Read thought-provoking articles here on competitive advantages, how to sell to many different markets, as well as the tips on selling your products or services on the Internet. Archives of previous week's articles are also kept here, so you won't miss anything, either. —(E.v.B.)

KEY NEWSGROUP **biz.misc** URL▶ http://www.gmarketing.com/tactics/weekly_prev.html

The Netrepreneur's Digest

Electronic Money Tree

Electronic Money Tree
Jump **5763**

What this rich site lacks in cool graphics it makes up for in content, which features many intriguing articles on Net marketing, promotion, and the use of technology for entrepreneurs. The tone here is one of encouraging success, but not at any cost. There is also a realization that those who read the Electronic Money Tree are not only members of the small business community, but of the entire Internet Community as well. So there are many words of caution here when it comes to Internet scams, spamming, and the inability on the part of some to wait for financial gratification. The writing here is quite professional, and must-read material for any entrepreneur or small business owner. —(J.P.)

KEY NEWSGROUP **alt.business.misc** URL▶ http://www.soos.com/$tree/

InteractiveAgeDigital

Daily Web Marketing News from Interactive Age

Interactive Age Daily Media and Marketing Report Jump **8080**

Here's a fresh daily newsletter on all that's happening on the Web of interest to Net marketers and advertisers. This online version of Interactive Age magazine gives you the latest on new Net product introductions, Net marketing information sources, insider company news, and more, including a complete archive of past online issues. A must for anyone in the marketing end of the Internet business. —(E.v.B.)

KEY NEWSGROUP **biz.misc** URL▶ http://techweb.cmp.com/ia/dailies/market.htm

---

Commerce with a Conscience

The Progressive Business Web Pages Jump **2231**

It's not easy being green (environmentally speaking) if you're in business, but these pages from the nonprofit Enviro-Link Network can help. You'll find links to businesses on the Internet that meet the organization's criteria for social responsibility and protecting the environment. You don't have to be an activist to buy from these firms, but if you're concerned about supporting companies that put principle over profit, this is a good starting point. While you're here, you also can browse the links to other socially responsible groups and resources, including publications, mailing lists, and government support agencies. —(L.S.)

KEY NEWSGROUP **alt.business** URL▶ http://www.envirolink.org/pbn/

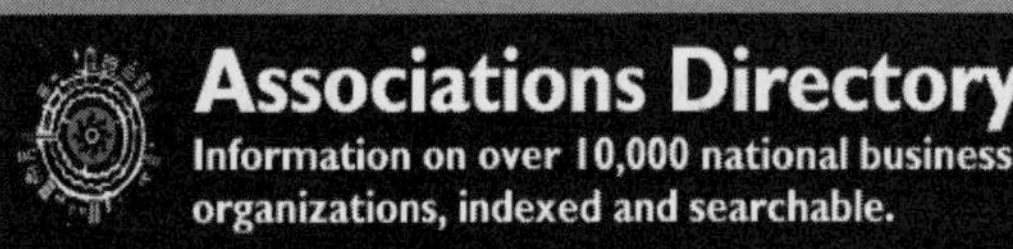

Associations Directory
Information on over 10,000 national business organizations, indexed and searchable.

Finding Trade & Industry Associations—Fast

NewMarket Forum Association Directory Jump **8081**

Trade associations can often be useful sources for industry research or sales leads, and here's a fantastic resource if you're looking for any professional or trade organization, a regional chamber of commerce, or one of over 10,000 other U.S. business organizations. Search here and you'll get all the basic information you'll need for contacting the association. If you run a business, or business-membership organization, you're also encouraged to add your details to this ever-expanding online trade directory. —(E.v.B.)

KEY NEWSGROUP **biz.misc** URL▶ http://www.newmarket-forum.com/assoc.html

---

Free Marketing Industry Profiles

MarketPlace Marketing Services Jump **5770**

This site, sponsored by MarketPlace Information Holdings, is a starting point for getting some basic market and industry information for your own business projects. What you get for free here are instant market analyses and profiles for 100 industries, access to a free marketing service network, free bookstore and a free online library, sponsored on this site. Membership is required, but it's also free. —(J.P.)

KEY NEWSGROUP **misc.entrepreneurs** URL▶ http://www.mktplace.com/home.htm

Entrepreneur's and Small Business Owner's Resources

Small Business Advancement Electronic Resource Jump **2049** 

The Small Business Advancement National Center is a government and privately-funded resource for research, training, consulting, and general information to support entrepreneurial and other small businesses. This growing site offers software, research, information bulletins and business contacts, as well as links to journals and other publications and articles of use to the small business. —(L.S.)

KEY NEWSGROUP **misc.entrepreneurs.moderated**
URL ▶ http://wwwsbanet.uca.edu/sbanet.html

▲ *Vintage advertisement for a money-making business, from* **BrettNews**, *at* Jump **1506**.

Starting a New Business

Big Dreams Jump **2070** 

This is a monthly newsletter on personal development and starting and succeeding in a small business. Written by Duncan Stickings, it includes common sense, good advice, helpful hints, and general support for the new entrepre-neur. It's not so much full of how-to as it is of things that make you look at your situation from a different perspec-tive, helping you find new opportunities and exploiting the opportunities you already have in front of you. —(L.S.)

KEY NEWSGROUP **misc.entrepreneurs.moderated** URL ▶ http://www.wimsey.com/~duncans/

Jupiter Communication's Market Intelligence for the Online Industry

Jupiter Communications Jump **5811** CONTENT

Jupiter is a New-York based research company that provides some of the Internet industry's most invaluable and authoritative information on the current and future state of online trends and interactive technologies. Although their customers usually include corporations in media, technology and entertainment, their Web site features excerpts from many of the content-rich reports they offer to these clients. Anyone interested in the future of the online world—and in the consumer-related aspects in particular—will find a wealth of information here. —(J.P.)

URL ▶ http://jup.com/

A Community for Small Business Entrepreneurs

American Express Small Business Exchange Jump **5760** 

Here's a great forum designed for entrepreneurs or small business owners looking for new business opportunities, advice and information. Features include Online Classifieds (where small businesses can advertise their products), a Business Network Directory (a quick way to find other like-minded services), as well as expert advice and a section on Business Planning and Resources, which contains a terrific library on online resources. And, best of all, the entire site is fully keyword searchable. —(J.P.)

KEY NEWSGROUP **misc.entrepreneurs.moderated** URL ▶ http://www.americanexpress.com/smallbusiness/

The Small Business Advisor

The Small Business Advisor

The Small Business Advisor Jump **5762** 

The Small Business Advisor is a content (and advertising)-loaded site that's updated nearly every day. While its on-screen ads make this site rather slow, once you've settled in you'll see that there is a wealth of information here, all of it very valuable to anyone involved in starting or operating a small business. At the heart is the "Advisor" section, where you'll find the archives for the Small Business Advisor Newsletter (you can subscribe to this free e-mail newsletter as well), state incorporation information, a piece entitled "Are You An Entrepreneur" (perhaps best read before going too far along), and information on obtaining a merchant credit card account. And you'll want to check out the sections on small business tax advice here as well. —(J.P.)

KEY NEWSGROUP **misc.entrepreneurs** URL ▶ http://www.isquare.com/

The Entrepreneur's Essential Resource

Cyberpreneur's Guide to the Internet Jump **2496**

When it comes to resources for entrepreneurs, it takes a lot of effort to separate the wheat from the chaff. This site does it for you. First created as part of a class at the School of Information and Library Studies at the University of Michigan, and written in its present form by Pamela Enyasi Wilkins and Suze Schweitzer, the links are carefully chosen, extremely well organized and clearly described. You can target sites by the type of Internet resource (newsgroup, mailing list, Gopher or Web), or browse an alpha-betical list. Either way, when you click on the resource, you're taken to a description of the site and a direct link. It's not as extensive as some other links lists on the Web, but that's because only the best sites are listed here. —(L.S.)

KEY NEWSGROUP **misc.entrepreneurs.moderated** URL ▶ http://asa.ugl.lib.umich.edu/chdocs/cyberpreneur/Cyber.html

Old Girls' Network

BBPW Metaguide Jump **2243**

Professional women can use this page as a ready reference to Internet business resources geared to their special interests. Maintained by Karen Schneider as part of the Barnard Business and Professional Women alumni group, it is similar to other business jumplists with two major differences. First, of course, is the emphasis on women's resources. More important, though, is that all the listings—even for the general resources—are very well annotated, so users will have more than a good idea of what's at the other end of the link. —(L.S.)

KEY NEWSGROUP **alt.business** URL ▶ http://www.intac.com/~kgs/bbpw/meta.html

Entrepreneur's Opportunities & News

Income Opportunities Jump **7313**

Income Opportunities ONLINE bills itself as the "original small business/home office magazine." And, if you're an entrepreneur or small business owner, you'll enjoy reading the latest news on business opportunities, advertised here in this zine's classified section. There's also info on finding the latest tips on new technologies, and inspiring profiles of other small business owners. Lots of links to Web business sites are offered as well. —(E.v.B.)

KEY NEWSGROUP **misc.entrepreneurs** URL ▶ http://www.incomeops.com/online/

Rich Entrepreneurial Resources

InterSoft Solutions - Commerce::Entrepreneurs Jump **7365**

InterSoft has created a no-nonsense Web site of rich resources for entrepreneurs. Those business people who love living on the edge can surf a great number of Web resources for entrepreneurs, find a compatible support organization, locate businesses catering to entrepreneurs and, for good measure, legal issues and resources related to entrepreneurs. As well, check out the bank and venture capital pages for the bottom line. —(E.v.B.)

KEY NEWSGROUP **misc.entrepreneurs** URL ▶ http://www.catalog.com/intersof/commerce/entrepre.html

Business at High Speed

Drive Electronic Magazine
Jump 5851

For Business At High Speed

Drive is a lively Web business magazine for the business professional who wants to keep up on the latest news and opinions, but doesn't have a whole lot of time to waste. The pieces are short and to the point, but professionally-written and illuminating. Among the self-help-related subjects covered are businesses that miss the boat by not moving quickly enough, life on the commuter train, office romances, how to better control your emotional responses in the workplace, and much more. —(J.P.)

URL http://www.drive-online.com/

Making a Life While Making a Living

Business@Home Jump 5765

This site, produced by Oregon Business Media, is committed to helping you make a life while you make a living. The thoughtful online features on this site document the radical restructuring that's occurring in the work force—and the definition of work—today. It provides you with news you can use in the wake of what they call the "workquake," and is of interest to everyone, not just work-at-home entrepreneurs. The operative world-view is one of leading mutli-layered lives, with emphasis on the notion that to be successful without "having a life" is no success at all. You'll find plenty of thought-provoking and timely articles here to help you find that balance. —(J.P.)

KEY NEWSGROUP misc.entrepreneurs URL http://www.gohome.com/

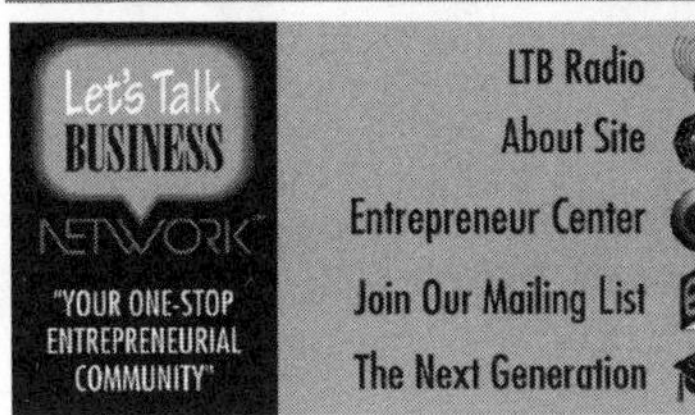

You Talk Business, We'll Listen

Let's Talk Business Network Jump 5766

The folks at the Let's Talk Business Network (LBTN) have put together a site that can serve as a one-stop site for entrepreneurs all over the Web. Along with great articles and tips, you find a unique marriage of radio and the Internet, since the folks at LBTN also happen to run the only nationally syndicated radio program focused on entrepreneurship, "Let's Talk Business." Here you'll find plenty of audio clips on topics ranging from franchising, personal growth, marketing, and more. —(J.P.)

KEY NEWSGROUP misc.entrepreneurs URL http://www.ltbn.com/

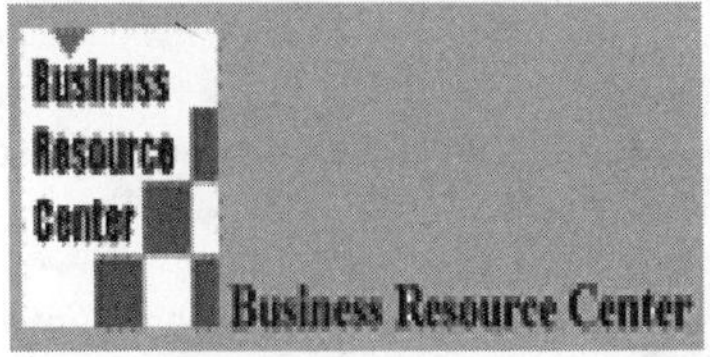

Starting and Succeeding in Small Business

Business Resource Center Jump 2074

Khera Communications, an organization that specializes in helping small businesses succeed, has developed this site of business start-up how-tos and good advice. It's a short course in starting and running a business, with sections on getting started, marketing, and management, as well as a section of useful miscellaneous articles. If you're looking for specific information, the entire site is also searchable by keyword. —(L.S.)

KEY NEWSGROUP misc.entrepreneurs.moderated URL http://www.kcilink.com/sbhc/

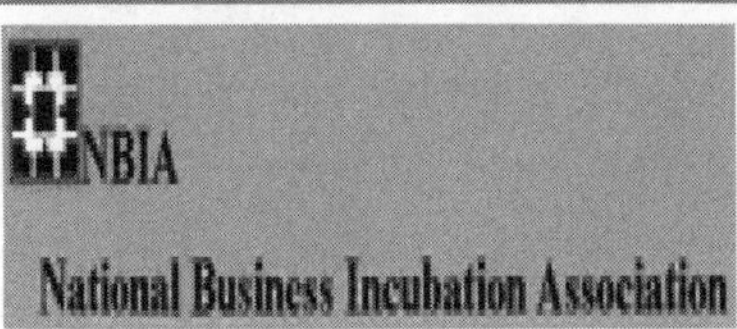

How to Hatch a Business

National Business Incubation Association
Jump 3675

So what's a business incubator? Business incubators support emerging businesses during their early, most vulnerable stages, promoting growth, technology transfer, neighborhood revitalization, and economic development and diversification. This site provides excellent information about the goals of this organization, which include an objective to build awareness of business incubation as a valuable business development tool, and also features some great links to useful Internet business and commerce sites. —(C.P.)

KEY NEWSGROUP alt.business.misc URL▶ http://ra.cs.ohiou.edu/gopher/dept.servers/aern/homepage/nbia.html

Internet Commercialization Directory

KnowledgeWeb, Inc. Jump 7253

This is a no-nonsense site covering all aspects of commercialization of the Internet, supported by KnowledgeWeb. Check out the Computer Events Directory for the latest information on technology conferences, exhibitions, seminars, and trade shows. Or, access the E-Commerce Directory that provides pointers to information on Internet-based financial transactions, and other related commercial information resources intended to help businesses to better utilize the Internet. —(E.v.B.)

KEY NEWSGROUP biz.misc URL▶ http://www.kweb.com/

publicity.com

How to Get Publicity for Your Company's Products

publicity.com Jump 5853

Ever wonder how all those guests keep ending up on all those TV shows? Well, you've come to the right place for the inside scoop. This site is an online publication that will give you tips on how to get publicity for your company's products or services, and how to get more bang from the the publicity you get. This site's creators, Media Relations, book hundreds of guests a year on radio programs and TV talk shows. So the aim here is to assist PR professionals and entrepreneurs in the art and craft of publicity. The editors of this site, Jason Kocina and Caroline Ruden, do a nice job of providing you with all kinds of useful publicity tips and other editorial features which look at the latest Web news from the standpoint of marketing and PR professionals. You'll enjoy this site's look behind the scenes of the PR biz, with its feature articles, interview tips, tricks, and other self-help advice. —(J.P.)

KEY NEWSGROUP URL▶ http://www.publicity.com/

BUSINESS WORLD

Online Business "How-To" Magazine

Marketing, Marketing, and More

Business World Table of Contents

Jump 7270

This online version of *Business World* magazine presents a number of interesting articles on all types of business topics from network marketing to mail order. You can browse present and past issues, visit the bookstore, post an ad, and read about marketing opportunities. A very solid, content-rich site. —(E.v.B.)

KEY NEWSGROUP biz.misc URL▶ http://www.mindspring.com/~jouver/bizworld/bizworld.html

Marketing News from Advertising Age

Ad Age - It's All About Marketing 7311

Welcome to the online version of *Advertising Age*—self-styled as "the preeminent content provider of marketing, advertising and media news, analysis and information." And they do live up to that statement here on the Web, too! Here you will read about the who's who of marketing and advertising, the latest news on who won what account, and who won what advertising award. As well, you can access an amazing amount of Web-based resources related to marketing and advertising: publications, statistical databases, corporation home pages, forums, and tip sheets. A great source for current advertising news and views. —(E.v.B.)

KEY NEWSGROUP biz.misc URL▶ http://www.adage.com/

Web Marketing Strategies

Chase Marketing Strategies Jump 5755

Larry Chase tells us, rather proudly as a matter of fact, that his firm is considered by many to have been the first ad agency to set up shop on the Web. Since then Chase has built a solid reputation helping companies understand how to best utilize the Web's marketing potential. More important to the rest of us, however, is the fact that this site is also home to the Web Digest for Marketers, (WDFM), one of the Web's oldest, most popular, and best sources of Net marketing advice and information, a must-read if you're involved in putting your business on the Internet. —(J.P.)

KEY NEWSGROUP **misc.entrepreneurs.moderated** URL ▶ http://www.chaseonline.com/

Cyber Marketing Discussion Lists

Marketing Lists on the Internet Jump 7342

CONTENT

Kim Bayne has collected hundreds of marketing-related e-mail discussion lists, freely-available on the Internet, that are extremely useful for small business owners. Kim also maintains a newsletter on cybermarketing, plus lists of trade publications, trade shows, and business resources. The scope of subjects covered by these lists are extensive—from advertising groups to biotechnology, and include e-mail subscription lists and moderated Usenet groups. For example, you can access the HTMARCOM List—an e-mail discussion group for high-tech marketing communicators in the computer and electronics industries. Anywhere marketing is discussed, Kim will link to that mailing list. —(E.v.B.)

KEY NEWSGROUP **biz.misc** URL ▶ http://www.bayne.com/wolfBayne/htmarcom/mktglist.html#index

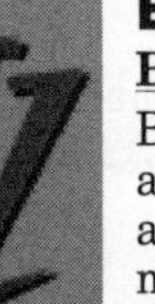

Blitz Media's Advertising Resource Center

Blitz Media Jump 7348

Boston-based Blitz Media has created an attractive site where media and advertising types are welcomed to read abstracts of articles from the national and regional press on media and advertising topics, plus numerous charts and tabular information on key media markets. You can also contribute stories about your own advertising hits and misses. The resource page has a lot of great and useful links for the media business. —(E.v.B.)

KEY NEWSGROUP **biz.americast** URL ▶ http://www.blitzmedia.com/

Marketing 101

Consumer Marketing Jump 2134

This primer on marketing to consumers outlines key concepts and activities the new marketeer must master to be successful. These pages pay particular attention to customer analysis and marketing strategy, but David Tyler plans to add additional information on marketing-plan implementation and advertising and promotion, as well as expanding the existing sections. Even in its current form, it covers the key concepts that often elude the new entrepreneur, and its outline form makes it easy to grasp and retain the ideas presented. —(L.S.)

KEY NEWSGROUP **alt.business** URL ▶ http://turnpike.net/metro/tuvok/index.html#outline

Selling to Japan

JETRO Jump 2617

CONTENT

Exporting to Japan is not impossible. It's not easy, but it can be done, and done successfully. What it takes, more than anything else, is an understanding of the Japanese market and economy, and the place to begin learning is here from the Japan External Trade Organization. This page will give you the information you need to get started, including Japanese government procurement information, Japanese economic news, market trends, information on business practices, and statistical data. —(L.S.)

KEY NEWSGROUP **alt.business** URL ▶ http://www.jetro.go.jp/

Web Newsletter for Editorial and Publishing Professionals

The Editorial Eye Jump 1589

Since 1978, the Editorial Eye has been giving advice to communications specialists and anyone else who cares about excellence in publications practices. Editor Linda Jorgensen realized a Web site "would reach people who might not otherwise hear of the publication." This 12-page monthly Web newsletter is a wellspring of ideas and encouragement for present and future writers and editors. The writing style, with topics like "Untangling the Web," "Dingbats Galore," "Researchers Who Glow in the Dark," doesn't lack for humor, yet presents important information for publishing and editorial professionals. Once you read the abbreviated articles, you'll be sending for a sample issue. —(H.L.)

URL ▶ http://www.eei-alex.com/eye/

Demographics of the Internet

The Internet Business Journal

Jump 5759

Of all the unanswered questions about use of the Internet, perhaps none has garnered more interest than the questions relating to who and how many are actually surfing the Internet at any given time. Figures vary, too widely to account for the standard "plus or minus" factors built into most surveys. In the hopes of helping you to answer these questions, The Internet Business Journal has collected a comprehensive index of the best Internet-accessible resources and reports on the demographics of the Internet. While many of these files do little more than document the difficulty in documenting the statistics, others go so far as to describe their findings as the definitive tally. A good starting point if you're looking for basic usage and market numbers for the Internet. —(J.P.)

KEY NEWSGROUP alt.politics.datahighway URL ▶ http://www.strangelove.com/ibj/marketing/demographi

Internet Business Facts

Economic FAQs About the Internet Jump 7484

Jeffrey K. MacKie-Mason and Hal R. Varian have compiled an extensive FAQ about "the economic, institutional, and technological structure of the Internet." The authors describe "the history and current state of the Internet, discuss some of the pressing economic and regulatory problems, and speculate about future developments." Detailed information on such topics as the problems associated with Web site usage accounting, economic problems for commerce on the Internet, and how Net-based electronic currency works, can also be accessed here. A dense, informative site. —(E.v.B.)

KEY NEWSGROUP alt.answers URL ▶ http://gopher.econ.lsa.umich.edu/FAQs/FAQs.html

Business Publications Net Index

Print Publications Related to Business Use of the Internet

Jump 7485

The Tenagra Corporation has created this informative site describing a great number of publications that help you learn how the Internet can be used for business purposes. Book reviews, articles, newsletters, journals and Web-based e-magazines are detailed. The authors of the site have also compiled a useful list of links to other Internet business-related sites. —(E.v.B.)

KEY NEWSGROUP biz.misc URL ▶ http://arganet.tenagra.com/Tenagra/books.html#dummies

CommerceNet

CommerceNet Jump 0066

A government and corporate consortium designed to give businesses a presence on the Web, CommerceNet features links to many corporate, business, and high-tech company Web sites. Most of the Web sites on CommerceNet belong to huge corporations, and we've found that these big company Web sites are, generally speaking, some of the Web's least useful and interesting Web sites. But if your business involves doing business with large corporations, CommerceNet is where you'll find them. —(E.G.)

URL ▶ http://www.commerce.net/information/information.html

Better Purchasing Management

The Purchasing Web of Articles Jump 2066 CONTENT

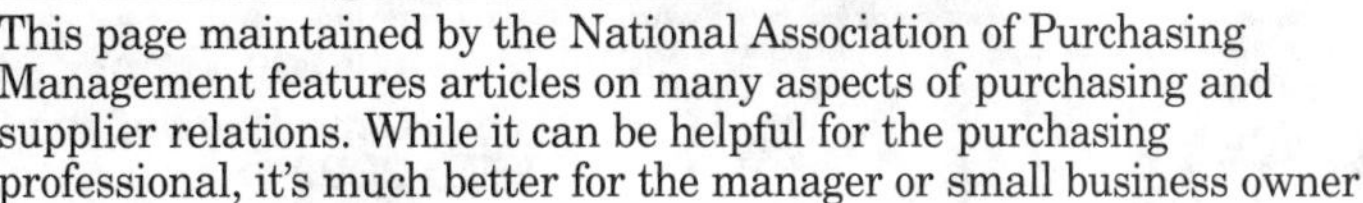

This page maintained by the National Association of Purchasing Management features articles on many aspects of purchasing and supplier relations. While it can be helpful for the purchasing professional, it's much better for the manager or small business owner who needs to know more about these aspects of running a business. —(L.S.)

KEY NEWSGROUP **alt.business** URL ▶ http://www.catalog.com/napmsv/pwhead.htm

Learn the Limits of Spam

Blacklist of Internet Advertising Jump 2014 CONTENT

If you're thinking of advertising on newsgroups or through e-mail, check this page established by Axel Boldt, which documents the infamous Canter & Siegel Net spamming incident and its aftermath (these two immigration services attorneys sparked a major Net controversy by posting an ad for their services on thousands of Net newsgroups, popularizing the word "spam," which, in Net parlance, describes the indiscriminate posting of junk advertising to irrelevant Net newsgroups). For starters, you'll get an idea of the boundaries of tolerance for spam. It very clearly describes how you can get on Net "blacklists" for various spamming offenses and, in the interests of fairness, offers suggestions of how a blacklisted person or company can strike back. Every entry has a description of the offense and, when applicable, a summary of the actions taken against them and their responses. —(L.S.)

KEY NEWSGROUP **alt.current-events.net-abuse** URL ▶ http://math-www.uni-paderborn.de/~axel/blacklist.html

Business Resources in Depth

IOMA Business Page Jump 2065 CONTENT

The main page provides one of the most comprehensive list of links to Internet resources, well organized by topic and subtopic and including links to articles, links to Web and Gopher resources, and a selection of links to current business news. It's easy to be overwhelmed by the depth of information available, but if you let that happen, you might miss some very useful stuff, such as The Institute of Management's newsletter articles covering a variety of business disciplines, including financial management, cash flow, benefits planning, inventory, and suppliers. —(L.S.)

KEY NEWSGROUP **alt.business** URL ▶ http://ioma.com/ioma/

Hooked on Phone Numbers: Mnemonic Calculator

PhonNETic Jump 2133 CONTENT

If you want one of those nifty mnemonic phone numbers that let your customers remember your number by remembering a simple word, Nikolay Uglov has written a CGI script (brought to Web life by Nick Sklavounakis) that will give you all the possible number combinations from that word. It's a great way to brainstorm different phone words, and gives you a head start in dealing with the phone company to secure the number. And if you're one of those people who hates hunting around the phone pad looking for the numbers that match the letters, Nickolay and Nick help you, too, with a word-to-phone number converter. —(L.S.)

KEY NEWSGROUP **alt.business** URL ▶ http://www.soc.qc.edu:80/phonetic/

Business in Canada Web Pages

Canada Net Pages Jump 2203 CONTENT

Business in Canada is as active on the Internet as business is below the 49th parallel, and these pages by Online Visions are an excellent resource for Canadian business and finance information. There's a well-designed search engine for locating businesses by company or individual's name, product classification, city, province, or stock symbol. You can locate career opportunities, mutual funds information, and real estate buyers and sellers. You can browse an online trade show with more than 100 exhibits, as well as links to the other interesting sites in Canadian Web space. You can even link to a Canadian Cool Site of the Week. What you can't do is absorb all these resources at one sitting, so bookmark it and keep going back! —(L.S.)

KEY NEWSGROUP alt.business URL ▶ http://www.visions.com/netpages/

Worldwide Recycling Resources

The Home Page of the Global Recycling Network Jump 2292

Organizations with machinery, materials or excess inventory to recycle, as well as those looking to buy, can use this database to post buy and sell offers, browse for bargains, or otherwise find a home for unwanted but usable items. This free service covers more than 100 countries and includes a free online newsletter covering current recycling news. —(L.S.)

KEY NEWSGROUP alt.business URL ▶ http://grn.com/grn/

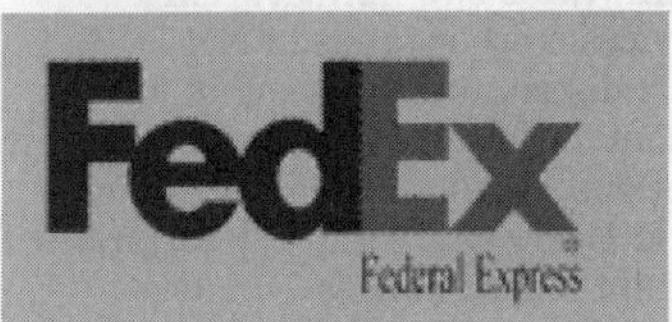

Follow that Package!

FedEx Airbill Tracking Form Jump 7112

Feeling nervous about the big business presentation you sent, via Federal Express, to your business partners? Will they receive them in time? Well, wipe the sweat off your brow and log onto to FedEx's tracking page. There you can track where your package or envelope is, anywhere in the world, anytime of the day. It couldn't be simpler— just type in your tracking number in the field provided and the status of the package will be displayed. —(E.v.B.)

URL ▶ http://www.fedex.com/cgi-bin/track_it

INTERNATIONAL TRADE LAW PROJECT

World Trade Documents

WTA/WTO & GATT 1994 Jump 7154

Need to know the regulations on shipping living plants across national boundaries? Visit here and download the Agreement on Sanitary and Phytosanitary Measures. The World Trade Agreement (WTA), World Trade Organization (WTO), the General Agreement on Tariffs and Trade (GATT) and more, all gathered under one electronic umbrella. Searching through these documents is a snap, thanks to the Law Faculty at the University of Tromso, Norway, which has established the online International Trade Law Project—an impressive collection of the full texts of these acts and agreements. —(E.v.B.)

URL ▶ http://ananse.irv.uit.no/trade_law/gatt/nav/toc.html

Manufacturer's Listings from the Thomas Register

Thomas Register Home Page Jump 3735

The Thomas Register of American Manufacturers is a valuable business resource that's now online. And, many of you who've used those big green books to locate suppliers of industrial products and services will want to link to this site. The Thomas Register Supplier Finder allows you to search on a product or service and retrieve information on the companies offering that product or service. As a special Web bonus, there's a set of mini-tutorials called "How to Buy It," which offers consumers a great way to find out what to look for when purchasing a variety of high-tech products. You can also get your own company listed in the Thomas Register by signing up online. And, since this is a commercial site, you can also order the complete set of books or a single CD-ROM, too. —(N.F.)

URL ▶ http://www.thomasregister.com:8000/home.html

Free Reads for the Computer Trade

The List of Free Computer Related Publications
Jump 2614 CONTENT

If you're involved in the computer business Jim Huguelet makes it easy for you to be sure you're getting the trade papers you need to stay on top on things. These are free magazines, although they are controlled circulation, meaning you need to obtain and answer a subscription questionnaire to be sure you qualify before they'll send you any copies. Each entry has a general description, specific content information and an overall rating, to give you a little guidance in choosing which publication to subscribe to. Of course, Jim tells you who to contact to subscribe, including phone numbers and online links, when available. —(L.S.)

BusinessWeek ONLINE
ENTER OUR SWEEPS!
Thursday Jan. 9
SIGN UP | BW CONTENTS | BW PLUS! | BW DAILY | SEARCH | CONTACT US | AD INFO
THE BEST...
Managers, entrepreneurs and products of '96: Shoes, wheels, & WebTV
UP FRONT
Smartest & dumbest '96 moves. Survey results. And a news trivia test
NIKKEI JITTERS
A flat budget, tax hikes, and 1% growth could pummel Japan's market
THIS WEEK
DAILY BRIEFING
Every business day: BW News Flashes, plus market info and insights
QUICK QUOTES
Market stats and lots more -- including your own Portfolio Manager
TRY MAVEN!
BW's Computer Buying Guide will make you a sharper PC shopper

OUTLOOK '97: AMERICA'S KEY INDUSTRIES
BusinessWeek
THE TOP 25 MANAGERS of the YEAR

▲ *BusinessWeek Online cover screen capture, from* **BusinessWeekOnline** *at* Jump **5717**.

KEY NEWSGROUP **biz.comp.services** URL ▶ http://www.soci.niu.edu/~huguelet/TLOFCRP/

Business Week on the Web

Business Week
Jump 5717 

McGraw-Hill's *Business Week* is one of the most respected names in business publications and they've brought their know-how to the Web in a big way. What you'll find here is the very latest in an online version that features all of the text from the paper edition, and much more, including some things you won't even find anywhere else! The latest issue is uploaded to this site every Thursday evening and includes both BW's U.S. and the International editions. Once online, you'll find everything from Daily Briefings, Quotes and Portfolios, Computer Buying Tips (their own Consumer Reports-style guide to computers), a company of the week (via Standard & Poor's Compustat) and enough feature-length articles to keep you up most of the night. And you can also sign up for the Insider Newsletter and receive up-to-date information via email —(J.P.)

URL ▶ http://www.businessweek.com/

Inventors on the Web

invent.html Jump 5106 CONTENT

Whether you're a workshop tinkerer or moonlight engineer, Inventus is a Web forum where you can present your inventions, ideas, speculations, and more. There are news and announcements for the inventor, including a list of new inventions, tips and guides, a look at the legal aspects of patent protection, and relevant news from around the world. For a list of inventions and products, check the "Shelves" section of this site. There are also other links to business, patent, and science information. A great Web resource! —(S.B.)

URL ▶ http://www.sgn.com/invent.html

Top Industrial and Manufacturing News Online

IndustryNet Daily - Industry's On-Line News Source Jump 7265 

There are a fair number of Web publications covering general business topics, but very few covering the important industrial and manufacturing industries. Industry.Net Daily covers the latest news and developments in manufacturing and industry, engineering and industrial automation, computers, and communications—all on a daily basis. Its regional coverage is superb. As well, international developments in manufacturing and engineering are also reported. —(E.v.B.)

KEY NEWSGROUP **clari.biz.industry.manufacturing** URL ▶ http://www.industry.net/daily

Entrepreneur's Web Magazine

Entrepreneur Magazine Online Jump **5764** 

One of the features on this site, the electronic version of the long-running *Entrepreneur* print magazine, is entitled "A Cut Above." You could say the same for the entire site, as a matter of fact. You'll find some great articles directed to entrepreneurs, to be sure, with a cross-section of national and international coverage. And the entrepreneurial marketing tips run fast and furious. What we like best, however, was the Net News section, which presents a handy list of dandy links for entrepreneurs. There's even a review of each, so you'll know where you're heading before you go there. And the selected sites are all as good as this one, too. Be sure to check out the site map here before heading too far because there really is a great deal of information here, and you'd hate to miss any of it. —(J.P.)

KEY NEWSGROUP **misc.entrepreneurs** URL▶ http://www.entrepreneurmag.com/

Capitalist Tool

Forbes Magazine 

Jump **5854**

This is it. The online version of *Forbes* is everything you've come to expect from the print version, plus a few added bonus features thrown in for good measure. We liked this site's layout, too. Instead of trying to duplicate the magazine, they kept it simple, with just one page per story. And there's a reader's forum, investment stats and advice, past issues archive, and fascinating tech articles from the *Forbes ASAP* supplements here as well. The entire site is searchable by keyword, and those with RealAudio can tune into the sound version of this site, too. —(J.P.)

KEY NEWSGROUP **alt.business.misc** URL▶ http://www.forbes.com/

Fortune Magazine on the Web

FORTUNE Jump **7274** 

Fortune, that icon of American big business and great-granddaddy of business publications, now has a very solid, well-done site on the Web. You can hobnob with the Fortune 500 and read all the business news, ideas, and solutions found in this very comprehensive online version of the well-known newsstand magazine. You can even hear the latest financial and business news of the day, updated frequently, through a RealAudio program at this site. Special issues can also be accessed. —(E.v.B.)

KEY NEWSGROUP **biz.misc** URL▶ http://www.pathfinder.com/

Inc. Magazine Online

Inc. Online Jump **5716** 

As a Web version of *Inc.* Magazine, Inc. Online delivers the goods on resources for "growing your small business." You'll find almost everything you'll ever need here, from in-depth, authoritative articles, tips and industry news, columns to help you sort out business fact from fiction, and an interactive bulletin board, and you can even read the current paper version online. And if you've got a few minutes to spare after all this (and it will take you a while!) you can even register for a free homepage on their site. —(J.P.)

URL▶ http://www.inc.com/

Success for Entrepreneurs

Success Jump **5861** 

Here's the Web version of the popular print magazine *Success*, offering all kinds of useful advice for entrepreneurs, small business owners, and sales pros. You can read the current issue of the magazine here—it's filled with great features and tips on working at home, selling your product, and spotting new market trends. The tone here is positive, supported with concepts and techniques that clearly emphasize the use of new technology. Back issues are also available, as is a bulletin board and special features such as "Franchise Gold" (a list of the best 100 franchise companies), and "The Source," a list of the best business-related Web sites. —(J.P.)

KEY NEWSGROUP misc.entrepreneurs URL▶ http://www.successmagazine.com/

Farm Business News & Talk

Farm Journal Today Jump 7299

How you gonna keep 'em down on the farm, after they've seen the Web? Easy. Send them to Farm Journal Today where farmers and other interested people can read the latest news on hogs, beef, crops and dairy concerns. You can also enter discussion rooms and chat about federal legislation and regulations, the weather, and other topics of agricultural interest. As well, you can surf to other Net resources, check commodity pricing, and contact online agricultural organizations. A great site! —(E.v.B.)

KEY NEWSGROUP alt.agriculture.misc URL▶ http://www.FarmJournal.com/

Form a Corporation Online

The Company Corporation Jump 2029

The Company Corporation, developers of this site, can help you incorporate your business in the United States or internationally, online, by phone, or by FAX, for as little as $119. Even if you don't want to take advantage of their services, there's good information here, enough to give you more than the basic whys and wherefores about incorporating. Online, there's information about the costs of incorporating in various states, an incorporation FAQ, plus a review of the different forms of corporations. You can also request a free guide to incorporating, too. —(L.S.)

KEY NEWSGROUP alt.business.mics URL▶ http://www.service.com/tcc/home.html

All about Doing Business on the Net

Tenagra Jump 3659

With the mad "I-gotta-get-my-business-on-the-Net" rush that's going on in commercial sectors these days, there's a growing tendency for businesses that are new to the Net environment to commit serious faux pas by failing to understand the culture of this new medium. The old adage "When In Rome..." applies here, too! Tenagra offers a serious collection of information that will assist the new Net entrepreneur in getting to know the territory. They specialize in "helping businesses establish their 'Net.Presence' using Net.Acceptable techniques..." An excellent resource! —(C.P.)

KEY NEWSGROUP alt.entrepreneur URL▶ http://arganet.tenagra.com/Tenagra/tenagra.html

Help Wanted & Careers

Help Wanted Metalist

JobHunt Jump 2527

This is one of the most comprehensive list of links to help wanted and other career-search resources, and one of the best maintained. Dane Spearing works hard to ensure that the links included are stable and useful for a wide range of job types and geographic areas. The online job listings are organized by general, academic, and science and engineering jobs, with additional links to newspaper classified ads, recruiting agencies, and newsgroup searches. In addition, Dane lists links where you can submit your resume and learn how to conduct a job search. A great feature of this page is that Dane has identified the best, the new, and the stale Web links, so you'll be able to use this list productively on your very first visit. —(L.S.)

KEY NEWSGROUP misc.jobs URL▶ http://rescomp.stanford.edu/jobs.html

College·Grad·Job·Hunter
Your Link To Life After College

Your Link to Life After College

College Grad Job Hunter Jump 5784

CONTENT

So you've fought your way through college and are ready to embark on a life-long career in . . . what? You might wake up one morning with the realization that you have to fight this battle on your own, but that's not necessarily the case. If you drop into the College Grad Job Hunter site you'll find actual proof that you're not alone. If you want to learn how to make yourself stand out in a crowded job market, check out the Job Search Prep section. It's filled with great tips and links. You can search for entry level jobs or learn the best ways to frame your resume. And there's also a great E-Zine and even Audio clips you can listen to! —(J.P.)

KEY NEWSGROUP **misc.jobs.misc** URL▶ http://www.collegegrad.com/

First Choice for a Second Career

Career Magazine Jump **5800** 

If you're about to change careers, or even if you're not, check out Career Magazine. With the job market in such a volatile state, there's no telling when you might need the advice you'll find here. You can begin with this site's job openings section. Everyday, this site's editors download all of the job postings from the major Internet employment-related newsgroups. You can also use their search engine to locate jobs by keyword. On this site's "Employer Profiles" page, you'll find links to the job pages of dozens of the top companies in the U.S., and you can upload your resume to the this site's online resume bank, and join in on this site's online discussion forums. —(J.P.)

KEY NEWSGROUP **misc.jobs.misc** URL▶ http://www.careermag.com/

Medical Job Search Database

MedSearch America Jump **5823** CONTENT

Increasingly the Internet is being used, by both employers and employees, in the area of employment. One of the newest to join the rank is the medical profession. With cutbacks now a daily part of medical life, employers are always on the lookout for better ways to find the best person for any new position. So not only will you find a listing of medical-related jobs listed here, but those interested can also submit resumes, with access to healthcare forum, employer's profiles and much more. —(J.P.)

URL▶ http://www.medsearch.com/

Life and Work in the Revolutionary New World Economy

Brave New Work World Jump **5849** 

Will occupations and traditional careers, as we know them now, still exist in the new information-based economy? If so, who will the workers be? This site, produced by Gary Johnson Communications, offers a unique take on the forthcoming brave new world of work. This is meant to be a source of information to perhaps alter our way of thinking about working in the new economy, while offering tips so that each of us might be better prepared for the constant changes ahead. At the heart is a every-changing collection of commentaries and news articles culled from around the world, meant to keep us abreast of the changes. And you'll also find many related reviews and site links. —(J.P.)

URL▶ http://www.newwork.com/

Best Bets for Job Searches

Job Search and Employment Opportunities Jump **2177** 

Save yourself a lot of time and frustration by visiting this site before you start searching the Internet for a job. Philip Ray and Bradley Taylor haven't just assembled a list of links, they describe each one in detail, so you know what type of service it is and what you can expect from the site. There also are tips on how to make the best use of the link, whether it contains job postings, resume services, or another job-related resource. The page is organized by categories—education, humanities and social science, business, government, science and technology—and because some of the best job resources aren't just on the Web, the authors have included Net-based Gopher and Telnet sites, too. Rounding out the resources here are guides for new Internet users and new job seekers. —(L.S.)

KEY NEWSGROUP **misc.jobs** URL▶ http://www.lib.umich.edu/chdocs/employment/

Help for Career (and Life) Changers

Jumping Mouse Online Jump **5855**

If you've ever spent a moment or two pondering the state of your life, you'll find plenty of food for thought at Jumping Mouse Online. The aim here is helping you to discover the art of reinventing yourself by changing your career or your life. All you need is the ability to believe that you can change your place in the world, by "thinking outside of the box." We agree! And the many real-life articles you'll find here will help you to do just that. You'll discover the world outside of work, how to turn an adventure into a career you'll love, tips on how to best tackle homeschooling for your children, help for at-home dads, and much more in this eclectic site, edited by Veronica Brown. —(J.P.)

URL▶ http://www.mindspring.com/~jpanddb/jmindex.html

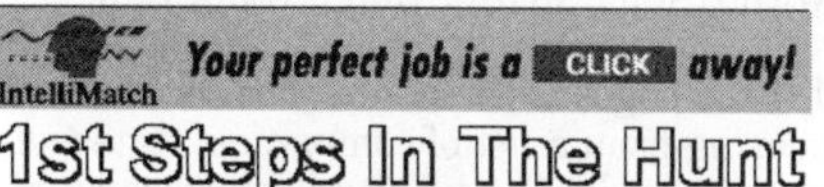

First-Step Net Job Pointers

1st Steps in the Hunt Jump **6757**

If you're looking for a more fulfilling career, you'll find this daily newsletter to be like having a personal career advisor by your side. Link here and tap first-hand knowledge on issues like using the Net to find a job, and how to prepare your resume for posting to the Internet. They'll even show you how to create an HTML resume to place on the Web, where the best summer jobs are, and how to write a winning cover letter. You'll also find one of the most comprehensive listings of Web job hunting links around today. Whether you're looking for jobs in the biological sciences, health services or any number of business professions, here's another useful starting point. —(L.T.)

KEY NEWSGROUP **misc.jobs.misc** URL▶ http://www.interbiznet.com/hunt/

E-Span Career Companion SM

E-Span's Career Searcher & Advice Site

E-Span's Career Companion

Jump **6883**

E-Span, one of the Web's first online employment sites, has created this new career aid that's designed for "upwardly mobile professionals." Whether you're a job seeker or you're satisfied with your present career but are looking for a different challenge, E-Span lets you search thousands of jobs in many different fields, from architecture to pharmaceuticals. You'll also be able to read their terrific guide on how to compose a winning resume, scan the latest employment news, find relocation tools (when you land the job of your dreams) and discover how to gain "the edge" with all of today's innovative, online job-hunting techniques. —(L.T.)

KEY NEWSGROUP **misc.jobs.misc** URL▶ http://www.caremercompanion.com

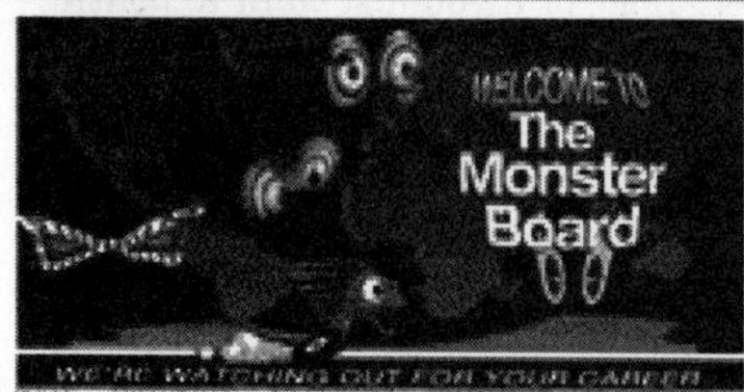

Jobs, Careers, and More . . .

The Monster Board Jump **2748**

Designed for both job seekers and employers, this is one of the most comprehensive career sites on the Net. For employers, there's human resources news and information, including tips for how to best advertise job opportunities, a section to post positions available, and a searchable database of resumes from job seekers. For the job seeker, there are similar services, and much more. Search for jobs by location, industry, company, discipline or any keyword, submit your resume or update one already online, or learn more about prospective employers, including their products and services, benefits programs and work environments. And then there's ROAR, a place where you can take a break and find out about music, movies and more, share job searching or other thoughts with others, ask career-related questions, or just vent about whatever's bothering you at the time. —(L.S.)

KEY NEWSGROUP **misc.jobs.misc** URL▶ http://199.94.216.72:80/home.html

Web Employment Opportunities

Interactive Employment Network Jump 0021

Executive recruiting firms have been actively and successfully using the Internet for some time now, posting job listings and providing career advice online. The E-SPAN Interactive Employment Network is one of the largest employment opportunities sites around. In addition to its large and extensive job library, containing career opportunities for a variety of employment positions searchable by job position and region, E-SPAN also features salary guides, career fair calendars, resume writing, and networking advice. A good Web stop with a wide variety of positions available—not just for computer programmers! —(E.G.)

KEY NEWSGROUP **misc.jobs.offered** URL▶ http://www.espan.com/

Job Hunting Made Easier

Online Career Center Jump 2002

Nonprofit (but with links to commercial resources), the Online Career Center offers information about and help with resume writing and posting your resume to the Net, employment events and recruiters, among other job-related topics. But the real jewel of these pages is the online jobs database. It gives you two choices: Search by choosing from a list of companies, states, or cities, or run a search from your own keywords. The job postings are current and, unlike some online ad services, not just limited to technical positions. —(L.S.)

KEY NEWSGROUP **alt.jobs, misc.jobs** URL▶ http://www.occ.com/occ/

Job Hunter's Resource

NCS Career Magazine Jump 2223

This page goes well beyond the usual help wanted listings to provide a well-rounded resource for job seekers. There are numerous articles to support your job search, including tips on resume writing and interviewing techniques, general news of interest to job seekers, and a weekly selection of articles taken from *The Wall Street Journal's National Business Employment Weekly*. Of most help, though, may be the online discussion forum. Job seeking can be a lonely affair, and this forum lets you network with others to discuss any aspect of the job search, workplace issues, and general employment-related topics. Even if you're not looking for a job now, this is a great site for keeping in touch with the market and building contacts for the future. —(L.S.)

KEY NEWSGROUP **misc.jobs.misc** URL▶ http://www.careermag.com/careermag/

Manage Your Career Online

CareerWEB Jump 3617

Looking for a new career? If so, or if you just want to polish up your resume, stop by CareerWEB, a network of career services and resources for today's high-tech work force. Whether you're an employer, a job candidate, a franchiser or recruitment-based company, you'll find something of interest here—from job opportunities to career fairs, from profiles of top employers to resume maintenance—CareerWEB has it all. You can browse through their many listings, and even nominate yourself if you think you're just the candidate a prospective employer is looking for. —(C.P.)

KEY NEWSGROUP **misc.jobs.misc** URL▶ http://www.cweb.com/

Starting Point for Career Searches

The Catapult Jump 2525

A collaborative effort of various college career offices, maintained by Leo Charette, this is an excellent starting point for a job or career search. Whether you're a recent graduate, or an experienced worker back in the job market, you'll find solid advice and pointers to everything you'll need to land the job you want. You can learn how to write effective resumes and conduct successful interviews, browse links to job ads, and even find out how to visit prospective employer companies via the Internet, so you can learn more about them before you apply for a job. The job listings and career guides are very comprehensive and well organized. If you can't find what you need here quickly and easily, it's probably not on the Net! —(L.S.)

KEY NEWSGROUP **misc.jobs** URL▶ http://www.wm.edu/catapult/resmdir/contents.html

Investment & Legal

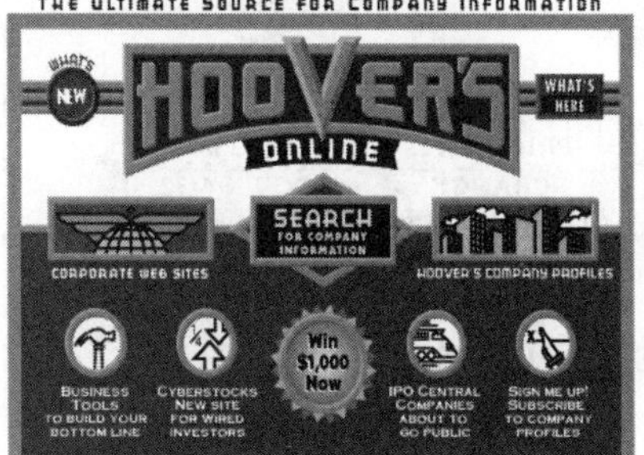

Hoover's Company Investment Database

Hoover's Online Jump 5721

Hoover's, Inc. is a seven-year-old business information company located in Austin, Texas. Through both books and online media Hoover's has fashioned a reputation by providing thorough and timely information on over 16,000 publicly-traded companys large and small. Online visitors can use Hoover's two searchable databases that are virtually without peer. The first is the Corporate Web Site database, which lists links to thousands of the largest corporations in the world. And this site's job database can be used to search for corporate job listings! And there's more, of course, including our favorite, the quick quote database. The really good information is for subscribers only (at a reasonable cost), but there's enough free information available here to make it worth your while, too. —(J.P.)

URL▶ http://www.hoovers.com/

Dictionary of Financial and Business Terms

Financial Encyclopaedia Jump 2030

This is more of a dictionary than an encyclopedia, but it is very useful nonetheless. You'll be able to easily find definitions and short explanations of virtually every term you encounter in business and finance, including computer-related topics. The most intriguing aspect of this site is that you can laud, complain, or contribute. Each entry has an electronic mail-to form you can use to tell Steve Bennett what you thought of the entry, and suggest additions to make it even more helpful. —(L.S.)

KEY NEWSGROUP **alt.business** URL▶ http://www.euro.net/innovation/Finance_Base/Fin_encyc.html

Just the FAQs on Investment

misc.invest.funds FAQ Jump 5724

Before heading out to make your first investment in a mutual fund, you might want to take a quick pit stop here at the **misc.invest.funds** FAQ (Frequently Asked Question) file. Like other Net FAQs, it's been created by Internet users as a service to help other Internet users. It ain't pretty, but if you've got questions, this FAQ's keeper, William Rini, has the answers. Who else will tell you: What is a mutual fund? What is a prospectus? It's the sort of thing you either know (because you already know) or you don't, because no one would ever give you a straight answer. But you'll find the straight dope here—plain, informative, and factual. —(J.P.)

URL▶ http://www.cis.ohio-state.edu/hypertext/faq/usenet/investment-faq/mutual-funds/faq.html

The Net's General Investment FAQs

USENET FAQs - misc.invest Jump 5725

The Investment FAQ (Frequently Asked Question) file is a collection of articles about investments and personal finance, including stocks, bonds, options, discount brokers, information sources, life insurance, and more, created by Internet users to help other users along the way. If you're a complete novice when it comes to investment information you've come to the right place. In a seven-part series, compiler Christopher Lott has put together a wonderful introduction to the world of investing. Our favorite section: Shorting against the Box, found in Part Six of the Investing FAQ (it means selling short securities that you already own, in case you were wondering). —(J.P.)

URL▶ http://www.cis.ohio-state.edu/hypertext/faq/bngusenet/misc/invest/top.html

streetEYE

2 Penn Plaza - Suite 1500
New York, NY 10121
(212) 292-5110

Investor's Search Engine

StreetEYE Index
Jump 5874

It's one thing to know what kind of investment information you want, but sometimes it's exceedingly difficult to find exactly what you need on the Internet. StreetEYE addresses these problems with a terrific search engine that's geared exclusively to the needs of investors and investment professionals. With StreetEYE you can search for brokers, investment managers and exchanges. There's also a great database for government sources and another devoted to personal finance. You can find all of the latest up-to-the-minute business and market news with StreetEYE's list of links. —(J.P.)

KEY NEWSGROUP **alt.business.misc** URL▶ http://www.streeteye.com/

DOW JONES 30 INDUSTRIALS

UP 37.93 TO 5,177.45

INDEX	CLOSE	POINT CHANGE		% CHANGE
20 TRANSPORTS	2,092.11	UP	5.85	+ 0.28%
15 UTILITIES	220.14	UP	2.04	+ 0.94%
65 COMPOSITE	1,730.78	UP	10.43	+ 0.61%

30-Year Bond

PRICED AT:	111 14/32
CHANGE	DOWN 6/32
INTEREST RATES	TO 6.041%

NEW YORK STOCK EXCHANGE

UP 2.19 TO 329.79

▲ *Daily stock market results, from* **FORTUNE** *at* Jump **7274**.

AAII's Web Tutorials and Resources for Individual Investors

American Association of Individual Investors
Jump 0223

If you're just getting started with a personal or family investment plan, the AAII Web site is one of the Web's best resources for giving you the information you'll need to get started. Whatever the investment topic, the AAII site takes you step-by-step through the basics of investing, with an extensive range of topics—from basic financial planning, to mutual funds, stocks, bonds, a reference shelf, and much more. If you're a complete investment novice, you'll also appreciate this site's extensive dictionary of investment terms. The AAII, which has long served thousands of individual investors since the early 1980s, has done beginning Web investors a real service with this site; if you're one of them, it should be your first Web stop for learning the smart investment information you'll need to know. —(E.G.)

KEY NEWSGROUP **misc.invest.stocks** URL▶ http://www.aaii.org/

Money Daily

Money's Tip of the Day

Money Daily Jump 5859

Money magazine has come up with a unique feature here in their Money Daily page. Their aim is to provide readers with one main money-saving story or idea a day. One day it might tell you how to save money on winter heating, and the next report might include a detailed report on the Federal Reserve Board. No matter the subject, the information here is timely and useful, and links to other useful Internet resources are also provided. The archive of daily features is available, and you can also browse other features like the "Money Business" Report and "Business Headlines." In fact, you'll find just about everything you've come to know and trust in *Money* magazine; only this one is updated daily! —(J.P.)

KEY NEWSGROUP **alt.business.misc** URL▶ http://pathfinder.com/money/moneydaily/latest/index.html

Market Talk

Market Talk's Investment Info

Market Talk Jump 5739

Money talks, but it does not always talk to you. Market Talk is about the market, all right, but it's more of a place to let your voice be heard, have fun, and make contact with other like-minded investors. Registration is free, and once you've registered you can join one of the three main discussion areas. Share tips and investment strategies on stocks and

IPOs (initial public offerings), and discuss specific markets and industries at this well-executed Web investment site. —(J.P.)

KEY NEWSGROUP **alt.business.misc 46** URL▶ http://www.markettalk.com/biz2/market_talk/webx/WebX.cgi

Barron's Online

BARRON'S Online Jump **6874**

Now you can access the most comprehensive investor's summary available anywhere. Not only will you find all the stories in Barron's venerable print version, but Barron's online edition lets you browse performance charts and daily news for virtually every public company. Their latest feature, Dossiers, not only furnishes quick stock quotes and market-shaking news, but also lists price/performance information on over 15,000 North American traded stocks and 7,000 mutual funds.—(L.T.)

KEY NEWSGROUP **clari.biz.market.news** URL▶ http://www.barrons.com

Dow Jones Investor Network

Dow Jones Investor Network Jump **6872**

Dow Jones has established a substantial Web presence, bringing their same grade of world-class global business and financial news reporting to their blue-chip Web site. Here you'll get the front page of The Wall Street Journal, plus many Web-only features, such as stock information databases and unedited interviews online from the world's foremost business managers such as Bill Gates, Jim Barksdale of Netscape, and Ted Turner. —(L.T.)

KEY NEWSGROUP **clari.biz.market.news** URL▶ http://www.djin.com/index.html

Quicken's Answers to Your Financial Questions

Quicken Financial Network Jump **5832**

Here is personal financial software giant Quicken's big financial information Web site, The Quicken Financial Network, which has a single mandate: To help people make better financial decisions. A tough job at the best of times, but this site is organized in such a way that you can easily find the kind of information you might be looking for. In this site's "Retirement Center," you can find out if you really are saving enough for your retirement years, with tips on how to save and plan for the future. And are you making the right investments? Check out the "Investment Center" to find out more about mutual funds and personal portfolios. Also you can post your own questions to this site's question of the day. —(J.P.)

URL▶ http://www.qfn.com/

Stock Smart™

Putting Investors Ahead...
Because It's *Your* Money™

Everyone's Stock Research Site

Stock Smart Jump **5818**

Stock Smart, "an independent advocate for truth on Wall Street," is an excellent, remarkable—and free—stock research and tracking service that allows you to follow stock, industry, and market trends in real time. Nothing is static here, thanks to the on-the-fly, Java-based recalculation of data, including the monitoring of the world's leading corporations, industry groups, and over 5,000 mutual funds and 8,000 stocks currently trading in the U.S.A valiant effort at providing world-class investment research data to everyone; not just the Wall Street market jocks who can afford it. —(J.P.)

URL▶ http://www.stocksmart.com/

Your Investment Wizard

InvestmentWizard Jump **6529**

So you can't afford the luxury of a daily Wall Street analyst's recommendations—this comes close—and it's free. Investment Wizard provides you with a

comprehensive set of research reports and recommendations on a full portfolio of stocks and mutual funds in today's investment market, and also contains a database of over 11,000 funds. —(L.T.)

KEY NEWSGROUP **misc.invest** URL ▶ http://www.ozsoft.com/iwhome.html

Helping to Empower the Online Investor

Investors Edge Jump **5833**

Show us an investor who isn't looking for an edge, and we'll show you someone who hasn't checked out InvestorsEdge. The key to sound investments is information, of course, and you'll find plenty of that in the InvestorsEdge database. For each company listed here, you'll find a comprehensive tabulation that includes a current stock quotation, 52-week price chart, annual reports (when available online), and more. Elsewhere, you'll find the latest stock quotes, business news of the day as well as the opportunity to set up your own personal portfolio to monitor up to 15 stocks and mutual funds. —(J.P.)

URL ▶ http://www.irnet.com/

High-Tech Investment Research

Silicon Investor - Home Page Jump **8031**

Silicon Investor leads new investors as well as seasoned stock pickers through the maze of young companies involved in the cutting edge of high technology. Access stock quotes and charts, and engage in real time, online discussions with other investors. You can also read the latest news from Silicon Valley, check out weekly market analyses, and access this site's collection of fascinating technology investment research reports. —(E.v.B.)

KEY NEWSGROUP **clari.biz.market.misc** URL ▶ http://www.techstocks.com/

Stock Investment Research from Zacks

Zacks Investment Research Jump **0232**

Zacks has long been a well-known investment research service to Wall Street pros and serious stock traders, and now they're a solid information source on the Internet. Although you have to pay extra to receive many of their in-depth stock analyses and reports, you can sign up here to receive a free 30-day trial to their subscription research services. Even if you don't want to pay extra, their "No Fee Zone" features many quite useful and free information features, including e-mail portfolio alerts, overviews of available company research reports, delayed quotes, and a unique "earnings surprises" ticker which is updated continuously. —(E.G.)

KEY NEWSGROUP **misc.invest.stocks** URL ▶ http://www.zacks.com/

Investment News and Resources from Kiplinger Online

Kiplinger Online Jump **6762**

Kiplinger's, a well-known business and investment newsletter and magazine publisher since 1923, is now on the Web. Link here and read Kiplinger's impressive investment and business news, opinion, and advice, access stock quotes, and view their lists of top-performing mutual funds, all updated daily (and sometimes throughout the day). There's also plenty of useful information for investment novices, such as FAQ files, and an extensive glossary of investor terms. —(L.T.)

KEY NEWSGROUP **misc.invest.funds** URL ▶ http://www.techstocks.com/

The Informed Investor

Mutual Fund Investor's Guide Jump **5740**

Since 1971 the Mutual Fund Education Alliance has been in the business of helping investors understand mutual funds. Their Web site continues this tradition, with even more information to help investors identify companies that sell funds directly to the public, without brokers (also known as no-load funds.) There are many special sections here, including a list of 40 mutual fund companies that sell directly to the public, helpful hints for the beginner, and a section entitled "Map Out a Plan," where you can develop your own personal asset allocation plan. There's also news and press releases and, perhaps the heart of this site, a Fund Quicklist, where you can identify which of the nearly 1,000 no-load or low-load funds might be right for you. —(J.P.)

KEY NEWSGROUP **alt.business.misc** URL▶ http://www.mfea.com

Mutual Funds Master Web Links

Mutual Fund Company Directory Jump **5741**

With so many mutual fund companies now on the Web, it was only a matter of time before someone—in this case, John Greiner—compiled a comprehensive listing of mutual fund companies, with their telephone numbers, and any other Web information that might be available. The list also includes some unit investment trusts and variable annuity companies, and other mutual fund-like investment vehicles. —(J.P.)

KEY NEWSGROUP **alt.business.misc** URL▶ http://www.cs.cmu.edu/~jdg/funds.htm

Mutual Fund Coffee Talk

Mutual Fund Cafe Jump **5743**

Visiting this site is much like strolling into your favorite cappuccino bar. Calling itself the "only Web site designed especially for mutual fund business and marketing professionals," this site strives to furnish the investment pros—and all the rest of us non-pros—with up-to-date information on industry trends, company updates, fund asset management, and much more. And you can also check their archives for past news as well. —(J.P.)

KEY NEWSGROUP **alt.business.misc** URL▶ http://www.mfcafe.com

Mutual Funds Resources, Commentary and Links

Mutual Funds Interactive-The Mutual Fund Home Page

Jump **0225**

CONTENT

Here's a site that once again proves that solid information will always win out over slick design every time. Martha Brill, a personal finance columnist for the *Boston Globe*, has put together a handy information clearinghouse for both novice and expert mutual fund investors. While it doesn't look has slick as many of the other investor sites out there, it more than compensates with its large selection of mutual fund expert commentaries, and its extensive collection of mutual fund site links, news, and other information resources. This constantly-updated site is a handy first stop for linking to many other funds-related sites and resources available, and includes its own database of extensive mutual fund background data and money manager profiles. —(E.G.)

URL▶ http://www.fundsinteractive.com/

All about No-Load Mutual Funds

100% No-Load Mutual Fund Council

Jump **2347**

Some mutual funds charge a fee whenever you buy or sell shares, similar to a brokerage asdfasdfasfdadsfasdfasdfasfasfasfdsacommission on stocks. No-load mutual funds do not, and that is one of their main attractions for investors. This site includes a general guide to investing in mutual funds, as well as specific information about investing in no-load funds. Also online are descriptions of the funds that are members of the Council, including info on their investment objectives, investment policies, and minimum initial investments. —(L.S.)

KEY NEWSGROUP **misc.invest.funds** URL▶ http://networth.galt.com/council/

MutualFunds Information from Morningstar

Morningstar Mutual Funds On Demand
Jump 6772

Investigate the funds that best suit your portfolio with these free reports. Thanks to INVESTools, you can read complete and unbiased summary analysis along with 500 statistics on the funds. Additionally, there's a slew of investor tools including searchable directories, newsletters, research resources and market news. If you'd like to view the reports off-line, you can download reports in their entirety and research them at your leisure. —(L.T.)

KEY NEWSGROUP misc.invest.funds URL http://www.investools.com/cgi-bin/Library/msmf.pl

Fast, Simple Stock and Mutual Fund Quote Searches

StockMaster.com Jump 5834

StockMaster has been serving investors on the Web since 1993, and their free, basic service allows you to type the symbol or name of the company or mutual fund, and the results are supplied in chart form, along with that company's current quote. Browse their extensive database using a variety of other search options, including top stocks, stocks by name, funds by name, or top funds. —(J.P.)

URL http://www.stockmaster.com/

Tracking the Stock Market

MarketWatch Jump 5887

Market Watch is a fee-based service that delivers the best and latest in real-time business news. The options are numerous, and include the ability to view real-time quotes for NYSE, AMEX, and NASDAQ exchanges on demand, create your own personal portfolios with the ability to track up to six personal portfolios, and receive real-time financial data. Not yet satisfied? How about the ability to search a database of over 8,000 companies, to trade online and—just for the heck of it—the latest sports scores as well. A popular stock-tracking site, produced by leading Net stock information provider Data Broadcasting Corporation. —(J.P.)

KEY NEWSGROUP alt.business.misc URL http://mw.dbc.com/

NASDAQ Over-the-Counter Stocks Site

NASDAQ Jump 6778

NASDAQ, the over-the-counter market listing many of today's fast-growing high-tech companies, provides you with a handy Web resource featuring up-to-the-minute market activity and charts, with daily composite NASDAQ index values. You can also search for full financial and background information on any NASDAQ-listed company, using this site's extensive database. —(L.T.)

KEY NEWSGROUP clari.biz.market.report.usa URL http://www.nasdaq.com/

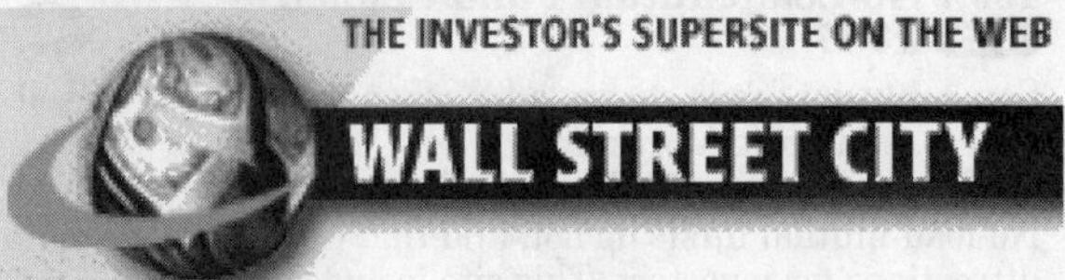

THE INVESTOR'S SUPERSITE ON THE WEB
WALL STREET CITY

Track Your Stocks at Wall Street City

Wall Street City Jump 6895

Want to research the market's top stock performers? Wall Street City by Telescan, Inc. is a great place to start your research. Not only will you find real-time stock quotes for 70,000+ securities, discussion forums, and a glossary of investment terms, but—most importantly—you'll find key background research materials. Take their research library, for instance. It's where to find out which stocks are the biggest gainers and biggest losers. And in the corporate headquarters section, you can select just about any corporation, then browse its current quote, a business summary, product and contact information. Features designed for more experienced investors include a mutual fund search engine, the ability to create your own custom stock ticker which delivers quotes on stocks you're already tracking, and market stats and commentary updated every business day at 6:30 P.M. —(L.T.)

KEY NEWSGROUP misc.invest.stocks URL▶ http://www.wallstreetcity.com/home.htp

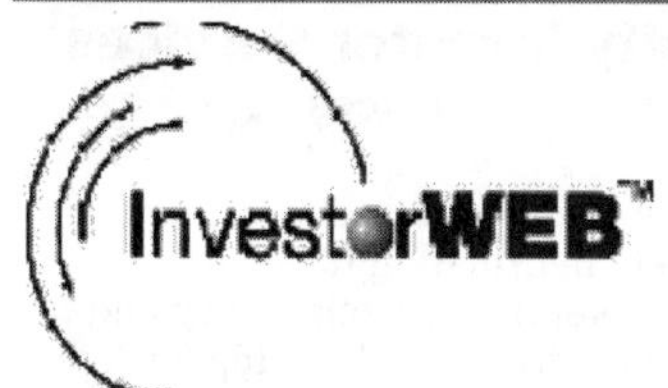

Investment Opportunities Exchange & Links

InvestorWEB Home Page Jump 7480

Got some dollars burning a hole in your pocket? Looking for an exciting, possibly "wild-'n-woolly" private venture startup investment? Well, why not search the information here at InvestorWEB? You can read up on a variety of companies, IPOs, and private equity opportunities. InvestorWEB also offers a number of investment newsletters, and hotlinks to other investment pages. For the beginner, the site offers (less risky) advice and other information you will need to help you make wise decisions on where to park your hard-earned money. —(E.v.B.)

KEY NEWSGROUP misc.invest URL▶ http://www.investorweb.com/

Investing in the Future

Investment Strategies for the 21st Century Jump 2244

The GNN Personal Finance Center, which hosts these pages, claims this is the first investment book to be published on the Internet. Author Frank Armstrong's experience as a portfolio manager and a technophile gives him some interesting insights on the effects of technology on investing in the future. What makes this site even more interesting is that feedback—positive or negative—is encouraged, and comments will be posted on this site as an ongoing dialogue of strategies and tactics based on the ideas presented here. —(L.S.)

KEY NEWSGROUP misc.invest URL▶ http://gnn.com/meta/finance/feat/21st/index.html

Investor's Info Center

Investment Research - Stocks, Commodities, Technical Analysis Jump 3718

Data Transfer Group of San Diego, CA, has put together a site filled with articles, discussions, data, statistics and information about investing of all kinds—stocks, commodities, futures, mutual funds and options. You'll find an 18-part series on the "Midas method" of technical stock analysis, The Holt Report, a daily list of indicators and market measures, articles on commodity futures, and an enormous list of links. The goal of the site is to "provide individual investors with actionable investment information," and we agree that their site would be a great Web starting point for getting access to the daily investment information you need. —(N.F.)

KEY NEWSGROUP misc.invest.stocks URL▶ http://www.thegroup.net/invest/ichome.htm

Your Online Personal Finance Guru

PersFin Digest Jump 2651

This online archive of Ira Krakow's PersFin Digest e-mail newsletter gives you access to past issues and, therefore, an essential resource for answers to most questions you may have about personal finance. Ira started the list for the same reason most people subscribe—to get answers to questions to help himself and to share ideas and experiences with other individuals. It covers everything from credit cards to stocks and bonds, and the information is both helpful and interesting. Keep in mind, though, that this is a list populated by regular folks, so the information here should be used to guide you toward making decisions, not taken as gospel. —(L.S.)

KEY NEWSGROUP misc.invest URL▶ http://www.tiac.net/users/ikrakow/

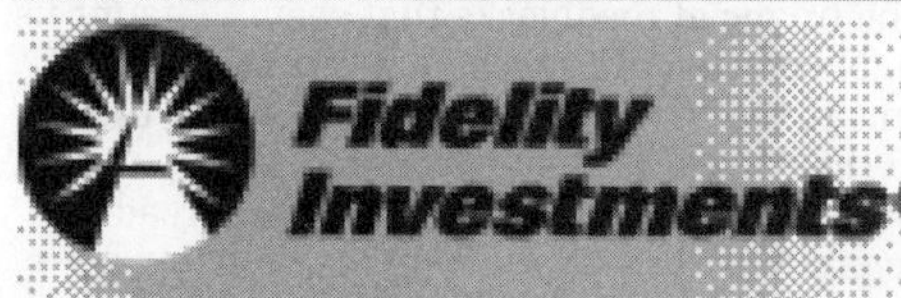

Fidelity's Investor Resources and Calculators

Fidelity Investments Jump 0224

Mutual fund powerhouse Fidelity has developed a Web site for both existing and prospective customers which, in addition to the usual corporate sales information, gives you a useful selection of worksheets to help you determine the amount of money you need to save each year to meet your retirement objectives, plus worksheets for corporate 401(k) retirement plans, market news, and commentary. This site also includes a wide range of other useful investor news and mutual fund information, and includes the company's Internet stock trading system for individual investors. —(E.G.)

KEY NEWSGROUP **misc.invest.stocks** URL▸ http://www.fidelity.com/

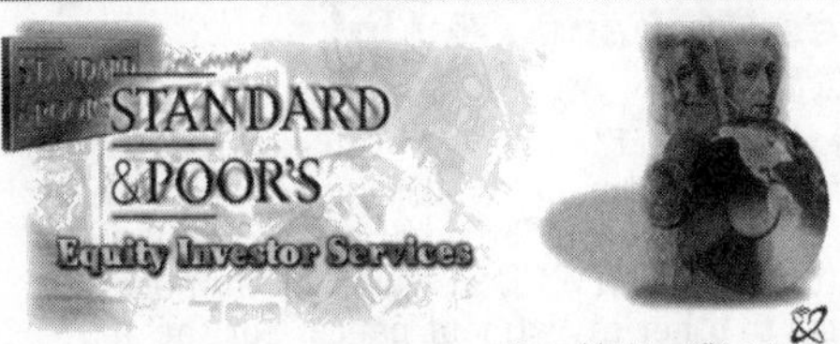

Standard & Poor's Equity Investor Services

Standard & Poor's Equity Investor Services

LINKS

Jump 6799

Standard & Poor's, a trusted name in the investment ratings world, now delivers the same timely information to you online. With continually updated stock market news, commentary and top stock picks, you'll find this site to be a frequent Web stop for top-notch investment information. The site features Standard and Poor's 500, MidCap 600, and SmallCap 400 index statistics, along with full company background information. S & P provides all this for free, but if you choose to register, which is also free, you'll get much broader access to the even more S & P information. —(L.T.)

KEY NEWSGROUP **misc.invest** URL▸ http://www.stockinfo.standardpoor.com

The Motley Fool

Investment Advice from Motley Fool

The Motley Fool

CONTENT

Jump 5720

The Motley Fools, who started out on America Online and attracted a huge following for their investment advice and forums, exist "to help you improve your investment returns" in the grand old style of "educating while amusing." They are dedicated to investing in stocks and only stocks. No risky options, futures or anything else. And you can find out why they adhere to this hard-and-fast rule and, hopefully, profit from it as well. The detailed investment approach is documented in their "13 Steps to Investing Foolishly" while the "Fool Portfolio" lists their real-life investment results every evening. For fun, check out Today's Pitch, and don't forget to read the Daily News sections, published every day at lunch and dinnertime. Whether you'll still be smiling if you follow the Fools' advice into a major stock market correction will remain to be seen, but hey—check out this site and make your own decision. —(J.P.)

URL▸ http://www.fool.com/

Help for the Individual Investor

Nest Egg Jump 2063

The online version of *Nest Egg Magazine* differs from many online versions of print publications in that you get the full articles, not condensed versions, and there are links within each article to the companies and resources mentioned. There's an archive of back issues, a link to thc Tradeline Performance Leader mutual fund charts, showing fund performance leaders over periods from one week to five years, and links to other personal investing resources. —(L.S.)

KEY NEWSGROUP **misc.invest** URL▸ http://nestegg.iddis.com/

How Can I Learn to Save?

Personal Finance Center Jump 5744

CONTENT

Sometimes it seems that all of life is geared toward overcoming the financial roadblocks that seem to haunt us at every turn. No matter your age or station in life, everyone seems to face the same concerns at about the same point in their lives. This site is geared to helping you to not only answer the questions, but to devise a roadmap that will help you plan for future financial concerns. Click on your age group and what you'll find is probably an accurate appraisal of where you are, financially, at that particular point in your life. You can learn how to minimize your taxes, plan for your children's education, buy or sell a house, and plan for you retirement. —(J.P.)

KEY NEWSGROUP **alt.business.misc** URL▸ http://www.ml.com/personal/

Money Talks Investment Magazine

Money Talks Jump **5742** 

Money Talks is a free investment magazine for investors interested in mutual funds, personal finance, equities marketplace, utilities and the retail industry. You'll find plenty of tips here, and columns written by "America's most respected financial writers." You can also take advantage of their instant access to stock quotes, also free of charge. And all of this information is updated on a daily basis! —(J.P.)

KEY NEWSGROUP **alt.business.misc** URL ▶ http://www.talks.com/

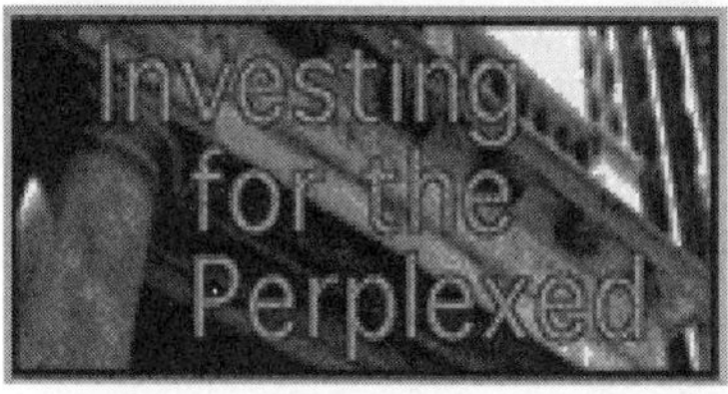

Straight Talk about Money

Investing for the Perplexed Jump **2382** 

Between the variety of investment vehicles, the extra fine print of a prospectus, and what's at stake for the small investor, high finance can quickly turn to high anxiety. Kelly & O'Sullivan Financial Services Group tries to relieve the anxiety with this page of articles and resources for people who want to invest, but don't know the ins and outs of stocks, bonds and whatever, and don't really care to learn. There's general information about investing, creating financial plans, establishing retirement plans, plus a quarterly newsletter. Taking advantage of this site can help you better utilize the other Internet-based investing resources. —(L.S.)

KEY NEWSGROUP **misc.invest** URL ▶ http://www.inch.com/~robertny/invest/menu.html

Concise Financial Market Reports

Weekly Market Summary Jump **2097** 

If you want graphics, there's nothing here. If you thirst for financial markets data, though, prepare to be quenched! Updated weekly, this report of market activity includes the top and bottom 10 performing industries, Dow Jones and other market averages, money rates, gold and silver prices, unemployment and inflation rates, and other pieces of useful information for the investor. The information is very concise, and if you want in-depth data, you'll have to look elsewhere. But if you need a quick take of the market and the economy, this is the place. —(L.S.)

KEY NEWSGROUP **misc.invest** URL ▶ http://www.gruntal.com/investments/wms.html

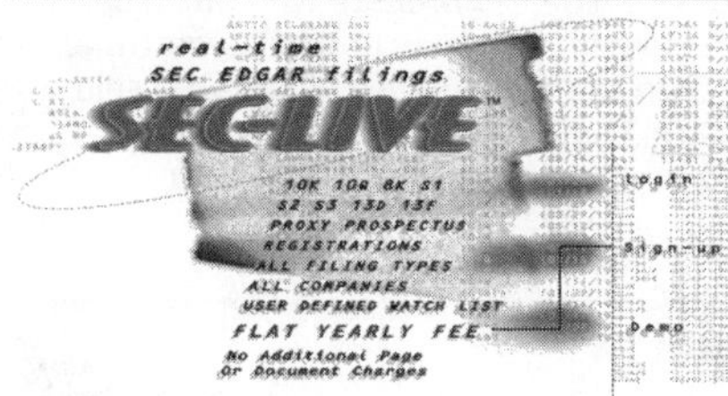

Fee-Based Public Company Investor Information from SEC-Live

SEC-LIVE Jump **5808**

This fee-based service provides real-time access to mutual fund filings submitted to the Securities and Exchange Commission's EDGAR System, for those of you power-curve investors who need the latest company news now. Subscribers can search and retrieve all current and historic data filed, and can construct a "watch list" of up to 15 companies or funds. When one of the organizations on your Watch List files a document through EDGAR, you receive an e-mail informing you of the transaction. Users can also add additional Watch List entries at an additional charge. Although the service is fee-based, you can sign up to get a few free sample reports, which makes it useful to sneak a free report now and then. —(J.P.)

URL ▶ http://www.seclive.com/

Smart Money Calculator Helps You Figure Major Life Decisions

Money Advisor Jump **5812** 

The goal of the Money Advisor is to help you make the right decisions about your finances, and they back this pledge with an interesting and quite useful array of on-screen calculators that can help you figure out everything from lease payments for a new car to costs of relocating once you've found a new job, and a "human life calculator" (yikes!) This site also features articles on money management (mortgage, legal, government and investing info, etc.) as well as links to other resources on the Web. —(J.P.)

URL▸ http://www.moneyadvisor.com/

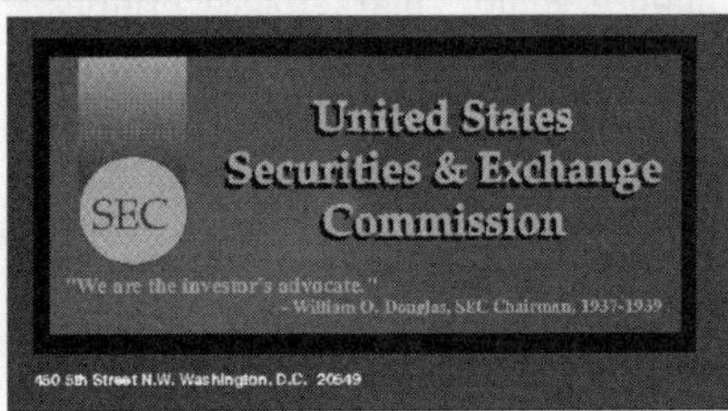

EDGAR: SEC Public Company information

Securities and Exchange Commission Jump 6588

Just a couple of years ago, companies and investors paid dearly to get the financial information on public companies you can now get for free over the Internet with the SEC's long-awaited EDGAR database. Investors can now go straight to the source with EDGAR, which contains every corporate financial document filed by every public company with the SEC. You can use EDGAR to get comprehensive financial information, news on significant developments, background information, and much more on the over 16,000 U.S. public companies required to file on EDGAR. An invaluable resource, and an important first step in your own personal investment research. —(L.T.)

KEY NEWSGROUP clari.biz.market.misc URL▸ http://www.sec.gov/

SEC Filing References

The R. R. Donnelley Library of SEC Materials Jump 2051

The folks at New York University's EDGAR Development Site, with the sponsorship of R.R. Donnelley, chopped two major SEC filing guides into hypertext-sized chunks for viewing on the Web. This is no mean feat, with literally megabytes of information in an easily navigable hypertext format. The guides are The SEC Filers Manual, and The R.R. Donnelley Guide to Filing Forms. Donnelley also sponsored the creation of the ASCII versions of the Securities Act of 1933 and the Exchange Act of 1934, both of which are also available here. —(L.S.)

KEY NEWSGROUP misc.invest. URL▸ http://edgar.stern.nyu.edu/sponsors/sponsors.html

Compare the Best Bank CD Rates

Bank-CD Rate Scanner Jump 3704

Here's a free service that allows Certificate of Deposit (CD) buyers to request quotes in order to compare rates and purchase FDIC-insured CDs. Why would you consider getting CDs over the Net? The CD brokers who put together this site tell us they have contracts with over 2,200 banks, all of which have varying CD rates at any given time. Let these experts do the research—they'll find the best rates—and you can reap the benefits. All of the CDs sold through this service are FDIC-insured, and there are no fees. There are also tips on long-distance banking, a frequently-asked questions document, and instructions for agents interested in joining the network. —(N.F.)

URL▸ http://www.wimsey.com/~emandel/BankCD.html

Determine Your Life Insurance and Retirement Needs

LifeNet Jump 0230

On the LifeNet site, you'll find a useful calculator that helps you estimate your life insurance needs, given your family's income, assets, net worth, and desired insurance benefit. According to *Fortune* magazine, the output you get from LifeNet's insurance calculator matched that of a recommendation made by an independent financial planner. This site also features one of the best glossaries of investment and insurance terms we've seen on the Web, and some interesting related articles on insurance and financial planning. —(E.G.)

URL▸ http://www.lifenet.com/

Check that Stock—and More

Security APL Quote Server Jump 2015

It's called a quote server, but it gives you much, much more, with lots of up-to-the-minute information. Type in the stock's symbol and this site returns the price, date and time of the last trade, the change in the price, the stock's volume that day, number of trades, the day's high and low, and the year's high and low. Don't know the stock symbol? Another search engine will tell you if you type the company name, plus it returns a list of Web links for the company. It's a great resource and an excellent starting point for doing your company investment research. You also can check activity of the major stock indexes and on the major exchanges, and the latest commodity prices. These are reported on a 15-minute delay. There are also graphs of hourly activity of the Dow Jones and Standard & Poor's indexes, reported on a 15-minute delay. —(L.S.)

KEY NEWSGROUP **misc.invest.stocks** URL▶ http://www.secapl.com/cgi-bin/qs

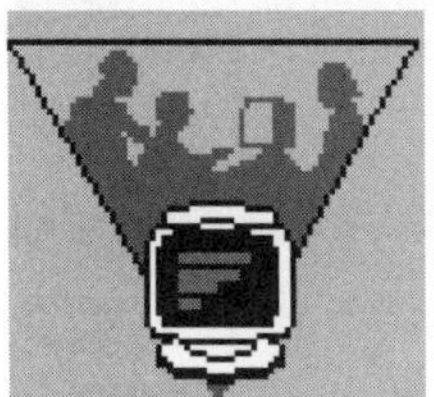

Corporate Financials Online

Corporate Financials Online Jump 6875

Each business day CFO publishes corporate news and the latest SEC filings online. Browse just-released financial reports from corporate giants like TRW, Motorola, IBM, Motorola and Coca-Cola.CFO's newest feature is "Insider Trading Comment," a must-read for news from the trading floor. From here, you can also connect to additional financial information links supplied by Reuters New Media, the Dow Jones Industrial Average, and Wall Street Opinion. —(L.T.)

KEY NEWSGROUP **clari.biz.market.news** URL▶ http://www.cfonews.com/

Bank Rate Monitor

Best Bank Loan and Savings Interest Rates

Bank Rate Monitor
Jump 0227

Here's a very useful—and free—service from the Bank Rate Monitor, which tracks the highest bank savings and interest rates, and the lowest credit card and mortgage rates. BRM tracks the best such rates across the country on a weekly—and sometimes even daily—basis. Needless to say, this is the first place you should go whenever you're shopping for places to park your money, picking a mortgage, or switching your credit cards. Their site also contains many informative current industry news features relating to selecting mortgages, car loans, and credit cards.—(E.G.)

URL▶ http://www.bankrate.com

Mortgage Tracking

Mortgage Market Information, Services, Inc.
Jump 7492

Need a daily dose of reality? Need to calculate your monthly mortgage payment? Want to follow the dips and rises of your mortgage rate? Come to Mortgage Market Information Services to learn all you want to know about mortgage rates and types of lending institutions. Read daily updates about mortgage news, trends and directions, and check out the real-estate and financial news, and surf to relevant Web links provided by this site's authors. —(E.v.B.)

KEY NEWSGROUP **misc.invest** URL▶ http://www.interest.com/mmis.html

Lowest-Cost Term Life Insurance from QuoteSmith

QuoteSmith Corporation-Term Life Insurance Quote Page
Jump 0231

CONTENT

This is the best way to get the lowest rate on term life insurance—without listening to sales pitches from insurance salesmen. QuoteSmith has been a well-known and experienced provider of term life insurance price comparisons in print form, and now they bring this service to the Web in this basic, but extremely useful, site. Simply enter your date of birth, and a couple of other general facts, and QuoteSmith generates comparative rates for the coverage you've selected from over 130 leading life insurance companies—with lowest-cost insurance providers listed first. Click on the cheapest quote's link, and you'll then see a nicely detailed insurance company ratings report, cost/benefits ratings analysis and company profile. There's even an application form for you to apply for coverage online. Couldn't be simpler! And no pesky insurance salesman will come into your home. —(E.G.)

URL▶ http://www.quotesmith.com/

ESOP and Equity Compensation

Foundation for Enterprise Development Jump 2072 

Here you'll find articles, references, and links about Employee Stock Ownership Plans, equity compensation, and generally helping your employees feel more involved in and committed to the organization's success. Be sure to check the Foundation newsletter and What's New links, as well as the case studies. They'll give you more information on the regulatory environment and other problems and prospects of implementing an ESOP. —(L.S.)

KEY NEWSGROUP alt.business URL▸ http://www.fed.org/fed/

Employee Stock Ownership (ESOP) Web Page

An Introduction to ESOPs Jump 2073 

Written by Jack W. Berka, Scott J. Adelson, and Ben A. Buttell, this guide to the ins and outs of Employee Stock Ownership Plans is an excellent source of information for the uninitiated. It takes you through all the steps and considerations of ESOPs and provides a bibliography and pointers to other resources if you want to know more.—(L.S.)

KEY NEWSGROUP alt.business URL▸ http://www.fed.org/fed/esop/

EE Bond Value Calculator

Find Out What Your Savings Bonds are Worth Jump 2656 

U.S. Series EE Savings Bonds continue to earn interest even after they've reached their face value. If you've got a shoebox full of bonds that you haven't done anything with, here's a nifty little online calculator that will tell you what they're worth. Just use the drop-down menus to select face value, month and year of issue, and the redemption month. In a flash, you'll find out what the bond is worth today. Unfortunately, you can't find out what it will be worth in the future, since MMR Software only includes calculations to the current year. If you want more, you'll have to buy their software, but it's inexpensive enough to be worth considering. —(L.S.)

KEY NEWSGROUP misc.invest URL▸ http://www.execpc.com/~mmrsoft/

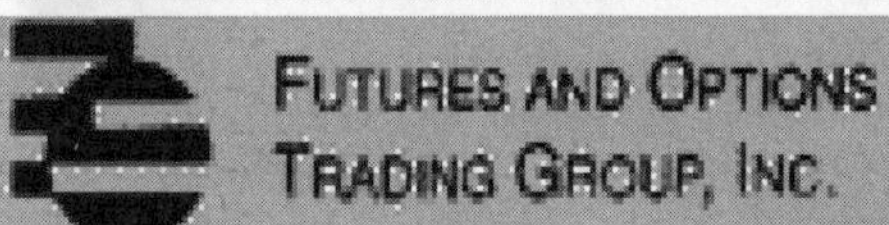

Futures and Commodities: Investments for the Strong and the Brave

Trading Financial & Agricultural Commodity Futures & Options Jump 2397 

If you've got nerves of steel and the instincts of a riverboat gambler, you might enjoy and possibly profit from trading financial options and commodity futures. They're complex trades, and can be very confusing, but the information here does a good job of sorting it all out. The key sections are the basic guides to options and futures trading, which include some basic rules to follow in determining what, when, and how to trade. You also can read the current and archived issues of the *Trade Plans Newsletter* for ideas, advice, and news of market happenings. —(L.S.)

KEY NEWSGROUP misc.invest.futures URL▸ http://www.teleport.com/~futures/

Grassroots Activism for Shareholders

The Shareholders Action Online Handbook Jump 2441 

The Shareholder Action On-Line Handbook

By Craig Mackenzie

It's easy for stockholders to feel they have no say in how a company is run. Too often, the only time they hear from their boards of directors is when the annual report comes out. But stockholders are the owners of a corporation, and if you think your companies aren't working in your interest, it's time to start acting like the owner you are—and take action! Even the smallest stockholder can have an effect, and if you want to learn how, just read this online book by Craig Mackenzie. It explains why you should take an interest, what to look for that can affect the value of your shares, and how to organize and take action. It was originally written for shareholders in the United Kingdom, so the descriptions of corporations and their organizations may not apply fully to their U.S. counterparts.

But the sections on taking action are appropriate for any country, and should be read by any and all stockholders. —(L.S.)

KEY NEWSGROUP **misc.invest**

URL▶ http://www.bath.ac.uk/Centres/Ethical/Share/

Learn to Price Options

Robert's Online Option Pricer! Jump **2052** CONTENT

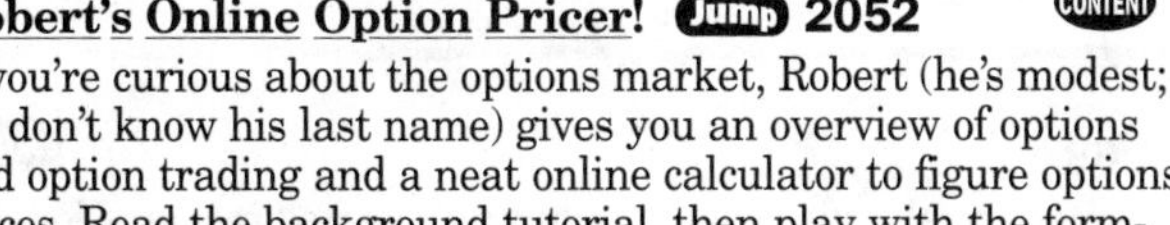

If you're curious about the options market, Robert (he's modest; we don't know his last name) gives you an overview of options and option trading and a neat online calculator to figure options prices. Read the background tutorial, then play with the form-based calculator. Once you've got the hang of it, you can use it to help you learn if you've got what it takes to trade options by pricing some test options and waiting to see how they do in the real daily market. —(L.S.)

KEY NEWSGROUP **misc.invest**

URL▶ http://slag.capmkt.com/robert/option-pricer.html

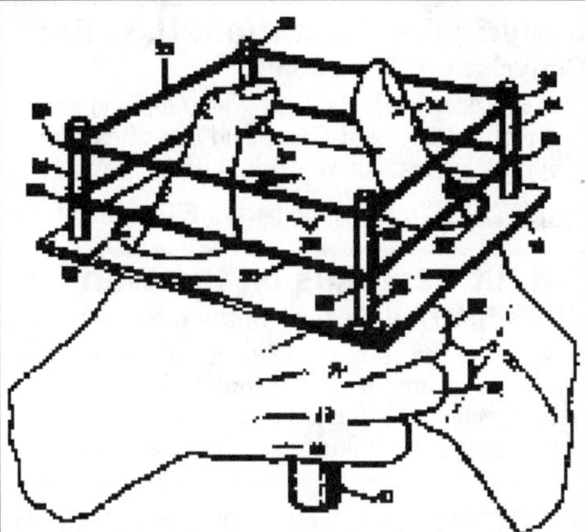

Thumb wrestling game ring

Patent Number: 4998724
Inventor: Hartman; Richard B.

Abstract

The game structure comprises a stabilising handle for gripping between interlocking hands of opponents engaged in a game of thumb wrestling. The stabilising handle provides for employing pressure generated by interlocking hands of opponents to stabilise and anchor the stabilising handle between players' hands. A game ring surface is joined to the stabilising handle. The game ring surface is stabilised and anchored upon the stabilising handle throughout competition. The game ring surface includes thumb holes for receiving the thumbs of opponents. Remaining fingers of opponents' interlocked hands grip the stabilising handle below the game ring surface.

▲ *Thumb wrestling ring patent idea, from* **STO's Internet Patent Search System** *at* Jump **2269**.

Investing in New Overseas Markets

The Emerging Markets Jump **5738** CONTENT

Looking for resources on investing in emerging overseas markets? You'll find plenty of background info and research here to answer your questions. This is a straightforward list of sources and links, all dealing with opportunities for investors in the "emerging markets" of Argentina, Brazil, Mexico, Venezuela, Chile, Peru, Colombia, and Bolivia. You'll find a section of security prices, a news and market journal, and financial markets research. Check out this site's EMC Newsgroup, a great forum to discuss "topics related to developing countries." —(J.P.)

KEY NEWSGROUP **alt.business.misc** URL▶ http://www.emgmkts.com/

Web Legalese for Selling Wares

Advertising Law Internet Site Jump **1545**

If you're selling your wares through the Internet, do you know all the legal rules? Can you use copyrighted graphics on your Web page? Find out at this comprehensive advertising and marketing site developed by Lewis Rose, law partner with the top Washington, D.C., law firm of Arent Fox Kintner Plotkin & Kahn. In these pages, you'll find principles, guidelines, rules, regulations, and other general advice about online marketing. If you have a question or want to discuss the latest slogan protection issue, for example, just ask in the discussion forum, where Rose and other professionals help you out. This site also points to articles, speeches, testimonies, trends and other advertising law, consumer protection, anti-trust, trade association sites. Still can't find what you need? Use the search engine. A must-read for anyone who's serious about developing Web sites! —(H.L.)

URL▶ http://www.webcom.com/~lewrose/home.html

Copyright Clearance Answer Center

Copyright Clearance Center Online Jump **7277** CONTENT

What's the law on reproducing an article that was written in the 1920s in an anthology? Are digital works covered by copyright? These and many other copyright questions are answered at the Web site of the Copyright Clearance Center (CCC), a not-for-profit corporation established by the U.S. Congress. You can read the latest regulations on photocopying, and reproduction rights governing the use of all types of art and printed works. It will also give you some pointers on easing the sometimes difficult path of obtaining permissions to reprint, copy, or reproduce. —(E.v.B.)

KEY NEWSGROUP **misc.int-property** URL▶ http://www.copyright.com/

Copyright Information: U.S. Copyright Office

Copyright Jump 0206 

The U.S. Copyright Office's Web (Gopher) site containing an extensive collection of informative articles on copyrights, copyright forms and classifications, copyright news, and other worthwhile items you can use to copyright your creative work. —(E.G.)

KEY NEWSGROUP misc.int-property URL ▸ gopher://marvel.loc.gov/11/copyright

Patent Searches on the Web

STO's Internet Patent Search System Jump 2269 

This site is the starting point in the patent search, and one that also gives you a regularly updated resource for patent news and laws. This online search engine can't replace a proper patent search, but it lets you retrieve patent titles by class or subclass code to give you an idea of what similar products and ideas are already protected. Also here are archives of articles from the Internet Patent News Service, information on subscribing to this free service, and an online reference to worldwide patent law. —(L.S.)

KEY NEWSGROUP comp.patents URL ▸ http://www.questel.orbit.com/patents/

Trademark Information & Resources on the Web

U.S. Trademark Law Jump 0207 

A useful Web starting point with many interesting links on the subject of trademark protection. Included in those are links to the U.S. Patent and Trademark Office's Web site, trademark application forms and trademark laws and decisions. —(E.G.)

KEY NEWSGROUP misc.int-property URL ▸ http://www.law.cornell.edu/topics/trademark.html

Law Resource Jumplist

P-LAW Legal Resource Locator Jump 2186 

Whether you're a professional lawyer or an individual looking for resources to help you understand the law, Kenneth Perry makes it easy for you to locate what you need. Updated regularly and organized by type of site, each link includes a detailed description to help you quickly find the right resource. Categories include legislative, general, topic specific, and statistics resources. If there's not a link, it's probably not on the Web. —(L.S.)

KEY NEWSGROUP misc.legal URL ▸ http://www.dorsai.org/p-law/

Updated Daily LAW JOURNAL EXTRA!

The Web Site for Lawyers

The Law Journal Extra Jump 5846 

Lawyers will love Law Journal Extra, but with all the legal issues filtering into our daily lives, the material on this site really will be of interest to everyone. The top stories featured here are taken straight from the daily headlines of the world of sports, entertainment and business—but from the legal perspective. And it's not only who is suing who, but the implications on other aspects of our lives are also addressed. In this site's "Practice Area" we learn the latest in the ongoing issues of intellectual property, and the laws guiding (or not guiding) the Internet. And this site's legal resources section provides a marvelous collection of links to government agencies, legal firms, and access to over 50 online legal libraries. —(J.P.)

KEY NEWSGROUP misc.legal.moderated URL ▸ http://www.ljx.com/

Law Books on the Web

The World Wide Web Virtual Library - Law Jump 7016 

A crazy driver nearly ran you down on the way home. Time to stop putting off writing a will. Log onto the World Wide Web virtual law library and search for instructions. While you're there, why not also dip into Peruvian, Israeli, Canadian law, as well as the wealth of U.S. legal documents, databases and libraries. —(E.v.B.)

KEY NEWSGROUP misc.legal URL ▸ http://www.law.indiana.edu/law/lawindex.html

News and Comment on Net-Related Legal Issues

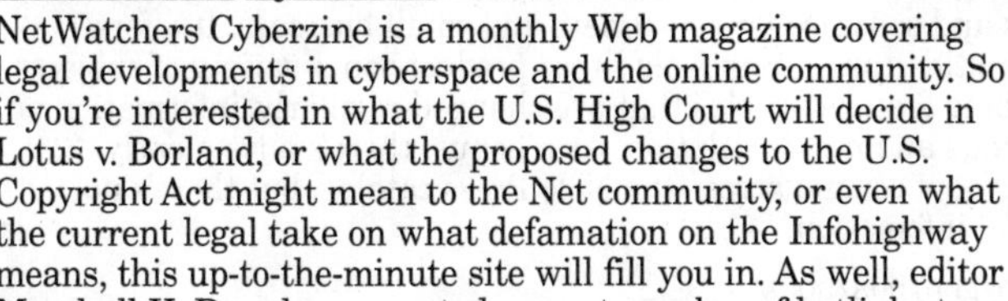

NetWatchers Cyberzine Jump 7381 CONTENT

NetWatchers Cyberzine is a monthly Web magazine covering legal developments in cyberspace and the online community. So if you're interested in what the U.S. High Court will decide in Lotus v. Borland, or what the proposed changes to the U.S. Copyright Act might mean to the Net community, or even what the current legal take on what defamation on the Infohighway means, this up-to-the-minute site will fill you in. As well, editor Marshall K. Dyer has mounted a great number of hotlinks to other law-related Web sites for you to explore. —(E.v.B.)

KEY NEWSGROUP **misc.legal**

URL ▶ http://www.ionet.net/~mdyer/front.shtml

Weird pyramid on the dollar

▲ *The "Great Seal," symbol from the U.S. One Dollar bill, from* **Washington University Image Archives** *at* Jump **0192**.

Lawyer's Corner

The Practicing Attorney's Home Page:Main Listing Jump 3705 LINKS

There's a tremendous amount of information for attorneys out on the Net. The problem is being able to quickly and easily find it. Internet Legal Services recognizes the need for cost-effective, easy access to legal resources, and has developed this links site to address this problem. Search or download from a wide variety of sources, including Net archives of the U.S. Code, Code of Federal Regulations, the Federal Register, environmental and litigation databases pending legislation, and much more. The goal of this site is "to help you use the Internet as an integral tool in your profession," and, if you're an attorney, we think you'll find they've done a wonderful job of it here. —(N.F.)

URL ▶ http://users.aimnet.com/~ils/main.html

Impress Your Lawyer

Legal Information Institute Jump 2012 CONTENT

Or depress the learned counsel. It all depends on how much your legal eagle likes your checking on things for yourself! Regardless, here's the Web's legal Jump Station, with links to legal content covering commercial law, securities law, taxes, intellectual property rights, disability and health, and virtually everything else that's important in operating a business. There's also a section covering legal issues of current interest, so you can bone up for cocktail party chit-chat. The links are updated continually, so while the amount of information on personal and family law is scant, it is growing. And if you can't find the link here, there are links to other sites where you probably will. —(L.S.)

KEY NEWSGROUP **misc.legal** URL ▶ http://www.law.cornell.edu/

Business & The Law

A World Wide Web Site Of

Reinhart | Boerner | Van Deuren Norris & Rieselbach, S.C.

Attorneys at Law

Legal Briefs

Business and the Law Jump 2131 CONTENT

This page by the law firm of Reinhart, Boerner, Van Deuren, Norris & Rieselbach serves as a good introduction to the everyday legal issues facing a business—or a successful person, for that matter—all written in a style that's relatively free of heavy-handed legalese. The main sections include intellectual property, trusts and estates, litigation, healthcare, and employee benefits, among others, and while each has articles written by firm members, you can skip them unless you want really in-depth information. Instead, read the questions-and-answers sections at the top of each heading. They'll give you the background you need to begin understanding the issues involved and to be a better, smarter legal consumer. —(L.S.)

KEY NEWSGROUP **alt.business** URL ▶ http://www.rbvdnr.com/

Do-it-Yourself Law

Self-Help Law Center Jump 2050

This page is maintained by Nolo Press, a publisher of legal self-help books and software for consumers and small business. It offers information taken from Nolo Press products on a variety of subjects, including feature articles that are changed regularly, information on laws that affect everyday life, and recent court decisions and new legislation. As a bonus, there's a frequently updated section of Nolo's favorite lawyer jokes. You can, of course, access the Nolo Press catalog, but there's no blatant commercialism on this page—just good, useful infomation. —(L.S.)

KEY NEWSGROUP **misc.legal** URL ▶ http://www.digital.com/gnn/bus/nolo/

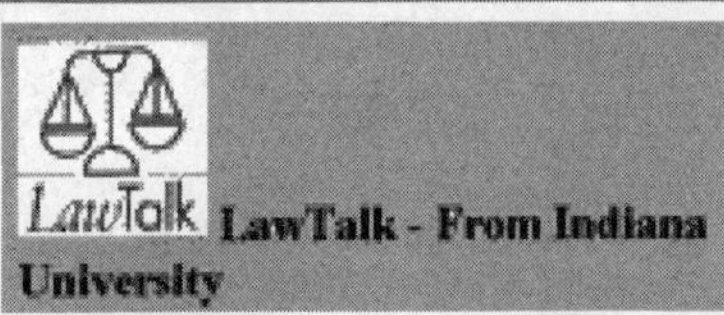

Listen to the Law

CONTENT

LawTalk Jump 2053

If you don't want to read the text stored on the Web's various law-related sites, try this one from Indiana University and listen instead. There are good selections of audio articles on business and personal finance law, criminal law, civil law, and amendments to the U.S. Constitution. There's a miscellaneous section, too, covering politically correct speech, among other things. —(L.S.)

KEY NEWSGROUP **misc.legal** URL ▶ http://www.law.indiana.edu/law/lawtalk.html

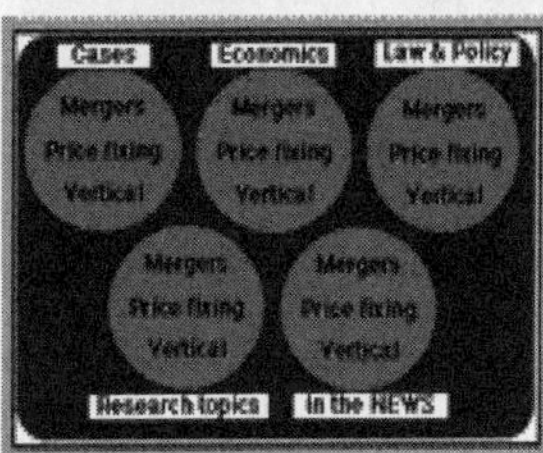

Antitrust Issues Web Site

CONTENT

Antitrust Policy Jump 2191

Antitrust issues are a combination of legal, economics, and public policy issues. Tim Kimosa of Vanderbilt University created these pages to help bridge the gap between the disciplines involved, and help practitioners and academics in each area of study understand how they interrelate. The information is organized into five main categories: antitrust cases, economics, law and policy, research topics and current antitrust issues in the news. The use of the Web's hypertext capabilities links the information in such a way that a lawyer, for example, can easily find the economic issues that affect the legal aspects of a given situation, or an economist understand the legal implications of a proposed merger that otherwise seems good for business. It's a rich resource for those deeply involved in this area, and a fascinating browse for anyone who's been watching small technology firms being gobbled up by corporate behemoths. —(L.S.)

KEY NEWSGROUP **alt.business.misc** URL ▶ http://www.vanderbilt.edu/Owen/froeb/antitrust/antitrust.html

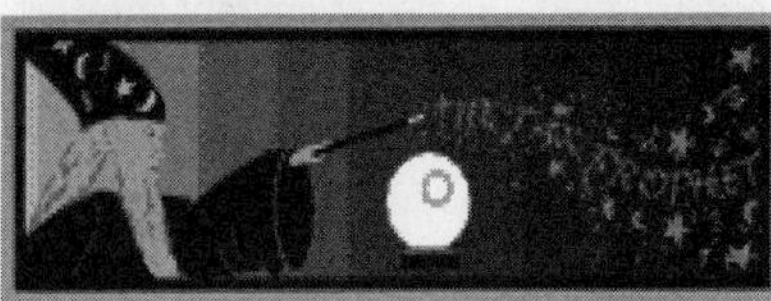

Tax News and Guidance

CONTENT

The Tax Prophet Jump 2418

Tax attorney Robert L. Sommers may not be the only tax expert online, but he's certainly among the most prolific. He's written so much for so long about taxation that he calls himself The Tax Prophet (and even registered this moniker as a trademark). So while you can't steal the name, you're welcome to help yourself to any of his newspaper and magazine articles. They're all online for download, as is his periodic newsletter. That keeps you up-to-date on IRS announcements, changes in tax laws, rumblings in Congress that can affect taxation, and other helpful information. There's even a tax fairy tale here, but you really have to look for it. —(L.S.)

KEY NEWSGROUP **misc.taxes** URL ▶ http://www.taxprophet.com/

Legal Resources

CONTENT

The SEAMLESS WEBsite Jump 3509

The SEAMLESS WEBsite is one of those special-interest Web pages that is so well done that you can't imagine that they've missed a single relevant topic or useful link! The brainchild of Kevin Lee Thomason, an enterprising California attorney, The SEAMLESS WEBsite offers an interesting collection of original articles on topics such as computer-

▲ *Early Electrolux vacuum cleaner advertising campaign vehicles, at* **http:/www.electrolux.se/elt2.**

generated evidence, consumer law, and cyberspace, as well as pointers to resources of interest to lawyers and other legal professionals. These include LawLinks, LEXIS Counsel Connect, the Internet Patent Search System and West's Legal Directory, as well as the Home Pages of law firms which maintain an Internet presence, and much more. —(C.P.)

KEY NEWSGROUP **misc.legal** URL▶ http://starbase.ingress.com/tsw/index.html

Virtual Marketplaces

Buying CDs on the Web

CDNow Jump **5729**

CDNow was one of the first retail music sites on the Internet to realize the full potential of the Web. First off the mark is not always the best, but in this case the adage is true. This site is clearly organized and so simple to use you'll find yourself searching for titles just for the sake of sticking around for a while. Their search engine is one of the best, and it's so simple it's truly a joy to use. And what is a search engine without content? CDnow has content to kill for. There is no indication here as to the actual number of items in their catalog, but the number must be immense. You can search for just about any title, no matter how obscure, and the odds are they will have it. Or they can get it for you. And we're not talking just CDs here, but vinyl, singles, videos, T-shirts, and more. They use the shopping basket approach, so if you find a title you want you can just drop it in and continue on. And you can also pre-order some titles. A great site for music lovers of any stripe. —(J.P.)

URL▶ http://www.cdnow.com/

Discount Music CDs Online

CD World Jump **0229** CONTENT

CD World is one of the Web's better online discount online CD stores, if you're looking to save $1-2 (or more) on music CDs. Although their site is not nearly as well-executed or fun to use as the Web's best-known music source, CDNow, we've found CDWorld's prices to be generally lower per item. And while it's not a terribly pretty or enjoyable site to use, their shipping is prompt and their prices are low, so you might want to do a little comparison shopping here, add in your shipping charges, then make your choice. CDWorld also sells videos and video games, also discounted. —(E.G.)

URL▶ http://www.cdworld.com/

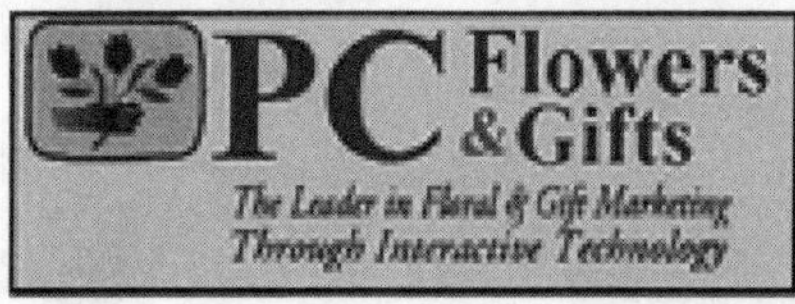

PC Flowers

PC Flowers & Gifts Jump 4516

COMMERCE

You know those interactive kiosks where you can ink-jet print your own personalized greeting card? Well this site goes one better—you can care enough to send the very best from the comfort of your own computer crib. That, plus flowers, balloons and other gifts. They'll even send you e-mail to remind you of your anniversary, mother's birthday, or any other important event you regularly forget. Is this a great country or what? —(T.W.)

URL▶ http://www.pcflowers80.com/

Buying Flowers Via the Web

1-800-Flowers Jump 5730

COMMERCE

Some things may change, but other things will always be with us. And one such thing is the need to send flowers. This very popular site, run by the folks at 800 Flowers, is a combination store and garden; the store includes a database of over 200 floral arrangements, any one of which you can order and have delivered by any of the 150 retail stores (or 800-Flower's 1,500 "partner florists"). The garden area includes seasonal specials, contests, and the locations of the stores themselves. —(J.P.)

URL▶ http://www.800flowers.com/

Lie-Nielsen TOOLWORKS INC.
Makers of Heirloom Quality Tools™

Makers of Heirloom-Quality Woodworking Tools

Lie-Nielsen Toolworks Jump 5828

You wouldn't think a photo of woodworking tools could inspire awe, but that's what happens here. This site serves as the online catalog for the Lie-Nielsen Company of Warren, Maine, and their line of hand-made woodworking tools, and we really do have to recommend that you drop in, even if you're not a woodworker. Once here you'll discover that this company, in business since 1981 and owned by Thomas Lie-Nielsen, manufactures planes, chisels, and other hand woodworking tools, modeled after fine vintage tools from the Stanley Tool Company.. You can browse the catalogue, pick out want you want, and order either online, or you can print out their order form. A fine example of a nicely-done, yet simple, online Web catalog site. —(J.P.)

URL▶ http://www.lie-nielsen.com/

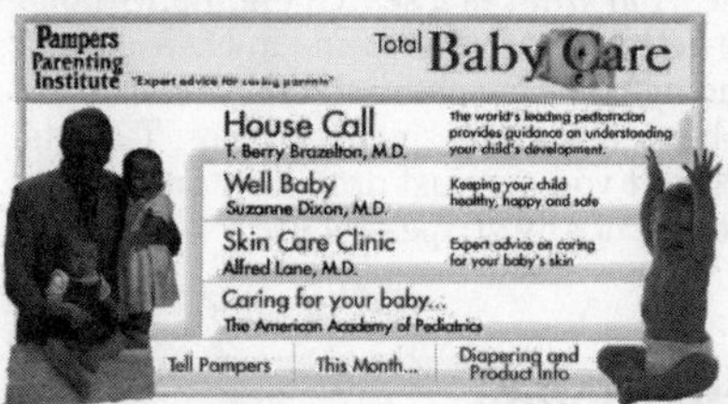

Baby Care Advice from Procter & Gamble

Pampers Total Baby Care
Jump 5787

Here's a commercial site, brought to the Web by Procter & Gamble, with all kinds of helpful and well-presented tips and information for new parents. Noted child care expert Dr. T. Berry Brazelton is the Doctor on call in the "House Call" section of this site and you'll find some great tips on everything from feeding your child to keeping track of their motor skills development, and more. Other editorial features on this site include Dr. Suzanne Dixon's tips on how to keep your child happy and healthy in the Well Baby Section, and other advice from the American Academy of Pediatrics. And, yes, the obligatory ads for Pampers are here, too, but it's all very low-key, and doesn't get in the way of the information that's presented here. —(J.P.)

KEY NEWSGROUP misc.kids URL▶ http://www.totalbabycare.com/

Free Stuff!

Freeshop Jump 5933

The Internet has become a great place to find free stuff, but the problem has always been finding the free items to begin with. Which is why Freeshop exists! If it's free and on the Web, you'll probably find it listed here. You can join the Freeshop club (for free, of course) for special offers, but otherwise you can feel free to browse their extensive database of items. All of the items are free, and some are demos or simple introductions to products. All are clearly marked, however, so you know what you'll be getting from the start. This site's "Browsing" section gives you the option of looking at items in a few dozen categories, including catalogs, clubs, clothing, jewelry, computers, electronics, education, training, entertainment, hobbies, and much more. —(J.P.)

URL ▸ http://www.freeshop.com/

Digital Craft Show

CraftShowPlace Jump 5865 CONTENT

Here's another one of those ideas that's just perfect for the Web—a virtual craft show. This is a place for artists from all over the U.S. to show their wares, and maybe even sell a few pieces online.You'll find the whole spectrum of arts and crafts here, with works from painters, photographers and pottery. The work you'll find here is what you'd see at any craft show, really, with a tendancy toward the tried-and-true over the experimental. The list of contributing artists is always changing, and you can order any of the items on display using the handy order form you'll find in each "booth." This is a site you might want to check once a month or so, just to see what's been added. —(J.P.)

KEY NEWSGROUP rec.crafts.misc

URL ▸ http://craftshowplace.com/

Handcrafted Hardwood Pens

by A. B. Petrow

This Fountain pen is supplied with a German made, gold plated iridium writing point. It can be used with either a standard short European cartridge (MontBlanc or Waterman), but it comes with a refillable cartridge for those who prefer to use their own choice of ink. As shown in Red/Black Dymondwood--$49.00

This Rollerball pen is suppplied with a gold plated writing tip and a high quality German made ink cartridge. The Rollerball pen writes a dark medium point line. Refills are available at office supply stores (MontBlanc Rollerball cartridge). This pen as shown in Walnut/Maple Dymondwood--$39.00

▲ *A.B. Petrow's handmade wooden pens for sale, from* **CraftShowPlace** *at* **Jump 5865**.

Shopping, Italian Style

A Weekend a Firenze Jump 5899 CONTENT

Now you can take advantage of the "global Web" with this chance to shop in Italy. Well, you don't actually have to leave home, but you will find a dazzling collection of intriguing, hand-crafted products from which to choose, all made in Italy. This is a virtual mall which includes products like custom frames, team shirts, books, dolls, and fine crystal, all crafted with Italian flair. —(J.P.)

URL ▸ http://www.nettuno.it/mall/

Buy a Star!

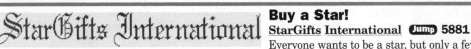

StarGifts International Jump 5881

Everyone wants to be a star, but only a few are chosen. Unless you want to buy one. A star, that is. You can buy just about anything on the Internet these days and we are here to tell you that you can now buy yourself—or your loved one—their very own star. You won't be able to put it in a jar or anything, but you will receive a personalized color certificate suitable for framing, and a poster-sized stellar map of the night sky with the star coordinates to help you find your very own star. All stars are visible either with the naked eye or through a telescope, and are located near major constellations. —(J.P.)

URL ▸ http://members.aol.com/rknetwork/stargifts.htm

The Wedding Registry

The Web's Wedding Registry

Town and Country Wedding Registry Jump 5896

Wedding registry comes to the Web in the form of the Town and Country Wedding Registry, produced by Hearst Publication's well-known print publication, *Town and Country*. This site serves a dual purpose. Guests of the prospective bride and groom can use this site's "Visitors Entrance" to see the details of the friend or family's registry. But of course too many gifts would not be good for the soul, so the

▲ *Web site advertising banner, from the Web site* Suck *at* Jump 7449.

editors of *Town and Country* have also included a few diversions for the congregated. So you might wish to "Ask the Experts," some questions you might have, or pick up some tips on wedding planning or honeymoons, even the latest horoscopes. —(J.P.)

KEY NEWSGROUP **alt.weddings** URL▶ http://tncweddings.com/index.html

Commercial Software for Downloading

Software Unboxed Jump **5915**

Here's an interesting variation on the downloadable shareware concept. At Software Unboxed, you have complete and free access to any number of software packages for Mac, Palmtops or Windows. Downloading is free, but you can't do anything with the software until you've paid the unlocking fee, which is in fact the cost of the software itself. Unlocking codes may be purchased from the software publishers, and can be sent to you via email, fax or over the phone. Insert the code and you've got a complete software package, just as though it had come in a box. This site also features demos of software programs, so you can try them before you buy. —(J.P.)

KEY NEWSGROUP **comp.misc** URL▶ http://www.unboxed.com/

INTERNATIONAL LANGUAGE DEVELOPMENT

Language Instruction You Can Hear

International Language Development Jump **5866**

Have you ever wanted to learn a second language but just never got around to it? Starting is always the hardest part, so the International Language Development folks have made it easy for you. They offer free language lesson samples in French, German, Japanese, Korean, Russian and Spanish. Just pick a language and you're ready to start your first lesson. Sounds like any other site so far, but the real compelling feature of this site is the ability to hear all of the words using RealAudio. So, if you wanted to learn German, for example, you can actually hear the words you're trying to learn as you go along. This is a great example of the extraordinary power of the Web to take a simple idea and turn it into something quite remarkable. —(J.P.)

KEY NEWSGROUP **bit.listserv.words-l** URL▶ http://www.ild.com/

New and Used Cars Marketplace

Auto Trader Online Jump **5869**

Forget about walking into that car lot and kicking the tires of that car you're thinking of buying. Join the million other visitors who've found motor manna at Auto Trader Online, the Web site that's brought to you by those same folks who make that handy little newspaper you find at grocery and convenience stores. You'll find over 250,000 new and used car classifieds here, most updated on a daily basis. You can search for used cars using the Auto Trader's wonderful search engine that uses your area code and other details to help you find the make and model of car you're looking for in your area. Or you can browse their database that's packed with everything you'll need to know about new cars (featuring over 40 manufacturers), or the listings of over 600 car dealers. And before you head off down the highway, don't forget to check out this site's links, devoted to car collectors and other cool auto sites. —(J.P.)

KEY NEWSGROUP **rec.autos.marketplace** URL▶ http://vision.traderonline.com/auto/

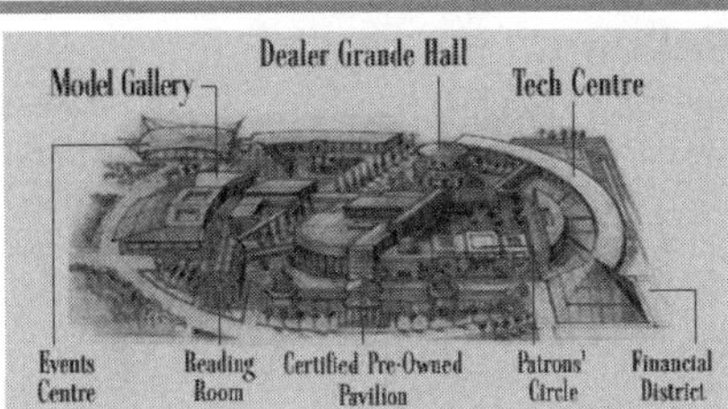

Lexus on the Web

Lexus Home Page Jump 5901

This official home page for luxury automaker Lexus offers a nice twist to the corporate promotional Web site, with a theme that revolves around a visit to its "Lexus Center of Performance Art." The art—and heart—of the site is the Lexus automobile, of course, and the data here is as detailed as you could hope for, and beautifully presented, with everything from the latest on new models to information on how to finance your new Lexus. You can read all the latest Lexus press releases in this site's "Reading Room," and, if you're already a Lexus owner, you can type in your vehicle identification number (VIN) to enter this site's special online discussion area. But since we can't afford to own a Lexus just yet, we can't actually tell you what you might find there! —(J.P.)

KEY NEWSGROUP **clari.biz.industry.automotive** URL▸ http://www.lexus.com/

Dr. Pepper's Web Site

Dr. Pepper Jump 5902

Dr. Pepper's home on the Web surely proves they can produce more than just another bland corporate promotional site. In fact, this magazine-styled site has some great exclusive features that might be found in some of the best Web news magazines around. Stories in recent editions have included features on Mars rocks and Nasa's search for life, the latest pro and college sports news, and some great trivia games. The site also includes an online discussion forum, contests, and more. —(J.P.)

URL▸ http://www.DrPepper.com/files/index2.html

AT&T Business Network℠ 

AT&T Business Network

AT&T Business Network Jump 6873

To promote themselves on the Web, AT&T supplies a valuable collection of the best business resources online. Here professionals can use the Web to their competitive advantage, with free access to the latest business news and links to this site's corporate or industry-specific reports. You'll also find such features as the Marketing Center, furnishing 1,000+ free reports, demographics research, and sound marketing advice, all viewable here. —(L.T.)

KEY NEWSGROUP **clari.biz.review** URL▸ http://www.bnet.att.com

Business Yellow Pages of the Web

WWW Business Yellow Pages Jump 2032

This list of links, compiled by Michael Walters and Diane Trippel of the University of Houston, is a real monster. It's easy to navigate, thanks to the organizational efforts of Chris Tillman of the Chinook College Funding Service, but when they say it includes every known business with a Web presence, they aren't kidding! If your business' Web site isn't there, you can get your link posted there by dropping a note to the editors. —(L.S.)

KEY NEWSGROUP **biz.misc** URL▸ http://www.cba.uh.edu/ylowpges/ylowpges.html

Business Yellow Pages of the Web

BigBook Jump 6686

BigBook is a colossal directory covering more than 11 million U.S. businesses, but it's much more than just another text-based Web business database. Search BigBook, and when you find the business you're looking for, BigBook draws a street map showing you how to get there. BigBook's business listings are also accompanied by customer ratings and reviews.You can search their huge database by business name, location or industry, and all of it's free. BigBook is also home to an sizable employment database. An innovative, useful Web site that's also a showcase for some of the Web's most exciting information and graphics display concepts. —(L.T.)

KEY NEWSGROUP **alt.business.misc** URL▸ http://www.bigbook.com

Let Your Fingers Do the Walking...

NYNEX Interactive Yellow Pages Jump 4510 COMMERCE

"Imagine filling your kitchen with almost 300 Yellow Pages directories!" That's the chilling thought that begins this incredibly useful (if you happen to live in NYNEX's service area) site. Imagine you want to find all the pet stores in New York City. Now, how about all of New York State, plus Connecticut and Rhode Island? You can do it with one simple visit to NYNEX's Web site. Even if you don't have a practical purpose, have fun! For instance: How many hair salons have the word "Mane" in their title? (The answer: 24, which is much fewer than we'd suspected, though many more than is absolutely necessary, don't you think?) —(T.W.)

URL▸ http://www.vtcom.fr/nynex/

Free Magazines!

MediaFinder Jump 6736

At first, MediaFinder's name may fool you, but here's the scoop—this is not a directory of reporters working in the media. It's a mammoth database offering the addresses, frequency of publication and specialties of thousands of newsletters, magazines, journals and catalogs. What's the big deal? With a single click, you can instantly request a free sample copy from most every publication listed here—and there are thousands upon thousands of publications specializing in every human interest—from fine arts to hardware. And, to make it easy for you, it's all searchable. With titles ranging from personal investment publications to fitness, you're sure to find a number of publications most suitable to your tastes—all free. —(L.T.)

KEY NEWSGROUP clari.biz.industry.print_media URL▸ http://www.mediafinder.com

World-Class Business Sites

Worldclass Jump 6619

Not only is this an excellent, daily-updated guide to the Web's finest business sites for over 70 countries, but each is accompanied by a full commentary. Worldclass features over 550 key business sites, each carefully chosen based on their usefulness for world commerce, timeliness, ease of use, and presentation. Each day Worldclass also delivers a featured site, a highlighted company site and global business headlines every Monday through Friday. Whether you're looking for market guides, import/export connections, government megasites, business dailies and magazines, ports and cargo, world stock markets or foreign investment resources, you're bound to find what you're looking for at the Worldclass site. —(L.T.)

KEY NEWSGROUP alt.business.import-export URL▸ http://web.idirect.com/~tiger/

Open Market's Commercial Sites Index

Commercial Services on the Net Jump 0069

A popular Web directory of many corporations, both large and small, having sites on the Web, is provided by Open Market, a company that provides businesses with assistance in developing commercial Web sites. You can search this extensive index or post your own company's Web site here—another no-cost way to spread the word about your company's Web site. —(E.G.)

KEY NEWSGROUP misc.entrepreneurs URL▸ http://www.directory.net/

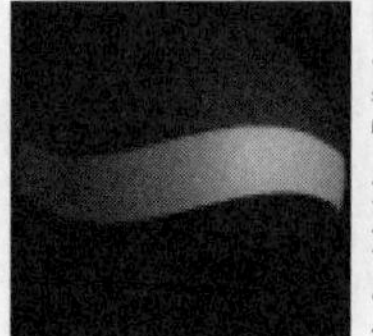

Pepsi's Web World

Pepsi World Jump 6665

The folks at Pepsi offer an entertaining home on the Web, combining movie previews, original interactive games and plenty of promotional giveaways. You can use the site for free, or register for free to retrieve even more goodies. The content here changes on a daily basis, but you'll always find the latest band interviews, many ongoing contests, and video game cheats. Try roaming the Terradome and play some exciting interactive games. If you're an artist, you can also submit your work to Pepsi's Syber Delix section, for the whole Web world to see. —(L.T.)

KEY NEWSGROUP rec.arts.movies URL▸ http://www.pepsi.com

How M&M's are Made...

M&M's Chocolate Mini Baking Bits Jump 8004

Here's where you can satisfy the question that's confounded all of us for years: Just how *do* they make M&M's? You'll not only find the answer here at M&M Mars' impressive commercial site, but you'll also find that the M&M's page is sure to delight. Although the title seems to suggest that the pages focus on just the baking bits, there's a lot more M&M's information here as well. You can send for a free recipe booklet, or drool over recipes such as Marbled Mocha Drops. Don't worry if you're new in the baking department—the Helpful Hints for Successful Baking page will help you out. Want to know more about M&M's? Then take the tour of their manufacturing process, read the M&M's FAQ (did you know M&M's have been around since 1941?), and link to other recipe and chocolate sites on the Web. —(E.v.B.)

KEY NEWSGROUP **rec.food.recipes** URL▶ http://www.baking.m-ms.com/index.htm

Internet License Plates

type_Document_Title_here Jump 8043

Do you hanker to receive e-mail from passing motorists? Well, it was only a matter of time before Internet e-mail and Web home page addresses became a sign of cool individual expression and, in this case, wired vehicular adornment. The folks at Internet Accessories want to make that possible. For a small fee, they will custom-print a license plate frame with your very own e-mail address or home page URL on it. If stuff like this is now available, we know that personalized T-shirts and baseball caps must also be out there, too! —(E.v.B.)

KEY NEWSGROUP **rec.auto.tech** URL▶ http://www.lookup.com/homepages/48618/plate.html

CyberAtlas: Trends on the Net

CyberAtlas Index Jump 8069

CyberAtlas, a solid Net industry news and trend-spotting site produced by TV research firm Nielsen and its partner, Internet ad auditor I/PRO, is a concise, fact-filled summary of vital research statistics and analysis of the Internet, and the marketing possibilities it offers. If you're wondering how big the Internet is, how fast it's growing, where all the Net's users are located, and a typical Internet user's gender, age, education and income, you'll find the answer here. Check out its coverage of such topics as future Net trends for business and marketing, the role of Intranets, the latest developments in commercial online services, and much, much more. CyberAtlas also features separate editorial sections relating to the latest trends in Internet technology, and Net developments for specific types of businesses. —(E.v.B.)

URL▶ http://www.cyberatlas.com

Spy Vs. Spy

Spy Zone Jump 6598

John Copen has designed a unique Web stop, exclusively for spies and spy buffs, that would make 007 get out his checkbook. Link to the Spy Zone and you'll get an eyeful of products suitable for corporate espionage, counter-intelligence, surveillance, and ultra high-tech detection. Professionals will find the latest technology in surveillance, techniques and tools here. Even if you're not a spy, there's plenty of sneaky-snoopy stuff here to get the goods on dishonest competitors, shifty employees and, yes, sometimes even cheating spouses. This site is so big it even features a Job Opportunities section. While most of Spy Zone's content is open to the general public, a few products are restricted to authorized law enforcement personnel, but most of the audio/video surveillance, discreet recording, FAX management, cellular phone locating, night vision, bug and lie detectors, body armor, bullet proof vehicles, and personal safety products foundd here are available to us civilians—for a price. —(L.T.)

KEY NEWSGROUP **alt.politics.org.cia** URL▶ http://www.spyzone.com/CCS1.html

Net Classifieds

The EPages Internet Classifieds

Jump 7267

Buying or selling a car, truck or motorcycle? Or perhaps you need a job, an apartment, Elvis memorabilia, or a ride from San Diego to Eugene, Oregon. The EPages Classifieds is one of many (and one of the better) such Net-based services providing free classified advertising for Internet users. You can search regionally or locally, or by subject. Trying to get away from a horrible boss, but don't want anyone to know? Well, don't worry, you can also post anonymously here. —(E.v.B.)

URL ▶ http://ep.com/

All Advertising, All the Time

Internet Advertising Site of the Day

Jump 2427

If you're the type that reads newspapers and magazines for the ads, or complains about those long interruptions between television commercials, check Tim Windsor's site. An award-winning copywriter and creative director, Tim crawls the Web looking at the various commercial sites that lately seem to be generating spontaneously. You can read Tim's capsule review of the site, and an insightful and witty snippet that helps you link with the right attitude (Editor's note: Even though Tim has stopped reviewing new ad sites, it's still worthwhile to stop here and read his archive of past reviews). —(L.S.)

KEY NEWSGROUP alt.business

URL ▶ http://www.charm.net/~windsor/todayad.html

▲ *1950s era film clips of television commercials, from* **Ad Age - It's All About Marketing** *via* Jump 7311

Bid & Buy: Web Auctions List

US Auction List Jump 2471

Auctions offer incredible deals on a wide variety of merchandise, as well as the opportunity to purchase collectibles and other rare items not often put up for sale. This site will link you to auction sites and related information on the Web that range from government sales to classic cars, with a brief description of each to help you find what interests you. If you're looking for good buys or rare merchandise, or you just enjoy seeing what types of unusual items are available, this is an excellent Web starting point. —(L.S.)

KEY NEWSGROUP misc.consumers URL ▶ http://www.syspac.com/~usaweb/auction.html

An Eclectic Little Web

MasterCard International Pointers Jump 2402

This is a prime example of how it should be done on the Web. The site is subtitled "A Webwide Collection of Cultural Treasures," and that's as good a description as any. The graphics are outstanding, with a level of quality and creativity that's not often seen. The content is excellent, as well. The main section is a collection of entertaining stories and fables that MasterCard wants you to add to as part of a worldwide collaboration to preserve and foster the tradition of oral histories. There's also a history of the Web, a tutorial on how to use it, and a good set of starter links. There's a commercial aspect since it's MasterCard's page, but it's unobtrusive and concentrates on service, not sell. —(L.S.)

KEY NEWSGROUP alt.culture.www URL ▶ http://www.mastercard.com/

Polaroid Online

Polaroid Home Page
Jump 7452

Step inside this site to get the latest news on what's happening at the Polaroid company, or take a nostalgic look at the past 65 years of its history, or even check out what's developing in the future. You can also read the latest online edition of *Test Magazine* that focuses on creative photographers at work. Or, browse through a gallery of current photographic work. As well, new products are highlighted, customer service contacts are given, and the latest developments on ISO 9000, photomacrography, and microscopy are detailed. —(E.v.B.)

KEY NEWSGROUP **rec.photo**
URL ▶ http://www.polaroid.com/homepage.htm

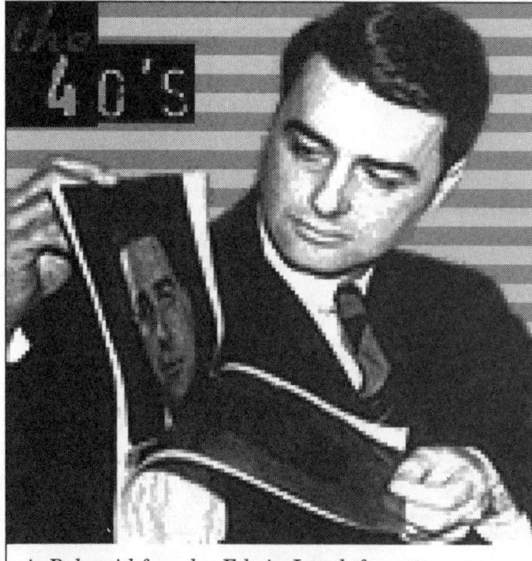

▲ *Polaroid founder Edwin Land, from* **The Polaroid Home Page** *at* Jump **7452**.

Good Looks at Top Commercial Web Sites

Interesting Business Sites on the Web
Jump 7482

Bob O'Keefe, the author of this site, has sifted through the Web to find the most interesting business sites available, with Bob's own reviews of the best ones he's found presented here. You can read about vineyards, hotels, car companies—large and small, from Coca-Cola to the Stash Tea Company. You can also read about the latest corporate legal tangles, financial services available online, and publishing and music companies. As well, browse through virtual catalogs and stroll through Bob's picks of the Web's best virtual malls. —(E.v.B.)

KEY NEWSGROUP **biz.misc** URL ▶ http://www.rpi.edu/~okeefe/business.html

Tickets, Get Your Tickets!

Ticketmaster Online Jump 3722

Where can I get tickets? What events are available? What dates will they be playing? All these questions can now be answered with one stop at Ticketmaster Online. Not only event schedules and information, but lots of other goodies too, like the Ticketmaster Store for T-shirts, or Backstage for interviews, chat and gossip, and daily news from the world of live entertainment. The Ticketmaster Spotlight has special offers and contests. Check out Ticketmaster Cares, which details the company's involvement with charities and community organizations. Development has already begun on online ticket sales. —(N.F.)

URL ▶ http://www.ticketmaster.com:80/

Never Forget an Important Date

Novator Internet Reminder Service Jump 2130

Now you can receive automatic e-mail reminding you of important birthdays, anniversaries, holidays, and other dates. All you do is complete the form with checkboxes for standard holidays, and fill-ins for your personal holiday and important events list. This is a commercial site, but the reminder service is free. The tradeoff is that with each e-mail reminder you also receive information about flowers, gifts, and other goodies you can buy from Novator to commemorate whatever occasion you needed reminding about. —(L.S.)

KEY NEWSGROUP **alt.consumers.free-stuff** URL ▶ http://www.novator.com/Remind/

Banking (with Real Money) Comes to the Web

First Virtual Jump 3656

Perhaps the only thing really standing in the way of full-blown commercial activity on the Web has been the issue of how to support the exchange of currency in a virtual world—but that's been a very big issue. It's all tangled up with security, accessibility, low cost, convenience and the ability to handle small-dollar transactions worldwide. But not for much longer! First Virtual has provided the final link for turning the flow of information into an industry.

Support for buyers and sellers is easy and inexpensive—it doesn't require any additional hardware or software—it's the 21st Century's version of Monopoly money that really gets you stuff! An extremely well-done site with loads of detailed information about how these concepts have been deployed into a working model ($2.00 for buyers, $10.00 for sellers to join, and a modest per-transaction charge). Now featuring a links page of merchants who trade in this new Web wampum. —(C.P.)

URL▶ http://www.fv.com/help/overall_map.html

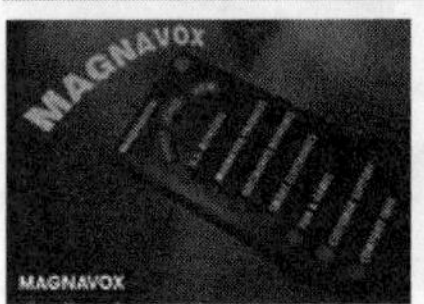

Magnavox Online

Magnavox Site Jump 7384

COMMERCE

Magnavox, makers of computer monitors, televisions, and other electronics, has established a very solid commercial site here. In fact, if you look closely at their TV commercials, you'll see this site's URL there, too! Of course, the main focus is the company—lists of retailers, in-depth description of products, pricing, company profile—the usual stuff. There's even a hot link to customer support. However, all is not Web self-promotion. You can read some original content articles on video and audio gear, and surf the many well-selected links provided here to Web sites on music, television, movies, games, and online magazines relating to the entertainment industry from this well-designed site. —(E.v.B.)

KEY NEWSGROUP alt.toys.hi-tech URL▶ http://www.magnavox.com/

The Sandal Dude

Rope Sandals Jump 0067

Whether or not you're a "Sandal Dude," you've got to admire Sandal Dude's moxie for being one of the Web's pioneering funky footwear purveyors. They've got six-strap sandals in tan, red, black, and denim—"last for years, even with daily use," plus two-strap sandals now on sale! We love you, Sandal Dude—and you will, too! —(E.G.)

URL▶ http://mmink.cts.com/mmink/kiosks/sandals/ropesandals.html

Shopping on the Net: Internet Shopping Network

Internet Shopping Network

Jump 0065

The Internet Shopping Network (ISN) is one of the Net's earliest and well-known online malls, featuring products of all types from more than 600 companies. Now a wholly-owned subsidiary of cable TV's famous Home Shopping Network, ISN features low prices on all kinds of brand name products and once you become a member (it costs nothing to join) you can access its many product listings. —(E.G.)

URL▶ http://www.internet.net/

QVC on the Web

The QVC Local Jump 4515

What happens when a shopping network climbs aboard a bus headed for all 50 states and decides to document it on the Web? Well, it's a lot better than you'd expect. This is one good-looking site. The same kind of thinking that goes into the design of a great magazine or print ad clearly went into this place as well. The premise is wacky, but simple: QVC's RV-cum-studio travels to all 50 states and finds neat stuff, cool places and not so surprisingly, stuff to sell you. Even though it seems under continuous construction, this site rates a visit now, and many return visits, as they move through the country. —(T.W.)

URL▶ http://www.qvc.com/

Real-Estate Property Locator

World Real Estate Listing Service Jump 2021

A public forum for buyers and sellers, the World Real Estate Listing Service organizes descriptions for properties for sale in the United States, Canada, Europe, and Australia. Whether you're an investor, an agent, or an individual looking to buy or sell, you can list your properties and view them here—the only costs involved are if you want to include a picture of the property in your listing. You can view properties by area (sorted by state or province and city) or in chronological order, to see what's been added since your last visit. There's also a link to other real-estate-related pages on the Web. —(L.S.)

KEY NEWSGROUP **misc.invest.real-estate** URL▶ http://interchange.idc.uvic.ca:80/wrels/index.html

Free Real-Estate Listings

ACCNET's Free Real Estate Listing Jump **2064**

You can list your residential or commercial property for sale here, for access by anyone on the Internet, or search through the listings if you're in the market for property. This is a free service and, unlike many such services, the sponsor is not trying to sell you something. It's just listings, and it's designed to deliver the maximum amount of content to the maximum number of people. Simple, straightforward forms are used to input listings and search, and the design of the system makes it quite fast. —(L.S.)

KEY NEWSGROUP **misc.invest.real-estate** URL▶ http://accnet.com/homes/

The Wired Cafe Site

Green Peppers Wired Cafe

"homestyle cooking in the heart of historic Gastown, Vancouver"

Green Peppers Wired Cafe - Vancouver, BC Jump **7269**

Green Peppers Wired Cafe is located in the heart of Vancouver, Canada's historic district Gastown—named after the lighting, not the effects of the cooking. If you are lucky enough to live in Vancouver, you can e-mail your order for breakfast, lunch or dinner. How could anyone resist Cyber Bites (fruit, croissants, etc.), or an order of Netscape eggs (Two fried eggs served on a corn tortilla with monterey jack cheese, salsa and cilantro). If you don't live in Vancouver, then you can e-mail your favorite home style cooking recipe to the Cafe—then, maybe it'll be featured on the menu the next time you surf by! —(E.v.B.)

KEY NEWSGROUP **rec.food. resturants** URL▶ http://www.canadas.net/peppers/

Translation Services for Business

The Translator's Home Companion Jump **2424**

English may seem like the de facto language of science, commerce and finance, but it's not as universal as English-speakers would like to think. With commerce becoming a global affair where even the smallest business has opportunities on the other side of the world, speaking the language of your markets is critical to success. This page is primarily a resource for professional translators, but it's also a good place for finding translation services or resources if you're a do-it-yourselfer. For those looking for help, the directory of translators and translation services is particularly good as a starting point. There also are links to online dictionaries and language education resources, with new links and services for translators and those needing their services added regularly. —(L.S.)

KEY NEWSGROUP **sci.lang** URL▶ http://www.lai.com/lai/companion.html

Advertise Your Business Web Site

NetSearch (SM) Jump **0059**

You can post a description of your business and list a hotlink to your company's home page free of charge with this well-done Web directory developed by American Information Systems, Inc. This allows any Web user who links to the NetSearch site to access information on your business by the keywords which you have supplied in your directory listing. —(E.G.)

KEY NEWSGROUP **alt.business.misc** URL▶ http://www.ais.net:80/netsearch/

Net Coffee Mugs

Cybermugs! Internet Mugs Jump **7206**

Well, here's an opportunity to combine two of your favorite addictions—caffeine and the Internet. Cybermugs is offering to sell 11-ounce mugs to hold your drink of choice while surfing. The three styles are emblazoned with the slogan "You can find me on the Internet!" You can chose between three other slogans for the other side of the mug—an example only a hard-core Webster would appreciate—"http://www.internet.mug/coffee/tea/caffeine.html." —(E.v.B.)

KEY NEWSGROUP **alt.drugs.caffeine** URL▶ http://www.webscope.com/cybermugs/

Amazon.com's Big Web Bookstore

AMAZON.COM Jump 5726

In under a year, the **Amazon.com** book site has done more to encourage Internet commerce than any other Web site. Why? Because consumers are far more likely to take a chance and buy a known commodity (like a book) online than any other product. And once they've made that all-important first Net purchase, consumers will then be more comfortable with buying other products online, too. Is Amazon.com the wave of the future in retail book distribution? Probably. Meanwhile, there is only one thing you really need to know about the Web's best-known online bookstore: You can search their online database of one million titles, which is pretty much any book currently in print. But this is not just an online bookstore, this is one of the best bookstores you'll ever experience. No more strolling the aisles, trying to remember the name of the author. Just go to **Amazon.com** and type it in the database (you don't even have to remember the full name), and you'll soon see a complete list of all books by that author, offered by Amazon. Each selection includes the price of the book, reviews, and sometimes even interviews with the author in question. Add the book to your virtual shopping basket, and you can arrange for shipment before you leave. There's also plenty of original book-related editorial features on the site, including the Book of the Day, Titles in the News, Hot Tips, feature articles and much more. —(E.G.)

KEY NEWSGROUP **alt.business.misc** URL▶ http://www.amazon.com

Free Stuff!!

The Best Things in Life (and the Web) Are Free!

Alt.Consumers.Free-Stuff Home Page Jump 2458

Maybe these aren't the best things in life, but, hey—everything included on this page is free and that kicks them up the list a bit. Marilyn J. Caylor created it because the newsgroup it takes its name from is bombarded daily with postings offering stuff that's either not free or totally useless. Discarded are offers for free brochures, recipes, and those get-rich-quick schemes that use free offers to disguise their attempts to sell you their questionable "secrets to success." And for those whose definition of "free" is strict, she separates the totally free stuff from the free stuff that asks a small shipping charge for delivery. The listings are updated at least once a week. Not as good as the daily newsgroup, but then again, the newsgroup doesn't find and polish the gems for you. —(L.S.)

KEY NEWSGROUP **alt.consumers.free-stuff** URL▶ http://gn2.getnet.com/~xinh/freestuff.html

Brown Trucks on the Web

UPS Jump 4501

COMMERCE

At this Web site, you'll find useful information from the men and women in the big brown trucks on rates and delivery times, plus the ability to track a package you sent, or are expecting. Very clean site. Very efficient site. A lot like UPS itself, actually. —(T.W.)

URL▶ http://www.ups.com/

Green Products

EcoMall Homepage Jump 1547

Environmental products and activism never seemed so exciting until now. Here's a colorful eco-oriented commercial site sporting clever representations of renewable energy, activities, eco-investments, environmental companies and products, and healthy restaurants. Not only can you find all sorts of information about each item, but there are scores of links to relevant articles on issues important to the earth. Do you know who the first environmental activist was? If so, you can win $$ by playing Cosmos, an eco-trivia game. And with every dollar won, you can invest it back into earth-wise products by purchasing something from the EcoMall. —(H.L.)

URL▶ http://www.ecomall.com/

(Real) Spam Hits the Net!

Show SPAM Gifts Jump 1588

COMMERCE

Despite the use of that most Net-notorious of terms, "Spam," this Web site is an honest-to-goodness online emporium for the real thing: Hormel's good old Spam and related promo products. Cheer up family and friends with everything from T-shirts to baseball caps emblazoned with that all-American Spam logo. There's even a cookbook so you can whip up a hearty batch of Spam, Spam, Spam, Spam, Spam, Spam, baked beans, and Spam. —(H.L.)

URL http://wolf.co.net/spamgift/index.html

▲ *Curious George rides his bike, from* **Welcome to FAO Schwarz** *at* Jump **7438**.

Toys Galore!

Welcome to FAO Schwarz Jump **7438**

COMMERCE

The wonderful world of toys—FAO Schwarz has created some lovely, animated pages reflecting their store and its merchandise. Both the young and the perennially young will enjoy browsing the online catalog full of building blocks, stuffed bears, dolls, puzzles and games. If you want more serious information on the company and the FAO Schwarz museum, they've got that too. If you can't wait to visit the real thing, they have posted addresses for their 30 stores. But admit it, what you really want to do is read their extensive "Barbie at FAO" section! —(E.v.B.)

KEY NEWSGROUP **rec.toys.misc** URL http://www.faoschwarz.com./faohome.html

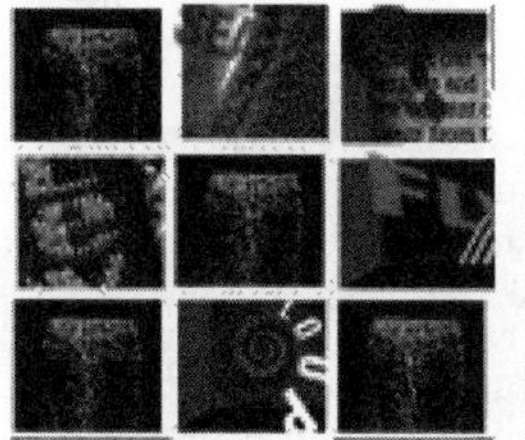

Levi's Home on the Web

Levi Strauss & Co. - Welcome! Jump **7259**

COMMERCE

If you believe that we have only one life to live, and that that life should be lived in denim, well, Levi Strauss has created the Web site for you! Page layout and cutting-edge Web graphics are extremely attractive throughout the site. However, if you have a slow modem, the flashing, multiple graphic-laden pages can load pretty slowly. However, once you're in, you'll learn about the company, read fashion and youth culture features and, of course, learn everything and more about those famous jeans. We especially enjoyed this site's "Jean-eology," which traced the history of the Levi's company. Did you know that belt loops weren't sewn on jeans until after World War I? —(E.v.B.)

KEY NEWSGROUP **alt.fashion** URL http://www.levi.com/menu

Upscale Catalog Shopping

Shopping2000 Home Page Jump **2092**

COMMERCE

There's good news and bad news at this site. The good news is that more than 40 leading retailers and direct merchants have online multimedia versions of their print catalogs here for you to browse. The bad news is that the graphics-laden pages take so long to load that you may figure out better uses for your money before you have a chance to drool over the goodies. The sluggishness starts with the main page, with image maps made of the covers of the online catalogs, and continues with some huge inline images on the catalogs themselves. Still, it's worth a visit, and judicious use of the "stop transfer" button on your browser can give you the text and links, and even some of the graphics. —(L.S.)

KEY NEWSGROUP **misc.consumers** URL http://www.shopping2000.com/

Cyber Publishers

The Eden Matrix Jump **7142**

The Eden Matrix Online Service, located in Austin, Texas, publishes and distributes underground, mainstream, and esoteric music (with titles like Machine Screw), magazines (such as *Thora-Zine*), comics (amuse yourself with Digital Ashcans), and periodicals (from architecture to UFOs). Eden Matrix carries over 1,000 items you can order. As well, for a small fee you can subscribe to the magazines of your choice. However, if you just want to visit this home page occasionally, you can do that, too. You can listen to an extensive collection of music and video sample clips, and check out your favorite band's touring schedule. You can also read selections from their immense offerings of e-zines and comics. —(E.v.B.)

KEY NEWSGROUP **alt.zines** URL http://www.eden.com/

Sony's Site on the Web

COMMERCE

Sony Online Jump 4027

This immense, well-executed site is the home of entertainment giant Sony. There's so much to do and see here it's hard to know where to begin. Among the information you can access are links for Sony music, movies, television, electronics products, software and video games, and much more. You can even take part in contests and win prizes directly from Sony. This site is graphically beautiful and loaded with fun resources, including downloadable multimedia files. —(R.B.)

URL▶ http://www.sony.com/

Sprint's Web Stop

Sprint Stop Jump 4502

Sprint has the most light-hearted site of the big three long-distance carriers (including MCI and AT&T). Its retro-diner look and feel carries through all of the handsomely-designed sub-areas, including even a live "lunch-counter" area where visitors are able to chat with specially scheduled guests. Overall, a very worthwhile rest stop on the Web. —(T.W.)

URL▶ http://www.sprint.com/

New Car Information Center

Dealernet Jump 0009

A well-executed, commercial Web site featuring several car dealerships and links to other Web sites for all leading car manufacturers, related automotive services, parts, boats, RVs, and other auto-related information. If you're not yet brave enough to buy a new car over the Internet, we understand, but this Web site can still provide you with intelligent answers to just about any new car-related question. While some may scoff at the idea of selling new cars over the Internet, Rood Nissan/Volvo of Lynnwood, Washington does a substanial Volvo parts business over the Internet already, plus, it actually sells quite a few cars over the Net, so this may be a harbinger of more big-ticket Internet business transactions to come. —(E.G.)

KEY NEWSGROUP misc.consumer URL▶ http://www.dealernet.com

Cadillac's Web Site

Cadillac Hard Drive Jump 4517

When we were boys, there were two types of people, those who lusted for Corvettes and those who aspired to Cadillacs. Either way, we suppose, GM was happy. Anyway, here's one for the heavy metal fans. You'll find information on Cadillac, of course—including a free interactive demo disk by mail, a list of local dealers and Cadillac accessories—plus information on yacht racing and golf, two demographically appropriate subjects for Cadillac's market segment. —(T.W.)

URL▶ http://www.cadillac.com/

Chryslers on the Web

COMMERCE

Chrysler Technology Center Jump 4500

Don't be put off by the seemingly unfriendly opening screen shaking you down for a "visitor badge." The Webmaster's tongue is clearly in his cheek, and it's optional anyway. But if you don't sign in, you won't see your name repeated back to you in every other sentence like any good salesbot is trained to do. A nice array of information on the company, plus cool photos and QuickTime movies of concept cars that you'll never own, but wish you could. —(T.W.)

URL▶ http://www.chryslercorp.com

Rent a Car Anywhere in the U.S.

Rent A Wreck Home Page Jump 3664

COMMERCE

Now this is leading edge. You may not find Hertz, Avis or National Car Rental on the Web (yet) but you'll see them scrambling as soon as word of this site gets out! Rent-A-Wreck has 400 locations in the U.S. and in eight foreign countries. Clickable maps guide you to the closest Rent-A-Wreck city, and offer some interesting and useful travel information, too! Great for the business or leisure traveler who doesn't have a fortune to spend on transportation. —(C.P.)

URL▸ http://www.charm.net/~ken/

Bullet-Stopping Locks

Master Lock Jump 4509

From the makers of the padlocks called "tough under fire" comes a Web site dedicated to home and personal security and, of course, Master Locks. Here, you'll find a great number of security tips for your home or business. Sure, it's designed to make you paranoid and go out and purchase a gross or two of Master Locks, but as a Web marketing tool, it's a far sight more informative than the Swedish Bikini Team. —(T.W.)

URL▸ http://www.masterlock.com/cgi-bin/c?master+idx

Snakeskin Boots Anyone?

G.C. Blucher Boot Co. Jump 7369

Round 'em up, ride 'em out—and don't forget to wear your boots. Cowboy boots, all the rage in country and city these days, have found a home on the Web at the G.C. Blucher Boot Company. Founded in June 1915, in Cheyenne, Wyoming, the company became known for the craftsmanship of its handmade boots. You can sample some of its wares, order a full catalog online, and read some of the fun, original stories thrown in to add a Western flavor. Interested in wowing your line-dance group with a pair of ostrich leather boots?—see them here. It's also fun to surf the country-western links to sites on Western art, rodeos, horses, cowboys and Indians, and country music. A content-rich, well-executed commercial site. —(E.v.B.)

URL▸ http://www.fn.net/business/boots.html

Brewer's Web Spot

Anderson Valley Brewing Jump 4512

Remember how in the movie "Miracle on 34th Street," the Macy's Santa sent the customers to Gimbel's sometimes? Well, this well-designed brewery site has a page of links to other brewers (i.e., competitors) with home pages on the Web. The holiday spirit lives on year-round at Anderson Valley. Of course, before you leave, you'll find a wealth of well-organized information on Anderson Valley's own products. Web designer Mark Felder-Allen has assured you'll have a great time at this virtual watering hole. —(T.W.)

URL▸ http://www.avbc.com/avbc/home.html

Nine-Alarm Chili Fun

Hot Hot Hot Jump 4518

You either love hot sauce, or you think Taco Bell's the kind of place to go for truly spicy food. For the first group, this is the place you've been looking for. Great graphics and a fine selection, even organized by firepower. This fun, great-looking site is Grand Central for those who really do like it hot. You can set up an account or order by credit card and burn away your tongue to your heart's content. —(T.W.)

URL▸ http://www.hot.presence.com/g/p/H3//

The radical change [MIT Media Lab Director Nicholas] Negroponte anticipates is a shift in the location of authority and creative intelligence from a few centralized sources of information and fun (media moguls, governments, games producers) to us, the digitally connected...

Negroponte's optimism in the face of the impending shake-down in the business of being human lies with the kids who wander happily in the non-geographic space of the Internet.

"While the politicians struggled with the baggage of history, a new generation is emerging from the digital landscape free of many of the old prejudices."

Amanda Leslie-Spinks, "Digital Technologies Are the Way of the Future," ***Calgary Herald***

Politics & Electronic Democracy

The blue-suited leaders of both political parties have not yet noticed the ground shifting beneath their shiny black shoes. Now that talk radio, the Internet—and now the Web—have put tremendous new political organizing power into the hands of individual citizens, things will never be the same for the current power structure.

Web Resources for Citizen Activism

One of the Internet's—and now the Web's—most exciting uses is the way ordinary citizens have used it as a communicating and organizing tool to effect grassroots change within the political process.

The Internet played its first significant role in the November, 1994 elections. Average citizens who, up until now, believed they had little or no power in the political process, helped to break the four decades-long political and legislative chokehold of an entrenched and unresponsive Congress. The Internet empowered 35-year-old Richard Hartman, and his wife Mary—two Spokane residents who heretofore had no involvement in politics—to organize an Internet-based grassroots effort that attracted campaign contributions from many ordinary citizens around the U.S. and played a significant role in unseating house speaker Thomas Foley in the November, 1994 mid-term congressional elections.

No matter their ideological beliefs, the Web provides ordinary citizens of all walks of life and political beliefs with a vehicle for instant communication to an audience of millions, any number of whom may join together to back political candidates, promote or lobby against political legislative efforts, or to organize and communicate among one another and the population at large to effect change within the system.

Web Access to Legislative Information

Your Congress has not been totally unresponsive in catching on to the power of the Web, however. House Speaker Newt Gingrich, no high-tech slacker himself, played a key role in getting Congress to establish a number of important Web sites, where you can get the complete text of proposed legislation before Congress, the latest status of congressional legislative activities, and direct e-mail access and contact information for members of Congress.

Tools for Spreading Conservative & Liberal Points of View

In general, a Web site can be the most powerful tool available to any individual who feels a burning need to express a strong political belief. There are also a large number of highly partisan Web sites covering politics from both ends of the political spectrum. However, judging from the number of Web sites, newsgroups, comments, and e-mail, conservatives seem to outnumber liberals, at least on the Net.

In addition to featuring many of well written, politically-oriented articles on a wide variety of partisan subjects, most of these kinds of Web sites can also give you instant access to a wide variety of related documents and news articles used by these Web site author/advocates to supplement the opinions they expressed on their sites. Whether or not you share the same views as the authors of the partisan Web sites, whether conservative/right or liberal/left, these sites are indeed a powerful new medium for the promotion of individual free speech.

Sites for Information on Current Events & History

The Web also provides a useful new medium for collecting information, photos, reports, and multimedia relating to a wide variety of current controversies. Whatever the issue, policy, or news event, someone has created a Web site that contains all kinds of relevant background information, news and updates to cover it. But beware: since anyone has the freedom to create a Web site on any subject, you must judge the credibility of that Web site's statements and news sources for yourself.

There are also a number of fascinating Web sites featuring in-depth information, oral histories and photographs. These include personal histories of World War II, Korea, and Vietnam veterans, providing the authors of these Web sites with a publishing forum for sharing their recollections, and providing you, the reader, with a fascinating look at history from the viewpoint of its participants.

Once the tools-in-trade of revolutionary struggle were (apart from guns and bandanas) handbills, loudhailers, secret jungle meetings and covert poster campaigns. The Zapatistas [a Mexican guerilla movement], however, have taken to spreading world consciousness about their battles via the Internet.

It was recently reported that in a raid by the Mexican police on Zapatista safe houses, more floppy disks were captured than guns. And the Zapatista leader, Subcommandante Marcos, is rarely to be seen without his laptop, tapping out his communiques. The disks are then transported to U.S. sympathisers, who put out the information on the Internet's World Wide Web and communicate them to various discussion groups.

"The Highwayman," ***The Guardian***

Citizen Political Resources

U.S. Federal Budget Online

Entire US Federal Budget Jump 6556

To date, no one had ever provided such a comprehensive Net-based record of U.S. government spending until the non-profit Institute for Better Education Through Resource Technology (IBERT) placed the entire U.S. Federal Budget on this site. Here you'll find a full compilation of federal budget line items, broken down by agency and activity. If you dig into the secondary levels of this resource, you'll find detailed budget itemization from every department of every agency, all presented in an easy-to-scrutinize fashion. —(L.T.)

KEY NEWSGROUP alt.politics.economics

URL ▸ http://ibert.org/

Thomas Paine Books

The LibertyOnline Thomas Paine Library Jump 5920 CONTENT

If you'd like to brush up on the background of one of the true legends of American history, you won't find a much better site than the Thomas Paine Library. Paine, whose writings were instrumental in the founding of the country, was an author and revolutionary activist who, we learn here, took part in three separate revolutions! You will find the text to three of his most influential works here: *Common Sense*, *Age of Reason*, and *The American Crisis*. The site is prepared in a style that takes advantage of your browser's frames capability, allowing you to skip around easily from section to section. You have the choice of continuing on to the next chapter, or returning at another time. Either way, it's well worth a visit to learn more about the man who, as John Adams said: "Without the pen of Paine, the sword of Washington would have been wielded in vain." —(J.P.)

URL ▸ http://libertyonline.hypermall.com/Paine/

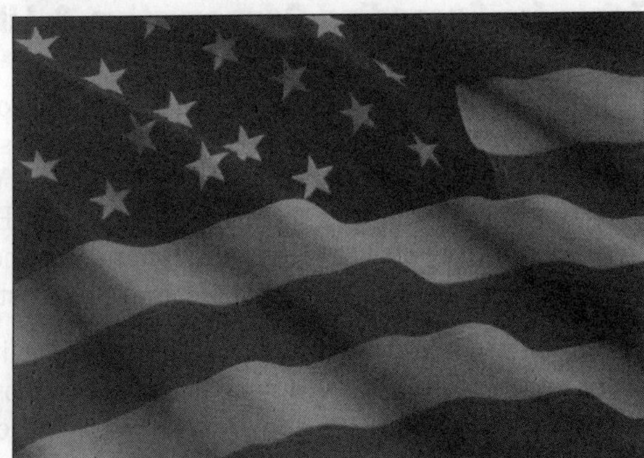

▲ *American flag photo, from* **Washington University Image Archives** *at* Jump 0192.

Mega Political Resources

The Political Scientist's Guide to the Internet Jump 7218

Are you a political junkie who needs a daily fix of information on politics, government at all levels, and law? Well, Peter Adams has scoured the Internet to pull together a truly amazing number of resources. Politicians, parties, and interest groups can be scrutinized. Political science libraries of the world can be searched. Election data can be downloaded. Major government documents and constitutions can be read. Feel lost? Take heart—Peter provides a guided tour to set your political feet on the right path. —(E.v.B.)

KEY NEWSGROUP talk.politics.theory URL ▸ http://www.trincoll.edu/pols/home.html

Comprehensive State and Local Governments Information

State and Local Government on the Net Jump 1544

If you want to find online government information about your state, or any other state, this is the place for you. This constantly updated site, compiled by Dana Noonan of Piper Resources, features complete listings of local and regional governmental contacts for all 50 states—the most comprehensive collection you'll see anywhere on the

Web. Not only can you find contacts for legislative and executive branches, and county/city information, you'll also find the national organizations serving state and local governments, think tanks, job banks, and executive session calendars. You can also search for specifics, like parks that have fishing access or water-rights laws. One of the most informative sites for your browser's bookmark file! —(H.L.)

URL http://www.webcom.com/~piper/state/states.html

Daily Election News from Around the World

Election Notes: Daily Worldwide Election News Jump 6884

A quick-loading site that furnishes daily election calendars, polls and returns from the entire world. When The Klipsan Press, creators of this site, covered the Russian elections, they didn't forget that other countries like Mexico, Bangladesh, and Iceland were holding elections at the same time, too. In keeping with its view toward global politics, you'll find the latest briefs, an upcoming election calendar (and, since weather affects voter turnout overseas, too) even International weather forecasts. —(L.T.)

KEY NEWSGROUP **alt.politics.elections** URL http://www.klipsan.com/elecnews.htm

Web-Based Political Documents Collection

Political Documents Jump 2390

When the 104th Congress was debating a new crime bill that would have given police the ability to search without a warrant, one congressman proposed an amendment to the bill—a verbatim copy of the Fourth Amendment, which protects citizens against such searches. It was soundly defeated, much to the chagrin of those voting against it when the amendment's source was revealed. If they had referred to Bill Dueber's page, they could have avoided the embarrassment. Here are links to online copies of the U.S. Constitution and other current and historical political documents that will keep you current with contemporary U.S. government laws and regulations, as well as help you learn about the roots of modern political thought. There also are links to international treaties and conventions, such as the Law of the Sea, human rights, conservation, and other subjects which directly and indirectly affect the everyday life of the planet. —(L.S.)

KEY NEWSGROUP **alt.politics.usa.constitution** URL http://www.cs.indiana.edu/inds/politics.html

 Iowa Electronic Markets

Betting on the Candidates

Iowa Electronic Markets Jump 2655

On the assumption that people will lie to pollsters without batting an eye, but always tell the truth when they put their own money down, the University of Iowa College of Business Administration has created this real-money futures market. Here you can buy and sell futures based on your feelings about a political candidate, or just see how the runners stack up against each other. The flaw in using this as an opinion poll is that it doesn't reflect how people will vote. Rather, it is based on how traders think people will vote. Regardless, it's a fascinating site to browse. Each market, including the presidential election, the party conventions, and others, includes a prospectus, current quotes and histories of price movements. There also are links to relevant Web sites, so you can do your own research before making a "buy." —(L.S.)

KEY NEWSGROUP **alt.politics.elections** URL http://www.biz.uiowa.edu/iem/index.html

Legislation 101

A Layperson's Guide to Congress Jump 2664

Actual work goes on in the U.S. Congress. Really. No joke. It may seem like all that the senators and representatives do is posture, call each other names, take lavish vacations paid for by lobbyists, and run for reelection, but there's real work going on (well, sometimes). If you're not familiar with how laws are made, this is an excellent introduction to the process, as simple and precise as the laws your leaders create should be, but never are. There's also a starter set of links if you want to know more about the legislative process, or track what's happening in Congress during the current session. —(L.S.)

KEY NEWSGROUP **alt.politics.usa.congress** URL http://www.we.com/lgc/

U.S. Congress Lesgislative Information

THOMAS: Legislative Information on the Internet Jump **0105**

CONTENT

THOMAS (named after Thomas Jefferson) is House Speaker Newt Gingrich's effort to make Congressional legislative information freely accessible to the public via the Internet. This well-executed Web site contains the full text of all versions of House and Senate bills searchable by key words or bill number, the full text of the *Congressional Record*, resolutions, and links to House member e-mail directories, calendars, and latest daily schedules. Information in THOMAS is updated regularly, with new features (like legislative summaries and chronologies) promised soon. —(E.G.)

KEY NEWSGROUP **talk.politics.misc** URL▶ http://thomas.loc.gov/

Local Election Coverage for Your State

ElectNet Jump **6729**

Sure there are many terrific election Web sites online, providing strong national focus. But ElectNet brings this coverage to a local level, and no one covers local elections like they do. This well-organized resource follows your state's candidates running for Governor, U.S. Senate, and Congress. This site starts with a clickable U.S. map, where you choose which state races to access. You'll then be launched to links for all relevant local politi-cal organizations, news, resources and election results available online, tailored specifically to your local area. —(L.T.)

KEY NEWSGROUP **alt.politics.elections** URL▶ http://www.e1.com/gov/

One Vote at a Time

Votelink Jump **1543**

Do you feel your voice isn't heard while Congress makes decisions you disagree with? Grassroots politics has always been an outlet for raising concerns; now it's commonplace on the Web. Here, you can register to vote weekly on world, national, and your own state and local issues—whether to raise taxes to reduce the federal deficit or eliminate all affirmative action programs, for example—and make a difference. Votelink staff tallies the votes and publishes them at the end of each week in digest form to news media, Congress, and the White House. You also have the opportunity to send feedback, provide suggestions for upcoming topics, and participate in town meetings by posting your comments in a public forum. Does it represent all the people? "No, just information seekers, thought leaders, and activists at thc cutting edge of the future," says publisher Alexia Parks, whose motto "Votelink: building a global mind, one vote at a time" might come true one day. —(H.L.)

URL▶ http://www.votelink.com/

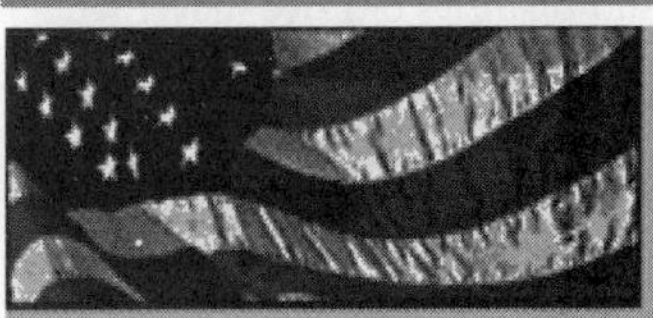

Congressional Directory

Contacting the 104th Congress Jump **2413**

Got a gripe about Congress, or an opinion you want to make sure your representative or senators know about? Or has hell frozen and you want to give your elected official a pat on the back? Whatever may prompt you to contact your leaders, Juan Cabanela maintains this site so you can find their phone and FAX numbers, addresses, and other helpful information quickly. Where available, he also links you to a Web page or e-mail address, and all listings are linked to the files on the appropriate Chamber's Gopher server. —(L.S.)

KEY NEWSGROUP **alt.politics** URL▶ http://ast1.spa.umn.edu/juan/congress.html

The Supreme Court in Action

Decisions of the US Supreme Court Jump **3520**

If you're a student of the Supreme Court, or if you're interested in watching how new law is made at the highest level—then come see the Justices at work! This site is one of several maintained by the Legal Information Institute at Cornell Law School, and it offers a summary of the last five years of decisions made by the highest court in the land. Indexed by year, and by the first and second parties, it's easy to find the decisions you're looking for. In addition to the text of decisions, this site offers the full text of historic Supreme Court decisions. —(C.P.)

KEY NEWSGROUP **clari.news.law.supreme**
URL ▶ http://www.law.cornell.edu/supct/

Know Your Politicians

Project Vote Smart Home Page Jump **2632** CONTENT

This volunteer organization works to compile factual information about the thousands of candidates running for office each election, especially those currently in power. They call it a Voter's Self-Defense System, and that's as good a description as any. Link to its Gopher server from this page, and you'll have access to biographical information and performance evaluations of the nation's governors and members of Congress. The performance evaluations are particularly interesting—the Project assembles ratings from various special interest groups and shows the rating given to the politician by that group, based on how often he or she votes in support of the group's positions. Find the groups that represent your views, and you'll have a quick reference to how well that politician represents your positions. —(L.S.)

KEY NEWSGROUP **alt.politics.usa.misc**
URL ▶ http://www.peak.org/vote-smart/

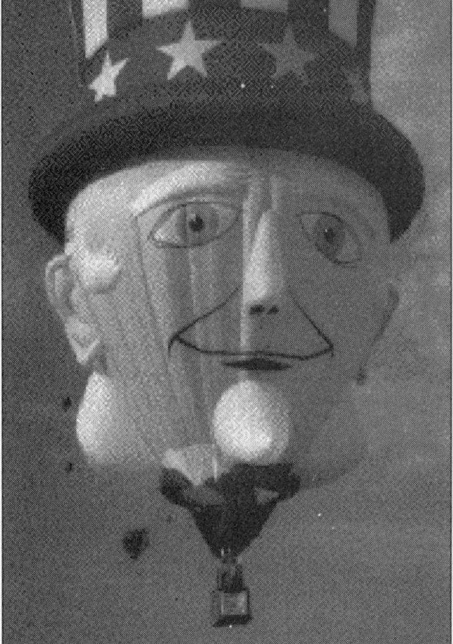

▲ *Uncle Sam hot air balloon, part of the collection of the Soukup & Thomas International Balloon & Airship Museum, from* **Cyberspace World Railroad Home Page** *at* Jump **2119**.

Information about the House of Representatives

US House of Representatives Home Page Jump **3521** 

Need to contact your congressman? Look no further—this is where you'll find him or her—and plenty of other great stuff, too! From information about bills and resolutions wending their way through Congress to up-to-the-hour reports about what's happening on the floor of the House, this site has anything you can think of that might be of interest on the topic of government. You can find the *Congressional Record*, the text of bills, schedules of legislative activities, info and maps for visitors to Capitol Hill, and educational documents concerning Congress and the entire legislative process . —(C.P.)

KEY NEWSGROUP **clari.news.gov** URL ▶ http://www.house.gov/

Documents Behind the News

Government Documents in the News Jump **7305** 

Ok, all you news junkies and grassroots activists—get your information straight from the source. Log on to the University of Michigan's Documents Center for official documents, statements by government officials, press releases, speeches and background papers from the United Nations, nongovernment organizations, the U.S. government, and other countries around the world. A great source for getting to the official documents behind today's news stories. —(E.v.B.)

KEY NEWSGROUP **misc.headlines** URL ▶ http://www.lib.umich.edu/libhome/Documents.center/docnews.html

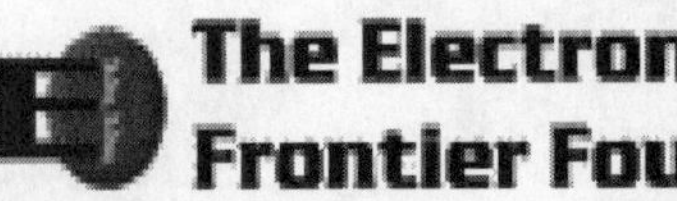

Internet Protectors

EFFweb - The Electronic Frontier Foundation Jump 7329

The Electronic Frontier Foundation (EFF), a nonprofit civil liberties organization, is on guard for you to protect privacy, free expression, and access to online resources and information. And at its site, the EFF provides a wealth of information on its activities through searchable archives and newsletters. You can also explore the Internet using the EFF's well-done guide to the Internet for Net novices, or take a virtual world tour of Cyberspace, featuring Aerosmith. You can also link into news and discussions on all the Internet's hot topics through links to pertinent Usenet groups. After exploring the serious stuff, you can also check out the EFF's collection of images, animations and sounds. A nicely-executed site by an organization that's truly a champion for the rights of all citizens on the Net. —(E.v.B.)

KEY NEWSGROUP **comp.org.eff.talk** URL▶ http://www.eff.org/

THE C-SPAN NETWORKS

Political Feed

The C-SPAN Networks Jump 7404

All of us who've become fascinated viewing the inner workings of government by watching C-SPAN can surf on over to the C-SPAN Web pages and find the latest news and views on the political process. Link here and check out daily program schedules, see what's up in the 1996 presidential campaign, read excerpts from the *Washington Journal*, hear speeches and other audio bits from C-SPAN programs, and read reviews of—what else?—politically-related books. You can also visit their Public Affairs Hotlinks Page for a direct connection to online political resources. For K-12 teachers, C-SPAN also offers a wide variety of lesson plans to help bring current events to the classroom. —(E.v.B.)

KEY NEWSGROUP **bit.listserv.politics** URL▶ http://www.c-span.org/index.html

Current House Floor Activities from C-SPAN

Current House Floor Activities Jump 6894

Integrate a live C-SPAN video image of the House floor, automatically update it every 20 seconds, and display text on what current legislation the House is debating on the floor, and you've got what's behind this site. You also get a birdseye view of daily House activities, schedule log, and what laws they're about to debate. Even when Congress is not in session, you'll get a snapshot of C-SPAN's live feed as it's being broadcast. —(L.T.)

KEY NEWSGROUP **alt.activism** URL▶ http://majoritywhip.house.gov/current/now.htm

propaganda

All about Propaganda

Propaganda Analysis Jump 2360

Say the word "propaganda" and images of totalitarians, fascists, and other undemocratic regimes trying to convince the world of their righteousness come to mind. But this maniupulative rhetoric is not limited to the Evil Empires of history. You encounter it every day, from politicians, advertisers, public interest groups, your spouse, and anyone else with an agenda that requires molding opinion to succeed. Whether it's a master manipulator or your best friend, knowing the history and techniques of propagandists can help you separate the fact from the bombast, enable you to better analyze situations, and base the decisions you make on fact rather than emotional response. To help you understand how it works, Aaron Delwiche reviews the common techniques of propaganda, including examples from today and the past. And if you study carefully enough, you'll not only be able to resist, you may even learn enough to become a master propagandist yourself! —(L.S.)

KEY NEWSGROUP **alt.politics** URL▶ http://carmen.artsci.washington.edu/propaganda/home.htm

Reforming Government

Char's Home Page Jump 2414

The Web outpost of the United We Stand America government reform group, this page maintained by Char Roberts keeps you up to date on UWSA and general news and activities of interest to people who want change

in Washington and elsewhere in the United States. There are almost daily Washington Updates from Joan Vinson, articles on government reform with links to third party and other like-minded groups, and special sections on immigration, welfare/entitlement programs, trade, and California issues. Even if you don't agree with UWSA, Char has created a useful resource for anyone who wants changes in the status quo of U. S. government. —(L.S.)

KEY NEWSGROUP **alt.politics.usa.misc** URL▸ http://www.emf.net/~cr/homepage.html

Protecting Your Right to Online Privacy

EPIC Jump **2570** CONTENT

With the online availability of adult-oriented entertainment, the fallout from the Oklahoma City bombing, and the general urge of government to control what they don't understand, the online privacy rights of individuals are facing serious threats. EPIC, the Electronic Privacy Information Center, maintains this Web site to help you stay current with the issues, monitor the actions of government, and alert yourself to actions you can take to protect your privacy. In addition to coverage of hot topics and issues threatening privacy rights, there is also an excellent interactive and links-rich guide to privacy resources on the Internet, and an online copy of the EPIC's regular newsletter covering electronic privacy issues. All the material here is updated frequently, making it the best source of privacy rights information available on the Net. —(L.S.)

KEY NEWSGROUP **alt.privacy** URL▸ http://epic.org/

Seattle Political Action

Seattle Community Network Jump **3585** CONTENT

Online since early 1994, the Seattle Community Network is a free, public computer network run by volunteers dedicated to "Democratic Technology for All." In that spirit, you'll find plenty of interesting things on this Web site—from the Peace & Justice Events Listing (a list of scheduled rallies, picketing and demonstrations on a wide range of issues) to useful Internet information and everything you can think of in between. Visit Seattle's Community Network—you'll be glad you did. —(C.P.)

URL▸ http://www.scn.org/

A Guide to International Trade

International Trade Law project - Ananse Jump **3637** CONTENT

For every student of international trade and for every American concerned about the effects, both positive and negative, of the balance of trade, NAFTA, etc., this comprehensive site is loaded with great information. Resources range from an index of NAFTA material available on the Internet, to model laws, information about WTO/GATT, ICC and U.N. initiatives, and much more. —(C.P.)

KEY NEWSGROUP **alt.politics.economics** URL▸ http://ananse.irv.uit.no:80/trade_law/nav/trade.html

Ending World Hunger

HungerWeb Home Page—We Can End Hunger Jump **2359** CONTENT

Hunger plagues one-fifth of the world's population. It's not an incurable disease, but it often seems so given its pervasiveness and tenacity. Originally designed by Daniel Zalik, these pages are now run by the World Hunger Program. While they are intended primarily for advocates, educators, researchers and field workers, there's also a browser's page that discusses hunger around the world and in the United States, with pointers to information on how you can help. If you wonder whether you can—or should—get involved, keep in mind that in the few minutes it takes to browse that Web site, more than 100 children will die from hunger. —(L.S.)

KEY NEWSGROUP **alt.activism** URL▸ http://www.hunger.brown.edu/hungerweb/

Electronic Environmental Watchdog

NRDC Web: State of Nature Jump 7179

If you're a serious advocate of environmental protection, you should read the federal Natural Resources Defense Council's timely newsletter—*State of Nature*. This succinct publication keeps you informed on what environmental bills are up for review and which have been vetoed, approved or passed in the House and Senate. You can also choose to have the newsletter delivered to you by e-mail. —(E.v.B.)

KEY NEWSGROUP talk.environment URL▶ http://www.nrdc.org/nrdc/field/state.html

Progressive Politics Resource Guide

The Progressive Directory Jump 4003

This site bills itself as "your one-stop guide to progressive organizations and resources," and it lives up to that statement. The Institute for Global Communications (IGC) brings you a link to progressive political resources from environmental issues to labor concerns. Updated current events, alternative news sources, and a directory of organizations are also included. —(R.B.)

KEY NEWSGROUP alt.activism URL▶ http://www.econet.apc.org/

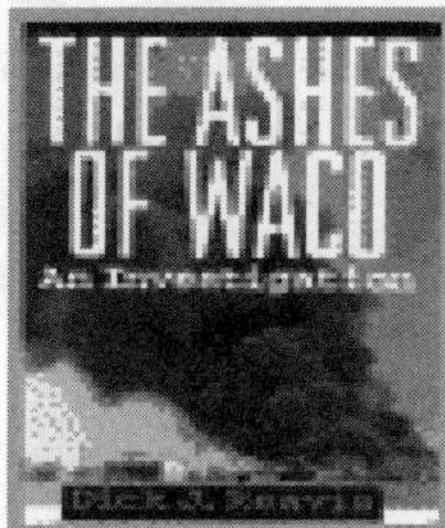

Koresh vs. the ATF

The Ashes of Waco Jump 2688

We may never learn what really happened at the Branch Davidian complex near Waco, Texas, but this site offers a good resource for those who wonder. Based on Dick J. Reavis's investigative book, *The Ashes of Waco*, you'll find a straightforward examination of the incident from both sides. Included are excerpts from the book, sound files from 911 and negotiation tapes, selected transcripts from the Congressional hearings, and a photo gallery. There's also a brief FAQ, and while you won't get all the answers, you will get the beginnings of a nonsensationalized overview of the situation. —(L.S.)

KEY NEWSGROUP alt.conspiracy URL▶ http://rampages.onramp.net/~djreavis/

Grassroots Tax Rebellion

Americans for Tax Reform Jump 2528

If you think your taxes are too high and want to do something about it, stop by this page. The Americans for Tax Reform is a conservative grassroots organization that opposes any further tax increases or reductions in existing deductions or exemptions. Their Taxpayer Protection Pledge was the precursor of the Republican Contract with America, and this group also led the fight against the proposed value-added tax. This site will tell you more about their programs and objectives, keep you posted on other tax topics, such as corporate welfare and the flat tax proposal, and alert you when individual action is needed to fight any other tax-raising proposal. —(L.S.)

KEY NEWSGROUP misc.taxes URL▶ http://www.sbsc.org/atr/1.html

Conservative Politics

Conservative Heavy Hitters

The Heritage Foundation Jump 7496

The Heritage Foundation embraces a number of issues and topics from a conservative point of view. The right to bear arms, balanced budget, the importance of religion in the life of the United States, trade and affirmative action issues. It is a content-rich site—you can read present and past issues of the Foundation's Policy Review which is "dedicated to rebuilding the institutions of American citizenship—families, neighborhoods, religious institutions, public and private schools, voluntary civic institutions, businesses, and local governments." All the familiar faces from the political right contribute to the journal. The Foundation also provides links to other Web sites of interest to conservatives, with issue-oriented essays from the president of the Foundation, calendar of events, electronic forums to discuss the issues of the day, and a well-stocked library of publications and other written resources.—(E.v.B.)

KEY NEWSGROUP **alt.society.conservatism**
URL ▶ http://www.heritage.org/

▲*The Jefferson Memorial at Cherry Blossom time, from* **JumpCity.**

Conservative Fun and Games

The Right Side of the Web
Jump 2188 CONTENT

Developed by Jeff Donels, this site includes the obligatory Newt Gingrich and Rush Limbaugh fan club pages, an online copy of the Republican Contract with America, pictures of the Gipper, an audio library, and other conservative fun and games. You can also read up on the latest issues of concern to the Right, post a comment to the Message Wall, and link to other conservative resources on the Web. This is a definite bookmark for conservatives, but it would do liberals well to visit, too, if for no other reason than to try to understand what the other side really thinks. —(L.S.)

KEY NEWSGROUP **alt.politics.usa.republican** URL ▶ http://www.clark.net/pub/jeffd/index.html

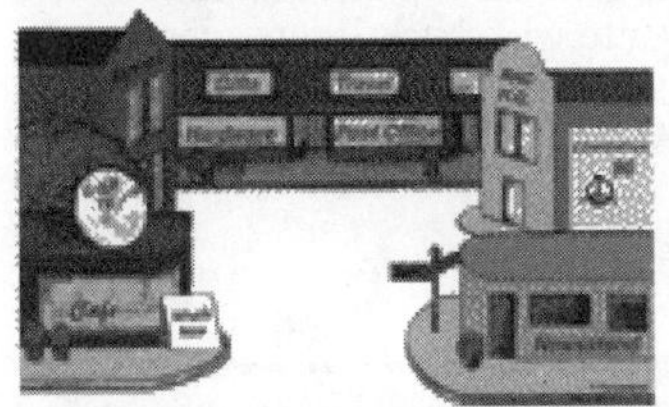

Republicans Having Fun?

GOP Main Street! Jump 2720 CONTENT

They took their sweet time about it, but the Republican National Committee finally has a Web site. The wait was worth it, though, as it's not just your typical political site. The GOP has created a virtual village, with a good-times attitude that makes it fun and useful to browse, even if you're a liberal. There's the School, which not only tells you about Republican policy positions, but provides a primer on running for office. There's the Newsstand, with online magazines and opinion columns. There's the Cafe, with chat rooms, and also GOP TV with video and sound clips from Republican-sponsored television shows. And, in the spirit of capitalism, there's the Gift Shop, filled with Republican trinkets you can buy and display to show your allegiance. —(L.S.)

KEY NEWSGROUP **alt.politics.usa.republican** URL ▶ http://www.rnc.org/

For Die-Hard Conservatives Only

The Conservative Link Jump 2597

LINKS

If you're a liberal, you'll likely hate these pages, but if you're a conservative, this is an excellent resource for finding what's available, not just on the Web, but across the Internet. The only thing Jeff Williams leaves out is links to newsgroups, but there are links to Web pages, to Gopher and FTP sites, and to e-mail lists. There also are sections on Liberal Lies, a mildly vitriolic list of links to leftist Web pages, and a small selection of links to conservative entertainers and celebrities. —(L.S.)

KEY NEWSGROUP **alt.politics** URL ▶ http://www.moscow.com/~bmdesign/tcl/conintro.html.

Jeffersonian Conservatism Online

One If By Congress, Two If By White House
Jump 7296 CONTENT

J.R. Wilson doesn't believe in big government or political parties. To further his cause—a belief in Jeffersonian Conservatism—he has set up these pages to advertise his book *One If By Congress, Two If By White House*, which examines a wide spectrum of current

societal problems that he feels are largely government-created. Wilson also provides links to what he (maybe only half jokingly) terms "enemy" pages and links to other conservative and government sites. —(E.v.B.)

KEY NEWSGROUP **alt.society.conservatism** URL▶ http://www.geopages.com/CapitolHill/1783/

All about Conservative Politics

Town Hall Jump **3692**

Town Hall is the first place on the Web where individuals and organizations can come together under what's touted as a "broad umbrella of conservative thoughts, ideas, and actions." This is where you'll find the who's who of the conservative movement, including the Heritage Foundation, Empower America, *National Review*, American Conservative Union, Family Research Council, Americans for Tax Reform, and many more. An active forum (requires preregistration to participate—may be a bit disconcerting and Big-Brother-ish for some of you) and bookstore with titles such as *Benchmarks: Conservative Principles for Rejecting Clinton Judges*, *Why Raising the Minimum Wage is a Bad Idea*, and *Thy Neighbor's Rap Sheet*. —(C.P.)

KEY NEWSGROUP **alt.society.conservatism** URL▶ http://www.townhall.com/

Conservative Politics for Generation X

CGX Jump **2447**

Liberal wags like to say that there's no such thing as a Young Republican. The implication is that Republicans are born old, and—aside from not being very funny—it's not very true. Likewise untrue is the perception that Generation X is comprised only of slackers who don't work, don't care for much besides their own angst, and, generally, don't have a clue. If you still have doubts, check out this page, based on a conservative newsletter written by two Generation Xers, Ehren Filippello and Paul Colligan. Aside from selected articles from the newsletter and an FTP site with back issues, young conservatives will find information about politics and general matters that affect their lives, links to conservative resources, and a good job bank. No matter what you think of the politics, these young people deserve a lot of credit for a well-thought-out and well-written page, an excellent resource for conservatives of all ages. —(L.S.)

KEY NEWSGROUP **alt.politics** URL▶ http://www.teleport.com/~pcllgn/cgx.html

For Newt Fans Only

The Newt Gingrich WWW Fan Club Jump **2540**

Here you'll find good things said about Speaker Newt Gingrich, from excerpts of his speeches, to the Contract with America and everything in between, courtesy of The Right Side of the Web. Catch up on his latest remarks to the press, check in with the Progress and Freedom Foundation, the sponsor of his cable TV show, and read the praise from other conservatives who've waited decades to have one of their own again in charge of the House of Representatives. You can even link to Gingrich's own page on the House of Representatives server to find out what legislation he's sponsoring. —(L.S.)

KEY NEWSGROUP **alt.fan.newt-gingrich** URL▶ http://www.clark.net/pub/jeffd/mr_newt.html

A Web Home for the Reagan Presidency

The Reagan Home Page Jump **4076**

This page, maintained by Brett Kottmann, is dedicated to resources and information on Ronald Reagan's presidency and political career. Resources here include information on the standard of living, tax cuts, social spending, income, deficit, debt, and other aspects of sociopolitical importance during Reagan's eight-year presidential term. You can also access the "Great Communicator" area to view speeches previously given by Reagan. Very informational, and a veritable shrine for Republicans and "Reagan Democrats" alike. —(R.B.)

KEY NEWSGROUP **alt.fan.ronald-reagan** URL▶ http://www.erinet.com/bkottman/reagan.html

Rush Limbaugh's "Undeniable Truths"

Undeniable Truth Generator Jump 5509

A bit of inspiration for Rush Limbaugh fans. Each time you access this site, it randomly displays one of Rush's 35 "Undeniable Truths." For more inspiration, click your browser's Reload button for another "Undeniable Truth." —(F.R.)

KEY NEWSGROUP **alt.rush-limbaugh** URL▸ http://www.acs.ncsu.edu/~nsyslaw/scripts/truths-nsyslaw

Rush Limbaugh on the Web

Rush Limbaugh Jump 2550

Fans of talk radio personality Rush Limbaugh will find all they could ever want here. In addition to the Limbaugh FAQ and station list, there are online versions of Rush's 35 Undeniable Truths and the 14 Commandments of the Religious Left, John Switzer's daily summaries of shows, and an extensive archive of sound bites from the radio shows. There even are links to send a FAX to Rush or, better yet—send e-mail to his CompuServe account. —(L.S.)

KEY NEWSGROUP **alt.fan.rush-limbaugh** URL▸ http://204.96.15.10/nat/pol/rush/

All about the Christian Coalition

Christian Coalition Home Page Jump 3645

This interesting site offers a Congressional scorecard, press releases, the ability to contact your congressional representatives and senator, a "Religious Rights Watch," info on education and seminars, and much more. A very well-done site—worth taking a look at, whether or not you subscribe to the politics. —(C.P.)

KEY NEWSGROUP **soc.religion.christian** URL▸ http://cc.org/

No Laughing Matter

How Can You Laugh at a Time Like This? Jump 7115

Bruce Madison, a self-styled middle-aged man who calls himself a Libertarian, publishes weekly columns on the Internet. He blasts conservatives and liberals alike. Madison enjoys puncturing the posturing, rhetorical balloons that are all too often sent aloft by politicians and other opinion makers. He also sends out warnings to us about abuse of power. A few of his recent titles: "Bruce Looks at the 'F' word," "Law and Disorder," "Gun Madness." He could become an addiction. —(E.v.B.)

KEY NEWSGROUP **talk.politics.misc** URL▸ http://www.skypoint.com/members/magic/bruce/howcanyou.html

Libertarian Access Point

World Wide Libertarian Pages Jump 2500

This is an excellent resource for anyone wanting a starting point for learning about Libertarian concepts and principles, as well as the best bookmark for Libertarians themselves. Mike Linskvayer's page is straight-to-the-point, very well organized, and covers every aspect of Libertarian thought and action. It begins with constantly updated news and information about and of interest to the movement, then flows into a smartly organized listing of Libertarian businesses, organizations, and people. The page ends with resources organized by newsgroups and mailing lists, important issues, and general links. News summaries, suggested links, and comments from page users are welcomed, and there's an online form to use for submissions of your own Web links. —(L.S.)

KEY NEWSGROUP **talk.politics.libertarian** URL▸ http://www.best.com/~au/wwlp/indexT.html

Libertarian Think Tank: Cato Institute Web Site

The Cato Institute

Jump 2501

The Cato Institute is the premier think tank addressing public policy issues from a Libertarian perspective. Unlike many such organizations, the Cato Institute does not isolate itself in an ivory tower to protect elitist thinking. It has an active program to involve the lay public in the discussion and formation of policy, evidenced by this Web site. You'll find information about the institute, its general activities and research programs, and online copies of the bimonthly *Cato Policy Reports*. *Policy Reports* is a journal of opinion and news of Cato Institute activities, congressional testimony, research, as well as other news and events that affect the shaping of public policy and is an excellent resource for keeping track of growing government and what's being done to control it.—(LS)

KEY NEWSGROUP **talk.politics.libertarian** URL▶ http://www.cato.org/main/

America's Third-Largest Party

Libertarian Party Jump **2502**

If you share the Democrats' ideal of equal rights and civil liberties for all, embrace the Republicans' affection for free markets and limiting government, but don't think either party really understands what these things are all about, the Libertarian Party may offer a viable alternative. This is Libertarian headquarters on the Net, and you'll be able to learn more about its philosophy, positions, and activities. If you want to get involved, there's membership information and an e-mail directory of local, state, and national party officials. Or if you just want to know what they think, there are online versions of the Party's campaign platforms and brochures that explain Libertarian views on important public policy issues. —(L.S.)

KEY NEWSGROUP **talk.politics.libertarian** URL▶ http://www.lp.org/lp/lp.html

Firearms & the Second Amendment

The Right to Keep and Bear Arms Jump **2531**

This page, maintained by David Putzolu, is specifically intended for the pro-Second Amendment faction, although the information here is useful for anyone involved in the debate over individual rights and gun control. There are philosophical essays in support of the right to keep and bear arms, news about existing and pending legislation aimed at controlling gun ownership, and articles on the meaning of the Second Amendment. This is not a comprehensive site, but it's one of the best overall for understanding this side of the issue and keeping up with current events, and there are links to other sites for those interested in further study of the issues involved. —(L.S.)

KEY NEWSGROUP **talk.politics.guns** URL▶ http://sal.cs.uiuc.edu/rec.guns/rkba.html

Current Controversies

Down with Big Brother!

Fight For Your Right to Electronic Privacy! Jump **7509**

Wired magazine maintains this index of articles and resources devoted to electronic privacy issues, including wiretapping, cryptography and the Communications Decency Act. Highlights include columns by the perpetually enraged and always insightful Brock Meeks, and links to organizations such as the Electronic Frontier Foundation and Computer Professionals for Social Responsibility. —(C.W.)

KEY NEWSGROUP **alt.privacy** URL▶ http://www.hotwired.com/clipper/index.html

Smoking and Nonsmoking Debates

Smoking from All Sides Jump **2697**

This is an attempt to assemble all the smoking-related links on the Web, whether they are pro- or anti smoking. Unfortunately, the anti smoking forces are either better organized or just more numerous, because this site, for all its efforts otherwise, looks more anti- than balanced. Still, it's one of the few places you'll be able to link to both sides of the issue, and one of the more comprehensive set of links you'll find, regardless of which position you take. —(L.S.)

KEY NEWSGROUP **clari.news.smoking** URL▶ http://www.cs.brown.edu/people/lsh/smoking.html

George Orwell Was Right

Newspeak and Doublethink Jump **2702**

Newspeak and Doublethink are terms coined by George Orwell in his novel *1984* to describe how he envisaged words being used to control and manipulate. This site takes off from that starting point to discuss how Newspeak and Doublethink have pervaded our lives and affect our thinking and attitudes today. It's something of a rant and highly political, but it's hard to determine what the political agenda is, beyond the obvious antigovernment/protection of the privacy/individualism theme. In other words, it's a site that challenges your thinking. —(L.S.)

KEY NEWSGROUP **alt.usage.english** URL▶ http://www.aloha.net/~frizbee/index.html

---

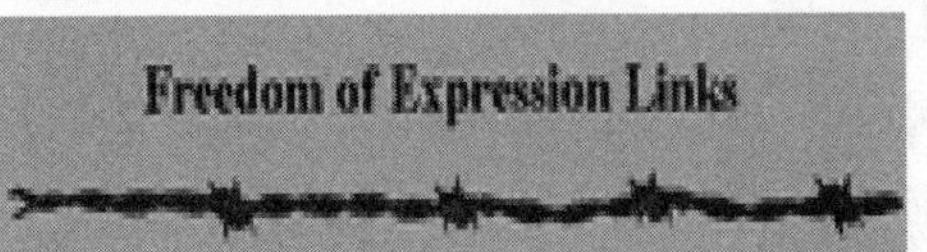

Internet Free Speech Links List

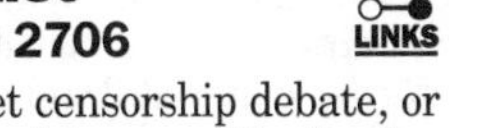

Freedom of Expression Links Jump **2706** LINKS

Before you jump headlong into the Internet censorship debate, or any censorship debate, browse the links on this page. It's clearly anti censorship, but you'll be able to see exactly why some people are so adamant about protecting free speech for everyone and everything, not just certain groups, ideas, or media forms. Compiled by Sandra Bernstein, the links are organized by general resources, documents, organizations, and newsgroups. It's far-ranging, covering everything from banned books to the human rights implications of censorship, and should be required browsing for anyone on either side of the censorship/free speech debate. —(L.S.)

KEY NEWSGROUP **alt.censorship** URL▶ http://insight.mcmaster.ca/org/efc/pages/chronicle/censor.html#Documents

---

Politics Gets Hip

Welcome to George Jump **2686** CONTENT

John Kennedy Jr.'s all grown up, and he's got himself a magazine. This Web site debuted at the same time as the print premiere of Kennedy Jr.'s *George* magazine, and it has potential. The main problem is too many too-large graphics. But your patience will be rewarded with regular departments, such as the Weekly Poll, the Political Trivia Quiz, plus some interesting articles, such as Madonna's "If I Were President." It may offend diehard politicos, but it's fun, and about time there was a lighter look at politics, at least one without any biting satire or sour cynicism. —(L.S.)

KEY NEWSGROUP **alt.politics.usa** URL▶ http://www.georgemag.com/

Internet Self-Regulation

Content Selection: PICS Jump **2707** CONTENT

PICS, the Platform for Internet Content Selection, is a section of the World Wide Web Consortium comprised of content providers, access providers, software vendors, and others involved in developing technologies that will enable users to control the kinds of material they and their children can access on the Internet. This site outlines the various methods under discussion, provides scenarios for their implementation, and includes pointers on how you can keep up-to-date on PICS and its activities to develop voluntary controls and put the decisions about what people can and cannot access in their hands, not the government's. —(L.S.)

KEY NEWSGROUP **alt.censorship** URL▶ http://www.w3.org/pub/WWW/PICS/principles.html

---

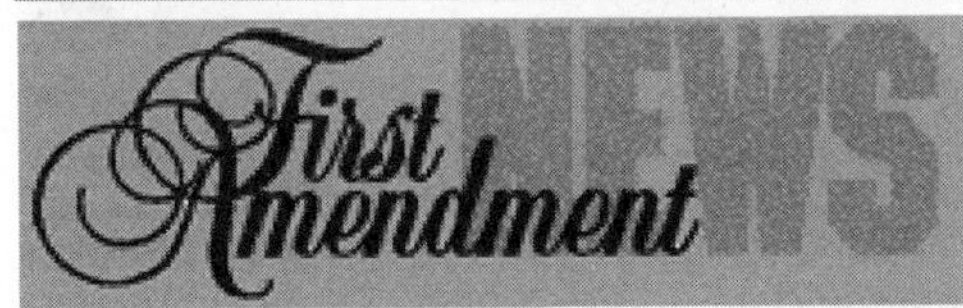

Freedom Newswatch

First Amendment News Jump **2737** CONTENT

First Amendment News, from the First Amendment Center at Vanderbilt University, is an online publication that acts as a clearinghouse of news, comment and events information related to the freedoms of speech, press, religion, assembly, and petition guaranteed by the First Amendment of the U.S. Constitution. Published monthly, it covers Supreme Court decisions, legislation, and other areas as diverse as school prayer and selling T-shirts on public lands. —(L.S.)

KEY NEWSGROUP **alt.society.civil-liberties** URL▶ http://www.fac.org/fanews/fanhome.htm

---

No More Censorship

Banned Books On-line Jump **1500** CONTENT

Feeling compelled to read a censored book or two? Find them historically described at this site, based at Carnegie-Mellon University. Exhibits here cover a wide variety of books that schools, libraries, and universities have banned over the years. As you read these book descriptions, you'll wonder why. Take "Grimm's Fairy Tales," for example.

Parents were concerned about the alcohol during the description of the heroine taking food and wine to her mother, so—zap!—many communities banned it from local schools. You can link to the actual text of these books, or download them for reading later. The site, created by Michael Witbrock, allows you to search for other banned books by author or title, and refers you to additional resources about censorship, including Internet material. Find out the latest government trends in censorship so you can decide how to cast your vote next time around. —(H.L.)

URL ▶ http://www.cs.cmu.edu/Web/People/spok/banned-books.html

▲ *Chimpanzee looking into the camera, from* **Bengt's Photo Page** *at* **Jump 3510.**

In Defense of Animals

Animal Rights Resource Site
Jump 1512 CONTENT

Ben Leamy and Donald Graft, two of the foremost experts on animal rights, have put together a comprehensive resource guide for those who want more information about animals and vegetarianism. No matter whether you're for or against meateaters, you can find out what the "movement" is all about, how to get involved, and why animal rights are important to a large segment of society. With special-interest articles ranging from "Are Pets Slaves" to "Feed Your Pet a Vegan Diet," these Web pages deal with this controversy in a fairly interesting way. In addition, the News section presents the latest environmental stories not normally found in mainstream publications. There are also a substantial amount of links to other animal- and vegetarian-related pages, along with quotes and poems about animals, which make this a worthwhile, well-rounded site. —(H.L.)

URL ▶ http://envirolink.org/arrs/index.html

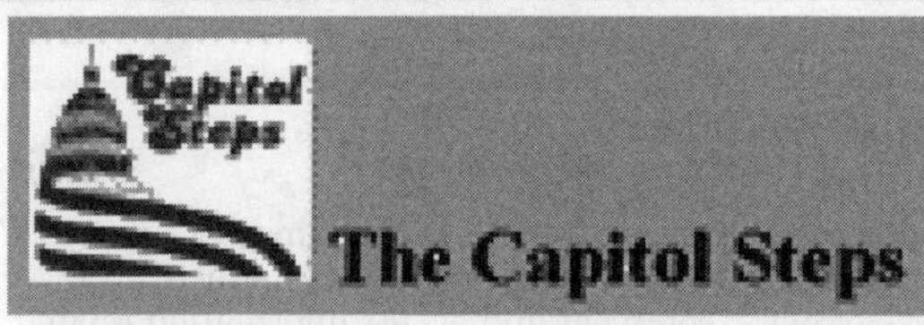

Political Satire from the Nation's Capitol

The Capitol Steps **Jump 2208** 

Billing itself as "the only group in America that attempts to be funnier than Congress," The Capitol Steps is a musical troupe that satirically kicks the seats of power. Most of the humor is based on American government, but the group occasionally moves to the international stage. Each week, a new audio clip is uploaded for your enjoyment. And since political satire works best when you have a solid knowledge of what it's poking fun at, the sound clips are accompanied by links to straight information about the subject. There's also an archive of greatest hits and some excellent caricatures for your further pleasure. —(L.S.)

KEY NEWSGROUP alt.politics URL ▶ http://pfm.het.brown.edu/people/mende/steps/index.html

Your Weekly Politics Fix

All Things Political **Jump 2596** 

If your tired of wading through the self-serving puff and postings from various wackos who think the Web is the perfect place to convert the political pagans of the world, bookmark this page for a weekly update of informative links and news on politics. You'll find a good selection of the latest additions to the political Web, as well as news on primary elections, links and analysis of speeches, and a weekly opinion poll. As good as these sections may be, the best part of the page is the search engine that lets you find political resources. It's actually four different search engines, one each for Web pages, Usenet discussion groups, *The Congressional Record*, and congressional bills introduced during the current session. —(L.S.)

KEY NEWSGROUP **talk.politics.misc** URL▶ http://dolphin.gulf.net/Political.html

Energy Department Secrets

The OpenNet Database Jump 2393

U.S. Department of Energy Secretary Hazel R. O'Leary sent shivers down the spines of secretive Washington wonks when she began a wholesale declassification of department documents, many which never should have been classified and some which have proved embarrassing or outright scandalous to the government, such as those related to radiation experimentation on humans during the Cold War years. Her commitment to openness reaches an apex with this searchable database of some 250,000 documents, and more are added all the time. Only a few of the documents are online, but there are instructions for ordering hard copies via e-mail. —(L.S.)

KEY NEWSGROUP **bit.listserv.govdoc-l** URL▶ http://www.doe.gov/html/osti/opennet/opennet1.html

John Birch Online

The New American Jump 2637

This is the online voice of the John Birch Society, so what you think of the content will depend on what you think of the John Birch Society. But if you're worried about, or entertained by, conspiracy theories, you'll be kept current with this twice-monthly Web e-zine. Keep in mind, though, that the attitude here seems to be that anything to the left of Ollie North is a threat to the world as we know it, so you've been warned. —(L.S.)

KEY NEWSGROUP **alt.conspiracy** URL▶ http://www.primenet.com/~tevans/newamericanindex.html

GOP Intramurals

Giles' GOP In-fighting Updates Jump 2627

The Republicans control both houses of Congress for the first time in decades, but all is not sweetness and light within the Grand Old Party. There's enough infighting, backstabbing and general factionalism to make a Democrat jealous. Douglas Giles prepares the articles here to keep you updated on the latest from the far-right side of the GOP, as well as to remind all of us that this faction, while vocal, does not necessarily represent the view of all Republicans. In fact, according to Giles, they are in the miniority. If nothing else, this page gives moderates, to say nothing of Democrats, some hope for the future elections. —(L.S.)

KEY NEWSGROUP **alt.politics.usa.republican** URL▶ http://www.webcom.com/~albany/infight.html

Conspiracy Central

Conspiracy, Control & ???? Jump 2535

This is rambling and sometimes confusing series of Web pages, but it's definitely worth a visit as a central point for learning about conspiracy issues and solutions. More important, since the Oklahoma City federal building bombing, it's one of the few Web sites to carry information on the militia movement. Almost every conspiracy theory is addressed: One World Government, Cold War Deception, FDA Tyranny, UFOs, and the Occult. There's also a section just for tracking the latest conspiracies. Each is a collection of articles on the given topic, and there also are links to related Web pages and newsgroups. If you feel compelled to act, there are articles about and links to groups taking stands against a particular issue, and here is where you'll find news and whatever links still exist to the militia

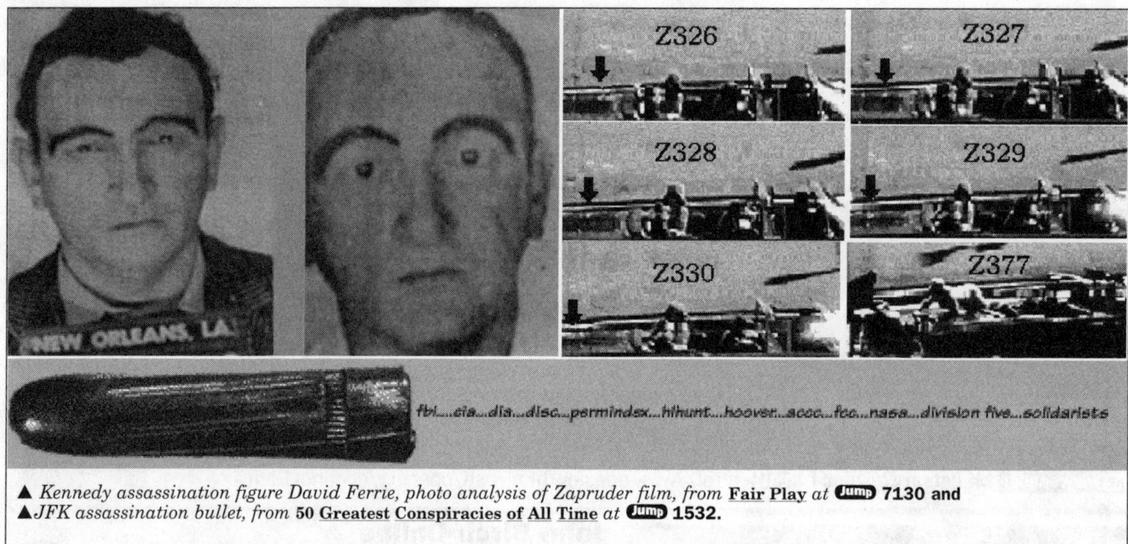

▲ *Kennedy assassination figure David Ferrie, photo analysis of Zapruder film, from* **Fair Play** *at* Jump **7130 and**
▲*JFK assassination bullet, from* **50 Greatest Conspiracies of All Time** *at* Jump **1532.**

movement. Keep in mind that what's here is not necessarily the opinion of the maintainer, known only as Sovereign, but an attempt to start you thinking about issues you might not otherwise address. —(L.S.)

KEY NEWSGROUP **alt.conspiracy** URL▶ http://www1.primenet.com/~lion/

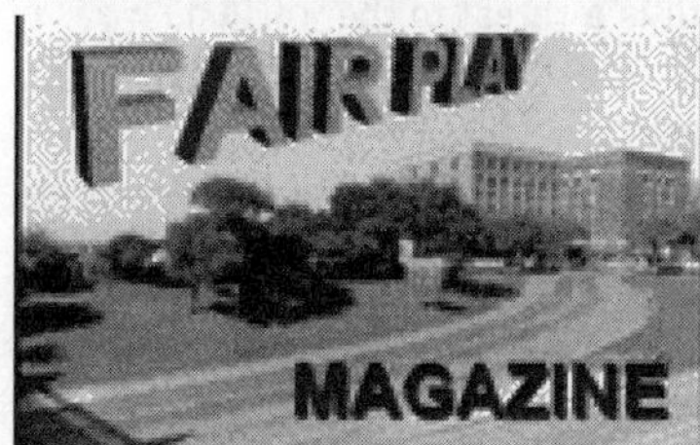

The JFK Assassination

Fair Play Jump 7130

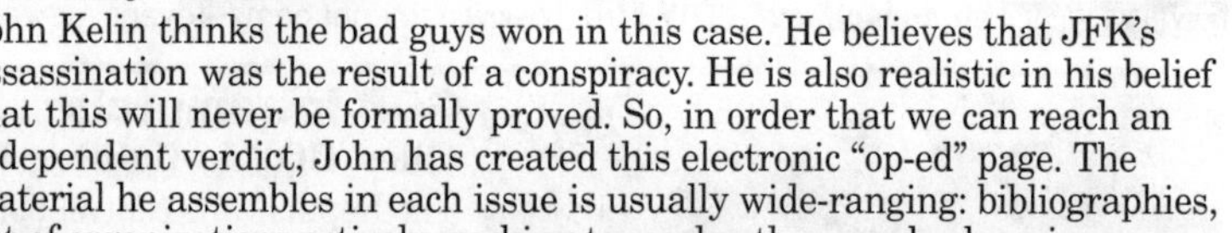

John Kelin thinks the bad guys won in this case. He believes that JFK's assassination was the result of a conspiracy. He is also realistic in his belief that this will never be formally proved. So, in order that we can reach an independent verdict, John has created this electronic "op-ed" page. The material he assembles in each issue is usually wide-ranging: bibliographies, list of organizations actively working to resolve the case, book reviews, graphics, and links to related sites. —(E.v.B.)

KEY NEWSGROUP **alt.conspiracy.jfk** URL▶ http://rmii.com/~jkelin/fp.html

British Anarchists

Freedom Press Home Page Jump 7148

CONTENT

This site is where you'll find anarchism with a British accent. Freedom Press, established in 1886, publishes the newspaper, *Freedom*, the quarterly journal, *The Raven*, and a number of other anarchist books and pamphlets. While browsing the site, you can read about the press's history and learn the true definition of anarchism (which is not quite as threatening as it is popularly perceived). While you can sample some of its wares online, you must contact the press for a complete book list. —(E.v.B.)

KEY NEWSGROUP **alt.society.anarchy** URL▶ http://web.cs.city.ac.uk/homes/louise/freehome.html

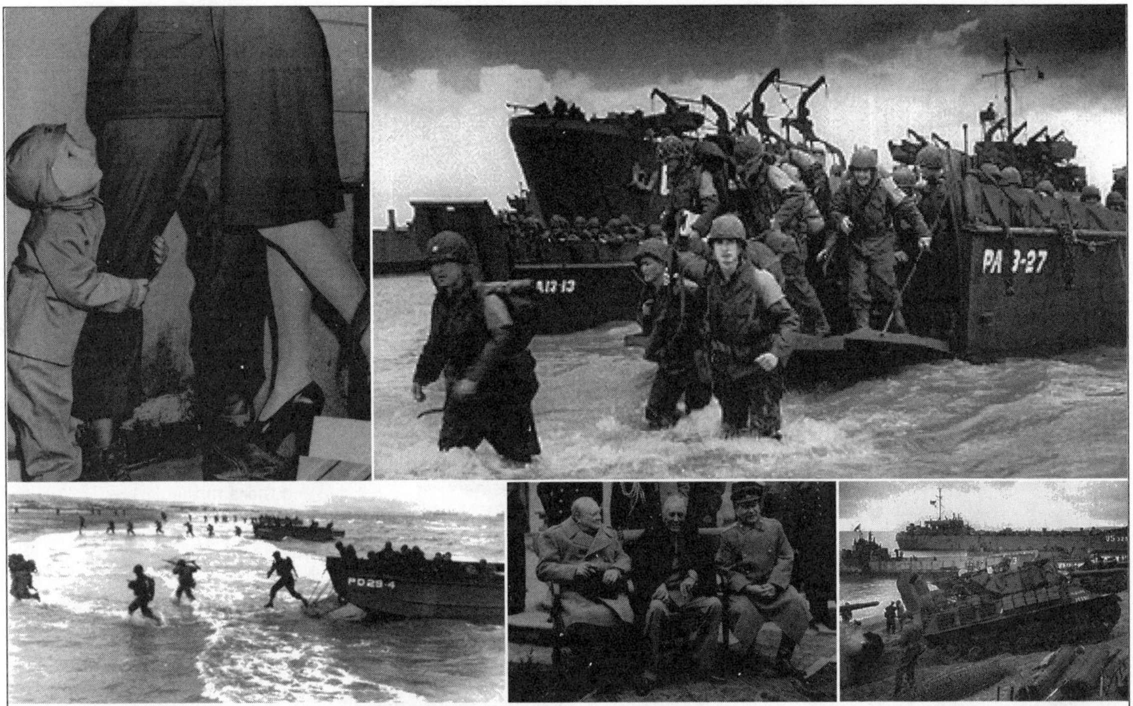

▲ *A photographic record of wartime and D-Day images from* D-Day *at* Jump **7128**.

History, Policy & War

All About Abraham Lincoln

Abraham Lincoln Online Jump **6691**

CONTENT

Flip a penny and Abraham Lincoln is in the palm of your hand. Flip over to this site and he's on your screen! Rhoda Sneller puts a great deal of time and effort into this Web resource, which features an online collection of President Lincoln's speeches, his writings, online discussions conducted by Lincoln admirers and Civil War buffs. Rhoda consistently maintains an intriguing "This Week in Lincoln History" segment. You can also find pictures of the era and the man in this site's photo gallery, as well as a splash of entertainment, with Rhoda's "Lincoln Impersonators" section. —(L.T.)

KEY NEWSGROUP **alt.war.civil.usa** URL▸ http://www.netins.net:80/showcase/creative/lincoln.html

World War II Archive Text, Photos, and Links

World War II Archive Jump **3680**

This neat site is a well-done project by the Patch American High School. Created to commemorate the 50th anniversary of VE Day, this site is full of photos, images of vintage recruiting posters, links to great Internet resources and much more. If you're interested in history, or are fascinated by those old wartime photos, stop by this site. You'll be glad you did (site is on a slow connection, so it can be difficult to reach—but worth your persistence). —(C.P.)

KEY NEWSGROUP **sci.military** URL▸ http://192.253.114.31/D-Day/GVPT_stuff/new.html

What's New? What's Cool? Handbook

(57 KB)

This is one of my dad's last drawings. Here's part of a letter from about the same time. - DR

Every night I crawl into my little sack and light up the last cigarette of the day and there in the dark with the wind whippin' around the tent flaps I think of you - of your hair and eyes and pretty face - of your lovely young body - of your warmth and sweetness. It isn't in the spirit of frustration but of fulfillment. I've known these things and knowing them and having them once, I have them forever. That wonderful look in your eyes when we'd meet after being apart for a few hours - or a few weeks - always the same - full of love. Ah, Betty Lou, you're the perfect girl for me - I love ya', Mama! - Rarey to Betty Lou, June 21, 1944.

▲ *Korean war buddies, from* Korean War Project Home Page *at* Jump 7124 *and* ▲ ▶ *photo of WWII pilot George Rarey and one of his last letters sent home to his wife Betty Lou, from* George Rarey's World War II Cartoon Journal *at* Jump 2508.

Online WWII History Lesson

D-Day

Jump 7128

The students at Patch American High School, located at the U.S. European Command Headquarters near Stuttgart, Germany, have created an outstanding Web page on the history of the World War II, concentrating on D-Day. You can see and hear the sights and sounds of that fateful day through photographs, audio files, and movie clips—all authentic. See German war footage showing Nazi troops marching into Paris, listen to speeches by Winston Churchill, and see photographs of the fateful landing on the beaches of Normandy. You can also study troop movements through the extensive collection of maps and battle plans on this site. —(E.v.B.)

KEY NEWSGROUP soc.history.war.misc

URL ▶ http://192.253.114.31/D-Day/Table_of_contents.html

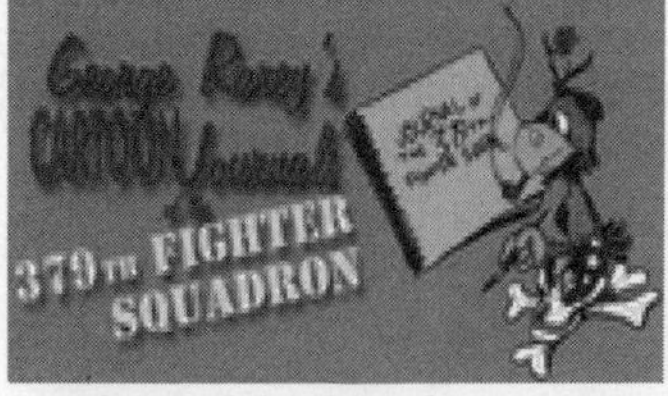

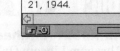

A Flying Artist's Eye View of WWII

George Rarey's World War II Cartoon Journal

Jump 2508

George Rarey was a commercial artist drafted into the Army Air Corps in 1942 and served in the 379th Fighter Squadron until a few days after D-Day, when he was killed in combat over France. He kept a daily journal of the life of a combat flyer, which his son, Damon, shares with us on this Web page. It's more than cartoons, though—there's text with each cartoon, contributed by surviving members of the Squadron or excerpted from Rarey's letters to his wife, Betty Lou. This page is one of those rare opportunities to get not only the facts about history, but a real feel for what it was like to be there. —(L.S.)

KEY NEWSGROUP alt.war URL ▶ http://www.nbn.com/home/rareybird/index.html

Remembering the Korean War

Korean War Project Home Page Jump 7124

Hal Barker, a photojournalist, writer, and designer, has created a well-written, graphically interesting, and comprehensive overview of the Korean War. The son of a Korean war veteran himself, Hal has scanned in photographs he took on a recent visit to Korea, historic photographs, maps of the country, and pictures of the soon-to-be-dedicated Korean War Veterans Memorial in Washington, D.C. He also gives an interesting account of this conflict and provides casualty lists, a directory of Korean War Veterans groups, and numerous links to Korean-related resources. He has created this page to say: "We have not forgotten." —(E.v.B.)

KEY NEWSGROUP **soc.history.war.misc** URL▶ http://www.onramp.net:80/~hbarker/

American History to World War I

The American Revolution and the Struggle for Independence Jump **2615** 

The title of this page is as above, the page heading says "From Revolution to Reconstruction," and the subhead says this hypertext project covers subjects up to World War I. Despite this confusion, this is an excellent resource for American history, and we're willing to give these people all the slack they want in their titles, given the amount of work it's taken to put this together. A collaborative project by many contributors, the basic text is taken from *An Outline of American History*, but there are many additional hyperlinks to HTML-formatted articles and documents to support the main text. Take it chapter by chapter, or browse and jump to areas that intrigue you. However you do it, it's a history course worth taking. —(L.S.)

KEY NEWSGROUP **soc.history** URL▶ http://grid.let.rug.nl/~welling/usa/revolution.html

Lest We Forget: World War II Dateline

50 Years Ago Jump **7111** 

John Davis has assembled an amazing amount of information on the events of the Second World War. His monthly columns, "50 Years Ago," which he distributes over the Internet, are archived here. Divided by month, these columns contain a day-by-day account of the major events of the war from April 1944 to June 1945. Davis has also compiled an extensive list of special collections, accounts, and recollections of the war, as well as other historical WWII resources available on the Internet. —(E.v.B.)

KEY NEWSGROUP **soc.history.world.war.ii** URL▶ http://www.webcom.com/~jbd/ww2.html

Holocaust Memories

Cybrary of the Holocaust Jump **1586** 

George Santayana said of the past that those who do not remember it are doomed to repeat it. Cybrary of the Holocaust is dedicated to guaranteeing that the slaughter of 9 million Jews, Catholics, Poles, Gypsies, homosexuals, disabled, and other "undesirables" is never forgotten. The site includes both its own learning materials and links to museums, information sources, and online education resources. This site's creator, Michael Declan Dunn, has created a compelling place that's hard to leave. —(H.L.)

URL▶ http://www.writething.com/cybrary

Vietnam: One Man's Story

Vietnam Memoirs Jump **7283** 

Richard Shand has dedicated this site to the men who served with him in his units, the "Dusters" and "Quad 50s," particularly the 5th Battalion 2nd Artillery. Except for the letters home he reproduces and the story "The Treasure," most of the accounts Richard presents are his first impressions on seeing Viet Cong dead, experiencing Saigon, or touring near the Cambodian border. Most were written in 1976. Richard also provides photographs from his tour of duty, plus links to other Vietnam-related pages on the Web. A sobering site. —(E.v.B.)

KEY NEWSGROUP **alt.war.vietnam** URL▶ http://marlowe.wimsey.com/rshand/reflections/vietnam/vietnam.html

A Veteran's Personal Vietnam War History

Images of My War Jump **7116** 

Ulf Heller has written some glimpses of the time he served in the army during the Vietnam War. He takes us from his jungle warfare training in Panama to his arrival in Vietnam, then through his tour of duty from July 1968 to January 1970. We see army life on the front lines, in the officer's mess, and on reconnaissance missions. Heller also offers his views on discipline and morale, technique and tactics, and on the foreign culture. Sobering, yet not trading on the horrific, Heller's memoirs make compelling reading.—(E.v.B.)

KEY NEWSGROUP **alt.war.vietnam**

URL ▶ http://www.ionet.net/~uheller/vnbktoc.shtml

The Gulf War

Operation Desert Storm Debriefing Book Jump **7125** CONTENT

The Gulf War has found an able chronicler in Andrew Leyden. At the time of the conflict, he began compiling information gained from his contacts on Capitol Hill and from military journals and the newspapers. Andrew gives us the background, the players, the military systems and equipment (missiles, aircraft, warships) involved—along with some interesting images. Supporting documents, such as United Nation's resolutions, executive orders, casualty lists, are also mounted. If his accounts have raised your interest, Andrew has also provided further Web links to other Desert Storm pages. —(E.v.B.)

▲ *Lincoln visiting the gravesites at Bull Run, from* **On-Line Images from the History of Medicine** *at* Jump **0186**.

KEY NEWSGROUP **soc.history.war.misc** URL ▶ http://www.nd.edu/~aleyden/contents.html

Military History through the Ages

EHAWK:mh:n_index.html Jump **7129**

Monte Turner and J.P. Hughes have designed and built an amazing forum for the study of military history from classical times, through the Napoleonic Wars, up to the Gulf War. Interested in the wars of the 19th century? Well, you can explore nautical military history—how the change in sails changed warships, for example—and read secondary sources on battles, link to online discussion groups, download bibliographies for further study, and see a collection of military graphics. The authors of this page want to provide the most comprehensive access to military history services on the Net—and they may have just done that. —(E.v.B.)

KEY NEWSGROUP **soc.history.war.misc** URL ▶ http://kuhttp.cc.ukans.edu/history/milhst/m_index.html

Civil War Photographs

The Civil War Chronicled in Photos Jump **3627**

The Library of Congress offers a large number of exhibitions to the public via the Net—one of the best is this exhibition of Civil War photographs. This collection of over 1,000 photos can be browsed or searched and contains fascinating images of military personnel, preparations for battle, and scenes from the aftermath of battle. The collection also includes portraits of both Confederate and Union officers and enlisted men. —(C.P.)

KEY NEWSGROUP **alt.war.civil.usa** URL ▶ http://rs6.loc.gov/cwphome.html

Liberal Politics

The Nation Online

The Nation Jump **5796** CONTENT

Established in 1865 by a group of abolitionists, *The Nation* remains one of the pre-eminent publications of the liberal left. You might not agree with everything you read here, but you will certainly be aware of the ideological positions taken by the writers on this site. Whether they're covering the latest political scandal, or taking a stand against an injustice here or abroad, the editors of *The Nation* have remained remarkably true to their own crusading orthodoxy. The digital edition carries on that tradition with a rich mix of articles, reviews and specials from the print version. You can also find out how to join *The Nation* electronic mailing list, and the archive is now searchable. This is still a fairly new addition to the world of online magazines, but it continues to grow with each issue. —(J.P.)

URL ▶ http://www.thenation.com

Progressives on the Web

The Left Side of the Web Jump **2538**

Although this page begins with a link to The Right Side of the Web (in the interest of fairness and balance), there's no denying that this is a page for liberals and those even further left. The links will take you to most every progressive/leftist organization on the Web, with an emphasis on those that serve to combat or otherwise inform you about "creeping fascism" in the United States. The page also provides links to current events considered important or threatening to progressive ideals, and topics include the perceived threat of militia movements in the U.S. Unfortunately, the links here don't represent a very good balance, although this is one of the only places on the Web you can link to FTP sites with pro-militia material. —(L.S.)

KEY NEWSGROUP **misc.activism.progressive** URL ▶ http://paul.spu.edu/~sinnfein/progressive.html

Cyberfeminism

Women Leaders Online Jump **1548**

The Women Leaders Online's agenda is to mobilize women to lobby against the GOP's Contract with America through the Internet. To show how powerful this medium is, within the first two weeks on the Web, they received over 1,000 responses of support, ranging from high-caliber professional women to students. This site is full of information about health, education, welfare reform, crime prevention, and constitutional rights. Taking into account the point of view of the sponsors of this site, the pages here dissect the radical right and conservative family values, and help women leaders organize grassroots political forces to challenge our political leaders and "antifeminism." You'll also be informed, through the Political Women's Hotline, about the latest political updates. It's a straightforward, straight-shooting site that gives you a chance to make a difference. —(H.L.)

KEY NEWSGROUP **alt.feminism** URL ▶ http://worcester.lm.com/women/women.html

Tracking the Democratic Agenda

Democratic National Committee Jump **2769**

The DNC makes it easy for party members and others to track important issues, as well as get involved in politics, through their home on the Web. If there's something happening in Congress or elsewhere in government that you should be aware of, you'll know about it as soon as the page loads, with the alert link that outlines the issue, talks about what you can do, and offers additional links to Web resources for more information. You'll also find the usual information about local, regional and national Democratic organizations and how to get involved, quick links to see what's new at the site, and a list of general resources of interest to political activists. —(L.S.)

KEY NEWSGROUP **alt.politics.democrats** URL ▶ http://www.democrats.org/

Grassroots Activity for Progressives

Macrocosm USA Home Page Jump **3728**

Macrocosm USA is a nonprofit clearinghouse for progressives. As grassroots activists, they show their concerns for the urgent social, political, and environmental issues of our time, and strive to present holistic approaches and solutions to these problems. Their mission is to compile and edit materials into handbooks, databases, a databank, and a newsletter. The organization maintains a database of over 6,000 organizations, periodicals, publishers and businesses, media contacts, and other resource guides. Sandi Brockway, the organization's editor and founder, feels the work of Macrocosm has a substantial impact on our society, as activism can be powerful. She cites several examples to clearly illustrate this impact. If you share these views, stop by this site to learn how and where to get involved. —(N.F.)

KEY NEWSGROUP **misc.activism.progressive** URL ▶ http://www.macronet.org/macronet/

Carrying the Banner of Socialism in America

DSA Intro Jump 2388

CONTENT

Socialists are not necessarily Communists. Nor are all Socialists wild-eyed Trotskyites. And they definitely aren't Anarchists. Confused? Drop by the DSA pages and you'll learn that, as far as these people are concerned, DSA's goal is to extend economic power to every citizen and to champion gender and social equality. There are other strains of socialist thought, and you'll find links to these, other leftist ideologies, and general politics, too. —(L.S.)

KEY NEWSGROUP **alt.politics.radical-left**

URL ▸ http://ccme-mac4.bsd.uchicago.edu/DSA.html

THE WHITE HOUSE
"I can count the changes I've made on one hand; I got elected."

▲*Clinton speechifying, via* **The Capitol Steps** *at* Jump **2208.**

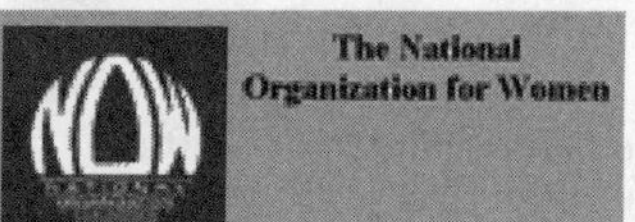

NOW

The National Organization for Women Home Page Jump 2163

CONTENT

While NOW is essentially a lobbying and support organization for women, this site is not merely a rallying point. Nor is it exclusively for women. In fact, a visit here by people unfamiliar with NOW and its activities can do much to break down the negative stereotype of activist women. There are clear, concise, and rational reviews of the important issues affecting women, with histories and background on the current state of affairs. Along with general information on NOW structure and activities, you'll find statements of NOW positions on these issues, recent editions of the organization's monthly newsletter, and links to other sites addressing women's issues. —(L.S.)

KEY NEWSGROUP **soc.women** URL ▸ http://now.org/now/home.html

Bad Subjects
Political Education for Everyday Life

Rethinking Leftist Politics

Bad Subjects Jump 2357

This online journal, and its associated e-mail discussion list, challenge not only capitalism as the basis for a political system, but also traditional leftist thought. It discusses issues such as multiculturalism and examines whether they are workable or merely banners that do more to separate people than bring them together. The primary focus is the application of political theory to everyday life, something many radicals (on the right as well as the left) tend to ignore when espousing their philosophies. Whether you agree or disagree, it's thought provoking, and if you want to contribute an article to this site, editorial guidelines and submission guidelines are online. —(L.S.)

KEY NEWSGROUP **alt.politics.radical-left** URL ▸ http://english-server.hss.cmu.edu/BS/BadSubjects.html

Left of Center: Liberal Politics

Liberal Information Page Jump 2369

CONTENT

Those who consider the Internet a bastion of liberal/radical kooks and rabble-rousers may be surprised to learn that while there are many resources for people of a liberal bent, there are very few sites that link them together. Or maybe not; except for the radical left, liberals rarely have been known as good organizers. Mike Silverman seeks to change this, and he's done a very good job. This site combines links to liberal resources with links to the right wing, not so much for balance as to keep liberals abreast of the nature and extent of conservative attacks on their ideals. Mike also takes some shots at the right, especially the radical right, but if you've seen any of the conservative pages on the Web, you know he's just returning their fire. —(L.S.)

KEY NEWSGROUP **alt.politics** URL ▸ http://falcon.cc.ukans.edu/~cubsfan/liberal.html

The Other Side of Newt

NewtWatch Jump 2542

This page is the balancer to the Newt Gingrich WWW Fan Club site. Billing itself as the first virtual political action committee, the page is dedicated to offering everything about Speaker Gingrich's past and current political record in support of those who think he's the worst thing to happen to Congress since the British attack on Washington during the War of 1812. Actually, it's not so rabid, but it certainly leaves few stones unturned, be it Gingrich's voting record, his contributors, the ethics complaints filed against him, or his personal finances. While NewtWatch is serious, there's a lot of humor on this page, especially the fill-out form that lets you send a "semi-personal" letter to the Speaker. —(L.S.)

KEY NEWSGROUP **alt.politics.usa.newt-gingrich** URL▶ http://www.cais.com:80/newtwatch/

Slowing the Rush

Anti-Rush Headquarters Jump 2551

It seems people either love Rush Limbaugh or hate him. There's not much middle ground, and Mike Silverman doesn't try to find any. With this page, he attempts to point out lapses in Rush's logic, with refutations of Limbaugh's 35 Unquestionable Truths and sections covering both sides of the Limbaugh vs. Fairness and Accuracy in Media contretemps. You'll also find pointers to other anti-Rush information, on and off the Net, and a way to comment on the pages, either pro or con. —(L.S.)

KEY NEWSGROUP **alt.rush-limbaugh** URL▶ http://falcon.cc.ukans.edu/~cubsfan/antirush.html

The Word According to Chomsky

The Noam Chomsky Archive Jump 7119

Jimmer Enders has compiled a comprehensive collection of the articles, interviews, lectures, reviews by and about Noam Chomsky. Chomsky is a philosophy and linguistic professor at MIT whom Enders also characterizes as "one of the most prominent dissidents writing in the United States today, a severe, impassioned and consistent critic of U.S. foreign policy." Enders also collects more than primary-source material—a number of related sites are also mounted. —(E.v.B.)

KEY NEWSGROUP **alt.fan.noam-chomsky** URL▶ http://www.contrib.andrew.cmu.edu:/usr/tp0x/chomsky.html

The Shadow Knows

Shadow Jump 7151

Shadow Press publishes a number of underground online and printed publications ranging from comic books (Squatter Comics, Killer Kop Komix) to underground self-help manuals (*The Complete Manual of Pirate Radio*, *Survival Without Rent*). However, these publications are only described here. To obtain the full text, you must mail a check. Shadow Press does support an online newsletter, MediaFilter, that covers a number of stories from a countercultural angle you're not likely to read in your morning newspaper. —(E.v.B.)

KEY NEWSGROUP **alt.zines** URL▶ http://MediaFilter.org/MFF/Shadow.html

Rainforest Altert!

Welcome to the Rainforest Action Network Home Page Jump 7182

The Rainforest Action Network, founded in 1985, works to protect tropical rainforests and the human rights of those living in and around these forests. The Network has taken itself onto the Net to coordinate its efforts further. To this end, you can surf to links of other environmental organizations—Greenpeace, Sierra Club, Student Environmental Action Coalition, and many others. As well, details of important conferences are listed, and tons of other relevant sites are provided, such as Mother Jones, EnviroWeb, Human Rights Home Page, vegetarian resources, and even music groups sympathetic to the cause. —(E.v.B.)

KEY NEWSGROUP **talk.environment** URL▶ http://www.ran.org/ran/

President Clinton

Whitewater on the Web

Whitewater Scandal Home Page Jump 0146 

Computer science student Preston Crow's compilation of relevant news, information and Web links on Clinton's albatross, the Whitewater affair. Contains Preston's own original written materials outlining and explaining Whitewater, a Whitewater timeline, current Whitewater news and links to many other Whitewater-related sites. —(E.G.)

KEY NEWSGROUP **alt.current-events.clinton.whitewater**

URL ▶ http://www.cs.dartmouth.edu/~crow/whitewater/whitewater.html

The Worst of Bill Clinton

Scandals of the Clinton Administration Jump 2552 

Preston Crow doesn't like President Clinton, and this page is designed to uncover and display every real or imagined scandal associated with him and his administration. There are sections on Whitewater, allegations of Clinton's drug use, a rather questionable Body Count list that tries to link the deaths of various of the President's friends to the man himself, and reviews of the other scandals and alleged scandals which have dogged Clinton since he was first running for the presidency. It's all interesting stuff, but you'll have to decide for yourself whether or not—and how much—to believe. —(L.S.)

KEY NEWSGROUP **alt.president.clinton**

URL ▶ http://www.cs.dartmouth.edu/~crow/whitewater/scandal.html

CLINTON,YES!

A Lone Web in the Political Wilderness

Clinton, Yes!
Jump 2624 

Just as in the real world, the virtual world is rife with well-organized vocal Republican and conservative groups, while the Democrats seem to be off in all directions with no focus. But not here. This page is unabashedly pro-Clinton, well-organized, and full of good information for Clinton supporters. You'll also find news of activities to support and alerts of activities to protest—assuming you agree with the premise of the page, of course. —(L.S.)

KEY NEWSGROUP **alt.politics.clinton** URL ▶ http://www.av.qnet.com/~yes/

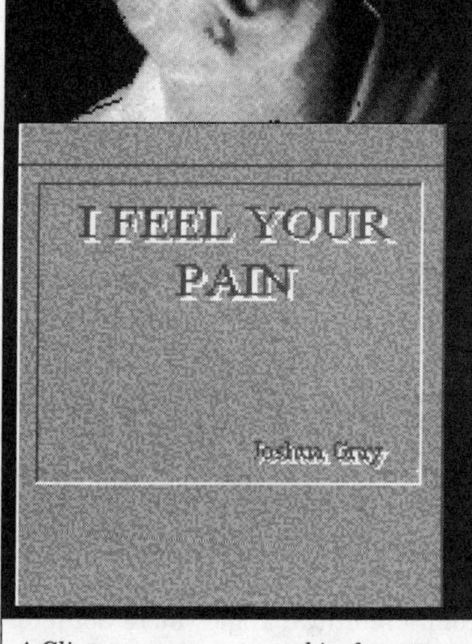

▲*Clinton monument graphic, from* **The Right Side of the Web** *at* Jump **2188.**

An Executive Tour

Welcome to the White House
Jump 5045 CONTENT

This "interactive citizen's handbook" allows you to view info on The White House, the executive branch, and the First Family. It also contains welcome messages from the President and Vice President, a guest book for you to sign, another place for you to leave comments, a "What's New at The White House," feature, and information on White House tours. —(S.B.)

URL ▶ http://www.whitehouse.gov/

Social & Support

The Web is as much a social phenomenon as a technological one. You'll find a wide range of Web sites offering information and resources to meet almost any medical, support, affinity, social, cultural, or religious subject.

Affinity, Support & Social Web Sites

New sites have sprung up all over the Web, reflecting the multi-faceted range of interests, affiliations, and shared concerns of millions of people around the world.

While there are sites for many lighthearted and socially oriented subjects, such as quirky Net "urban folklore sites," and culturally-oriented sites that supply information on countries around the world, perhaps the most useful Web sites are the ones devoted to providing information, resources, and support for those suffering from various personal health conditions—and their friends and families.

These Web sites provide comprehensive, useful information, news, advice, and referrals to medical and health resources, online support groups, excerpts from medical journals available on the Net, and other background reading material on the site's specific health or support-related topic. In many cases, these Web support sites have been created by people who are actually experiencing the medical conditions or other personal problems addressed by their Web sites—which only adds greater credibility to the information and personal advice these authors provide in their Web sites.

Unfiltered, Unedited, and Unwaveringly Opinionated Support Info

As with most of the information presented on the Web, medical and personal support information is often free of the editorial filtering you'd find in magazine articles or news stories about the same topic, since many authors of support Web sites will often provide you with their unvarnished, pull-no-punches advice and opinions on these sensitive topics. When it comes to medical support Web sites, there also seems to be a far greater and more varied amount of information

Members of support groups historically forge relationships over coffee and conversation. Now, participants in online 12-step programs like Alcoholics Anonymous or Overeaters Anonymous may never know a computer colleague's first name, just a catchy handle, much less see a face. There are hundreds of support groups sharing intimacies and swapping advice online for problems ranging from chronic fatigue syndrome to cancer, from the trials of widowhood to multiple personality disorder. Messages are zapped back and forth between anywhere from 2 to 20 people. Sometimes, the chat focuses on one topic; other times, it is like a big cocktail party in which several conversations can be heard, or read, at once.

Lisa W. Foderaro, "I'm O.K. You're O.K. We're Online,"
The New York Times

Not surprisingly, the Internet is a vast reservoir for medical and fitness information. In January, the Centers for Disease Control & Prevention announced the availability of Morbidity and Mortality Weekly Report and other CDC publications online. Written for medical professionals, MMWR reported the first AIDS cases in 1981 and the outbreaks of Legionnaires' disease and hantavirus. You can find the reports by sending e-mail to lists@list.cdc.gov or by using a World Wide Web browser such as Mosaic to connect to the CDC. Meanwhile, the National Cancer Institute is among the outfits putting together a World Wide Web server over the Internet.

Edward Baig, "The Medical Hot Line in Your PC," ***Business Week***

available than that found in conventional print or broadcast media on such topics as unconventional treatments, the role of nutrition as it affects certain health conditions, and the personal accounts of patients who have dealt with these personal medical crises.

Individually-authored support Web sites are also useful in that their authors, who may be contacted instantly by by electronic mail, are usually quite happy to provide you with additional, useful information and advice on your specific problem, based on their personal experience.

Religious & Culturally Oriented Web Sites

If you're interested in learning about other countries and cultures around the world, the global nature of the Internet has fueled the creation of many Web sites that provide fascinating information and multimedia resources, helping to promote interest in the many varied cultures around the world. There are also many sites providing in-depth religious information and pointers to large Net-based repositories of information on nearly all of the world's religions. These sites, which also include sites about philosophy, can put you at the center of a vast array of informative, thought-provoking information on all the world's religions, and expose you to a broad spectrum of new philosophical beliefs as well.

Affinity & Social Groups

CyberMom Dot Com

CyberMom Dot Com Jump 6502 CONTENT

CyberMom Dot Com is a content-rich, fully interactive Web site devoted to the skills and challenges of being a parent in the 90s. Its rich graphical layout replicates a home, complete with a kitchen, vanity, basement for the kids, a chat porch and various nooks and crannies filled with even more informative online features. The editors of this professionally-executed site have spared no effort in providing a rich array of articles on child-raising issues, health care tips for kids, recipes, time-saving advice for moms, and more. But this site's best feature are its many online forums, where real moms can exchange helpful tips and support on a seemingly endless range of subjects—and you can join in, too. —(L.T.)

URL▶ http://www.thecybermom.com/

▲ *Teatime on the Web, vintage photograph image file, from* **geekgirl** *at* Jump **1504**.

Women on the Web

FemInA Jump 2699 LINKS

This site's maintainer, A. Wilson, claims this is the first comprehensive Web directory of resources exclusively for and about women and girls. Categories range from art to writing, with entertainment, health, and politics among the ones between. You can browse at your own speed or, if you're looking for something specific, use the search engine. It may not be the first, as claimed, but it certainly is among the most comprehensive and easy to use. —(L.S.)

KEY NEWSGROUP soc.women

URL▶ http://www.femina.com/

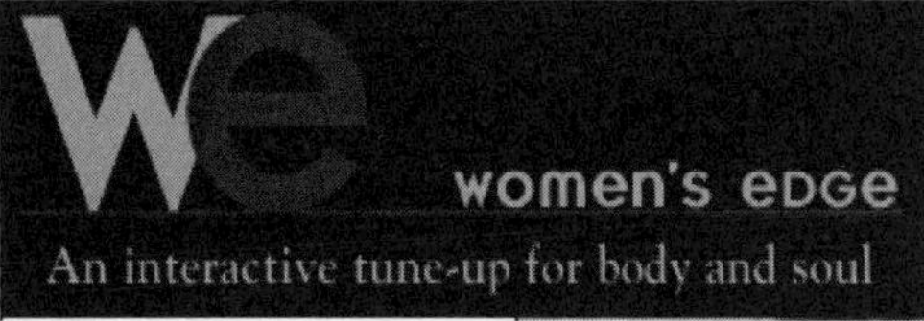

Help for Women's Body & Soul

Women's Edge Jump 5789 CONTENT

If you've ever wondered what happened to all those women's magazines that used to give you tips and columns about health and nutrition, we think maybe they've been reincarnated on the Web. We've found one, one of the best in fact, that does all of the above without the menacing guilt-inducing feminist propaganda that seems so fashionable these days. Subtitled "An Interactive Tune-up for Body and Soul," Women's Edge is a breath of fresh air. There are at least half a dozen features per issue, each with great articles on body and soul, as well as links and recipes. And the main sections link to sub-sections, like the House of Natural Healing, Nutrition Central, Weight Loss Central and, of course, Children's Central. This is just the sort of place where many women could spend an hour or two. —(J.P.)

KEY NEWSGROUP soc.women URL▶ http://www.womensedge.com/

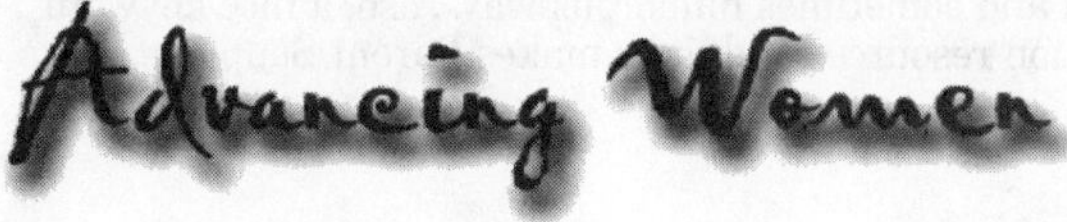

Women Joining Together

Advancing Women Jump 5835 CONTENT

Advancing Women serves as a network to help women join together to face challenges in the workplace and beyond. In this way, they hope to help women share each other's common goals and concerns. They have done this in a number of ways, most prominently in documenting the advances that some women have already made. You can read all about these notable women here, but what we liked the best were the reports featured in the International Network of Advancing Women, which documents the life and times of women around the world who have excelled in many fields. —(J.P.)

URL ▸ http://www.advancingwomen.com/

Are You a Concerned Net Citizen?

CPSR's Home Page Jump **1573**

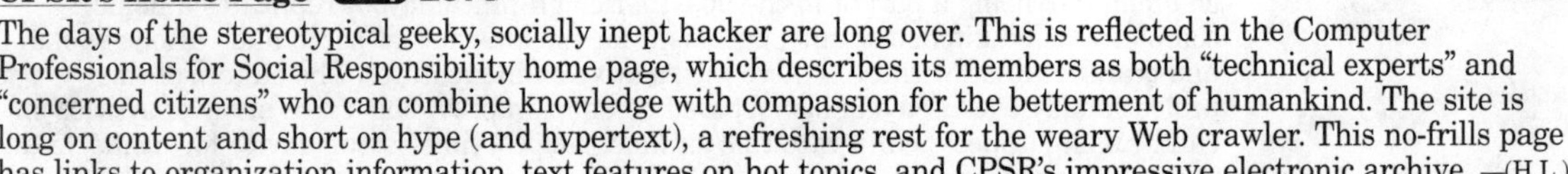

The days of the stereotypical geeky, socially inept hacker are long over. This is reflected in the Computer Professionals for Social Responsibility home page, which describes its members as both "technical experts" and "concerned citizens" who can combine knowledge with compassion for the betterment of humankind. The site is long on content and short on hype (and hypertext), a refreshing rest for the weary Web crawler. This no-frills page has links to organization information, text features on hot topics, and CPSR's impressive electronic archive. —(H.L.)

URL ▸ http://www.cpsr.org/lib/htdocs/home.html

Communicating in a New Net Culture

CMC Magazine Jump **3732**

CONTENT

Communications by computer raises many issues beyond the technical. What are the social implications of this emerging online culture? What changes must be made in the field of journalism to use this exploding new media? How will government intervention affect the way we've come to communicate? Computer-Mediated Communication (CMC) Magazine attempts to get to the heart of these issues, with compelling feature articles, news, and reviews. Visit this site for a unique perspective of the ever-changing online world of computer communications. —(N.F.)

URL ▸ http://sunsite.unc.edu/cmc/mag/current/toc.html

Links for Kids by Parents

Steve and Ruth Bennett's Family Surfboard

Jump **2708**

There are many, many Web pages dedicated to links for kids and families, but relatively few of them are compiled by parents for parents. This site is, and if it didn't merit special attention for that reason, its content and organization does nonetheless. In addition to sites with engaging content, the Bennett's list activity sites where children can entertain themselves, or be joined by their parents for online fun. There aren't a lot of links here, which is a nice change from these types of lists, especially since each one carries a rather detailed explanation, as well as the date it was added or updated by the Bennetts. —(L.S.)

KEY NEWSGROUP **misc.kids** URL ▸ http://www.sjbennett.com/users/sjb/surf.html

ParentSoup

ParentSoup

Jump **6608**

A slick, well-executed site that's also an excellent example of how the Web can be used to link people together with their shared interests, Parent Soup also contains a rich array of original editorial features on many aspects of the art, science, and guesswork of raising a child. What's especially noteworthy about Parent Soup are its extensive online forums, where parents can talk about a wide range of child-raising issues, and trade advice and answers on such topics as children's health problems, child psychology, emotional issues and more—all of which are treated here in a very down-to-earth and sometimes humorous way. Also, a nice keyword search feature to this site's many online parenting information resources and links makes Parent Soup one of the Web's best resource for parents. —(L.T.)

KEY NEWSGROUP **misc.kids** URL ▸ http://www.parentsoup.com

Customized Advice for Parents

ParentTime Jump 5792

It really is the most important job in the world. And with all the children in the world it seems remarkable that parents so often feel as though they are alone in their concerns about bringing up children, but that is often the feeling we have. If you're looking for proof that this is not the case, look no further than the wonderful ParentTime site. This is a parent site with a twist, and a great twist it is. The first time you sign on to this site you'll be asked to answer a few simple questions, having to do with your status (expectant parent, parent, step-parent, etc.) followed by your child's age. Then you'll be taken to a page that's geared to those two variables, where your thoughts and concerns will be at the forefront. A great idea, and the information on the pages is wonderful, too. You'll also want to check out the library, the bulletin board, and some fun features like "Baby Name of the Day," and "Book of the Day," and "Recipe of the Day." —(J.P.)

KEY NEWSGROUP **misc.kids** URL▶ http://pathfinder.com/ParentTime/Welcome/

News, Advice, and Support from Family Planet

Family Planet Jump 5795

If you're looking for a news source with a "family-friendly" difference, you might want to check out Family Planet. You'll find many current news stories here, all right, but with an interesting twist: StarWave, creators of this site, selects and presents news and features from the standpoint of their importance to you as a parent. You can also browse Family Planet's other features, such as advice and holiday suggestions, and join in online forums on family-related topics. There's are also game features for kids, more parenting advice and "Kids Only" feature to round out this slick and content-rich site. —(J.P.)

URL▶ http://family.starwave.com/

Jewish Parenting, with Purpose

Jewish Family & Life Jump 5830

Family life seems to be under attack from all fronts these days, and no less so in the Jewish family. This site is dedicated to helping parents impart traditional family and religious values and allowing for discussions of what constitutes such in this day. There are many articles here dealing with the subject, from the meaning of Hanukkah, to such questions as: "are Seinfeld and friends healthy for Jewish families?" Regular features include holidays, health, food, advice, media and an online message board. —(J.P.)

KEY NEWSGROUP **soc.culture.jewish** URL▶ http://www.jewishfamily.com/

Parents Helping Parents

ParenthoodWeb Jump 5657

One of the most difficult things to deal with when raising a child is that feeling of isolation. No matter how urgent the question or need, it's just so difficult to get out and find what you need with a child to care for. That's why places like ParenthoodWeb make so much sense. Now you can log on and ask a question, join this site's interactive forums and express your opinions, all without leaving the house. This site is all about "parents helping parents"— sharing advice that the experts forget to tell you, or asking a question of the many experts who can be contacted here. —(J.P.)

KEY NEWSGROUP **alt.parenting.solutions** URL▶ http://www.parenthoodweb.com/

Baby Boomer Central

Bill's Baby Boomer Pages Jump 6611

Take note Boomers—now there's a home on the Web just for you, full of nostalgia and resources for all those born between 1946 and 1964. You can thank Bill Hogsett, who shares your birth roots, since he was born on June 13,

1946. Let Bill welcome you to a ever-increasing counter displaying how many Boomers have turned 50 to date, and some intriguing stories such as: "Boomers Read Menus, Not Labels," and "ATM's—Sure we use them!." Other features adorn this site as well, like a Baby Boomer TV crossword puzzle, census data, boomer financial advice, and The BoomerPhile, full of articles, stories, poetry and other items written with boomers in mind. —(L.T.)

URL ▸ http://www.xmission.com/~seer/Hogsett/boomers.htm

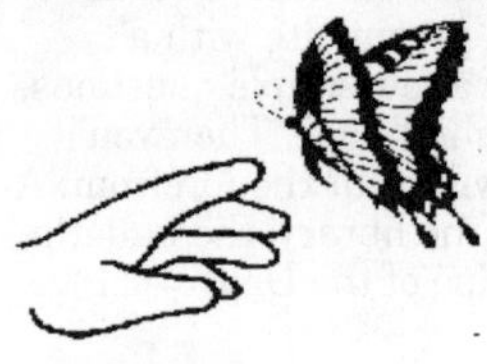

Educated Self-Help Advice for Parents

The Wonder Wise Parent Jump 6656 CONTENT

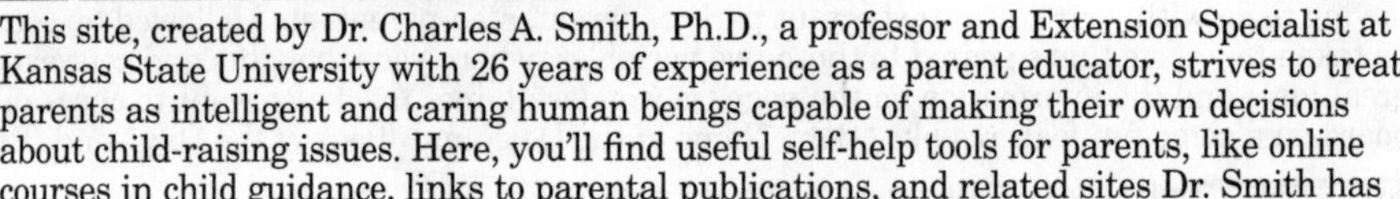

This site, created by Dr. Charles A. Smith, Ph.D., a professor and Extension Specialist at Kansas State University with 26 years of experience as a parent educator, strives to treat parents as intelligent and caring human beings capable of making their own decisions about child-raising issues. Here, you'll find useful self-help tools for parents, like online courses in child guidance, links to parental publications, and related sites Dr. Smith has selected for you. —(L.T.)

KEY NEWSGROUP **misc.kids** URL ▸ http://www.ksu.edu/wwparent/wondhome.htm

News & Chat for the 40-Plus Set

Maturity USA Jump 6879 CONTENT

Designed for those aged 50-plus, this new magazine publishes informative articles about financial, health and travel issues. Designed to be graphically easy on the eyes, you'll also find a virtual community where participants discuss mid-life and senior matters in their global chat room. Browse a supply of Will Rogers' humor and Burma-Shave jingles. Or gain insider knowledge on the news that's affecting you daily, such as the latest Medicaid changes, new treatments for prostate cancer, or how the healthcare industry is wasting money. —(L.T.)

KEY NEWSGROUP **clari.news.aging** URL ▸ http://www.maturityusa.com

Post Announcements of Your Group's Next Big Event

Worldwide Events Database Jump 3707 CONTENT

Got an event you'd like to tell the world about? Here's a great way to do it. The Worldwide Events Database allows you to post events of all types to the Web, at no charge. An easy-to-use form is provided to allow you to fully describe your event, and allows others to read all about it. Looking for a particular event? You can search by location, date, keyword, or phrase. Or, look through the entire list of events by category—there's Arts and Festivals, Crafts, Hobbies, Sports, Conferences, and more! Internet Productions, Inc. has created a terrific resource for event sponsors, participants, and travelers. —(N.F.)

URL ▸ http://www.ipworld.com/events/homepage.htm

College Student's Virtual Hangout

What's New at T@p On-line Jump 7241 CONTENT

T@p On-line is a Web zine that speaks to college students across the United States. You can chat in the virtual dorm, log into video music jams, follow college teams, and read reviews and views on music, art, the Net, and current events. Need to unburden yourself? Well, you can do that here too by venting to t@phead. Need money for school? You can also find tips on loans and jobs at this site. —(E.v.B.)

URL ▸ http://www.taponline.com/tap/new.html

Teen Delight

Welcome to FishNet Jump 7376 

FishNet, a nicely-executed site created especially for teenagers, contains a number of interesting resources, such as the College Guide, which provides users with links to more in-depth college sites and e-mail communications links to college placement advisors, and access to interesting college-related articles. You can also check out KnowBase, a database of articles of interest to teenagers, and StreetSpeak, a place where you can discover the jargon of the streets, or add your own slang. There's also

Read Edge, an electronic magazine that covers opportunities for teenagers, news, book reviews, and more. Or how about interacting on Threads, a bulletin board where teens can exchange news and views. And to top it all off—why not cruise this site's Moola Mall, where you can investigate educationally-oriented products and learning opportunities. —(E.v.B.)

KEY NEWSGROUP **alt.kids-talk** URL▶ http://www.webpress.net/jayi/

Happy Birthday to You!

World Birthday Web (WBW) Jump **0037**

What a great idea: Tom Boutell's World Birthday Web lets you post your name and birthday to see your name displayed when that happy day comes! While you're at it, you'll also see the names and e-mail addresses of other Netters who also share your birth date. —(E.G.)

URL▶ http://sunsite.unc.edu/btbin/birthday

Family Activities & Advice

Family World Home Page Jump **2173**

This collaborative effort of 30 members of Parenting Publications of America starts with a compilation of activity calendars for parents, children, and families, making it the perfect response to the inevitable weekend lament: "There's nothing to do!" If it stopped there, it would be a worthwhile bookmark, but it goes on to give you a selection of features covering travel and recreation, fashion, health, education, child development, general parenting tips, and book reviews. Use it as a general resource, but be sure to visit every month when new additions are listed on the main page. —(L.S.)

KEY NEWSGROUP **misc.kids** URL▶ http://www.family.com/indexTX.html

---

Case Western Reserve University
Habitat for Humanity

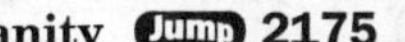

Building a Better World: Habitat for Humanity

Habitat for Humanity Jump **2175**

If you're looking for a way to help your community, want to see some tangible results of your efforts, and you enjoy physical labor, Habitat for Humanity may be for you. Begun in 1976, this organization builds and rehabilitates homes, then sells them to low-income families for the cost of the materials, using mortgages that are kept low because they don't include interest or profit. This page, maintained by the Case Western Reserve University chapter, tells you what it's all about and how to get involved—as well as where to get involved—with its listing of chapters worldwide. —(L.S.)

KEY NEWSGROUP **alt.activism** URL▶ http://www.cwru.edu/0/activities/habhum/home.html#index

---

Finding Love on the Web

Web Personals (Personal Ad Listings)
Jump **2180**

Find your soulmate with this free service from Internet Media Services (a different company with the same name as this book's publisher; not affiliated in any way with the publisher of this book). It has Web-based personal ads features, letting you browse ads by category or search with keywords. But then there's the Love Hound, a unique feature that lets you key in some search criteria, then have matches e-mailed to you. Rounding out the page is an online forum, where you can discuss various aspects of dating and relationships. The service is "semi-moderated," meaning that the owners screen submissions to this site to ensure that ads and postings meet some basic criteria and keep wackos at a minimum. —(L.S.)

KEY NEWSGROUP **alt.personals.ads** URL▶ http://www.w3.com/date/

Friends from Around the World

The E-mail Club Jump **5145**

Looking for electronic pen pals over the Net? This page promotes the E-mail Club, a mailing list of new friends worldwide. This page tells you a little bit about the club, contains a link to member profiles, and provides info on

how to become a member. Moderated by veteran "Netizen" Stewart Ogilvy, this is touted as one of the highest-quality moderated mailing lists on the Net. —(S.B.)

URL▶ http://www.emailclub.com

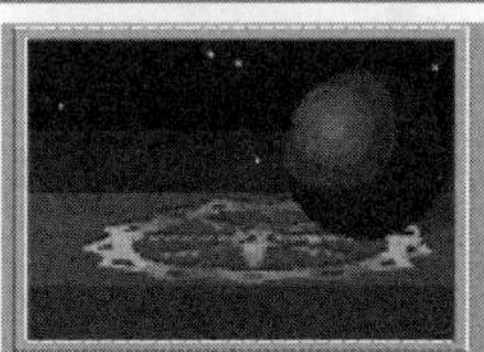

A Journal of Consciousness

The Weaver at Communique.com Jump 2385

This fascinating online journal touches on all aspects of religion, ancient and contemporary, the paranormal, and even science—with its coverage of psychology and psychotherapy. If it has to do with the Web of Life (as opposed to the Web of Internet!), and how we interact with it, you'll find it here. Unlike other Web-based magazines, back issues aren't archived separately. They are collected and organized like a real Web page, coherently by subject, so you can always visit the archive and read about specific topics of interest. Contributions and comments are welcomed, and there is an online form to make communicating easier. —(L.S.)

KEY NEWSGROUP **talk.religion.misc** URL▶ http://www.hyperlink.com/weaver/index.htm

Weekly Parenting Advice

The National Parenting Center Jump 2625

The National Parenting Center offers information and advice about rearing children from pregnancy to adolescence. Each week, they publish new articles from their newsletter, one article for each age group—pregnancy, newborn, infant, toddler, pre-school, preteen, and adolescence—all written by experts in the field of child rearing and cover topics that can help you be a better—and saner—parent. —(L.S.)

KEY NEWSGROUP **misc.kids** URL▶ http://www.stpt.com/TNPC/

Midwives' Information & Resources

Midwifery Jump 7036

Searching for a career that has growth potential and is also in at the beginning of things? Have a look at the midwifery page for news and views of the profession, conferences, e-mail contacts, and other Web links. —(E.v.B.)

KEY NEWSGROUP **misc.health.alternative** URL▶ http://www.csv.warwick.ac.uk:8000/midwifery.html

Info for Nonprofit Organizations

Welcome to Impact Online Jump 7187

Impact Online is dedicated to connecting people to nonprofit organizations and nonprofits to one another, over the Internet. Every month a social issue is featured, in addition to the usual interactive material on nonprofits in general. Press releases and volunteer opportunities and events are also presented. Impact Online has also developed an online course that helps nonprofits use Internet technology, which is also informative for Net novices, too. —(E.v.B.)

KEY NEWSGROUP **alt.activism** URL▶ http://www.webcom.com/~iol/

American Indian Web Resources

Tribal Voice Jump 7209

Tribal Voice seeks to be "an uncensored, blunt, and direct outlet for the native American heart." In addition, this site is dedicated to creating a tribal cyberspace network. To this end, Tribal Voice lists extensive native American and American Indian resources and groups Web sites of interest by subject and geographic area. Links are also provided to important conferences, festivals, concerts, etc. —(E.v.B.)

KEY NEWSGROUP **alt.native** URL▶ http://www.tribal.com/

News and Views for Women

Women's Wire Jump 2678 

The keystone of this site is current news of interest to women, taken from the UPI wires and updated daily, and that's a good enough reason to bookmark it. But there are a few other features that bear attention, such as the Back Talk section. Here you'll find a weekly thought, quote, or news item, and an opportunity to post your feelings about it. Each week, a new item and the better comments from the previous week are posted. The Question Authorities section is also excellent. Here you can post questions and read the responses from experts in business, investing, the Internet, health, and other areas. Rounding out the site is a very good list of links to women-owned businesses, women's organizations, and other relevant sites. —(L.S.)

KEY NEWSGROUP **soc.women** URL▸ http://www.women.com/

Feminists Online

Feminist Majority Foundation Jump 2679 

This is the place for feminists on the Web, a combination news, watchdog, action and support site. There are sections covering urgent issues and how individuals can become involved, plus news, events, and support services. You can also access information on better health, succeeding in the workplace, safety, and women's sports, books, and film. If you can't find the information you need by browsing or using the search engine, or if you want to find out more about a subject, there's links to online resources to help you research specific topics. —(L.S.)

KEY NEWSGROUP **soc.feminism** URL▸ http://www.feminist.org/welcome/welcome2.html

Online Networking for Women

Virtual Sisterhood Jump 2681 

Virtual Sisterhood is a global, completely online organization dedicated to promoting the women's movement via electronic communcations. Chief among their objectives is educating women in how to utilize electronic communications to advance the women's movement. Current initiatives include establishing a global resource directory, helping women develop Web sites, and mobilizing volunteers interested in helping digitize the movement. —(L.S.)

KEY NEWSGROUP **soc.feminism** URL▸ http://www.igc.apc.org/vsister/

The Urban Cyberstation

EURweb Jump 5843 

EURWeb stands for Electronic Urban Report, one of the best places on the Web for African-Americans to meet, chat and find out all the latest news on the greatest stars. You'll find plenty of exclusives here from the cream of the entertainment world, featuring the likes of Lionel Richie, Vanessa Williams, and more. Join the chat area and maybe you'll meet the mate of your dreams. Have you heard a rumor about a soap star? Send it in to Scopes, Soaps & Trivia. And don't leave without checking out this site's photo gallery. You can even submit your own photo if you want. —(J.P.)

URL▸ http://www.eurweb.com/

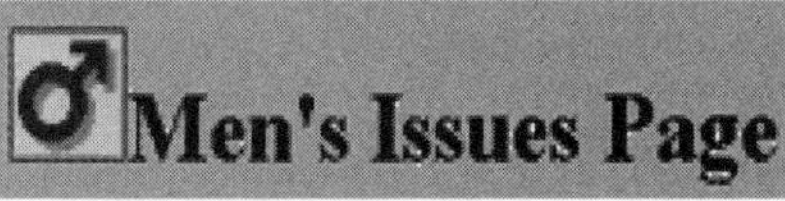

Men Have Rights, Too

Men's Issues Page Jump 2456 

Without minimizing the difficulties women have in an admittedly male-dominated society, the fact is that men don't have it all that well. It has become much too easy for men to be unjustly accused of sexual harrassment, discrimination, and domestic violence, and all too convenient to ignore the fact that men, too, suffer these crimes. With this page, David R. Throop provides men with links to support resources, organized by topics. In addition to coverage of the more sensationalistic issues, there also are good resources here on men's health, employment, and personal growth. It's an excellent resource for any man trying to deal with changing expectations and perceptions in contemporary society, and a good place for any woman to gain a little perspective on how things look from the other side. —(L.S.)

KEY NEWSGROUP **soc.men** URL▶ http://www.vix.com/pub/men/index.html

Creating a Country

Oceania—The Atlantis Project Jump **2745**

Ever wanted to chuck it all and just start your own country? These people did, and they're doing something about it. Oceania is the name of the planned nation-state, and since they assume no one will sell them land to create the new country, they're planning to build it out of concrete and steel in the Caribbean Sea. For the time being, though, the country and its culture are completely virtual, but that doesn't mean these folks aren't serious. It's a fascinating concept, with a real plan behind it, and you can check in every now and then to see how they're progressing. Or, spend a little more time and learn about the project from its inception, and join up. —(L.S.)

KEY NEWSGROUP **alt.culture.virtual.oceania** URL▶ http://oceania.org/

The Peace Corps

Peace Corps Jump **4514**

There was a time when one of the most noble decisions any young American could make would be to join the Peace Corps. Today, such a decision would be just as noble—and useful—but far less likely. This site keeps the fire burning with information about the Peace Corps, reasons for its existance, and, yes, even information on how to join. Not a slick or beautiful site, but full of worthwhile content, to be sure. —(T.W.)

URL▶ http://www.clark.net/pub/peace/PeaceCorps.html

Caring & Support

Medical News Online

Your Health Daily Jump **8013**

R&D Laboratories produces this site, which is distributed online by The New York Times' syndication division, where you get a rundown of the week's top medical stories. Alcoholism, food allergies, asthma—you name the condition, and you'll find information on it here. You can read today's latest news, and then switch over to the medical and health news database and search for more information by topic or keyword. You can also participate in R&D's online discussion groups to ask questions and share information with medical professionals who are active on this site. —(E.v.B.)

KEY NEWSGROUP **bit.listserv.mednews** URL▶ http://nytsyn.com/medic/

Multimedia Medical Reference Library

Your Own Private Medical Library

The Multimedia Medical Reference Library Jump **8533**

Picture in your mind a library devoted to medicine and health. Is it dusty, dark, and difficult to find what you want? Well, you used to be right. Now it looks just like your Web display screen. This is a database of links and it's massive. But instead of the Dewey Decimal System, it's arranged by medical topics, which link you to the many medical resources on the Web. It's also searchable, although the engine will only link you to the general topic page, and not the resource itself. Even so, there's plenty to see here, some of which lives up to the title of multimedia: sound, still pictures, and movies (for those of us with the right software or hardware). And that's something the old med school libraries could never do. —(R.B.)

URL▶ http://www.tiac.net/users/jtward/multimed.html

■ Social & Support

Alice in Medicineland

Go Ask Alice Jump **8535**

Hunting for a healthy diversion? Hop on over to Alice, a medical site written with wit and irreverance. The health topics addressed here have a college campus flair, which isn't surprising, since it's located at Columbia University's Web Server. There's no real rhyme or reason to this site; it's in a question and answer format that's arranged in what seems to be chronological order. Although the information is sound, it's definitely offbeat. You'll find answers to everything from how to deal with a seriously depressed roommate, to the causes of a missed menstrual cycle. It's worth a trip because it *is* a trip. —(R.B.)

URL ▶ http://www.columbia.edu/cu/healthwise/alice.html

State-of-the Art Medical Treatments

Centerwatch
Jump **8511**

If you're interested in cutting-edge treatments for just about any disease, this extensive Web database probably has what you're looking for. You can search for new treatments by disease categories, or look for research centers located near you that are conducting experimental studies. This site provides a notification service, too. By listing your e-mail address and specifying the type of disease you're interested in, you'll recieve updates on new treatment trials when they're listed on the site. It's important to note that this is not a governmental service, and that the lists of clinical trials are provided by the research centers themselves. Some prominent centers aren't listed, but more are being added regularly. —(R.B.)

URL ▶ http://www.centerwatch.com/

Mayo Clinic Health Information Site

The Newstand: Mayo Online Health Magazine
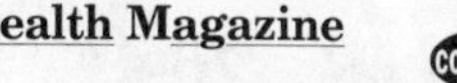
Jump **8539**

When you're cruising the Web for health information, the most important thing is to make sure that what you're reading is from a reliable source. Not much to worry about here—it's the Mayo Clinic we're talking about, after all. And this electronic newsletter is a "best in class" for the Web. Monthly articles cover many health topics in a very readable style. "Hot Topics" include features on new developments in the health field. In addition to this site's extensive FAQ list, you can even send in a question to be answered by a Mayo physician. Individual responses aren't given, but it might be chosen to be added to the FAQ list. Check in monthly for lots of new and accurate information. —(R.B.)

URL ▶ http://healthnet.ivi.com/hnet/common/html/pubs.htm

Dial-a-Disease

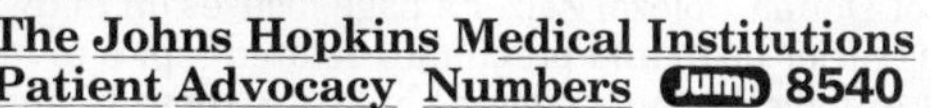

The Johns Hopkins Medical Institutions Patient Advocacy Numbers Jump **8540**

Although there are other phone directories on the Web, this site is the quickest guide to organizations related to medicine, and the most comprehensive. Alphabetical listings point to societies that either offer support, or to gov-ernmental resources for many diseases. Some even have Web sites, too—and you can link to them from here. —(R.B.)

URL ▶ http://infonet.welch.jhu.edu/advocacy.html

Helping Hand for Depression Support

Depression Central Jump **5801**

Won't find any wallowing in pity here at Depression Central. Although this site is not intended to act as a substitute for professional diagnosis, it does serve as a wonderful starting point for anyone who might want to survey the many aspects of clinical depression. You may wish to begin with this site's great introductory section on mood disorders. The articles are excellent, covering in great detail many topics related to depression, and the selection of books and videos on the subject are also very helpful indeed. The other sections include depression in the elderly and children, genetics of depressive illnesses, post-partum depressions and premenstrual dysphoria. And there are links to many other related sites as well. —(J.P.)

KEY NEWSGROUP **alt.support. depression** URL▶ http://www.psycom.net/depression.central.html

Welcome to
Dr. Ivan's DEPRESSION CENTRAL

Resources for Depression Sufferers

Dr. Ivan's Depression Central Jump **8514**

This is the most comprehensive site for anyone interested in depression, from psychiatrists to anyone with a passing interest. Information on this site runs the gamut from the super-technical to, "you've-got-a-friend" support. You'll find a comprehensive list of links conveniently grouped under large topical headings, and technical research papers are also available. This site provides great information on many aspects of depression and other mental illnesses including links to personal home pages of people who suffer from depression. —(R.B.)

URL▶ http://www.psycom.net/depression.central.html

Help for Depression Sufferers

Depression Resources List Jump **7322**

Dennis Taylor has compiled an extensive list of links to newsgroups and Web pages devoted to all sorts of depression-related resources. You can find information on different depressive problems such as panic attacks, manic-depressive episodes, cognitive disorders, and seasonal depression. Reference books, samples of prose and poetry by fellow sufferers, and information on antidepressant drugs can all be accessed from this page. —(E.v.B.)

KEY NEWSGROUP **alt.support.depression** URL▶ http://earth.execpc.com/~corbeau/

Heart Support

Heart Link Home Page Jump **7326**

Heart Link, a British independent support group, offers practical help, advice, and comfort for heart patients, their families and caregivers. This comprehensive site presents information on heart conditions, and descriptions of treatments, medicines, and surgical interventions. The site also offers real-time counseling, lists of reference works, news of recent research findings, and links to other heart-related Web sites. —(E.v.B.)

KEY NEWSGROUP **sci.med** URL▶ http://www.ibmpcug.co.uk/~rwall/

Childbirth Jumplist

Midwifery, Pregnancy and Birth Related Information Jump **2590**

While most of Donna Dolezal Zelzer's page focuses on midwifery and homebirth links, there are enough links to sites covering other birth and pregnancy related topics to make this an excellent bookmark for anyone interested in these topics. Among the more general links are those to nutrition and pregnancy, high risk situations, alternative health resources, and general resources for parents. The links are well organized, with a separate page for each heading, and quite extensive. Donna also updates the links regularly, so you can be sure of having a quick guide to the latest information. —(L.S.)

KEY NEWSGROUP **misc.kids.pregnancy** URL▶ http://www.efn.org/~djz/birth/birthindex.html

Promoting Better Mental Health

Metuchen Psychological Services Home Page Jump **2245**

Psychologists Timothy M. Bogen and Marsha Lesowitz have made it easier for people to find information and resources on mental health issues. There are articles and general resource links covering mood disorders, obsessive-compulsive disorders, substance abuse, physical abuse, youth and parenting, and other issues. They've specifically concentrated on consumer information, making it a very useful site, and one that avoids the confusing technical coverage of these topics that can leave a person even more troubled and confused. —(L.S.)

KEY NEWSGROUP **alt.support** URL▶ http://www.castle.net/~tbogen/mps.html

Links for the Psyche

School Psychological Resources Online Jump 8517

Despite this site's name, there's much more than school resources to be found. Here you'll find links to almost any pschological or learning disorder. You won't just find descriptions of illnesses, either. It contains a very complete list of professional organizations, support for parents, journals, and pamphlets. You won't possibly be disappointed with the vast collection of psychology-related Web sites featured here. —(R.B.)

URL▶ http://www.bcpl.lib.md.us/~sandyste/school_psych.html

Sexual Abuse Support Index

Sexual Assualt Information Page Index Jump 2563

This is an excellent reference and jumplist to Internet resources covering sexual assault, abuse, and recovery. Virtually every topic is covered, from child abuse and date rape, to men's issues. Site organizer Chris Bartley also includes links to counseling resources, victim compensation information, and prevention and crisis centers. If you don't find what you need, contact Chris—there's much information not yet added to the index, and Chris will search the pending files and send you pointers if you ask him. —(L.S.)

KEY NEWSGROUP **alt.sex.abuse.recovery** URL▶ http://www.cs.utk.edu/~bartley/saInfoPage.html

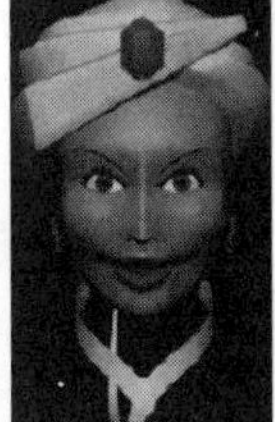

Menopause Support Group

Power Surge Jump 5815

Power Surge is a support network created for women experiencing menopause, and was created by Alice Lotto Stamm in 1994, after she found herself confused with the new feelings and changes that so dramatically overtook her life. Although the focus of this site is the discussion about menopause, including issues such as hot flashes, estrogen deficiency, insomnia, depression and more, it is also a place to put everything into context. In this light, the site explores how these things affect the other aspects of a woman's life, and how open discussions can help to take the issue "from the closet," and "into the living room." —(J.P.)

URL▶ http://members.aol.com/dearest/index.html

Sleep Disorders Support Page

Sleep Medicine Home Page Jump 2248

This page goes beyond insomnia, snoring, and sleep apnea to cover virtually every sleep disorder known, and certainly all those represented by Internet resources. It begins with links to related newsgroups and ends with listings of sleep clinics. In between, the resources covered include a list of specific sleep disorder resources, treatment information, professional associations, foundations, federal and state information, and book reviews. As comprehensive as it is, new resources are always being added to the Internet, so if you know of an item that's not there, you can submit it. —(L.S.)

KEY NEWSGROUP **alt.support.sleep-disorder** URL▶ http://www.cloud9.net/~thorpy/

Good Healthy Advice

Healthwise Jump 1509

If you have serious health problems, consult your physician. But if you're curious or concerned about health issues, Healthwise is here to help. Sponsored by the Health, Education, and Wellness program of Columbia University Health Service, a team of professional and peer educators are "committed to helping you make choices that will contribute to your personal health and happiness, the well-being of others, and to the planet we share." They've assembled a comprehensive, FAQ in hypertext format, along with articles and links to relevant material. Through Alice, a metaphor for the health-care team, you can anonymously e-mail questions about relationships, fitness and nutrition, drugs, sex, alcohol, and stress. Presented in an easy-to-use, intuitive format, you can also search for previous topics by entering key words. The search engine returns lists of responses that match. Find out about upcoming workshops and conferences by reading Alice announcements, or participate online in a number of discussions on a wide variety of health-related topics. —(H.L.)

URL▶ http://www.columbia.edu/cu/healthwise/

Health News for Women

Women's Health Hot Line Home Page Jump 2236 

Here you'll find news on women's health issues, such as hormone therapy for menopause and breast cancer screening. You'll also find helpful guides on choosing a primary care physician and other topics. But being a newsletter, the information is not very comprehensive, and the pages don't take full advantage of the hypertext medium. So, if you want more information on a topic, you'll have to look for yourself. Still, you'll get a well-written and informative monthly news digest, one that serves as an excellent starting point for keeping current on these health topics. —(L.S.)

KEY NEWSGROUP **soc.women** URL▶ http://www.soft-design.com/softinfo/womens-health.html

Coping with Down's Syndrome

Down Syndrome WWW Page Jump 2233 

Compiled from contributions by members to the Down's Syndrome mailing list, this page provides family members of Down's Syndrome children with with abundant resources. Included are helpful articles written by parents and professionals, activity and educational resources, and a list of support organizations and conferences. It's a new and growing page, and if you want to be involved, the best way to start is to join the Internet mailing list, by using the instructions you'll find here. —(L.S.)

KEY NEWSGROUP **alt.education.disabled** URL▶ http://www.nas.com/downsyn/

Making Children More Street-Smart

Safe-T-Child Online Jump 2704 

This site offers guidance and advice for parents on how to help their children learn to protect themselves from abduction and other dangers on the streets. Beginning with a quick questionnaire that will let you determine your child's "street smarts," and through a variety of resources available online, you'll be able to help your children protect themselves, without necessarily instilling fear in them. The site includes an online newsletter for parents and teachers with tips and updates on child safety, with a new feature each week. —(L.S.)

KEY NEWSGROUP **misc.kids** URL▶ http://yellodyno.safe-t-child.com/

SIDS Support & Resources

Sudden Infant Death Syndrome (SIDS) Network Jump 3717 

Sudden Infant Death Syndrome (SIDS) kills 7,000 babies a year—a staggering statistic. The goals of the nonprofit, voluntary Sudden Infant Death Syndrome Network, Inc. are three-fold: To eliminate SIDS through the support of SIDS research projects; to provide support for those who have been touched by the tragedy; and to raise public awareness of SIDS through education. Bringing their organization to the Internet helps make SIDS information available to millions of people. At this enormous site, you'll find facts about SIDS, tips for reducing the risk for SIDS, "We Remember with Love"—a heartfelt tribute to babies who've been lost to this condition, grief information, and a tremendous number of links to related sites. —(N.F.)

URL▶ http://www.eskimo.com/~pageless/home/sidsnet/

The Other Side of Dyslexia

Dyslexia: The Gift. Information for Parents and their Children Jump 7295 

This site is described as an online information center dedicated to the positive side of a "learning disability,"as well as to remedial therapies and teaching methods suited to the dyslexic learning style. It is maintained by the Davis Dyslexia Association International, located in Burlingame, California. Here you will learn about dyslexics from another, little-known perspective—about their ability to be visual, multidimensional thinkers. Dyslexics are said to be intuitive and highly creative, and excel at hands-on learning. The pages are rich in information on teaching techniques to surmount difficulties in reading and they also point to other dyslexia-related Web resources and organizations in North America. —(E.v.B.)

KEY NEWSGROUP **alt.support** URL▶ http://www.parentsplace.com/readroom/dyslexia/index.cgi

Breastfeeding Your Baby

La Leche League International Jump **8518**

New moms with new babies often need new information...especially about breast feeding. La Leche is an organization dedicated to the breastfeeding mom, and their site reflects their attitude: educational with a healthy dose of encouragement. You can find Web sites (and phone numbers) of local chapters, information on becoming a trainer, and even articles on breastfeeding and the law. La Leche says that although breastfeeding is a natural process, it doesn't come naturally. Maybe not, but the available pamphlets and "mother to mother" support offered here make this page a natural choice for interested couples. —(R.B.)

URL▶ http://www.prairienet.org/llli/

Parent's Resources

PARENTS PLACE.COM — the parenting resource center on the Web Jump **7317**

ParentsPlace.com

A world of parenting news, views, tips, and advice has certainly been gathered here. Need information on pregnancy, breast-feeding, babies, the challenges of raising teenagers, parenting twins, step-parenting, single parenting, children's health and education, family activities? Or perhaps you'd just like to chat with other parents, and then shop by traveling the links to many catalogs and online stores also available here. —(E.v.B.)

KEY NEWSGROUP **alt.parenting.solutions** URL▶ http://www.parentsplace.com/index.html

Foster Parent Center

Foster Parent Newsletter Jump **6675**

Foster parents will truly appreciate this unique online newsletter written by Barbara Leiner. You'll find a useful collection of articles, resources and issues relating to the care of foster and at-risk children. Meet and share experiences with other present and prospective foster parents or obtain valuable advice from articles like "Welcoming the Stranger," "Question Checklist for Placements," or get creative ideas from this site's "Simple Activities for Younger Children" guide. If you're already a devoted foster parent or you're thinking about becoming one, you'll take great comfort in knowing that Barbara has created this informative site just for you. —(L.T.)

KEY NEWSGROUP **misc.kids** URL▶ http://www.westworld.com/~barbara

Child Development Tips for Parents

The National Parent Information Network Jump **2168**

This site is intended not just for parents, but for anyone who works with children and child development. The section of "Short Items Especially for Parents" is particularly helpful with information about child care, children and the media, helping children learn at home, teen issues, and other topics. There's also an online edition of "Parent News," a publication dealing with issues about and affecting parenting, and links to the AskERIC information clearinghouse and digests, other parents' resources, and ideas for community involvement. —(L.S.)

KEY NEWSGROUP **misc.education** URL▶ http://ericps.ed.uiuc.edu/npin/npinhome.html

When Kids Are Troubled

Facts for Families Jump **2172**

This online version of the American Academy of Child and Adolescent Psychiatry's pamphlet series provides parents with concise, up-to-date information about general and specific problems children and teens—and their parents—may encounter. Among the topics covered are depression, children and divorce, drug use, learning disabilities, and discipline. It's a good place to check when you think your child may have a problem but you don't know how to begin dealing with it, as well as to browse for insights into the issues of parenting. —(L.S.)

KEY NEWSGROUP **misc.kids** URL▶ http://www.med.umich.edu/aacap/facts.index.html

Support for Families & Friends of Alcoholics

Al-Anon and Alateen Jump 2263

The most difficult aspect of dealing with alcoholics is that there's nothing you can do if they don't want to help themselves. Even if they do, your options are limited, and the problems of coping with a person in recovery still remain. Al-Anon is a group organized on the same principles as Alcoholics Anonymous, but instead of support for stopping drinking, it's support for those who have to deal with an alcoholic, whether or not that person is trying to stop. Alateen offers the same support, but specifically for teenagers living in an alcoholic family. This site will help you determine if either of these groups is for you, and shows you how to get involved. —(L.S.)

KEY NEWSGROUP alt.support URL▶ http://solar.rtd.utk.edu/~al-anon/

Comprehensive Info on Infertility

Resolve Jump 8519

Millions of couples struggle to conceive a child. Not everyone succeeds. But anyone with difficulty will find help, information, and support on this subject from this organization and their Web site. Basic facts—and myths—about infertility are explained here, in easy to understand language. For those with a deeper interest, Resolve's other services are explained, including member-to-member support, a telephone helpline, and physician referrals. This site is a very good introduction to a very sensitive topic. —(R.B.)

URL▶ http://www.resolve.org/

Understanding and Treating Infertility

Chapter 11 Jump 2511

People coping with infertility and seeking an understanding of what causes it and how it can be treated will receive an excellent overview of these topics at this Web page. A chapter from the book *Bone Marrow Transplants—A Book of Basics for Patients* by Susan L. Stewart on the effects of BMT on fertility is only a small part of the text available here. The chapter begins with an explanation of the steps toward pregnancy, drugs and other treatments that can cause infertility, and the various treatment and pregnancy options available. There also is guidance on how to choose a reproductive assistance program, dealing with the emotional aspects of the process, and adoption as an option to infertility. —(L.S.)

KEY NEWSGROUP alt.infertility URL▶ http://nysernet.org/bcic/bmt/bmt.book/chapter.11.html

Attention Deficit Disorder Support Group Online

Children and Adults with Attention Deficit Disorder 

Children and Adults with Attention Deficit Disorders (CH.A.D.D.), a nonprofit, parent-based organization, has created these Web pages to support families and advance advocacy concerning A.D.D., and to encourage public and professional education. A wealth of information on A.D.D. can be downloaded—from how to treat those suffering from it, to lists of contacts all over North America, and to sources of online help. —(E.v.B.)

KEY NEWSGROUP alt.support.attn-deficit URL▶ http://www.chadd.org/

ADD Information & Help

Attention Deficit Disorder WWW Archive Jump 2600

Meng Weng Wong has assembled a wide variety of excellent information on attention deficit disorder (ADD), making it an essential resource for anyone concerned with ADD. There's a very detailed FAQ in hypertext format, an article describing the criteria for determining whether someone has ADD, followed closely by an article on the dangers of self-diagnosis, and pages discussing how to cope with ADD. There also are links to home pages of ADD mailing lists, including a list for parents of children with ADD. You'll also find occasional news here that relates to ADD and its treatment, but most of the attention is paid to collecting articles and other information to help people understand the illness and cope with it day to day. —(L.S.)

KEY NEWSGROUP alt.support.attn-deficit URL▶ http://www.seas.upenn.edu/~mengwong/add/

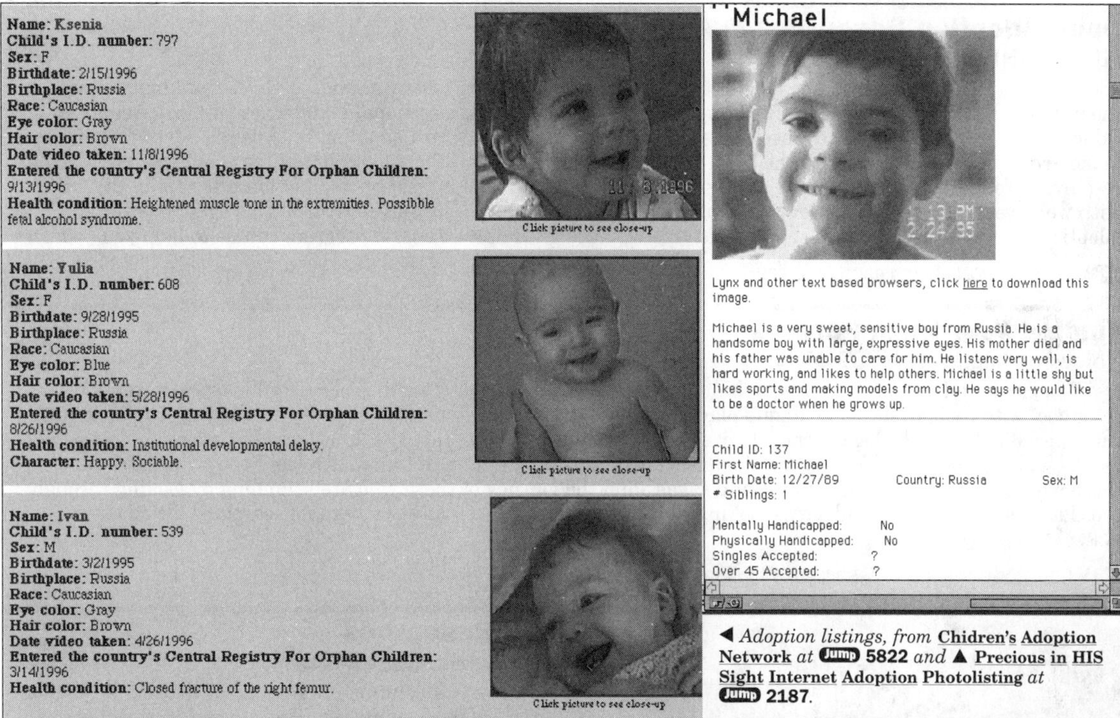

Name: Ksenia
Child's I.D. number: 797
Sex: F
Birthdate: 2/15/1996
Birthplace: Russia
Race: Caucasian
Eye color: Gray
Hair color: Brown
Date video taken: 11/8/1996
Entered the country's Central Registry For Orphan Children: 9/13/1996
Health condition: Heightened muscle tone in the extremities. Possibble fetal alcohol syndrome.
Click picture to see close-up
Name: Yulia
Child's I.D. number: 608
Sex: F
Birthdate: 9/28/1995
Birthplace: Russia
Race: Caucasian
Eye color: Blue
Hair color: Brown
Date video taken: 5/28/1996
Entered the country's Central Registry For Orphan Children: 8/26/1996
Health condition: Institutional developmental delay.
Character: Happy. Sociable.
Click picture to see close-up
Name: Ivan
Child's I.D. number: 539
Sex: M
Birthdate: 3/2/1995
Birthplace: Russia
Race: Caucasian
Eye color: Gray
Hair color: Brown
Date video taken: 4/26/1996
Entered the country's Central Registry For Orphan Children: 3/14/1996
Health condition: Closed fracture of the right femur.
Click picture to see close-up
Michael
Lynx and other text based browsers, click here to download this image.
Michael is a very sweet, sensitive boy from Russia. He is a handsome boy with large, expressive eyes. His mother died and his father was unable to care for him. He listens very well, is hard working, and likes to help others. Michael is a little shy but likes sports and making models from clay. He says he would like to be a doctor when he grows up.
Child ID: 137
First Name: Michael
Birth Date: 12/27/89
Country: Russia
Sex: M
Siblings: 1
Mentally Handicapped: No
Physically Handicapped: No
Singles Accepted: ?
Over 45 Accepted: ?

◀ *Adoption listings, from* **Children's Adoption Network** *at* Jump **5822** *and* ▲ **Precious in HIS Sight Internet Adoption Photolisting** *at* Jump **2187**.

International Adoption Resources

Internet Adoption Photolisting Jump 5923

CONTENT

There are more and more resources on the Internet for parents wanting to adopt children from countries other than the United States. This site differs from some of the others we've seen in that it's devoted almost exclusively to the children themselves. You will find touching pictures of all the children available for adoption, along with a detailed family and personal history of each child. The children themselves live in a number of countries, including Brazil, China, India, Korea, Romania and—by far the most—Russia. The database is sorted by country, age of child, adoption agency, and date. —(J.P.)

KEY NEWSGROUP **alt.adoption** URL ▶ http://www.adoption.com/

Adoption for Children from Russia and South America

Children's Adoption Network

Jump 5822

CONTENT

Adopting a child can be a confusing business under the best circumstances, but what if you are trying to adopt a child from another country? This is a common experience now, and sure to become more so. An option for help is available here at the Children's Adoption Network, an agency which helps with adoptions of children from South America and the former Soviet Union. The site features a touching photo database of children available for adoption, accompanied by birth and medical information for each child. Their trained staff will help you with all the necessary documentation and other legal requirments. And of course the site contains information on the children themselves. —(J.P.)

URL ▶ http://204.252.125.34:80/can/

Open Adoption Resources & Advice

adoptionHELP! Jump 3715

adoptionHELP! is a great resource for those thinking about adopting a baby as well as those thinking of having their child adopted by another family. Brought to you by the nonprofit National Federation for Open Adoption Education, this site focuses on counseling, education, and support. ("Open adoption" means the adopting parents make arrangements directly with the birth parents). Questions about the adoption process are answered, and resources are shared in an open and caring environment. This is the largest open adoption program in the USA with well over a decade of experience and offices across the country. The success rate of this agency—over 100 adoptions in the last 4 months—shows what this well-designed and extensive program can do to help you. —(N.F.)

URL ▶ http://www.webcom.com/~nfediac/

Finding Your Birth Parents

Voices of Adoption Jump 3720

Here's a site for adoptees who are searching for their biological roots. It's also a place for biological parents to reconnect with their pasts. This unique place on the Web is dedicated to all those who are digging deeper to find that special link—the biological one. Denise Castelluci, the creator of this site, knew of other adoption pages available, but none quite like the one she envisioned—one with a human face and voice. Follow the journeys of those who have searched, with stories and sagas. Join the journey of those who are searching by looking through the classifieds, which cover adoptees looking for birth families as well as birth parents searching for adoptees. —(N.F.)

URL ▶ http://www.best.com/~savage/adoption.html

Adoption Resources

AdoptioNetwork Jump 2438

AdoptioNetwork is a volunteer organization that helps anyone involved in the adoption process. The site includes content offering guidance to birth mothers who are considering giving their children up for adoption, advice for adoptees looking for their birth parents, and information for people seeking to adopt children, including info on the process of starting infant, open, and subsidized adoptions. There are lists to public and private adoption agencies, links to state adoption regulations, postadoption assistance, and other resources. There also are lists of pointers to resources not on the Internet, making this as complete a site on adoption as you're likely to find anywhere. —(L.S.)

KEY NEWSGROUP alt.adoption URL ▶ http://www.infi.net/adopt/

Adoption in Russia

Adoption of Russian Children Jump 5778

With the introduction of new adoption regulations in Russia, it is now possible for parents from outside the country to adopt many of the children now living in orphanages. This site, run by a Russian adoption agency that has completed over 70 such adoptions since 1993, provides helpful advice to sorting out all the rules that must still be observed. Prospective parents can read a number of useful online guides to the process here. You'll also find pictures of some of the children recently adopted, and you can arrange to see videotapes of some of the children available for adoption. It should be noted that most of the paperwork must be completed by an adoption agency in the U.S., but contact information is also provided. —(J.P.)

KEY NEWSGROUP alt. adoption URL ▶ http://www.cris.com/~Rusadopt/index.html

Fighting Child Abuse

National Child Rights Alliance Jump 2516

Founded by survivors of child abuse and neglect, the National Child Rights Alliance goes beyond the standard definition of abuse. In addition to the usual definition that covers family situations, it also defines child abuse as the neglect of children and their rights by society at large. This page features articles on the history and philosophy of NCRA, and within them you'll find stories of abuse, information on recovery, and ways to help protect the rights of all children. —(L.S.)

KEY NEWSGROUP **alt.sexual.abuse.recovery**
URL ▶ http://www.ai.mit.edu/people/ellens/NCRA/ncra.html

Parents' Guide to Child Sexual Abuse

Child Sexual Abuse Jump **2562** 

Child sexual abuse can take many forms, and many children are unable to directly communicate that they have been abused. This guide from the Sexual Assault Crisis Center of Knoxville, Tennessee, starts with a basic introduction to child sexual abuse issues, with an emphasis on the signs to look for if you think you know a child who is being abused. There's also guidance on how to understand the child's feelings, as well as a list of things you should—and should not—do once you suspect, or have evidence of, abuse. —(L.S.)

KEY NEWSGROUP **alt.sexual.abuse.recovery**
URL ▶ http://www.cs.utk.edu/~bartley/sacc/childAbuse.html

Netscape: Bouncing Back

Back Forward Home Reload Images Open Print Find Stop

Location: http://none.coolware.com/health/good_med/BouncingBack.html

What's New? What's Cool? Handbook Net Search Net Directory Newsgroups

BOUNCING BACK

A Woman Discovers Holistic Medicine and Wins her Battle against Cancer

By Kristina G. Dykes

Tina Pacheco was 28, happily married, and just recuperating from the birth of her second child when she noticed a lump on the front of her neck.

"I didn't know what it was so I immediately made an appointment with my doctor to find out," She says. "At first the doctors suspected a problem with my thyroid as I was feeling run down, losing weight, and had a lump located in that area. Personally, I thought that the fatigue was just a side effect from having another child to take care of. I never really thought it would be anything serious."

After numerous tests, Tina's doctors convinced her to have a biopsy performed on the inflamed area. The biopsy results concluded that she did not have a thyroid problem. Instead, she was told she had Hodgkin's disease. "Hodgkin's disease? Isn't that an old person's disease?" she thought.

Hodgkin's disease is usually a chronic, progressive, sometimes fatal disease of unknown origin. It is marked by inflammatory enlargement of the lymph nodes, spleen, and often the liver and kidneys. "It is a fibrosis cancer that attacks target groups-kids in their early teens and adults in their late twenties and fifties," Tina explains. Although she had a grandmother and grandfather die of cancer, she didn't think it could happen to her. "Especially," she says, "when everything was going so well in my life."

Immediately after she was told she had Hodgkin's, Tina wanted to find out more about the disease and what she, personally, could do about it. "I became somewhat of an information sponge. I didn't want to procrastinate; I wanted to devise some sort of game plan as soon as possible," she says. "I went to libraries, bookstores, and health food stores. In addition to finding cancer books, I also got books on holistic medicine, vitamin supplements, and nutrition."

▲ *Shared experiences, from* **Good Medicine Magazine** *at* Jump **2522**.

Alcoholics Anonymous: Electronic Support

Information About AA/AA Related Literature Jump **7135** 

Phil W. has assembled a great amount of literature, links, and contacts for anyone wanting to know more about Alcoholics Anonymous, or for those who would like online support. He publishes personal articles that are sometimes sad, sometimes humorous, sometimes informational, but always compelling. Phil has also entered the text of a number of AA-related books and pamphlets. Conferences and events are detailed. As well, a worldwide list of contact numbers are given. Need to talk to someone online? Phil also discusses online meetings and pertinent IRC channels on the Net. —(E.v.B.)

KEY NEWSGROUP **alt.recovery** URL ▶ http://www.moscow.com/Resources/SelfHelp/AA/

Twelve-Step Resources

The Recovery Home Page Jump **2339** 

This page brings together links to Internet resources for the various 12-step programs for recovery from addictions, as well as programs for families and friends of people in recovery. There's also an excellent, and growing, archive of recovery literature covering the programs in general and their specific steps. Visit often, as the links and content both are increasing and improving. —(L.S.)

KEY NEWSGROUP **alt.support** URL ▶ http://www.shore.net/~tcfraser/recovery.html

Divorce 101

Legal Net—Family Law Jump **2513** 

Mark Ressa, a California attorney, has written a basic introduction to the legal steps involved in a divorce. It's not a detailed explanation, but it covers every step of the process, from the original petition for divorce, through discovery, disclosure, negotiated settlements, and trial. For anyone contemplating a dissolution of marriage, this is a good site to visit before contacting a lawyer. It will help you understand the process and will help you decide what questions you'll need to ask an attorney so that you can better understand the specifics as they relate to your case. —(L.S.)

KEY NEWSGROUP **alt.support.divorce** URL ▶ http://www.legal.net/family.htm

the Divorce Page

Divorce: Support at the End of Relationships

The Divorce Page
Jump 2764

CONTENT

Talk to someone who's been through a divorce, and they'll probably say it was the most traumatic experience of their life. It's painful, ugly, unfair to both spouses, and even more so to the children, if any are involved. Dean Hughson has been through it, and one way he has coped is with this page of articles and links to provide support for others going through it, too. It doesn't take sides; virtually all of the material is applicable to either party, except, of course, for the separate listings of resources for men and women. There's much here for dealing with the details of the process, but it's geared more to recovering from the experience and moving on, and the advice and suggestions in this area can be priceless, if they're followed. —(L.S.)

KEY NEWSGROUP **alt.support.divorce** URL▶ http://www.primenet.com/~dean/

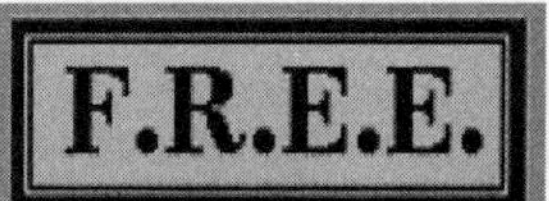

Support for Divorced Fathers

Fathers' Rights and Equality Exchange Jump 2514

There are numerous groups to support single mothers, but very few to support single fathers. This site, maintained by one of those few, Father's Rights and Equality Exchange (FREE), offers articles, referrals, and other pointers for fathers looking for assistance in parenting, child support, and related issues. There's an excellent set of articles on child support and false allegations of domestic violence, and a link to an FTP site with more articles on these and other topics covering various men's rights issues. There's also advice on how to write your elected officials, join FREE, and otherwise take an active role in working toward more equitable treatment of fathers. —(L.S.)

KEY NEWSGROUP **bit.listserv.free-l** URL▶ http://www.vix.com/free/index.html

Child Support and Custody Issues

Single Dad's Index Jump 2515

This should be the primary bookmark for men involved in child custody and divorce issues, both for reference and to stay on top of news and events. Part of David R. Throop's Mens' Issues Pages, it's one of the most extensive single-topic collections of articles of any kind. You'll find general articles covering child-support issues, plus news about government activities and support group initiatives. There's an informative section covering the economics of child support, with statistics and interpretations of that data from the men's perspective. A similarly extensive and helpful group of articles covers visitation and divorce-settlement topics. —(L.S.)

KEY NEWSGROUP **alt.dads-rights** URL▶ http://www.vix.com/men/single-dad.html

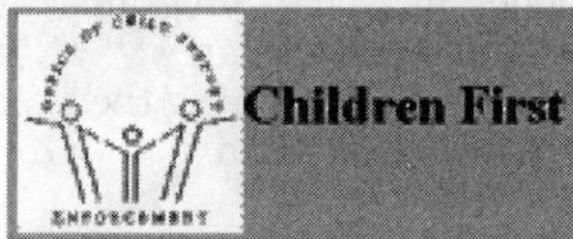

Help with Child-Support Problems

Child Support Home Page Jump 2561

The home of the Office of Child Support Enforcement of the Department of Health and Human Services, this page will help you keep current with changes in child-support laws while linking you to information to help you deal with deadbeat dads and moms. The listings of state enforcement offices is very helpful, with information on enforcement policies and procedures, as well as contact information. There also are several reports online, the best of which describes the various methods of identifying assets and collecting payments. —(L.S.)

KEY NEWSGROUP **alt.child-support** URL▶ http://www.acf.dhhs.gov/ACFPrograms/CSE/ocsehome.html

The Right to Smoke . . .

Smoker's Rights and Tobacco Issues Page Jump 5921

To everything there is a season, and to every issue there is a countervailing opinion. And there aren't many issues as divisive today as the rights of non-smokers versus the right of smokers. This site presents the opinions of those who choose to smoke, a voice that is not nearly as vocal as their counterparts. Although the page is still in its early stages, it will soon have much more information on subjects as diverse as state laws regarding smoking, editorials on the right to choose, feature articles, and links to many other smoker's rights pages. —(J.P.)

URL▶ http://www.lava.net/~pontes/smoke/smokenf.html

Help to Stop Smoking

Smoking Cessation: Nicotine Anonymous Jump 2623

A 12-step group offering support and help for people who want to quit smoking, Nicotine Anonymous offers this Web page to help people start down the road to empty ashtrays. There's an explanation of how the group's program works, a history of the organization, and contact information. Unfortunately, there's no interactive assistance here, but it is one of the more successful organizations available to help those who want to quit, and membership is free. —(L.S.)

KEY NEWSGROUP **alt.support.smoking-stop**

URL▶ http://www.slip.net/~billh/nicahome.html

▲ *Smoker lights up, from* **Ad Age - It's All About Marketing** *at* Jump **7311**

Support to Stop Smoking

Alt.Support.Stop Smoking Home Page Jump 2694

This is one of the best places on the Internet for anyone who wants to stop smoking, as well as for people who want to stay stopped. There are helpful FAQs and a link directly to the newsgroup, as well as an archive of the best articles from the **alt.support.stop-smoking** newsgroup. Learn how to change your thinking about cigarettes, how to deal with the many causes of relapses, and find out how others have found healthful ways to channel their obsession for smoking. —(L.S.)

KEY NEWSGROUP **alt.support.stop-smoking** URL▶ http://www.swen.uwaterloo.ca/~bpekilis/ASSS/asss.html

Up in Smoke, Down to Business

The QuitNet Jump 8527

Smokers and non-smokers rarely agree on tobacco topics. But anyone who wants to quit, learn about the subject, or join the fight against tobacco companies will agree on this Web site. The news section includes "Highlights"—anti-smoking news articles—and "Lowlifes," where you can read about recent developments by the "enemy." Quitting Tools features interactive forms to determine how addicted you are, and reasons why you smoke. It also provides quitting advice and a calendar for quitting. You can find a searchable form listing other smoking (actually, anti-smoking) links, too. Surfing this web site could probably qualify as an anti-smoking technique too—you're always using your hands to click! —(R.B.)

KEY NEWSGROUP **alt.support.stop-smoking** URL▶ http://www.quitnet.org/

HIV Resource Index

The World Wide Web Virtual Library—AIDS (and Related Topics) Jump 2365

This page will link you to Internet resources on all aspects of HIV, AIDS, and related topics, be they social, political, or medical. The best way to start is to take advantage of the quick access to the sci.med.aids FAQs available here. For more detailed information, you can then link to the various databases or investigate the BBS systems and document archives listed here. Not all the links are described in as much detail as they could be, but this remains the best index of these resources available on the Web. —(L.S.)

KEY NEWSGROUP **sci.med.aids** URL▶ http://www.actwin.com/aids/vl.html

A New Look at AIDS

Reappraising AIDS Jump 7139 

The Group for the Scientific Reappraisal of the HIV/AIDS Hypothesis has created this online newsletter to disseminate information on new research that often runs counter to established medical opinion on the connection between HIV and AIDS. Past issues are archived here, as well as links to other AIDS resources on the Net, and a roundup of recent news on the disease are also provided. —(E.v.B.)

KEY NEWSGROUP **sci.med.aids** URL▶ http://aspin.asu.edu:80/~jvagner/aids/

Allergy Resources Page

Welcome to the Online Allergy Center Jump 2035 

Allergies can be difficult to treat, and, according to Dr. Russell Roby, the patient often needs to self-treat to control symptoms. So he created these pages to provide background information and help for allergy sufferers. You can browse and learn how to treat the more aggravating symptoms, get information on food allergies, and read the latest news on allergies and their treatment. Every month, new articles and features are added, so if your watery eyes don't keep you from reading the screen, it's a good idea to check back regularly! —(L.S.)

KEY NEWSGROUP **sci.med** URL▶ http://www.sig.net/~allergy/welcome.html

Information Center for Seniors

Senior Site Jump 6514 

Whether you're a senior, or you're an adult son or daughter who's taking care of your elderly parents or grandparents, you'll find Senior Site to be a rich information resource. There's information here on senior medical issues, health and exercise, and numerous online discussion forums covering topics like financial security for seniors, self-help for specific health conditions, advice from experts, online classifieds, social forums, and scores of other online features. —(L.T.)

KEY NEWSGROUP **clari.news.aging** URL▶ http://seniors-site.com/

Caring for Elderly Parents

One caretaker to another Jump 5799 

Her name is Elaine and for the past five years she has been trying to help those who help others. She has a father who is 90 and legally blind and a mother, who at 87, is frail and fully dependent. She does what she has to do to care for them, but she also understands that there are times when every caregiver wants to give up. Elaine has been there, and as a service to others who are taking care of elderly parents, she posts many helpful and practical bits of advice and support for the daily home care of seniors with medical problems. Her articles are full of the kind of practical advice that can only come from personal experience, and Elaine also generously offers her e-mail address so you can share your concerns and comments on this topic. —(J.P.)

URL▶ http://pw2.netcom.com/~lehdoll/caretaker1.html

Help for Care of Aging Parents

ElderCare Help Page Jump 6542 

If you're caring for an aging parent, you'll appreciate this fine health care information resource, created by Laura Beller. With subjects covering timely issues like Social Security, Medicare/Medicaid, home health agencies, nursing homes, plus information on elder care service providers around the U.S., Laura's page can help you deal with this emotionally traumatic, and sometimes perplexing, health care issue. Access Laura's "Ask the ElderCare Lady" section, a weekly online question-and-answer column, addressing questions like "does a reverse mortgage make sense for a retired couple?," or join others in this site's online discussion forums. —(L.T.)

KEY NEWSGROUP **clari.news.aging** URL▶ http://www.mindspring.com/~eldrcare/elderweb.htm

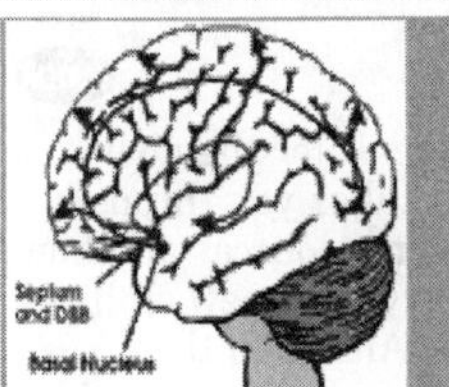

Alzheimer's Research Resources

Alzheimer Web Home Page Jump 7136 

David Small has primarily designed this page as a resource for researchers in the field of Alzheimers, and secondarily for those wanting to know more about the disease. Answers to frequently asked questions about the disease are posted. There are also links to research laboratories, researchers, and healthcare-related employment opportunities. The page is rich in reference materials: some full-text articles, book reviews, a database of important papers, research grant and patent information, and links to related Web resources. Want to network? A conference calendar is also presented. —(E.v.B.)

KEY NEWSGROUP **alt.support** URL▶ http://werple.mira.net.au/~dhs/ad.html

Asthma Answers

alt.support.asthma FAQ: Asthma—General Information Jump 2554 

Keeping in mind that the intent is to provide general information, not medical advice, this is an excellent source for finding common questions and answers about asthma. Maintained by Patricia Wrean and written by her and other contributors to the **alt.support.asthma** newsgroup, it explains the different types of asthma and asthmatic conditions, as well as other lung ailments, such as emphysema, bronchitis and pneumonia. The information on treatment and medications is also quite good, and there's a separate, more comprehensive medications FAQ here to download.—(L.S.)

KEY NEWSGROUP **alt.support.asthma** URL▶ http://www.cco.caltech.edu/~wrean/asthma-gen.html

Prostate Cancer Information, Treatments, & Resources

The Prostate Cancer InfoLink Jump 3712 

Cancer affects all of us in one way or another—whether we ourselves get the disease or know of someone who does. Prostate cancer is one of the most common forms of cancer in males, making this site all the more valuable. The Prostate Cancer InfoLink goes a long way toward providing us with the vital, frequently updated information we need, and perhaps some peace of mind. Here you'll find diagnosis and treatment sections, current news, "Ask Arthur," a forum where you can post questions, and prevention insights. Learn how to contact support groups, share your experiences with others, and link to other related sites. —(N.F.)

KEY NEWSGROUP **alt.support.cancer** URL▶ http://www.comed.com/Prostate/index.html

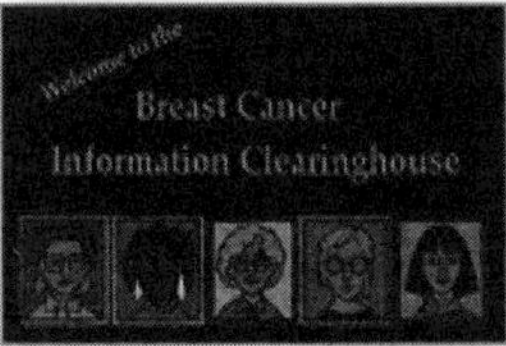

Breast Cancer: Helpful Information & Advice

Breast Cancer Information Jump 0022 

A comprehensive, Web site developed by the New York State Education and Research Network containing a full range of information and support services for breast cancer patients. Features include information on prevention and early detection, counseling, coping with a breast cancer diagnosis, treatment options, unconventional treatments, and more, including links to other important cancer-related Web sites. —(E.G.)

KEY NEWSGROUP **alt.support.cancer** URL▶ http://nysernet.org/bcic/

Cancer Prevention, Treatment, Research and Support

University of Pennsylvania—OncoLink Jump 2348 

This highly-recommended site is a rare exeption to the "you can't be all things to all people" rule, because no matter what your interest or need about cancer—as patient, physician, caregiver, family member or friend—it's here. The list of cancer FAQs—25 and growing—is a good place to start, but if there's a specific area you want to investigate, there are even more detailed resources covering general issues and specific cancer types, their progressions, treatment, research, and support groups. The support sections cover not only pain management, caregivers, and suggestions of how patients, families and friends can cope with the disease, but also information about and links to support groups and the role of spirituality in cancer treatment. —(L.S.)

KEY NEWSGROUP **alt.support.cancer** URL▶ http://cancer.med.upenn.edu/

Cancer Resource Search Tutorial

NCCS Guide to Cancer Resources Jump **2391**

Even with the various jumplists and search engines, finding things on the Internet can be difficult for the novice, so Marshall Kragen wrote this tuturial to help fellow cancer patients and survivors learn how. It takes you through the process of locating and accessing information, introducing you to general and specific cancer resources and how to use them. Each section of the tutorial includes links to the resources discussed, so you can try your new skills as you learn them. Along the way, he provides hints and tips on how to best use a given resource. Although the tutorial is specifically geared toward cancer issues, anyone learning to use Internet resources for almost any subject can also benefit from it. —(L.S.)

KEY NEWSGROUP **alt.support.cancer** URL▸ http://www.access.digex.net/~mkragen/cansearch.html

Cancer Information: National Cancer Institute

NCI Cancer Net Database Main Index Jump **0113**

CONTENT

This invaluable Web site for cancer patients and their families contains a comprehensive array of informational text files covering a wide variety of issues for all forms of cancer. These include cancer fact sheets arranged by type, information on dealing with the effects of various forms of cancer, up-to-date research news, cancer screening, drugs and prevention summaries, and a host of other useful information resources. This site is also fully keyword searchable for fast access to specific cancer information files. —(E.G.)

KEY NEWSGROUP **alt.support.cancer** URL▸ http://imsdd.meb.uni-bonn.de:80/cancernet/cancernet.html

Myeloma Support

International Myeloma Foundation

Jump **2310**

Myeloma is an incurable bone cancer where blood plasma cells grow uncontrollably. The International Myeloma Foundation helps support research toward improved treatment and a cure, and promotes communication among patients for mutual support. In addition to information about the disease, research activities, and related information, you'll find a patient-to-patient directory to foster communication, an online newsletter that features patient-contributed articles, and an e-mail hotline to ask questions about myeloma and the foundation. —(L.S.)

KEY NEWSGROUP **alt.support.cancer** URL▸ http://www.comed.com/IMF/imf.html

Cancer Info from the Patient's Perspective

CancerGuide: Steve Dunn's Cancer Information Page Jump **2364**

This page differs from the Web's other resources for cancer patients in that it is maintained by a cancer patient, Steve Dunn, and concentrates on how patients can do their own research into their disease and evaluate available treatments. What's more, there is a good deal of original material here that you won't find elsewhere, including Steve's essays on cancer fundamentals, alternative therapies and clinical trials of experimental treatments, and a tutorial on how to use the many online resources available. Overall, the information is well organized and easy to get to, especially with the Tour Guide that gets you quickly to your areas of interest. —(L.S.)

KEY NEWSGROUP **alt.support.cancer** URL▸ http://bcn.boulder.co.us/health/cancer/canguide.html

Mega Cancer Information Archive

The Medical Information Archives

Jump **8026**

Unfortunately, there's no doubt that cancer, in many, many different forms, is extremely prevalent today. Few families have not been touched by it. As well, the state of many health care systems makes it imperative that patients inform themselves about treatments and options. Medinfo has mounted just such a resource. It is the central access location for all the online cancer discussion list archives available on the Internet. For example, the entire contents of CancerNet are now integrated into the cancer-related lists, as well as the contents of the Cancer-L List. You can search the various archives, and post messages directly to the appropriate newsgroup. —(E.v.B.)

KEY NEWSGROUP **alt.support.cancer** URL▸ http://www.medinfo.org/

Fighting Cancer with Nutrition

American Institute for Cancer Research Online

Jump 8515

"You are what you eat." Now, stop and think: Do you really want to be a greasy hamburger? We didn't think so. The best part of this site is what's available for free. A free newsletter on the latest news on diet and cancer. Free recipes with cancer-fighting ingredients. And even a free callback service to answer specific questions by a registered dietician. All in all, an excellent place for information that's vital to everyone interested in a healthy lifestyle. This site is sponsored by the American Institute for Cancer Research, which is a clearinghouse for everything related to diet and cancer. They support medical research, publish newsletters, and promote healthy eating habits. Best of all, they're a great resource for anyone with an interest in this topic—professionals and consumers alike. —(R.B.)

URL ▸ http://www.capcon.net/aicr/

Fight and Survive Cancer

Can.Survive - Amanda's Home Page Jump 6711

Amanda Gee, cancer survivor and creator of this vast links site to a vast library of cancer information, presents a touching resource for those who are fighting cancer, and their families. From Amanda's page, patients and family members seeking an online community experience can link over to OncoChat, an Net-based, real-time discussion and support group. Patients can also discover how to take part in clinical trials or gain insight into the history of chemotherapy, including its methods of treatment and psychological and physical side effects. This site has links to many excellent and informative cancer information resources—from basic layman's information to in-depth medical resources for doctors. Amanda's site also features inspirational stories from strong-willed patients who are waging their daily battles with cancer. —(L.T.)

KEY NEWSGROUP alt.support.cancer URL ▸ http://www.avonlink.co.uk/amanda/

DIABETES MONITOR™

Diabetes Self-Help

The Diabetes Monitor Jump 8543

Here's a great example of how a locally-produced site can outdo the big national Web sites. The Diabetes Monitor is a bright and interesting site which should be on every diabetic's bookmark list. Here you'll find great educational material on diabetes, including diet and medications. Complications, coping, self-monitoring, and research are all covered. There's a companion site called Diabetes on the Web, which contains lots of links to diabetes-related Web sites. Because this site is based in Kansas City, there is definitely a local flavor to some of the postings. Even so, the depth and breadth of the information that's presented blows away any national site you might find. —(R.B.)

URL ▸ http://www.castleweb.com/~monitor/with.htm

Essential Information on Diabetes

Patient Information Documents on Diabetes

Jump 2505

You'll find everything you'll need to understand diabetes, its treatment and research into a cure at this site by the National Institute of Diabetes and Digestive and Kidney Disease of the National Institutes of Health. Written specifically for patients, these documents do a good job of avoiding the medical mumbo-jumbo that confuses more than enlightens. But, when confusion can't be avoided, there's also a diabetes dictionary. You shouldn't need it, though. The sections explaining insulin- and non-insulin-dependent diabetes are clearly written, describing the diseases and what causes them, how they affect the body, and how to live with those effects. There's also coverage of diabetic eye disease, professional and voluntary organizations, and statistical data about the disease and its sufferers. —(L.S.)

KEY NEWSGROUP misc.health.diabetes URL ▸ http://www.niddk.nih.gov/DiabetesDocs.html

Diabetes and Kids

children with DIABETES (TM)

Jump 7389

Children with DIABETES, the online magazine for kids who have insulin-dependent diabetes, and their families, is the Web's best repository for juvenile diabetes-related information and support. Kids can explore the children's corner, which explains how parents feel about the disease, how to cope with school, holidays, summer camp and, of course, the daily reality of blood tests and shots. Medical information, contact addresses for medical and research experts, food tips, a bulletin board where diabetic kids can exchange notes, and many other great resources can be found. Links to other diabetes-related sites are also provided. —(E.v.B.)

KEY NEWSGROUP misc.health.diabetes **URL▶** http://www.castleweb.com/diabetes/index.html

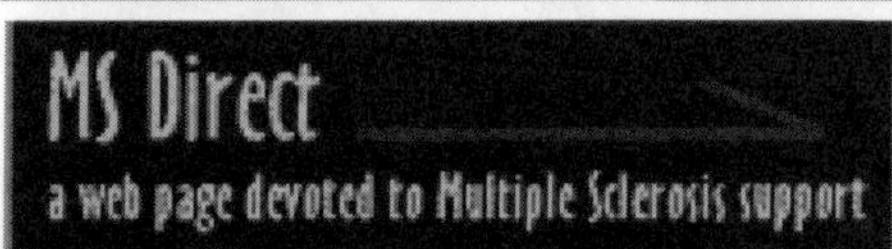

Multiple Sclerosis Support Source

MS Direct **Jump 2509**

This is a growing list of links to Internet information and support resources for persons with multiple sclerosis. Dean Sporleder, whose wife is affected by MS, takes great care in his links descriptions, so you will know exactly what is at the other end, be it a major resource or a single menu item. They're conversational, too, not the cold, dry descriptions you find on most Web links pages. The links are updated frequently, so this is a good place to check regularly to find new resources easily. If you have a resource you think should be added, e-mail the information to Dean. —(L.S.)

KEY NEWSGROUP alt.support.mult-sclerosis **URL▶** http://www.aquila.com/dean.sporleder/ms_home/

Information for the Chronically Ill

ChronicIllnet Home **Jump 7290**

ChronicIllnet provides information on chronic illnesses including AIDS, cancer, Persian Gulf War Syndrome, autoimmune disease, Chronic Fatigue Syndrome, heart disease, and neurological diseases. The site is designed for researchers, patients, laypeople, and physicians. The latest research and treatments are presented, a discussion forum is available where researchers and others can share discoveries, conferences are announced, and other resources are presented. This rich site is sponsored by the California company, Calypte Biomedical Corporation. —(E.v.B.)

KEY NEWSGROUP alt.support **URL▶** http://www.calypte.com/

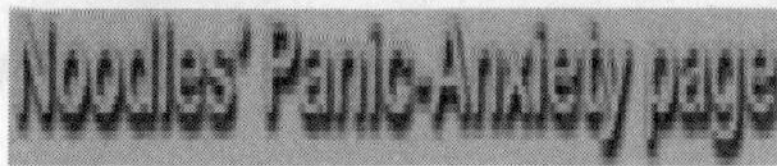

Help for Sufferers of Anxiety & Panic Disorders

PANIC-ANXIETY

Jump 7383

If you've ever suffered from an anxiety-related disorder, you'll certainly be happy to find these pages. They are suffused with the good news that these types of disorders are among the most treatable of all psychological conditions. You will find information on debilitating anxiety, panic attacks, phobias, obsessive thoughts, and/or depression. As well, read about different medications, support-group contacts, nonmedical treatments such as relaxation techniques, good nutrition, coping skills, and exercise. You can also access related resources, read "tales from the frontlines," and participate in an interactive bulletin board with fellow sufferers. —(E.v.B.)

KEY NEWSGROUP alt.support.anxiety-panic **URL▶** http://frank.mtsu.edu/~sward/anxiety/abw.html

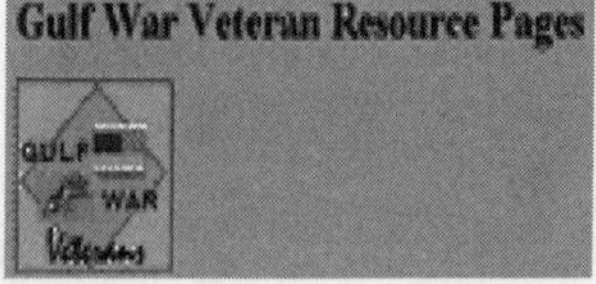

Gulf War Syndrome Support Site

Gulf War Veterans Resource Pages **Jump 2161**

More than 50,000 veterans of the Persian Gulf War suffer a variety of ailments, the cause of which cannot be explained. It's called Gulf War Syndrome, and many feel it is the result of Iraq's use of chemical weapons. Grant Szabo, assisted by a handful of other volunteers (including this book's own top reviewer, Lee Stral), assembles support and information resources for Gulf War vets and others interested in helping those who suffer the syndrome. Here you'll find a description of the problems, what's being done (and what's not being done), news, links to support organizations and other information. It's a massive set of pages, but it's very well organized and easy to navigate, so you can browse or find specific information with equal ease. If you just want to find what's new, the updates section tracks the ongoing additions for quick access. —(L.S.)

KEY NEWSGROUP **soc.veterans** URL▶ http://www.ides.com/Gulf_War/gulf.html

Giving the Gift of Life

TransWeb—Organ Transplantation and Donation  Jump 2378 CONTENT

Transplants have saved thousands of lives, given sight to the sightless, and, in general, hope to the hopeless. It seems new advances are made every day, in surgical techniques, anti-rejection drugs, and the types of transplants that can be successful. Based at the University of Michigan Medical Center, TransWeb is an international resource for patients, donors, families, physicians, and others involved in transplantation. There are excellent question-and-answer sections, news, information on support and service groups, essays on patient and family experiences with transplantation and donation, political and legislative updates, and links to related sites. Virtually anyone can be a donor, and few of us can say we couldn't be a recipient. If for no other reason than "just in case," visit this site.—(L.S.)

KEY NEWSGROUP **bit.listserv.transplant** URL▶ http://www.med.umich.edu/trans/transweb/twhome.html

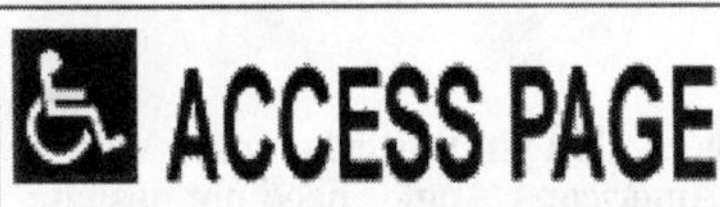

Computer Access for People with Disabilities

NCSA Mosaic Access Page Jump 2485 

This is a key resource for learning about Internet access for people with disabilities, as well as for those who work with them. Part of the Mosaic Access Project, the short-term goal of this page is to help identify the barriers which prevent or limit Internet access by those with disabilities, with the long-term objective of developing methods to overcome those barriers. The content begins with a general overview of the issues of computing, access and disabilities, and goes on to review the situation as it relates to a specific disability, computing platform and Internet resource. Anyone who believes that the Internet should be available to everyone but hasn't considered the unique difficulties of people with disabilities, can gain a new perspective by browsing these pages. —(L.S.)

KEY NEWSGROUP **misc.handicap** URL▶ http://bucky.aa.uic.edu/

Audio Descriptions for the Blind

Audio Description Jump 3663 

Audio Description is a free narration service that attempts to convey the visual images of theater, media, and museum exhibitions, which the sighted person takes for granted, for people who are blind or have impaired vision. It's a wonderful use of technology that helps bring an additional dimension to experiences that would otherwise be inaccessible to those who are visually impaired. Sponsored by the National Endowment for the Arts, this site is presently under construction, but seeks to provide links to other Internet-based resources for the disabled, as well as to a range of published material and conference notes on this important subject. Interesting sample audio description files are also available for downloading. —(C.P.)

URL▶ http://www.tmn.com/Artswire/www/ad/home.html

Help Find the Missing Children

National Center for Missing and Exploited Children Search Jump 8006 

The National Center for Missing and Exploited Children provides a service which unfortunately, has become more necessary in today's world. The Center has mounted an extensive database of missing children information that can be searched by name, city, state, age, and other criteria. They have also included multiple contact numbers if you think you've seen a missing child. Links are also provided to the Children At Risk Web page. —(E.v.B.)

KEY NEWSGROUP **alt.missing-kids** URL▶ http://www.missingkids.org/search.html

Lost & Missing Children National Database

GEMS - Missing Kids Jump 4004 

The Global Electronic Marketing Service brings this site to you as a public service to help find lost or missing children. In conjunction with the National Center for Missing and Exploited Children, this site gives you access to its missing children database, which includes pertinent information, as well as online photos. It also offers links to related information and tips to prevent your child from being abducted. An excellent demonstration of the public service use of the Net. —(R.B.)

KEY NEWSGROUP alt.missing-kids URL▶ http://www.gems.com/kids/index.html

Cultural News & Pages

South Africa: All about the African National Congress

African National Congress Home Page Jump 3581 

The ANC is the majority party in the Government of National Unity. It came to power after South Africa's first democratic elections in April 1994. This Web server offers access to the ANC Gopher, as well as e-mail services to each of the ANC's Members of Parliament. Other interesting things on this server are links to all other servers in South Africa, and an organized listing of Internet resources arranged by category. —(C.P.)

KEY NEWSGROUP soc.culture.africa URL▶ http://www.anc.org.za/

Es Muy Caliente

Entretengaze 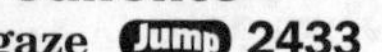 

Hot music, hot movies, and hotheads combine in this cyberspace Web station created by and for Hispanic Americans. Anglos need not despair, though, since the site is in English, and the entertainment crosses cultural boundaries. You can download samples of the latest Latino music, download and upload Quicktime video clips, lounge or party in the virtual bar, and exchange opinions with angry, and not so angry, cyberpunks. And don't miss the interactive, multimedia soap opera, chronicling the adventures of three Latino women in and around Cyberland. —(L.S.)

KEY NEWSGROUP rec.arts.misc URL▶ http://bluepearl.com/bluepearl/entertainment/entertainment.html

Pueblo Indian Culture

Indian Pueblo Cultural Center Jump 7018 

If you're thinking of visiting the American Southwest, why not bone up on the area's native-American culture? To learn more about the 19 Pueblo communities, read the offerings presented by the Indian Pueblo Cultural Center. For example, read about the Zuni's love of color and their tradition of fine crafted jewelry. —(E.v.B.)

KEY NEWSGROUP alt.native URL▶ http://hanksville.phast.umass.edu/defs/independent/PCC/PCC.html

World Wide Aboriginal Server

NativeWeb Jump 7060 

Language, literature, and cultural information on Aboriginal groups from the Latin American Maya to the Scandinavian Sami to the Oklahoma Cherokee are presented, accompanied by illustrations, at this site. As well, information and links to other Native organizations, publications, and reference bibliographies are also offered. —(E.v.B.)

KEY NEWSGROUP soc.culture.native URL▶ http://ukanaix.cc.ukans.edu/~marc/native_text.html

Rhythmic Gumbo Culture

Cajun/Zydeco in Baltimore & Washington Areas Jump 7098 

Get that down-home feeling when you explore these hot Louisiana pages. Despite the title, Cajun resources are given for most of the United States—where to go to listen and dance to this good-feeling music, schedules of Cajun music groups, plus lots of Louisiana links. An added benefit is the large file of instructions on how to dance the Cajun Jitterbug—hip turns, the sweetheart slide, and more. Let the bon temps roll! —(E.v.B.)

KEY NEWSGROUP alt.culture.cajun URL▶ http://www.bme.jhu.edu/~jrice/cz.html

Religion & Philosophy

Religious Resources

Finding God in Cyberspace Jump 2166

Despite the lightness of this Web site's title, this is a list of links to scholarly resources covering religion, including Christianity, Judaism, Islam, and Buddhism. John L. Gresham Jr., director of the Sterling (Kansas) College library, has created an impressive document, with links to online journals, discussion groups, and FTP sites, and additional information on how to use them. This is a selective list, but it is nonetheless quite comprehensive, espec-ially for the serious student of theology.—(L.S.)

KEY NEWSGROUP talk.religion.misc URL▶ http://www.dur.ac.uk/~dth3maf/gresham.html

Catholicism Resources

Religious Resources on the Net Jump 2557

While there are links to other religions here, virtually all the links and on-site content relate to Catholicism. Compiled by James A.A. Tucker, there are links to prayers, the Catholic archives at American University, a collection of papal letters listed according to the pope, spiritual quotations, the Dominican and Franciscan home pages, and a list of patron saints. While everything about Catholicism may not be featured here, this is an attractive and well-organized page, with links that will get you to everything. —(L.S.)

KEY NEWSGROUP bit.listserv.catholic URL▶ http://convex.cc.uky.edu/~jatuck00/Religion/Religion.html

Monks Sing

Gregorian Chant Home Page Jump 5085

CONTENT

This page was designed to support research on all traditions of medieval Christian liturgical chant. It includes a Gregorian Chant tutorial, and links to scholarly projects in chant research, Biblical studies, liturgical studies, medieval studies, and more. Unfortunately, however, audio clips are not currently available because of copyright protection issues. —(S.B.)

URL▶ http://www.music.princeton.edu:80/chant_html/

The Promise Keepers Movement

Promise Keepers Jump 5927

Promise Keepers is a multi-denominational religious movement, and a burgeoning male-centered cultural trend in itself, dedicated to "uniting men through vital relationship to become godly influences in their world." Begun in 1990, Promise Keepers believe that Christian growth begins by making seven promises: for example, "A Promise Keeper is committed to honoring Jesus Christ through worship, prayer, and obedience to His Word, through the power of the Holy Spirit." This is the organization's official site, and you can read more about the Promise Keepers movement, surf to other Promise Keepers home pages, tap schedules of events, and link to more information on this rapidly-growing movement. —(J.P.)

URL▶ http://www.promisekeepers.org/index.htm

Gospel Web Center

Gospel Communications Network Jump 7278

Read the Word here! Gospel Communications Network (GCN) has gathered a large number of online Christian resources on its extensive Web pages. You can read about youth ministries, and check out the offerings of Gospel Film Inc. a company that distributes Bible information via film and software packages. You can also read a Bible quote of the day, and use the links provided to surf to other Christian sites on the Web. —(E.v.B.)

KEY NEWSGROUP soc.religion.christian URL▶ http://www.gospelcom.net/

Christians Online

First Church of Cyberspace Jump 7382

In what surely must be another Web "first," the First Church of Cyberspace brings Christianity online through the sponsorship of the Central Presbyterian Church of Montclair, New Jersey. It uses the latest Internet software and techniques to bring its message to the Net. For example, it uses RealAudio, Netscape's latest animation techniques and creative graphics to enhance its music, sermons, and its multimedia Bible. Virtual parishioners can read movie reviews, browse in inspirational art galleries, and participate in online, real-time church services.—(E.v.B.)

KEY NEWSGROUP **soc.religion.christian** URL http://www.execpc.com/~chender/

Judaic Hotlist

Judaism and Jewish Resources Jump 2576

Judaism is as much a culture as a religion, and this page will link you to the many Internet resources covering both aspects of Jewish life. Andrew Tannenbaum maintains this rich list of links that covers everything from Jewish studies to Yiddish culture to communities, organized by resource type and subject. Each link is carefully annotated to help guide you through the dozens of resources available, and the What's New section makes it easy to keep track of resources as they become available. A nice touch is this site's virtual "scavanger hunt." There are no prizes, but it's an entertaining way to familiarize yourself with Judaism and the resources available on the Internet. —(L.S.)

KEY NEWSGROUP **soc.culture.jewish** URL http://shamash.nysernet.org/trb/judaism.html

The Secret of the Scrolls

Dead Sea - Introduction Jump 2724

The Dead Sea Scrolls were discovered a half-century ago, but they have been shrouded in secrecy and only recently have parts of them become available to the public. The subject of intense scholarly debate, they are expected to provide a great deal of insight into Jewish life two millennia ago, as well as the development of early Christianity. This online exhibition includes fragments from the Scrolls, as well as background information on them from the Library of Congress. It tells the story of the discovery of the Scrolls, uses archaeological discoveries to discuss life in the region during the time they were written, and discusses the challenges facing scholars as they try to reconstruct the documents from the thousands of fragments they have found. You can either view the entire exhibit, going through each section as it is presented at the Library of Congress, or use the hyperlinked outline to jump to areas of specific interest. —(L.S.)

KEY NEWSGROUP **sci.archaeology** URL http://sunsite.unc.edu/expo/deadsea.scrolls.exhibit/intro.html

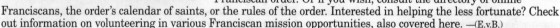

Franciscans around the World

Franciscan Files Jump 7065

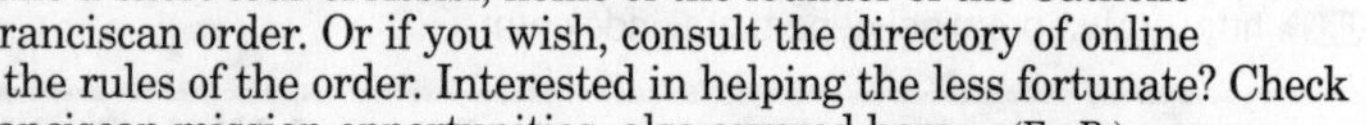

Take a short tour of Assisi, home of the founder of the Catholic Franciscan order. Or if you wish, consult the directory of online Franciscans, the order's calendar of saints, or the rules of the order. Interested in helping the less fortunate? Check out information on volunteering in various Franciscan mission opportunities, also covered here. —(E.v.B.)

KEY NEWSGROUP **bit.listserv.catholic** URL http://listserv.american.edu/catholic/franciscan

Egyptian Christians

The Christian Coptic Orthodox Church of Egypt

Jump 7062

The Coptic Church, established in 200 A.D., has made many contributions to Christianity—many of which are detailed here. In addition to a comprehensive

history lesson, you can also access religious images, prayers, hymns, and daily lessons, as well as read up on your favorite saint, the history of monasticism, and other church history. —(E.v.B.)

KEY NEWSGROUP **bit.listserv.catholic** URL▶ http://cs-www.bu.edu/faculty/best/pub/cn/Home.html

About Islam & Muslims

Islamic Texts and Resources MetaPage
Jump **2578**

This page contains resources, articles and texts covering Islamic thought and Muslim culture and tradition, as well as the basic tenets of the religion itself. Introductory material includes the soc.religion.islam FAQ and online copies of pamphlets by The Institute of Islamic Information and Education. Next, you can link to explanations and indices of the *Qur'an*, Islam's holy book, articles on Islamic thought, and a page of resources covering Islamic language, art, and culture. —(L.S.)

KEY NEWSGROUP **soc.religion.islam** URL▶ http://wings.buffalo.edu/student-life/sa/muslim/isl/isl.html

Buddhists Connected

Buddhist Web Jump **7069**

This site electronically connects the 31 major Buddhist temples in Korea. In addition, FTP and Gopher sites are listed, online Buddhist studies centers around the world, such as the Jeonggak-won, are linked, and pertinent newsgroups are compiled. —(E.v.B.)

KEY NEWSGROUP **soc.religion.eastern** URL▶ http://www.dongguk.ac.kr/DGU/College/Kyongju/Budcul/Budweb/

Web Time Out

INTERLUDE Jump **7419**

The folks at Interlude want "to bring to your Internet experience a few moments of peace, composure, and mental expansion." So enter this site ready to take some time out, and perhaps do some meditating. Then, why not surf to other peaceful meditation sites, as well as use the links to sites representing many religions of the world and other spiritual paths. As well, you can access health and wellness sites and online publications related to spiritual quests. —(E.v.B.)

KEY NEWSGROUP **alt.meditation** URL▶ http://www.teleport.com/~interlud/

The Philosophy of Ayn Rand

Objectivism on the WWW Jump **5925**

Objectivism is a philosophy that was originated by novelist and philosopher Ayn Rand, author of such classics as *Atlas Shrugged* and *The Fountainhead.* The central tenets include the notions that: Reason is man's only means of knowledge, rational self-interest is the objective ethical code, and that laissez-faire capitalism is the objective social system. There is plenty of detailed information on extensive Web links and contents page by Diana Brickell, including essays, letters and other information on Rand, as well as links to other related Net resources. —(J.P.)

URL▶ http://artsci.wustl.edu/~diana/objectivism/

Objectivism Information Center

Objectivism Home Page Jump **0024**

This is a volunteer-developed Web site for readers of Ayn Rand's popular writings and novels, including *Atlas Shrugged* and *The Fountainhead*, which frame her philosophy of objectivism, stressing the importance of rational self-interest and antigovernment laissez-faire capitalism. This well-done site contains a helpful introduction to objectivism, essays, an extensive bibliography of Rand's books and related works, as well as objectivist fiction and poetry. —(E.G.)

KEY NEWSGROUP **alt.philosophy.objectivism** URL▶ http://www.vix.com/pub/objectivism/home.html

Life Views

The Asphalt Philosopher Jump 7333

Roland H. Johnson III, a sociology professor, is a self-styled asphalt philosopher—with insights gained on the road of life. Roland loves to share his thoughts on life, marriage, middle age, teaching, and love, and not necessarily in that order. This site is under construction, but if you enjoy reading another person's take on the big and little questions of life, then by all means, come and meet Roland. —(E.v.B.)

KEY NEWSGROUP **alt.consciousness** URL▶ http://www.myriad.net/ROLAND/

Spiritual Rest Stop

The Haven Jump 2758

Hani readily admits that not much goes on at this site, but that's why he maintains it. Compared with most Web pages, even those that address spiritual issues, it's a soothing, restful stop in cyberspace, although not without useful content and links. Most interesting and challenging is the section on transpersonal psychology, which, as it sounds, is a melding of spirituality with traditional psychology. But you don't need to be challenged if you don't want. Just browse, relax, and explore according to your own spiritual or religious bent. That's really what this site is about. —(L.S.)

KEY NEWSGROUP **talk.religion.misc** URL▶http://sfbox.vt.edu:10021/H/hshabana/index.html

Thoughts on The Human Condition

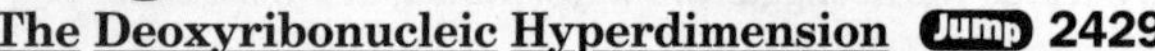

The Deoxyribonucleic Hyperdimension Jump 2429

A curious, deep thinker named Dimitri maintains this site which combines links to essays on philosophy, religion, and politics with the goal of helping people think about their place in the universe, as well as in the world. It defies a direct description, which, in all likelihood, is the point. After all, the human condition itself defies simple description. The idea of this site is to introduce you to what non-mainstream thinkers say about this rather broad topic, and to stimulate your own thinking. There are sections on Alan Watts, the psychologist with strong roots in Eastern philosophy, shamanism, general philosophy, political thought, and even the end of the world (as we know it). Beyond this is a very good and quite extensive list of links to other sites covering politics, philosophy, fringe groups of one sort or another, and links to some really nifty general Web pages. Even if you skip the main section, the links to other related Web sites are worth a bookmark for this page. —(L.S.)

KEY NEWSGROUP **talk.philosophy.misc** URL▶ http://www.intac.com/~dimitri/dh/deoxy.html

Let Your Love Light Shine

° Prelude to Angelnet ° Jump 7377

Lots of peace, love, and harmony swirling around the graphically attractive pages of Anglenet. The flashing title bars are amusing to watch as they develop, and the multimedia elements are equally fun to see. You can read stories about angels, listen to the unearthly song of the dolphin, and read Web zines dedicated to the gentler aspects of life. There are also numerous links to sites on massage, yoga, New Age art galleries, and much, much more. Don't miss a chance to enter the altar and rub the magic lamp. —(E.v.B.)

URL▶ http://alive.mcn.org/angelnet.html/

New Age Thinking

School of Wisdom Home Page Jump 2431

Wisdom is defined here as the "knowledge behind the knowledge" that gives one the ability to live in a chaotic world. The first page of this site offers a practical example, with the link to the site's table of contents virtually hidden at the bottom of a very long page. Just treat it as your first lesson, because this site is worth the effort for its different take on New Age philosophy. There is some very interesting content relating law, politics, and science to New Age thinking, as well as some very thought-provoking and thought-challenging articles—for example, read one of its articles, "The Wheel or Metapolitics, Wisdom and the Internet." —(L.S.)

KEY NEWSGROUP **talk.religion.newage** URL▶ http://www.webcom.com/~metanoic/wisdom/welcome.html

Hobbies, Special Interests, & Travel

There are thousands of sites along the Web with plenty of information, advice, and contacts to suit most any hobby or special interest. The Web is also a vast storehouse of useful, money-saving travel and vacation advice, too.

Collecting, Crafts, Hobbies and Other Special-Interest Infomation on the Web

There's an overwhelming volume of hobby, collectible, and special interest information all over the Web, much of which has been created by talented Web site creators, whose individual obsessions drive them to broadcast their hobby and special interest information on the Web.

If you love to cook, fly kites, fish, hunt, sew, or fly airplanes, or anything else, there are Web sites for these—and many other—hobbies and special interests. Filled with lots of practical advice, these sites reflect the best of the American spirit of ingenuity and self-sufficiency that's very much alive on the Web.

The spirit of community that pervades the Internet is also reflected in its hobby and special interest-related Web sites. In addition to the useful information they contain, authors of these sites, via electronic mail, can also provide you with useful tips and advice on your hobby and special interest, whether you're a total novice or you're already fully involved in the hobby.

Wise And Money-Saving Travel, Vacation, & Dining Advice

Travel topics are also popular on the Web. Notable among these are Web sites featuring traveler's recommendations and other insider's tips to help you save money on air fares, accommodations, car rental, etc., and can provide you with specific advice on places to go and local sites of interest, plus insights on local customs in the foreign countries you plan to visit.

Every day, it seems, someone adds a new travel stop on the Web. Hotel companies. Tourist offices. Travelers themselves.

But to get to the information, cyber-travelers must either know and type in the often-cryptic (and very unforgiving of typos) "hypertext transfer protocol" or http address, or get there through another site that offers a link to it.

The unifying site will be called the United States Travel and Tourism Information Network. A prototype is already up (http:/www.colorado.edu/USTTIN/home.html). By next year, a fuller version will give travelers a single Web site where they'll find detailed information on every state and city in the nation.

Gene Sloan, "New Tourism Web Site to Ease Cyberspace Journey," *USA Today*

Arts

▲ *Sistine ceiling by Michelangelo, showing a portion of the Creation scene from Genesis, from* Index of/Multimedia/Pics/Art/ *at* Jump 0161 ▲ *Museum visitors viewing a painting, from* Santa Barbara Museum of Art/ *at* Jump 5088.

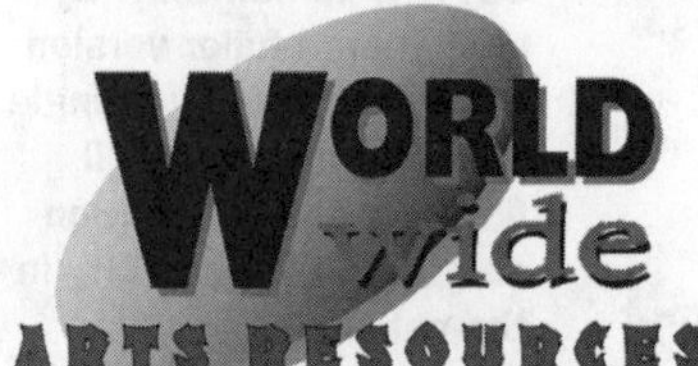

World Wide Arts Resources

World Wide Arts Resources Jump 6516

Art enthusiasts of all types will find World Wide Arts Resources to be a handy links repository to visual arts information on the Web. With over 9,000 resources, all searchable by keyword, you'll be able to access the major and minor art museums around the world, plus their schedules, events, and festivals. Links to sites covering the performing arts, antiques, related art resources and publications are posted here, too. Searching for Web info on a particular artist? Find it here on this site's index. —(L.T.)

KEY NEWSGROUP **rec.arts.fine** URL▶ http://www.concourse.com/wwar/default.html

Links to Online Web Art, Exhibitions & Images

Online Exhibitions, Images, etc. Jump 0041

A great Web jumping-off point for viewing some of the Web's most interesting art and visual images. Australian Jim Croft has put together this nice jump page containing links to the best image collections available on the Web. Examples of Web links contained here include the Vatican art exhibit at the Library of Congress, the Dead Sea Scrolls, Smithsonian art and nature exhibits, and dozens of other Web-based image collections. —(E.G.)

KEY NEWSGROUP **alt.binaries.pictures** URL▶ http://155.187.10.12/fun/exhibits.html

Fine Arts Resources Web Site

The Fine Art Forum WWW Resource Directory Jump 0162

Web jump site by Jane Patterson features links to many events in the arts, individual artist's home pages, commercial galleries on the Web, photograph exhibits, electronic art journals, and much more of interest to artists and art lovers around the world. —(E.G.)

KEY NEWSGROUP **rec.arts.fine** URL▶ http://www.msstate.edu/Fineart_Online/art-resources.html

Dali Exhibit Online

WEBCOAST PAGE TAMPA BAY SALVADOR DALI Jump 7424

Here's an extensive collection of the works of the master of surrealism, Salvador Dali. In all, 159 images from the Salvador Dali Museum Collection in St. Petersburg, Florida, have been scanned in here—ranging from paintings and drawings to watercolors. You can also read a short biography of the artist, learn more about the museum, and surf to other Dali links from this site. —(E.v.B.)

KEY NEWSGROUP **rec.arts.fine** URL▶ http://webcoast.com/Dali/collection.htm

Fulfilling Warhol's Vision

Warhol's Famous for Fifteen Minutes
Jump 2692

File this one under useless but poignant. Just click and you'll link to some previously unknown personal home page, thus helping to fulfill Andy Warhol's prediction that someday everyone will be famous for 15 minutes. The link, of course, is updated every quarter hour, and you can add your page to this list of the soon-to-be-shortly famous. —(L.S.)

KEY NEWSGROUP **alt.culture.www** URL▶ http://www.grapevine.com/warhol/warhol.htm

Andy Warhol Web Museum

The Andy Warhol Museum Home Page
Jump 1523

Andy Warhol, possibly the most influential artist in the latter half of this century, left a legacy of contemporary and pop art, now archived in a downtown Pittsburgh, Pennsylvania, museum that showcases his talent. You can see samples of the 500-work collection on a tour through the seven floors, featuring everything from numerous self-portraits, to Marilyn Monroe and paintings of branded food items, including the infamous deadpan wit of the Campbell's soup can. Each Web page is dedicated to one floor, with maps and archive notes. See how Warhol depicted his life throughout his career, finally culminating in the sixth floor's "success" and the seventh floor's "fame, fortune, and fashion" exhibits. The site also describes other aspects of the museum, such as the well-stocked gift shop, from which you can order online, and membership information. Guaranteed you'll spend more than 15 minutes here! —(H.L.)

URL▶ http://www.usaor.net:80/warhol/

Interactive Art Gallery Finder

Find Arts Jump 5146

On this nicely designed interactive site created by Webmaster Alejandro Eluchans, you can locate artists, commercial designers, and art galleries by entering various search terms. Search for composers, printmakers, sculptors, potters, as well as painters, graphic artists, illustrators, photographers, and filmmakers, among others. You can search by discipline, media, style, subject, name, or location. The search form has nice pop-up menus to make it easy to set the search criteria. Viewers can access artists' home pages, view their artwork, and contact them directly or through their galleries or dealers. Another nice feature is a complete list, organized by country, of artists who have a link to this page. If you are an artist, you can (for a fee) build a Web site here. There's also a revolving exhibit by various artists, from this site, with links to the artists' home pages. —(S.B.)

URL▶ http://www.find-arts.com/

Virtual Studio & Painting Pointers

Welcome to Barbara Safran Studios Jump 3711

Barbara Safran, a professional artist for nearly twenty years, has opened a studio in Cyberspace. Some of her best works are on display here, beautiful paintings that are available as reproductions, which you can also order online. Find out about Barbara's education, exhibits, collections, and philosophies at this site filled with her gorgeous art. Barbara also shares her talents in "The Artist's Corner," where you'll find lessons on techniques such as painting with watercolors. Art on the Net—it's a natural. Spend a day at Barbara's studio from the comfort of your own home. —(N.F.)

URL ▶ http://lydian.csi.nb.ca/safran/

Ansel Adams Web Photo Exhibit

UCI Bookstore Ansel Adams Home Page Jump 0098

A wonderful tribute to the famous Western landscape photographer, this Web site features photographs taken by Ansel Adams from a project commissioned by the University of California in 1963. Exhibition features many Adams photographs of University of California campuses, its natural reserve system, agricultural centers, and field stations. In addition to its beautiful on-screen photos, this site also features informative accompanying text and background material on this project and exhibition. —(E.G.)

URL ▶ http://bookweb.cwis.uci.edu:8042/AdamsHome.html

Le WebLouvre, Paris

Louvre Art Web Site

Web Louvre: Bienvenue Jump 0099

Nicolas Pioch's popular and well-done Web page features paintings, descriptive background text, period music sound files, travelogue, and commentary on art at France's famous Louvre Art Museum in Paris. Nicolas takes great pains to tell you he's not associated with The Louvre (he says he got a nasty letter from their attorneys but he's not deterred), but since these paintings are in the public domain, we'll just write off the Louvre's lawyer's complaints as typical Gallic cultural protectionism! Anyway, Nicolas has done a great job putting this site together—it's very educational too! —(E.G.)

URL ▶ http://sunsite.unc.edu/louvre/

Chesley Bonestell Art Gallery

The Art of Space Exploration

Chesley Bonestell Gallery Jump 1522

Space—still a mysterious place. Yet it was captured at its best, before space exploration actually began, by Chesley Bonestell, one of the most renowned artists of space flight and astronomy. Some say his paintings changed the future of space exploration. If you're unfamiliar with Bonestell's work, first read his illustrated bio. Then go on the tour of Bonestell's paintings. Created by curator Katheryn Humm as an educational resource, the renderings reveal his ability to foresee the future when he first painted them in the 1940s and 1950s. The star series, Mars, Earth, Saturn, and the Moon all appeared in major scientific publications, which led to his collaboration with Arthur C. Clark and other scientific and space flight moviemakers. The combined detailed high-resolution images and text, including Bonestell's accompanying notes, are linked to NASA documents so you can explore topics that interest you the most. —(H.L.)

URL ▶ http://www.secapl.com/bonestell/Top.html

History of Printmaking

prints.html Jump 1535

CONTENT

Australian National University Fine Arts professor Michael Greenhalgh has created an interactive student tutorial on the history of artists' prints and printmaking. With 2,800 digitized images from the first century to the present, from religious art to secular, and from modern art to pop art, this site is for anyone wanting to learn more. The presentations include close-ups of prints you select to show engraving techniques, and you can read the history of and comments about the prints as well. The Web pages are well organized—you can access the artwork by clicking on the artist names, the name of the work, the category, or the genre. You can also link to Greenhalgh's other projects: architectural research, technology—even an essay on the advantages and disadvantages of artists using computers to render their masterpieces. —(H.L.)

URL ▶ http://www.ncsa.uiuc.edu/SDG/Experimental/anu-art-history/prints.html

The Tole & Decorative Artist's Web Site

ToleNet.com Jump 5825

The original tole paintings were pictographs or stone carvings of animals and flowers, the kind you might see on ancient stone walls. In time, the paintings evolved into small works of art that explored religious themes or even the kind of folk art drawings that are now so popular, using a variety of styles and materials. This site is a terrific place to begin if you want to learn the history of this form of painting, or want to actually learn how to create the works of art yourself. In the "Beginner's Guide to Tole Painting," you will learn the supplies to use, as well as a complete history of the various styles, complete with many stunning samples. You can also subscribe to a newsletter that boasts a membership of over 875 painters world-wide, and who also offer advice and encouragement free of charge. —(J.P.)

KEY NEWSGROUP rec.arts.find URL▶ http://www.tolenet.com/

Southwestern Art

Santa Fe Fine Art Jump 1541

CONTENT

Santa Fe, New Mexico, is known for its collections of some of the best southwestern art in the world. You can see the area's finest representatives of today's photographers, painters, sculptors, and printmakers here. An interesting, well-designed, clean site, you'll find about 20 full-page, quick-loading works of each artist, along with media and size descriptions and artist comments about each piece. Find information on purchasing and future shows and how to contact the artists through the Santa Fe Fine Art Association's listings. For more, check out the links to the Southwestern Artist's Web site and other relevant information. —(H.L.)

URL▶ http://www.sffa.com/

Art Treasures

World Art Treasures Jump 7091

Imagine how influential Jacques-Edouard Berger has been. He so dedicated his life to the pursuit of art and beauty and to lecturing and writing on his discoveries that after his untimely death, his friends set up a foundation to honor his memory and continue his work. You will see the results of Berger's lifework by viewing a portion of his collection (over 125,000 slides) and writings that the foundation has brought to the Internet when you explore the World Art Treasures site. Examine the art of Egypt, China, Japan, and many other countries online, and, for a time, touch Berger's spirit. —(E.v.B.)

KEY NEWSGROUP rec.arts.fine URL▶ http://sgwww.epfl.ch/BERGER/

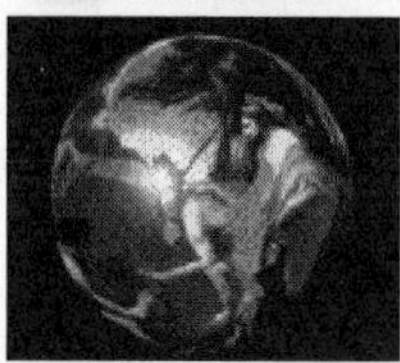

Contemporary Classicism in Art

Net in Arcadia Jump 7210

Net in Arcadia is a virtual museum dedicated to contemporary classicism—mainly painting. So far, this site is exhibiting the works of Alfred Russell and his students. These painters are exploring the Western figurative tradition, and often refer back to classical painting in their own works. Poussin is a major influence. This is a lushly illustrated site and is rather restful after surfing the neon post modern cyber art that seems to be the Web's usual fare. —(E.v.B.)

KEY NEWSGROUP rec.arts.fine URL▶ http://www.parnasse.com/net.in.arcadia.html

Online Dutch Art

Bas Van Reek Art Building Jump 7222

Bas Van Reek, a Dutch artist, has created a lush, electronic gallery where he exhibits his innovative and beautiful art—many pieces are well-rendered silk screens. Bas has constructed the gallery for great ease of movement and contemplation of his prodigious output. You can ride the Web "elevator" from the painting gallery to the electronic art floor, through the third floor where guest artists exhibit their work, then on to the multimedia floor, and, finally, into the gift shop, where you can order Bas's work. Don't miss a trip to the cellar where Bas keeps some cool links to other interesting Web sites. —(E.v.B.)

KEY NEWSGROUP **rec.arts.fine** URL ▶ http://www.xs4all.nl/~basvreek/

Stonework & Gargoyles Galore!

Walter S. Arnold / Sculptor home page Jump **7231**

Walter Arnold wields a mean chisel. He has gathered a number of his beautiful stone carvings and sculptures together for our enjoyment. Don't miss the gargoyles! As well, Walter demonstrates his skill with fireplace carvings, entry panels, public sculpture, architectural ornaments, and portrait busts. He also takes you deeper into his craft through the files he's posted on stone carving tools and techniques, history of stonecutters and their North American union, and Italian and English carving techniques. Lots of links and some of Walter's off-the-wall humor are also provided. —(E.v.B.)

KEY NEWSGROUP **rec.arts.fine** URL ▶ http://www.mcs.net/~sculptor/home.html

Cartooning Tips on the Web

CorelNET - The CARTOONIST Online! Clip2ns Jump **6015**

Jim Phillips is one of the first commercial cartoonists to use CorelDRAW to create cartoons. His work has been featured in *The Toronto Sun*, *The Ottawa Sun* and *The Calgary Sun*, and now he's sharing his knowledge of computer-generated cartooning with all of us at this terrific site. Stop by the classroom for traditional techniques, learn how to come up with ideas, and actually watch the process of a cartoon being developed. You can order clip art in CorelDRAW.CDR format, and even trade stories with other budding cartoonists in the "Cartoons Online" section. Best of all, there's lots and lots of Jim's work here. Let Jim share his expertise in this fascinating process! —(N.F.)

URL ▶ http://www.corelnet.com/corelnet/toons/toonhome.htm

The Artist's Imagination

Erik Johnson's Virtual Gallery Jump **7426**

Enter the imagination of Erik Johnson when you access his virtual Web gallery, featuring over 400 of his drawings and other artwork that spans, as Erik points out, the surreal to the silly, from pen and ink drawings to computer images. We especially enjoyed flipping through the virtual pages of his sketchbooks—the largest section of his gallery. Erik notes that the sketchbooks "chart my progress as an artist and as a person." —(E.v.B.)

KEY NEWSGROUP **rec.arts.fine** URL ▶ http://phidias.colorado.edu/vgallery.htm

The Art of the Next Generation

GEN ART - Home Page Jump **7431**

GEN ART, or "art of the next generation," is a not-for-profit organization dedicated to connecting young artists, audiences, and professional opportunities—whether through exhibitions, online programs or community involvement. GEN ART is based on both American coasts. You can browse through artists' creations in the interactive catalog, surf to Web pages that support the GEN ART effort, meet some of the artists in the "party pages," and read about current exhibitions and the group's other efforts. —(E.v.B.)

KEY NEWSGROUP **rec.arts.fine** URL ▶ http://www.genart.org/home.html

äda Floating

ada in flux, an evolving journey Jump **7467**

äda in flux is a site that defies definition—it's an art gallery, a dialogue between body and mind, and a collection of artists with a vision of the urban experience. For example, think about this explanation of one section of the site: "What we are experiencing now is that the self is joined to various networks of selves and is projected and thrives within a chain of bodies." See for yourself. —(E.v.B.)

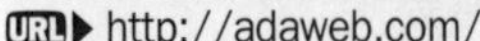

URL ▶ http://adaweb.com/

Art Online

The Electric Gallery Jump 7170

Enjoy the art from the Amazon, Haiti, or folk art from Europe, America, and the Caribbean? Or is art depicting the powerful emotions of blues and jazz more to your liking? You can wander through the various wings of the Electric Gallery and see it all—either in thumbnail GIFs or full-screen JPEG images. If you fall in love with one of the many posters, prints or serigraphs, you can even order a copy here, too. —(E.v.B.)

KEY NEWSGROUP **rec.arts.fine** URL▶ http://www.egallery.com/egallery/homepage.html

Surreal Art Online

Strange Interactions Jump 7233

John Jacobsen's online art exhibit will take you on quite a trip through his artist imagination. His works include oil and acrylic paintings, drawings, woodcuts, etchings, and lithographs—all on display on this site. As John explains: "My work is representational but surreal, perhaps best described as an attempt to recreate vivid yet bizarre dream-states through visual art." Move over, Dali! —(E.v.B.)

KEY NEWSGROUP **rec.arts.fine** URL▶ http://amanda.physics.wisc.edu/show.html

Digital Clicks

Sam Laundon - Photographs Jump 7235

Sam Laundon, a Boston photographer, has set up a wonderful exhibit that demonstrates the wide range of his photographic skills honed over a 25-year career. You can browse through his collections of black-and-white and color landscapes, architectural pics, Boston street scenes, and black-and-white portraits. He also presents examples of his art photography—mainly digital portraits and still-life images. Give your eyes a treat and visit this site. —(E.v.B.)

KEY NEWSGROUP **rec.photo** URL▶ http://www.tiac.net/users/slaundon/

Antiques & Collectibles

Antique Collector's Paradise

Antiques Jump 1514

Collecting antiques can be confusing—there are many guidelines and techniques you need to learn to get the most for your money. Gordon and Yvonne Cariveau, the owners of Antiques Oronoco in Rochester, Minnesota, present a primer to start you off on the right foot. The Web pages deal with items commonly purchased and sold at antique shows, auctions, flea markets, and shops around the United States "to acquaint the unfamiliar with some things they might want to collect and learn about." And that they do! Their comprehensive index describes each type of antique, from dolls to stoneware to—well, you name it. They not only tell you what to look for, but also how to select a dealer, find the right shows, and negotiate prices to reduce your risks as you venture into this field. The site also links to reference books for those who wish to gain a more in-depth knowledge of a particular type of antique. You'll be inspired to start tomorrow! —(H.L.)

KEY NEWSGROUP **rec.antiques** URL▶ http://www.ic.mankato.mn.us/antiques/Antiques.html

Welcome to The Collectors Network

Web Haven for Collectors

The Collectors Network Jump 7089

Have a little inner voice continually saying, "I want, I want?" Come to the Collectors Network and meet others with similar cravings. Gemstones, folk art, clocks, beer steins, dolls, toys—even glass lamp shades, for heaven's sake—are all gathered in this giant cyber flea market. Links to information on a number of collectibles are provided. Buy-sell-trade files span the world—you just might find a buyer for Aunt Tilly's horseshoe collection here, too! —(E.v.B.)

KEY NEWSGROUP **rec.collecting** URL▶ http://www.xmission.com/~patco/collect.html

THE GLITTER BOX
Collectible Designer Jewelry for Discriminating Tastes

Vintage and Costume Jewelry Shop

The Glitter Box Jump **0236**

All vintage jewelry collectors know what it's like getting up at 5:30 on a Saturday morning to be first at an estate sale that may or may not have what you're looking for. But sign on to the Web any day and time of the week, and you'll have access to a huge inventory of collectible jewelry from all over the country—and the world! The Glitter Box site, maintained by Sheila Pamfiloff, is one of the best sites out there for jewelry collectors, and also provides links to other great vintage jewelry sites. Pieces for sale are listed, along with nice, clear photos that really let you see what the jewelry looks like. Sometimes, items are even put up for "auction," so you can place a bid online. You can also put something on hold, or you can try the time-honored technique of "making an offer," or asking questions about the jewelry you already own. —(E.G.)

KEY NEWSGROUP **rec.antiques** URL▶ http://www.crl.com/~pamfil/GLITTER.HTM

Timepiece Collector's Heaven

TimeZone Jump **8083**

TimeZone is a Web site devoted to collectible watches, clocks, and timepieces galore. You can view pictures of timepieces, browse a directory of watch and clock dealers, buy a watch, even join in on this site's online forums. The TimeZone people have also collected some of the most interesting information on time that you can find on the Internet. Learn about time-related software, surf the interesting collection of links, check the time all over the world, whether in Barbados, Malaysia, the Yukon, or Mongolia. Take some time and read a great story on this site by Mark Twain, entitled, "My Watch." —(E.v.B.)

KEY NEWSGROUP **alt.horology** URL▶ http://www.timezone.com/

The Daguerreian Society

The Daguerreian Photographer's Society

The Daguerreian Society-Homepage Jump **6722**

The photographic daguerreotype image process was created in the late 1820's by Louis Jacques Mande Daguerre, and this site presents a large gallery of these Nineteenth-century portraits, along with modern works of photographic art done in this process. The Daguerreian Society, creators of this site, takes great pride in presenting these images to you online, and they also take the history, science, and art of daguerreotype very seriously indeed. Along with the galleries, you can access a historical bibliography, view an illustrated description of the process, check an updated events calendar, and link to other historical photo-related sites. —(L.T.)

KEY NEWSGROUP **rec.photo.advanced** URL▶ http://java.austinc.edu:80/dag/

Stamp Collecting Tips & Info

Joseph Luft's Philatelic Resources on the Web Jump **2144**

Ignoring the irony of being so close to e-mail, the traditional post's most dangerous enemy, Joseph Luft has assembled a comprehensive list of Internet links for stamp collectors. From here you can link to general and country-specific resources, postal authorities, and other collectors' home pages, as well as the stamp collector's FAQ and newsgroup. There are also links to dealers and downloadable stamp images. —(L.S.)

KEY NEWSGROUP **rec.stamps.collecting** URL▶ http://www.execpc.com/~joeluft/resource.html

Collectible Newspapers

History Buff's Home Page Jump **2727**

Considering how important a contemporary record can be to understanding history, and how important a free press has been to America, the name of this page is not a misnomer. But it's primarily for those who are interested in American journalism and newspaper collecting, although there is extensive American history and American publishing history research information here, as well as links to other sites covering American history. But as the online edition of the Newspaper Collectors Society monthly magazine, its emphasis is on collecting more than history. To that end, there's a primer on collecting, a price guide for old and historic newspapers, and information on how to buy and sell. —(L.S.)

KEY NEWSGROUP **rec.collecting**
URL ▸ http://www.sojourn.com/~topdog/historybuff.html

The Wonderful World of Barbie

Plastic Princess Page
Jump **1518** CONTENT

Who would've thought grown adults would enter the world of collecting Barbies, sometimes with such vengeance that you forget who it was Mattel really created America's favorite doll for. Zoli Nazaari-Uebele, an avid "doll-collecting maniac," teaches you the dozen or so themes for collecting Barbies, from Happy Holiday to Department Store special Barbies (and don't forget Ken, Skipper, and Midge). This is a plethora of resource links to videos and movies, miscellaneous tidbits, periodicals, books, a picture gallery to help you identify Barbie eras and outfits, and a glossary of terms (TNT only means Twist 'N Turn here). But the real fun starts with Barbie's Freak Circus—Barbies and Kens you won't see on store shelves, dressed as hackers, postal assassins, killers, gang members, and even O.J. and Nicole Simpson—tasteless but timely. If you're truly bored after that, you'll just have to resort to the interviews with a wide range of plastic personalities. —(H.L.)

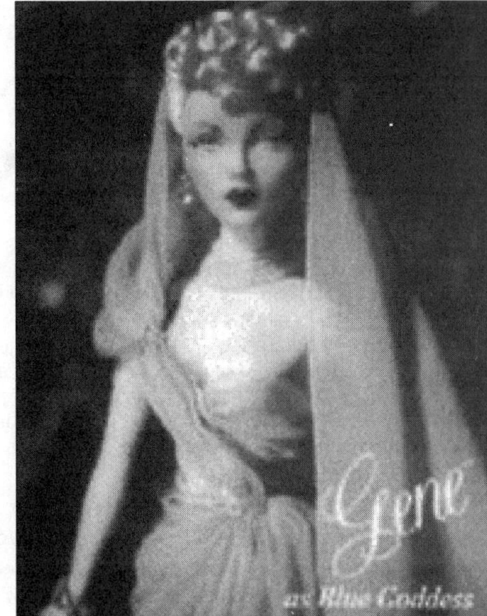

▲ *Collectible Gene´ doll, from* **The Plastic Princess Page** *at* Jump **1518**.

URL ▸ http://deepthought.armory.com/~zenugirl/barbie.html

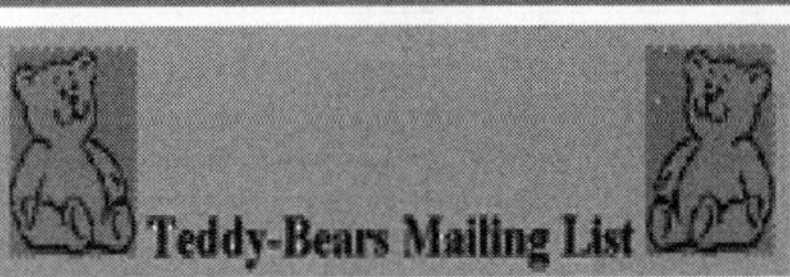

Teddy Bear Fanatics on the Web

Teddy-Bears Mailing List WWW Service Jump **2222** 

The Web home of the Teddy-Bears Mailing List, these pages will satisfy anyone from the serious collector to the recreational cuddler. Andreas Oesterhelt has included a browseable version of the mailing list discussion so you can easily track threads of interest and has added a standard list archive, FAQs, a history of teddy bears, patterns for making your own friends, and a general collection of teddy-bear-related texts, too. Any bear lover is welcome to contribute, and help is, in fact, needed. —(L.S.)

KEY NEWSGROUP **rec.collecting** URL ▸ http://www.rhein.de/Mailing-Lists/teddy-bears/

Home Base for Postcard Collectors

The Postcard Page Jump **2395** CONTENT

Most people use postcards to make their homebound friends jealous, but some people collect them. For collectors, Marcel Marchon's pages are a must bookmark. As concise as a postcard message, yet as full and rich as the most beautiful card image, these pages begin with the official postcard collector's FAQ, a document for beginners as well as long-time collectors. Marcel also includes links to other postcard pages and resources, including Postcard People and trading lists. For people interested in the more personal aspects of card collecting, there's also *The Inquiring Collector*, a feature maintained by Paul Engelberg that starts and recaps a thread from the mailing list that focuses on how people got started collecting, why they like a particular type of postcard, and other personal insights into collecting and collectors. —(L.S.)

KEY NEWSGROUP **bit.listserv.postcard** URL ▸ http://www-iwi.unisg.ch/~mmarchon/postcard/index.html

Coin Collectors' Home Page

Coins Jump 2574

You can read collecting FAQs and some of the better articles posted to the **rec.collecting.coins** newsgroup or link to other coin sites from here, but that's just the beginning, and the contents are growing. Perhaps the best feature is the Grading Coins section, where you can try your hand at grading, leave your comments, and see how they stack up against other graders. There's also a section where you can help others identify coins, or upload an image of a coin you need identified. Also interactive are the coin price database and want/have list. It's already a great page, and Frank Chlebana has ambitions to make it even better. But he can't do it alone, and any help he receives from volunteers will be greatly appreciated. —(L.S.)

KEY NEWSGROUP **rec.collecting.coins**
URL ▶ http://zow00.desy.de:8000/~chlebana/coins/coins.html

▲ *Collectible KORDA silver pin made for the 1940s movie "The Thief of Baghdad," from* **The Glitter Box** *at* Jump **0236**.

U.S. Coin Collectors' Page

E Pluribus Unum
Jump **2575**

Michael Caver's two favorite hobbies are coin collecting and the Internet, and if this Web page is any indication, he's at the top of both. There's a heavy emphasis on U.S. coins, as the page's title would suggest, but there's information here for any other collector, too. There's the latest coin news, an online and downloaded guide to grading coins, a collection of writings about coins and collecting, and a selection of coin collector software available for download. A nice set of links to other coin sites, organized by organizational, personal, and commercial, is here too. (L.S.)

KEY NEWSGROUP **rec.collecting.coins** URL ▶ http://atheist.tamu.edu/~ratboy/Coins/coins.html

Money of the Emerald Isle

Irish Coins and Banknotes Jump **7078**

John Stafford-Langan's well-designed, informative, and illustrated page has put Irish money collecting on the cyberworld map. See pictures of the earliest coinage used in Ireland, read about Irish currency history, browse an online catalog, and join the Numismatic Society of Ireland. As well, follow the money trail through a series of other links listed here. —(E.v.B.)

KEY NEWSGROUP **rec.collecting.coins** URL ▶ http://www.hursley.ibm.com/Ireland/coins/coins.html

Desktop Doodads

The International Paperweight Society Jump **7077**

Say, did you know that the most expensive paperweight in the world recently sold for $258,000? The inner worlds of paperweights—from the intricate to the floral to the bizarre—are explored at this site. The International Paperweight Society provides the newbie or the seasoned collector alike with an interesting array of information on what to collect, contacts, and paperweight trivia. —(E.v.B.)

KEY NEWSGROUP **rec.collecting** URL ▶ http://www.armory.com/~larry/ips.html

A Tasty Hobby

Robert's Candy Wrapper Collection Jump 7082

Anyone for a Wunderbar? Imagine, eating your way through the world's candy bars and collecting the wrappers as trophies. Robert Batina is doing his best to build the largest candy wrapper collection in the world. So far he's collected candy bar wrappers from the U.S., Canada, Australia, and Germany, which he has listed alphabetically. Send him a wrapper and your name will be posted on his page. Sweet immortality. —(E.v.B.)

URL▶ http://www.infinet.com/~rbatina/other/candy.html

▲ *The Holyoke Merry-Go-Round, from* Carousel! *at* Jump 7208.

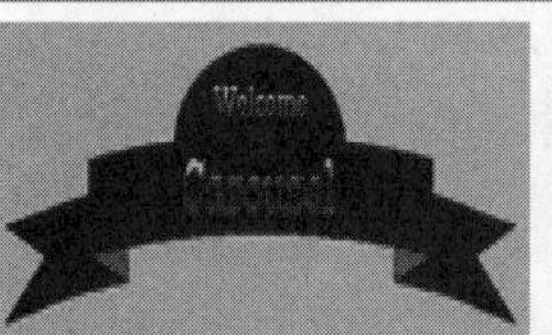

Very Merry-Go-Rounds

Carousel! Jump 7208

R.E. Burgess has grabbed the brass ring with this site. It's chock full of pictures, sound bites, history, and hot links to carousel-related sites. Where else could you enjoy hearing band organ clips, read poetry about merry-go-rounds, or even visit various museums and sites dedicated to everyone's all-time favorite amusement ride? Burgess goes a step further and lists a number of resources for the collector: periodicals, reference works, music sources, restoration experts, and dealers in antique carousel figures. —(E.v.B.)

KEY NEWSGROUP **rec.parks.theme** URL▶ http://www.access.digex.net:80/~rburgess/

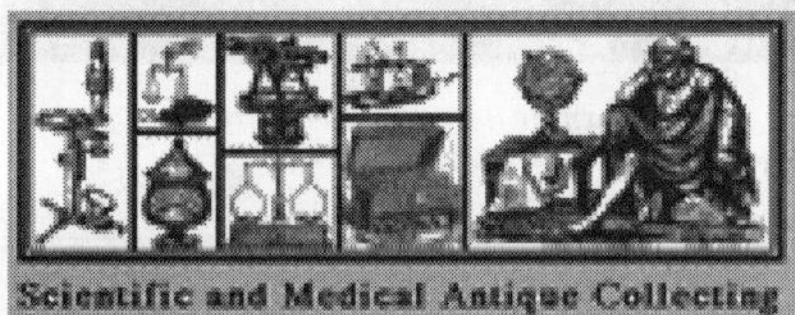

Old Slide Rules, Anyone?

Scientific and Medical Antique Collecting System Jump 7086

Have a mania for antique electrotherapy devices? Sundials? Surgical instruments? If so, Thomas E. Jones has all the files to satisfy the appetites of the hungriest scientific and medical antiques collectors. In addition to buy-sell files and descriptions of antique equipment and devices, Jones has provided information on dealers, reference books, and online museums. Think you've found a real treasure? Confirm your find by contacting one of the many experts he lists. —(E.v.B.)

KEY NEWSGROUP **rec.antiques** URL▶ http://www.duke.edu/~tj/sci.ant.html

Crafts, Gardening & Do-It-Yourself

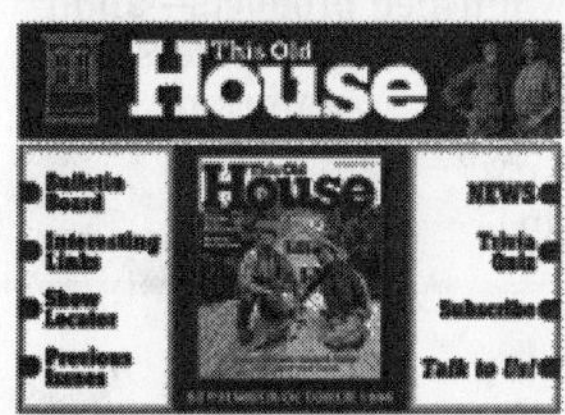

Home Fixer-Upper's Haven

This Old House Jump 2753 CONTENT

The online version of the magazine based on the popular PBS program, the This Old House page is a terrific resource for home repair do-it-yourselfers. In addition to detailed articles from the bimonthly magazine that offer instruction on techniques and tools for home renovation, you'll find info about the current season's project, a bulletin board to post and answer home repair questions, and general news about the program. —(L.S.)

KEY NEWSGROUP **alt.home.repair** URL▶ http://www.pathfinder.com/

Woodworker's Reference Site

rec.woodworking tidbits
Jump 2560

This page offers amateurs and professionals alike quick access to all the important woodworking infomation they would want. James Roche makes available the general **rec.woodworking** FAQ, as well as FAQs on hand tools, motors, and electrical wiring. There also are pointers to sources of equipment reviews, information about wood bending, toy safety, and woodworking for kids, as well as images and links to other woodworkers' pages. —(L.S.)

KEY NEWSGROUP rec.woodworking
URL ▸ http://www.cs.rochester.edu/u/roche/wood.html

Furniture & Interior Designers Web Site

The World Wide Web Virtual Library: Furniture and Interior Design
Jump 0158

A Sweden-based Web links page containing many valuable links and information resources, graphics files, electronic publications and suppliers for furniture builders and designers, interior design planners and architectural interior designers. —(E.G.)

URL ▸ http://www.i3.se/furniture.html

Home Improvement Resources

Home Ideas
Jump 7505

Thinking about tackling a home improvement project, but don't know where to start? Home Ideas lets you enter information about your project, you can then receive free catalogs and product brochures by snail mail. You can also browse back issues of Home Mechanix by issue or keyword. Plentiful links let you jump to other home improvement-related sites. —(C.W.)

KEY NEWSGROUP misc.consumers.house URL ▸ http://www.homeideas.com/

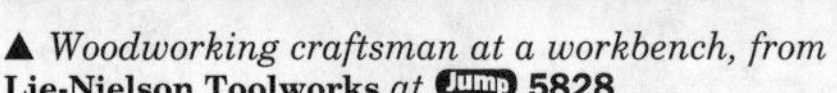
▲ *Woodworking craftsman at a workbench, from* **Lie-Nielson Toolworks** *at* **Jump 5828**.

Let the Chips Fall Where They May

Woodworking (and Hiding) in the Garage **Jump 7106**

CONTENT

Power up those sanders and explore this woodworker's page. Design and craft a chair, compare tools, exchange tips on furniture design, and view finished products—all in wood. Woodcarvers also have a place on this page, alongside furniture restorers, lumber suppliers, and moisture meters. Numerous links to other woodworking sites are given, as are back issues of woodworking magazines.—(E.v.B.)

KEY NEWSGROUP rec.woodworking URL ▸ http://www.iucf.indiana.edu/~brown/hyplan/wood.html

Gardening Reference Web Site

Books That Work Garden Encyclopedia **Jump 2405**

This online version of Steve Ettlinger's book covers more than 500 different items, from soil and pesticides to tools and decoration. You can use it to learn new gardening techniques, increase your knowledge about specific topics, or just browse. The pages are very well organized, with each chapter divided into hyperlinks covering general and specific information on the subject. There also are two search engines, one that will return full documents, the other designed for browsers who only have a general idea of what they want to find. —(L.S.)

KEY NEWSGROUP **rec.gardens** URL▶ http://www.btw.com/garden_archive/toc.html

Gardener's Web Jumplist

The Garden Gate on Prarienet Jump **2125**

Here are the roots of great gardening. A comprehensive series of pages of links to virtually every gardening resource on the Internet, this site by Karen Fletcher is organized for browsing as well as for finding specific references. There are links to resources on indoor and outdoor gardening, gardening FAQs, plant lists, glossaries, virtual garden tours, and gardening software, all with descriptions that let you know what's at the other end. The "What's New" links let you keep up with recent Web additions, and the "Garden Spider's Web" gives you quick access to the best of the best gardening-related features on the Web! —(L.S.)

KEY NEWSGROUP **rec.gardens** URL▶ http://www.prairienet.org/ag/garden/homepage.htm

Hydroponic Gardening Info & Resources

Hydroponics, Hydroponics, Hydroponics Jump **2396**

You don't need a large plot of land to have a vegetable garden. You don't even need dirt, either. With hydroponics, all you need is a nutrient solution, some lights, and you're on your way. It's not quite that simple, but this site by Inter Urban Water Farms will give you the information you need to understand how hydroponics works and how to get started. There's a general introduction and FAQ, advice on nutrients and lighting, links to other online resources and the hydroponics e-mail discussion list archives, plus an online mall of indoor gardening products. If you've got some empty space and a taste for vegetables year-round, check it out. The results can be quite impressive, since hydroponics, unlike soil gardening, gives you the ability to adjust the nutrients used to grow the plants so you can give each variety the mix it needs for optimal growth. —(L.S.)

KEY NEWSGROUP **rec.gardens** URL▶ http:/ /www.aloha.com:80/~virhol/

Plants: Displays & Information Resources from NYBG

The New York Botanical Garden Jump **2410**

With more than 250 acres, the New York Botanical Garden is one of the largest in the world, and these Web pages bring you virtually every square inch. With pictures and text, you can take guided tours through the rose, rock, herb, and other gardens, visit the Garden Complex for ideas and tips for your own garden, or learn about the special collections of trees and shrubs, bulbs, orchids, and other plants. Also online is information about the NYBG's research and education programs and a section of plant information with monthly planting tips and specific information about various plants. —(L.S.)

KEY NEWSGROUP **rec.gardens** URL▶ http://www.pathfinder.com/

Gardener's Answer Page

Hoticulture Solutions Series Jump **2487**

Is there a better source for answers to gardening questions than an agricultural college? If there is, it can't be much better than this site from the Cooperative Extension Service of the University of Illinois School of Agriculture! Here you'll find guidance and answers for all types of plants, with sections covering flowers, trees and shrubs, fruits, vegetables, and houseplants. There are separate sections for dealing with pests and choosing and using the proper soils and fertilizers, as well as a helpful glossary of terms. Use this resource not only when you have a problem to solve, but before you start any part of a new garden, and you'll see your thumb turn green before your eyes! —(L.S.)

KEY NEWSGROUP **rec.garden** URL▶ http://www.ag.uiuc.edu/~robsond/solutions/hort.html

Home Orchid Gardening Tips

The Orchid House Jump 7052

Once the expensive hobby of the rich, orchids are now affordable and available to a wide range of indoor gardeners. To help beginning and experienced orchid fanciers, Jerry Bolie has assembled cultivation notes on each major orchid family, listed suppliers, and judging categories for the competitive-minded, and even includes a short story featuring orchids, written by H.G. Wells. —(E.v.B.)

KEY NEWSGROUP **rec.gardens.orchids**

URL ▸ http://sciserv2.uwaterloo.ca/orchids.html

▲ *Cute origami dragon, from* **Joseph Wu's Origami Page** *at* Jump **7009**.

Strawberries on Parade

The Strawberry Facts Page

Jump 7054

Yummm. Be careful, you might start drooling on the computer keys as you read through the illustrated jams, drinks, and desserts recipes. Jenni Mott, however, doesn't just stop here. She also includes exhaustive cultivation and harvesting tips, graphics with strawberry themes—even songs about this luscious fruit.—(E.v.B.)

KEY NEWSGROUP **rec.food.cooking** URL ▸ http://www.wimsey.com/~jmott/sbfacts/

Origami Tips & Tricks

Joseph Wu's Origami Page Jump 7009

Joseph Wu, a graduate student at the University of British Columbia, has created a paper-folding extravaganza. If you have a four-foot-square piece of paper handy, you can learn how to fold it into a large lobster. You can also browse a photo gallery of Wu's original creations, download folding directions for a number of other models, check a world-wide list of origami clubs, surf the links of a host of great origami home pages, or even read a paper on molecular origami—the folding of molecules! —(E.v.B.)

URL ▸ http://www.cs.ubc.ca/spider/jwu/origami.html

Busy Fingers

The Online Knitting Magazine Jump 7093

Dig out those knitting needles, find some yarn and log on to *Emily Way's Online Knitting Magazine*. Soon your fingers will be itching to knit, as you read helpful hints on color and technique, study the work of contemporary designers, and download intricate as well as beginner patterns for sweaters, socks, hats, and scarves. You can search further afield in Emily's list of bulletin boards, mailing lists, and available computer programs—all for the knit-one, purl-one crowd. —(E.v.B.)

KEY NEWSGROUP **rec.crafts.textiles** URL ▸ http://www.io.org/~spamily/knit/

All about Quilting

Welcome to the World Wide Quilting Page Jump 2271

What began generations ago as a simple craft with the practical objective of keeping warm on cold nights has evolved into a true art form. Whether you practice the craft or the art or you just admire beautiful work, there's something here for anyone interested in quilting. Sue Traudt has brought together everything from patterns and instructions for quilting to software for quilters. In between, there's a history of quilting around the world, information about quilting exhibitions, descriptions and resources for various fabrics, a bulletin board of hints and tips, and lots of pictures of beautiful quilts. Spend some time familiarizing yourself with each section to take best advantage of this resource and then use the handy What's New section to keep track of this site's growing store of information. —(L.S.)

KEY NEWSGROUP **rec.crafts.textiles.quilting** URL▶ http://quilt.com/MainQuiltingPage.html

Driving, Cars & Racing

CAR AND DRIVER BUYERS GUIDE

Car and Driver's Buyer's Guide

Car and Driver's Buyer's Guide

Jump **6567**

Sure you recognize the name, but did you know that you can browse Car & Driver's well-known annual buyer's guide online? Car and Driver's Buyer's Guide allows you to search by make, model, manufacturer or price range. You can also browse all of their database categories at your own freewheeling pace—Economy, Luxury or Sports Car, Station Wagon, Van or Pickup Truck. This site also features in-depth reviews for each model, from Car & Driver's top-notch road test editors. —(L.T.)

KEY NEWSGROUP **rec.autos.driving** URL▶ http://www.caranddriver.com/

The Web's Monster Site for Car Buffs

The Auto Channel

Jump **5889**

If cars, trucks, or anything else with wheels are your thing, you'll flip for the Auto Channel. The first thing you'll want to do is check out the site map. This is the only way you can possibly hope to see everything this site has to offer. From there you can choose from literally dozens of options. Click on this site's "Motorsports" link, for example, and you can pick among links to trucks, stock cars, open wheel, motorcycles, and more. You'll also find information on magazines, parts and repairs, RV's, classic cars and new vehicles. This is one exhaustive (and exhausting!) site. —(J.P.)

KEY NEWSGROUP **rec.auto.sports.misc** URL▶ http://www.theautochannel.com/

Car Buff's Dream Site

All Things Automotive Jump **2693**

The title isn't an overstatement. This page will link you to virtually everything automotive, including enthusiasts pages, manufacturers, dealers, FAQs, and mailing lists. It's well organized, but there are two problems. The first is that it doesn't link you to newsgroups, and while this isn't a serious omission, it's an obvious one. The second is that all the links are on a single page. This wouldn't be so bad if there were links back to the top of the page from each section, but there aren't, and it makes browsing difficult. Generally, though, if you want to keep on top of what's new in automotive resources, or are looking for something specific, this is an excellent starting point. —(L.S.)

KEY NEWSGROUP **rec.autos** URL▶ http://www.webcom.com/~autodir/

Drivers, Start Your Engines!

NHRA Online Jump **1551**

This is where the rubber meets the road. Opening with a high-tech funny car graphic, the National Hot Rod Association shows you its stuff: the latest racing news and results, valuable statistics and data, important contacts and phone numbers, membership information, and a sneak peek at articles and news from the current issues of National DRAGSTER, the weekly newsmagazine of the NHRA. You'll find TV and racing schedules and a photo gallery of the greatest association racing stars and feats (yes, even a few crashes for the voyeur). Drag racer quotes comprise the most humorous aspects of this site. For example: "I saw Elvis at a thousand feet," muttered John Force, winner of five Winston Funny Car championships, as he crawled from the wreckage following

▲ *Porsche 911 off-road racer, photo by Patrick Martin, from* **Off-Road.com** *at* Jump 5926.

his spectacular 1992 Mid-South Nationals fire and crash. Sure to make fans yearn for the smell of burning tires at their nearest local track. (H.L.)

URL▶ http://www.goracing.com/nhra

Indy 500 Racing News

SpeedNet Jump 3724

From the auto racing capital of the world—Indianapolis, Indiana—*The Indianapolis Star* and *The Indianapolis News* have joined forces to bring you SpeedNet, your home for auto racing information. With its coverage of Indy cars, NASCAR, NHRA, Formula One, and regional racing circuits, racing fans will have plenty to keep them occupied. Follow top stories, schedules, and events, as well as your favorite racers. See this year's Indy 500 pace car, peruse the archives, even jump into one of the forums to have your say. —(N.F.)

URL▶ http://www.starnews.com/speednet/

The Ultimate Automotive Info Site

AutoSite Jump 5777

If you're in the market for a car, or even if you just wish you were, you'll love AutoSite's Ultimate Buyer's Guide. We're talking new cars, with tons of information on buying a new car, including dealer invoice prices, datasheets, information on the latest rebates and incentives, how to calculate your loan payments, and more. You can check how much your trade-in is worth, or read the tips on buying (or selling) used cars. Other sections of this site tell you how to keep your car in top shape, and provide links to valuable consumer protection advice as well. —(J.P.)

KEY NEWSGROUP rec.autos.marketplace URL▶ http://www.autosite.com/

Classic & Exotic Car Central

The Special Car Journal Homepage Jump 5121

The Special Car Journal is a new online service for classic and exotic car owners and enthusiasts. Here you'll find a dealers' directory, links to other automotive Web sites and a list of car-related newsgroups. There's also a classifieds section, that lists over 850 classic and exotic cars. As a special bonus, check out the link to information on the new Mercedes-Benz E Class autos. —(S.B.)

KEY NEWSGROUP **rec.autos.antique** URL▶ http://specialcar.wwa.com/

Motor Trend Magazine Online

Motor Trend Jump **6891**

Its name is instantly recognizable, but the online difference is advance sneak peeks of Motor Trend's Buyers Guide, Car of the Year, and constantly-refreshed news coming to you live from the automotive capitals of the world. If you can't visit daily, you'll find reoccuring monthly features like test drives on cars hot off the assembly line, the latest truck technologies, and behind-the-scene tours of major car factories on this site that's as good as its print counterpart. —(L.T.)

KEY NEWSGROUP **rec.autos** URL▶ http://www.motortrend.com/

No Lemons Here

THE CARPLACE Jump **7385**

Looking for a new or late model car? Then tool over to Robert Bowden's pages. Here you can read one of Robert's weekly reviews of a new car model, or browse past reviews looking for a car that might suit you. Robert also reviews components and mounts lists of top-ranked cars. Have a beef about your new car? Then, take advantage of the feedback corner and add your comments. —(E.v.B.)

KEY NEWSGROUP **rec.autos.driving** URL▶ http://www.cftnet.com/members/rcbowden/

Saturn Car Owners' Web Site

Saturn Server Jump **0017**

Saturn makes a nice little car that's developed a real cult following, as evidenced by this neat Web site for Saturn owners put together by Mike Huang, Gary Aulfinger, and Michael Fischer. It contains loads of Saturn car specifications, products, information on Saturn, the company, even pictures of Saturns posted by their owners to this Web site. Also featured are Saturn product reviews, a comprehensive FAQ (Frequently Asked Question) file, plus plenty of tips—like how to install a custom stereo—and much more. —(E.G.)

URL▶ http://www.physics.sunysb.edu/Saturn/

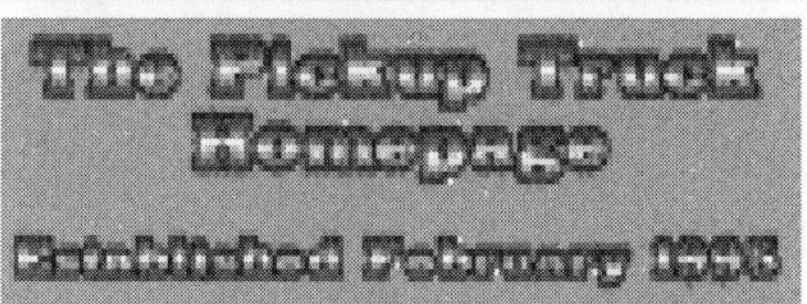

Four Wheeling Fun

The Pickup Truck Home Page Jump **2353**

With trucks accounting for nearly half the vehicles sold in the U.S., it's a wonder that there are not more Web pages devoted to them. With the high quality of his Web site, Michael Levine more than makes up for the dearth of truck-related sites on the Web. Although there are lots of pictures, he's careful not to overload your modem, so the pages come through with good speed. In between the pictures, there's the latest pickup truck news, details about manufacturers and their lines, and special sections for truck racers and off-roaders. You'll also find pictures of celebrities and their pickups, and a Reader's Pickup Truck of the Week that could feature yours if you submit a photo and other information. —(L.S.)

KEY NEWSGROUP **rec.autos** URL▶ http://thunder.met.fsu.edu/~nws/buoy/

The Ultimate 4X4 and Off-Roader's Site

Off-Road.com Jump **5926**

When these folks say "off-road" they really do mean off-the-road. As the picture on the home page shows, why drive on the road when you can use your four-wheel to climb a cliff?!? This extensive off-roader's site brings you up-to-date on all the latest outings, including the ever-popular dune runs and other races and contests. Further on, you'll find a bevy of links to other off-road topics, including an off-road products area, with many links to vendors, an off-road store, and racing news. You'll also find some cool photos and an extensive calendar of upcoming events. —(J.P.)

KEY NEWSGROUP **rec.autos.4X4** URL▸ http://off-road.com/

LandRover Home Page & Information Site

Land-Rover Jump **4051**

Although not an "official" company site for these upscale, four-wheel-drive sport utility vehicles, Lloyd Allison has provided a dream site for anyone interested in these Land Rovers. You'll find tons of pictures of Land Rovers throughout history up to the current models. There's also plenty of information and specifications as well as links to other Net resources pertaining to Land Rovers, plus Web links to many general automotive resources as well. —(R.B.)

KEY NEWSGROUP **rec.autos** URL▸ http://www.cs.monash.edu.au/~lloyd/tildeLand-Rover/index.html

The Lead Foot's Page

The Speed Trap Registry Jump **7118**

Traveling to Pennsylvania—or anywhere else in the U.S.—and have a tendency to keep your pedal to the metal? Perhaps you should check the speed-trap registry page to see where all the possible speed traps exist along your route. Andrew Warner thinks the police have better things to do than entrap unwary motorists in order to "increase fine revenues." He's collected information on locations in all 50 states and parts of Canada where the police are likely to lurk. Oh, yes, Pennsylvania. Watch out on I-83 just south of York. —(E.v.B.)

KEY NEWSGROUP **rec.autos.driving** URL▸ http://www.nashville.net/speedtrap/

Motor Scooter Fans' Page

The Original Motor School Home Page Jump **2472**

They may not have the macho of Harleys, but Vespas and other motor scooters boast their own unique cult following. Mr. Mark knows this, and he shares his enthusiasm with others who enjoy riding, collecting, and restoring these little vehicles. There are listings of clubs, rallies, and races, and tips on restoring and customizing scooters, with photos of scooters and their restorers. There's also a growing list of information and links to motor scooter information around the world. —(L.S.)

KEY NEWSGROUP **alt.scooter** URL▸ http://weber.u.washington.edu:80/~shortwav/

Motorcycling News & Resources

Motorcycle On-line Jump **0088**

An excellent resource for motorcyclists, Motorcycle On-line is a superbly-designed Web site featuring extensive original material, a new motorcycle models database, online motorcycling how-to articles, graphics, downloadable video clips and more, all executed in an highly professional manner. —(E.G.)

KEY NEWSGROUP **rec.motorcycles** URL▸ http://motorcycle.com/motorcycle.html

Motorcycling Enthusiasts' World

Markolf Gudions' Motorcycle Page Jump **2372**

Markolf Gudions starts his page with an audio clip to get you in the mood, and follows that up with pictures and descriptions of his bikes, links to racing pages, and more pictures. But for the true motorcycle lover, he has a comprehensive page of links that should not be missed. They are organized by country, so no matter where you are or where you're going, you'll be able to find people who share your interests. There also are links to magazines, safety organizations, clubs, events, and anything else that's motorcycle-related on the Web. —(L.S.)

KEY NEWSGROUP **rec.motorcycles**
URL ▶ http://jupiter.lfbs.rwthaachen.de/~markolf/Motorcycles.html

Motorcycle Rock 'n' Roll

Whip It! Jump **7121** 

The Montreaux Media Corporation has gathered a lot of off-road motorcycle rally, race, and cross-country competition information. Like to see photos of riders leaping high in the air as they clear small chasms on their bikes? Check out the photo galley of high action pictures. As well, you can read race results, upcoming events, latest bike information, guides to trails and tracks, other competition results, and a host of related files. Itching to ride? Whip on over to this page and virtually participate in a Supercross series! —(E.v.B.)

KEY NEWSGROUP **rec.motorcycles**
URL ▶ http://www.visualradio.com/whipit/

Webbin' Harleys

World Wide Glide Jump **7107** 

All you Harley fans out there, tool on over to Zipgun Beauregard's extensive Harley-Davidson page. Here you'll learn to decipher the Harley alphabet soup of model designations over the years. For example, from 1932 to 1972, the initial letter "G" indicated that this machine was a "Servicar Three Wheeler." Contract a serious case of the "I-want-its" as you look through the numerous bike photos. The gospel of sparkplugs and gap settings, tuning for all engine types, and tool kits for the road are extensively described. But all is not points and carbs here. Zipgun also presents, through satire and essay, the biker's view of freedom of the road, restrictive laws, and ruminations on the future of motorcycling. You can also roam through a host of other motorcycle-related Web sites and resources —(E.v.B.)

KEY NEWSGROUP **rec.motorcycles** URL ▶ http://www.halcyon.com/zipgun/wwg/wwg.html

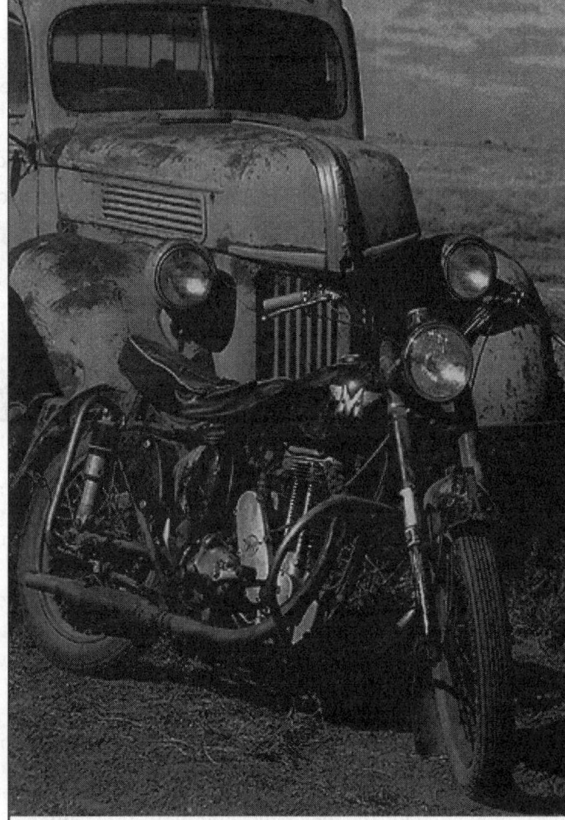

▲*1951 Matchless G80, used to herd sheep in the Australian Outback, from* **Off-Road.com** *at* Jump **5926**.

Hog Heaven (or, Easy Rider Comes to the Web!)

Harley-Davidson Stamford Jump **3660** 

As a Harley corporate executive was once heard to say: "The most solid marketing franchise is one where your customers tattoo your logo on their arms." There may be no group more loyal to a brand than those folks dressed up in leathers and helmets—and they now have a place on the Web! If you're a Harley-Davidson enthusiast, this site is a must-see. You'll find product information, a gear shop, images, sounds, parts, event listings, a Buells & Racers' Corner—this page even talks to you while you're browsing! An ongoing contest invites submissions of photographs for use in the Web site, with a free Harley-Davidson t-shirt for all those whose photos are selected for use! —(C.P.)

KEY NEWSGROUP **rec.motorcycles** URL ▶ http://www.hd-stamford.com/

BMW Motorcycle Repair

BMW K-Bike Motorcycle Home Page Jump 7123

Own a BMW K series motorcycle? Have we got a page for you! Walt Dabell has assembled an amazing amount of information. You can learn how to fix a flaky speedometer, set the timing on a K75, do a rear spline lube, and much, much more. Walt has also mounted links to other BMW pages and has allowed some information in on R1100 models. Motorcycle accident statistics, other bike pages, and even the motorcycle tire code table are also presented here for your interest. —(E.v.B.)

KEY NEWSGROUP **rec.motorcycles** URL ▶ http://www.cms.udel.edu/~walt/BMW.html

Flying & Aviation

The Web's Aviation Information Center

Landings Jump 5928

If it has anything at all to do with aviation, you'll find it here at Landings, the Web's one-stop resource for aviation. There are an astounding number of links here, from airports, flying clubs, organizations and publications to news, aviation events, home-building, FAA regulations, service difficulty reports, airworthiness alerts, and weather reports. This site also includes links to several important aviation-related search engines, including plane registrations, the Certified Pilot Database, Aviation Medical Examiner's Database, The Airmen's Information Manual (AIM), and others. This is the definitive aviator's site on the Web, and more information is being added all the time. —(J.P.)

KEY NEWSGROUP **rec.aviation.misc** URL ▶ http://www.landings.com/aviation.html

Aerospace Adventures

AIR&SPACE Magazine Jump 5123

On this, the Smithsonian Institution Air and Space Museum's online magazine and home page, you can check the museum's current exhibitions, explore the online magazine, and much more. There are links to other aviation-related Web pages, featured space pages, subscription info for the magazine, and many other links as well. —(S.B.)

URL ▶ http://airspacemag.earthlink.net/

Dimitriy's Aviation Database

AirPage Jump 5142

Dimitriy Levin puts out a lot of effort to continuously update this database that includes information on a vast range of airplanes, from World War I to modern times, and extensive coverage on helicopters, too. Entries have a brief description, history, technical data, and at least one photograph. In addition, there are databases of engines and weapons, and you can even vote on the world's best aircraft and view a list of all aircraft makers by country. If your Web browser has background viewing capability, you'll also be able to see a backdrop of various planes on the main page. —(S.B.)

URL ▶ http://trex.smoky.ccsd.k12.co.us/~dlevin/air/air.html

Flying Photos & Movies

Aviation Image Archives Jump 2289

From hang gliders to space vehicles, if there's an image of it archived on the Net, you'll find it with this list of links by Günther Eichhorn. He's scoured the Net, examining archives all over to give you good descriptions of what each holds, making it easy for you to know where to look or to find the specific aviation-related images you want. —(L.S.)

KEY NEWSGROUP **rec.aviation.misc** URL ▶ http://adswww.harvard.edu/GA/image_archives.html

Into the Wild Blue Yonder

GeZi's Aviation and Piloting Page Jump 7251 

The avid aviator, GeZi, is determined to make all white-knuckle flyers into happy pilots with his enthusiastic pages on the wonder of flying. He presents a collection of stories—real and fictional—on the many facets of flying, and illustrates them with his own photographs. —(E.v.B.)

KEY NEWSGROUP **rec.aviation.misc** URL▸ http://www.gezi.com/gzworld/ng.html

Jane's Aerospace & Armaments

BTG Jane's EIS Jump 2229 CONTENT

Jane's has a well-deserved reputation as the premier resource for complete, impartial information on defense armaments, military and civil aviation, and aerospace technology. Use a keyword search and the return will give you all available links that have the search string anywhere in the text. Choose an item, and you'll not only get just the basic facts and figures, but also a development history, a description of the armament and electronic systems, and pictures of the item. This demonstration site doesn't offer the complete text of the Jane's volumes, so the defense ministers of the world still will have to pony up the bucks for real copies. But for a military buff, a Tom Clancy fan, or anyone curious as to what the Pentagon is spending all that money on, this is a bookmark for you. —(L.S.)

KEY NEWSGROUP **rec.aviation.military** URL▸ http://www.btg.com/janes/

Pictures, Poetry—and Planes!

CYBERSPACE.COM Aviation Image Archive  Jump 2316 

This is not the largest collection of aviation images available on the Web, but most of the hundreds that are available are archived here, enough to make this site unusual in the world of Web image archives. More important, Michael Brunk also makes available original color and black-and-white images that you may not find elsewhere, plus a compilation of aviation poetry. Images are archived by category, with new images kept in a separate category for quick review. —(L.S.)

KEY NEWSGROUP **rec.aviation** URL▸ http://www.cyberspace.com/mbrunk/aviation.html

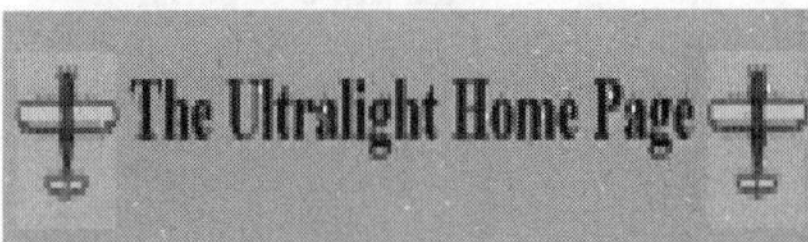

Small Fly

Ultralight Home Page Jump 2327 

It would seem that with so many aviation-related sites on the Web, there would be several covering ultralight aircraft. Surprisingly, there aren't, and so far only this one by Jon Steiger organizes and presents information for the general ultralight community. The ultralight FAQ is here for beginners, along with more detailed information on regulations, safety, and maintenance. There's also an events listing, with an online submission form, organized by location and date. As it's a relatively new page, submissions of all types are needed and encouraged. —(L.S.)

KEY NEWSGROUP **rec.aviation.ultralight** URL▸ http://www.cs.fredonia.edu/~stei0302/WWW/ULTRA/ultralight.html

Paraglider's Landing Spot

World's First Paragliding WWW Server—Big Air Jump 2558 

Kinsley Wong not only has compiled all the information you'd want about paragliding, but just in case he missed something, he's included an extensive set of links to related Internet sites. Every list here is comprehensive, from the contests and events, to schools, to equipment specifications. There's even information on new developments in the design of these parachute-like gliding devices. Of course, there's also an extensive picture gallery and an address book of paraglider pilots if you want to get in touch with others who share your interest.—(L.S.)

KEY NEWSGROUP **rec.aviation.misc** URL▸ http://www.housing.calpoly.edu/html/paragliding.html

Homebuilt Aircraft Info & Resources

Home Built Page Jump 2111

Take a little Wilbur and Orville, add a splash of Chuck Yeager and a pinch of pre-Vegas Howard Hughes, and you've got the home built aircraft hobbyist. Experimental by nature (and FAA regulation), building an airplane from a kit takes knowledge, patience, and fortitude. If you've got it, Kevin Walsh has the pointers you need get on with it. There's information on kits and plans, much of it from people who are currently building planes from them, powerplants, design software, as well as technical reports and a hyperlinked version of FAA regulations. There's also background information on clubs and newsletters, books and magazines, and a list of other homebuilders on the Net. —(L.S.)

KEY NEWSGROUP **rec.aviation.homebuilt** URL▸ http://www.mit.edu:8001/people/krwalsh/Homebuilts/homebuilt.html

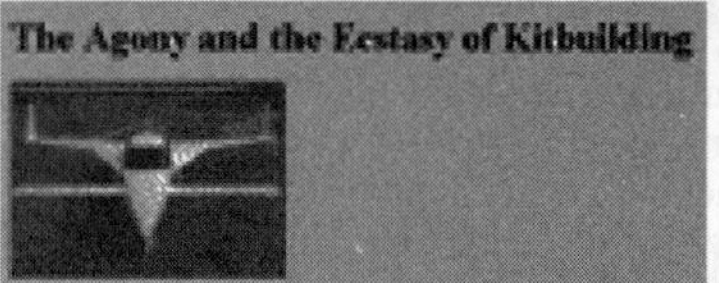

Diary of a Mad Home-Built Aviator

Building the Velocity 173 Kitplane Jump 2112

Subtitled "The Agony and the Ecstasy of Kitbuilding," this first-person account by G.A. Venkatesh will take you through the entire process, from deciding to build the plane to the takeoff—but you'll have to wait for that, since this ongoing saga has not yet reached that point. Even if you have no interest in building airplanes, this is an interesting journey for anyone considering a project of considerable scope. It doesn't matter if it's an airplane, a house, a quilt, or a stamp collection. The struggles and rewards are quite similar, and with this diary you can get pointers on how to persevere as you get a feel for the process of executing and completing such a massive project. —(L.S.)

KEY NEWSGROUP **rec.aviation.homebuilt** URL▸ ftp://flash.bellcore.com/pub/venky/www/Velocity.html

Above the Crowd: Balloonists' Resources

Ballooning Home Page Jump 2110

The first piloted balloon lifted from Earth in 1783, and the beauty and majesty of these aircraft have awed and fascinated generation after generation. Ballooning captured Jeff Pestun, and he's created a Web site that has something for the novice, the expert, and even those with only a passing interest. There's a well-written backgrounder on ballooning, covering history, physics, modern design, competition, and what's involved in a typical flight. There also are listings of upcoming competitions and other ballooning events, extensive links to e-mail discussion lists, ballooning and general aviation pages, and an image archive. —(L.S.)

KEY NEWSGROUP **rec.aviation** URL▸ http://www.cs.hope.edu/~pestun/balloon/balloon.html

Food, Drink & Recipes

Talk Back to the Star Chefs

Star Chefs Jump 5841

This site, featuring profiles, recipes, and discussions with some of the best chefs in the world, has the look and feel of a very fine, glossy cookbook. You know, the kind you look at in the bookstore but you don't buy because they cost more than a good meal. Well, fear not. This site's free. And besides, when was the last time your cookbook answered one of your questions? Join the fun with your own complaints or observations about service, tools of the trade or other topics. And, of course, there's the food element too, with recipes, great features on cooking secrets, regional restaurant coverage, and much more. –(J.P.)

KEY NEWSGROUP **rec.food.cooking** URL▸ http://www.starchefs.com/

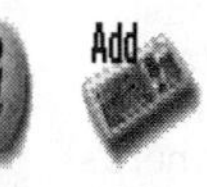

Finding and Rating Restaurants

DineSite Search Engine Jump 6880 CONTENT

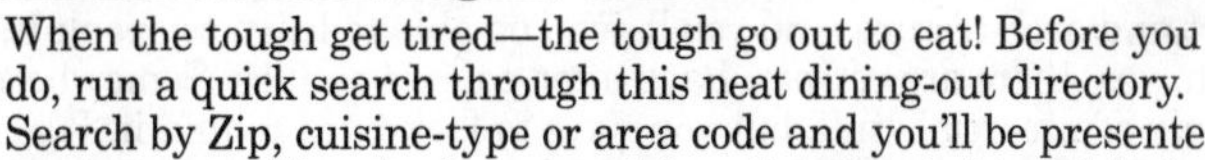

When the tough get tired—the tough go out to eat! Before you do, run a quick search through this neat dining-out directory. Search by Zip, cuisine-type or area code and you'll be presented with the reviews, ratings and menus from matching restaurants. There's also a special section devoted to celebrity restaurants, including Michael Jordan's. If you work in the restaurant business, their Restaurant SupplySite, a central directory of wholesalers, equipment and employment opportunities, can also be searched here. —(L.T.)

KEY NEWSGROUP **rec.food.restaurants** URL▶ http://www.dinesite.com

Worldwide Restaurant Guides

Dining Out on the Web Jump 2155 LINKS

If you travel, you know the hardest part is finding the really good restaurants. John Troyer has solved the problem. He says he created this list because he's insane, but greatness often comes out of insanity, and this is a great list of links. He includes the expected comprehensive restaurant guides, but then the insanity really sets in. He has tracked down most every dining-out guide on the Web and organized them by state and city for U.S. restaurants, and by country for international dining. Unfortunately, even John's insanity has its limits, and he's looking for someone to help maintain the list, or even take it over. —(L.S.)

KEY NEWSGROUP **rec.food.restaurants** URL▶ http://www.cmpharm.ucsf.edu/~troyer/diningout.html

An Epicurean Delight

Epicurious Jump 2675

You'd think the publishers of *Gourmet* and *Bon Appétit* magazines would take food and drink seriously. Well, they do, but they also know how to have a good time. Beginning with the campy, 1950s graphics, and carrying through with an attitude that's pure fun, Epicurious proves that playing with your food is not necessarily a bad thing. There are recipes, restaurant reviews, sample menus, and all the other items you'd expect to find in an online magazine about food and drink. But there's also a lot of tongue in cheek, such as Victual Reality, which offers such highlights as an imprint of Julia Child's hand. There's also a comprehensive list of tips and tricks for eating various foods without slopping on, or otherwise embarrassing, yourself as you do it. Of course, there also are online versions of *Gourmet* and *Bon Appétit*, and lots of straight, very helpful information, another example of how a commercial Web site can have fun while taking care of business. —(L.S.)

KEY NEWSGROUP **rec.food.drink** URL▶ http://www.epicurious.com/epicurious/home.html

Gourmands Online

Great Food Online Jump 5890

Great Food is a retail gourmet food store for people who love fine food. Guess that would include all of us! You can do all your shopping right here in this site's "Gourmet Food Store," where you'll find links to many companies that sell special coffees, sauces, meats, seafood, and more. Enjoy great recipes from visiting chefs, or register on this site to win great prices. If you know what you're looking for, you can head straight to the list of related site links. And the real food lovers can register for "Great Food Online News Bites," where you'll receive e-mail notices of special updates and special sales. —(J.P.)

KEY NEWSGROUP **rec.food.cooking** URL▶ http://www.greatfood.com/

Mama Mia! Whatta Web!

Ragu Presents Mama's Cucina Jump 2145 COMMERCE

This is a commercial site, but it doesn't look like one. It's maintained "by your fellow Netheads" at Ragu (you know, those spaghetti sauce folks) and the shared sensibilities show. Beginning with the URL (**www.eat.com**) and continuing throughout, it's presented in the voice of the archetype Italian mama—wise, warm, inviting, informative, humorous, and just plain fun. You'll find some wonderful family stories, a section on Italian art and architecture, and you'll even be able to learn to speak Italian. Oh, yes, there are recipes. Page after page of recipes. Somewhere there's truly commercial stuff, but you have to look hard to find it. It's clear that the primary purpose of these pages is to entertain, and if you don't visit, you'll be missing one of the better good-time Web sites around! —(L.S.)

KEY NEWSGROUP **rec.cooking** URL▶ http://www.eat.com/

▲ *New York's Little Italy, from* **Ragu Presents Mama's Cucina** *at* Jump **2145**.

Kraft Kitchen Ideas

Kraft Interactive Kitchen

Jump **5906**

Kraft sees their Interactive Kitchen commercial Web site as an evolving concept; the information you find online today will be supplemented with the new, and the old will be added to the database. And what they have already is pretty darn impressive for a purely commercial site. You can pick and choose between tons of recipes, and tips on cooking, entertaining, and feeding those kids. And there are features as well, such as an ongoing special called "Kraft Simple Answers," a great place to check for quick and easy meal ideas. —(J.P.)

KEY NEWSGROUP **rec.food.cooking** URL▶ http://kraftfoods.com/

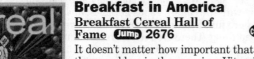

Breakfast in America

Breakfast Cereal Hall of Fame Jump **2676**

It doesn't matter how important that first meal of day may be, most of us still go for the cereal box in the morning. Vitamin fortified, sugar enhanced, often nutritionally questionable, it's a tradition, or a habit, few break willingly. If you're one of those who refuses to let go, this page from Scott Bruce and Bill Crawford is for you. Each month there's a new inductee into their Breakfast Cereal Hall of Fame, as well as other interesting bits and pieces of cereal culture. Learn about Marky Maypo, why cereal costs so much, or how to create cereal fashion statements, if you'd rather, er, wear—than eat—your breakfast. It's fun, and appropriately irreverent. —(L.S.)

KEY NEWSGROUP **alt.cereal** URL▶ http://198.3.117.222/index.html

Weight Watcher's Treasure Trove

Fatfree: The Low Fat Vegetarian Archive Jump **2725**

If you're on a low-fat diet and complain of bland, boring, and repititious meals, try this site. There are more than 2,000 low-fat vegetarian recipes here, with more added each week. Compiled by Michelle Dick, these are nutritious and tasty dishes that even meat eaters can enjoy. The searchable archive includes recipes in more than 50 categories, organized by dish, meal, and regional cuisine. You can browse the archive, just check the new recipes or, if you don't know what you're in the mood for, click on the random recipe link and be surprised. Also here are the USDA Nutrient Database, plus various FAQs and general information about low-fat and vegetarian eating. —(L.S.)

KEY NEWSGROUP **rec.food.veg** URL▶ http://www.fatfree.com/

Culinary Recipe Delights

Welcome to RecipeNet Jump **3733**

RecipeNet, the Online Cooking and Recipe Information Network, is a unique approach to cooking and recipe collection. There are recipes and feature stories in the Side Dishes section. This site's Main Dishes section describes many of the products and services available, such as RecipEmail, a subscription service which will deliver recipes right to your Net mailbox. The Take Out Menu highlights a particular food interest—this month it's The Zucchini Gazette, which includes a variety of zucchini recipes available for purchase. The Desserts section has a great glossary of commonly used cooking terms, as well as interesting monthly discussions. —(N.F.)

KEY NEWSGROUP **rec.food.cooking**
URL▶ http://www.indi.net/welcome.html

Big Recipes Collection on the Web

Recipe Archive Index Jump **7050** CONTENT

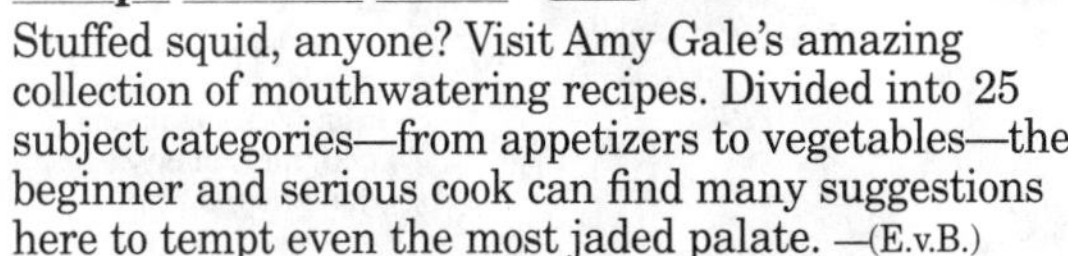

Stuffed squid, anyone? Visit Amy Gale's amazing collection of mouthwatering recipes. Divided into 25 subject categories—from appetizers to vegetables—the beginner and serious cook can find many suggestions here to tempt even the most jaded palate. —(E.v.B.)

KEY NEWSGROUP **rec.food.cooking**
URL▶ http://www.vuw.ac.nz/who/Amy.Gale/recipes/

Jellophile's Jell-O Recipes

Jell-Ophile #2 Jump **0101** CONTENT

Chaz Baden's comprehensive Web page devoted exclusively to Jell-O recipes...everything from Jell-O salads to frozen ice pops and alcoholic Jell-O shots! Remember, there's always room for Jell-O—even on the Web! —(E.G.)

URL▶ ftp://ftp.netcom.com/pub/hazel/www/jellocook.html

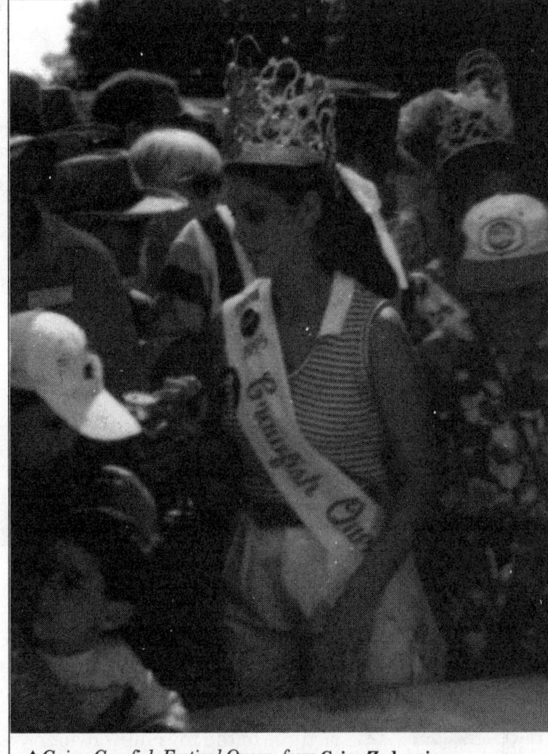

▲*Cajun Crayfish Festival Queen, from* **Cajun/Zydeco in Baltimore & Washington Areas** *at* Jump **7098**.

Cajun, Creole & N'Awlins Culture

The Gumbo Pages Jump **2399** CONTENT

You'll find a very good resource here for keeping track of what's happening in the New Orleans and southern Louisiana music and culture scene, but the real reason to visit Chuck Taggart's pages is the Creole and Cajun Recipe Page. Forget about the Cajun food craze of the 1980s and prepare to introduce yourself to real Cajun and Creole cooking—spicy, hearty and lots of fun. Chuck includes ample background to understand the cultural roots of these cuisines, excellent descriptions of their main ingredients and how to use them, and all the recipes you'll need for any meal, from appetizers to desserts. —(L.S.)

KEY NEWSGROUP **rec.food.cooking** URL▶ http://www.webcom.com/~gumbo/

Home Canning Made Easy

Home Canning Online Jump **5903** CONTENT

Home-canning has experienced a revival of late, but it's still somewhat difficult to find reliable information on the subject. You'll find everything you need here at Home Canning Online by Bernardin, Ltd., of Toronto, Canada. At the heart of the site is Home Canning Magazine, a handy and extensive guide to the fundamentals of home canning, a reference area, and a great archive of back issues. All of the information is available in English and French. Back on the main page is a link to the virtual cookbook of the recipes section, which includes a searchable index. And if you're stuck, or just want to chat with a fellow canner, take a moment to check out this site's home canning forum. —(J.P.)

KEY NEWSGROUP **rec.food.cooking** URL▶ http://www.home-canning.com/

Time Warner's Virtual Kitchen

Virtual Kitchen Jump 6885 CONTENT

If the kitchen is your favorite spot to be, you'll like this new resource from Time Warner. The Virtual Kitchen whips up new ideas in cooking, drinks, and eating in general. You're bound to come up with new culinary ideas, such as this site's soufflé, Cajun, and fondue recipes. Or browse reviews on who makes the best sipping wines. There's also a very handy seafood primer, with expert tips on proper handling and preparation techniques. —(L.T.)

KEY NEWSGROUP **alt.creative.cook**

URL ▶ http://pathfinder.com/twep/kitchen/

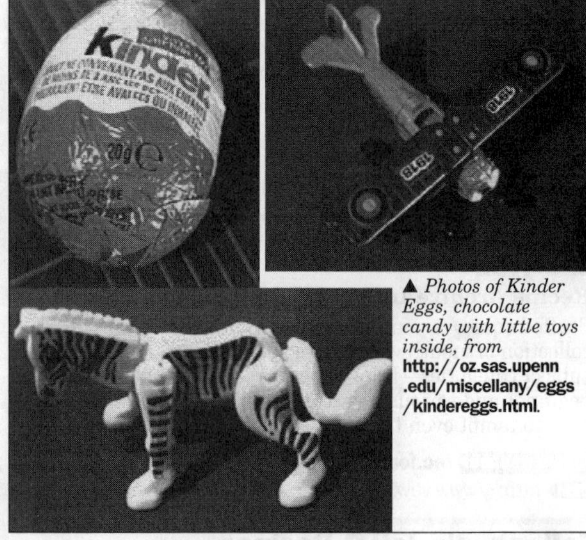

▲ *Photos of Kinder Eggs, chocolate candy with little toys inside, from* **http://oz.sas.upenn.edu/miscellany/eggs/kindereggs.html.**

KinderEggs Kult Kandy Korner

KinderEggs? Jump 7323

Good things come in small packages, so Ranjit Bhatnagar believes. He has devoted this Web page to those German treats—KinderEggs. These small, hollow chocolate eggs are exciting to open—what neat toys inside? A zebra, a Holstein cow, an airplane with a rotating propeller, or many more trinkets. For Ranjit, every package promises surprise and delight for the young and the young-at-heart. He also provides links to other KinderEggs pages, and some neat pictures of the toys he's obviously eaten a lot of chocolate to get to. —(E.v.B.)

KEY NEWSGROUP **rec.toys.misc** URL ▶ http://moonmilk.volcano.org/miscellany/eggs/kindereggs.html#kenews

A Dieter's Nightmare (or a Chocolate Lover's Dream Come True!)

Recipes to be Approached with Reckless Abandon Jump 5060 CONTENT

This page is full of sinful, delightful chocolate dessert recipes. Each recipe has a difficulty rating using the star method (as in movie reviews), a photograph or illustration of the finished dessert, and a complete list of ingredients and step-by-step instructions. Everything from your basic brownie to a White Chocolate Mocha Napoleon is covered here. A dieter's nightmare and a chocolate lover's dream come true! —(S.B.)

URL ▶ http://www.godiva.com/recipes/chocolatier/index.html

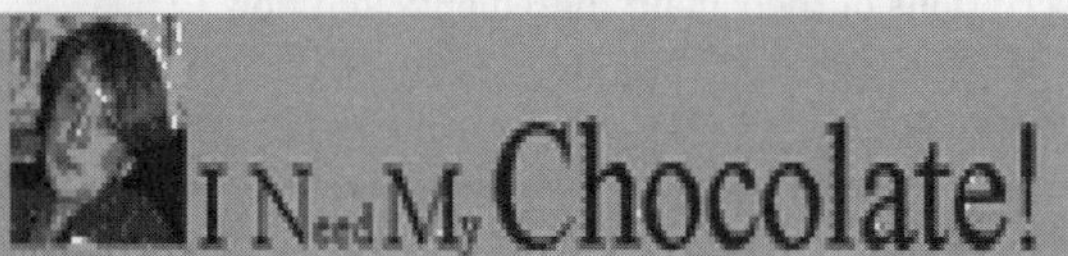

Chocolate Lovers' Web Pages

I Need My Chocolate Jump 2158

Forget what they say about bread, the most important food (to some) is chocolate...just ask Shellie Holubek. So far, she's the only chocolate lover who's found the time to leave her favored treat long enough to put up a real Web page. There are links to some of the better chocolate sellers' pages, but the real reason to visit is for the chocolate recipes. —(L.S.)

KEY NEWSGROUP **rec.food.chocolate** URL ▶ http://www.qrc.com/~sholubek/choco/start.htm

If You Knew Sushi . . .

Welcome to the World Wide Sushi Restaurant Reference! Jump 2340

Sushi is an acquired taste, but once acquired it's hard to stop tasting. Using the **alt.food.sushi** newsgroup as the starting point and main resource, John Maraist has compiled a comprehensive listing of sushi restaurants and restaurant reviews, so sushi lovers will be able to satisy their cravings anywhere in the world. The entire site is well organized and easy to navigate, especially the glossary section. Here, John has divided the glossary into sections that make it much easier to use than most. You can browse through general terms, or jump directly to glossaries for fish, fruit, vegetables and seaweed, spices and seeds, noodles, mushrooms, and beans and bean products. If there's not a specific heading, go to the "Other" section, and you're likely to find what you need. —(L.S.)

KEY NEWSGROUP **alt.food.sushi**

URL ▶ http://wwwipd.ira.uka.de/~maraist/Sushi/

▲ *"Happy Kids" vintage peanut butter jar label, from* **Brett News** *at* Jump **1506**.

Homemade Sushi Tips

Rolling Your Own Sushi
Jump **5035** 

This page contains some really great info about sushi, whether you're addicted or just a beginner. It covers sushi-related terminology, equipment you need to roll your own, how to prepare rice for sushi, and several other topics related to sushi-making. The creator of this Web page, Mark "Hutch" Hutchenreuther, even includes some nifty graphics of how to place the sushi ingredients for proper rolling! Read this page—and remember to buy really fresh fish—before you invite all your friends over for homemade sushi! —(S.B.)

URL ▶ http://www.rain.org/~hutch/sushi.html

Icelandic Fish

Icelandic Fisheries Laboratory Jump **7013** 

The Icelandic Fisheries Laboratory server (surprise, surprise!) presents a wealth of information on fish in Icelandic waters. Not only that, but you can browse through some mouth-watering fish recipes. After sampling these items, you can wear off the virtual calories by going on the illustrated tour of the island thoughtfully provided by the Lab. —(E.v.B.)

KEY NEWSGROUP **rec.food.cooking** URL ▶ http://www.rfisk.is/

What's Cookin'?

KETCHUM KITCHEN Jump **7254** 

Something sure smells good over at the KETCHUM KITCHEN Web site! The professional foodies here will answer all your cooking questions—from the definition of bouquet garni to how to substitute dried herbs for fresh. Seeing as how this is, after all, a commercial site sponsored by the Ketchum public relations firm, a food product from one of their clients is featured here every week. The friendly cooks employed to provide content for this site also share recipes and tips and insights into cooking and baking. Seasonal food information is also presented, and cookbooks are reviewed. Very solid! —(E.v.B.)

KEY NEWSGROUP **rec.food.cooking** URL ▶ http://www.recipe.com/

All about Cheese

CheeseNet Jump **2331** 

Surprisingly, this page is not based in Wisconsin, but in Oregon, and whether the proud denizens of the Dairy State will retaliate remains to be seen. For now, everything you would want to know about cheese is here. Kyle Whelliston starts with an overview highlighting the diversity and versatility of cheese, moves on to its history and manufacture, and wraps it up with a glossary of terms. Of course, there are pictures of cheese and cheesemaking, and recipes, too. Contributors not only get the pleasure of seeing their submissions on the Web, they also get rewarded with a CheeseNet sticker. —(L.S.)

KEY NEWSGROUP **alt.food** URL▶ http://www.efn.org/~kpw/cheesenet.html

Vegetarian Jumplist

Vegetarian Pages Jump 2157

There's a bit of content here, in the form of a glossary and list of definitions, but Geraint Edwards' real contribution to online vegetarians is his comprehensive list of links. The recipe links by themselves, especially the fat-free recipe links, make it worthwhile for anyone to visit, but the focus is on vegans, and he fulfills that with links to nutritional information, and various vegetarian organizatons. —(L.S.)

KEY NEWSGROUP **rec.food.veg** URL▶ http://catless.ncl.ac.uk/Vegetarian/

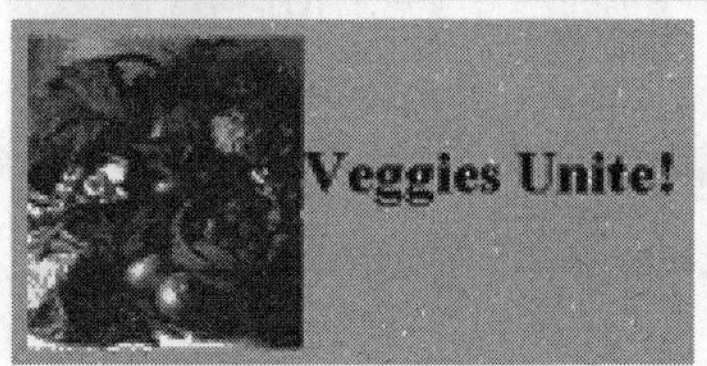

Vegan Recipes

Veggies Unite! Jump 2162

This massive searchable database holds more than 1,500 vegetarian recipes. If you want to browse instead of using a keyword search, Yvette Norem also lets you view the recipes by category, and alphabetically. If these 1,500 recipes aren't enough, there are links to other recipe databases, along with links to general health, medical, and nutritition sites (if you actually need reasons why you should eat your veggies!). —(L.S.)

KEY NEWSGROUP **rec.food.recipes** URL▶ http://www-sc.ucssc.indiana.edu/cgi-bin/recipes/

Brewing Central

Beer InfoNet Jump 2759

Beer drinkers and home brewers will find a ready resource here for just about everything they would want or need to know about beer. Maintained by John Lock, this is the home of the **rec.food.drink.beer** FAQ, the BrewStarter resource for those who are interested in starting their own microbrewery or brewpub, the Beer Periodicals List, comprised of magazines, newspapers, and club newsletters, and the Beer Classifieds, a free service for commercial enterprises in beer and beer-related businesses. John also maintains the WWW Virtual Library's Beer and Brewing Index, one of the most comprehensive site listings available, so that's here, too. What's not here, and it's as refreshing as the first draft from newly cleaned vats, is excessive graphics, silly backgrounds, or blinking text. It's pure content, neatly organized and easy to use, especially with the site's search engine. —(L.S.)

KEY NEWSGROUP **rec.food.drink.beer** URL▶ http://www.beerinfo.com/~jlock/

Beer Lover's Magazines

Beer Periodicals List Jump 2007

If you like to read while you quaff, this list of beer-related magazines will point you in the right direction. Maintained by John Lock with the aid of Jim Dorsch, Tom Dalldorf, and Paolo Viotti, the list is organized by type: general interest, homebrewing, professional brewing, and club. Each listing provides a description of specific editorial coverage, along with subscription information. If the publication has an Internet presence, a link is provided as well. John needs help in maintaining the lists, especially with infomation on non-U.S. magazines. So if you know of any that aren't listed, use the online form to submit the information. —(L.S.)

KEY NEWSGROUP **alt.beer** URL▶ http://www.mindspring.com/~jlock/beermag0.html

Home Brewer's Paradise

The Brewery Jump 2115

There are beer drinkers, there are people who drink beer, and then there are those who brew their own. If you enjoy real beer and have never tried home brewing, you should. This page is a great starting point, and it's even better for the experienced brewer. Karl Lutzen maintains the site, with contributions from a host of like-minded people. It opens with a link to the Cat's Meow, perhaps the largest repository of home brewing recipes on or off the Web, and continues with an index of online articles about brewing, downloadable beer brewing software and information files, and background on tasting and evaluating beer. There's also an information database of beer-related clubs, suppliers, events, and articles that you can comment on and add to as you view them. —(L.S.)

KEY NEWSGROUP **alt.beer** URL▶ http://alpha.rollanet.org/

▲ *A round of java, from* **Ragu Presents Mama's Cucina** *at* Jump **2145**.

You Can Almost Smell the Beans

Over the Coffee Jump **2294** 

If you drink decaf with lots of cream and sugar, skip this page. But if you really like coffee, don't miss it. Tim Nemec maintains this page based on the contributions of participants of the various coffee newsgroups, offering a reference and opinions about the various beans and blends, roasting and brewing techniques, and equipment available to coffee lovers. There also are images, poems, and various musings about life and coffee, perfect reading with your morning cup or afternoon break. —(L.S.)

KEY NEWSGROUP **rec.food.drink.coffee** URL▶ http://www.infonet.net/showcase/coffee/refdesk.html

Coffee Info on the Net

The All-New Ode to Coffee Jump **5032** 

This page starts off with a great citation circa 1850 about the godliness of coffee drinkers–really! Next, you'll want to check out some of the links on this page. One of them is Java Jive, a guide to café-speak (a glossary of sorts to help you muddle through the difference between caffé latté and cappuccino, and how to order exactly what you want). Also look at the list of "wired" coffee houses—the ones that let you use their Internet connection (for a fee, of course) while you sip your coffee. —(S.B.)

KEY NEWSGROUP **rec.food.drink.coffee** URL▶ http://www.flightpath.com/Brento/AnOdeToCoffee.HTML

For Wine Connoisseurs

Wine Home Page Jump **2194** CONTENT

If you partake of the fruit of the vine, you can enhance and share your pleasure through Jarrett Paschel's wine page. Most interesting is the extensive and interactive Tasting Archive, where you can read the wine tasting notes of others and add your own. It's an excellent way to discover new wines, and let others know about your notable finds. There's also a Virtual Tasting Group, where you can participate in group tastings via the Internet, an archive of *Bud Starr's Wine Net* newsletter, and reviews of Washington state wineries. —(L.S.)

KEY NEWSGROUP **rec.food.drink** URL▶ http://augustus.csscr.washington.edu/personal/bigstar-mosaic/wine.html

Wines Across the Country

American Wine Jump **2457** CONTENT

It's been some time since wine snobs wrinkled their noses and sighed mightily at the mention of any wine not from France, but that same snobbery often denies the fact that good American wine is available from anywhere beyond California. This online magazine takes wine lovers across America, introducing them to the wines, wineries, and people of this rapidly growing domestic industry. Each month finds new articles about wine in America, including profiles, reviews, and regional reports covering every part of the country. The writers take a different approach from most wine magazines: they consider wine an everyday drink that can be enjoyed by everyone, not merely the self-avowed connoisseur. It's a refreshing change. —(L.S.)

KEY NEWSGROUP **rec.food.drink** URL▶ http://www.deltanet.com:80/food/wine/

Wine School

SWE Home Page Jump 5034 LINKS

This is the home page of The Society of Wine Educators (SWE), dedicated to the advancement of wine education. The page contains links to highlights from wine conferences as well as a wine glossary, and a Web-based Virtual Library of Wine. In addition, a link to an online wine-related newsletter is included. —(S.B.)

URL▸ http://ramey.chem.oxy.edu/

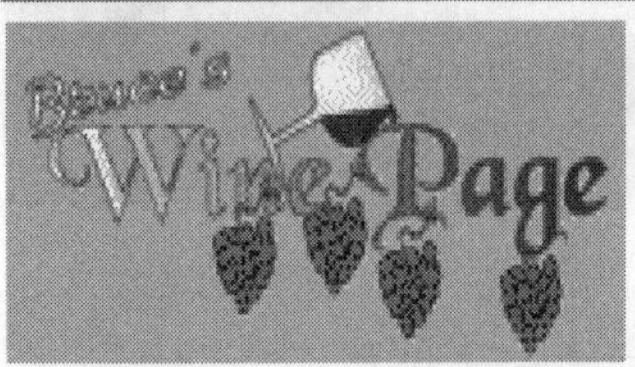

World of Wine Web Links

Bruce's Wine Page Jump 7186 LINKS

Bruce Skinner seems to be on excellent terms with the grape—in liquid, fermented form, that is. He has collected a large number of interesting wine sites on the Web. You can shop in wine stores, visit vineyards, and participate in wine forums and mail lists. The serious lover of wine can also download newsletters, read FAQs on winemaking, and check prices of favorite wineries before surfing off into the many other links Bruce thoughtfully provides. —(E.v.B.)

KEY NEWSGROUP alt.food.wine

URL▸ http://www.pcix.com/wine/index.html

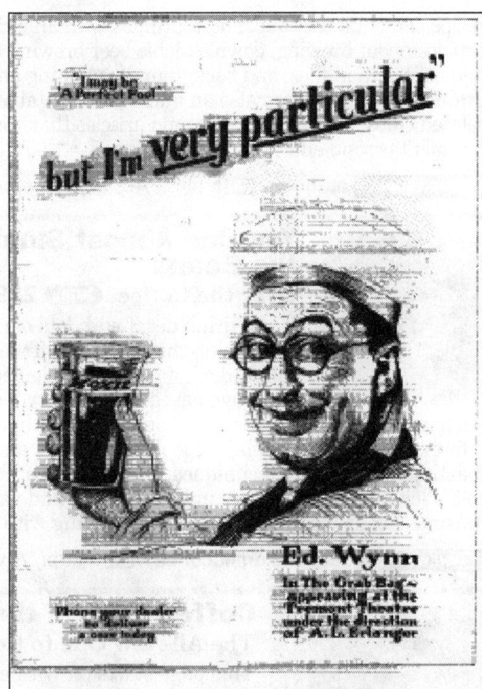

▲ *Cheers from Ed Wynn in an old Moxie advertisement, from* **The Moxie Home Page** *at* Jump 2196.

Site for Wine Enthusiasts

WineZone Jump 8016 CONTENT

This polished commercial site offers news about wines and wineries around California's Napa Valley, Sonoma County, and Pacific Coast region. Discover the new blends being offered by various wineries featured in the Zone. Read articles written by wine connoisseurs, download recipes and suggestions for the good life, and explore the wineries, and related tourist links, of the region online. —(E.v.B.)

KEY NEWSGROUP rec.food.drink URL▸ http://winezone.com/

Good Wine for a Good Price

Robin Garr's Wine Bargain Page Jump 2304 CONTENT

Wine reviewer and columnist Robin Garr brings his considerable expertise to bear on finding good wines for less than $10 a bottle. The reviews are brief, but informative, and new reviews are added frequently. There are two important bonuses here, not counting Robin's list of wine links. First, if you have a question about wine, you can ask it from this page. Robin tries to respond to all questions within 24 hours. Second, you can access his online Quick Wine Tasting Course, an excellent series of articles that takes the snobbery out of wine drinking. For those of you with larger budgets, there's also a link to reviews of higher-cost, but still reasonably priced, quality wines. —(L.S.)

KEY NEWSGROUP rec.food.drink URL▸ http://www.iglou.com/why/wine.html

Drinks Galore

Bartending in the 21st Century 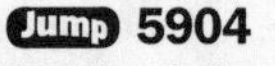 

Jump 5904 CONTENT

Here's the site you've all been waiting for: the definitive bartender's guide on the Internet. Know a drink but don't know how to make it? Check out this sites "Recipes A to Z" section. Want a drink by flavor? Well, check out "Select by Flavor," and then you can browse through the wine drinks, punch drinks, coffee, and even hot drinks. And then if you still have strength, you might want to head over to the great collection of beer, liquor, wine, and related sites. And before you leave, don't forget to raise a glass to bartender Steven Foster, who has done a great job with this site.—(J.P.)

KEY NEWSGROUP **alt.parties** URL▶ http://www.mixdrinks.com/

Scotland & Scotch Whiskey

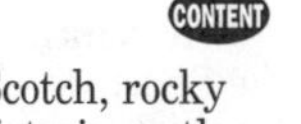

Welcome to Scotch.Com Jump **5089**

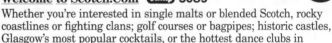

Whether you're interested in single malts or blended Scotch, rocky coastlines or fighting clans; golf courses or bagpipes; historic castles, Glasgow's most popular cocktails, or the hottest dance clubs in Edinburgh, **scotch.com** is your departure point for an exciting journey of exploration and discovery. An amazing and very informative journey for the Scot in you! —(S.B.)

URL▶ http://scotch.com/

Ya Gotta Have Moxie

The Moxie Home Page Jump **2196**

Long before there was Coke or Pepsi, there was Moxie. One of the first nerve tonics or soft drinks, the taste was so strong and distinctive that "Moxie" became synonymous with strength of character. To this day, it's defined in the dictionary as "spunk" or "guts," in addition to "soft drink." Ira Seskin is a lively writer, so you don't have to be a collector of Moxie memorabilia to enjoy these Web pages. Stop by, and he'll tell you about Moxie's history, show you wonderful graphics of old ads and promotional materials, and let you know what's happening with Moxie today (Hint: it's still being made!). —(L.S.)

KEY NEWSGROUP **rec.collecting** URL▶ http://www.xensei.com/users/iraseski/

A Home for the Cigar Lover

CONTENT

The Tobacconist Jump **4063**

This site, maintained by Ken Mortensen, is a great Web resource for finding information on the world of cigars. The site is split up into three areas each containing different resources. The Cigar Shoppe contains links to other cigar-related resources on the Web. The Humidor gives you information on cigar types and cigar manufacturers. Finally, The Smoking Room presents reading material about the smoking of cigars. A true home for those who love to puff! —(R.B.)

KEY NEWSGROUP **alt.smokers.cigars** URL▶ http://www.law.vill.edu/~kmortens/humidor/

High-Tech Hobbies

Here's The Gadget Guru

COMMERCE

The Gadget Guru Jump **4519**

Lots of consumer electronic buffs would love to have Andy Pargh's job. Pargh, best-known for his appearances as The Gadget Guru on NBC's Today Show, and his syndicated newspaper column of the same name, serves up a fact-filled, comprehensive and keyword-searchable site, packed with reviews of all kinds of new products—from stereos, computers and cameras, to motorcycles and household appliances. Andy's product review archive provides knowledgeable, feature-filled writeups of all the latest new products, plus daily updates. Andy does a wonderful job of filling you in on the features, pros, cons, and tech details of the latest products, often before they hit the market--so you can be a more well-informed electronics consumer. —(T.W.)

KEY NEWSGROUP **alt.toys.hi-tech** URL▶ http://www.gadgetguru.com

Shortwave Radio

The Shortwave/Radio Catalog

Jump 3507

The original purpose of the Shortwave/Radio Catalog was to provide the shortwave hobbyist with informative and useful links to Internet resources on the topic of shortwave radio. In the months since this page made its debut, it has grown to include much, much more. Maintained by Pete Costello, the Shortwave/Radio Catalog has become a jumping off point for Internet resources that offer a myriad of audio files, pictures, graphics, software, and interactive online programs—and it now includes info on other radio types, such as medium wave, FM, and satellite broadcasting, as well as pointers to clubs and equipment suppliers. —(C.P.)

KEY NEWSGROUP rec.radio.shortwave

URL ▶ http://itre.uncecs.edu/radio/

While mother and her guests relax,
the Space Cadets blast off noiselessly!
Earphones are attached to the helmets.

▲ *Gadget promising quiet TV viewing, from* **The PM Zone** *at* Jump **2355**.

German Shortwave Radio

Deutsche Welle Radio and TV

Jump 7017

Guten tag! Welcome to the German shortwave radio service—Deutsche Welle. If you're a shortwave fan, you'll love reading program previews, technical transmission specs and news reports, and analyses presented in four languages (your choice)—German, English, Spanish, and French. —(E.v.B.)

KEY NEWSGROUP rec.radio.shortwave URL ▶ http://www-dw.gmd.de/english/index.html

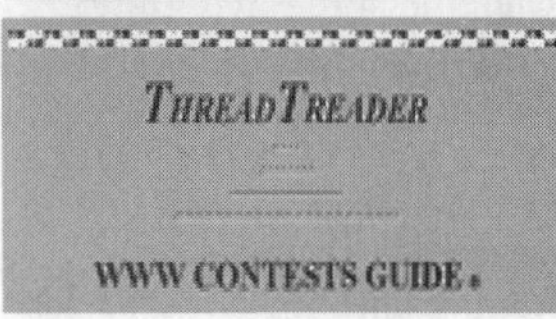

Amateur Video Editing Tips

Videonics Video Editing Resource Page Jump 7454

Videonics, a leading manufacturer of editing gear for amateur videographers, has created a rich site—both in content and in visual interest. You can learn about video editing and the postproduction process through the articles on simple and advanced video editing techniques posted here. As well, the company has provided additional sources you can access on the Web. Read about the seminars and products offered by this company, as well as supportive user's groups and newsletters. And tap into their video editing list server, which facilitates sharing hints, asking questions, and exploring ideas with other professionals. A super site for aspiring videographers! —(E.v.B.)

KEY NEWSGROUP rec.video URL ▶ http://www.videonics.com/

Hobbies: Miscellaneous

Guide to Contests on the Web

ThreadTreader's WWW Contests Guide Jump 2446

Perhaps the best aspect of the commercialization of the Web is that merchants, in their quest to draw attention and visitors to their sites, have begun a never-ending series of contests offering cash and merchandise as prizes. The odds of winning may be long, but most are fun and all of them cost you nothing except a little time. Michael J. Soltys makes it very easy to find and play these contests so that cost can be kept to a minimum. The contests are listed alphabetically and by category, and each is described so you can decide if it's your type. Michael also makes it easy to stay on top of the contest scene with sections on the current month's new offerings, and approaching deadlines for other Web contests. —(L.S.)

KEY NEWSGROUP alt.consumers.free-stuff URL ▶ http://www.4cyte.com/ThreadTreader/contest.html

You May Already Be a Winner!

Sweepstakes Online! Jump 2703

The people who maintain this site are in the business of providing data and other information for the die-hard sweepstakes entrant and contest participant. But they have free information available here, too. There's a Sweepstakes of the Week listing that lets anyone get started in what has become anything from a profitable hobby to an obsessive lifestyle for many, as well as a page where visitors can share their sweepstakes tips. Better for Web surfers, though, are the listings of the many sweepstakes and contests you can enter right on the Web. It's kept up-to-date, so checking regularly will keep you on top of what's happening. —(L.S.)

KEY NEWSGROUP **alt.consumer.free-stuff** URL▸ http://www.seanet.com/Vendors/sweeps/swon.html

North American Lottery Results

Welcome to InterLotto - On-Line Lottery Information Service Jump 3745

Here's the place to be to get results on all North American lotteries—all U.S. state lotteries, as well as those in Canada—updated daily. No more calls to those 900 number services—lottery results are now just a mouse click away! There are also links to many international lottery pages, such as those for Australia and Great Britian. —(N.F.)

URL▸ http://www.interlotto.com/

Dance Links Web Site

Dance Directory Jump 0159

Marv Vandehey's neat dance-related Web jump site has many links for devotees of specific dance styles. From this site, you can jump anywhere from the "Harvard Radcliffe Ballroom Dance Club Home Page" to the "Santa Barbara Country Dance Society," the "Ithica Swing Dance Network," and "Ernesto's Tango Page!" A Wide World of Web links for any dance interest. —(E.G.)

KEY NEWSGROUP **rec.arts.dance** URL▸ http://www.cyberspace.com/vandehey/dance.html

Totally Fresh

SB's Break Dancin' Home Page Jump 7096

Yo! This high-energy page is compiled by break dancin' Steven Berke. Get that 1980s feeling when you read his lingo page. Learn the moves through text and downloadable movies. Soon you'll be windmillin', backspinnin', uprockin' all over the house. Not enough? Read about the music and the history of break dancing, and view 1980s graffiti before you moonwalk out the door. —(E.v.B.)

KEY NEWSGROUP **rec.arts.dance** URL▸ http://rowlf.cc.wwu.edu:8080/~n9344199/bd/bd.html

Hola! Tango!

Tango Dance Notation Argentina Argentine Jump 7097

Stick a rose behind your ear and let's tango! S. Koppenhoefer, a Swiss enthusiast, has created a multimedia tango page. In addition to book and video lists, discography files, a calendar of tango events, and a fascinating history of the dance, there are movies, movies, movies of Claudia, Romeo, Pepito and Maria interpreting this sensuous dance. As well, there are lots of photos of various tango artists, a file on the latest method of movement notation (learn new steps!), and biographies of the greats. —(E.v.B.)

KEY NEWSGROUP **rec.arts.dance** URL▸ http://litwww.epfl.ch/~shawn/tango/

Hoofers on the Web

Tap Dance Home Page Jump 7099 

Feet get itchy when you watch a tap dancer? Well, time to pull on some tap shoes and shuffle, break, and stomp along with page creator Paul Corr. He has assembled all the information you need to get those feet moving: detailed notations of traditional tap steps, lists of teaching and entertainment videos, lists of clubs, glossaries, biographies, clips of tap performances, history of the dance—even when to celebrate National Tap Dance Day in the U.S.—it's May 25. —(E.v.B.)

KEY NEWSGROUP **rec.arts.dance** URL▸ http://www.hahnemann.edu/tap/#INDEX1

Dance, Dance, Dance

The US Swing Dance Server Jump 7101 

Remember the Shag? The Boogie Woogie? The Jitterbug? Want to learn these dances or relive past dance glories? Check out the instructions on over 40 swing dances. A tip: If you're learning the Sugar Push, think water skiing when you push and pull your partner as you swing around the dance floor. In addition to getting you up and bouncing, this page presents a calendar of dance events, lists of music, a few video clips, tips on technique, as well as definitions of all the varied styles of swing dancing. —(E.v.B.)

KEY NEWSGROUP **rec.arts.dance** URL▸ http://www.cs.cornell.edu/Info/People/aswin/SwingDancing/swing_dancing.html

Virtual Squares

Western Square Dancing Jump 7103 

Swing your partner and allemande right onto this comprehensive Web page where everything you ever wanted to know about square dancing and calling are presented. Have a partner handy? You can practice such basic calls as the ladies chain, reverse flutterwheel, load the boat, and box the gnat. There are over 50 to choose from. As well, you can read a guide to correct square-dance behavior, obtain information on clubs and organizations, and link to other services such as electronic mailing lists and calling schools. Out of breath? Stop and read the amusing Bugs Bunny episode Sour Belly Trio, that's also here. —(E.v.B.)

KEY NEWSGROUP **rec.arts.dance** URL▸ http://suif.stanford.edu/~rfrench/wsd/

The World of Fashion

ELLE Magazine Jump 7428 

Ah, ELLE Magazine, trés chic, n'est pas? If keeping up on fashion's hot trends is one of your life priorities, explore the well-executed online version of this popular print publication. Read the "runway reports" to see what's in and what's out, check out ELLE's fashion tips, and then use ELLE's bulletin board to share your thoughts on fashion. As well, you can stroll through the Model Gallery and meet the beautiful women who model the latest fashions. After you've exhausted ELLE's offerings, you can surf its hot links to the Web's fashion sites. —(E.v.B.)

KEY NEWSGROUP **alt.fashion** URL▸ http://www.ellemag.com/member/

Fashion News, Views & Advice

@fashion Jump 2690 

Here's the place to plug into the latest trends, get to know the top designers, pick up a bit of gossip, and generally keep up to date on the ever-changing fashion scene. It's all here, in a site updated at least monthly with well-written features that rival the glossy magazines. Along the way, you'll also get some excellent fashion advice from Jeanne Beker, be able to participate in online discussions, and even question the fashion experts. Each month, Debbie Steinberg, who produces the site, also points you to some of the other interesting fashion sites on the Net. Whether your idea of fashion is haute couture, ready-to-wear, or someplace in between, you'll find this site worth checking regularly. —(L.S.)

KEY NEWSGROUP **alt.fashion**
URL ▶ http://www2.pcy.mci.net/fashion/tbd/index.html

Fashion's Internet Central

Fashion Internet
Jump 6707 CONTENT

Packed with pictures, resources and in-depth articles on the garment world, Fashion Internet is a first-rate site for coverage of the fashion world. Read how a high-end discount shopper describes the "thrill of the kill," or the clueless guy's guide to buying a suit. Reviews of recent season fashion shows from Richard Tyler, John Bartlett and Nautica, among many others, can be found here. And from here, you can open the doors to the designer Web showrooms of Bill Blass, Donna Karan, Joan & David, or Natori, to name a few. In addition to this site's editorial fashion coverage, articles on related subjects, such as perfumes, and skin and fitness, are also featured. —(L.T.)

KEY NEWSGROUP **alt.fashion** URL ▶ http://www.finy.com/

Fashion News & Trends

Fashion Page
Jump 2160

Want to keep up with the latest fashion trends? Couldn't make it to the Paris shows? Never fear, for Linda Stretton is your eyes and ears in the world of fashion. Not only does she cover the shows and the scene, she offers up helpful advice on accessories, styles, and how to wear them (with fashion tips for men, too). With the help of editor Jake Commander, she writes in a conversational style that makes it seem as if you've run into Linda at a one of those chi-chi cocktail parties instead of the Web. Coverage includes the prevoius, the current, and the next seasons, items on more esoteric fashions, and reviews of other fashion media. She doesn't take the subject as seriously as it may sound, but she is serious about providing good information. —(L.S.)

KEY NEWSGROUP **alt.fashion** URL ▶ http://www.charm.net/~jakec/

▲ *Fantastic fashion for the stylish, from* **Geek Chic** *at* **Jump 7477**.

What's in Fashion?

Welcome to Fashion Net **Jump 7196**

Fashion Net is fun to browse, whether your constant apparel is denim or silk. You can read the latest news from fashion centers of the world. You can find links to the pages of models, photographers, stylists, and makeup artists on Web. If you're employed in the fashion industry, Fashion Net provides a showcase for your work, the latest industry news, available jobs, and, soon to come, virtual fashion shows. —(E.v.B.)

KEY NEWSGROUP **alt.fashion** URL ▶ http://www.triple.com/fashion-net/

Roots Lists

Genealogy Toolbox

Jump 2626

With more than 550 links, and growing all the time, Matthew Helm's page should be the primary resource for both amateur and professional genealogists. It's very easy to use, too, divided into 13 sections to keep the section lists manageable. Among those sections are general guides and indexes, geographical resources, groups and associations, professional resources, software, and heraldry. There's even an index of surnames contained in databases and family histories on the Internet. And, as with any good links page, there's a what's new and history page to make it easy for you to keep track of additions and deletions. —(L.S.)

▲ *Old photos, part of a genealogical record of a family, from* The Genealogy Home Page *at* **Jump 2128**.

KEY NEWSGROUP **soc.roots** URL▸ http://ux1.cso.uiuc.edu/~al-helm/genealogy.html

Counting Back the Generations

Genealogy Resources on the Internet **Jump 8067**

Chris Gaunt has pulled together some great resources for scaling that family tree, by identifying scores of useful mailing lists, Internet newsgroups and other Net genealogical features. The alphabetical organization of his resources is comprehensive, and easy to use. For example, you can look up genealogical links by ethnic group, find the right archive to search for information, choose what state resources are useful in your search, and even get to U.S. census data. —(E.v.B.)

URL▸http://wwwpersonal.umich.edu/~cgaunt/gen_web.html#COMM

Help for Genealogy Enthusiasts

The Genealogy Home Page **Jump 2128**

Because of its ability to let people access other people and resources worldwide, the Internet has drawn professional and amateur genealogists in droves. This site is the root of the genealogists' tree, with links to anything and everything related to the topic. There are links to help sources and guides, libraries, general and specific resources, online information, software, maps, and commercial services. And what would a special interest page be without links to newsgroups, mailing lists, and others sharing the interest on the Net? They're here, too. The pages are updated frequently, and you can track the latest changes and additions through the What's New section. But given the depth of resource links, you just may want to browse this site regularly to keep up to date. —(L.S.)

KEY NEWSGROUP **soc.genealogy.misc** URL▸ http://ftp.cac.psu.edu/~saw/genealogy.html

Family History Resources

TREASURE MAPS - the "How-to" Genealogy Site

Jump 8068

The folks at Treasure Maps, publishers and creators of this site, are dedicated to helping you trace your family history. Follow their easy-to-understand "Five Steps to Getting Started on your Family History," or take the tutorial on using the U.S. Federal Census data, or even learn how to use the Mormon Church's online guides to their vast genealogical archives. Family history is not all sitting in dusty archives, straining your eyes over nearly illegible county records—you also learn here how to properly do tombstone rubbings! Don't forget to subscribe to their free monthly e-mail genealogy newsletter. —(E.v.B.)

KEY NEWSGROUP **alt.genealogy** URL▸ http://www.firstct.com/fv/tmaps.html

Genealogical Roots Reference

Everton's Genealogical Magazine Online Edition Jump 2420

Everton's claims to be the largest genealogical magazine published, with some 300 pages per issue. The online version is somewhat smaller, but it's free and includes features not in the print edition, such as links to online sites covered in the articles and a special e-mail from the reader's section. Each issue carries news, a calendar of genealogy-related events, reports on Web sites, and a feature on the genealogy of a specific family or ethnic group, in addition to other articles to help amateur and professional genealogists alike. If you don't want to spend time online reading each monthly edition, you can download the HTML files and browse at your leisure offline. —(L.S.)

KEY NEWSGROUP **soc.genealogy.misc** URL▶ http://www.xmission.com/~jayhall/ghonline.html

Genealogical Names Search Site

Churchyard/Orr Family Museum (Genealogy) Jump 5097

This is a translation of parts of the genealogy compendium *Our Family Museum* by James Nohl Churchyard into HTML format. Over 360 different family names and 835 different individuals are indexed. The main regions of origin are England, Quebec, France, the Rhineland (Germany), Ulster, New England, New York, and the middle states. Contact information for the author is provided. Is your name here? —(S.B.)

KEY NEWSGROUP **soc.genealogy.surnames** URL▶ http://uts.cc.utexas.edu/~churchh/genealgy.html

Social Security Death Index Genealogical Search Site

Ancestry's Social Security Death Index (SSDI) Search Jump 5651

Here's another useful Net resource for your genealogical searches. The Death Master File (DMF) from the Social Security Administration (SSA), contains over 50 million records created from SSA payment records. Each file includes (if available) information on the decedent: last name, first name, state in which the record was issued, birth date, last known residence and any lump sum payment. To search the database, one simply fills out the form, adding as much information as possible, and the results will appear in seconds. Although the SSA does not have a death record for everyone, this is a very impressive database. —(J.P.)

KEY NEWSGROUP **soc.genealogy.misc** URL▶ http://www.infobases.com/ssdi/

Finding Friends on the Net

International Penpal Page Jump 2129

If it does nothing else (which is highly unlikely!), the popularity of the Internet and e-mail is bringing back the threatened art of letter writing and revitalizing the hobby of pen pals. Jill Lampi has created a short, but very sweet, page of links and resources to help you get started and expand your list of e-mail correspondents. She includes both snail-mail and e-mail penpal lists and resources, but the snail-mail listings are by far the more extensive, with both general and special-interest lists described. —(L.S.)

KEY NEWSGROUP **soc.penpals** URL▶ http://www.mbnet.mb.ca/~lampi/penpal.html

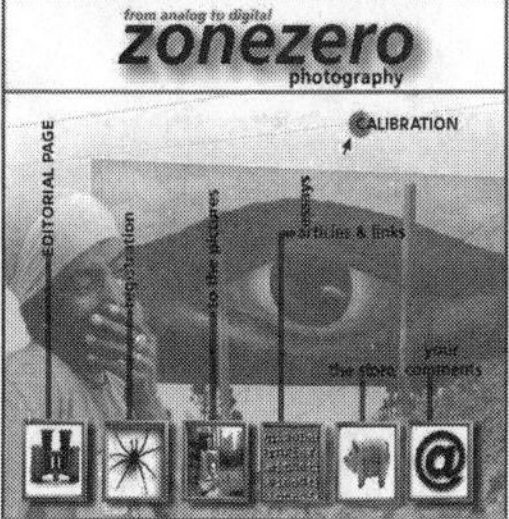

ZoneZero Photography

ZoneZero Photography Jump 6735

If you're very serious about photography, you'll be impresed by the content offered here by the folks at ZoneZero, best known for their fascinating catalog of heavy-duty photo equipment and techniques. Professionals and advanced amateurs alike will find articles and essays discussing such topics as the future of photojournalism, and the latest advances in documentary photography. Photo enthusiasts of all skill levels will also delight in viewing the hundreds of cultural images taken in both black and white and color film, by some of the world's top photographers. —(L.T.)

KEY NEWSGROUP **rec.photo** URL▶ http://www.zonezero.com/

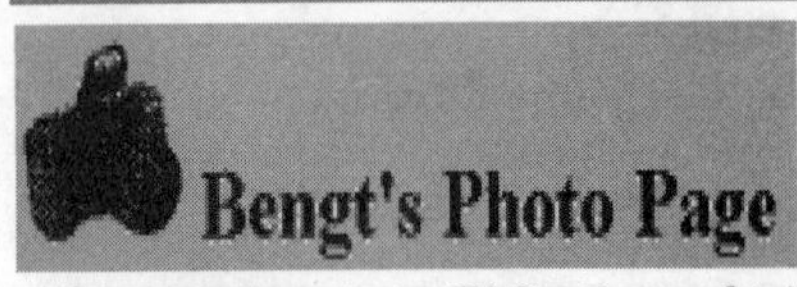

Photography Resources

Bengt's Photo Page Jump 3510

Swedish photographer Bengt Hallinger has put together what easily qualifies as "the" Web resource for the amateur or professional photographer. This site offers fascinating links to photo exhibitions, archives and contests, FAQs, tips and tricks, the **rec.photo** newsgroup hierarchy, a selection of individual photo pages, and a number of commercial operations, as well. If you've got a question about film or lenses, darkroom techniques, or framing—this is the page to come home to! —(C.P.)

KEY NEWSGROUP **rec.photo** URL▶ http://math.liu.se/~behal/photo/

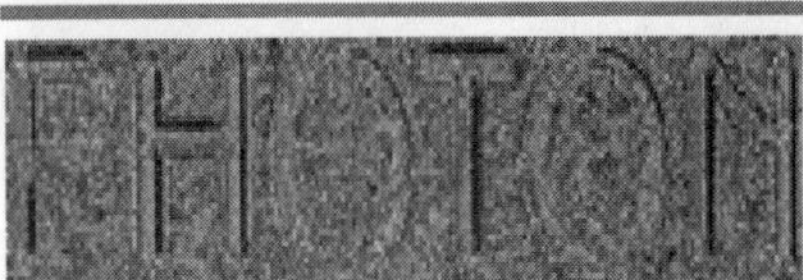

Photography as Art

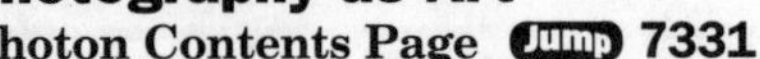

Photon Contents Page Jump 7331

Photon magazine, published in Britain, is full of wonderful articles on what it describes as the art and science of light—in other words, photography. You can read, in the online edition, about equipment (cameras, lenses, enlargers), the interface between digital photography and computers, or even pointers on the life of a freelance photographer. As well, individual photographers and their works are often featured. One of the value-added features is the Virtual Model Agency, where real model agencies can mount information and photos of their models, and studios can also advertise their workshops or group shoots. You can post a classified ad for equipment or look for photo assignments here, too. —(E.v.B.)

KEY NEWSGROUP **rec.photo.advanced** URL▶ http://www.scotborders.co.uk/photon/photon.html

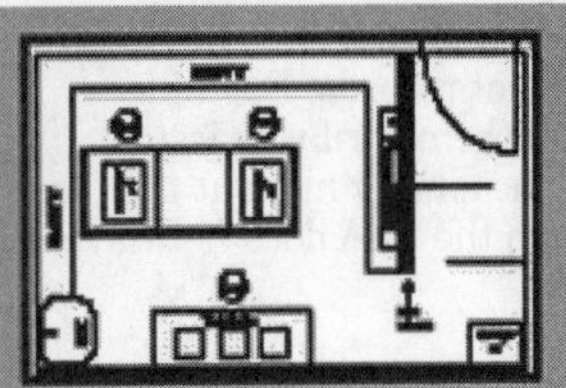

Photo Darkroom Guide

The Photography Center Jump 2594

This site deals exclusively with black and white film developing and printing for the beginner and the intermediate photographer. Maintained by Adam Block and the Photo Club of the University of Miami, there are instructional guides for film and print processing, as well as many helpful hints and tricks. If you're just getting started, the Quick and Easy sections of the film and print processing guides tell you everything you need to know to learn the basics. Once you've mastered those, you can spend more time with the extended guides to hone your skills. —(L.S.)

KEY NEWSGROUP **rec.photo** URL▶ http://www.ashe.miami.edu/ab/photo.html

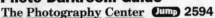

Fast and Easy Horoscope Index

EasyScopes
Jump 5870

They call this the one-stop Zodiac guide, and that's just what it is. And it's so simple it's a wonder no one has thought of this before. What Jochen Savelberg has done is collect together a couple dozen of the best astrology sites from around the world and grouped them together for daily, weekly or monthly readings. All you do is pick your sign, sit back, and choose which of the columns you want to read. And that's not all—there's also a bookstore and a chat area here, too. —(J.P.)

KEY NEWSGROUP **alt.astrology** URL▶ http://stars.euregio.net/joe/zodiac/

Your Daily Horoscope

Jonathan Cainer's Zodiac Forecasts
Jump 2282

Each day, Jonathan Cainer of Britain's Daily Mail newspaper tells you what the stars hold for you. Just click on your zodiac sign and Jonathan's forecast for that day appears. If you want to learn more about a sign of the zodiac, there's a nice, but brief, description of each, along with a good set of links to other Web sites with astrological information. —(L.S.)

KEY NEWSGROUP **alt.astrology** URL▶ http://www.metawire.com/stars/index.html

A Weekly Horoscope

Horoscopes/Astrology: Weekly Cyber-stars from John James Jump 2283

If you want some guidance before venturing into your week, John James consults the stars to give you some hints. His weekly horoscopes highlight the problems and prospects indicated for you, and, combined with a daily horoscope, give you as much astrological insight as you can get without a personal chart. John also has an interest in dreams, and he welcomes e-mail from readers sharing theirs. —(L.S.)

KEY NEWSGROUP alt.astrology URL▶ http://www.dircon.co.uk/networks/stars.html

Your Future Is in the Cards

Tarot Jump 2324

Tarot is like any other fortune-telling device—what you get out of it depends on what you put into it. That's clear with this tarot-generating page, as Jonathan Katz admonishes you to "strive to understand how the cards fall for you this day." Since there's no ersatz Gypsy to interpret the cards for you, you need to do it yourself, but at worst, Jonathan's Tarot page is good fun, and it may even trigger some insights for you. The full Keltic reading is best, especially if you read the tarot FAQs that are also here. If you're in a hurry, there's also a much quicker three-card reading. —(L.S.)

KEY NEWSGROUP alt.tarot URL▶ http://cad.ucla.edu/repository/useful/tarot.html

Magic, Mysticism, & the Occult

Anders Magick Page Jump 2322

From ancient druids to contemporary practitioners, from alchemy to voodoo, if it's mystic, ritualistic, or paranormal—and on the Web—Anders Sandberg's page will link you to it! The links aren't limited to fringe groups, either. Anders includes Eastern religions, organizations such as the Freemasons, and the New Age movement side by side with the satanists and pagans. There's even a section of humorous "magick" links, so whether you're serious about this or seeking entertainment, you'll find your pointers. —(L.S.)

KEY NEWSGROUP alt.magick URL▶ http://www.nada.kth.se/~nv91-asa/magick.html#gen

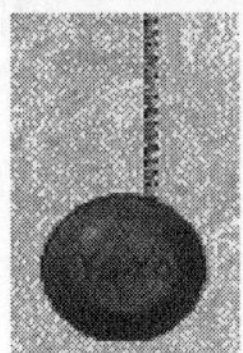

Yo-Yos Make a Comeback

World of Yo Jump 2722

Once the world's most popular toy, the yo-yo has fallen on hard times. There was a slight resurgence with the Smothers Brothers "Yo-Yo Man," but that didn't last long. Now, though, it appears that there's another comeback in the works, with attendance at yo-yo events increasing, sales of yo-yos showing signs of life, and, yes, Web pages. This one has information about events and competitions, tips on basic yo-yo tricks, and a link to the history of this simple, yet engaging toy. —(L.S.)

KEY NEWSGROUP rec.toys.misc URL▶ http://www.socool.com/socool/yopage.html

Cyber Lighthouse Exhibit

Bill's Lighthouse Getaway Jump 7436

William A. Britten is obviously a connoisseur of lighthouses. He has mounted a great collection of photographs, history, and information on American lighthouses from the Great Lakes to the Outer Banks to the California coast. William tells us which ones are endangered either by the elements or by human neglect, and how you can join various efforts to preserve these beacons of the sea. He also provides contact information for lighthouse societies throughout North America. —(E.v.B.)

KEY NEWSGROUP alt.architecture URL▶ http://www.lib.utk.edu/lights.html

Juggler's Home on the Web

Juggling Information Service Jump 2098 CONTENT

If you juggle, or want to learn how, Barry Bakalor maintains these pages of information and links to juggling resources on the Internet. With the aid of other jugglers around the world, he gives you hints and tips, selected articles from juggling magazines, lists of juggling festivals, FAQs, links to jugglers' home pages, and information about the International Jugglers Association. For the more scholarly juggler, there's an article on the mathematics of the art. There's even juggling software here, to help you hone your skills and create new juggling patterns. Hup! Ho! —(L.S.)

KEY NEWSGROUP **rec.juggling** URL ▶ http://www.hal.com/services/juggle/

▲ *Juggler and juggling pins, photo from* **Juggling Information Service** *at* Jump **2098**.

All about Castles

Castles on the Web Jump 7437 CONTENT

Ted Monk has been obsessed with castles from an early age. He has created these pages to mirror this continuing interest in what he terms an "age of heraldry, chivalry, and the romance of another place in mind." Browse through his extensive collection of photographs and links to individual castle Web sites—from Nagoya Castle to Panicale, Peel Castle to Prague Castle. In "Castle Quest," you can post your questions on castles, and Ted will answer to the best of his ability. Don't worry if you don't know the correct terms for the parts of a castle: Ted has mounted a glossary for your use. A wonderful site! —(E.v.B.)

URL ▶ http://fox.nstn.ca/~tmonk/castle/castle.html

Homes Away from Home

Motel Americana Jump 7450 CONTENT

Andy and Jenny Wood have created a site celebrating the independent roadside motel—which they feel is slipping into obscurity. Read excerpts from their "road trips," and view the photos of motels this couple has visited. For some, these motels were havens from the storms of driving, or a memory of family togetherness playing a game of Go Fish on a lumpy motel mattress; you're encouraged to add your family's vacation motel memories here as well. After the nostalgic tour of neon signs and low-rise architecture, surf the other Net resources the Woods have gathered on motels. —(E.v.B.)

KEY NEWSGROUP **rec.travel** URL ▶ http://oak.cats.ohiou.edu/~aw148888/motel.html

High-Powered Model Rockets

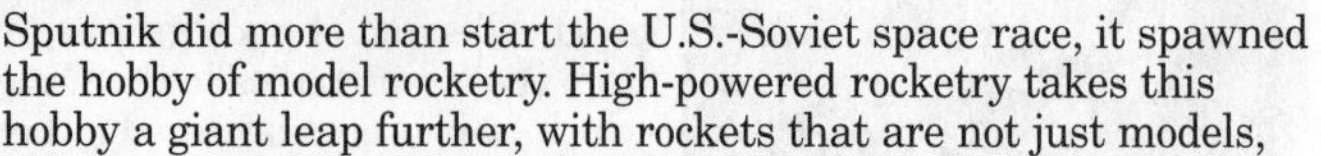

SEDS High Powered Rockets Page Jump 2099 

Sputnik did more than start the U.S.-Soviet space race, it spawned the hobby of model rocketry. High-powered rocketry takes this hobby a giant leap further, with rockets that are not just models, but small-scale versions of the real things. The difference between a high-powered rocket and a standard model rocket is in size and power and the fact that you need to clear the high-powered launch with the FAA. For the beginner, there is information about the sport, a glossary of rocketry terms, information about SEDS activities, and links to other rocketry Web pages. For the more advanced rocketeer, there are links to space model plans, software to assist design, and pointers to finding high-powered rocketry equipment. —(L.S.)

KEY NEWSGROUP **rec.models.rockets** URL ▶ http://seds.lpl.arizona.edu/rocket/rocket.html

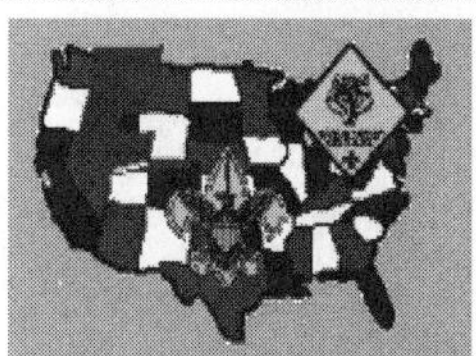

Scouting's Main Campsite

U.S. Scouting Front Door Jump 2543 CONTENT

This very well-organized site has everything the active Scouter or merely curious would want to know about Scouts and Scouting. There are separate sections for each of the different types of Scouts, from Cub to Explorer, as well as Girl Scouts and the Order of the Arrow honor society. Within each subpage, there's an explanation of what that group is about, how you advance through the group and up a level, and recommended activities, guides, tips, and other information to build skills and have fun. With the links to newsgroups, mailing lists, FTP sites and other related resources, this site is all you need to get started—and keep going—with Scouting. —(L.S.)

KEY NEWSGROUP **rec.scouting**

URL▶ http://www.cais.com:80/newtwatch/

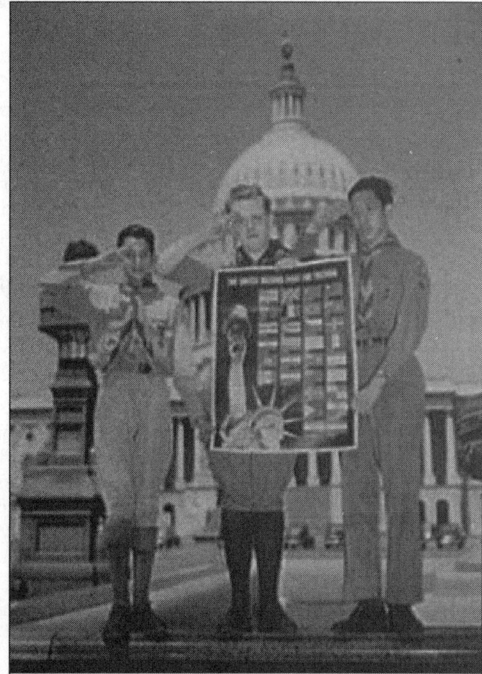

▲ *Boy Scouts in front of the U.S. Capitol, from* **Library of Congress WWW Home Page** *at* Jump **0100**.

International Scouting Resource

The InterNETional Scouting Page Jump 2541 LINKS

Even with the terrific U.S. Scouting resources available elsewhere on the Web, no Scout should skip this page. Maintained by David Jansen, it offers links to Scouting pages, troops, resources, and activities around the world, a good way to find new ideas and keep up with what's new on the international Scouting scene. The links include listings of Scout camps around the world, online Scouting books, and links to general pointers of interest and help. There's also a Web link to ScoutNet, the official electronic link for Scouting maintained on FidoNet. —(L.S.)

KEY NEWSGROUP **rec.scouting** URL▶ http://www.strw.leidenuniv.nl/~jansen/scout/

Kite Flying Heaven

Kite Flier's Site Jump 2107 CONTENT

Even if you don't fly kites yourself, you can't help but be impressed by the beauty, creativity, and imagination of the kite designs in the image gallery here. If you do fly kites, this is your home page. There are features on interesting people, articles by kiters on various aspects of kite design, art, and sport, and links to other kite-oriented Web pages. The archives themselves are remarkably well organized. Andrew Beattie and his cohorts put a great deal of time into organizing the various FAQs by subject and reformatting them from standard text to hyperlinked pages, each with a table of contents. The result is one of the easiest-to-navigate archive sites on the Web. —(L.S.)

KEY NEWSGROUP **rec.kites** URL▶ http://twoshakes.kfs.org:80/kites/

Up, Up, & Away

Cyber-Kites Home Page! Jump 7075 CONTENT

If building and flying kites is your kind of hobby, drift on by Daryl Erwin's page. Here you can see the kites he has made, read about competitions, and subscribe to kite magazines around the world. Still high? Then float through the other kite-flying home page links he has thoughtfully provided. —(E.v.B.)

KEY NEWSGROUP **rec.kites** URL▶ http://derwin.wlu.ca/kites.htm

Cryptography Information Center

The Cryptography Archive Jump 3502 

Nca uyo drea sthi? Od uyo ecar? If the answer to both of those questions is yes, then you're probably one of those folks who fools with the CryptoQuote in the morning paper. If you're fascinated by cryptography and cryptoanalysis, the Quadralay Cryptography Archive is a must-see. This site offers pointers to every major archive of cryptographic material on the Net—even one run by the NSA itself. No joke! And it's loaded with detailed information about crypto standards that range from DES to the Clipper Chip and everything else in between. Cool graphics, too! Ese uyo ether. :-) Oh, if you haven't figured these mini ciphers out by now, here's a hint: just move the first letter in each word to the last position, instead. See it now? This cipher technique is known as a simple transposition. Fun, isn't it?! —(C.P.)

KEY NEWSGROUP **sci.crypt** URL▶ http://www.quadralay.com/www/Crypt/Crypt.html

LEGO's Home on the Web

Official LEGO World Wide Web Site Jump 5929 

While the LEGO site is primarily dedicated to children, adults will certainly enjoy the history of the company and related news that's presented here. And they can certainly feel free to leave their kids alone here to wander about the site as well. A special feature here lets your kids create their own LEGO home page, where they can use LEGO pieces as links to their favorite sites. They can also download wallpaper, screensavers and even watch a Quicktime movie. —(J.P.)

URL▶ http://www.lego.com/

Treasure Hunting Tips

International Treasure Hunters Exchange
Jump 2246 

This is the Web's only site devoted to the adventure of treasure hunting. Whether you scour the beaches with a metal detector, or search the deep sea for shipwrecks, you'll be able to exchange messages with others who share your interest, read true stories from other adventurers, and even learn about and buy equipment over the Net. There's also treasure hunting news, a research guide with pointers to agencies to help with research, maps, and permits, and excerpts from *Treasure Quest magazine*. —(L.S.)

URL▶ http://www.treasure.com/

X Marks the Spot

TreasureNet Jump 5059 

If you are interested in treasure or treasure hunting, TreasureNet is where you should be. There are many links here, including ones to products and services related to treasure seeking (maps, of course), a list of "TreasureNet'rs" (Net users who are also treasure hunters), Treasure News, and Special Events. And even if you're not interested in hunting for long lost treasure, be sure to check out the section on treasure stories for some good tales. —(S.B.)

URL▶ http://www.halcyon.com/treasure/

Big Game Fishing

Saltwater Fishing Home Page Jump 2451 

Whether you put out to sea or cast from surf, this page gives you the resources you need to better enjoy saltwater fishing. There are fishing reports, advice on better angling offshore or in the surf, fish stories and pictures, and links to equipment manufacturers and dealers. It's also the place to share your tips and stories, and contributions are encouraged. Just send them to Webmasters International, which maintains this site for the benefit of all sport fishers. —(L.S.)

KEY NEWSGROUP **rec.outdoors.fishing.saltwater** URL▶ http://wmi.cais.com/saltfish/index.html

Rocky Norway

Norwegian Rockhound Jump 7081 

Rockhounds never die, they only petrify—so says the Norwegian Rockhound, Hans-Jorgen Berg, designer of this page. Get out your rock hammer and your long underwear and go rockhunting (even in minus-20 degree weather) with Berg. Along the way, he'll show you pictures of minerals and entertain you with news and rumors about the Norwegian rockhunting scene. —(E.v.B.)

KEY NEWSGROUP sci.geo.geology

URL ▶ http://www.uio.no:80/~hansjb/index.html

Fly-Fishing Tips

Trout Tales Jump 2644 

The emphasis is on fishing in the Colorado area in Dennis Smith's monthly online newsletter, but there's interesting stuff here for any fly-fisher, too. The articles on fly-tying will be particularly useful, and the articles on fishing in the various rivers in the area include tips applicable to most any locale. Mixed in are tales of personal successes and failures with rod and reel, general trout fishing hints and tips, and a swap shop for buying, selling and trading fishing gear. —(L.S.)

KEY NEWSGROUP rec.outdoors.fishing URL ▶ http://www.inetmkt.com/bobs/ttalesag.html

▲ *Bass man on the Web, from* **FLIES Page** *at* Jump 7092.

Fly-Fishing Tips & Resources

The Virtual Flyshop Jump 2100 

Before you pull on the waders, try casting around this Webspace for information about one of life's more serene sports. Although Greg McDermid is adding some commercial features, the main purpose of these pages is to be the fly-fisher's primary Internet resource, and it lives up to that billing in quality as well as quantity. There's an online magazine, a how-to section for those who tie their own flies, information on fishing trips, and a good selection of links to other fly-fishing sites and angler home pages. —(L.S.)

KEY NEWSGROUP rec.outdoors.fishing.fly URL ▶ http://rmii.com/~flyshop/flyshop.html

Fishing in Iceland

Angling Club Lax-A Jump 7049 

If a fly-fishing holiday in Iceland is your dream, troll on over to this Web site. Information on every Icelandic river, maps of fishing sites, club details, and general information on Icelandic angling are posted. Pictures of happy fishermen and women with the day's catch can also be viewed. —(E.v.B.)

KEY NEWSGROUP rec.outdoors.fishing URL ▶ http://www.ismennt.is/fyr_stofn/lax-a/uk/anclub_uk.html

Virtual Fly Tying

FLIES Page Jump 7092 

Spinner wing tying, hackle fly swisher, streamer dressings—"huh," you say. Read Nic Blackwell's page on fish-fly tying, and you, too, can talk that talk. And learn how to tie the fishing lures to end all fishing lures. Along the way you can also learn the difference between dry to wet dressings and the newest methods of fly tying. As well, you can watch a movie on fly fishing, check out Nic's fishing album (do we believe everything we see?), and explore other fishing sites that Nic has selected. —(E.v.B.)

KEY NEWSGROUP **rec.outdoors.fishing.fly** URL▸ ftp://ftp.geo.mtu.edu/pub/fishing/from_nicb/flys.htm

Scientific Casting

The Physics of Fly Casting Jump **7095**

Now here's a really serious fisherman. Jeff Kommers, at MIT, naturally, is studying the physics of fly casting. He's developed a model based on a theory of mechanics that you can wade through. As well, why not watch the movies he's assembled on the motion of a fishing line during a typical cast. Need more? Then scan the articles Jeff has entered from other scientific fishermen. —(E.v.B.)

KEY NEWSGROUP **rec.outdoors.fishing.fly** URL▸ http://www.mit.edu:8001//people/kommers/fly.html

Jeff Cooper's Shooting, Hunting and Cultural Commentaries

Jeff Cooper Commentaries
Jump **5758**

Jeff Cooper is widely recognized as the father of modern combat pistol shooting. Over the years, Cooper's many original techniques in pistol shooting revolutionized the use of the handgun in combat, law enforcement, and personal protection. As an author of some of the field's most popular shooting books, and editor-at-large at the magazine *Guns & Ammo*, Cooper has also become known for his "Commentaries," in which Cooper adds his own recent personal experiences, hunting stories, and political opinions to his usual discussion of the use of firearms "in the social context." The Commentaries are collected here, dating from 1993 to the present. —(J.P.)

KEY NEWSGROUP **info.firearms** URL▸ http://www.concentric.net/~mkeithr/jeff/index.html

All about Guns & Gun Ownership

rec.guns FAQ Home Page
Jump **2533**

Every gun owner, from target shooter to hunter, novice to expert, should bookmark this page for quick reference. Very well organized by FAQ maintainer David Putzolu, you can jump quickly to FAQs (Frequently Asked Question files) on gun safety, pointers on what to look for when purchasing firearms, a glossary and acronym dictionary, and a section listing recent additions and updates. A compilation of all the various FAQs from the Net's **rec.guns** newsgroup is also available, presented as a single document with hyperlinks to specific topic areas. You'll also find archives of sounds and images, downloadable Postscript target files, and links to related pages, including one that lists people for novices to contact if they want to use firearms safely . —(L.S.)

KEY NEWSGROUP **rec.guns** URL▸ http://www-sal.cs.uiuc.edu/rec.guns/

THE Gun Owners' Home Page

NRA.org (National Rifle Association Home Page) Jump **2534**

The National Rifle Association is much more than a group that lobbies on behalf of the rights of gun owners, but this page is devoted almost exclusively to the political issues surrounding firearms ownership. There's a section of alerts, news, and other timely articles; information on state and federal firearms laws; and listings of current and proposed laws that affect Second Amendment rights. You'll also find sections devoted to women's issues and general firearms issues that don't fall into any of the specific categories. —(L.S.)

KEY NEWSGROUP **talk.politics.guns** URL▸ http://www.nra.org/

Railroading Today

Cyberspace World Railroad Home Page Jump **2119**

Railroads are very much alive, if not well, in the United States, and quite healthy in other parts of the world. If you want to find out what's happening in the world of rails, just stop at these pages maintained by Daniel S. Dowdy. They begin with news and features, updated at least monthly, covering all aspects of using and running railroads. Continue down the main page and you'll find sounds and images, clip art, railroad fonts and logos, timetables, links to historical information, FAQs, and links to other railroad Web pages. This is an attractive, well-designed, and content-rich Web site, and another example of how graphics can be used as an integral, not an intrusive, part of a Web page. —(L.S.)

KEY NEWSGROUP **rec.railroad**
URL▶ http://www.mcs.com/~dsdawdy/cyberoad.html

▲ *Bad day at the train station, from* **Washington University Archives** *at* Jump **0192**.

Everything about Railroads

Railroad-Related Internet Resources
Jump **2149** 

The best part of this railroad enthusiast's page is the Link of the Week, an ongoing compilation of resources that don't fit anywhere else. It could be information about earthquake-ravaged railroad lines, or a new monorail link, but whatever it is, it's probably not easily found elsewhere. The links to other railroad-related pages are very well described and extremely well organized: General, Regional, Railroad-related, Single Railroad, Indexes, and Photoessays are among the categories. The rest of this site, maintained by Robert Bowdidge and based, partly, on Matthew Mitchell's **rec.railroad** FAQ, is equally comprehensive, but not as well organized. Still, you'll find maps, railroad schedules, newsletters, databases, links to sounds and images, and most anything else you could want relating to railroads. —(L.S.)

KEY NEWSGROUP **rec.railroad** URL▶ http://www-cse.ucsd.edu/users/bowdidge/railroad/rail-home.html

Jumping a Freight Train, Hobo-Style

Train Hopping Jump **2120** 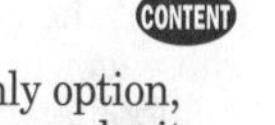

Hobos jump onto moving freight trains because it's their only option, next to walking, to get from here to there. But there are those who it consider it an attractive vacation option and still others who view it as a sport. For those in the latter categories, this site (maintained anonymously, for the obvious reason that train hopping is mostly illegal!) has all the how-tos and wherefores you need. There are instructions on what to take along, where to catch rides, what cars are best to jump into, and some miscellaneous hints, such as a useful guide to how train brakes work. There also are image galleries, railroad maps, and a resource listing, including instructions on how to join the train hopping e-mail discussion list on the Net. All that's missing is info on wireless computer communications, so you can surf the Web while you ride the rails! —(L.S.)

KEY NEWSGROUP **rec.railroad** URL▶ http://www.catalog.com/hop/

Steam Train Enthusiast's Site

Steam Locomotive Information Jump **2146** 

Unfortunately, steam locomotives are fast becoming extinct, but Wes Barris is doing what he can to keep them alive with this page. There's plenty of information here, from general specifications to wheel arrangements, plus the expected links to related pages. The real gem here, though, is Wes's tours of steam locomotive museums. He's your virtual tourguide, telling you about the museums and the locomotives on exhibit and including thumbnail images of the trains themselves, with links to download larger-sized versions of the image, if you want. —(L.S.)

KEY NEWSGROUP **rec.railroad** URL▶ http://www.arc.umn.edu/~wes/steam.html

▲ *Old train photos, via* Virtual Image Archive *at* Jump 7315.

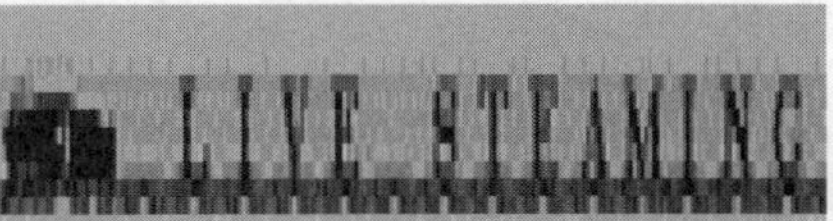

The Little Engine that Could

Live Steaming Jump 7079 

Don your engineer's hat and chug around Live Steaming, where live steam and model engineering hobbyists can find all the model railway information they need to stoke their hobby. Coming events, club information, sale items, and links to other railroad sites are listed by enthusiast Ron Stewart. Love to chat about rolling stock? Don't miss the tech talk file. —(E.v.B.)

KEY NEWSGROUP rec.models.railroad URL▶ http://mindlink.net/Ron_Stewart/livsteam.html

Modelmakers' Reference Page

rec.models.scale Home Page Jump 2122 

This is a relatively new page maintained by Daniel Koehne for the scale modeling newsgroup, but what's there already is impressive. Instead of the usual newsgroup archives, Daniel has put up a very well-organized reference, ideal for novice and expert alike. Never used an airbrush? Dip into Tools and Techniques for a tutorial. Want some input before sinking big bucks into that superkit? Check out the reviews section. There's also a color FAQ to help you get the right paints for that French Mirage—and avoid making a mistake when building the Israeli version. The pages are growing, and need input from all modelers, so if you have any tips, tricks, or suggestions, Daniel's included an e-mail form to make them easy to submit. —(L.S.)

KEY NEWSGROUP rec.models.sc URL▶ http://meteor.anu.edu.au/~dfk/scale_model.html

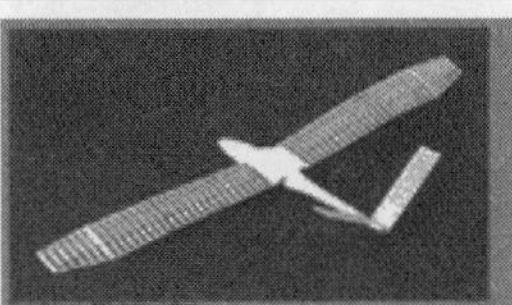

Fly like a Bird

Ornithopters Jump 7104 

Page creator Nathan Chronister says that ornithopters are smack dab in the mainstream of the trend towards increased biological functioning of machines. Evidently hundreds of other ornithopter hobbyists agree. They design, build, and fly ornithopter (plane) models that imitate a bird in flight—in short, they flap their wings. Rubber bands are a major component in the physics of ornithopter aerodynamics and mechanisms. Read how to do it, and see how it's done through descriptions and plans, videos, and computer animations. Hooked? Download information on the Ornithopter Modelers' Society and start flapping! —(E.v.B.)

KEY NEWSGROUP rec.aviation.misc URL▶ http://www.bucknell.edu/~chronstr/

Fireworks Info

Tom's Pyro Page Jump 2123 

Personal ownership and use of fireworks is illegal in most states, but with the proper licensing and safety precautions, there are plenty of opportunities to view pyrotechnics. Tom Dimock has created a page of links and information resources on fireworks that will ease the craving of any fireworks afficianado. The calendar of exhibitions and competitions lists North American events, there are links to other pyro home pages and some very useful and interesting information on using, making, and exhibiting fireworks, contributed by the Western New York Pyrotechnic Association. —(L.S.)

NEWSGROUP rec.pyrotechnics URL▶ http://tad1.cit.cornell.edu/Tom/Pyro/MyPyro.html

Web Fireworks

Pyrotechnics Jump 1515

Say the word "pyrotechnics" and conjure up Stephen King images of lawbreakers setting random fires. But, as Finnish enthusiast Petri Pihko points out, pyrotechnics refers to the art, craft and science of fireworks—stars, rockets, and shells, as in those July Fourth displays. From its first inception as a craft in China during the first century, the art of pyrotechnics has grown to worldwide proportions and organizations with thousands of members. Organizations, including the not-as-creative Pyrotechnics Home Page, literature, and other resources, are linked here. This site is bursting with photos (some slow to load) of different pyrotechnic configurations and effects, with brief descriptions of each. After reading these pages, you'll be able to impress your friends by identifying each type of fireworks during the next July Fourth extravaganza! —(H.L.)

URL▶ http://cc.oulu.fi/~kempmp/pyro.html

Pet Care & Advice

Your Web Guide to Pets

Acme Pet
Jump 5892

Pet lovers rejoice! Acme Pet has hit the Internet, and the Net will never be the same. This is a great pet site, a terrific place to hang out with pets—and other humans. At the heart of Acme Pet is "Acme Pet Times," a online magazine that rivals anything we've seen elsewhere, pet-wise or otherwise. You'll find some great feature articles here, along with health tips, special reports, contests, a "Pet Public Library," as well as links to chat rooms, bulletin boards and more. You can also explore this site's pet guides, where you'll find tons of information on canines, cats, birds, horses, fish, and exotic pets. —(J.P.)

NEWSGROUP rec.pets URL▶ http://www.acmepet.com/

The Web's Site for Pet Lovers

PetStation
Jump 5831

They call it PetStation, but for pet lovers they could just as easily have called it "Pet Heaven." This is a virtual pet store on the Web. At the heart of PetStation is "PetStation Realms," a sort of best-of area for pet news. Each realm, with names such as the "Bird Barn," "Cat Cabana," and "Fish Fair," each contain great articles and tips on pet care. Further afield you'll find some monthly attractions like the pet photo of the month, an online talk forum, and more how-to tips for pet lovers. And our favorite spot, "PetStation Kids," a site rated "KG-13," where parents are only allowed when in the company of kids 13 or under! —(J.P.)

NEWSGROUP rec.pets URL▶ http://petstation.com/

No Kitty Litter Here

Cat Fancier's Home Page Jump 1526

This group of ailurophiles—cat breeders, exhibitors, and veterinarians—have put together the ultimate Web site for cat fanciers. Orca Starbuck and Marie Lamb designed these feline Web pages with easy-to-use indexes and a plethora of links to other Web-based feline resources. Here, you'll find fascinating facts, humor, disease information, a large bibliography, vet advice, rescue and shelter news, and show schedules from the Cat Fancier's Association. Does your tabby have unusual habits? Compare them to others in the online pet forum. Are you contemplating getting a kitten but don't know what breed is right for you? Check out the library of cat pictures and in-depth descriptions of over 60 breeds (a Cymric,

Munchkin, or Oricat may just be the breeds for you). And if you decide to enter your new pet in a show, find out how at this ever-changing Web site. —(H.L.)

KEY NEWSGROUP **alt.pets.cats** URL ▶ http://www.fanciers.com

Border Terriers Home Page

Border Terriers Jump 4065 CONTENT

This site gives you all sorts of resources about the Border Terrier dog breed, as well as links to other general dog-related information. Sam Carrier maintains this page, where you can consult "The Border Terrier Guide," find out about other people interested in the breed, and even link to specific sites dealing with other terrier breeds. A nice site for the dog lover in you! —(R.B.)

KEY NEWSGROUP **rec.pets.dogs**

URL ▶ http://wwwtest.cc.oberlin.edu/Personal/Dogs/BorderTerriers.html

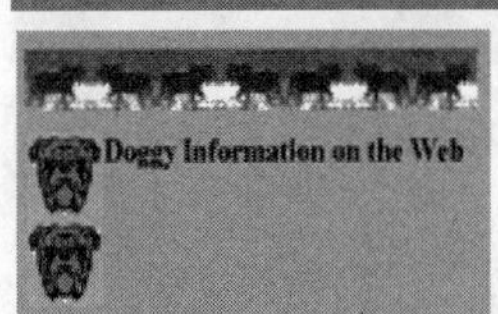

Pooch Pages

Doggy Information on the Web Jump 2276  LINKS

If you're looking for Fido FAQs, start with this page! Wilfred LeBlanc has links to FAQs for specific breeds, as well as general canine compilations. He also has collected links to dog and dog owner home pages, humane groups, and dogs as assistants to the disabled. This Web site excels, though, with its links to more esoteric topics, including Bulldog Haiku, an online novel about a dog, and a link to the dog genome project. —(L.S.)

KEY NEWSGROUP **rec.pets.dogs**

URL ▶ http://www.io.com/user/wilf/dogs/doggy_info.html

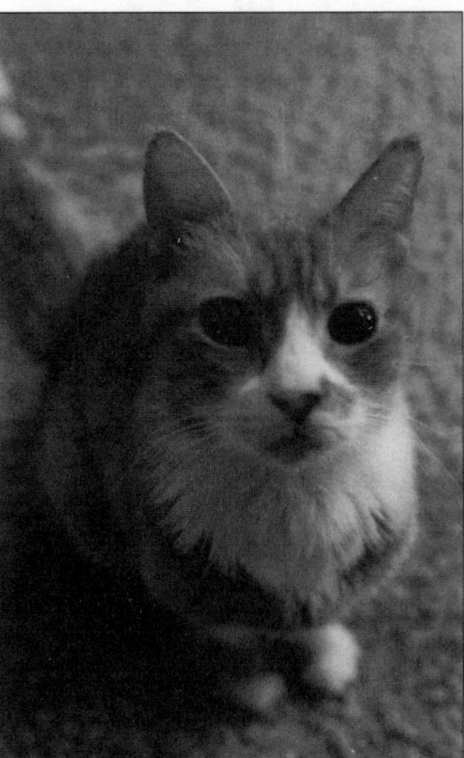

▲ *Boots the cat, from* **JumpCity**.

Bowser Browser

The Dog WWW Homepage Jump 2277 CONTENT

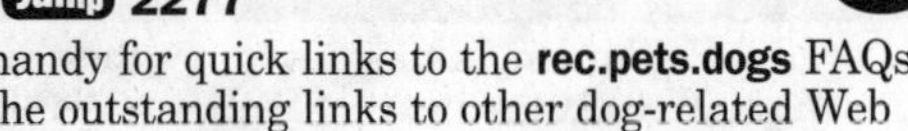

Keep a bookmark for this page handy for quick links to the **rec.pets.dogs** FAQs and newsgroups, as well as for the outstanding links to other dog-related Web pages as compiled by Cindy Tittle Moore. But the best thing about this site by Bryan Schumacher is the way you can search for and "fetch" Web pages and pictures of dogs. He's created the search engine to let you use keywords to narrow the search, or use a list of breeds to quickly retrieve pages of links. Even if you have no interest in dogs, visit this page anyway, for an example of clean design, judicious and effective use of graphics, and general Web browser friendliness. —(L.S.)

KEY NEWSGROUP **rec.pets.dogs** URL ▶ http://www.sdsmt.edu/other/dogs/dogs.html

Health Care for Pets

Internet Vet Column Home Page Jump 2275 

Regular readers of the **rec.pets** newsgroups already know about Jeff Parke. He's a veterinarian who answers questions and gives general pet health care advice to Internet pet owners through his e-mail-distributed column. Cindy Tittle Moore edits and maintains this archive of Jeff's columns, an excellent resource on all aspects of pet care. You can browse the columns issue by issue or use the subject index to quickly locate infomation on a specific topic. —(L.S.)

KEY NEWSGROUP **rec.pets** URL ▶ http://www.io.com/user/tittle/ivc/homepage.html

Pet Advice & Tips

Dr. Jim's Virtual Veterinary Clinic Jump 2408

Talk radio listeners are already familiar with Dr. Jim, aka veterinarian Jim Humphries. Now he brings his advice and tips for healthier cats, dogs, and other animals to the Web. Topics are based on questions from listeners, so they deal with the everyday but still perplexing problems faced by any pet owner. New articles appear every week, and they cover all aspects of pet care, so it's likely that even if you don't have a specific problem with your pet, you'll find some helpful advice anyway. —(L.S.)

KEY NEWSGROUP **rec.pets**

URL ▸ http://rampages.onramp.net:80/~drjim/#Dog2

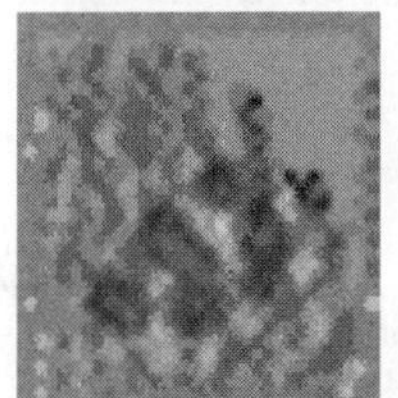

Aquarium Archive

FINS: Fish Information Service Jump 2593

Freshwater or ocean, tropical or temperate, if it has to do with fish and aquariums, you'll find it at Mark Rosenstein's FINS page. The archive begins with general FAQs from the aquarium newsgroups, as well as a FAQ for reefkeepers, and includes information on disease diagnosis and treatment, plans for aquarium projects and catalogs of fish and marine invertebrates. There also are archives of the more interesting discussions from aquarium newsgroups, images and movies, and links to related sites on the Internet. —(L.S.)

KEY NEWSGROUP **rec.aquaria** URL ▸ http://www.actwin.com/fish/

▲ *Trixie, a Jack Russell pup, from* **http://www.lucy-the-dog.com/index.html.**

Fish & Aquaria

The Amazing Fish Cam Jump 3505

LINKS

Not only is this page way cool, but it offers an amazing selection of pointers to the FINS Fish Information Service, all the relevant newsgroups that cover fish, plus info on the care and feeding of same. The "Fish Cam" is a camera that points toward a 110-gallon aquarium—with a real time JPEG image available so you can see just what the resident puffers and tangs are up to. A swimmingly fun page! —(C.P.)

KEY NEWSGROUP **alt.aquaria** URL ▸ http://buarc.bradley.edu/wwwvl-ham.html

Freshwater Aquarium Fish

CHOP: Cichlid Home Page Jump 2592

Cichlids are popular freshwater aquarium fish, and this page by Eric Gracyalny provides all you need to know about selecting and caring for them. Each entry includes information on each type's appearance, origin, and care, some with additional information on breeding. You can browse the database by genus name if your Latin is up to snuff, or by common name or point of origin. The last is useful if you want to simulate a natural community of fish who commonly live together. Supplemental information also exists for the benefit of the user. There's also information on freshwater fish diseases, and a reference section of textbooks on cichlids. —(L.S.)

KEY NEWSGROUP **rec.aquaria** URL ▸ http://trans4.neep.wisc.edu/~gracy/fish/opener.html

Aquarium Database on the Web

The Krib (Aquaria and Tropical Fish) Jump 2599

This is an excellent starting point for finding information and resources about aquariums, tropical fish, and related topics. You can either search by keyword or browse by subject. Among the subjects covered are planted tanks, raising tropical fish, raising your own live food, tank chemistry, tank hardware and design, and diseases. The information here is general in nature, and Erik Olson has added links to the various **rec.aquaria** FTP sites so you can get more indepth information if you want. —(L.S.)

KEY NEWSGROUP **rec.aquaria** URL▸ http://www.cco.caltech.edu/~aquaria/Krib/index.html

Polly Wanna Cybercracker?

UAS Home Page Jump 7090

CONTENT

Has your parrot been misbehaving? Link to the Up at Six Aviaries Home Page to download a primer on parrot training. While there, you can explore the extensive files on parrots of all kinds, suppliers, breeders, newsgroups, and discussion lists. Still not enough to feed your hobby? Up at Six also features tons of bird pics, lists reference books and available software for the bird fancier, and much, much more. —(E.v.B.)

KEY NEWSGROUP **rec.pets.birds** URL▸ http://www.rt66.com/ftp/users/upatsix/uas.htm

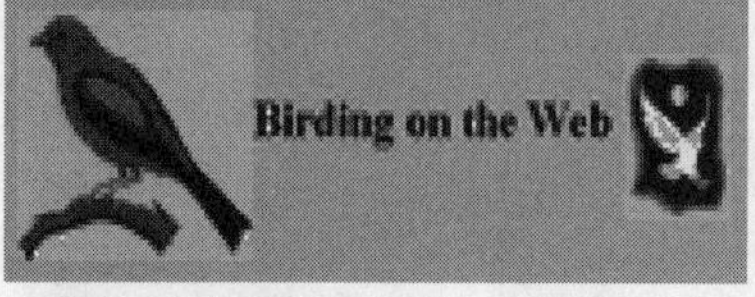

Birdwatching News & Resources

Birding Jump 2346

From reports of hot bird sightings to birdwatching newsletters and checklists, avid birders will find whatever they can think of—and much they didn't—at Jack Siler's pages. The Bird Chat section includes digests and ongoing discussions, plus FAQs and information about books, CD-ROMs, and birdwatching tools. Then there are announcements of festivals and other activities, online editions of newsletters from birdwatching organizations, photo galleries and book reviews, and checklists of birds of various regions and countries. It would all be overwhelming, except that it is so well organized that finding and accessing what you want is a simple matter. And in the unlikely event that what you need is not here, there are links to related sites that can fill the few holes in content at this one. —(L.S.)

KEY NEWSGROUP **rec.birds** URL▸ http://compstat.wharton.upenn.edu:8001/~siler/birding.html

Rat Cousins

Brian's Hedgehog Page Jump 7188

Anyone can have a cat—check out this site for a different sort of pet. Brian MacNamara obviously loves hedgehogs—you know, those walking hairdos with an attitude (but watch out for those sharp quills!). Brian has posted pictures of his own pet hedgehogs, as well as links to other enthusiast's pages. You can also find out the latest news on raising the little critters and on their adaptability as pets. He is also slowly building a directory of Canadian hedgehog breeders. —(E.v.B.)

KEY NEWSGROUP **rec.pets** URL▸ http://www.pci.on.ca/~macnamar/velcro.html

Sailing & Boating

Schooners & Tall Ships Directory

SchoonerMan

Jump 5793

Is there anything as grand or glorious as the sight of a tall ship sailing into the harbor? Well, perhaps it is an acquired taste, but once so acquired it does tend to stay with you forever. If schooners and tall ships are your thing, you'll spend many a grand hour touring this site, which also includes many links for active sailors as well. You might want to start with the twin sections of Tall Sailing

Ships A to G and Ships H to Z, where you'll find profiles of some of the best. There's also sections on boatbuilding, seafaring explorers, lighthouses, navigation, sea stories and more. And there are literally dozens of other links as well. —(J.P.)

KEY NEWSGROUP **rec.boats**
URL▸ http://www.novagate.com/~schoonerman/

▲ *A sailing schooner, from* Schooner Man *at* Jump **5793**.

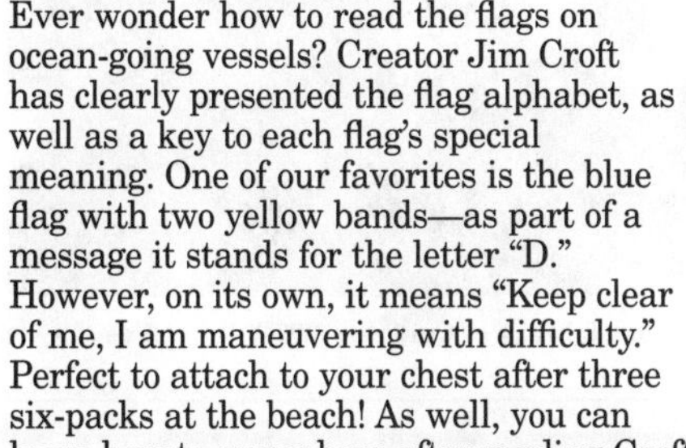

What Is That Sailor Saying?

International Marine SignalFlags Jump **7007** CONTENT

Ever wonder how to read the flags on ocean-going vessels? Creator Jim Croft has clearly presented the flag alphabet, as well as a key to each flag's special meaning. One of our favorites is the blue flag with two yellow bands—as part of a message it stands for the letter "D." However, on its own, it means "Keep clear of me, I am maneuvering with difficulty." Perfect to attach to your chest after three six-packs at the beach! As well, you can learn how to semaphore after reading Croft's comprehensive tutorial. —(E.v.B.)

URL▸ http://155.187.10.12/flags/signal-flags.html

Sail Away, My Viking Lad

Viking Navy Jump **9503** CONTENT

Peter Sjolander has a serious interest in Viking sailing. He has built a 3-foot working model of a Viking sailing ship (you can view it from many angles) that he takes on tour and tests for speed and maneuverability. Read his essays on Viking sailing, and view his sketches of oar placement and sail design. Want to see the boat in person? Download Peter's traveling schedule. Intrigued? Well, come on board. You are invited to join the Viking Navy and share Peter's hobby firsthand. —(E.v.B.)

KEY NEWSGROUP **rec.boats** URL▸ http://www.digalog.com/peter/viknavy/vikhome.htm

Travel & Tourism

Fodor's Travel Advice Site

Fodor's Jump **5731** COMMERCE

Fodor's publishes 11 travel guidebook series and more than 200 titles to destinations all around the world. In bringing their expertise to the Web, the editors have put together a nifty collection of facts and figures that will help any would-be traveler. The hotel and restaurant indexes are extremely useful—just click on the country or city and you'll find a great list of choices. The Departure Lounge is a bulletin board where travelers can get and give advice. The "Personal Travel Planner" allows you to create your very own mini-guide to destinations around the world, while the "Get Ready Before You Go" section gets down to the nitty gritty with a currency converter, a section on world weather and recent government travel advisories. And the FAQ even tells you how you can become a writer for Fodor's. Overall, one of our best picks for super travel advice. —(J.P.)

KEY NEWSGROUP **rec.travel** URL▸ http://www.fodors.com

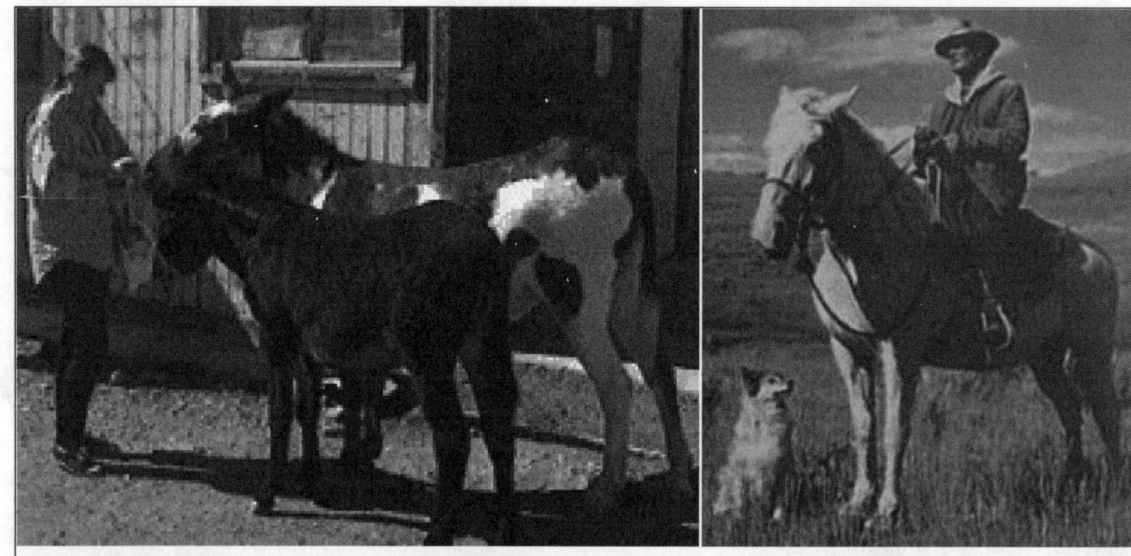

▲ *Feeding the wild burros, from* Route 66 *at* Jump 2070 ▲ *Shepherd on horseback, from* Library of Congress WWW Home Page *at* Jump 0100.

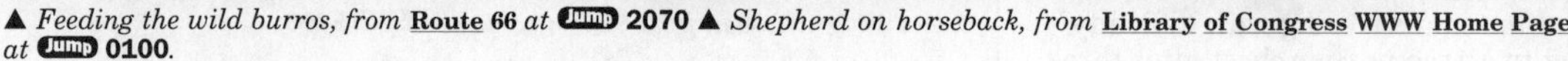

Travel Reservations for the Do-It-Yourself Traveler

Travelocity Jump 5829

CONTENT

If you are looking to plan your next vacation on your own, you might want to visit Travelocity as a good first step. This is one of those future-at-your-fingertips sites; after looking through the offerings here, you'll wonder why you ever left the planning to anyone else. To help you plan your trip, Travelocity has access to schedules from over 700 airlines, 50 car rental companies, and reservation capability for 28,000 hotels, and an online travel chat area. Not a bad start. Add to that a database of over 1,700 maps, photos, video/sound clips, plus details on golf courses, restaurants, and entertainment spots–all searchable–and you have a virtual encyclopedia of travel information. —(J.P.)

KEY NEWSGROUP **rec.travel.misc** URL▶ http://www.travelocity.com/

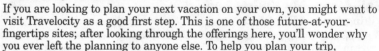

theTRIP.com the FLIGHT

the FLIGHT — the AIRPORT — the RIDE — the HOTEL — the CITY

The Business Traveller's Ultimate Resource

TheTrip.com Jump 5856

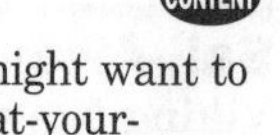

The Trip is a Web site for business travelers that, among other things, allows you to track a flight that's actually in the air. You can also make travel reservations here with this site's secure server, check flight availability, check out the airport guide, and get information on ground transportation and hotels. There are city guides and links to other resources on the Web, too. You can also register for a free e-mail newsletter that tracks bargain air fares. —(J.P.)

KEY NEWSGROUP **rec.travel.misc** URL▶ http://www.thetrip.com/

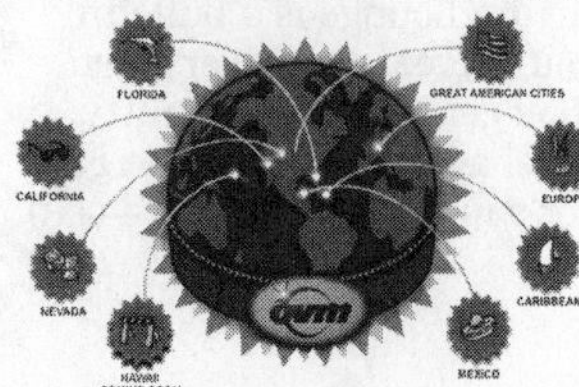

One-Stop Travel Reservations

Online Vacation Mall Jump 5868

CONTENT

Need a vacation, but too tired to visit the travel agent at the local mall? Well, why not visit the Online Vacation Mall instead. No need to get dressed or anything. And you could be out the door and on your way to the airport before your hair dries. No, really. This is a wild site. And it really is as big as a mall. The only difference being if you get lost here, you only have to hit the back button. We're talking trips to dozens of travel spots, travel "steals of the week" packages, sightseeing tours, online reservations (you can also modify or cancel a reservation), and much more. Reservations and purchases can also be made securely on this site. —(J.P.)

KEY NEWSGROUP **rec.travel.misc** URL ▶ http://www.onlinevacationmall.com/

Airline Ticket Reservations Made Easy

TripWeb Jump **5914**

Here's a online airline reservations system that's so simple you can book your own flight within a few minutes—all online. TripWeb is a real-time airline reservation system that utilizes one of the largest reservation systems in the world. All you need to do is give you city of departure and arrival, date and airline (if you have a preference) and click a button. You are given a multitude of choices (non-stops are given top berth) and you can then book your flight, and pay for it (securely) if you choose. Tickets can be sent directly to your home or, with some airlines, they can be sent electronically. —(J.P.)

KEY NEWSGROUP **rec.travel.misc** URL ▶ http://www.tripweb.com/

Internet Airline Reservations

Reservations.com Jump **5884**

Imagine being able plan and book airline tickets over the Internet! Well, the sytsem is still a bit on the rusty side, but Reservations.com has almost made the idea a reality. The plan is simple enough: you register with them (usual name, address, etc.) and then they walk you through a step-by-step reservation system. Using the system itself is a bit on the tedious side, but the site features best-priced fares lists, vacation previews, and secure transactions. —(J.P.)

KEY NEWSGROUP **rec.travel.misc** URL ▶ http://www.reservations.com/

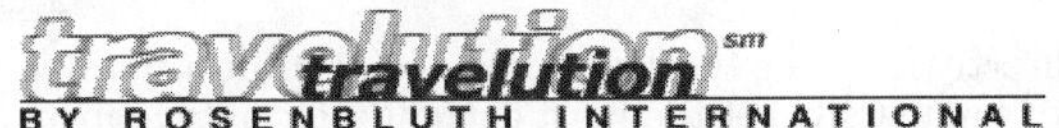

Easy Travel Reservations

Travelution Jump **5885**

It's getting to the point that you won't even have to leave the house when you go on vacation! We'll just sign on, book the tickets, and leave the actual flying to someone else. But for now we have a nifty alternative from Rosenbluth Travel, in their nifty Travelution site. The registration is quick and painless, and the options easy and rewarding. To help you plan your vacation, you are offered a number of alternatives (single, family, etc.) and then you're offered a number of packages. A great site for planning—and booking—a vacation. —(J.P.)

KEY NEWSGROUP **rec.travel.misc** URL ▶ http://www.rosenbluth.com/

TravelWeb's Online Travel Reservations

TravelWeb Jump **5897**

TravelWeb is dedicated to making your life easier, with its easy-to-use database of hotel and travel information. And it couldn't be easier to use: Click on an icon and you can use their extensive database to either search for a particular hotel, or browse through the database. The hotel search engine works on the same principle, with extra attention given to the location of the hotels. Another feature is this site's "Business Traveler Resource Center," where you can browse through a host of business services chosen exclusively for the busy executive. Here you'll find great links to news items, travel services, catalog shopping, and special offers just for TravelWeb users. —(J.P.)

KEY NEWSGROUP **rec.travel.misc** URL ▶ http://www.travelweb.com/

Travel Connections

TravelFile Jump **8071**

TravelFile is an online destination information service that links you to tourism offices and travel suppliers worldwide. TravelFile provides an easy-to-use keyword search form that helps you look for bed-and-breakfasts in southern California, or golf links in Arizona. It also supports an extensive calendar of events, a database of tour operators, convention facilities, cruise lines, museums and in-depth features, such as a comprehensive listing of current ski conditions in North America and Europe. —(E.v.B.)

KEY NEWSGROUP **rec.travel** URL ▶ http://www.travelfile.com/

The Directory of Web Restaurant Directories

The ULTIMATE Restaurant Directory
Jump **6532**

LINKS

The ULTIMATE Restaurant Directory gathers together many different restauarant Web review directories, giving you a single point from which to select your next dining destination, for a big night out in your town, or an upcoming trip to a different one. Use it to locate a restaurant by cuisine, type, zip code, state, or country. —(L.T.)

KEY NEWSGROUP **rec.food.restaurants** URL ▶ http://www.orbweavers.com/ULTIMATE/

Outdoors Travel Tips & Info

GORP—Great Outdoor Recreation Page
Jump **2139**

Outdoors types will love this page of links to what to do and where to go in the great outdoors. Organized to make the task of finding the travel info of interest to you quick and easy, the links here are organized by locations, activities, and ideas for travel. Locations links also are organized by type and geography. There are links to information about outdoors gear and food, travel newsstands and bookstores, clubs, associations and other nonprofit travel groups, as well as general travel resources. This is definitely the starting point for the outdoors traveler, especially since it's updated weekly to keep it one of the most current travel links pages on the Web. —(L.S.)

KEY NEWSGROUP **rec.travel** URL ▶ http://www.gorp.com/default.htm

Tourist Information Searcher

Tourism Offices Worldwide Directory Jump **2394**

The best way to start planning a trip is to get information directly from the tourism bureaus of your destinations. Even though their primary objective is to sell you on visiting, you usually get the most current information about the sights and accomodations, and often there are special offers you won't easily find elsewhere. With this Web searcher, you can retrieve addresses and phone and fax numbers for the country bureaus you want from the hundreds available. For the United States and Canada, you can also search by state or province and city. If your browser doesn't support forms, you can browse a text version of the list. —(L.S.)

KEY NEWSGROUP **rec.travel** URL ▶ http://www.mbnet.mb.ca/lucas/travel/tourism-offices.html

Resources for Asian Travels

TravelASIA Jump **5508**

The place for planning (or dreaming about) your next trip to Asia. Includes links to pages for 17 Asian countries including China, Vietnam, India, and Nepal. You'll find current travel information, weather charts, visa requirements, first-hand accounts of Asian travels, and many beautiful photos. —(F.R.)

KEY NEWSGROUP **rec.travel.asia** URL ▶ http://silkroute.com/silkroute/travel/index.html

Traveler's Companion

Conde Nast Traveler Jump **3716**

Conde Nast Traveler, the magazine, has been around for sometime. Now it's on the Web. It's "a source of worldly, opinionated travel advice, albeit in a whole new, constantly updated, infinitely interactive forum." Beautifully done with great photos and graphics, you can look to this site's "Great Escapes" for information on more than 150 beach and island destinations around the world. Check out the "Beach and Island Finder," your guide to thousands of attractions, hotels, and restaurants. There are also travel forums, an index, and Stop Press, your source for late-breaking travel news. Solid, useful, and well designed. —(N.F.)

KEY NEWSGROUP **rec.travel** URL ▶ http://www.cntraveler.com/

Travels to Disney Vacation Spots

The Ultimate Disney Link Page LINKS
Jump 2648

This isn't an official Disney page, but it's maintained by a member of the Walt Disney World staff, so you can count on it being as current and informative as any links page you can find. Sterrett has collected and organized links to official Disney Web pages, available FAQs, and pages maintained by Disney's numerous fans with access to Web servers. Since Sterrett works at the Orlando park, the information on Walt Disney World is very comprehensive and helpful, covering everything from hours and admission prices to information on the cast to facts and updates on the various attractions. There's even Orlando travel information, too. —(L.S.)

KEY NEWSGROUP **rec.arts.disney**
URL▶ http://www.america.com/~dcop/disney/dcop.html

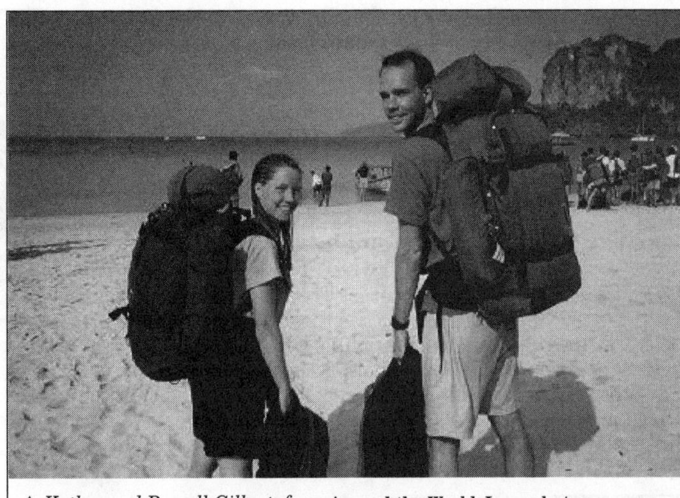

▲ *Kathey and Russell Gilbert, from* Around-the-World-Journal *at* Jump 2242.

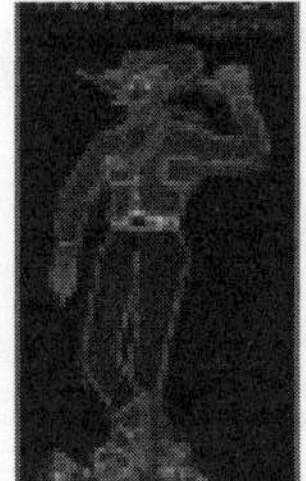

Web Travel Guide

TravelASSIST - TravelASSIST MAGAZINE Jump 3723

Whether you just like to travel from the comfort of your favorite chair or you actually get up and go, TravelASSIST MAGAZINE is the place to see. Published monthly, you'll find travel articles, photo essays, and destination and planning information. TravelASSIST brings the travel agents and specialists right to the site, so you can get started right away planning your trip. If you're a travel professional, you can be added to the listing at no charge. Back issues are available as well. Great ideas, great information, and a great Web travel treat! —(N.F.)

KEY NEWSGROUP **rec.travel** URL▶ http://travelassist.com/mag/mag_home.html

Travel Bargains from John Hart

TravelGram Jump 7240

John Hart just loves a travel bargain. And, lucky for anyone with itchy feet and limited funds, he also likes to publish his findings on the Web. Browsing through his pages will save you money, for example if you decide to take up Northwest Airlines's latest seat sale, or book in with one of Hart's finds on ski lodge vacation package deals, or put together a never-to-be-forgotten trip to the Australian Outback on a cut-rate Quantas flight. Hart also provides a complete set of airline toll-free reservation phone numbers, as well as a tour of related sites on the Web for armchair travelers. —(E.v.B.)

KEY NEWSGROUP **rec.travel** URL▶ http://www.csn.net/~johnhart/tfb.html

Watch the Air Miles Accumulate

WebFlyer, Sponsored by InsideFlyer Magazine!
Jump 7280

If you're counting your frequent flyer miles until you've earned a free ticket out of town, you can stop by this very content-rich site and see if your frequent flyer club is doing its job. You can read the Frequent Flyer, the online version of the hard-copy magazine, to get inside news on the best memberships (and any that are in trouble) or find out about the underhanded activities of some air travel coupon brokers. Travel the many links to frequent flyer programs such as American Advantage, Finnair Plus, or LatinPass to see what's on offer. Soon you'll also be able to calculate your own air miles here, or learn where the best seats on any plane are. But the tips are best: learn the shortcuts to managing your miles, get help claiming your awards, and you can also find out how to recover air miles from a bankrupt airline. —(E.v.B.)

KEY NEWSGROUP rec.aviation.misc
URL▶ http://www.insideflyer.com/

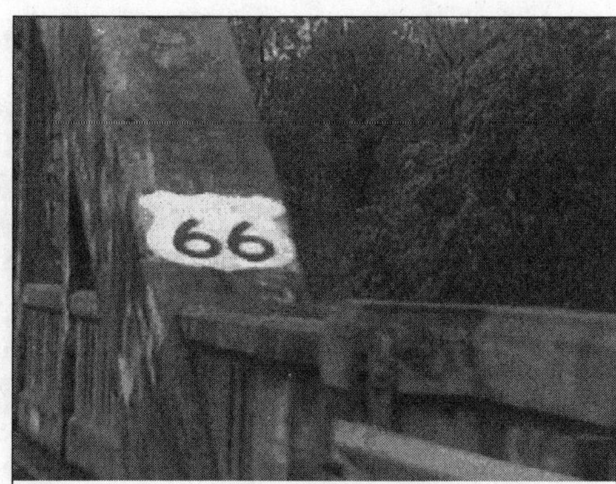

▲ *Bridge preserved by the Kansas Route 66 Association, from* **Route 66** *at* **Jump 2103**.

Web Travel Agency

Internet Travel Network - Travel Reservations and Information **Jump 7412** CONTENT

The Internet Travel Network has created a unique site through which you can book your travel arrangements online, which links to a travel agency near you—very convenient for checking up on tickets and other travel needs. When you register at the Web site, which is free, you create a personal account that allows you to research your trip using a direct feed to a real-time reservation system, and then complete your booking online. —(E.v.B.)

KEY NEWSGROUP rec.travel **URL▶** http://www.itn.net/cgi/get?itn/index/

Travel Tips on the Cheap

Student and Budget Travel Guide **Jump 2101** 

Even if you don't need to watch your pennies, this is a great resource of travel information. Well organized and attractively designed, you can browse by subject, or alphabetically. Tatiana Falk and Lara Friedman have done an outstanding job, starting with an excellent "how to use these pages" guide and continuing through a comprehensive list of topics of interest to novice and experienced traveler alike. Tips on where to go, how to get there, what to eat, and what to do are all covered here. And if your budget is so tight it hurts, there's even a section of resources for armchair traveling. —(L.S.)

KEY NEWSGROUP rec.travel **URL▶** http://asa.ugl.lib.umich.edu/chdocs/travel/travel-guide.html

Staying Healthy on the Road

Travel Health Information **Jump 2102** 

Nothing puts a damper on a vacation like a good case of malaria, or even a bad cold. This page, maintained by the International Travelers Clinic of the Medical College of Wisconsin, gives you the basics, from what to take in your traveling medical kit to how to deal with motion sickness. But its real value is for those traveling to developing countries, where diseases most of us have forgotten about still pose dangers. With vaccination information and current reports on the status of infectious threats in various locales, you can prepare before you leave and ensure a healthy trip. —(L.S.)

KEY NEWSGROUP rec.travel **URL▶** http://www.intmed.mcw.edu/ITC/Health.html

Virtual Kicks on Route 66

Route 66 **Jump 2103** 

Even those who don't remember George Maharis, Martin Milner, and that cherry Corvette easily become enrapt by Route 66, the icon of America's love affair with the automobile and the open road. Replaced by the Interstate Highway System and ignored by current maps, Route 66 is no longer the country's primary Chicago to Los Angeles highway, but it still exists, and this is your map and guidebook to traveling it. A testament to its allure, the mother of all Route 66 pages is maintained not by an American, but by a Belgian, one S. Frantzen. There's excellent content here, especially in the descriptions of the road and its sights, but it's best used as a compilation of Route 66-related Net resources. Everything from books and articles to maps and advice is covered. Even so, there's much that can be added, and contributions are gratefully accepted. —(L.S.)

URL▶ http://www.cs.kuleuven.ac.be/~swa/route66/main.html

International Travel Advisories & Info

U.S. State Department Travel Warnings Jump 2104

Each entry on this U.S. State Department-sponsored Web site includes a brief description of the country, its entry requirements, medical facilities, and the location of American embassies and consulates. There's also information on crime, drug penalties, and warnings about any special dangers that may exist, of course, but for basic information about a destination, this is a perfect starting point. As a bonus, you can even download maps and flags of each country. —(L.S.)

KEY NEWSGROUP rec.travel URL▶ http://www.stolaf.edu/network/travel-advisories.html

The Font of Travel Information

Rec.Travel Library Jump 2105

This is no mere Net file repository. Instead of links to file directories, these pages give you a tool to navigate through all the excellent information available on the vast **rec.travel** newsgroup archives, as well as links to tour operators, travel agents, and other helpful travel resources. Basic information is organized by region and country, with additional pages organized by topic: general travel information, activities and sports, air travel, general books and publications, cruise reviews, health, and hostels. There are several mirror sites, so to spread the server load, give yourself the fastest Net connection, and choose the one closest to you. —(L.S.)

KEY NEWSGROUP rec.travel URL▶ ftp://ftp.cc.umanitoba.ca/rec-travel/README.html

Planning Your Dream Trip

Round-the-World Travel Guide Jump 2138

What avid traveler doesn't dream of an around-the-world trip? If you've been thinking about such a trip, and don't know how to start, or even if you're an experienced traveler, Marc Brosius has created the online reference for you. Every conceivable area is covered—from the major decisions you must make about the trip before planning it to packing, safety, and even how to deal with the home folks when you've returned. In between, Marc covers the various modes of transportation available to you, money matters, accommodations, health, personalities, and international communications tips. Even if you're only going across the state or country and not around the world, the tips here are definitely worth a browse. —(L.S.)

KEY NEWSGROUP rec.travel URL▶ http://www.digimark.net/rec-travel/rtw/html/faq.html

A Traveler's Journey

Around-the-World Journal Jump 2242

Lots of people dream of chucking it all to hit the road, but few actually do it. Russell Gilbert did, and here he shares his record of his nine-month, 26-country journey. He shares his experiences and insights for those planning to travel to any of his destinations, and includes a nice selection of photos from the trip for those who prefer armchair travel. If you want to learn more about a particular city, Russell also includes links to detailed information. And as a bonus, he created a table with country-by-country expenses, providing a good reference point for figuring your costs to visit any of these 26 countries. —(L.S.)

KEY NEWSGROUP rec.travel URL▶ http://russell.webtravel.org/atwj/

Hostel Accommodations for International Travelers

The Internet Guide to Hostelling Jump 2148

Hostels provide inexpensive accommodations to budget travelers, and this guide, written and edited by Darren K. Overby, provides all the information the novice or experienced hosteller needs. Since many hostellers also are backpackers, there's information on that subject, too. Use the well-organized frequently asked questions section as your basic reference, then move on to the *Worldwide Hostel Guide* to find hostels around the world. For backpackers, there's a guide to transportation and a reference list of guidebooks written specifically for backpackers. Contributions, reviews, tips, and other information from visitors to this Web site is encouraged. —(L.S.)

KEY NEWSGROUP rec.travel URL ftp://ftp.crl.com/users/ro/overby/hostel.welcome.html

Travelers' Language Tips

Foreign Languages for Travellers Jump 2142

It's not Berlitz, but this site will help you learn key words and important phrases to help you communicate in 10 languages as you travel. Michael C. Martin has compiled basic words and phrases for dining, transactions, travel, and shopping including sample sound clips to help you perfect your accent. Once you've mastered the basics here, he provides links to other pages for more advanced study on all kinds of languages, as well as links to online translation dictionaries. —(L.S.)

KEY NEWSGROUP rec.travel URL http://insti.physics.sunysb.edu/~mmartin/languages/languages.html

Travel Sights & Sounds from Russell Johnson

Russell Johnson—Travel Media

Jump 2297

CONTENT

Each month, travel journalist and photographer Russell Johnson uploads some of the more interesting travel articles and photographs you'll find on the Web. Sometimes there's even a special treat, like the sound file of Eskimo throat singing or the article about Sri Lanka that includes an interview with science fiction legend Arthur C. Clarke. Always, the articles and photos take you beyond the usual travel destinations, letting you experience the world through the eyes and ears of a seasoned traveler and experienced journalist. —(L.S.)

KEY NEWSGROUP rec.travel URL http://www.travelmedia.com/index.html

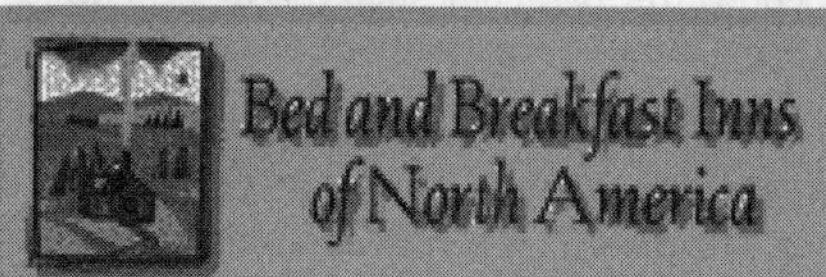

The Comforts of Home

Bed and Breakfast Inns of North America

Jump 2367

If you prefer the atmosphere and comfort of a home to that of a hotel, this page will provide information on bed and breakfast accommodations throughout North America. Each listing includes a photo and description, a list of distinctive features, and information about rates and reservations. This is not a review site. The information is provided by the inn itself, so read these listings as you would any promotional brochure. —(L.S.)

KEY NEWSGROUP rec.travel URL http://fohnix.metronet.com/cimarron/

Traveling on the Cheap, around the Lonely Planet

Lonely Planet's WWW Site

Jump 2439

Maureen and Tony Wheeler wrote their first travel guidebook in 1973 after trekking their way from England to Australia by car, bus, boat, train, and thumb. From that first book came Lonely Planet, their thriving publisher of guides for people who prefer backpacking and other low-cost travel, and this site offers you condensed, online versions of those books, too. The writing is lively and informative, offering information you don't find in your standard travel guide, such as how to avoid the $6 capuccino in Japan, what Charles Darwin did in Australia, and other tidbits to help the adventurous move off the beaten path. There's also one of the best online guides to staying healthy on the road, with advice for predeparture planning and information on specific maladies a traveler can encounter. As a bonus, the folks at Lonely Planet sift through the thousands of post cards they receive from their readers to give you an added resource for travel tips and advice. You can find out how to buy their books, too, but it's very clear that this site is here to help you, not to sell. —(L.S.)

KEY NEWSGROUP rec.travel URL http://www.lonelyplanet.com.au/lp.htm

Review of Bed & Breakfasts in California

California Bed & Breakfast Jump 4073

The folks at Net 101 bring you this site, which provides details on bed & breakfasts all around the state of California. Information contained on this site is quite comprehensive and serves also as a brief travelogue to the state. The database is split into geographical sections and includes over 600 listings for bed & breakfasts in California (including name, address, phone, and for most, the number of rooms available). A great guide if you're traveling to the Golden State. —(R.B.)

KEY NEWSGROUP alt.california URL▶ http://net101.com/BBCA/

Whole USA Travel & Tourism Information Center

See the USA in Your Virtual Chevrolet Jump 0010

CONTENT

A big Web jumping-off point for state-by-state travel and tourism information files. Links on this site range from conventional state tourist agency material to the far funkier (and much more interesting) state travel files created by talented individual Web contributors. There's a broad and eclectic collection of travel material available from this site—everything from *MotherCity Coffee:* Reviews of Seattle Coffeehouses to Smithsonian and the National Zoo, *Cynthia Seller's Cape Cod Travel Guide*, and *Todd D. McCartney's Very Unofficial Guide to Walt Disney World*. A great Web starting point for any summer vacation in the good old U.S. of A.! —(E.G.)

KEY NEWSGROUP rec.travel URL▶ http://www.std.com:80/NE/usatour.html

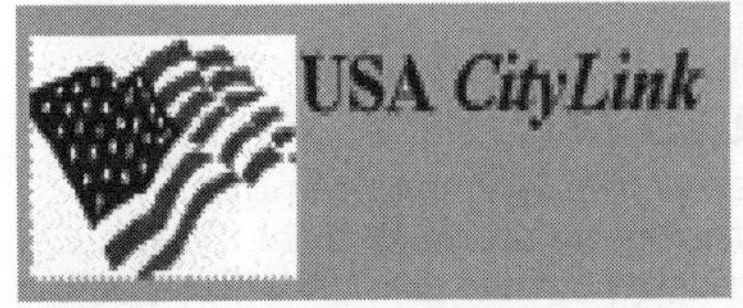

City Pages

The USA CityLink Project Jump 2307

If want specific information about a specific U.S. city or state, the CityLink Project page is the place to look. The project aims to be the most comprehensive listing of city and state information on the Internet, and the listings are growing quickly. You'll be able to link to pages of vital statistics, chamber of commerce information, and travel and entertainment guides. Be prepared to spend some time when you visit here: if you don't get hooked on browsing the cities, you'll likely find enough interesting links within the links to keep you busy for some time. —(L.S.)

KEY NEWSGROUP rec.travel URL▶ http://www.NeoSoft.com:80/citylink/

See Where You're Going Before You Get There

City.Net Jump 4059

If you're looking for local Web sites for any city, anywhere in the world, this is the place! The City.Net page is unique, not only in its quality, but quantity, too. There are Web links from here to literally thousands of towns, cities, and geographic areas around the world, even descriptions of specific areas of towns. From Antarctica, to Europe, North America, and everywhere in between, you can look up a place by keyword and get images and details on travel, entertainment, local business and government, and community services. —(R.B.)

KEY NEWSGROUP rec.travel URL▶ http://www.city.net/

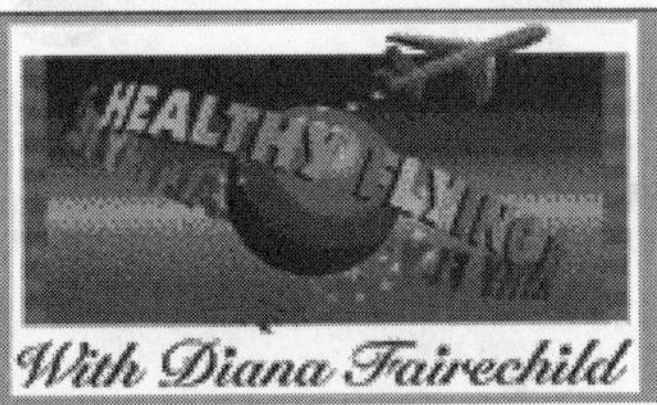

Travel Tips for the Jet Set

Healthy Flying with Diana Fairechild Jump 5014

This Web page is described by the author, Diana Fairechild, as "an interactive hypertext column created to help jet travelers fly." Look for articles on special meals available from airlines and how to get them, packing, jet lag, dehydration, and adjusting to timezones. If flying is in your future, make this Web page your first stop! —(S.B.)

KEY NEWSGROUP rec.travel.air URL▶ http://www.maui.net/diana/

Travel Tips for America's Paradise

U.S. Virgin Islands Tourist, Vacation, and Business Guide
Jump 5092

The U.S. Virgin Islands Tourist, Vacation and Business Guide features recreation, hotel, real estate, yacht charter, restaurant, and event information. There's also a monthly giveaway contest of a one-week vacation for two in the American Paradise and commercial sponsor information. You can even find out the current local weather forecast. —(S.B.)

URL ▸ http://www.usvi.net/

European Tourism Center

The European Tourist Information Center Jump 6610

Have a European vacation or business trip in mind? If you're planning travel to France, Ireland, Italy, Switzerland, Liechtenstein, Austria, Spain, Scandinavia, or the UK, you'll want to link here before packing your bags. What you'll discover are rail schedules, a subway navigator, the "Money Abroad FAQ," worldwide airlines links, weather, and Euro traveler's health tips. A noteworthy feature of this site is its exclusive listing of European MasterCard & Visa-ATM networks, mapped out on a country-by-country basis, to make finding cash overseas a snap. —(L.T.)

KEY NEWSGROUP rec.travel.europe URL ▸ http://www.iol.ie/~discover/europe.htm

Virtual France

The Travel Channel Online Network - Spotlight -France Jump 7415

Ah, c'est si bon. A guided tour of Normandy, France, courtesy of Spotlight—the online presence of the Travel Channel Cable Network. Spotlight features information, television schedules, and hyperlinks that often focus on a specific event, holiday, destination, or activity—in this case, France. Learn before you go about the climate, a bit of history, location of the U.S. embassy—even a small collection of useful phrases. —(E.v.B.)

KEY NEWSGROUP rec.travel URL ▸ http://www.travelchannel.com/spot/spot.htm

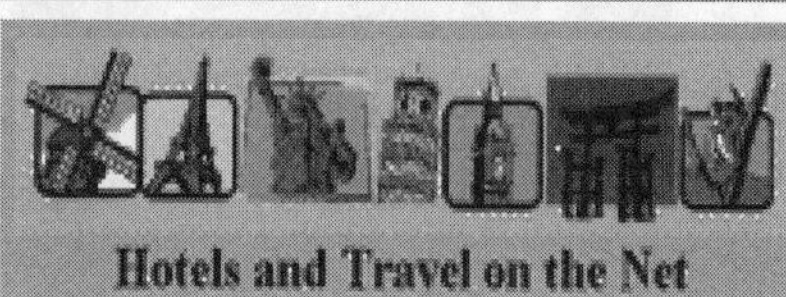

Quick Web Links for Business Travelers

Hotels and Travel on the Internet
Jump 2392

Busy travelers can quickly link to the pages of airlines and both chain and independent hotels around the world from this page. There also are links to resorts, cruise lines and tours, as well as helpful resources such as the *CIA World Factbook*, exchange rates, and general travel-related information. The site is offered as a public service, but virtually all the links are to commercial pages. So while it's useful to all travelers, it's best suited to the business traveler who needs information fast and isn't concerned about getting the best deal on transport or accommodations. —(L.S.)

KEY NEWSGROUP rec.travel.marketplace URL ▸ http://www.webscope.com/travel/homepage.html

Adventure Travel

Salmon Spawning Ground Jump 7022

Lynn Solomon is an adventurous world traveler whose goal is to visit all the sites on the UNESCO World Heritage List. She not only provides interesting links to other sites related to travel and maps, but she also publishes well-written travelogues of her various trips on her Web site. We especially enjoyed her account of visiting the breathtaking Moreno Glacier in Argentina. —(E.v.B.)

KEY NEWSGROUP rec.travel URL ▸ http://www.cco.caltech.edu:80/~salmon/

Fly Vintage Air

Air Cruise America Jump 7379 COMMERCE

Air Cruise America advertises its "nostalgia tours" in its vintage DC-3s on these pages, but the company also presents some interesting facts and information. You can read a history of the plane and browse through a photo collection of the same. Links to other tourism and aviation Web sites are also provided, as well as news related to historic planes. You can also get information about the DC-3/Dakota Historical Society and the World Airline Historical Society. Still interested? Then browse through Air Cruise's library of DC-3 books, get the addresses of where other DC-3s fly, and access lists of interest to the airline memorabilia collector. Still can't get enough? Join the DC-3 Net mailing list or the Airline-Memorabilia discussion list. —(E.v.B.)

KEY NEWSGROUP **rec.aviation.misc** URL▸ http://www.webcom.com/aca/

Road Trip Vacation Helper

Freeways by Alamo Rent A Car Jump 2448 COMMERCE

You don't need to rent a car to benefit from the information here. You don't even need to be taking an auto trip, although the resources on this site, produced by the Alamo Rent-A-Car folks, are geared specifically to those driving during their vacations. You do need to check this site, though, if you're looking for travel hints, tips, and suggestions. There's a section of games, puzzles, and ideas for keeping the kids amused and quiet on long trips, news about popular destinations, and suggestions and travel routes for scenic, historic, and just purely pleasant drives. There are also forums for you and other drivers to post their suggestions for places to go, things to see, and how to get there by car. —(L.S.)

KEY NEWSGROUP **rec.travel** URL▸ http://www.freeways.com/fun/index.html

Adventure Travel in Thailand

Lost Horizons Home Jump 5153 COMMERCE

Lost Horizons is an American-based travel company specializing in adventure travel—not your ordinary, run-of-the-mill resort or hotel-type vacations. This Web page illustrates, by way of some nice photos, a Thailand dream adventure: scuba diving, snorkelling and boating on sparkling waters, walking in the rain forest, snoozing on the beach, and much more. There's also info here on what adventure travel is, other things to do in Thailand, and (but of course!) how you can contact Lost Horizons to begin your trip. —(S.B.)

URL▸ http://www.gdserv.com/hps/lh/

News, Info, & New Web Media

The Web has emerged as a completely new and exciting broadcast media form, giving anyone who creates a Web site a forum for publishing and self-expression to an audience of millions. The Web also gives you real-time, anytime access to a wide variety of news and current events information.

...the Web will grow the same way that desktop publishing has with the proliferation of personal computers.

At first, novice publishers mixed fonts and styles "just because the technology was there and they could," he said. Eventually, though, people tired of the jumbled look and settled for a more mainstream, professional-looking product.

"I see every man, woman and child on this planet having their own Web page, because the process of creating a page is so easy," said Steve Berlin, 33, a computer consultant in Cupertino...

P.J. Huffstutter, "Wacky Web Wonders Whet Wiseacre Whims: Compilation of Totally Useless Internet Sites is Based in San Diego," *The San Diego Union-Tribune*

The New Web Media: Accessible, Individualized, and Powerful

One of the most exciting developments this year has been the emergence of the Web as a new form of media, that, unlike other, older media, such as newspapers, magazines, radio, or TV, tips the balance of broadcasting power toward the individual. That's because anyone who knows how to create a Web site (it's an easy thing to do) and has a few dollars a month to rent space on a Web server can use the Web as his or her own publishing and distribution medium.

Anyone can be a Web publisher, broadcaster, or record company executive, bypassing traditional "Old Media" publishing and distribution structures, and taking their information and creative content directly to the end consumer. It no longer takes a printing press, a record or video store, broadcast network, or the associated expense that used to be required to publish information, music, or multimedia. Now, any aspiring writer, artist, musician, photographer, film producer, or publisher can use the Web to reach an audience of millions. And this is exactly what's happening, as thousands of talented, creative people are building Web sites to publish their works online. Self-publishing Web authors, musicians, and artists in the "New Media" will succeed as long as they employ the same high professionalism, production values, and editorial discipline long employed by the "Old Media" they are helping to displace.

Examples of Web self-publishing take many different forms, and include Web-based magazines, complete with written articles, commentaries, reader feedback, original photos, and art and graphics; counterculture-oriented 'zines, featuring the offbeat and sometimes humorous impressons of their talented authors/publishers; and an increasing number of sites making use of the Web's multimedia capability—bands and recording artists with Web-accessible songs (sometimes even complete, downloadable albums), and movie makers, who also provide downloadable versions of their works via the Web.

It's a fascinating thing to see these new Web media sites emerge and expand in ever-increasing numbers. And once methods are developed to provide these talented publishers and artists with a means to receive payment or advertising support for their work over the Web (this, too will happen soon), there's no doubt that many of these talented creative types will turn their Web sites into profitable businesses. Who knows—maybe there's a chance that the next century's William Randolph Hearst of the Web might be some Web site builder with a site listed in this chapter!

Freelance new media trend spotters don't dare take their eyes off the San Jose Mercury News. Under executive editor Bob Ingle, the Merc has become a place where some of the best and brightest people in the newspaper business are trying to figure out where the industry might go from here.

So, when the paper announced in January that it was mounting a Home Page on the World Wide Web, it was time to sit up and browse.

...How is the Merc's Web site doing so far? According to Bill Mitchell, one day alone during the first week of live service brought 115,000 page accesses to the site, although there is no way to know exactly how many users that represents. But we do know that it's a good idea to keep your eye on the Merc.

Michael Conniff, "Mercury Center cites Web opportunity," ***Editor & Publisher Magazine***

Instant News and Information on the Web

The emergence of this exciting Web-based "New Media" hasn't caught everyone in the conventional newspaper, magazine, record, or other old-line publishing business flat-footed, however. A good number of big media companies have also established a beachhead on the Web, providing Web-adapted versions of their publications and media products, with varying end results.

The more successful newspaper and magazine-sponsored Web sites make the fullest use of the Web's information access and visual presentation capabilities, acknowledging the fact that the Web version of their conventional media product is a different undertaking that must conform to the new realities of this new media form. For example, Web users expect to see information updated on these sites frequently, sometimes even throughout the day; in this respect, a Web site is more like a radio station than a print product. Also, as communication speeds increase along the Web, the use of multimedia such as video or sound clips is also coming into wider use.

If you're looking for up-to-the-minute news of the day, weather information, sports, or business news, or if you're intrigued by the new media creations that have taken root and blossomed all along the Web, you'll spend many informative and fascinating hours of your Web time accessing these informative and thought-provoking sites.

News & Information

The New York Times
ON THE WEB

The New York Times on the Web

Electronic New York Times Jump 8062 

The New York Times, which has long been an important online resource for librarians and professional online researchers on costly, proprietary online services, took its time to join the move to the Internet. Its new site, now available free of charge to all Web users (you'll have to endure a clunky one-time registration setup, however) gives you all the content you've come to expect from this news heavyweight, in a solid, serious, and extremely useful site that's probably one of the Web's very best content resources. Not only is the full text of each day's Times—including most of its classifieds—presented in easy-to-access fashion, but there's also a superb full-text archive of the paper that's accessible by a professional-grade keyword search feature. You could spend hours searching for articles of interest, sorted by date, size, or relevancy. The Times site takes information access a step further, offering a number of well-travelled online discussion forums for talk of current issues, controversies, and attitudes. A true information delight for all—professionals, business owners, executives, families, students—the *Times* has done itself proud with this unassuming yet powerful information access tool for the Internet. —(E.G.)

KEY NEWSGROUP **alt.journalism** URL ▸ http://www.nytimes.com/

USA Today's Web Site

USA Today Jump 2654 

USA Today brings the flashy graphics and quick-read articles of its print edition to the Web in this attractive, easy-to-navigate site. In many ways, it's better than the print version, since many of the articles here include links to previous articles on the same subject, as well as background information. There's also a sometimes intriguing section covering interesting Web sites and online events. Its features sections for News, Sports, Money, Life and Weather, a hotlink to sports scores, the Snapshot statistics factoid, and even a crossword puzzle. —(L.S.)

KEY NEWSGROUP **misc.headlines** URL ▸ http://www.usatoday.com/

The Washington Times Online

The Washington Times Jump 8040 

Here is the Web version of the *Washington Times*, presenting news from a conservative point of view. Their site features a daily, full-text feed of news and editorials from this small but up-and-coming paper. The *Times* site is a scrappy paper which has, of late, outscooped its much larger, more famous, and more liberal competitor, the *Washington Post*, on a number of important political stories. —(E.v.B.)

KEY NEWSGROUP **misc.headlines** URL ▸ http://www.WashTimes-weekly.com/

The Wall Street Journal Hits the Web

The Wall Street Journal Interactive Edition
Jump 7491 

Money & Investing Update, a top-notch site created by the venerable *Wall Street Journal*, covers global markets and the top stories in business and finance. It draws on the contents of the *Wall Street Journal*, *Asian Wall Street Journal*, *Wall Street Journal Europe* and news from the Dow Jones newswires. You can surf this site for free, obviously, but if you want extended coverage, you must pay to subscribe. One of the nice features of the site is its Company Briefing Books that "provide highly graphical reports on companies, including stock performance charts, financial overviews, the latest news, and press releases." —(E.v.B.)

KEY NEWSGROUP **biz.misc** URL ▸ http://update2.wsj.com/welcome.html

CBS News: Up to the Minute

CBS News: Up to the Minute
Jump 5614 

Stop in at this site once, and you might feel compelled to visit on a regular basis. The folks at CBS have hit upon something here with the special news features on this site, updated on a regular basis. Main links include: what's new with the Space Shuttle, movie reviews, developments in Cyberspace, the latest in women's medicine and parenting information. —(J.P.)

URL▸ http://uttm.com/

MSNBC January 9, 1997
WORLD COMMERCE SPORTS SCITECH LIFE OPINION WEATHER
BREAKING NEWS: Explosions rock Tel Aviv. Details to come.

Greg Marinovich / AP

Mideast peace talks close to caving in
Frank Sinatra hospitalized after apparent heart attack
The longest ride down: an MSNBC report on Challenger disaster

▲ *News page, from* MSNBC *at* Jump 5733.

NEWS.COM: CNET's Internet and Industry News

Welcome to NEWS.COM! Jump 0221 

CNET, a well-financed, California-based Web news and information service, which has rapidly become one of the Web's top sites, has now launched its feature news service for those of us working in the Internet and high-tech fields business. This site is so good, however, that you don't have to be in this industry to enjoy it. This site's attractively-designed, accessible screen layout, combined with its well-selected choices of each day's top industry and tech news stories, make it an enjoyable way to learn more about the Net and high-tech business. NEWS.COM also happens to feature one of the best and juiciest "rumor mill" sections, too. Be careful when you click here, though—you'll be tempted to link to CNET's other fascinating information features! —(E.G.)

URL▸ http://www.news.com/

CNN Interactive
U.S. NEWS | WORLD NEWS | BUSINESS | SPORTS | SHOWBIZ | POLITICS | WEATHER | TECHNOLOGY | FOOD & HEALTH | STYLE
Contents | Search | Welcome Page | Help

CNN's Breaking News, with Sound & Video

CNN Interactive Jump 2646 

It took CNN awhile to get themselves on the Web, but this page demonstrates that the wait was well worth it. The main page gives you the latest news, updated as it breaks throughout the day, along with QuickTime movies for those of you who miss seeing, as well as reading, the news. When you go to the individual articles, you'll find additional information, such as statements from the newsmakers and more sound and video clips. The site is fully searchable, and articles are archived for those who don't check in every day and want to catch up, or follow the development of a specific story. About the only thing missing is a sound clip of James Earl Jones, telling you "This is CNN." Maybe soon. —(L.S.)

URL▸ http://www.cnn.com/

Investor's Business Daily
"For People Who Choose To Succeed"

Investment News from Investor's Business Daily

Investor's Business Daily
Jump 5722 

The *Investor's Business Daily* was founded in 1984, and now has a daily readership of over 800,000. They have done that by providing what they call "highlighting potential winning stocks before they receive widespread attention." You can read the latest version here, as well as take a tour of the print version of *Investor's Business Daily* online. And of course you can check out the information on subscribing to the print publication, too. —(J.P.)

URL▸ http://www.investors.com/

News, Info, & New Web Media

Bloomberg Business & Investment News

Bloomberg Personal Jump 5723

If you are looking for straight-ahead business facts and figures, this is the place for you. The latest DJIA's are posted right at the top of the page and the rest of the data are just click away, providing you with all the information you've come to expect from watching Bloomberg PERSONAL on TV. You can check out the World Equities, U.S. Treasuries, Foreign Exchange and more in the World Section. There's also the latest headline news and Financial Analysis, Who/What/Where/When sections, and more. —(J.P.)

URL http://www.bloomberg.com/

CNNfn: Financial News

CNNfn Jump 6531

A top choice for Web business and financial news, CNN's Financial News Network provides comprehensive coverage of the business world in CNN's typically thorough and information-rich style. Features hourly updates on the Dow Jones Industrials, late-breaking business news, market reports and personal investment features. Also features a handy entry blank for getting 15-minute-delay stock quotes. —(L.T.)

KEY NEWSGROUP **clari.biz.market.news** URL http://www.cnnfn.com/

All Politics, All the Time

Time/CNN AllPolitics Jump 6575

If you're looking for comprehensive up-to-the-minute political coverage online, this collaborative news effort between media giants Time and CNN offers a fully searchable, continuously updated site, with news, analysis, and a fascinating archive of political and issue polling results. Also featured are excerpted commentaries from *Time* magazine, interview transcripts, and moderated, online political talk forums. —(L.T.)

KEY NEWSGROUP **talk.politics.misc** URL http://AllPolitics.com

The Latest Political News from PoliticsNow

PoliticsNow Jump 5814

PoliticsNow is a combination of two great political sites, ElectionLine and PoliticsUSA, which have joined forces to provide what they hope will be the best one-stop site for political news on the web. A joint effort of ABC News, *The Washington Post*, *National Journal*, *Newsweek,* and *The Los Angeles Times*, the editors of this site have fashioned a site that lives up to its promise. Many of the news articles on this site include online forums, so you can respond to the latest stories, too. A nicely-executed site that provides an always-current overview of the latest news in today's politics. —(J.P.)

KEY NEWSGROUP **talk.politics.misc** URL http://www.politicsnow.com/

Wired Political News

The Netizen - Impolitic Jump 8064

Irreverent, topical, hard-hitting political commentary defines The Netizen, a high-energy portion of HotWired — *Wired* Magazine's popular site. One of The Netizen's high-profile offerings is Impolitic, a column written by John Heilemann, a former Washington correspondent for *The*

Economist. In addition to his other HotWired pieces, he has now become The Netizen's "boy on the bus" for political campaign coverage and commentary. —(E.v.B.)

KEY NEWSGROUP **talk.politics.misc**

URL ▸ http://www.hotwired.com/netizen/

MSNBC's TV and Web News

MSNBC

Jump 5733 CONTENT

As the newest mammoth Net news sites, MSNBC, the joint effort of Microsoft and NBC, certainly has its work cut out for it. While some have suggested that the last thing the TV world needs is another source for the same old news, few doubt that Microsoft would become involved with such a cash-drinking cow were it not at least modestly hopeful for a successful conclusion. Time will tell, of course, but there are few disparaging words one can say about this Web site. It is clean and concise, to be sure, and the news is generally not much more than three minutes old. The special features include the ability to design your own personal front page capable of displaying the news headlines you want to see, or you can select an MSNBC affiliate in your area for local news. Download their Web toolkit and you can also receive a personalized MSNBC Web page sent to your e-mail box for a customized news feed. —(J.P.)

URL ▸ http://www.msnbc.com/news/default.asp

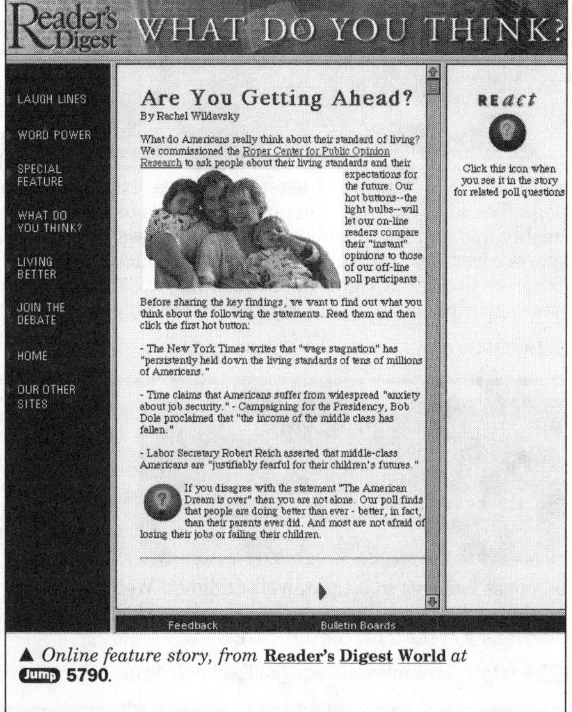

▲ *Online feature story, from* Reader's Digest World *at* Jump 5790.

News from Capitol Hill from Roll Call

Roll Call Online Jump 6633 CONTENT

Roll Call, the daily newspaper of Capitol Hill, now offers the latest inside news coverage of Congress and politics that's a handy Web stop if you like to follow politics with rabid intensity. Explore the people, politics and processes shaping the legislative battles on today's issues. The site features a handy congressional database, an election map providing complete coverage of every Senate and House race, including sneak peeks at future races. If it's happening in Washington, you'll get a birds-eye view of it here. —(L.T.)

KEY NEWSGROUP **alt.politics.usa.congress** URL ▸ http://www.rollcall.com

Mercury Center Web: *San Jose Mercury News*

Mercury Center Main Menu Jump 0203 CONTENT

Many other local newspapers who want to go up on the Web will have to try very hard to top the *San Jose Mercury News* in this stellar Web news effort! A well-designed site featuring nicely detailed graphics, the Mercury Center Web presents the full texts of the daily print version of the *San Jose Mercury News* plus computer-related features and an intriguing personal news service called *News Hound*, which sends you articles from a wide variety of news sources by electronic mail, according to the keywords and subjects you select, at a modest extra charge of about $10 per month. Also includes search capability of the *Mercury News* classified advertising section and wire service news. —(E.G.)

URL ▸ http://www.sjmercury.com/main.htm

NandO.net: Raleigh News and Observer Web Site

Welcome to NandO.net Jump 0091

While the Web publishing efforts of many big conventional newspapers, magazines, and other media outlets are, quite frankly, mediocre uses of Web publishing, the *Raleigh News and Observer*'s NandO.net is an innovative, exciting, and extremely well-executed news, sports, and features Web page. The folks at NandO.net obviously devote considerable time, effort, and creativity to this Web site, giving you freshly updated and crisply written daily news summaries, business features, entertainment news and features, sports coverage, and editorial cartoons produced in a graphically pleasing and Web-friendly format. The *News and Observer* is doing it right—and that's why we recommend it to you—and as an example to other potential newspaper publishers jumping onto the Web. —(E.G.)

URL ▸ http://www.nando.net/welcome.html

The Digital Missourian

n/a Jump 0117

The Journalism School at the University of Missouri is one of the country's best, and this student-created news Web site lives up to this school's fine reputation. The Digital Missourian, or DIGMO, makes excellent use of the Web as a new media form, featuring well-written national and world news, features, sports news, and business features in a tight, well-designed Web format. Its colorful graphics and icon buttons are worth the trip all by themselves and the students here show that they most definitely have what it takes to become the major Web journalists of the 21st century. —(E.G.)

URL ▸ http://www.missouri.edu/%7Ejschool/digmo/

News Junkie's Connection

NewsLink Jump 2237

This page lets you keep track of the newspapers, magazines, and broadcast outlets that offer free resources on the World Wide Web. There's also a section of special links that features resources for journalists and timely media-related events pages, such as the NCAA Basketball Tournament. Maintained by Eric Meyer, a journalism teacher at Marquette University and founder of NewsLink, the list is fairly comprehensive. It does need some work, especially in the magazine section, and Eric depends on visitors to help keep all the sections growing. But for the true news junkie, that's a benefit of this free service, since the greatest fun is in sharing your discoveries. —(L.S.)

KEY NEWSGROUP alt.journalism URL ▸ http://198.137.186.91/newslink/index.html

WEBWEEK™

Web Week's News of the Web

Web Week Jump 5734

Web Week, published by Mecklermedia, a major publisher of Net-related print products and sponsors of the mammoth Internet World trade show, is the place to go if you want to find out what is happening on the business side of the Web world.If you're interested in breaking into the Net industry, or if you already run a commercial Web site, there is much to read here, and all of it presents a rather remarkable picture of the real complexity of this Web world. There's plenty too, on the world of America Online and other commercial online services, of course. Other sections, which include late-breaking news, feature articles, marketing and commerce, intranets, industry news and an opinion section make Web Week a must if you need to follow the latest trends in the business of the Internet. —(J.P.)

URL ▸ http://www.webweek.com/

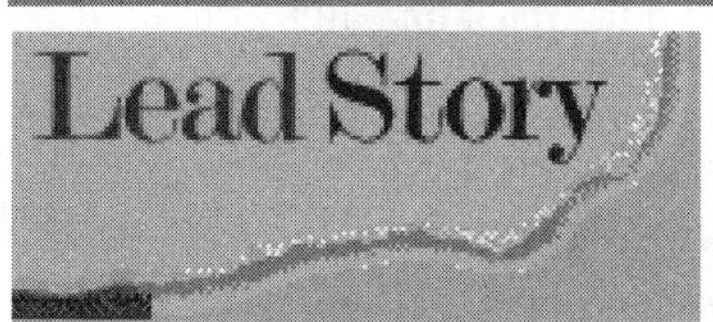

Quick News for Business Professionals

Lead Story Jump 5876

Lead Story is AT&T Business Network's site that brings you a detailed look at the major business story of the day. Each days the editors of Lead Story pick one story that they think will be of particular interest to business professionals, or anyone else who wants more than just a quick skimming of the day's headlines. Recent topics have included the role of technology in business, the encryption debate, and the TV rating system. Once you've read the story of the day you can also join others for a round of debate in the discussion forum. Past daily stories are indexed, and you can also read about the issues that will be covered in future editions. —(J.P.)

URL ▸ http://www.bnet.att.com/leadstory/

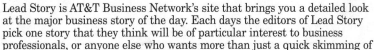

Business News on Demand

News Alert Jump 5886

We still remember the old days when we would be watching television and the announcer would break into the program to tell us to stay tuned for a special announcement. You just knew it had to be bad news. Now you can get your own personal news alerts from News Alert (at a modest additional charge). You won't find anything quite so anxiety-inducing here, but if you want to register, you can configure your account to deliver the latest in business and general news. This is real-time data, with 15-minute delayed stock quotes, charts and reports, and other news from Reuters, BRIDGE News, BusinessWire, and more. —(J.P.)

KEY NEWSGROUP **alt.business.misc** URL ▸ http://www.newsalert.com/

National Geographic on the Web

National Geographic Jump 6878

The venerable *National Geographic* has launched an online adventure your whole family will want to explore. This exceptionally designed site is loaded with the beautiful photos of world people and places you've come to expect from the print version of the *Geographic*, plus fascinating maps and special Web editions of National Geographic and Traveler Magazines. There's even a special Web magazine just for the kids, entitled "The World." National Geographic's online features include coverage of Incan ice treasures and South African park landscapes. And there's also a nice collection of interesting historic maps here, too. —(L.T.)

KEY NEWSGROUP **rec.travel** URL ▸ http://www.nationalgeographic.com/

OMNI Magazine

OMNI Magazine Jump 6730

Omni, the slickly-produced pop-science and science print magazine, is no longer available on paper—it's now being published exclusively on this site. Check out articles like "The Yearly Brain Olympics" or "Primordial Soup in Cyberspace." You can also join online discussion forums on Galileo, artificial life, and real-world mad scientists here. Links to science fiction sites and OMNI's weekly picks for coolest science site are here as well. —(L.T.)

KEY NEWSGROUP **sci.misc** URL ▸ http://www.omnimag.com/

Reader's Digest on the Web

Reader's Digest World Jump 5790

If you're expecting *Reader's Digest*'s Web site to be staid and stagnant, all earth tones and muted opinion, you are in for a surprise. Indeed the staple of doctor's offices since the beginning of time has hit the Web in a big way. We're talking glossy, brash and opinionated, an interactive melting pot that just doesn't quit. You'll find all the familiar old features of its print version here, like Laugh Lines ($400 for your story), Word Power, and Living Better. But you'll also find great Web-only articles, an online discussion forum, and searchable archives. Now that *Reader's Digest* is online, does that mean the Internet is really here to stay? —(J.P.)

URL ▶ http://www.readersdigest.com/

Read All about It!

The HomeTown Free-Press Home Page Jump 5148

Here's a geographical index to over 500 sites providing local news and event information for communities around the world. Sources include newspapers, radio/TV stations, as well as civil and civic organizations. You can link to newspapers or magazines from Cannes, France, to Kailua-Kona, Hawaii, to Sarasota, Florida and many more places, all around the world. —(S.B.)

URL ▶ http://www.well.com/user/niche/hometown.htm

Little Planet Times Kids' Newspaper

Little Planet Times Jump 6732

Parents and children alike will find this newspaper, by and for kids, to be a thoroughly entertaining Web experience. The goal here is to promote reading, writing, and communication skills for grades K-5. All ages will have fun reading the many articles written by young children. Tiny explorers can make new friends on this site's interactive forum, or catch the latest on movies for kids. Kids can also stop by and say "hi" to Owly Bear, Little Planet Time's librarian, who teaches kids the importance of reading good books. —(L.T.)

KEY NEWSGROUP csn.ml.kids URL ▶ http://www.littleplanet.com

The SenseMedia Surfer: Hypertext Web News & Links

The SenseMedia Surfer Jump 0208

A hip, well-executed Web news, information, and links page featuring an eclectic collection of Web links and a nifty hypertext search engine that lets you keyword search a couple of dozen major news-based Web sites to get all the news that fits your particular search keyword. Also features "Get a Job!," a section where Web page designers and multimedia folks can post their resumes and pictures in HTML format free of charge. A funky Web site that's making some of the most innovative use of Web hypertext links that you'll see on the Web! —(E.G.)

URL ▶ http://sensemedia.net/surfer

Media Watchdogs

Media Watch Home Page Jump 2337

If you're confused by the increasingly blurry line between reporting and advocacy, or, just on general principle, take what you read or see on TV with more than a grain of salt, visit these pages. Michael Ernst links you to media watchdog groups, both in the U.S. and internationally, general media criticism, and alternative news and information sources that go beyond soundbites to dig deeply into the issues surrounding the news. He also has an excellent set of links to Internet resources covering censorship, as well as links to general journalism resources. —(L.S.)

KEY NEWSGROUP alt.journalism.criticism URL ▶ http://theory.lcs.mit.edu/~mernst/media/

Online Funnies & Editorial Cartoons

The Daily Internet News Collage: Comics Jump 2660

The Daily INC is an online daily newspaper comprised of links to online news sources, including Reuters, *USA Today* and the NandO Times. Maintained by Prashant Babu Buyyala, it does a very good job of it, with an attractive design and excellent use of graphics, but that's not the reason it's recommended. What sets it apart is a very comprehensive set of comic strip and editorial cartoon links. You can link and download each individually, as part of a group or, if you've got the time and inclination, all three dozen or so at once. If you can't get through the day without your daily Dilbert, Peanuts, or a poke at politics, this is your page. —(L.S.)

KEY NEWSGROUP **rec.arts.comics.strips** URL▶ http://www.rhythm.com/~prash/inc/comics.shtml

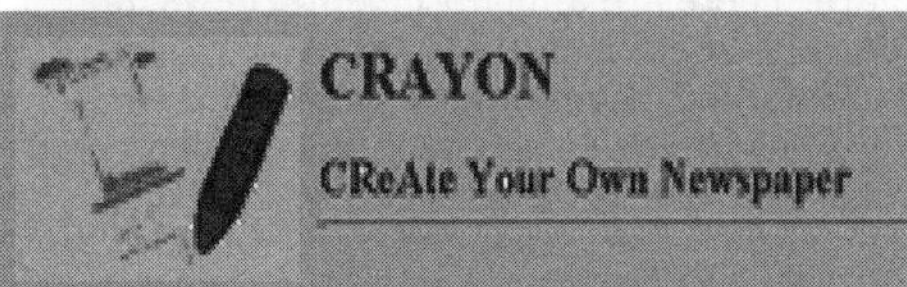

Create Your Own Newspaper

CRAYON Jump **2220** 

You can get daily Web delivery of the best online news, weather, and features with this creation of Jeff Boulter. Just fill in the form, checking the online news and features you want to read, and a customized newspaper, in the form of Web page, is created for you. Save it to your hard drive, create a bookmark, and every time you use it you'll get a fresh paper. Jeff makes it easy for you to choose your news, organizing the selection of daily updated resources into sections: News, Weather, Business, Technology, Entertainment, Sports, and Comics. There's also a place here to submit your suggestions for additional Web links for Jeff to add to this site. —(L.S.)

KEY NEWSGROUP **alt.journalism** URL▶ http://sun.bucknell.edu/~boulter/crayon/

Behind the Headlines

Hot News/Hot Research Jump **2334** 

Despite the seemingly endless number of links to news on the Internet, the depth of information available often is limited. Nora Paul helps you get behind the headlines by offering links to research and other background information on each week's top news story. With each link comes an extended description of its contents, making it easy for you to zero in on those aspects of the story that interest you most. Suggestions for links are always welcomed, as are suggestions for the Hot News item to be featured. —(L.S.)

KEY NEWSGROUP **alt.news-media** URL▶ http://www.nando.net/prof/poynter/hrintro.html

Disaster Preparedness Info & Resources

Federal Emergency Management Agency Jump **2387** 

This is Disaster Central, courtesy of the federal government. If you want to be prepared in the event a disaster strikes, learn how to get help after a disaster; or, check the latest news on the major disasters making the headlines. If you want facts about earthquakes, floods, hurricanes, tsunamis, or any other overwhelming act of nature, there are fact sheets and photo files to keep you busy for quite a while. You can browse leisurely, or, if a tornado is bearing down on you, jump to the Master Index and quickly find what you need! —(L.S.)

KEY NEWSGROUP **clari.news.disaster** URL▶ http://www.fema.gov/homepage.html

Disaster News

Disaster Information Network Jump **2530** 

When disaster strikes, the Internet is fast with news and general information on the event. The problem has always been that the resources are scattered, and by the time you hunt them down the news is old. The Disaster Information Network does the searching for you, providing the best spot to go first for news of major natural or man-made disasters anywhere in the world. Sponsored by Internet Direct and Telekachina Productions as a public service and maintained by Matthew Grossman and Jason Ayers, the page starts with the latest bulletins about the latest disasters. After that, there's a comprehensive list of articles from various Internet resources, so you can get more background on the event, or catch up if you've not been following developments. There's also information on non-Internet information sources, so you don't have to limit yourself to what's available here if you want still more information. —(L.S.)

KEY NEWSGROUP **alt.current-events** URL▶ http://www.disaster.org/

Dealing with Disaster

Illinois CES Disaster Resources Jump 2747

Although this site is maintained by the Illinois Cooperative Extension Service, it provides information and resources about preparing for and coping with disasters wherever you are. There are announcements, news, and other information about current disasters, including weather reports and the latest Federal Emergency Management Administration updates. You'll also find a good selection of information on how to prepare for a disaster, what to do after, and how to get assistance or help others, as well as a good selection of links to emergency management networks and other resources, both for coping with and tracking disasters. —(L.S.)

KEY NEWSGROUP **clari.news.disaster** URL http://www.ag.uiuc.edu/~disaster/disaster.html

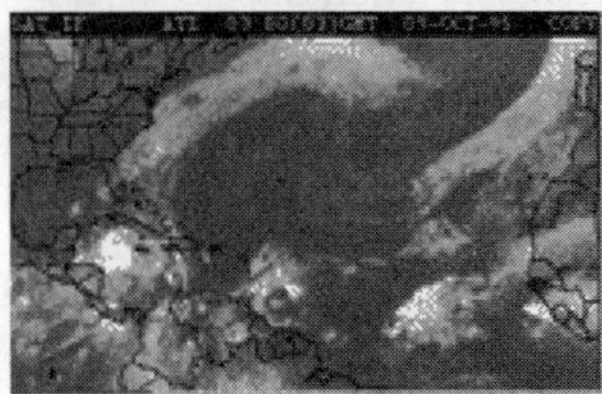

Today's Hurricane News

Hurricane Watch Jump 2729

We've seen one of the worst, if not the worst, years for hurricanes in history. Just when one passes through, it seems another is set to hit, and it looks like a pattern that may be with us for awhile. To help you keep track, Ryan Scott opens this page with the current satellite photo of the Atlantic and lets you download the current tracking map to show you the predicted paths of active storms. He also provides links to the various weather servers offering additional imagery and weather advisories, so you can quickly try a different Net server when the one you want is overloaded, a frequent situation when storms are approaching the U.S. coast. —(L.S.)

KEY NEWSGROUP **sci.geo.meterology** URL http://www.netcreations.com:80/hurricane/

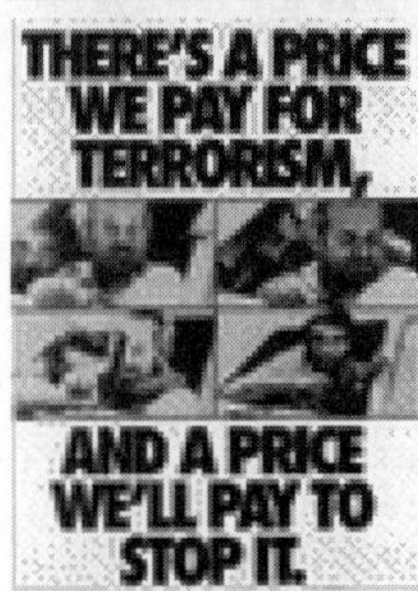

Terrorist Watch

Counter-Terrorism Rewards Program Jump 3670

Whether you know it or not, the U.S. Department of State Diplomatic Security Service sponsors a Counter-Terrorism Rewards Program. In fact, the reward money played a major role in the capture of a Ramzi Ahmed Yousef, who now awaits trial for his alleged role in the World Trade Center bombing. This site offers fascinating details about a number of documented terrorist attacks, including the 1985 hijacking of TWA 847, and the 1988 bombing of PanAm 103 over Lockerbie, Scotland—complete with full-color wanted posters of those sought for these crimes. Any information about the whereabouts of these criminals is sought, with privacy guaranteed for all those who contact the FBI or State Department. This page is a tribute to those who have been murdered, and an excellent use of the global medium of the Web to collect information that could lead to the capture of those responsible. —(C.P.)

KEY NEWSGROUP **clari.news.terrorism** URL http://www.clark.net/pub/heroes/home.html

News of New Medical Research and Breakthroughs

Medical Breakthroughs Jump 5783

Gone are the days when we were content to cull our medical knowledge from prime-time TV shows. With new strains of new diseases apparently cropping up all the time, it has become increasingly important to at least be aware of what might be lingering around the next corner. The problem has always been finding the latest news that's something better than the usual sensationalized TV news segment. This top-notch site, professionally produced and updated daily by Ivanhoe Broadcast News, who gathers their information from the world's leading medical centers and research labs, is certainly worthwhile. You won't find anything alarmist here, but you will find some remarkable updates on pressing issues such as the ongoing war against tuberculosis, and the dramatic turnaround in the ability of antibiotics to fight our battles for us. —(J.P.)

KEY NEWSGROUP **bit.listserv.mednews** URL http://www.ivanhoe.com/

Modern Healthcare Today

Modern Healthcare **Jump** 6580

Modern Healthcare Today provides a concise rundown of daily business news in the healthcare industry, contributed by 26 reporters from six news bureaus across the nation. Even for those of us not involved in the health care field, this site provides informative coverage of the business of health care, and the role of government and corporate involvement in shaping legislation and the future of the industry. Other regularly-updated features rounding out this site include Technology, Washington Report, Financial Information, Marketing, Medical Groups, Outpatient Services, and Healthcare Systems. —(L.T.)

KEY NEWSGROUP clari.biz.industry.health URL▶ http://www.modernhealthcare.com/iconpage.html

Viruses & Epidemics News & Info

The Hot Zone **Jump** 2580

This is as much a current events site as it is a science site, one that tracks news of virus outbreaks and epidemics while it links you to sources of more information about virology. If you had this site bookmarked during the past year, you would have had one of the better sites for tracking news of the Ebola virus outbreak in Africa. Although Chris Johnson emphasizes current news, he also has links that will give you background on viruses in general, and efforts to control viral outbreaks and improve health conditions worldwide. —(L.S.)

KEY NEWSGROUP bionet.virology URL▶ http://mixer.visi.com/~chris/hotzone/

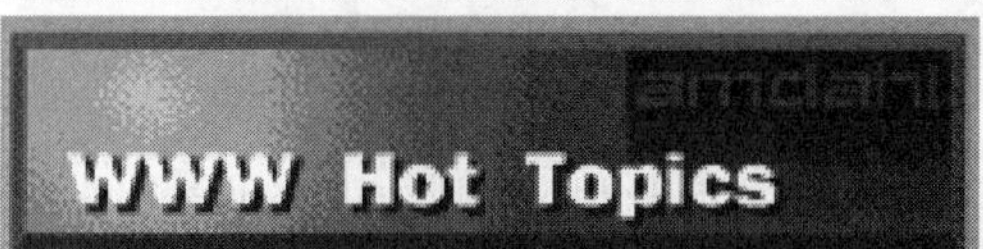

Good News on the Web

Amdahl's WWW Hot Topics **Jump** 2587

Check this page for current events coverage that others miss. You won't necessarily find the headline topics—no bombings, no murders, no epidemics—but you won't find any other Web site that covers timely happenings that make you feel as good. Among the recent events covered are the America's Cup (OK, we lost, so it's not really good news), the next and immediately past Space Shuttle missions, and news about the *Star Trek: Voyager* television show. There's also an archive of past hot topics, as well as links to other Web pages that cover current events, such as the National Press Club. —(L.S.)

KEY NEWSGROUP alt.current-events URL▶ http://www.amdahl.com/internet/hot.html

Multimedia Media News

MMWIRE Online **Jump** 7258

Multimedia Wire has designed these pages for multimedia and interactive entertainment professionals. The pages contain information on associations, upcoming conferences, and employment opportunities. You can also browse in MMWIRE's financial information and statistics databases. Commentary from industry experts is also presented. As well, you can subscribe to the MMWIRE electronic newsletter. —(E.v.B.)

KEY NEWSGROUP comp.multimedia URL▶ http://www.mmwire.com/

Entertainment Megasite

Entertainment Network News **Jump** 2755

If you're looking for entertainment news and links covering just about everything, this could be your Web site. Relatively new, it is nonetheless very comprehensive, with links to sites covering movies, television, radio, music, video, software, computers, 'zines, and children's entertainment, plus late-breaking entertainment news. A joint project of Metronews and the SC Foundation, the plan seems to support the site with sponsorships, but the fact that they say all proceeds will go to the National Children's Coalition indicates that this will be a family-oriented site that can be an excellent starting point for safely exploring the Web. —(L.S.)

KEY NEWSGROUP clari.living.entertainment URL▶ http://www.slip.net/~scmetro/home.htm

THE REPORTER
Boxoffice at record pace

Your 24-Hour Entertainment News Source

The Hollywood Reporter Jump 6650

Need the latest buzz in film, television and music news? Let Hollywood Reporter be your entertainment news source, with its excellent, full-text, around-the-clock news site. Here's where you'll find a continually-updated news feed from the entertainment and media worlds, the latest box office earnings, who's doing the latest movie deals, what's happening on the multimedia entertainment front, as well as the usual personality news and puffery. —(L.T.)

This Day in History

Born:

- **Janet Leigh** (1927), *Psycho* actress; mother of Jamie Lee Curtis
- Sylvester Stallone (1946), he'll always be Rocky to us
- Nancy Reagan (1921), former actress and First Lady
- Maximillian (1832), emperor of Mexico for three years, then executed
- Merv Griffin (1925), TV producer; talk show host
- Pat Paulsen (1927), comic; 1968 presidential candidate

1535: English statesman and scholar Sir Thomas More, unable to bear the thought of Henry VIII as the religious leader of his country, is executed on Tower Hill.

▲ *The day in entertainment history, from* **Mr. Showbiz** *at* Jump **2622**.

KEY NEWSGROUP **clari.living.entertainment** URL▶ http://www.hollywoodreporter.com

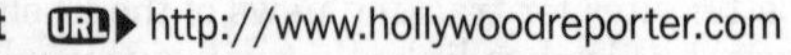

Entertainment World News

THE BIZ: THE ENTERTAINMENT CYBERNETWORK Jump 7465

THE BIZ is an online trade publication that focuses on individuals making the entertainment industry move—from film, television, video to music, cable TV, radio, publishing, multimedia, stage, and game development. Read in-depth interviews with these creative individuals. Check out the daily news updates, regular columns about the entertainment industry, the list of who's who in the industry, and the entertainment industry resource guide. —(E.v.B.)

KEY NEWSGROUP **clari.living.entertainment** URL▶ http://www.bizmag.com/

Entertainment News & Reviews

Mr. Showbiz Jump 2622

Here's a way to get the latest—and we mean today's—news from the world of popular culture, in an entertaining and engaging format. Mr. Showbiz will satisfy even the most voracious with news, reviews, and gossip. Many of the sections are updated daily, but even if you've gotten all of today's stories, there's still plenty to do here. You can talk back to Mr. Showbiz or the entertainment industry in general, and maybe see your comments on this page. Or you can go to this site's chat area and share your views with other entertainment fans. Informative, interactive, always up to date—this is one of those sites that really takes advantage of the Web, and you should take advantage of it, too. —(L.S.)

KEY NEWSGROUP **rec.arts.misc** URL▶ http://web3.starwave.com/showbiz/

The Lowdown from Entertainment Weekly

Entertainment Weekly Jump 3682 CONTENT

Who won at Cannes? Who is Nicole Kidman, anyway? For show-biz, entertainment and "inside-scoop" addicts everywhere, Entertainment Weekly's online version is even more fun than the glossy edition you'll find at the newsstand—and you can even download those images right to your own machine! Well worth adding to a hotlist of weekly publications that you can read online, although the high level of activity at this site can impact its speed. But who's complaining—it's fun, it's "free," and it's Netscape-enhanced, with animation! —(C.P.)

KEY NEWSGROUP **clari.news.entertain** URL▶ http://www.pathfinder.com/

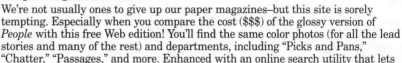

People Now Online!

People Magazine Jump 3681 CONTENT

We're not usually ones to give up our paper magazines–but this site is sorely tempting. Especially when you compare the cost ($$$) of the glossy version of *People* with this free Web edition! You'll find the same color photos (for all the lead stories and many of the rest) and departments, including "Picks and Pans," "Chatter," "Passages," and more. Enhanced with an online search utility that lets you do a keyword search against any of the Time-Warner online magazines! An extremely busy site, and the graphics can be slow-loading, but definitely worth a regular visit! —(C.P.)

URL▸ http://www.pathfinder.com/

Premiere Magazine's Entertainment Web Spot

Premiere Magazine Jump 6670 CONTENT

Premiere Magazine's online edition offers compelling articles and information on the hottest new movie releases, movie news and Hollywood celebrity profiles. Premiere's site also features a daily rundown of news items, along with behind-the-scenes coverage of movies now shooting in Hollywood's backlots. Action-movie buffs will love gliding over to Shot-by-Shot, which explains the secrets behind special effects and stunts. Downloadable movie clips and press kits are another key feature you won't find in the print version...and, did we mention this one's free? —(L.T.)

KEY NEWSGROUP rec.arts.movies URL▸ http://www.premieremag.com/hfm/index.html

African-American Entertainment News

Electronic Urban Report Jump 6662 CONTENT

Supplying an exclusive feed on black entertainment and culture, this daily news offering provides the latest on African-American celebrities, events and issues. Get the scoop on the latest with Janet, Prince, Snoop, Whitney, Anita, Denzel, Shaq, TLC, Babyface, Salt-N-Pepa and many others. An additional bonus includes a fully searchable archive of all back issues and info on receiving this site's free e-mail newsletter update —(L.T.)

KEY NEWSGROUP soc.culture.african.american URL▸ http://www.leebailey.com/EUR.htm

CourtTV Hits the Web

CourtTV Home Page Jump 7320 CONTENT

Now made famous by such high-profile court cases as the Simpson trial, CourtTV, a 24-hour-a-day, 7-day-a-week legal news cable network, brings civil and criminal trials into your living room, accompanied by attorney commentators who explain the proceedings. This experience has now been transferred to Cyberspace. At this rich, continually updated site, you can read CourtTV's program schedule, court documents, and transcripts of legal proceedings that you may have watched on this channel. As well, you can access many practical legal tips, lists of legal resources, play legal games, and enter discussion groups about the law. For example, you can read up on all the current cases that have anything to do with computer or technology trials, find out what's going on in the Supreme Court, browse through legal information of interest to small business owners, and more, much more. And if you have a legal question, there is a place where you can submit it to CourtTV's panel of experts. —(E.v.B.)

KEY NEWSGROUP misc.legal URL▸ http://www.courttv.com/index.html#Top

Gallup Polls on the Web

The Gallup Poll Jump 5768 CONTENT

When you read news stories like "Public Satisfied With Way Things are Going" you might have a pretty good idea that the Gallup people have something to do with it—who else would ask such a question? Gallup takes polls, you see, and their results are considered by some to be the most accurate appraisal of the public mood. This is a great site if you want to read the latest findings, be they the revelation that "Cats and Dogs Reign as Pampered Family Members," or that "One Fourth of Americans Still Smoke, But Most Want To Give Up The Habit." —(J.P.)

URL ▶ http://www.gallup.com/

Finding Any Event, Around the World

EventSeeker
Jump 5649

You know of an event taking place somewhere in this vast world...but can't quite pinpoint the when and where of it? How do you go about looking up such information? You go to EventSeeker! You can search their database by various methods, including date or country. Included in their database are trade shows, conferences, recreational events and more. And if you have an event you'd like to sponsor, you can enter it into their database, too. —(J.P.)

URL ▶ http://www.eventseeker.com/

Electronic Versions of Print Publications

Electronic Newsstand Jump 5083

The Electronic Newsstand carries complete articles from over 250 magazines, periodicals, journals, and books on many topics from business and technology to recreation. The page claims that you can browse for free and subscribe to the hard copy version of the publication at a discount. Check out "Today's Feature," or access information by subject. There is also a search feature available on this info-packed Web site. —(S.B.)

URL ▶ http://www.enews.com/

The Camera Clicks in Fort Worth

Allen Rose's Daily Work Jump 7207

Allen Rose is one busy Texas photographer who works for the *Fort Worth Star-Telegram.* He has archived his work here—you can choose to see what he's captured every day of the week, or if you're really interested, his past work is also offered. And it's all here in living color. Browsing through his weekly collection gives you a slice of life of the Fort Worth area. —(E.v.B.)

KEY NEWSGROUP rec.photo URL ▶ http://www.metronet.com/~arose/today/workhome.html

Sports News the Way You Want It

S.C.O.R.E. Jump 2658

The NandO Times, one of the first and still one of the best online newspapers, now allows fans to create personalized sports news pages with S.C.O.R.E., its Specially Configured Online Reader's Edition. Maintained at no cost to the user on NandO's server, you can save yourself the time and trouble of browsing through NandO's sports server, or create separate bookmarks for all the sports and teams you want to track. You can change your page at any time, and include links to the NandO news and entertainment servers, making your personal sports page an entry point into the NandO network. —(L.S.)

KEY NEWSGROUP clari.sports.misc URL ▶ http://www2.nando.net/SportServer/SCORE/

ASIA, INC. ONLINE

Asian Business News & Finance

Asia, Inc. Online Jump 7487

Asia, Inc. Online is billed as the first online Asian business magazine. Although this Web site contains articles from current and past issues of the newsstand edition of *Asia, Inc.*, you can also read exclusive articles prepared just for the online edition, investment information from regional financial experts, discussion forums, and an archive of selected articles from Asia, Inc. After you've finished absorbing all the business and financial news, then surf through the many links (listed by country and by subject) to other Asia-related sites on the Net. —(E.v.B.)

KEY NEWSGROUP clari.biz.market.asia URL ▶ http://www.asia-inc.com/

Asian Business News

Singapore Business Times Jump 3721 

"News and views you need to do business in Asia. Online and on time." That's the motto of the Singapore Business Times' Web site, and there is indeed a wealth of information here to help you do just that, from breaking news to features and editorials. The Shipping Times section includes Air & Land Transport news, along with the Shipping Times Guide. The Focus section discusses property and construction, personal finance, advertising news, and more. Corporate/Financial News covers specific company information. And there's a Views/Lifestyles section and a forum to add your comments. If you do business in Asia, this is a good starting point for accessing the region's current business news. —(N.F.)

URL▸ http://www.asia1.com.sg/biztimes/

BBC News, Schedules, & Information

The BBC Home Page Jump 0218 

The BBC maintains this large, well-designed, and well-organized Web site featuring extensive descriptions of TV and radio programs, summaries of upcoming program broadcasts, and news on the BBC's latest activities in the online world. If you're a shortwave radio listener of the BBC in the U.S., you'll especially like its program schedule of BBC Radio's World Service. —(E.G.)

KEY NEWSGROUP soc.culture.british URL▸ http://www.bbcnc.org.uk/

News from the *London Sunday Telegraph*

Electronic Telegraph Jump 0234 

Conservatives often accuse the U.S. mainstream media of ignoring or downplaying important news of the controversies surrounding the Clinton administration. Some conservatives have even pointed to media sources outside the U.S., such as the *London Sunday Telegraph*, as providing better coverage of these stories than our own media. The *London Sunday Telegraph*, and, most notably its Washington correspondent, Ambrose Evans-Pritchard, have often been way ahead of the U.S. media in coverage of such Clinton controversies as Whitewater, the Vince Foster case, the Paula Jones sexual harassment case, the Mena connection, and other stories. On this, their the online version of the *Telegraph*, you'll see all such related news, plus their coverage of U.K. news as well, updated on a daily basis.—(E.G.)

URL▸ http://www.telegraph.co.uk/

Canadian Media

The CBC Homepage Jump 5113 

The Canadian Broadcast Corporation's Web page is full of useful information if you live in Canada or have access to Canadian media. There are links here to English TV and radio, Radio Canada International, Newsworld and French Services, schedules, CBC celebrity bios, and even an archive, with historical video you can download and view. You can navigate through all the available links on this site via an interesting and easy-to-use CBC Web site map that's shaped like a flow chart. —(S.B.)

URL▸ http://www.cbc.ca/

An Experiment in Electronic Newspapers

The Winnipeg Free Press Jump 3583 

The Winnipeg Free Press and Red River Community College have undertaken a pilot project to put the newspaper online. And they've done a smashing job! This Web site offers a peek into day-to-day life in Canada, with plenty of interesting news stories—some written by Red River students—photos, and much more. —(C.P.)

URL▸ http://www.mbnet.mb.ca:80/freepress/

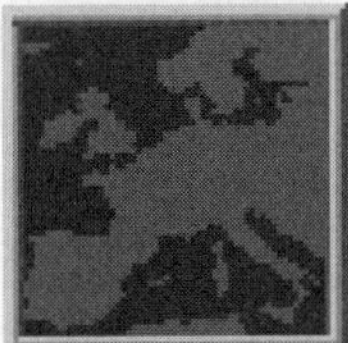

Your News Link to Europe

PanWorld NEWSLINK Jump 6644

PanWorld's Newslink is as comprehensive as a news index gets, linking you to every available European news source online. Seeking the latest stories from Europe, Asia, and Africa? You'll find the source you need here in less than a minute. By providing the latest feeds on sports, world politics, entertainment, science, culture, and weather from every corner of the world, a daily visit here keeps you abreast of the latest newsbreaking events around the world —(L.T.)

KEY NEWSGROUP clari.world.europe.union URL▶ http://www.panworld.com/paneuro.htm

Israel News Summary

IS Line Jump 0217

Daily news summary compiled from various Israeli news services covers Israeli politics, Israeli/Palestinian peace talks and conflicts, and provides additonal detail not usually found in U.S. media coverage of the Middle East. —(E.G.)

KEY NEWSGROUP soc.culture.israel URL▶ gopher://israel-info.gov.il:70/1m/new/isline

Nikkei Net: Business News from Japan

Nikkei Net Jump 6801

The creators of the Nikkei Stock Average deliver comprehensive daily Asian business news from this site, a collaborative effort of over 1,000 reporters from top Japanese newspapers, including *The Nihon Keizai Shimbun* and English-language *Nikkei Weekly*. You'll find full-text articles covering Asia's economy, export, and technology trends. —(L.T.)

KEY NEWSGROUP clari.biz.market.asia URL▶ http://www.nikkei.co.jp/enews/

News from Japan

Shima Media Network Jump 7059

All the news, "from exclusive sources without censorship or filtering from government or news agencies," that's fit to launch into cyberspace from Japan, is available here. News is updated weekly and is accompanied by photographs, and augmented by business information, conference schedules, plus a list of hot links to other Asian Web sites. —(E.v.B.)

KEY NEWSGROUP soc.culture.japan URL▶ http://www.eccosys.com/SMN/

Russia Today

Russia Today Jump 6779

When events in Russia are taking their usual twists, and turns, you'll find the format of this resource changing hand-in-hand. Russia Today is a comprehensive reference to the latest Russian political, business, and financial news. You'll find Russian TV programming schedules, and the latest election polls and results. If you're planning a personal trip there—here's a good site for up-to-date Russian news, and insight. (L.T.)

KEY NEWSGROUP alt.current-events.russia URL▶ http://www.russiatoday.com

Electronic News at Your Fingertips

ClariNet Home Page Jump 7215

Who hasn't dipped into at least one of ClariNet's extensive offerings of news topics, gathered from the wires of AP and Reuters—from computers to the economy to the environment? Well, at this site you can explore even more of its electronic news offerings—excerpts from stock reports, the latest business news, or even the latest Bizarro cartoon. ClariNet also provides interesting Net sites to discover, as well as listing job opportunities at its parent corporation. —(E.v.B.)

KEY NEWSGROUP clari.net.announce URL▶ http://www.clarinet.com/index.html

Computer News from CMP Publications

CMP's TechWeb Jump 1565

CMP, an elder statesman in the world of computer and business publishing, has produced a simply grand Web site. Run, don't walk, to TechWeb, where you'll find an amazing array of buttons and links to an arcade of interactivity. You can see a good deal of content from CMP's 16 publications—all business-, computer-, and Internet-related, and find out about the latest and greatest technology, mergers, ups and downs in today's business world. Make sure you also use their search engines to check their archives of back articles —(H.L.)

URL ▶ http://techweb.cmp.com/current/

Technology Online

Technology Online Jump 6562

Not only does Technology OnLine feature an infinite range of daily computer and technology news, it also provides a birds-eye view of the business relationships taking shape in the computing world. Once you've read the latest developments, you can link to thousands of major computer vendors, and read the latest press releases from high-tech companies. This site also provides access to hundreds of free catalogs, software, and subscription offers as well. —(L.T.)

KEY NEWSGROUP comp.infosystems.www.announce

URL ▶ http://www.tol.mmb.com/

New York Times Daily Computer News

Computer News Daily Jump 3719

The *New York Times* Syndication Sales Corporation, a leader in news service around the world, has developed Computer News Daily, a fabulous source of timely news, features, and columns on the world of computers. Think about it: computer news in one place, from one source updated on a daily basis and available FREE! If you're in the industry, put this one on your bookmark list, and you'll not only keep up with the computer news you may be missing, but you'll save time in the process. —(N.F.)

URL ▶ http://nytsyn.com/

Tracking the Business of Technology

Upside Home Page Jump 2636

Upside is a technology business magazine. Rather than covering hardware and software, it covers the people and companies shaping the application of technology, analyzes the state of the digital revolution, and probes the impact of technology on business and society. This online version of the publication does not offer the complete contents, but it offers a very good selection, including the lead stories and interviews. You can subscribe online and, if you qualify, even get a free subscription to the hard-copy edition. —(L.S.)

KEY NEWSGROUP comp.society URL ▶ http://www.upside.com/

Red Herring's High-Tech Industry Review

herring.com Jump 5756

From the publishers of the *Red Herring* high-tech business magazine comes herring.com, a terrific resource for those in the high-tech field. There's plenty to see here, including an Entrepreneurs Resource Center, containing useful information and sharp analysis in this section's many featured articles, and links to other resources. This site also features There's also news and analysis, company profiles and a great Web directory featuring relevant links to many important high-tech sites. And don't forget to sign on for the free online newsletter Red Herring Direct, a free online technology business update. —(J.P.)

KEY NEWSGROUP alt.business.misc URL ▶http://www.herring.com

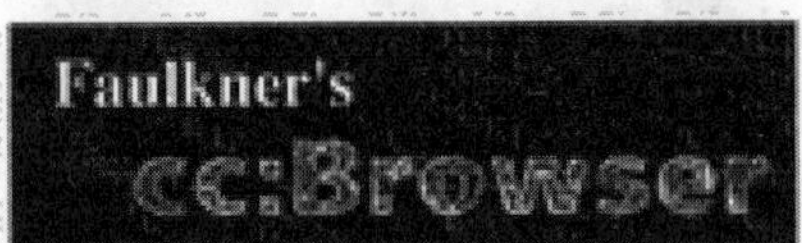

Information Provider

Faulkner's cc:Browser Jump 7161

For over 30 years, Faulkner Information Services has been a leading-edge provider of information and research on the computer and communications industries. To keep us all surfing on the curl of this information wave, this site offers articles on the latest happenings on the Net through its online newsletter, *CyberScape*, as well as weekly news bites on the computer industry, and the biweekly *News Flash* for a fuller treatment of such issues as the latest layoffs at the big computer companies, what company is merging with whom, and other hot high-tech topics. —(E.v.B.)

KEY NEWSGROUP **clari.tw.computers** URL▶ http://www.faulkner.com/#toc","clari.tw.computers

Online Publishing Tech News

The Cole Pages Jump 5131

A useful news and information source for anyone in the online publishing business, *The Cole Pages* are a monthly newsletter on technology, journalism, and publishing. You can also access *The Cole Digest,* which updates you on Web and Internet news, *The Cole Newswire,* which covers online publishing technology, and *The Cole Papers*, featuring stories from newspaper history. —(S.B.)

URL▶ http://colegroup.com/

Internet & Computer Industry News & Features

c|net online front door Jump 7410

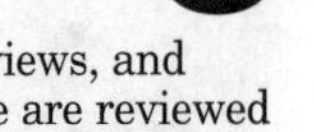

An extremely content-rich, well-designed site covering Internet news, views, and reviews. For example, e-mail software, Web sites, and browser software are reviewed in depth. Feature articles cover the hot Internet topics of the day and well-known columnists give informed opinion on a variety of Net-oriented subjects. Perhaps you'd rather browse through "software central," which contains thousands of programs. Go ahead. Having a problem? Never fear, c|net also posts e-mail and phone numbers for the leading hardware, software, and peripheral vendors support services. —(E.v.B.)

KEY NEWSGROUP **alt.answers** URL▶ http://www.cnet.com/

ZDNet Computer News

ZD Net Jump 5718

Computer publishing megaforce Ziff-Davis calls this "the most trusted computer site." And we can tell you that this is about as complete a computer news and information site as you're likely to find. This aspires to be a one-stop site for all your computer needs, and that's why you'll find a little bit of everything, from a straightforward guide to buying a new PC, news on the latest software—including games, utilities and CD ROMs, all the latest industry news, and much more. And if you don't find what you want here (unlikely as that may seem) you can use the searching tool to search all of the Ziff-Davis computer magazines. —(J.P.)

URL▶ http://www5.zdnet.com/

Seidman's Internet Views

Seidman's Online Insider Jump 8035

Opinionated and knowledgeable Net watcher Robert Seidman puts the Internet under his insightful scrutiny here, providing his unique view of the Internet's newest technology, company news, and industry announcements from one end of the Net to the other. See what Seidman thinks—you can read each weekly issue online, check his archive of past columns, or have them e-mailed to you for future reference. —(E.v.B.)

KEY NEWSGROUP **clari_matrix.news**

URL▶ http://techweb.cmp.com:80/net/online/current/columns/seidman/online_insider/

Internet News Daily

Netrepreneur News **Jump 8034**

Daily, Netrepreneur News monitors the mainstream media and trade magazines for news related to the Internet and commercial online services, and then distills the stories into bite-sized pieces. You can easily keep up-to-date on the latest news of Net commercialization by reading this site's summaries of leading stories. To track a topic in-depth, the News also provides archives of its coverage under subject headings, such as Marketing, World Wide Web, or Technology, and also features book reviews and specially-commissioned interviews with Net business luminaries. —(E.v.B.)

KEY NEWSGROUP clari_matrix.news

URL▸ http://www.conceptone.com/netnews/netnews.htm

Morning's at seven;
The grass is dew pearled;
God's in his heaven,
All's right with the world!

If you want to start a small business, pick one that caters to the rich. There will always be rich people who will indulge their whims. Today more than ever.

I'm amused by people and their cellular phones. I have a neighbor, a young business woman, who regularly backs out of her garage as I'm leaving on my morning walk. No sooner does she get started down the street than she picks up her cellular phone and makes a call. Now why couldn't she have made that call in the house before leaving? Are we so driven that every minute must count, that none can be wasted in relaxation or just driving our car and observing the beauty of the morning?

Having briefly watched not only the top rated TV shows, but the ones near the bottom, I've come to the conclusion that the shows I might like won't last very long.

White water men

▲ *Ken Sadler shares his opinions, from* **THE PASSING SHOW**, *at* **Jump 7359**.

Internet & Multimedia News for the Digital Age

Welcome to DigitalPulse **Jump 7418**

DigitalPulse takes, well what else?—the pulse of the digital world—from online services to multimedia companies to cable television. Read daily headlines of what's happening in high tech. After catching up on the news, surf the Net on the links DigitalPulse provides to great sites for kids, hardware and software company home pages, and to the online versions of such publications as *Information Week*, *Interactive Age*, *Technology Review*, or *Multimedia Wire*. This is yet another solid, value-added Pathfinder site from Time Warner. —(E.v.B.)

KEY NEWSGROUP alt.answers **URL▸** http://pathfinder.com/

IN, AROUND and ONLINE

What's New in Commercial Online Services

Online Service Industry **Jump 7134**

Robert Seidman produces a thoughtful weekly newsletter that reports the news from AOL, Compuserve, Prodigy, Apple, Microsoft, and all their electronic cousins, aunts, and neighbors. Robert interviews company spokespersons, gives considered opinions on the events he reports, and even uploads the latest stock quotations for these companies. After you read Robert's newsletter, you can explore the links he provides to many of their home pages. Still want more? Explore the lists of commercial online newspaper services and a directory of online publications too. —(E.v.B.)

KEY NEWSGROUP alt.bbs.internet **URL▸** http://www.clark.net/pub/robert/home.html

Multichannel News: Cable & High-Tech Business News

Multichannel News Online **Jump 6794**

Here's your weekly fix for the latest cable television and technology news. Multichannel delivers insight and industry views, and thoroughly examines hot new innovations such as cable modems. You'll find links to many online cable TV industry resources, track telecom stocks, and browse Nielsen's latest cable ratings. A great daily news site for those who work in and around the cable and telecom industry. —(L.T.)

URL▸ http://www.multichannel.com

What's the Latest News from the Net?

Edupage.new Jump 7132 CONTENT

Here's a useful news summary which covers the latest Net and telecom-related news stories. Published by Educom, a Washington, D.C.-based consortium of colleges and universities which are seeking to "transform education through the use of information technology," this news summary page is updated three times a week. Despite the rough presentation, the editors of this page provide snippets of newsworthy information technology items—very broadly selected from a wide range of journals and newspapers—that you need to know to stay in the know. —(E.v.B.)

KEY NEWSGROUP **bit.listserv.edtech**

URL ▶ http://www.educom.edu/edupage.new

Myself, I plan to take full advantage of the virtual world.

I'm particularly excited about interactive television. I'm biting my nails, waiting for it to arrive. In preparation, my telephone, my computer, and my television are negotiating a merger that, if successful, will cause them to move into one corporate headquarters called a set-top box that will sit on top of my television. With this box I will control my virtual world. My home will no longer be a place where I store dirty laundry and eat dinner standing over the kitchen sink. It will become a conceptual space where magical things occur.

I'm already cultivating a strong emotional bond with my television so we will be on the same wavelength when the excitement begins. My television, which now is just a stupid box that sits in the living room doing nothing most of the day, is going to be a busy center of commerce. Besides video on demand, it will provide me with sex on demand, food on demand, shopping on demand--well, you get the idea.

My only fear is that I will become petulant, standing in front of my television, stamping my foot, saying, "I demand pizza, I demand an espresso machine." There could be no limits to my cravings.

Practically anything I want will be at my fingertips. I think I will cease to leave my house or deal directly with people, except for the delivery guys bringing the food I'm going to demand. This will be good because people carry germs and frequently say irritating things. With my new toys I can just click my remote and have someone else do my bidding. I won't have to do too much shopping though. If I never go out, I don't really need new clothes, do I?

▲ *A different view of the Interactive Age, from* **Sam Johnson's Electronic Revenge**, *at* Jump 7399.

A Rational Look at the Online Pornography Controversy

The Cyberporn Debate Jump 2667 CONTENT

The July 3, 1995, issue of *Time* magazine carried a cover story alleging rampant pornography on the Internet. It sparked a debate that still rages, mostly because people still believe the *Time* story was factual. It wasn't. The story was based on very flawed research, and the article itself was biased toward sensationalism instead of journalism. This page, part of the respected Project 2000, offers excellent critiques of the debate, as well as a link to the original article and a means for you to add your comments. However you feel about the issue, you owe it to yourself to get the facts behind the story, before making a final judgment. —(L.S.)

KEY NEWSGROUP **alt.internet.media-coverage** URL ▶ http://www2000.ogsm.vanderbilt.edu/cyberporn.debate.cgi

Wired Attacks the Net Porn Scare

HotWired: Pornscare Index Jump 2668

This is HotWired's take on the *Time* magazine cyberporn debacle. In the HotWired tradition, it's as edgy as it is informative, going after *Time*, Philip Elmer-DeWitt who authored the article, and Martin Rimm who conducted the highly questionable research study used by Elmer-DeWitt to write the story. But, considering the site's opening quotation of Elmer-DeWitt describing the Rimm study and his article that opens the site—much of it may be bogus, error-ridden, or just plain wrong—it's hard to blame them. In addition to in-depth analysis of the controversy and its fallout, there's also an interview with Elmer-DeWitt, in itself reason enough to check out this site. —(L.S.)

KEY NEWSGROUP **alt.internet.media-coverage** URL ▶ http://www.hotwired.com/special/pornscare/

The Start of the Cyberporn Debate

Time Magazine Cyberporn Cover Story Jump 2669 CONTENT

This is it. This is an online version of the July 3, 1995, *Time* magazine cover story that sparked the great cyberporn debate, complete with illustrations many consider as, if not more, pornographic than what is purported to be available on the Internet. If you read this before going to the various sites that dissect the article and the research study it is based on, keep in mind that even Philip Elmer-DeWitt realizes much of it is wrong and wrongly presented—and he wrote it. —(L.S.)

KEY NEWSGROUP **alt.internet.media-coverage** URL ▶ http://www.pathfinder.com/

Who's Not Working

Strike Page! Jump 2674

This page provides information about union strikes worldwide, either ongoing or threatened. Each listing describes the issues involved, the union's strategy, and any news about the strike and prospects for settlement. Edited by Hilary Diamond, it's clearly pro-labor, so it's not so much a page of news and information as it is a way to promote solidarity and communicate the positions of labor unions to other unions and the general public. —(L.S.)

KEY NEWSGROUP **clari.news.labor** URL▸ http://www.igc.apc.org/strike/

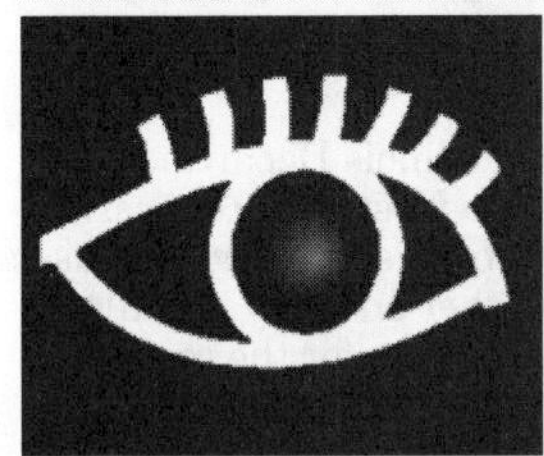

Big Brother, Conspiracies, and Alternative Media Views

Big Brother Home Page
Jump 5805

This alternative news-reporting and links page is dedicated to sticking it to a government (ours) they claim is constantly sticking its nose into the lives of everyday citizens (us). Freedom is at stake, they say, and they are determined to restore the government to the original intent of the Founding Fathers. The creators of this site offer a boatload of articles and links, most of which, we are told, have not been reported (or at least grossly under-reported) in the mainstream press. The topics include the scandals of the Clinton Administration, stories profiling the underlying threat of one-world government, and related content, from sources of varied reliability. —(J.P.)

KEY NEWSGROUP **alt.conspiracy** URL▸ http://www2.vivid.net/~gnc422/

Conspiracy and Alternative News from ParaScope

ParaScope News Home Page Jump 0221

The Net has become fertile ground for thousands of Web sites and newsgroups documenting all kinds of alleged government plots, conspiracy theories, UFO sightings, alien abductions, and the like. While many of these sites are as nutty as you would think they'd be, the Internet does provide a forum for dissemination of news and information which certainly would not be available in mainstream broadcast or print media. ParaScope is one such alternative news and information source, edited by Charles Overbeck, and it's every bit as well-designed, produced, and executed as any major conventional newspaper web site. ParaScope sits squarely on the fence between the plausibly believable and the absurd, covering all kinds of unconventional theories, stories, and events. These range from the down-to-earth, such as the use of millimeter-wave scanners (which can be used on street corners to literally "see through" people for concealed weapons or drugs) and their threat to individual liberties, to the typical UFO, Bigfoot, and alien abduction fare that's commonly found all over the Net. You'll have to be the judge as to how much of this content you'd prefer to take seriously. That said, ParaScope may be right for you if your looking for a polished, well-designed alternative news site. —(E.G.)

KEY NEWSGROUP **alt.conspiracy** URL▸ http://www.parascope.com/index.htm

The 60s Yet Survive: Mother Jones Web Site

Mother Jones Jump 2332

Back in the days when the spirit of the 1960s still flourished in America, *Mother Jones* was just one of many radical leftist magazines exposing the wrongs of greedy capitalists and dishonest government. Today, with that spirit all but dead, *Mother Jones* remains, not quite as radical but still focused on exposing abuses of power and identifying and offering solutions to the problems afflicting contemporary society. You can keep abreast of its activities and opinions while contributing your own with this online, interactive version of the magazine. Plus, you can read online articles from the magazine itself. —(L.S.)

KEY NEWSGROUP **alt.motherjones** URL▸ http://www.mojones.com/

weatherOnline!: The Web's Big Weather Site

weatherOnline! Jump 6668

WeatherOnline! has now established itself as the Web's monster weather site, just about every U.S. forecast available, along with superbly-executed full-screen maps, graphics, weather tools, ski reports, rainfall/climate summaries, agricultural, and offshore water forecasts. Whether you're in Freeport, Maine or San Francisco, California—you'll find the weather info you need here. —(L.T.)

KEY NEWSGROUP **clari.news.weather** URL▸ http://www.weatheronline.com/

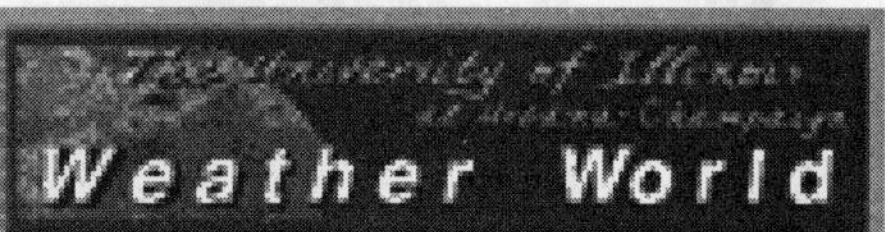

The Weather Machine

Welcome to Weather World Jump 2238

This is the Web version of the University of Illinois Department of Atmospheric Science's Weather Machine, the most comprehensive and up-to-date weather resource on the Web. There are numerous color satellite images, surface maps, forecast maps, animations, and daily forecast and weather advisory text files. The resources are arranged by region, state, and city for the U.S., with slightly-broader breakouts for the rest of the world as well. Most of the data and imagery is updated hourly, so this is the place to get the latest, as well as the best, weather information. —(L.S.)

KEY NEWSGROUP **sci.geo.meteorology** URL▸ http://www.atmos.uiuc.edu/wxworld/html/top.html

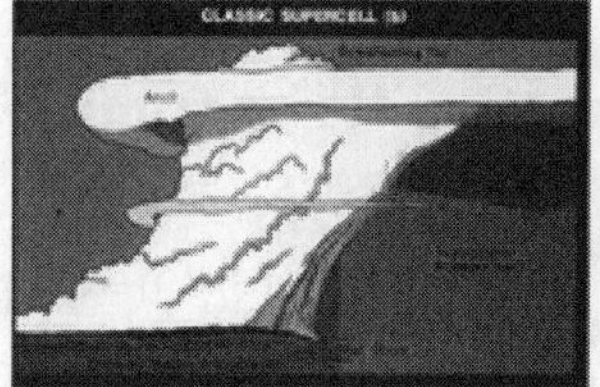

Tornado & Storm Warnings

NWSFO Norman WWW Home Page Jump 5140

A great weather resource for those of you living in the hurricane and tornado-prone areas of the Midwest and the South. Nicely put together by Steve Nelson, this site describes the functions and mission of the main office of the National Weather Service, located in Norman, Oklahoma. You can learn about the duties of the NWS, the services it offers, how its forecasting tools work, its research activities and applications, and contact information. There's a FAQ, the latest news at NWS, and a list of related Web sites, too, plus a featured page that includes an illustrated severe weather safety guide and storm spotter's guide, with amazing storm photos and graphics. —(S.B.)

URL▸ http://doplight.nssl.uoknor.edu/nws/

News for and by Journalists

The American Reporter Jump 1558

The American Reporter is a five-day-a-week electronic "newshare" owned by the writers whose work it features. Joe Shea, editor-in-chief, founded the site to give journalists around the world an opportunity to have a financial stake in their own work and to earn equity for the correspondent in profits from advertising and subscriptions, and income when their stories sell to other newspapers. The straightforward style makes this site strictly content-oriented, with a heavy dose of national and international late-breaking stories and commentary about society's role in shaping the news. Additionally, searchable archives, articles about cyberspace, selected press releases, humor and opinion pieces, reprints from other publications, letters to the editor, and links to sports, business, and weather round out this interesting cyberpaper. The American Reporter has no political, corporate or other affiliation. If you're a journalist, or simply interested in good journalism, definitely pay a visit here. —(H.L.)

URL▸ http://www.newshare.com/Reporter/today.html

Finding News Sources Around the World

netMEDIA Jump 6672

A good first stop to locate Web-based newspapers, magazines, television and radio stations around the globe should be here. This expanding links site features links to over 400

media outlets in Africa, Australia, Austria, Belgium, Brazil, Canada, China, Costa Rica, Ecuador, England, France, Germany, The Netherlands, India, Ireland, Italy, Japan, Mexico, Norway, Peru, Poland, Russia, Scotland, Sweden, Switzerland, Singapore, South Korea, Slovak Republic, Slovenia, Spain, United Kingdom...had enough? —(L.T.)

KEY NEWSGROUP **clari.news.top.world** URL▶ http://www.gopublic.co.at/gopublic/media/

The Newspaper Industry's Bible

Editor & Publisher Home Page

Jump 2765

CONTENT

Those print publications that don't adapt to new media will find themselves close to their ends, so the bible of the newspaper publishing industry is on the Web, too. E&P's Web edition gives you the insider's view of what's going on with newspapers and magazines, and even on the Internet, beginning with Steve Outing's five-days-a-week column and continuing with breaking news on the business of news. There are good links, too, for journalists looking for sources on the Net, what newspapers are doing in the online world, and, by jumping to the E&P Web Edition, additional news and features taken from the print version. —(L.S.)

KEY NEWSGROUP **alt.journalism.print** URL▶ http://www.mediainfo.com/edpub/

Journalism Resources from the National Press Club

NPC Home Page

Jump 7205

The National Press Club, based in Washington, D.C., has entered the online world with an extensive site that covers information on the NPC itself, and broad-based online resources for journalists and news junkies alike. You can listen to speeches given at the NPC from 1990 on, access a number of newsgroups related to journalism, and search an index to journalism periodicals, or you can even match wits with professional copy editors. Allied associations, such as the National Association of Broadcasters, American Communication Association, Society of Environmental Journalists, are also linked here. —(E.v.B.)

KEY NEWSGROUP **misc.headlines** URL▶ http://town.hall.org/places/npc/

Media News

Media Daily Jump 7448

If you're a media watcher, here's another electronic newsletter devoted to daily updates on all kinds of media, from magazines to online services. In Media Daily, read about the Village Voice's 40th anniversary and its Web page, or what media types were laid off in the federal government, or even the latest on the Book-of-the-Month Club. If you want to track a story, use the Media Daily archives. You can also participate in its active forums, give an opinion on the day's news, or check out jobs wanted and offered in the "opportunities in media and marketing" forum, or see what's happening in the many industry forums such as online services, electronic publishing, and a host of other interesting discussion groups. —(E.v.B.)

KEY NEWSGROUP **alt.zines** URL▶ http://www2.simbanet.com/simba/m_daily/media.html

The New Web Media

Slate

Slate Jump 5931

After a rocky start (pun intended), Slate, the high-profile Web political, news, culture, and comment magazine is finally beginning to find its footing. At the outset, Microsoft and editor Michael Kinsley fell victim to a media-inspired wish-fulfillment for failure. Under the glare of the spotlight, few could have survived with their vision intact. But we are pleased to report that the death of Slate was indeed exaggerated, and all concerned have persevered to produce a Web-magazine that may indeed prove to be ground-breaking in concept. The articles are far-reaching and intelligent, provocative and timely. There is little pandering to the common denominator, and thankfully the smug elitism so popular with the Web's in-crowd is also largely missing. —(J.P.)

URL ▶ http://www.slate.com/TOC/current/contents.asp

SITO Online Art Collective

SITO
Jump 5728 CONTENT

A wonderful, award-winning art site which truly pushes the technical boundaries of the medium of Web-based collaborative art, SITO "is a place for image-makers and image-lovers to exchange ideas, collaborate and, in a loose sense of the word, meet." It is the Web's best-known art collective, except that it's also a place for artists—and those who enjoy art—to gather together to discuss the latest and the greatest. So what will you find here? There are three main areas: SYNERGY (the collaborative art projects), THE ARCHIVES (hundreds of individual artists' images divided up by category), and EXHIBITS (Web-based specialized art-displays). You also can spend hours exploring HYGRID, the endless linked-art and culture project that's been developed in part by Jon van Oast (who, incidentally, is the developer of this book's own Web site, JumpCity). And the art itself? It is everything you'd expect from a collective—part daring, part experimental and, of course, the parts that leave you breathless. —(J.P.)

HyGrid Walking Cyclone

Base image by Ranjit Bhatnagar on 11 Feb 1996.
Other HyGrid pieces by Ranjit Bhatnagar.

Haven't you been here before?

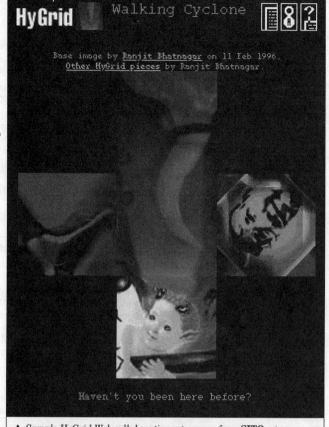

▲ *Sample HyGrid Web collaborative art screen, from* SITO, *at* Jump 5728.

URL ▶ http://www.sito.org/

All the (Netly) News . . .

Netly News Jump 5735 

When it comes to tracking the "culture" and the big movements of players behind the growth of the Net, the Netly News is a very thought-provoking (and funny) indeed, and the perpetrators, Joshua Quittner and Noah Robischon, have but one Netly Mission: "If it happened online, it's Netly News." And since the online world has been rather busy of late, you can expect to find just about anything here, from a satire on Reverend Bill (Gates, that is) to leting the air out of current Net fads (both technical and human) and generally raising as much of a fuss as possible on $1.50 a day (and that's *their* overhead, not ours). Oh, and there's a discussion list you can join as well at this site, originally developed as a counter to *Wired* Magazine's attitude-enriched Suck site (see Jump 7449). —(J.P.)

URL ▶ http://pathfinder.com/

Literate Web Magazine

SALON Jump 8037

David Talbot, editor of the hip Web e-zine SALON, wants his publication to howl with creative honesty. SALON features the usual political and social commentary found in most Web magazines, but with the added bonus of good writing, insightful commentary, and occasional wit. Interviews, movie, television and book reviews, and all kinds of columns and topics are treated in a knowledgeable, literate manner. —(E.v.B.)

KEY NEWSGROUP alt.zines URL▶ http://www.salon1999.com/

Stay Current

The Today Page Jump 7140

LINKS

Obviously Howard Jones is an up-to-the-minute kind of guy. He has assembled a page of comprehensive links to Web sites that change daily. So you can check out the latest weather photos, read, if you're so inclined, the day's BBC TV listings, your horoscope, whose birthday it is today, and discover what the cool Web site of the day is. Want more? OK, the Dilbert cartoon changes daily, as do the listings of the *Voice of America News*. —(E.v.B.)

KEY NEWSGROUP alt.cul ture.internet URL▶ http://www.vossnet.co.uk/local/today/index.html

Adding the Spiritual to the Everyday Roles of Life

American Spirit Newspaper Jump 5848

The American Spirit is an educational—and uplifting—Web newspaper published with the goal of educating people about the spiritual and self-help sides of their everyday living and work, be it in areas of finance, the economy, family, health issues, and more. The paper edition is published by Sterling Rose Press in the San Francisco Bay Area, and their Web site carries on in that tradition. This site tries to broaden your perspective, with articles about a wide (and seemingly strange) range of subjects, from wiser use of credit cards, to the benefits of trance states. An example is the recent feature on harvest traditions, where we learn that, despite what city-dwellers might think, such traditions still have a strong part to play in the lives of many people around the world. Not as nutty as it all may seem, because the material is well-written, useful, and pulled together in a convincing manner. —(J.P.)

URL▶ http://www.celestia.com/alpha/SRP/

Web Magazine for Disgruntled Workers

Disgruntled Jump 5850

So you're fed up and you're not gonna take it anymore? Who you gonna call? Disgruntled, of course. This is the place where you'll discover that you're not alone in the working world—there are others out there just as disgruntled as you are. The articles here are as negative as you might expect, which is not a bad thing; the stories come from all walks of life, and while some of the pieces are indeed whimsical in nature, such as: "DISGRUNTLED Offers Readers Tips On How To Spend Their Minimum Wage Raise," many articles really do shed light on the plight of those who work for a living. The tone here is honest, and sometimes profane, so it is not recommended for younger readers (or many *employers*, for that matter). —(J.P.)

URL▶ http://www.disgruntled.com/

What's New at the WELL

The WELL Jump 0214

One of the earliest and still one of the most popular and active private conferencing systems is the San Francisco-based WELL (which stands for Whole Earth 'Lectronic Link) started by Stewart Brand, the man who started the *Whole Earth Catalog*. The WELL is an "online community" of conference discussions on a wide variety of subjects, much like a private version of the Internet's USENET newsgroups. If you've become an Internet newsgroup junkie, you might be interested in joining The WELL to access their wide array of interesting private conferences for a modest additional subscription charge. This Web site features The WELL's online conference descriptions, the latest WELL news plus a handful of The WELL's funky Web tips and events. —(E.G.)

URL ▶ http://www.well.com/

KidNews: News By and For Kids

KidNews Jump 6537

KidNews delivers the latest current events for kids, and, what makes this site unique is that it's written exclusively by and for them. Children all over the Internet are free to submit their stories for inclusion, and Educators are invited to use the stories offered online for their teaching purposes. Filled to the brim with sweet kid-written features like "What the Hay-Go For a Ride!," "Homeschool is Cool!," and "How to Have Fun in the Snow," to newsworthy coverage of important issues like "Police Explain New Helmet Law," here's a site where your kids can post their stories, too. You'll also find educational narratives such as "History Spoken Here," and "WWII and the Depression," along with rainy-day guides like "How To Build your own Birdfeeder." A must for children, teachers, and parents alike. —(L.T.)

KEY NEWSGROUP **csn.ml.kids** URL ▶ http://www.vsa.cape.com/~powens/Kidnews3.html

A Fine Family Site

The Faherty Web Front Door Jump 7421

Ring the Faherty's front door bell and meet some really nice folks at this site, created by the Faherty family themselves: John (Dad), Denise (Mom), and kids Kristen, Andrea, Joey—and even Felix (the cat). They're obviously a nice online family who uses the absolute latest Net design tricks in implementing their site. Their front door (great graphics) is a multimedia treat—hear the windchimes, pet the cat! After the introductions, why not surf around exploring each member of the family's favorite Web links. Then check out the Faherty's Web site pick of the day and multimedia site of the week. You won't want to leave this friendly bunch of people, but going out the "back door" of their site is nearly as fun as entering its front door! —(E.v.B.)

KEY NEWSGROUP **alt.answers** URL ▶ http://www.alternate.com/~fart/index.html

Lauren's Web Page

What is this complete and utter craziness? Jump 5909

Although we didn't discover Lauren's last name but we can tell you that she is 13 years old and she's created her own Web page. And it's a wonderful page for surfers young or old. At the heart of Lauren's site is her daily journal entitled "Through the Eyes of Ruby," where we read all about Lauren's "So Called Life." She is witty and very observant of many of the details in life that us adults now take for granted. And you'll also want to visit her link pages, including the wonderfully named "Linkos," and the many music links. And you can't leave without checking out the links in her "RiDe them WaVeS" section. —(J.P.)

URL ▶ http://www.vvm.com/~lbane/lbane.html

What Was That Again, Dave?

DaveNet '96 Jump **8078**

Dave Winer, best known for his popular commentaries on DaveNet at the HotWired site, enjoys controversy, whether it's generated by his tinderbox opinions on the campaign trail, Microsoft, the Internet, the Queen of Soul, Aretha, or whatever topic takes his fancy. His essays are thought-provoking, flame-attracting, funny, and often tongue-in-cheek. DaveNet is never dull—come on over and refresh those tired brain cells. —(E.v.B.)

KEY NEWSGROUP **talk.politics** URL▶ http://www.hotwired.com/staff/userland/davenethome.html

David Siegel's World on the Web

David Siegel's Home Page Jump **7228**

Computer graphic artist, writer, and typeface designer David Siegel has assembled a graphically beautiful, informative, and creative set of Web pages that are, without a doubt, one of the best-designed Web sites around. He not only provides Web graphic design tips, including some outstanding new Web page style concepts, but for filmmakers and game designers, David has posted his nine-act story structure program. As well, you are treated to quite an array of David's excellent writing—from nonfiction pieces, such as his discussions of the myth of protein and calcium, to short stories. He's also in the process of creating a Frank Lloyd Wright page—so stay tuned! —(E.v.B.)

KEY NEWSGROUP **comp.graphics** URL▶ http://www.best.com/~dsiegel/home.html

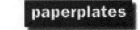

Toronto Zine

....paperplates.... Jump **7243**

Bernard Kelly and a host of creative friends in Toronto, Canada, have crafted a rather neat Web zine. Featuring poetry, short stories, essays, book reviews, film reviews—all hip, all very urbane. The graphics are fun and the layout is eye-catching. —(E.v.B.)

KEY NEWSGROUP **alt.zines** URL▶ http://www.hookup.net/~beekelly/

It Was a Dark and Stormy Night . . .

The Dark Pool Jump **7268**

The Dark Pool is an amazing Web hypertext narrative created by Canadians Janet Cardiff and George Bures Miller. They lead you on a fascinating exploration of magic, unreality and reality, accompanied by voices from the past, disembodied bird wings, and washing machines. Very strange, very beautifully illustrated, very intriguing. It has also been mounted as an exhibit at the Walter Philips Gallery in Banff, Alberta. —(E.v.B.)

KEY NEWSGROUP **misc.writing** URL▶ http://www-nmr.banffcentre.ab.ca/WPG/DarkPool/index.html

Connected Chat

Cyber Babble Jump **7356**

Rich Atkinson, creator of Cyber Babble, has put together a colorful, interesting collection of reviews (the usual games, music, and art), feature articles on software, and an amazing collection of action figures. Into this interesting mix, Rich also throws in great Macintosh links, and lists of the best Web sites to visit. You can also enter one of Rich's contests before you leave the site. —(E.v.B.)

KEY NEWSGROUP **alt.zines** URL▶ http://www.kernel.com/usr/rich/CyberBabble.html

As One Man's World Turns

THE PASSING SHOW Jump **7359**

Ken Sadler has a keen interest in life as it unfolds in front of him—the passing show. Every two months, Ken issues a series of observations, and short short stories on life around him—garage sales, cars he desires, the neighbor's

yards, religion—you name it. The pieces are pithy, sometimes humorous, and always interesting—on the small scale. —(E.v.B.)

KEY NEWSGROUP misc.writing URL▶ http://www.Europa.com/~kbsadler/passingshow.html

Spike Webb Home

Spike Webb Home Jump 5646 

Like the old weekly adventure shows of old comes Spike Webb, a self-proclaimed mix of Sci-Fi and campy detective. Spike's Web is devoted to explaining and having fun with the Internet. Each week Spike teams up with two other super sleuths to "fight the evil and greedy criminals" who abuse the Internet. There's a new episode of the adventure published every Friday. And drop by on Tuesday for a technology rant, which provides a forum for two opposing sides to many computer-related issues. And there's even a fan club! —(J.P.)

URL▶ http://www.spikewebb.com/

Freedonia

www.freedonia.com Jump 5772 

There is plenty to see here on this interesting, satirical and beautifully designed site by Carl Steadman, co-creator of the well-known Suck site. You might start with the section having to do with "Satirical Intent for the Amusement and Edification of Both Fanciers and Detractors of the Feline Specie." Or, perhaps you prefer "Kid A In Alphabet Land: An Abecedarian Roller Coaster Ride Through The Phallocentric Obscurantism Of Jacques Lacan." Whew! And of course there is the "Panic Encyclopedia: The Definitive Guide to the Postmodern Scene," and prose from Carl. And lest we forget, you can also pop into the "placing" site (see review elsewhere) at Jump 5771. Enjoy! —(J.P.)

URL▶ http://www.freedonia.com/
zines (Web) Web (zine)

Chris Abraham's Personal Web Page

my room Jump 7375 

Chris Abraham, Renaissance man, is, depending, we guess on the time of day, a photographer, a poet, fashion designer, literati, scuba diver, multimedia writer, and owner of a beloved Mercedes named Gertie (after Gertrude Stein, of course). An interesting guy, Chris. And if you want to know more about him, well stick around and surf through pages devoted to his travels, his many interests, his online and offline life. His pages are attractive and the graphics (mostly his own photographs) are creatively used. —(E.v.B.)

KEY NEWSGROUP misc.creativity URL▶ http://www.artswire.org/Community/chris/home.html

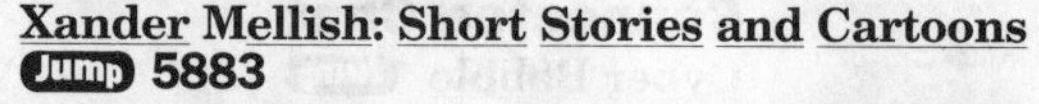

Xander Mellish: Short Stories and Cartoons

Xander Mellish: Short Stories and Cartoons Jump 5883 

Xander Mellish is a talented author and cartoonist who originally published her stories on telephone poles and laundromats around New York City. But a cleanup of NYC streets followed, forcing the author to take up residence on the Internet. Which is where we find her. The site features much of the same work that so captured the hearts and minds of New Yorkers. As you'll discover here, her stories and artwork are minimalist in nature, each conveying a rare insight into everyday life that is quite remarkable. The stories capture your imagination—about a woman pining for his husband who is fighting a war in Europe, or the seemingly mundane tale of businesspeople eating lunch in their office. Even more remarkable, of course, is her determination to carry on no matter what the odds, no matter what obstacles were placed in her way (NOTE: This site contains some material which is not suitable for children). —(J.P.)

URL▶ http://www.users.interport.net/~xmel/

Commentary at Large

Sam Johnson's Electronic Revenge Jump 7399

Sam Johnson's Electronic Revenge, published by Silly Little Tomte Publications, is an online magazine that features new writers and seemingly anyone else with a well-written opinion. The editor, Derek Davis, encourages his contributors to "exchange opinions, expound on their favorite obsessions, challenge orthodoxies, uphold universal truths, advocate offensive causes, devise cures for social ills, engage in pointless silliness, and rattle the cages of the mighty." This Web zine, named after the famous British wordsmith Samuel Johnson, covers the arts, politics, society, and cultural issues. —(E.v.B.)

KEY NEWSGROUP **alt.zines** URL▸ http://pobox.com/slt/sam.home.html

Winn's Weekly Opinion

Winn's World Wide Web Weakly Weekly Jump 7402

Philip Winn is editor and chief writer on this weekly zine that's often filled with his rants on the events of the day. Read his thought-provoking essays on Mac versus DOS, or what if men did all the housework and women ran all the businesses, or even on how to become a writer. —(E.v.B.)

KEY NEWSGROUP **alt.zines** URL▸ http://www.winn.com/w6/index.html

Aussies on the Web

Matilda in Cyberspace Jump 7063

Tony Barry is the moving force and, not incidentally, the editor of this monthly newsletter—*Matilda in Cyberspace*. Devoted to Internet events and issues related to Australia, the newsletter presents articles by a number of contributors on such topics as computers in school, community access, and new sites. —(E.v.B.)

KEY NEWSGROUP **aus.computers** URL▸ http://snazzy.anu.edu.au/Matilda/start.html

Meet Marius

Marius Watz' WWW Pages Jump 7226

Marius Watz's pages range over a number of topics of great personal interest: architecture, artificial life, Hakim Bey, the NEXUS project, computer art, cyberspace, graphic design, and virtual reality. You will find links and other documents in each of these categories. Or, as Marius writes: "It will contain personal statements, manifestos and agitprop." For those fans of the FutureCulture Net mailing list, you can read its FAQ, check out the personalities on the list, and read excerpts from the list itself. —(E.v.B.)

KEY NEWSGROUP **alt.culture.internet** URL▸ http://www.uio.no/~mwatz/

Charlie on Parade

Charlie's Place Jump 9504

Charlie Stross has one busy keyboard. At Charlie's Place, you are treated to a smorgasbord of his writings from a collection of his rants, to essays on civil liberties in cyberspace, to his fictional offerings. Along the way, he discusses why he doesn't include images on his pages—a hint: he is devoted to content. As well, you can keyword search his entire site using his own text search engine. —(E.v.B.)

KEY NEWSGROUP **alt.prose** URL▸ http://www.tardis.ed.ac.uk/~charlie/index.html

Small-Town Texas

The Round Top Register Jump 7447

The Round Top Register, the online newspaper from Round Top, population 81, the smallest incorporated town in Texas, is great fun. Not only will you read about the celebrations (bet you didn't know it was celebrating its 125th year of incorporation), you can also catch up on other hometown news. Christopher K. Travis, the editor, records the latest news out of Round Top, details of the classical music festival, or the 25th anniversary of the

Shakespearean festival, in addition to other goings-on about town. Not to be missed for a real small-town experience. —(E.v.B.)

KEY NEWSGROUP **alt.zines** URL▶ http://www.rtis.com/reg/roundtop/

Newspapers in the Age of the Net

Newspaper Association of America Jump **1561**

The explosive growth of electronic media has a profound impact on the newspaper industry. The Newspaper Association of America (NAA) site helps journalists and newspapers stay ahead of the curve by disseminating electronic media information and providing a forum of idea exchange among newspaper professionals. As a nonprofit organization representing over 1,500 member newspapers in the U.S. and Canada, this site focuses on marketing, public policy, industry development, and newspaper operations. The well-organized, easy-to-use NAA pages discuss key issues such as "The Microsoft Network—win or no-win for newspapers?" and "Does Microsoft have designs on cybermedia newsgathering?" There are numerous hotlinks to all Web newspapers, industry-related events, reports of previous conferences, including a brief on how to attract dollars in political advertising. The best resources here for the beginner are their online publications, including "Facts About Newspapers"—the industry's key statistical reference—and their jobline. —(H.L.)

URL▶ http://www.infi.net/naa/

Web Magazine for Farmers & Rural Residents

Progressive Farmer Online
Jump **3744**

Progressive Farmer, the agricultural business and lifestyle print magazine, now reaches about 650,000 farm families throughout the southern and midwestern United States. Now it will reach many more with this Web version of its publication. Stories cover typical farming issues, such as crops and livestock. But *Progressive Farmer* also covers issues important to rural families—such as the environment, rural healthcare, and farm safety. Sign up for the free Progressive Farmer e-mail newsletter. A wonderfully colorful, fact-filled Web magazine. —(N.F.)

KEY NEWSGROUP **alt.agriculture.misc** URL▶ http://www.pathfinder.com/

Scanning the Best of the Print Media

Live from the Free World: Mr. Media!
Jump **7238**

Magazine subscription salespeople must adore Mr. Media. Mr. Media, or Bob Andelman when he's at home, scans an amazing number of magazines to produce his weekly Web site. Not only are you treated to Mr. Media's weekly column on any media topic or person in the news, but he also delivers a lot of snippets from a diverse selection of periodicals from *Fusion* magazine to *Oxford American* magazine to the latest from Marvel Comics. An accomplished journalist, Mr. Media doesn't stop at the hard copy world, but also reports on the latest Web sites that catch his interest. Be warned that Mr. Media could also be called Mr. Graphics—the numerous GIFs he includes make his pages pretty slow loading on a slow Net day. —(E.v.B.)

KEY NEWSGROUP **alt.journalism** URL▶ http://www.mrmedia.com/mrmedia/

The Web's Most Wanted

Silent Witness Jump **0212**

You saw it here first: the 21st century's Web equivalent of the "wanted poster," Silent Witness was created by the Phoenix, Arizona, Police Department to give all Net surfers broad access to the gallery of bad guys who've committed crimes in the Phoenix area. Contains listings of crimes and suspects wanted—including Web-based mug shots. Not the happiest place to see, but certainly an innovative use of the Net as an information dissemination tool. —(E.G.)

URL▶ http://www.getnet.com/silent/

Net Users Write Their Own Online Book

FAQs of LIFE Jump 8009

Gennera, Knab & Company, an advertising and marketing communications agency, has mounted a site that collects FAQs of Life—pithy observations on the pitfalls and joys of navigating the road of life. Imagine you are giving advice to "a 21 year old about to embark on the one-way street of adulthood", and then let loose all those life lessons you wish someone had told you before you had to learn them the hard way. Here you'll find out the proper way to tip skycaps, why some think that people should never marry, and more in this innovative site described by its authors as "the first book entirely composed by Net surfers." —(E.v.B.)

KEY NEWSGROUP **soc.culture.misc** URL▶ http://www.interaccess.com/faqslife/

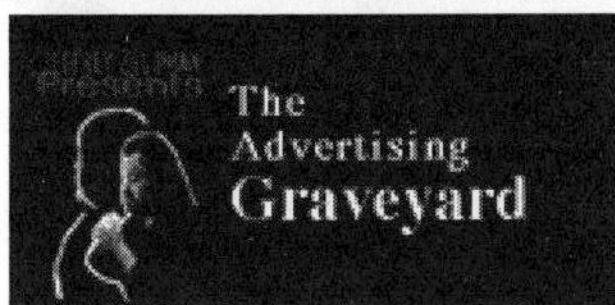

Adman's Tales

JZ Presents: The Advertising Graveyard Jump 7335

Jeffrey Zeldman, a copywriter with a, shall we say, unique sense of humor, has created a page that features ads and campaigns that never made it out the door for many reasons—clients were frightened of them, focus groups hated them, or the boss just said no. If you are in the ad business and have a dead ad, send it to Jeffrey and he will bury it with full honors in his advertising graveyard. You can also check out his gallery of other projects including a description of his work in designing and setting up the Warner Brothers' Batman Forever Web pages. You can also see what you think of his rather different set of icons you are allowed to borrow for your own Web pages. Other links, music files, and works of fiction can also be viewed here, on this well-designed site. —(E.v.B.)

URL▶ http://www.zeldman.com/ad.html

Interactive Multimedia Industry Zine

Welcome to CLiCK 1.0 Jump 7354

You'll enjoy browsing through CLICK—a solid, jazzy, Australian Web magazine focusing on the people, ideas, and products connected with the spread of interactive multimedia on CD-ROM, the Internet, the Web, and the evolving broadband services. Read the latest ideas on interactivity design and the new media business—one issue has already spotlighted writing for multimedia. CLICK describes itself as a "cultural space in which new media practitioners and thinkers can talk in real time, test ideas, and learn new techniques." The feature writing is top-notch, the observations and predictions on interactive mass media are worth a look, and the pages themselves are a visual treat. —(E.v.B.)

KEY NEWSGROUP **comp.multimedia** URL▶ http://click.com.au/

CyberWire Dispatch by Brock N. Meeks

CyberWire Dispatch by Brock N. Meeks Jump 0125

A well-known presence on the Net for his irreverent writing style, Brock Meeks bears the distinction for being the first person ever sued for libel for something he wrote on the Internet (a suit that he eventually won), and here is where you'll find his CyberWire Dispatches, his pull-no-punches, Net insider's look at current Internet goings on, government policy, Net people, business on the Net, etc. It's enjoyable reading, and it gives you a good overall look at the people and events that are shaping the future of the Internet. —(E.G.)

URL▶ http://cyberwerks.com:70/1/cyberwire

Professional Journalist's Public Web Channel

Medicine and Poison: Doug Fine Unedited Jump 7476

Doug Fine, a professional journalist, has collected a number of his writings—published and unpublished—here. You can read his thought-provoking article on the Alaskan anti-government movement (which was rejected at the last minute by a well-known, hip Net culture magazine) about conservation of mountain gorillas in Rwanda, profiles of notables, excerpts from his novel, or even his take on the Oklahoma bombings. Enjoy some food for the mind on these attractive pages. —(E.v.B.)

KEY NEWSGROUP **alt.journalism** URL▶ http://www.well.com/user/fine/

FUSE Interactive Font Web Magazine

FUSE Jump 0018

Web-based interactive magazine featuring new and intriguing typographic font designs contributed by Web graphic designers. *FUSE* "is an interactive magazine that sets out to challenge our current ideas about typographic and visual language in an age of ever-changing communications technology and media." Features visually stimulating font and graphics designs. —(E.G.)

URL ▶ http://www.worldserver.pipex.com/fuse94/fuse94.html

College Multimedia Web Zine

TRINCOLL JOURNAL Home Page Jump 7294

The Trincoll Journal, billed as the Internet's only weekly multimedia magazine, has been published on the Web by students at Trinity College in Hartford, Connecticut, since 1993. The Journal, focused mainly on a student audience, incorporates video, sound, and graphics in its articles, which are embedded in a sophisticated layout. Essays, poetry, video clips, photo essays, film reviews, best of the Net picks, and humor pieces are enjoyable to read, hear, and see. —(E.v.B.)

KEY NEWSGROUP alt.zines URL ▶ http://www.trincoll.edu/tj/trincolljournal.html

Around the Virtual World

WorldVillage's Multimedia Cafe Jump 7297

A lot of the WorldVillage may still be under construction, but what we've seen will certainly draw us back. Shopping, religion, research links are all available, and great software reviews can be read. Fire up your phasers and enter the Gamer's Zone for some R&R from the day's work. In the schoolhouse, read articles written by educational professionals, reviews of the latest books relating to education, and browse the archive of highly rated shareware educational titles. —(E.v.B.)

KEY NEWSGROUP alt.zines URL ▶ http://www.worldvillage.com/wv/cafe/html/cafe.htm

Essays on Technology

Frank Beacham Jump 7433

Frank Beacham's newspaper column, "Questioning Technology," distributed by ALTERNET of San Francisco, can be found here. Frank asks such thought-provoking questions as: "Will humanity be the roadkill on the information superhighway? Will the Net become a truly democratic medium for a diversity of information and opinion or will it become a corporate dominated 'cyber-mall' glutted with advertising and propaganda?" If his take on technology and culture interests you, read his current and past columns here. You can even see and listen to his multimedia presentation "Tools for the Revolution." —(E.v.B.)

KEY NEWSGROUP sci.philosophy.tech URL ▶ http://www.beacham.com./

Internet Surveys

PCS Survey-Net Jump 7442

Survey-Net is a substantial Web center for information, opinions, and demographics gathered from the Net community. You can also add your two cents to other Web surveys, also conducted here. Want to find out what your colleagues say about Net sex, shareware use, the future of Internet shopping, or even find out who uses the Internet and for what purposes? The numbers and opinions are here. And don't be afraid to participate—Survey-Net assures the confidentiality of your answers. —(E.v.B.)

KEY NEWSGROUP alt.cyberspace URL ▶ http://www.survey.net/

suck.

Cutting-Edge Web Media Criticism

Suck Jump **7449**

Suck, an excellent Web zine with an offensive name and a definite attitude, is put together by Carl Steadman and Joey Anuff, two extremely opinionated Net watchers who provide knowing criticism and must-read, inside observations on the current state of the Web. It's also our own wild card choice for one of the best new Web media sites around. Steadman and Anuff define Suck as "an experiment in provocation, mordant deconstructionism, and buzz-saw journalism." Here's an example of what awaits you: "A certain amount of copycat-ism is spread around as all these johnny-come-latelies and johnny-came-early-but-just-smelled-the-coffees dig in the same gold mine for the precious Web resources to put in their indices." And this well-designed incendiary device is archived and updated daily. Enjoy! —(E.v.B.)

KEY NEWSGROUP **alt.zines** URL ▸ http://www.suck.com/

SUCK.

"a fish, a barrel, and a smoking gun"
for 9 January 1997. Updated every WEEKDAY.

Hit And Run LXVI

The editors of *Time*, that quintessence of conventional wisdom in print, have sent an early valentine to Salon1999, the web's own pretender to the equivalent online throne, naming them Best Website of The Year. This neat handing of the baton

▲ *Sample editorial feature from the Web zine* Suck, *at* Jump 5728.

The World According to Gilder

Gilder Articles Index Jump **2189**

Will it be a sleek superhighway, or a pothole-ridden back alley? Will it change the way we interrelate, or merely make things easier? And what will happen to newspapers and television? George Gilder addresses these and other questions in his *Forbes* series that attempts to help readers prepare for the technological and cultural impact of the information superhighway. This is an important and useful perspective, providing background and insights often missing from the hype that finds its way to the popular media. —(L.S.)

KEY NEWSGROUP **alt.culture.internet**

URL ▸ http://www.seas.upenn.edu/~gaj1/ggindex.html

HotWired: The Wired Magazine Home Page

Welcome to HotWired: Are You a Member?

Jump **0064**

Highly recommended as a sneak preview of the future of advertiser-supported Web sites and an excellent model for Web page designers, this site is brought to you by *Wired,* an innovative magazine covering the online and high tech world. Every bit as innovative and visually stunning as its hard-copy version, *HotWired* is one of the few sites to combine cutting-edge graphic design with reader interaction, since readers may post comments to specific topic "threads"—a truly interactive form of "Letters to the Editor." *HotWired* is also one of the first Web sites to feature display advertising in the form of discreet "strip ads" at the top of its pages, each of which are "clickable," linking to that advertiser's own Web page. —(E.G.)

KEY NEWSGROUP **alt.wired** URL ▸ http://www.wired.com/

Net Surfer Digest: News from the Net

Net Surfer Digest Home Page Jump **0096**

A hip, well-written and well-designed Web magazine produced every week and published by Arthur Bebak, Net Surfer Digest features interesting Web and Internet news, links to interesting

Web sites, originial features, hardware and software product news and much more from its highly professional editorial publishing staff. Highly recommended, especially for its extensive coverage of useful info for Macintosh users! —(E.G.)

URL▶ http://www.netsurf.com/nsd/index.html

Cybersight's Interactive Web Site

Cybersight Jump 0109

Internet Marketing, Inc.'s, hip and innovative Web site with lots of links to neat Web culture sites on the Net, plus an interactive user survey feature where you can vote on your own most and least favorite Web sites and view survey results and their links to Web sites on a wide variety of subjects. An attractive and visually interesting Web site that makes extensive use of the interaction of its Web visitors! What you'll like about this site is its interesting lists (and links) of most and least popular Web sites for a wide variety of subjects and funky Web culture features. Highly recommended! —(E.G.)

URL▶ http://cybersight.com/cgi-bin/cs/s?main.gmml

MIT MediaLab: Fishwrap Electronic Newspaper

Fishwrap Main Page Jump 0126

Features a number of originally-written Web page publications from students at MIT's MediaLab and Web-based versions of tradition MIT print publications like *The Tech*, MIT's student newspaper. —(E.G.)

URL▶ http://fishwrap.mit.edu/

Howard Rheingold's Web Site

Howard Rheingold Jump 0165

Personal Web page for Howard Rheingold, Net visionary and author of the popular book *The Virtual Community.* Features online versions of *The Virtual Community,* recent texts, articles and reviews which make for interesting and thought-provoking reading on the subject of Internet online discussion groups as a form of community, and other interesting Net-related topics. —(E.G.)

URL▶ http://www.well.com/www/hlr/

Desktop Video Conferencing on the Net: CU-See Me

CU-See Me Jump 0180

Web home page for Cornell University's pioneering Internet desktop video conferencing project, CU-See Me. On this site, Macintosh and Windows Net users having video capture boards, simple video camcorders and conventional Internet connections can use CU-See Me software to try desktop video conferencing with other CU-See Me users on the Net. Although video image quality is small and not great, sound quality is better, which gives CU-See Me high marks, according to users. If you have the basic setup to try it—for example, Mac users need any color Macintosh, a low-end video capture card like VideoSpigot and any consumer video camcorder—we've heard CU-See Me is a fabulous way for you to become a desktop video conferencing pioneer, engaging in live video hookups with other CU-See Me users on the Net! —(E.G.)

URL▶ http://magneto.csc.ncsu.edu/Multimedia/Classes/Spring94/projects/proj6/cu-seeme.html

Ted Nelson: The Father of Hypertext

Xanadu Home Page Jump 0182

This Web site is a must if you're interested in learning more about the history and underlying concepts surrounding the use of hypertext links on the World Wide Web. The Xanadu Project is a sort of online think tank created to develop and promote the ideas of Ted Nelson, the widely acknowledged creator of the hypertext concept. As you may already know, hypertext is the term used to describe the "sideways linking of information"—that is, the idea of clicking on a term or word within a text paragraph and then being able to instantly jump to other text related to that subject. It was Ted Nelson who started the whole ball rolling back in 1960, when he coined the term "hypertext," and subsequently wrote a number of groundbreaking books on the subject. On this site, you'll see a number of excellent articles which go a long way to explain the concept of hypertext, Nelson's ideas for fully distributed online hypertext-based publishing distribution, access and payment methods, and Nelson's important underlying philosophy, which stresses free and open access to all information over the Net. An excellent way to become familiar with the fascinating history and concepts underlying the World Wide Web. —(E.G.)

KEY NEWSGROUP **alt.hypertext** URL▸ http://www.aus.xanadu.com:70/1/xanadu

Vannevar Bush: As We May Think

As We May Think Jump **0204**

Denys Duchier's Web page reprint of scientist Vannevar Bush's July 1945 article published in the *Atlantic Monthly* and hailed by many as the blueprint for information access via the World Wide Web. In this fascinating article, Dr. Bush "calls for a new relationship between thinking man and the sum of our knowledge," by urging scientists and inventors to create machines which can aid man in better understanding the sum total of all human knowledge and experience. The underlying philosophies expressed in this article can now be seen in modern-day inventions like the Internet, distributed online computing, hypertext links, and computer-based information storage and retrieval methods. Required reading for those of you who are interested in learning more about the philosophical underpinnings of modern networking and computer technology. —(E.G.)

KEY NEWSGROUP **alt.hypertext** URL▸ http://www.csi.uottawa.ca/~dduchier/misc/vbush/as-we-may-think.html

Woodstock '94: The Web Site

Woodstock '94 Multimedia Center Jump **0215**

1969's original Woodstock was, itself, the first "multimedia event" of its generation, spawning record albums, a movie, books and endless generational navel-gazing on the part of aging former hippies. The next generation's Woodstock '94 happening attempts to one-up its parent with high-tech stuff like this interesting Web site, which was used at Woodstock '94 as the global Web link for this event and sponsored by the San Francisco-based online conferencing system, The WELL. Lots of flashy Web graphics, event and concert info, real-time impressions, stories, and event gossip. —(E.G.)

URL▸ http://www.well.com/woodstock/

Cyberscene Journal

Viro-Vision Jump **2356**

This journal is for the "hunters and gatherers" of the Internet, with news, articles, and links updated at least monthly and often more frequently. Unlike some online journals which treat visitors like new pledges during fraternity Hell Week, *Viro* considers you a member in good standing, and wants to help you get the full benefits of that membership. Each issue keeps you current with the latest news of the Web and Internet technology, popular media, and art. You can also check out *Viro*'s latest rants on whatever is bothering him at the moment, and the Geek of the Week, which profiles a fellow cyberjunkie. There also are tons of links to new sites, *Viro*'s enduring favorites, and the seedier side of the Web. —(L.S.)

KEY NEWSGROUP **alt.culture.www** URL▸ http://www.PrimeNet.Com:80/~virogen/

Welcome to Infobahn Home Page

Infobahn - a Different Kind of Internet Zine Jump **3618**

INFOBAHN examines the Net from a cultural and intellectual point of view, focusing on policy issues, business, lifestyles, technology, and the arts. *INFOBAHN* doesn't offer how-to info or lists of Web sites—they focus on the big picture, complete with investigative reporting, commentary, essays and analysis, accompanied by original art and photos. —(C.P.)

KEY NEWSGROUP **alt.culture.www** URL▸ http://www.postmodern.com/

Op-Ed, Web-Style

WebRunner Jump 7159

The folks at *WebRunner* want to disseminate thoughtful essays throughout the Internet. To do this, they have established a monthly e-zine dedicated to considered, well-written opinion pieces that strike "a balance between the anarchistic scramble of the newsgroups and the cautious formalism of the traditional media." They are actively soliciting essays from eager, opinionated cyberwriters—but, alas, are not offering fees yet. —(E.v.B.)

KEY NEWSGROUP soc.culture.usa URL ▶ http://www.access.digex.net/~web/

The Ghost in the Computer

The McLuhan Probes Jump 7172

The Nova Scotia College of Art and Design and the Herbert Marshall McLuhan Foundation have collaborated to create a Web site to spread the work of Marshall McLuhan, the communications visionary, around the world. Still under construction, the site hopes to be able to offer a generous sampling of his work, which includes 600 articles, 75,000 letters, 13 books, and a wealth of audio and video tapes. To best explore the first issues of McLuhan Probes, the online publication of the Foundation, use Adobe Acrobat Reader software. —(E.v.B.)

KEY NEWSGROUP sci.philosophy.tech URL ▶ http://www.mcluhan.ca/mcluhan/

Multimedia Midwestern Style

OMNIBUS:EYE at the Northwestern U. Dept. of Radio/TV/Film Jump 7216

The OMNIBUS:EYE Project at Northwestern University is a diverse project that focuses on the production and study of digital media. The Web offerings of this project are incredibly diverse. You can explore numerous fascinating individual projects, read the project's online newsletter, browse the Chicago art scene and enjoy seeing individual artist's works. Not enough? Hang on to your hat—the Project has posted nearly 1,000 links to film, video, TV, multimedia, conferences, theater, and cinema-related sites. —(E.v.B.)

KEY NEWSGROUP comp.multimedia URL ▶ http://www.rtvf.nwu.edu/index.html

Net Discussions

The Internet Roundtable Society Jump 7217

The consultants at the Internet Roundtable Society host the *Roundtable Interview*—an hour of interactive chat with notable scientists, authors, politicians, and policy makers. If you miss an interview, don't worry, you can read transcripts of past encounters. As well, the Internet Roundtable Society has established the WebChat Broadcasting System, which consists of "stations" based on Usenet newsgroups, Web sites and subject topics. The Society provides the software to facilitate this online talk. So limber up your fingers and chat online—it couldn't be easier. —(E.v.B.)

KEY NEWSGROUP alt.culture.internet URL ▶ http://www.irsociety.com/

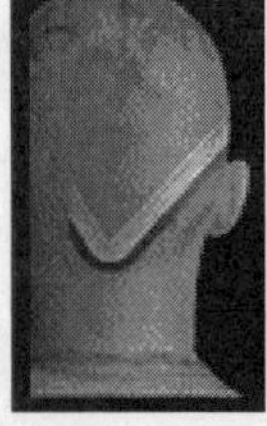

Weirdly Fascinating Web Zine

Are you worthy of joining cyberblack? Jump 7358

Well, what can we say about cyberblack?—first, it's an alternative zine to end all zines. It's dedicated to exploring the avant-garde, accompanied by some pretty eye-catching graphics. And it's not without humor: if you click on the option saying you are not worthy of joining cyberblack, you are immediately connected to the home page of the Canadian conservative political party—the Reform Party. —(E.v.B.)

KEY NEWSGROUP alt.zine URL ▶ http://www.cyberblack.com/public/en/membr.html

Creatively Strange Site

Kingswood Kranium Home Page Jump 7478

Kingswood Kranium is a well-written Web magazine that bills itself as "your one-stop Web site for the strange, the unbelievable, the blatantly untrue." It is divided into some fun sections: Synapses (puzzles and perplexing factoids), Optic Nerve (links to strange images and photos), Spinal Cord (where hotlinks are found to other humorous or otherwise interesting Web pages). Or how about Brain Tumor: "a compilation of misunderstandings, misinformation, and general misconceptions that can only be explained by a large mass of foreign material in space usually occupied by thinking tissue." A lot of fun! —(E.v.B.)

KEY NEWSGROUP alt.zines URL▶ http://www.kingswood.com/

Biting Web Humor & Cultural Commentary

HITCH OnLine Jump 7391

HITCH OnLine describes itself as a "Journal of Pop Culture Absurdity," and aims at many targets in each bimonthly issue using the weapons of satire and sarcasm. For example, read "Deconstructing Mentos," its humorous mock-analysis of those way-strange TV commercials for Mentos mints. As well, for comic relief, we guess, each issue contains the FBI's Fugitive of the Month. You can also finds lots of funny fillers, video, music, and e-zine reviews, plus cartoons, and links to other humor-related Web sites (this is not a site that is suitable for children or teens). —(E.v.B.)

KEY NEWSGROUP alt.slack URL▶ http://www.ionet.net/~twilken/hitched.shtml

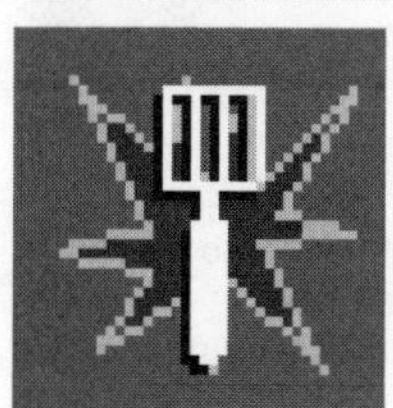

Spatula City

n/a Jump 0036

Spatula City is the cute and inventive Web page creation of Stefan and Jenny Gagne, who let their imagination and graphics talents run wild in this ersatz parody of an imaginary business Web site, "Superior Spatula Technology" (where else could you "buy" the "Hefty Mon Spatula" to make pancakes two feet wide!), funny fiction and sound files, all produced with a wonderful sense of good humor. Give them an "A" for wit, imagination, and Web page design style (sorry, as if you needed to be told by now, none of Spatula City's spatulas are available for sale). —(E.G.)

URL▶ http://www.wam.umd.edu/~twoflowr/

Doctor Fun

The Doctor Fun Page Jump 0071

A popular Net feature, David Farley's Doctor Fun cartoons offer humorous, high-tech and sometimes bizarre daily comics in the vein of Bizarro and Gary Larson's famous "Far Side" cartoons. Drawn by David Farley, a computer guy at the University of Chicago Library, Doctor Fun has become a popular Net staple and an example of how the Net has allowed "content creators" (cartoonists, writers, graphic artists, etc.) to bypass traditional publishers and other channels, bringing their own works directly to the consumer. We think you'll enjoy your daily Doctor Fun cartoon fix and highly recommend you make this a part of your daily excursion on the Web. —(E.G.)

URL▶ http://sunsite.unc.edu/Dave/drfun.html

The BORDERLINE

More Web Satire

The BORDERLINE Netazine Homepage - Cartoon, Animation, Humor and Satire Jump 1505

If you're in a cynical mood, turn to Gabe Martin's humor Netzine—a blend of the dark side and the absurd. Combining oddball news headlines, a monthly newsletter offering musing about such subjects as what kind of animal a "salisbury" is, and the "second daily Internet cartoon in the known world," Martin's depictions of everyday life are reminiscent of Matt Groening's "Life in Hell" and Gary Larson's "The Far Side." Martin isn't averse to stunts, either: you have a chance at winning $1,000 and an original T-shirt if you put a link to the *BORDERLINE* on your Web page. The downside is that each cartoon is too large for one screen, so you have to scroll down to see the punchline. But it's worth it. —(H.L.)

URL ▶ http://www.cts.com/~borderln/index.html#top

Fig Newtons
i placed a stack of fig newtons in a ziploc bag, which i then put in my handlebar bag. i looked at her looking at me. she wasn't happy that i was going bicycling with victoria. i looked down at the opened package of fig newtons. "these are a good source of protein and carbohydrates," i said.

▲ *Personal story from the Web zine* placing; d, *at* Jump 5771

Zine for Thought—And Fun!

BRETTnews Home Page
Jump 1506 CONTENT

Created by Brett Leveridge, this Webzine embraces the art and journalistic style of the 1950s, but with the edge of today's topics: films, music, sports, horoscopes, and tongue-in-cheek advice columns for health and relationships. Weekly updates of cable movies and what's new on the Infobahn round out this entertaining site. You'll be caught up in reading one of his best pieces—replete with photos and outlandish humor—the tale of The American Odyssey, an account of Leveridge's four-month, 48-state, 23,000-mile journey across the states. Leveridge doesn't forget to put in a plug for subscriptions, watches, and T-shirts, but he does offer you a free print version of his work through snail mail. A well-designed and attractive layout and pointers to other interesting sites make it well worth your while to stop by. —(H.L.)

URL ▶ http://www.BRETTnews.com

Comedy with a Wallop

Citizen Poke Jump 1507 CONTENT

An interactive, monthly Webzine, *Citizen Poke* touts itself to be the fastest-growing and only full-blown humor magazine on the Internet. And funny it is. With topics ranging from sexual harrassment trading cards, O.J. Cliff Notes, The Seven Sins of Childhood, and Ten Steps to Beating Jury Duty, just to name a few, Amherst students Josh Koppel and Seth Mirick are on the pulse of the latest trends. If you feel you're just as funny as they are, send in your work, whether it be graphics, photos, cartoons, articles, reviews, parodies, or satire. The only glitch to this site is that to read the 'zine, you must download the 20-plus pages, full of pictures and text, which takes time, depending on your modem speed. But while you're waiting, take their weekly survey to find out, for example, if you're right for the right, write letters to the editor, or sign up on their mailing list for announcements and bits of humor. Then laugh out loud once you read the printout...you'll be back. —(H.L.)

URL ▶ http://www.amherst.edu/~poke/

PANIC encyclopedia

Panic Encyclopedia: The Definitive Guide to the Postmodern Scene

Panic & Anxiety Disorders in the Postmodern World

Panic Encyclopedia: The Definitive Guide to the Postmodern Scene
Jump 1524 CONTENT

Feeling anxious and stressed out? Then this is the site for you. Authors Arthur and Marilouise Kroker believe we live in a panic culture, "a floating reality, with the actual as a dream world, where we live on the edge of ecstasy and dread, between delirium and anxiety, between the triumph of cyber-punk and the political reality of cultural exhaustion." *The Panic Encyclopedia*, designed to educate the masses about the growing awareness of true panic disorder and its remedies, is chock full of frenzied and reflective retrospectives from A to Z (thus the encyclopedia reference) written for the postmodern audience. You learn how today's society affects our lifestyles. You'll be pulled into reading almost every entry, including ones for Panic Elvis, who is "invited to come on down for one last retro-appearance as a memory residue," or Panic Quiet (where noise invades the social field), Panic Jeans (your identity, that is), and more. Not an easy site to pin down, but it's sure to evoke an emotional response; whether it's one of frenzy or reflection is entirely up to you. —(H.L.)

URL ▶ http://english-server.hss.cmu.edu/ctheory/panic/panic_contents.html

British Political & Social Satire

Gateway to the Eye Jump 2611 CONTENT

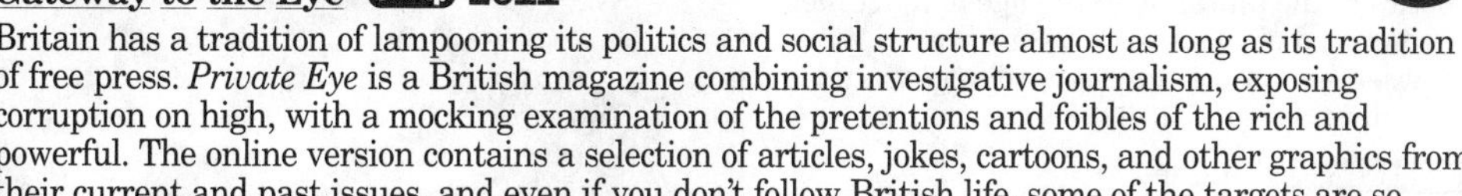

Britain has a tradition of lampooning its politics and social structure almost as long as its tradition of free press. *Private Eye* is a British magazine combining investigative journalism, exposing corruption on high, with a mocking examination of the pretentions and foibles of the rich and powerful. The online version contains a selection of articles, jokes, cartoons, and other graphics from their current and past issues, and even if you don't follow British life, some of the targets are so universal that you'll have no trouble getting most of the points and punchlines. —(L.S.)

KEY NEWSGROUP rec.humor URL▶ http://www.intervid.co.uk/intervid/eye/gateway.html

An E-Zine for the Times!

Electric Chip! Jump 3691 CONTENT

If you're looking for an excellent example of Web publishing at its best, visit *Electric Chip*. This is an absolutely original, brilliant e-zine—just the kind of thing the Web is made for. You'd never find this on a newsstand, but it's delightfully apropos to the new Web media. Hilarious reviews, incredibly clever take-offs—you haven't seen an Web e-zine until you've seen *Electric Chip*. Newly updated with a Netscape-enhanced look—this one is a gem! —(C.P.)

URL▶ http://www.interaccess.com/users/chip/

Have a Problem? Ask a Puppet!

Punchy Advice Jump 7213 CONTENT

Need advice on matters of the heart, your budget or on interacting with society at large? Well, jump over to *Punchy Advice*, where a cast of hilarious characters—based on real-life puppets—will set your heart, your bank account, or your social life in order. For example, Bradley, a rather nerdish accountant, will set you straight, well, in a manner of speaking, on any topic you send to him. But you don't have to confine your questions (which are easily sent via an interactive form) just to Bradley. Leo Brodie, creator of the puppets and this innovative and engaging site, presents 10 other characters who dispense advice here as well. —(E.v.B.)

KEY NEWSGROUP soc.couples URL▶ http://www.pacificrim.net/~lbrodie/punch/advice.html

Reinventing Democracy in the Net Era

The Red Rock Eater Jump 1562 CONTENT

Q: What is big and red and eats rocks? A: A big red rock eater (from Bennett Cerf's *Book of Riddles*). Phil Agre, a professor of Communications at the University of California, San Diego, developed "The Network Observer," a monthly Internet "red rock eater" newsletter about computer and social networks and people getting together to decide how to run their lives. "TNO is my own small contribution to the reinvention of democracy in a new technological world," Agre says. This eclectic, simple Web site offers advice on how to run online newsletters, information about how to use the Net; articles on the Net community, privacy, and politics of technology; recommended books and periodicals; archives of previous issues; and even music (Bruce Springsteen is a favorite). Last, but not least, if you want to receive TNO in your own e-mail box, Agre tells you how. —(H.L.)

URL▶ http://communication.ucsd.edu/pagre/rre.html

The Thinking Person's Web Zine

SPEED Home Jump 7417 CONTENT

Speed is a high-octane zine that's definitely not designed for intellectual lightweights. As editor Benjamin Bratton noted in the first issue, Speed hopes to foster a "different kind of conversation about contemporary life and politics, a forum composed of many different voices that in the past have not often been heard alongside one another...part of what we hope to accomplish in this, and in future issues, is to circumvent these structures toward the discovery of new objectives, languages and understandings that might produce better and more public ways of thinking about technology, media and society."

So if in-depth exploring of issues such as "the myths of electronic living," or "the politics and poetics of the fantastic in the age of machines" is your kind of reading, put your Web browser—and your mind—in high gear and roar off to Speed. —(E.v.B.)

KEY NEWSGROUP alt.zines
URL▶ http://www.arts.ucsb.edu/~speed/

▲ *The Kaleidospace Home Page, from* **Kaleidospace**, *at* Jump **4017**.

Literary Thoughts from PBoT

PBoT Jump **5826** CONTENT

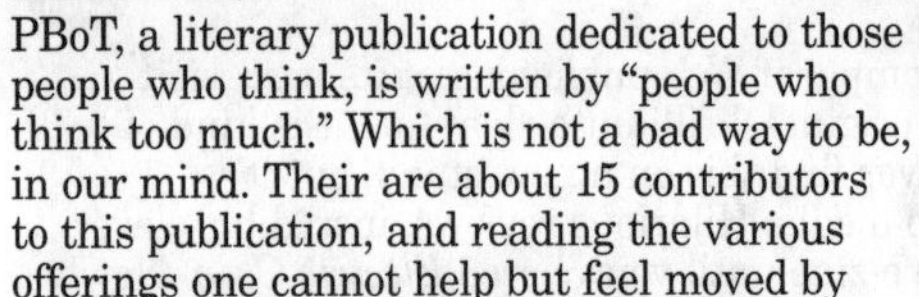

PBoT, a literary publication dedicated to those people who think, is written by "people who think too much." Which is not a bad way to be, in our mind. Their are about 15 contributors to this publication, and reading the various offerings one cannot help but feel moved by the intimate reflections that so perfectly capture the tribulations of day-to-day life. There is an archive filled with past postings, and the contact link allows readers to contact the writers directly to offer comments. —(J.P.)

URL▶ http://www.pbot.com/

Alternative Opinion

Z Magazine Jump **7160** CONTENT

Z Magazine is the online version of an alternative journal that covers a wide range of topics from cultural to economic, foreign affairs to ecology, current events to political organizing and sexual politics. Z's Web site offers a selection of provocative articles written by heavy-hitting opinion makers such as Noam Chomsky, Edward Herman, Barbara Ehrenreich, and many others. You can also participate in interactive chat on the content of these articles and surf over to the home pages of Z's staff and contributors. —(E.v.B.)

KEY NEWSGROUP alt.politics.radical-left URL▶ http://www.lbbs.org/ZMag.htm

An E-Zine for Thoughtful People

The Utne Lens Jump **2641** CONTENT

Long before Generation X became the darling demographic and 'Zines used the term "alternative" to mean it's now acceptable to write poorly and spell worse, there was true alternative journalism. It meant socially conscious and responsible reportage and opinion that challenged the establishment and offered solutions instead of angst. There remain some representatives of this endeavor, and The Utne Reader is one of the better examples. Now, they bring their commitment to content, context, and community to the Web, but this is not just a Web version of the magazine. It also focuses on the issues important to the growth and use of the Internet, while fostering a sense of community and free exchange of ideas. In addition to offering news, the Lens publishes opinions and pointers to more information about contemporary issues and challenges, and features an online forums, where visitors can offer their own opinions and interact with each other. The site is attractive, well organized and easy to navigate. Just don't expect to hit and run when you visit. The content forces involvement, and you won't get its full value unless you commit the time needed to think about what's here. —(L.S.)

KEY NEWSGROUP alt.culture.internet URL▶ http://www.utne.com

Cool Site for Women

The Cybergrrl Webstation Jump 2701

Cybergrrl is the online alter ego of A. Sherman, and she's created a terrific site for and about women. But while it's clearly pro-women, it's definitely not anti-men. Much of the material here is gender irrelevant and worth regular visits by anyone. You can browse the HiLites section that covers what's new at the site, delve into special-interest modules such as those covering business and health resources for women, or jump to the Surf page and see what interesting sites Cybergrrl has found on the Web. There's also a section for Webgrrls, a Cybergrrl spinoff for women Web professionals. The site is updated regularly, and at least monthly, so the information and resources are always kept fresh. —(L.S.)

KEY NEWSGROUP soc.women URL▶ http://www.cybergrrl.com/cg.html

Stuff You Never Learned in School (and That You Really Need to Know!)

Tripod Jump 2762

Once upon a time, there were things called general interest magazines. They came in the mail or appeared on the newsstand every month or so, full of all sorts of useful and entertaining stuff that didn't necessarily fall into a single category. There aren't many, if any, left in print, but they're making a comeback on the Web. Tripod is one of them, and their "Tools for Life" slogan is indicative of the broad range of topics they cover. Better still, its features are updated at least weekly, and sometimes daily. Each day, for example, there's an interview with an interesting person, along with links to news, weather, special features, surveys, and contests. Weekly, there's a new feature on some aspect of living, be it health, personal finance, entertainment, politics, or other category. Tripod also features interactive services you can use to design a resume, plan a trip, search for movie reviews, or contact a medical expert. Most of the content seems geared to younger people, but it serves just as well for the young at heart. And given the breadth of content here, even aging hearts should check in regularly. —(L.S.)

KEY NEWSGROUP clari.living URL▶ http://www.tripod.com/

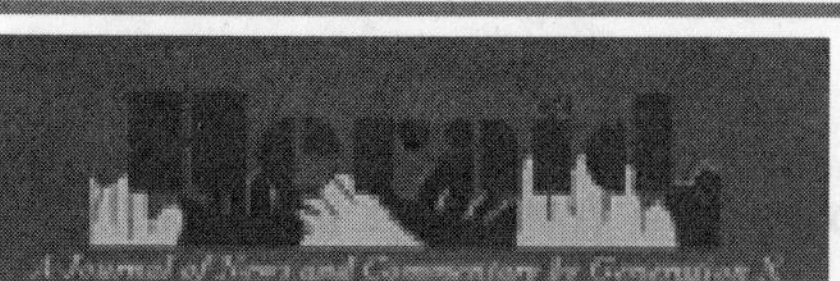

Generation X Web Newspaper

The Internet Herald Home Page Jump 3727

The Internet Herald is "A Journal of News and Commentary by Generation X," rather fitting since this site is brought to you by students of the University of California at Berkeley. This site is filled with news, opinions, stories, music coverage, opinions, poetry, jokes, opinions, politics, and . . . well, more opinions! It's attracting quite a bit of attention, too, with several interviews, reviews, and feature stories published in the last few months. Check out the user-nominated Stud and Putz of the Month, and submit your own ideas, stories, and articles. Your opinions are welcome as well. —(N.F.)

URL▶ http://server.Berkeley.EDU/herald/

Made with Real Fruit Juice

placing: d Jump 5771

We'd like to be able to tell you—succinctly or otherwise—the meaning of this site. And it's not like we're searching for the meaning of life here, but that quest might actually be easier. So we'll tell you what we have here and then you can go there and decide what it is. Start off on the site and you'll find a picture of a commercial product accompanied by an ironic real-life personal vignette on the product. Not just any product, mind you, but the kind of ordinary, branded grocery product you never really think about all that much (which, when you think about it, gets us closer to the meaning of this site after all). When you've finished browsing, hit the arrow and you'll arrive at the next vignette. And so forth. A strange and interesting use of Web space, created by Carl Steadman, co-creator of the equally innovative—but certainly less mysterious—Suck site. —(J.P.)

URL▶ http://www.placing.com/

FEED: Media & Culture Commentary

Welcome to Feed Jump 7247 

New on the Web zine scene is FEED—dedicated to debating the issues of the day, with articulate, thoughtful commentators—many of whom are well-known, heavy hitters on the media scene. It is a visual treat as well—although the pages sometimes load like electronic molasses. Some of the topics recently covered include: patenting genetic material, the relationship of public space and consumerism, the backlash against affirmative action, and a host of other thought-provoking items presented in true multimedia fashion accompanied by sound and video clips. —(E.v.B.)

KEY NEWSGROUP alt.zines URL▶ http://www.feedmag.com/

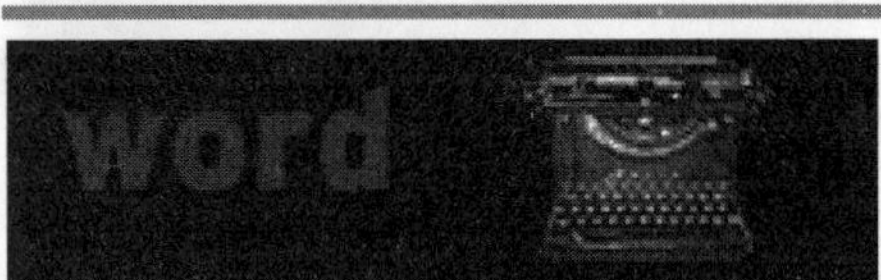

The Word's Out

WORD Jump 7260 

WORD is a Web hip Web literary review that's attracted much attention for its spark and originality. Counter to much Web content, the features are some of the longest we've read in a long time. And the number of articles and images is quite impressive. World trade, skater dudes, recipes, skinheads, drugs—you name it, Word might just cover it, in addition to the usual music and movie reviews you'll find on many other Web zines. —(E.v.B.)

KEY NEWSGROUP alt.zines URL▶ http://www.word.com/index.html

Ex-Students View the World

The Cyber Maze Jump 7357 

PPSA was formed as a college club at Michigan Technological University in 1983. Now these bunch of people (rocket scientists, lawyers, computer experts, teachers and politicians) have joined together to share what they term "an honest, yet irreverent way of looking at the world." See what you think, as you read accounts of members' road trips, check out the photos they took along the way, read essays on art, life, and the Internet, and laugh at some of their humor pieces published here. —(E.v.B.)

KEY NEWSGROUP alt.zine URL▶ http://www.mxm.com/ppsa/index.html

Threaded Excerpts from the Best of the Net

Threaded: Contents Jump 7362 

Threaded collects articles on entertainment, politics, and society from the far reaches of the Net and features a wide spectrum of viewpoints, ideas, and personalities. It covers topics such as new bands, movie reviews, privacy on the Internet, and American politics. Geez, you'll even find a primer they found on lock picking, and an anarchy guide for high-school students—presumably this site's creator's way of tweaking the procensorship forces on the Net. —(E.v.B.)

KEY NEWSGROUP alt.zines URL▶ http://village.ios.com/~paulchiu/threaded/threaded.htm

Culture L.A. Style

PIG Intertainment Jump 7398 

Those creative people at PIG seem to be twentysomethings at work and play in Los Angeles. They offer up an electronic mixture of digital art, underground L.A. art and photography, interviews with actors and singers (who can resist the article, "RuPaul Speaks Out"???), and other entertainment items. But, hey, it's not all fun and games here. Advice is also forthcoming in the self-help section. You can learn how to best turn 30, how to meet women, and how to break up with women. As well, lots of cartoons and lampoons to tickle even the most staid funny bone. Also, there are contests to be played and prizes to be won. So, head to this West Coast Webzine and be prepared to be entertained. —(E.v.B.)

KEY NEWSGROUP alt.zines URL▶ http://pigweb.com/

Atlantic Monthly Takes to the Web

The Atlantic Monthly Jump 7406

The Atlantic Monthly, a part of American culture since 1857, brings its hard-copy edition to the Web. Excerpts from current issues and material written specifically for the online edition focus on the usual *Atlantic Monthly* topics: politics, society, the arts, and culture. However, this site is not just a clone. The newsstand edition is supplemented by specially written, multimedia-enhanced material. You can hear poets published in the magazine read their works. You can read sample chapters from books reviewed in the hard-copy magazine, download some pretty classy recipes, and preview the latest events in the arts. —(E.v.B.)

KEY NEWSGROUP **alt.zines** URL▶ http://www2.TheAtlantic.com/Atlantic/

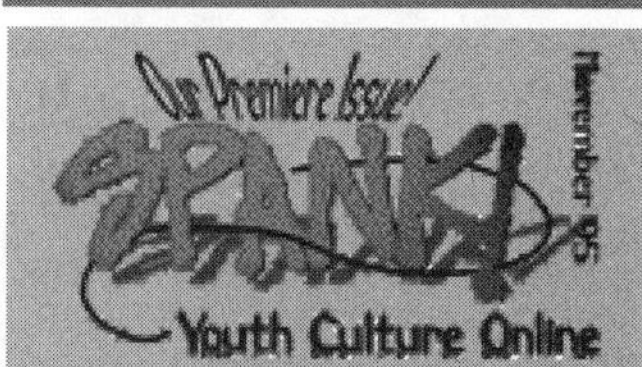

Canadian Youth Culture Zine

Spank! Table of Contents Jump 7427

Spank!, a hip Calgary, Alberta, Web zine, bills itself as "youth culture online." Read interviews with young artists, singers and actors, check out features on such topics as the rites of body piercing, high school/university tips and information, and fashion flashes from the street. The usual Web reviews of youth-oriented music, film, and books can also be found. —(E.v.B.)

KEY NEWSGROUP **alt.zines** URL▶ http://www.cadvision.com/spank/

Explore Realms of the Imagination

Realms Title Jump 7455

The Realms is nice, creative urban narrative designed and written by Annette Weintraub. You are taken through different realms of consciousness, the Roof, the Streets, and Subterranean, using the metaphor of the city. The episodes of this journey through urban life are illustrated by Annette's arresting digital images. —(E.v.B.)

KEY NEWSGROUP **misc.writing** URL▶ http://artnetweb.com/artnetweb/projects/realms/realmstitle.html

Latino Culture Online

Electric Mercado Jump 7459

Electric Mercado, a colorful Web magazine, showcases the rich Latino culture. Music in Brazil, Mexican recipes, Cuban artists and writers, and much, much more is available at this bilingual site. For example, youth issues and interests, language issues in the United States, events and celebrations of interest, and links to many Spanish and Latin American sites on the Web are presented against a jazzy graphical background. —(E.v.B.)

KEY NEWSGROUP **soc.culture.latin-america** URL▶ http://www.mercado.com/

Inquisitor Magazine

Inquisitor Magazine

Jump 0019

Web site for *Inquisitior,* a hard-copy 'zine that "strives to look beyond the hype and trendiness of current 'Cyberculture'." Contains excerpts from recent issues and previews of upcoming features. *Inquisitor's* Web site features many eye-catching on-screen graphics and is, in our opinion, a fine example of Web page information presentation, too. —(E.G.)

URL▶ http://mosaic.echonyc.com/~xixax/Inquisitor/

InterFace Magazine

InterFace Magazine Jump 0048

A well-written, well-designed, and highly innovative Web (and hard copy) magazine "created expressly to allow 'creative' human beings a place to showcase their skills and talents, focusing on the 'CREATIVE' use of technology." Edited by Robert McCourty, this excellent Web magazine features profiles of companies and individuals who utilize technology in a creative manner, plus excellent and innovative computer art submitted by talented Web contributors, uploaded stories from readers, intelligent commentary on the current and future state of the Net, selected Web hot links, and featured columns. We highly recommend this professional Web publication, an excellent model for publishing a Web-based magazine! —(E.G.)

URL▶ http://www.dataflux.bc.ca/v3/interface/

Artists for Revolution through Technology on the Internet: ARTnet

IAMfree Information Jump 0199

An innovative Web "museum space" devoted to helping artists in all media—graphics, pictures, sound and words—present their works to the public through the Internet. The ARTnet site features some of the most creative visual art seen on the Net, including digital design and ideas by Dave Parmley, photographs by Mark Johns and "The Dance of Antoine," by performance group The Slowest Train in the World, the "first-ever music album created exclusively for the Internet." A nicely executed and visually appealing Web site, it proves once again the revolutionary impact the Web and the Internet have on traditional communication channels—in this case, allowing artists to bypass galleries, museums and art dealers, and present their works directly to the public. —(E.G.)

URL▶ http://www.artnet.org/iamfree/IAMFREE/html/info.html

geekgirl

i'm a geekgirl!

me too!

HI THERE!

Women Are Geeks, Too

geekgirl Jump 1504

An Australian Webzine designed for women, geekgirl is a first of its kind—devoted to remapping international cyberculture with a feminist bent. While entertaining and irreverent, this 'zine defines new terms for cyberchix; for instance, you learn that "cyberfeminism" is an alliance between women, machinery and the new technology. Eclectic is the word here. Women feel safe discussing Net issues in The Electronic Salon, a place they could post discussion papers, ideas and interests in a flame- and harassment-free environment. Off-the-wall interviews with the likes of authors Kathy Acker and Noam Chomsky are combined with the Electronic Witches and Virtual Sisters cyberbooths. There are also primers on cryptography and the criminal justice act, and links to other electronic 'zines. A must-read for everyone interested in what women throughout the world are up to these days. —(H.L.)

URL▶ http://www.next.com.au/spyfood/geekgirl/

Big Brother Is Watching

50 Greatest Conspiracies of All Time Jump 1532

Opening with a whimsical background of eyes, Jonathan Vankin and John Whalen have designed a clever site to get you to buy their book of the same name. And you just might, after reading excerpts, both humorous and serious. They've added new possible conspiracies: is Diane Sawyer really Watergate's "Deep Throat"? Did the government drop noxious nerve agents and mustard gas during the Persian Gulf War? Find out here. Listen to Ed Wood's favorite TV psychic and coffin-sleeper, Criswall, share predictions of the future. Maybe they're outlandish, but they're a hoot to read. If you're jittery about whether the government has your number, go through the Big Brother Checklist, an inventory of surveillance devices and other ways the government can spy on you, and explore links to other relevant sites. There's even a parody of cigarette companies trying to gloss over the facts, with great graphics. They've even included the top 10 underrated stories of the year—sure to make you look over your shoulder! —(H.L.)

KEY NEWSGROUP alt.conspiracy URL▶ http://www.webcom.com/~conspire/

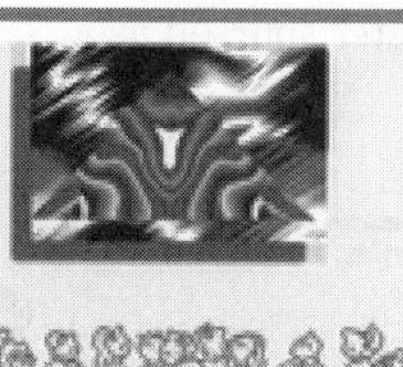

Photographs of Robert Altman

Homepage- Robert Altman Communications Jump 1533

Photographer and filmmaker Robert Altman has been dubbed the "official" photographer of the 1960s and 1970s scene in the San Francisco Bay Area. This site not only reprises his work of that era, but shows you what he's up to now. Remember his photos of such musical denizens as Mick Jagger, Janis Joplin, Jerry Garcia? Writers and wits Ken Kesey or Abbie Hoffman? How about Groucho Marx and Joe Montana? Bands, Berkeley, and ballrooms are all featured prominently here. If you were around during that volatile time, you'll definitely smile with nostalgia! This Web gallery is set up well—a set of instructions informs you how to view the photos to maximize your modem speed (the photo groups do take awhile to load). One of the best attractions here is Altman's personal scrapbook, where he writes a photo column in journal style and shares a collection of his latest work. —(H.L.)

URL▸ http://www.cea.edu/robert/x.index.html

Meeting Place of Ideas

The Hub Jump 1538

The "Hub Tub," a British-based meeting place for people and ideas, is a way to submit your artistic work for critique or locate collaborators to help you with projects you're working on in the realm of visual arts, film, performance, writing, sound, or multimedia. Become part of the directory of resources, which links to e-mail and Web addresses, phone numbers, and skill sets of Hub members. You can download floppies of other works or share your own, and vote to determine which floppies make it to Hub Heaven each month, like "Great Moments on Film: Jaws," a QuickTime animation, or "The London Zoo," an interactive postcard collection. (Beware that some files take as long as 20 minutes to download.) Creators Richard Gooderick and Russell Knights also include tools and training material, and Hub Happenings, a valuable source of events and submission information. Find links to literary agencies, employment opportunities, and other sites relevant to the arts here, too. —(H.L.)

URL▸ http://www.ace.mdx.ac.uk/Hub/Hub_out.html

African-American Perspectives: An Online Journal

Meanderings Jump 2320

This online magazine covers art, culture, and politics, and, although it's written from an African-American perspective, it holds interest for anyone. Article topics have included the state of affirmative action, black conservatives, Rosa Parks, short stories, and music and movie reviews. This magazine is truly interactive—readers can post comments directly from the articles, and see them with editor Cuda Brown's response in the next issue. —(L.S.)

KEY NEWSGROUP soc.culture.african.american URL▸ http://www.webcom.com/~sppg/meanderings/me.shtml

A Magazine on the Net & About the Net

Cyberkind Jump 4006

"*Cyberkind* is the chronicle of a new society—the Networld," and the *Cyberkind* site is an online magazine brought to you by DreamTech Enterprises. It contains fiction, nonfiction, poetry, and images all pertaining to the subject of the Net and/or computer networking. Editor Shannon Turling has put together quite a nice collection of information in a graphically pleasing style. —(R.B.)

KEY NEWSGROUP alt.zines URL▸ http://sunsite.unc.edu/shannon/ckind/title.html

A Virtual City on the Web

Downtown Anywhere Jump 4015

Brought to you by Downtown Anywhere, Inc., this site is set up as though it were a virtual city. Just click on the link for the area you're interested in, be it the newsstand, museum, sports arena, etc., and you're off to more

resources and/or link for that topic. You can shop, send a fax, read the paper, and even register yourself as a "citizen." Some of these services cost money, but most of it is totally free. —(R.B.)

KEY NEWSGROUP alt.culture.internet URL▶ http://www.awa.com/

Independent Media & Film on the Web

Reel Access Home Page Jump 4045

This site is dedicated to allowing independent film producers and other media creators show their work to an audience via the Web. Alan Eyzaguirre brings you this page, which contains many resources as well as links to related information. You can check out the feature presentation (usually a multimedia work), access a discussion area, or go to the different "studios" where other works are available. —(R.B.)

URL▶ http://www.best.com/~ake/cgi-bin/reel.cgi

Survival Research Laboratories' Home Site

Survival Research Laboratories Jump 4075

This is the home site for the famous techno-art (or "creative technicians") group Survival Research Laboratories (SRL). Maintained by Eric Paulos, this page contains all sorts of resources pertaining to this group "dedicated to redirecting the techniques, tools, and tenets of industry, science and the military away from their typical manifestations in practicality, product or warfare." You can get info and view images and clips from their shows, find out about recent and upcoming events, browse through their catalog, or even read an interview from *Wired* with founder Mark Pauline. —(R.B.)

URL▶ http://robotics.eecs.berkeley.edu/~paulos/SRL/

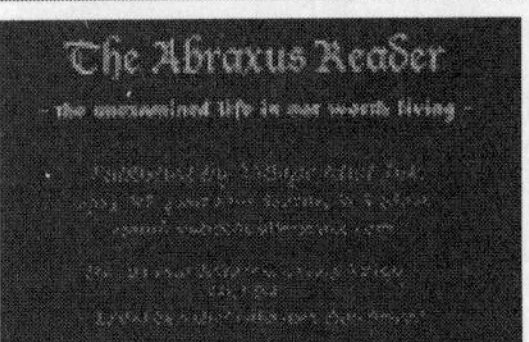

Online Literary Magazine

The Abraxus Reader Jump 5053

The Abraxus Reader is an online literary magazine that contains the literary talents of Internet contributors. Poetry, fiction, essays, and translations are all on display here. You can check out the current issue, back issues, a humor section, feedback, the publication's sponsors, and the excellent Prometheus Literary Database, which can connect you to hundreds of books, stories, and excerpts. Contact Abraxus with your suggestions via e-mail. Plans for a CD-ROM-based anthology are also underway. —(S.B.)

URL▶ http://www.cyberspace.com/vidiot

Send an Electronic Postcard on the Web

The Electric Postcard Jump 7003

Want to keep in touch with a friend, but don't have the time to write a letter? The Postcard Store has lots of choices to type your "wish you were here" on. Fancy a colourful Van Gogh or a supercool New York City shot in black and white—all are freely available here! Simply click on your postcard choice, type in your message and the recipient's e-mail address. The program then notifies your friend to pick up the postcard, all electronically via the Web. —(E.v.B.)

KEY NEWSGROUP bit.listserv.postcard URL▶ http://postcards.www.media.mit.edu/Postcards/Welcome.html

Time Warner's Excellent Web Adventure

Welcome to Pathfinder Jump 7110

A brilliant example of outstanding Web page media design and execution, those helpful people at Time Warner have designed Pathfinder, an excellent Web site that allows you to easily surf through a number of their products: *TIME, Vibe, People, Entertainment Weekly, Sports Illustrated, Fortune,* and many more publications. Eventually, they want to make it extremely easy to swim through this huge company. E-mail addresses for the Pathfinder employees are extensively listed for maximum feedback. —(E.v.B.)

URL▶ http://www.pathfinder.com/

Hidden Agendas

CAQ Jump 7167 

CAQ, or Covert Action Quarterly, is an e-zine that presents the "other side of the news." Get facts and opinions on the events and issues from a different perspective than you normally read in the newspaper or see on the evening news. Back issues include the rise of citizen militias, inside the FBI, workings of the CIA, and other hair-raising articles written by contributors such as Allen Ginsberg, Howard Zinn, and Jack Colhoun. —(E.v.B.)

KEY NEWSGROUP **alt.activism** URL▶ http://MediaFilter.org/MFF/CAQ_Contents.html

Wisconsin E-Zine

Slack Home Page Jump 7169 

Slack Online is a monthly e-zine published in Madison, Wisconsin. Its content mirrors the hard-copy version of this alternative/underground periodical that covers local, national, and international issues, literature, fine arts, entertainment, and sports. The text is often accompanied by art and cartoons; past issues can also be read. As well, you can read reviews posted by the editors and other interested readers on available shareware and freeware found on the Net. —(E.v.B.)

KEY NEWSGROUP **alt.zines** URL▶ http://www.msn.fullfeed.com:80/slack/

New York Electric

Urban Desires Jump 7198 

Urban Desires, begun in the living room of a New York couple, Kyle and Gabrielle Shannon, has rapidly become one of the favorite e-zines on the Web. Subtitled "an interactive magazine of metropolitan passions," Urban Desires is quite beguiling. Well written, very New York-hip in its graphics and content, and with excellent Web page design, this e-zine is a real trip. You can surf through pieces on art, music, food, theater, style (of course, it's New York), and travel. The articles are enlivened with music, sound, and video clips. Don't miss this one. —(E.v.B.)

KEY NEWSGROUP **alt.zines** URL▶ http://desires.com/pub.html

Tune in, Turn on, Tune Out

The Timothy Leary and Robert Anton Wilson Show
Jump 7199 

Dimitri has brought Timothy Leary ("revolutionary avatar of the mind") and Robert Anton Wilson ("important scientific philosopher") together because "they just belong together, dammit!" You are invited to explore Leary's works through commentary by Dimitri, and through hot links to video clips, audio samples and other Leary pages. Wilson's material is a little less extensive, but also includes reviews, links to other Wilson pages, and excerpts from his extensive writings, such as his science fiction, and his new *Journal of Futurism and Heresy*. —(E.v.B.)

KEY NEWSGROUP **alt.consciousness** URL▶ http://www.intac.com/~dimitri/dh/learywilson.html

Happening Toronto

eye.NET Jump 7200 CONTENT

eye demonstrates that the image of Toronto, Canada, has certainly evolved from the gray, "everything closed on Monday" sort of place, into a vibrant, leading-edge city. eye covers the city—especially cultural Toronto: its music, theater, and films. As well, eye contains a healthy commentary section on the latest issues such as gay rights, environmental controversies, and other burning topics in the city. But, first things first, eye also reports on the best bars, restaurants, and bands. —(E.v.B.)

KEY NEWSGROUP **tor.general** URL▶ http://www.interlog.com/eye/

A CD Affair

Metzger Associates: As the Web Turns Jump 1557 

This humorous and intriguing weekly soap opera, the first of its kind on the Web, has developed a cult status, clearly demonstrating a clever way for a commercial Web site to sell without being obvious. Developed by Bret Clement, written by Lance Jones, and illustrated by Sherrie Lotito of Metzger Associates—a PR firm in Boulder, Colorado—this weekly saga weaves client names into the story through hypertext links. With episodes called "Ring Around the Collar," "Bring on the Hounds," and "Bowling with Pinheads," the cast of characters sweat through weekly, continuous challenges, as in episode 40: "Snooks beheld the woman, draped in ethereal heaps of gauzy and filmy fabric. He seemed to remember exchanging pleasantries, and found himself seated on a chenille sofa, a mint julep dripping icy perspiration down the side of his hand." No doubt about it. You'll be returning next week! —(H.L.)

URL ▸ http://www.metzger.com/soap/2pinecliff.html

The Freedom of Art

The Open Scroll Jump 3741 

The Open Scroll is "dedicated to the freedom of art in the pursuit of passion, brilliance, and insanity." This monthly publication airs a variety of opinions through poetry and prose. The editor elicits contributions from readers in the hopes of furthering the cause of freedom of speech. And freedom of speech is quite evident at this site! You'll find poems, stories and opinions (political and otherwise), as well as featured guests (this month—Rush Limbaugh!). Your voice, your opinions, and your ideas are what The Open Scroll is looking for. —(N.F.)

URL ▸ http://www.hooked.net/users/scroll/

Buzznet Music & Culture Web Zine

WELCOME TO BUZZNET Jump 7355 

Buzznet is a pretty funky zine. Full of hip reviews of the alternative music scene, films, art and fashion. As well, you might even find a feature on soapbox derbies, rock climbing, even political essays on Ross Perot—really! The graphics are in-your-face, and so is the writing. —(E.v.B.)

KEY NEWSGROUP alt.zines URL ▸ http://www.buzznet.com/

Anathema Sez

Ana Sez Jump 5820 

Ana Sez, a story about teenage students, is a new writing experiment produced exclusively for the Web. It's sort of like the old serials you may have seen on TV when you were a kid, where a story is told in small segments over a month or two. Here the new episodes arrive Tuesdays and Fridays, with each "episode" running 3-4 pages in length. The story on this site began as a short story, soon outgrew that form and, while it might have seemed destined to become a novel, author and site editor Gage Steele thought serialization to be a more manageable means of achieving that end. You can join the story at any point (past episodes are always available) and you can also join the fun at "Sez What?!," an online message center where you can meet this site's cast members, staff, and other Web readers just like yourself, to read and post public notes. —(J.P.)

URL ▸ http://www.sonic.net/~anathema/

WAXweb Hypermedia Page

WAXweb Home Page Jump 0039 

David Blair's independent film, *WAX or The Discovery of Television Among the Bees,* can claim credit for being the first movie ever "broadcast" over the Internet in 1993. David Blair's new project is this intriguing hypertext-based version of *WAX,* which allows you to add to the story line of the movie and view and/or listen to video and audio clips of the film on your very own computer. A pioneering and innovative use of the Web for those of you who like to stay on the cutting edge of media culture! —(E.G.)

URL▸ http://bug.village.virginia.edu/

The Web's Melrose Place: The Spot

The Spot Jump 7388

The Spot, on one level, is a beach house inhabited by a number of attractive twenty-somethings. On another level, it's a slickly (and expensively) designed "episode" Web site, which was recently named the "Cool Site of the Year" in a Web-wide survey. The creators of this site, ad agency Fattal & Collins, have mastered every trick in the book to turn the Web's unique features—its interactivity, graphics display, and nonlinear story presentation capability—into a stunningly innovative site with stories and characters that many first-time visitors actually believe are true. You meet the characters who live or have lived at The Spot, and then you add to the story—which has elements of reality, fiction, and the paranormal all jumbled up into one interesting narrative. You can jump right in, or read all the past episodes (including private diary entries and letters) to see where to lead the plot. Sound and video files enhance the experience—which may also be described as somewhat voyeuristic. Great graphics add to the innovative, yet in our opinion, exploitive, nature of this site. (NOTE: This site is not suitable for children.)—(E.v.B.)

URL▸ http://www.thespot.com/

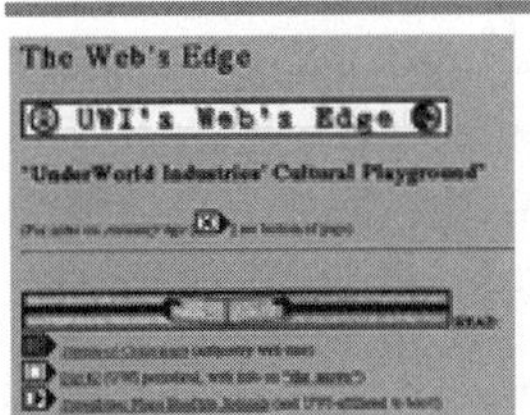

UnderWorld Industries Web's Edge

UWI's Web's Edge Jump 0047

We were so impressed with this site, we hired its developer to help us create ours! Jon Van Oast's Web site stands out as our choice for one the most innovative, best-designed Web sites. A creative and skilled Web page designer, Jon's Web site features links to other innovative electronic 'zines, experimental music pages, avant-garde typography, weird stories and Jon's excellent personal Web picks. Jon's funky and delightful writing style bolsters his excellent Web page design skills and is worth the visit all by itself! All in all, we think this is the Web site other Web page designers should go to for instruction and inspiration. Highly recommended! —(E.G.)

URL▸ http://kzsu.stanford.edu/uwi.html

Truly Interactive Fiction

The Round Robin Storybook Jump 2425

Round robin storytelling involves one writer starting a story, then handing it off to another to continue, who then hands it off to another. Sometimes a new author takes an existing story and creates a new branch with its own round robin. The results can be quite interesting, and always entertaining, whether you participate as writer or reader. Jenni Mott maintains this page for both, and includes information on how to get involved. If a story interests you, check the rules to see if there's an opening for a writer. If there's no vacancy, see if you can create a new branch. If you're still stymied, Jenni even tells you how you can start a new story. —(L.S.)

KEY NEWSGROUP **rec.arts.int-fiction** URL▸ http://www.wimsey.com/~jmott/RoundRobin/strybook.html

Portrait of the Artist As a Young Byte

Virtual Beret Archives Jump 2225

This is an interesting, interactive experiment focusing on the perception of artists in the online environment. Artist Sarah Smily conceived this site, maintained by fellow artist Patrick Jordan, that invites anyone—whether an artist or not—to create fictional artists, describe them, their works, and their berets. The idea of describing the beret is based on the reasonable assumption that people's hats reflect their personalities and outlooks, and the virtual beret of the fictional artist will give the reader a special insight. Sarah also posts monthly project updates and musings concerning her experiences with the Net, art, and related topics. It can be a strange, yet compelling, page that followers of art, culture, and cyberspace are well advised to visit. —(L.S.)

KEY NEWSGROUP **alt.culture.internet** URL▶ http://www.rp.csiro.au/~pjordan/VirtualBeret/

An Art Gallery for Graffiti

Art Crimes Jump 4013 

An interesting Internet art gallery with a somewhat different subject. Graffiti is the art form here, and Susan Farrell has put together an elegant and visually stimulating collection of photos of city graffiti around the U.S., and the world. You can click on thumbnails of pictures to display them in a larger format. The graphics are categorized by city, and there's also a link to the FTP server so you can download any of the images you'd like to have. —(R.B.)

KEY NEWSGROUP **alt.graffiti** URL▶ http://www.gatech.edu/desoto/graf/Index.Art_Crimes.html

Independent Artists on the Internet

Kaleidospace Jump 4017 

The Kaleidospace site brings you an area in which you can view, listen to, and even order some of the works of various types of artists. From the well-known (Thomas Dolby) to the unknown, all forms of art are represented here, including video, music, fine art—even comedy. A wide variety of content and a load of interesting images, video, and sound make this a site at which you can spend a lot of time. —(R.B.)

KEY NEWSGROUP **alt.artcom** URL▶ http://kspace.com/

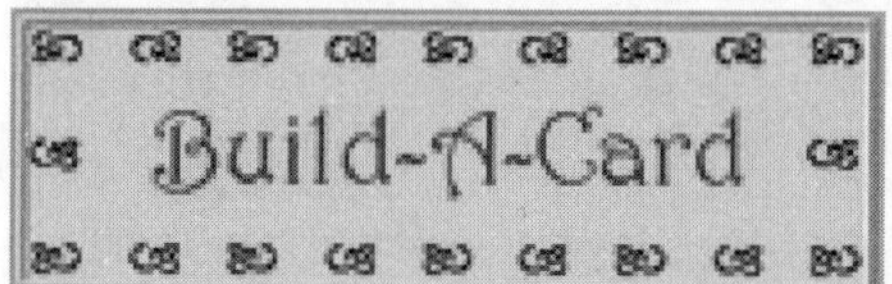

Care Enough to Send the Best: Web Greeting Cards

Welcome to Build-A-Card Jump 4050 

Brought to you by Maximized Online, this is one of the neatest sites you'll find on the Web. As it says on the page: "Build-A-Card lets you mix pictures and text to create a Web-based greeting card. Each card gets its own URL, which can be sent to friends, loved ones, or others you want to 'receive your card'." That's right, interactive greeting cards! Now you have no reason to be late in sending a card for a birthday or other special occasion, because now you can send it from your computer, free, with this very cool service! —(R.B.)

URL▶ http://infopages.com/card/

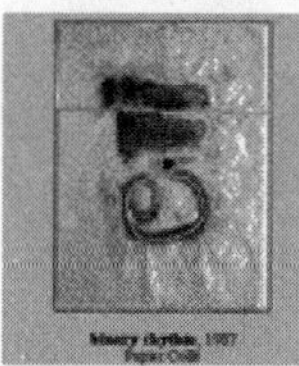

Art on Parade

Lin Hsin Hsin Art Museum Jump 7061 

This multimedia extravaganza focuses on the Singapore artist Lin Hsin Hsin. Not only can you view her prodigious output of sculpture, painting, and other creations, but you can also read her poems, listen to her musical compositions, and see video clips of the artist herself. Like her work? Don't forget to visit this site's virtual souvenir shop on your way out and purchase a copy of her publications. —(E.v.B.)

URL▶ http://www.ncb.gov.sg/lhh/

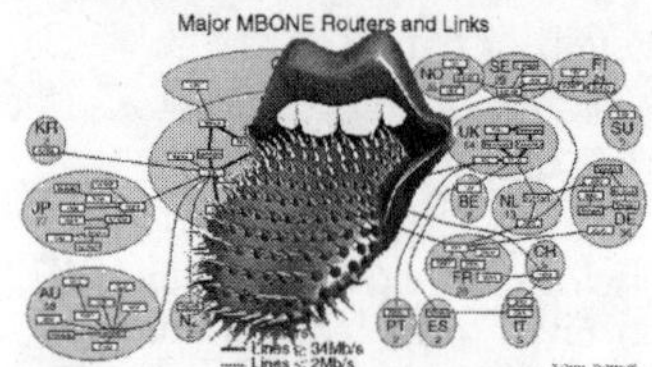

Rolling Stones Concert Live Video Web Page

The Stone Bone Connected to the Mbone Jump 0127 CONTENT

Mick Jagger (reputed to be a big-time Net surfer himself) and the Rolling Stones made a bit of Web history in November 1994 by broadcasting one of their live concerts over a network of high-speed links on the Web called the Mbone. Accessible only via this high speed link and on fancy SUN workstations, this concert was the first live digital video broadcast ever made across the Internet. This Web site is a summary of that event with links to technical tidbits on the broadcast. Unfortunately, none of this video feed is available to those of us (most of us) who don't have access to this fancy equipment, but, since digital video over the Internet is most certainly a future thing, reading about it here will give you an idea of things to come. —(E.G.)

KEY NEWSGROUP **alt.rock-n-roll.stones** URL▶ http://www.stones.com/mbone/

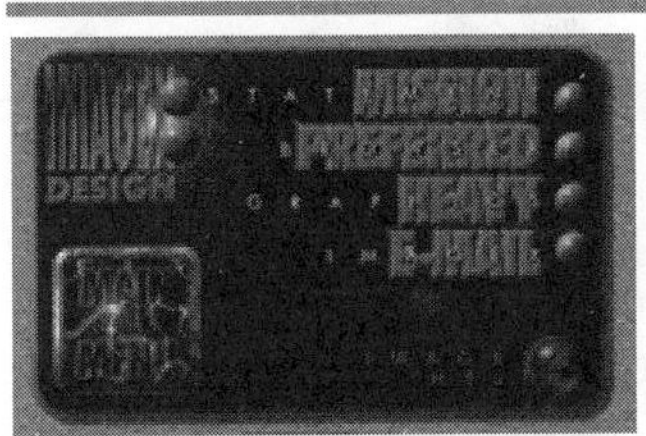

Computer Art Deluxe

Imagex Design Jump 7211

The creative folk at Imagex Design have created colorful, well-designed pages that take computer art along innovative paths. The group has mounted an extensive portfolio of their work that can be browsed at your leisure—meaning that some of the files take a looooong time to load! However, they are considerate and warn you when a large file is coming up. They do not confine themselves to the Web, but also do a lot of traditional design work you can also view. —(E.v.B.)

KEY NEWSGROUP **comp.multimedia** URL▶ http://sandpiper.rtd.com/~imagex/newindex.html

The Arts Online

basilisk Jump 7221

basilisk is a quarterly e-zine, full of great graphics and interactive material, that expends its considerable creative energy on film, architecture, philosophy, literature, music, neuroscience and perception. Serial novels, critiques of recent architectural projects, reviews of alternative music are only a few of its hip features. Intriguing essays into the mind also excite the neurons. Give yourself some digital food for thought and visit this site! —(E.v.B.)

KEY NEWSGROUP **alt.artcom** URL▶ http://swerve.basilisk.com/

Christopher Penrose Original Music Web Site

After the Taj Mahal: New Music by Christopher Penrose Jump 0197

Innovative Web page features original works by musician Christopher Penrose and demonstrates how many innovative, Net-savvy musicians are using the Web to distribute their music directly to listeners, bypassing traditional record label and radio station distribution channels. —(E.G.)

URL▶ http://crca-www.ucsd.edu/TajMahal/after.html

Paul Haeberlie's Digital Graphic Notebook

Grafica Obscura Jump 7224

Computer graphic artist Paul Haeberlie has put his notebook online. It contains technical notes (such as how to modify photographic lighting), pictures (a large gallery of digital pictures), and essays (background on the Futurist Programming movement). As well, you can learn step-by-illustrated-step, how to make a folded paper sculpture or how to create really great images for HTML documents. For the professionals, take a look at his thoughts on the properties of light and image merging. —(E.v.B.)

KEY NEWSGROUP **comp.graphics** URL▶ http://www.sgi.com/grafica/

Klubs, Kalendars, & Musik

HalluciNet Jump 7168

If psykoRappers, cyberRavers, and other neuroKultists turn your particular crank, HalluciNet is for you. Subtitled "an online entertainment resource for SoKal," this site has extensive listings of klubs, bands, and items (musik, films, komputers) for sale or trade in southern California–all "c's" seem to be banned from this site. As well, you can watch clips, er, klips, from Miramax films such as *Tank Girl,* or listen to new bands such as Mad Love. For a deeper exploration of this intriguing site, the Webmasters advise that you use Adobe Acrobat–er, Akrobat–Reader software. —(E.v.B.)

KEY NEWSGROUP **bit.listserv.allmusic** URL▶ http://hallucinet.wwa.com/

A businessman based in the Caribbean has come up with a plan to run a casino accessible worldwide by use of a computer modem—a concept likely to have mass appeal in this wager-a-minute, hi-tech society.

Due to be launched on May 15, the idea is the brainchild of Warren Eugene, the 34-year-old president of the Internet Online Offshore Casino and Sports Book.

"I see a really big vein here," said Eugene, who believes that if only a tiny portion of the Internet's estimated 20 million users check in, he'll soon be running the largest casino in the world—staffed by just three people and a handful of very powerful computers.

Mark Hughes, "Your Bets on the Net," *South China Morning Post*

Chapter 8: Entertainment & Media

Whatever your interests in books, music, TV, or the movies, there's someone out there who's created a Web site to satisfy the fan in you. What's more, entertainment-related Web sites, because they're created by devoted (even obsessive) people, are sometimes even more entertaining than the Web sites which have been created by the big-media movie studios, networks, publishers, and other owners of these forms of entertainment themselves.

Fan-Related Media Entertainment Web Sites

There are hundreds and hundreds of fan's Web sites for just about every author, film, musician, singer, music group, movie, or TV show—from beyond-the-fringe cult features and characters, to blockbuster movies and prime-time shows. What most of these sites have in common is the fact that someone, usually a rabidly enthusiastic (some might say obsessed) fan, has either written or assembled tons of interesting background information, notes, news, graphics, photos, sound/video clips, and the like relating to your favorite character or media attraction into one single place on the Web—providing you with more information than you'd probably see anywhere else.

Games, Humor, and Cartoons

Game-playing has long been a favorite Net activity, so it's no surprise that it's also taken hold on the Web. There are Web sites devoted to players of all games of all kinds—from conventional board and strategy games to commercial and video and computer games, Internet-based multi-player games, arcade games, and much more. Lots of game-playing tips, cheats, comments, free downloadable game software, and more are available all over the Web.

Books & Language

Direct Links to Book Publishers on the Web

Publisher's Catalogs Home Page Jump 0011

A one-stop jump page with links to scores of book publishers on the Web compiled by Peter Scott of The University of Saskatchewan Libraries. This Web page gives you fast and easy access to the individual Web sites of many of the world's leading publishing companies. In many cases, these publisher Web sites feature a publisher's extensive catalog of books, catalog and backlist offerings, announcements of upcoming books and even online Web book ordering capabilities. Also features offerings from many technical, scientific, and specialized book publishers. —(E.G.)

URL ▶ http://duke.usask.ca/~scottp/publish.html

Hitchhiker's Guide to the Galaxy Home Page

Hitchhiker's Guide to the Galaxy Home Page Jump 0163

Jan Paul Davis' Web jump site is for the many Net fans of the humorous science fiction writings of Douglas Adams, best known for the *Hitchhiker's Guide to the Galaxy*. Features many links to fun sound files featuring material and characters from The Guide, excerpts, short stories, and Net newsgroup links. —(E.G.)

KEY NEWSGROUP alt.fan.douglas-adams

URL ▶ http://www.galcit.caltech.edu/~jdavis/hhgttg.html

The Slot: The Spot for Copy Editors

The Slot Jump 5864 CONTENT

We've all heard of copy editors, but what exactly do they do? Find out here in this wonderful site created by veteran newspaper copy editor Bill Walsh. Walsh has been a copy editor for a couple of decades, and after years of sharing his knowledge of writing and editing in various print media, he has brought his passion for words to the Web. And words really are his passion—especially those used wisely. So we learn in "The Curmudgeon's Stylebook," a great writer's reference source for tips on punctuation, capitalization, spelling, style, quotations, and much more. And don't pass up the chance to read some of Walsh's sharply-worded editorials in his "Sharp Points" section. This is where Walsh vents his disdain for those who ignore the basic rules of writing, whether on the Internet or off. —(J.P.)

URL ▶ http://www.theslot.com/

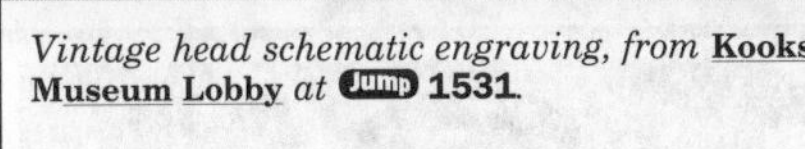

Vintage head schematic engraving, from **Kooks Museum Lobby** *at* Jump **1531**.

Take it from the Word Wizard

Word Wizard Jump 5873

Lovers of words will want to unite at the home of the Word Wizard. The Wizard in question is Cabinet Derek Erb, a wordsmith who not only lives for words, but has a keen sense of playfulness that is truly invigorating. Among the highlights are word games that feature new words and snappy quotes, contests (with some pretty neat prizes), and our favorite spot, "Coining it," where you'll find the latest in newly-coined words. They might not be in the dictionary yet, but if they're all right with the Word Wizard, that's good enough for us. —(J.P.)

URL ▶ http://wordwizard.com/

English Language Usage Resources

Keith Ivey's English Usage Page Jump 2171

Language is dynamic. New words are added, old words take new meanings, and syntax itself evolves. English is particularly changeable, with new words being created by commercial enterprises and society's various subcultures that either add excitement to, or debase communications, depending upon your point of view. If you want to stay abreast of what's "correct" today, Keith Ivey's page is your starting point. There are links to various dictionaries, jargon files, and usage FAQs, all related to the use of our common language. —(L.S.)

KEY NEWSGROUP alt.english.usage URL ▶ http://cpcug.org/user/kcivey/engusage.html

The Languages of the World

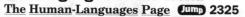

The Human-Languages Page Jump 2325

Tyler Jones may want to change the page title to "The Humanoid-Languages Page," since he's included Klingon among the links. But this small inaccuracy aside, his efforts in bringing together resources for language study is notable. There are links to translation dictionaries, study aids, linguistic guides and references, multilingual resources, and books and literature, along with commercial resources and language-related events. Many languages are covered, but many are not. Tyler needs volunteers to help accumulate links, as well as to translate the page introduction into languages other than English. —(L.S.)

KEY NEWSGROUP sci.lang URL ▶ http://www.willamette.edu/~tjones/Language-Page.html#edu

Web Reading Room

Books On-Line, Listed by Author Jump 2422

Readers are leaders, they say, and you can hone your leadership skills by linking to this page of great writing by great writers. This isn't a catalog; these are links to full text or HTML versions of the best books in the history of the written word, courtesy of Carnegie-Mellon University. From philosophy to science fiction, bibles to manifestos, poetry or prose, the selection is outstanding, and represents the great thinkers and storytellers of all time. —(L.S.)

KEY NEWSGROUP rec.arts.books URL ▶ http://www.cs.cmu.edu/Web/bookauthors.html

Castle Aphrodesia

Castle Aphrodesia Jump 5648

Castle Aphrodesia is "dedicated to those weaving the threads of love into magnificent literary tapestries to titillate and arouse the imagination." In other words, this is a place for those who enjoy the magic of words. Once you pass through the main gate, you'll enter the village, where you will find surveys, message boards, games and other "interactive goo." And that's just the beginning! In the castle proper, be prepared for a dozen or so other links, taking the adventurer to places such as Bard Heaven, where you can join in the celebration of storytelling, or take A Roll in the Bower for an interactive Medieval fantasy, or journey to The Turret, for general information for writers. And there is much more. —(J.P.)

URL ▶ http://www.tallahassee.net/~conroye/aphrodesia/index2.html

Lewis and Alice's Great Adventures

Lewis Carroll Home Page *Illustrated* Jump 8017

William Maury Morris II has created a stunningly beautiful site focusing on the classic children's fiction written of Lewis Carroll. The pages contain illustrated, full text editions of *Alice's Adventures in Wonderland*, *Through the Looking Glass* and the *Hunting of the Snark*. Many of the over 100 illustrations were drawn by Morris himself.

Reading through these classics is a feast—visually and intellectually. And soon they will be an aural feast, as Morris plans to add sound files to this exquisite mix. —(E.v.B.)

KEY NEWSGROUP bit.listserv.literary URL▶ http://www.cstone.net/library/alice/

Information for Tolkien Books Fans

The J.R.R. Tolkien Information Page Jump 4020

Eric Lippert has worked since November of 1993 to put together this site which offers a remarkable list of links to Tolkien resources around the world. Everything and anything you want to know or find out about Tolkien and his works is linked here. Resources include: FAQ's, mailing list info, newsgroups, graphics, online texts, societies and newsletters, and even special downloadable Tolkeinesque fonts. —(R.B.)

KEY NEWSGROUP alt.fan.tolkien URL▶ http://herald.usask.ca/~friesend/tolkien/rootpage.html

The World of Mark Twain

Mark Twain Resources on the World Wide Web Jump 4069

Created by Jim Zwick, this page is a collection of links to all sorts of information pertaining to the great American author Mark Twain. There are connections to exhibits, electronic texts, scholarly studies, syllabi, and resources for teachers—even a section with links to information on how Twain has affected our popular culture. This site is a "must" bookmark for anyone interested in this classic American writer. —(R.B.)

KEY NEWSGROUP bit.listserv.literary URL▶ http://web.syr.edu/~fjzwick/twainwww.html

Generation-X Meets Bill Gates

CONTENT

Microserfs Home Page Jump 1550

Microserfs are those young, bright engineers that work at the kingdom of Microsoft. Douglas Coupland's book of the same name describes their lives, environment, and most of all, their attachment to and sometimes irreverence for the largest employer in Washington state. This site relays passages from the book, read by Matthew Perry of *Friends*, and reveals the book's hidden messages. Are you distraught about the death of Generation-X? Take Coupland's advice: "It's still a good policy to continue defying labels." Don't miss the Girl's Guide to Geeks or Douglas Coupland's own home page, which includes bios and transcripts from his online chats. Most entertaining, however, is the link to the Holy Temple of Bill—a page devoted to Microsoft's founder and CEO. Photos, interviews, stories, humor, and articles bedeck this special area. Also included are serious links to the company, the 60-building "campus," current Microsoft jobs and products, as well as links to Seattle-related sites. —(H.L.)

URL▶ http://www.metatec.com/~dmorford/MicroSerfsHome.html

Help Write the First Book Authored Online

FAQs of Life Jump 2713

Just about everyone has some lessons they've learned in life that they'd like to share. And even those who don't think they do will likely have some pearls of wisdom that someone will find helpful. This page is about sharing those lessons and casting those pearls, and creating the first book written completely online. The topics so far range from how much to tip a doorman to Zen-like meditations on the meaning of friendship, so if you don't think you have anything to contribute, think again. Anything that has anything to do with living in the real world is welcomed.—(L.S.)

KEY NEWSGROUP talk.philosophy.misc URL▶ http://www.interaccess.com/faqslife/

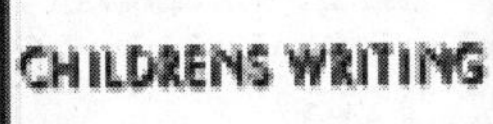

RESOURCE CENTER

Writing Children's Books

Welcome to CWRC! Jump 1546

If you've always dreamt of writing for kids, or even if you've already published in the field, this is the place for you. Publishers Jon Bard and Laura Backus offer a wealth of information to help you accomplish your goals: marketing tips, publisher insider secrets, how to use the Internet for research and networking, the latest children's best-sellers, and even how to write a rebus (placing written words with pictures). Don't miss the library of "how-to" information and a comprehensive glossary. You can also find links to other great Web resources and ideas. Be sure to download free stuff, like a career starter demo, or digests from the Children's Book Insider newsletter, or join the e-mail discussion group, where you can discuss issues, share ideas, and solve problems with peers and professionals. —(H.L.)

URL▶ http://www.mindspring.com/~cbi/welcome.html

But Will He Be as Funny as Ford?

Dave Barry for President Jump 2653

Maintained by Dave Barry fan Jen, this is the virtual headquarters for the humorist's latest campaign for leader of the free world. It would seem to be a very grass-roots movement, since all of Barry's material is copyrighted and, therefore, none of it appears here. Instead, denizens of the **alt.fan.dave_barry** newsgroup offer up their suggested platform, as well as recommeded positions on issues ranging from NAFTA to official White House snack. —(L.S.)

KEY NEWSGROUP **alt.fan.dave_barry** URL▶ http://www.wam.umd.edu/~meercat/Dave_Barry_96

From Sri Lanka to Rama

Arthur C. Clarke Unauthorized Home Page Jump 2689

Arthur C. Clarke is one of the most honored and prolific science fiction authors. Best known for co-writing the screenplay for *2001: A Space Odyssey*, he's written some 60 books, and his influence goes far beyond the SF community. As a scientist, for example, he created the concept of placing communications satellites in geostationary orbit, the basic idea behind the success of today's global communications capabilities. This page, maintained by Reinaldo A. C. Bianchi, will tell you more about Clarke's science fiction and science fact, including interviews on a variety of topics. —(L.S.)

KEY NEWSGROUP **rec.arts.sf.misc** URL▶ http://www.lsi.usp.br/~rbianchi/clarke/ACC.Homepage.html

The Sharpest Wit in the English Language

The Wild Wilde Web

Jump 2715

No one in the history of English literature combined wit, personality and talent as Oscar Wilde did. Lover of and participant in scandals, speaker of dangerous thoughts, and never afraid of challenging the comfortable, his reputation sometimes overshadows his art. Here you'll learn about the life of this most interesting person, along with a list of his works in print and a bibliography for reading more about him. Even if you're not interested in Wilde and his work, stop by for samples of his wit. Updated regularly, these snippets are some of the most humorous and biting commentaries on manners and mores you'll ever read. —(L.S.)

KEY NEWSGROUP **bit.litserv.literary** URL▶ http://www.anomtec.com:8001/oscarwilde/

If You Liked That Book, You May Like This One . . .

SF RIYL Page Intro Jump 2730

Many authors write in similar styles, but that's not to say that they copy each other. Rather, it means that if you liked one author, that could indicate you'd like another, and that's what this page is about. Maintained by Chris Sterritt, it's for science fiction fans to share their observations about what other readers may enjoy. Each entry connects one author and book to another. Find an author you like and you'll be given an idea of what another reader thinks you'll like about a different author, as well as what you may dislike. It's a collaborative effort, and needs contributors, so if you're a reader who likes to share, stop by and add your suggestions. —(L.S.)

KEY NEWSGROUP **rec.arts.books.reviews** URL▶ http://metro.turnpike.net/C/chriss/http://metro.turnpike.net/C/chriss/'

Looking for a Good Book?

Ed's Internet Book Reviews Jump 2731

Forget the bestsellers lists and try Ed Bell's compilation of book reviews by Net contributors. They're not limited to technical book reviews, although you'll find those here, along with general fiction, science fiction and fantasy, mystery, business, politics, religion, new age, and science. When you jump to a specific section, you can read reviews by title, or by reviewer if, after a few visits, you find someone whose opinions you trust. You can also become a reviewer yourself—just follow the online guidelines. —(L.S.)

KEY NEWSGROUP **rec.arts.books.reviews** URL ▶ http://www.clark.net/pub/bell/review/book_review.shtml

The Book on Spenser

Beer and Bullets—The Spenser Page

Jump **2733**

Robert B. Parker has created something of an industry with his Spenser character, a Marlowe-esque character with fists of iron, the soul of a poet, and no first name. With his penchant for cracking wise, waxing philosophical, and cooking gourmet, he's one of the more interesting denizens of detective fiction, and this page gives longtime fans and newcomers alike all they would want to know about Spenser and his buddies, antagonists, and world in general. You'll also find summaries and bibliographic information about all the Spenser stories, including simply wonderful annotated guides to the literary allusions Spenser/Parker sprinkles through the adventures, and the best lines in each book. —(L.S.)

KEY NEWSGROUP **rec.arts.mystery** URL ▶ http://mirkwood.ucc.uconn.edu/spenser/spenser.html

Stories for Children, and Grownups, Too

Realist Wonder Society Home Page Jump **2766**

The folks who maintain this Web page call it a whistle stop of imagination between way stations of reality, and that about sums it up. It's a place to take a breath and relax with fairy tales and fables for children and adults, poetry and art, and general thoughts about creativity, imagination, and life. The graphics are outstanding, the tone soothing, and the content delightful. New material is added every two weeks, and if there's not enough for you here, there's also a list of links to other pages that serve to stimulate your imagination. —(L.S.)

KEY NEWSGROUP **alt.prose** URL ▶ http://www.rrnet.com/~nakamura/

Ink Spots for Young Writers

Resources for Young Writers Jump **6639**

If you have a budding Hemingway on your hands, put your aspiring young writer's creative efforts to work through the latest in online writing contests and Web sites looking to publish your youngster's work on this interesting site. Your kids can read all about how a book is made, and access many other helpful kid-written tips and tutorials. Whether your child is writing a simple short story or a screenplay, this site will encourage and guide them through every step of the creative writing process. —(L.T.)

KEY NEWSGROUP **alt.usage.english** URL ▶ http://www.interlog.com/~ohi/inkspot/young.html

A Directory of and Resource Center for Freelancers in the Fields of Communication

Directory and Resources for Freelance Writers

Freelance Online Jump **5782**

Freelance Online has quickly become one of the single best Net resources for writers. The layout is clean and precise and the content surpasses many other subscription-based books and magazines. Yes, all this and it's free too. Writers can submit their profile if they wish, with the hopes that it might be seen by any of the many publishers looking for writers. There's a forum for discussion of writing-related topics and a resource area containing some wonderful links to other related writer's sites. There's also a jobs section, where you'll find a couple dozen job postings, mostly freelance (but sometimes other), from book and magazine publishers across the U.S.—(J.P.)

KEY NEWSGROUP **misc.writing** URL ▶ http://haven.ios.com/~freelans/

Authorlink Book Publisher's Site

Authorlink

Jump 6892

Why do editors reject books? It's a question most every author has asked themselves at one point or another. At Authorlink, it's answered by Thomas Colgan, an editor with Berkley Publishing in New York. Created by Multimedia Strategies of Dallas, Authorlink is of value to writers, or anyone in the publishing industry, and it's where you'll find the latest publishing news, links, upcoming book releases, conference listings, literary contests and more. A click on its market links section leads you to editorial guidelines from publishing houses like Dell and Pocketbooks. Here, you'll also discover a library of insights from editors, agents, and authors, with useful articles on what to do after signing a contract, common questions (and answers) about literary agents, and advice for aspiring young writers. —(L.T.)

KEY NEWSGROUP **misc.writing** URL▶ http://www.authorlink.com/

Crime Writer's Online Help Center

INTERNET CRIMEWRITING NETWORK

Jump 7246

Martin Roth and his crime-writing friends have created a fantastic site designed to assist and entertain television, film, and fiction crime writers and anyone else interested in true life blood and gore. This site is incredibly rich with facts, references, writing tips, and other pretty neat stuff. Got writer's block, need a researcher? Well, enter the Crimewriter's crisis intervention center. Or, perhaps you need expert advice on a point of law or forensic lab terminology. Don't hesitate, drop a line to the many police officials and lawyers who are willing helpers in the Interrogation Room. As well, you can advertise your own writing work in the Wanted! section. —(E.v.B.)

KEY NEWSGROUP **misc.writing** URL▶ http://www.hollywoodnetwork.com:80/Crime/

Great Online Reading

The Reader's Corner: Mystery, Romance and Fantasy Jump 7403

Readers and writers of mystery, romance, and fantasy fiction will enjoy this rich site. The pages are associated with The Automated Pen, a company that is "building a collection of electronic genre fiction: mystery, romance, and fantasy, for sale on the World Wide Web." Mystery fans can read articles on such diverse topics as The Modern American Female Detective, Law Enforcement in History, or Historical Detectives. Those with a more romantic turn of mind can read articles on Victorian Escape versus Modern Technology, contrasts between the Regency and Victorian Eras, or Victorian Books of Romance, Fantasy, and Adventure. Book excerpts are also to be found. —(E.v.B.)

KEY NEWSGROUP **misc.writing** URL▶ http://www.quake.net/~autopen/

Finding Great Books for Kids

Children's Literature Home Page

Jump 7441

ParentsPlace.com publishes the Children's Literature newsletter to help adults find the best children's books available. The "cream of the crop" is reviewed here out of the more than 5,000 children's books published each year. You will also find reviews of electronic books and multimedia, as well as profiles of prominent authors and illustrators. If you have a specific title or author you're searching for, ParentsPlace makes it easy—just search their online database of reviews. The subject areas are wide—from animals to native people to family relations to famous 20th Century women, to the tough issues of the day. —(E.v.B.)

KEY NEWSGROUP **misc.kids** URL▶ http://www.parentsplace.com/readroom/childnew/index.html

For Lovers of Pop Culture

Hype! International

Jump 2183

If you seriously enjoy the hype, kitsch, and camp of pop culture this is your site. Specific areas covered include comics, movies, television, nostalgia, and video games. It's done with a combined sense of reverence and humor, an almost breathless enthusiasm, and a clear understanding that even the worst of pop culture can be fun if approached with the right attitude. Though the topics may not be taken too seriously, the site is, with well thought-out content and new additions almost every day, including interactive polls, nostalgia trips, and links to new sources of pop culture on the Web. —(L.S.)

KEY NEWSGROUP rec.arts.misc URL▶ http://www.hype.com/

Danielle Steel's Home on the Web

Danielle Steel

Jump 6899

The queen of NBC's mini-series has written 37 best-selling novels. And a click over to Ms. Steel's site lets you read the first chapters of all 37 books, starting with 1977's *Passion's Promise*, to her latest release, *Silent Honor*. Scroll through her site and you'll find that she has nine (!) children, and you'll also check out a "day in the life of Danielle Steel." Here, you can follow Ms. Steel around on one of those days, view personal photographs (including her way-cool house and antique car collection), read some exclusive online poems, and play her monthly trivia contest for your chance to win a limited edition set of her novels. —(L.T.)

KEY NEWSGROUP rec.arts.books URL▶ http://www.daniellesteel.com

▲ *Cast of the 1960s TV show "The Time Tunnel," from* Hype! International *at* Jump 2183.

Mark Twain Web Site

n/a Jump 0166

CONTENT

Mark Twain was a lover of the "high tech" of his day. In fact, he invested (and lost) most of his fortune trying to develop a newfangled automatic typesetting machine. If he were alive today, we think he'd have a lot of clever and insightful things to tell us about the Web—and we bet he'd have one heckuva Web page, too! This site, created by Mark Twain fan, Alan Eliasen features a nice selection of Twain's travel stories and other journalistic writings, plus links to the complete text of other Twain works, including full-text, Net-based online books (like *The Adventures of Tom Sawyer* and *The Adventures of Huckelberry Finn*) stored on The Guttenberg Project. —(E.G.)

URL▶ http://hydor.colorado.edu/twain/

All about Books

Bookwire: The First Place to Look Jump 1501

Bibliophiles, this is your kind of place! Stop here to find everything you want to know about books and more! These pages, updated daily, give you the latest and greatest information around, from the newest titles and authors, book reviews, online catalogs, and late-breaking book industry, to lawsuits and copyright issues for print and online publications. Find over 225 book publishers and links to library catalogs and related sources. Even Mort Gerberg gets into the act, providing cartoons related to the publishing industry. If you want to find out about your favorite book publisher, author, or even friend or relative in the biz, stop by the People Page. Here, you even get the opportunity to send in announcements, URLs, and photos of those they missed. Publishers Weekly, Bookwire's sponsor, even offers you the opportunity to subscribe to their publication online. —(H.L.)

URL▸ http://www.bookwire.com/

Tolkien Books Web Page

J.R.R. Tolkien Information Page Jump 0168 

Eric Lipper's extensive Web links page featuring scores of comprehensive text files and links of interest to devoted readers of Tolkien works such as *The Hobbit* and *The Lord of the Rings Trilogy*. It contains many Tolkien FAQs, mailing list links, links to Tolkien-based role playing games, Tolkien language links, electronic newsletters, Tolkien graphic files, fonts, and family trees. A wealth of resources for Tolkien enthusiasts! —(E.G.)

KEY NEWSGROUP rec.arts.books.tolkien URL▸ http://csclub.uwaterloo.ca/u/relipper/tolkien/rootpage.html

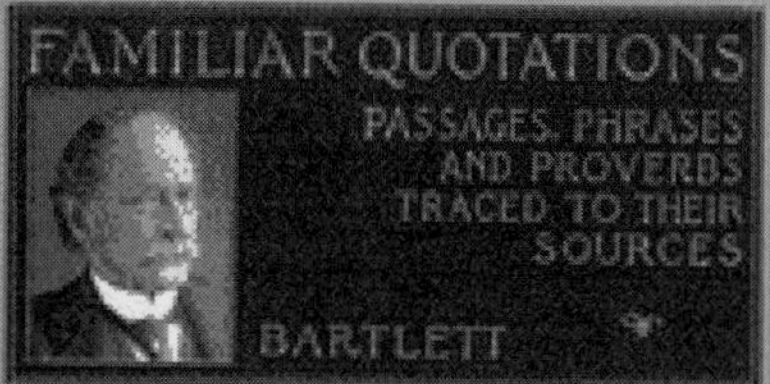

The Original Bartlett's Quotations

Bartlett, John 1901, Familiar Quotations Jump 2228 

This is an online version of the ninth, and last, edition of the original *Bartlett's Familiar Quotations*. As such, you won't find 20th-century references, but you will find most anything you need from the ancient Greeks through 19th century literature, including both the Old and New Testaments. Put online by Columbia University's Project Bartleby, you can find the quotation or passage you're looking for by browsing through the alphabetical authors' listing, or by using a keyword search. —(L.S.)

KEY NEWSGROUP alt.quotations URL▸ http://www.columbia.edu/~svl2/bartlett/

The Superior Nerd Perseveres

I-Ching Jump 2004 

The *I-Ching*, or Book of Changes, is an ancient Chinese text that strives to help one understand the forces that affect our lives and explain how "the superior man perseveres" in the face of struggle and change. Jonathon Katz has done aficionados and the curious alike a great service in letting them forego the handful of sticks or half-dozen coins needed to determine the hexagram which will disclose enlightenment in favor of a mouse click. While the commentaries are not as extensive as those in the actual book, the text used is taken from the Wilhelm/Baynes translation, considered the definitive English version of this insightful book. He also accepts submissions from those who have studied and interpreted the *I-Ching* themselves. —(L.S.)

URL▸ http://cad.ucla.edu/repository/useful/iching.html

Published Authors on the Web

Internet Directory of Published Writers Jump 2212 

If your favorite authors are online, you can find them through this database. Stephan Spencer makes it easy with alphabetical and categorical listings for browsing, or with keyword searches that will return the listings with hypertext links. Since only those writers who submit their information are included here, you can be pretty sure that if there's an e-mail link, they won't mind being contacted by fans and others interested in their work. —(L.S.)

KEY NEWSGROUP misc.writing URL▸ http://www.bocklabs.wisc.edu/ims/writers.html

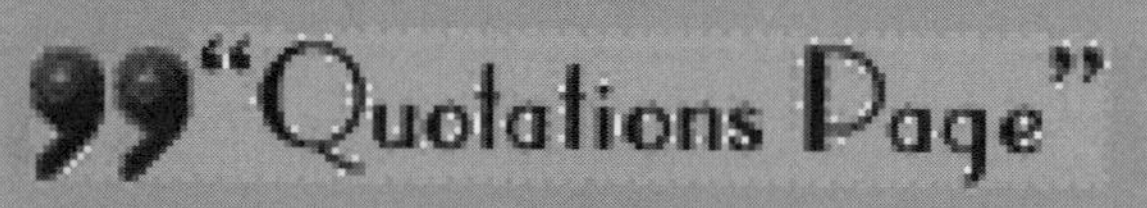

Witty & Wise Quotations

Michael Moncur's Quotations Page Jump 2253 

Michael Moncur collects quotations, mostly humorous. Here you'll find more than 1,000 of his favorites, along with a search engine to help you sort through and locate the ones of most interest to you. If you don't want to search, you can try Michael's Quotes of the Day, which randomly selects four new quotes each morning. And if you're insatiable, his random quote generator will choose three different quotes from his database each time you access it. If that's still not enough, he thoughtfully includes links to other online quotations databases, including humorous and movie quotes databases, and an FTP directory if you want quotes to go. —(L.S.)

KEY NEWSGROUP alt.quotations URL▶ http://www.xmission.com/~mgm/quotes/index.html

Quotations from All Over

Welcome to loQtus Jump 7038

Jason Newquist has assembled a quotations collection to cover almost every aspect of life. Some from arty types, some from scientific types, some from the famous, and others from the not so famous. Browse, choose and use—impress your friends and family with an apt turn of phrase. —(E.v.B.)

KEY NEWSGROUP alt.quotations URL▶ http://pubweb.ucdavis.edu/Documents/Quotations/homepage.html

Book Lovers' Web Site

BookWeb Home Page Jump 2260

People who point to the new electronic media and tut-tut that the printed book is dying rapidly need only visit sites like BookWeb to learn better. For bibliophiles who need no convincing, this informative and entertaining site gives you the latest book news straight from the American Booksellers Association. Beyond book news, there are features highlighting specific genre and topics, author interviews, regional best seller lists, and calendars of upcoming author tours and book reviews. If you like puzzles, try the monthly contest based on page content, with a bookstore gift certificate as the prize. There's an update on the state of New Media, too, but this Web site really is for those interested in "Old Media"—and it fulfills the purpose quite well!—(L.S.)

KEY NEWSGROUP alt.books.reviews URL▶ http://ambook.org/bookweb/

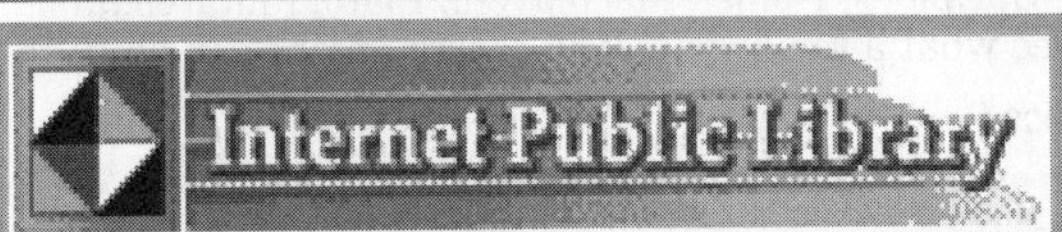

Virtual Bookstacks

The Internet Public Library Jump 2303

It's a real library, with most everything you'd expect to find at a stone and mortar library, with the possible exception of that wizened person at the desk who shushes and shoots nasty looks when you start enjoying yourself too much. Developed by the School of Information and Library Studies at the University of Michigan, you can browse here, but the best way to learn about and access the IPL's resources is to take the online tour. You'll find out about Internet training courses, special youth services and fun programs, the long list of reference links, and the library's search capabilities. For library professionals, there's also a separate section of professional development resources. —(L.S.)

KEY NEWSGROUP rec.arts.books URL▶ http://ipl.sils.umich.edu/

What If? Fiction

Usenet Alternate History List Jump 2612

What if the South had won the Civil War? What if the Nazis had won World War II? What if the Cubs hadn't choked in 1969 (Well, that may be just too fantastic!)? If you enjoy playing such what-if games, you should enjoy reading the answers in the form of alternate history, fiction that starts with the "what if" premise and tells a plausible story of how history may have changed. Robert Schmunk's list covers a wide variety of topics and genres, describing each story, essay, or novel on the list. And if your interests are more academic, there are a few good essays on alternative history writing, as well. —(L.S.)

KEY NEWSGROUP alt.history.what-if

URL▶ http://thule.mt.cs.cmu.edu:8001/sf-clearing-house/bibliographies/alternate-histories/

Vocabulary Builder

A.Word.A Day Jump 2361

Were you the kid who used to read the dictionary for fun? If so, this Web version of the A.Word.A.Day mailing list created by Anu Garg will appeal to you. Each day, a new word, its definition, and usage commentary is posted here. The list's archives are here, too, so if one word a day isn't enough, you'll have months and months to browse through, cogitate upon, and winnow the hours. —(L.S.)

KEY NEWSGROUP alt.usage.english URL▶ http://www.wordsmith.org/awad/

Language References & Fonts

Yamada Language Guides Jump 2426

This site, created by the Yamada Language Center of the University of Oregon, combines language guides and references with an archive of non-English language fonts. Close to 100 languages are referenced here, organized alphabetically and geographically. And no matter where you start with a language, each page includes links to other pages on this site, or the Net, covering that language. There are fonts for both Windows and Macintosh computers, although there are more for the Mac. Each font page includes a sample and tips for using them, and there also are tips for representing a language without a special font with the standard English keyboard. Topping it off is an annotated listing of language-related Net newsgroups that includes all available newsgroups for each specific language. —(L.S.)

KEY NEWSGROUP sci.lang URL▶ http://babel.uoregon.edu/yamada/guides.html

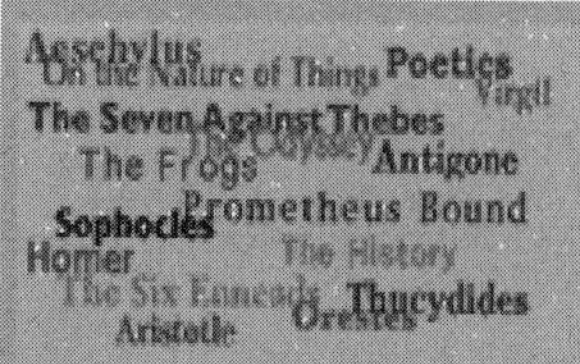

Search the Classics

The Tech Classics Jump 2430

You can find online texts of classic literature at various sites around the Internet. But what if you're looking for a specific topic within the text? Researchers, term-paper writers, arguers, and anyone else looking for specific citations now have the means to do so with the outstanding search engine at this site. Written by Dan Stevenson, a student at Massachusetts Institute of Technology, you can search classic texts by whole or partial keywords using Boolean operators. A variety of works by 17 authors are here, including Aeschylus, Aristotle, Euripides, Homer, Machiavelli, Plato, Plutarch, and Virgil. Even if you don't care about the writing, stop by and see what a really good Web search engine can do.—(L.S.)

KEY NEWSGROUP sci.classics URL▶ http://the-tech.mit.edu/Classics/

Frodo Lives!

The Hypertextualized Tolkien FAQ Jump 2432

Bilbo Baggins, the wizard Gandalf, and the other personalities, races, and happenings of Middle-Earth, and the locale for J.R.R. Tolkien's tales of fantasy and adventure are the basis for most all of today's warriors-and-wizards-type fantasy fiction and role-playing games. And no matter how good today's offerings are, Tolkien remains the master. To help fellow fans get the most out of the books, Niels Olof Bouvin created this HTML version of the Tolkien FAQ, the definitive reader's reference on the Net. You'll be able to learn more about Tolkien and his works, the various inhabitants of Middle-Earth, and the history of this unique world. It's all very well organized, with internal links within each section to aid navigation. And what would a FAQ page be without links to related sites? Incomplete, and this page isn't! The links list is very comprehensive making this the main bookmark for any Tolkien fan. —(L.S.)

KEY NEWSGROUP rec.arts.books.tolkien URL▶ http://www.daimi.aau.dk/~bouvin/tolkienfaq.html

Douglas Adams Fans' Information Site

The Douglas Adams Worship Page Jump 4047

Nathan Hughes brings you this site devoted to information on popular science fiction/fantasy author Douglas Adams. Adams' "Hitchhiker's Guide to the Galaxy" and it follow-ups have garnered him an active and large following, and this site is proof. You can get FAQ's, other works by Adams, related documents, fan club information, and more here. —(R.B.)

KEY NEWSGROUP alt.fan.douglas-adams URL▶ http://www.umd.umich.edu:80/~nhughes/dna/

Antiquarian Books

ABAA booknet/rmharris ltd Jump 5118

The Antiquarian Booksellers' Association of America's Web site features links to 448 U.S. booksellers, 75 of whom are already online. Here you can search by specialty and location, access online catalogs and other bookseller services, check

out the ABAA Newsletter, and link to library catalogs worldwide. There's also a list of book fairs around the country. The online research and book information is among the most extensive available anywhere on the Web. —(S.B.)

URL ▶ http://www.abaa-booknet.com/

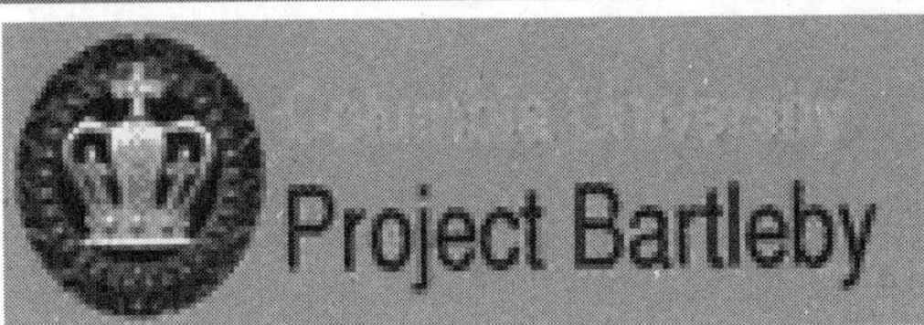

Great Classics of Literature on the Web

Project Bartleby 
Jump 5047

This ever-expanding project is a great literary source. "The Public Library of The Internet" features some great books that have been translated to online life. Such classics as *Leaves of Grass* by Walt Whitman, *Poems* by Oscar Wilde, and *Bartleby The Scrivener* by Herman Melville are featured here, online. There are also the presidential addresses of every president from George Washington to George Bush. You may also listen to a recorded welcome and there is a way to search for info as well. —(S.B.)

URL ▶ http://www.cc.columbia.edu/~svl2/index.html

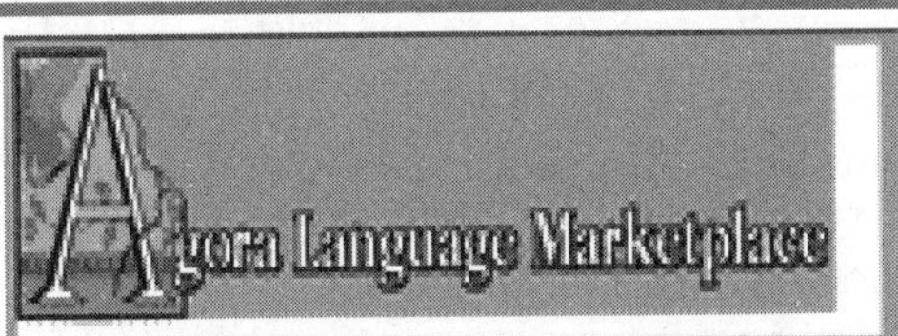

Linguistic Help

Agora Language Marketplace Jump 5049 

Agora is a buyer's guide for language materials and a source of information for language professionals. Selections include a publishers' directory, Agora Publishing Group listing, language schools and study abroad, calendar information, professional workshops, events, and employment information. There are links to receive their newsletter, weekly updates on their top features, and a study abroad section—especially useful if you want to go to school overseas. —(S.B.)

URL ▶ http://www.agoralang.com:2410/

A Thought a Day

The Commonplace Book Jump 7203 

If you like to collect striking quotes, this is the place for you. This page is an electronic version of the often intensely personal collection of quotes, originally called commonplace books, that we have all made at some time in our lives. It's wonderful to browse: Hunter Thompson on deadlines, Jack London on the search of soul, Gene Wolfe on sanity, Borges on dying, and on and on. You are encouraged to submit your favorites—so don't be shy, dig out those old notebooks! —(E.v.B.)

KEY NEWSGROUP **alt.quotations** URL ▶ http://sunsite.unc.edu/ibic/Commonplace-Book.html

How to Get Your Book Published

CROW Story and Idea Exchange Jump 1511 COMMERCE

How many times have you started your great American novel? If you've finished it, how do you contact the right publisher? Or, if you're a publisher, how do you manage that "slush pile" of writer submissions? Kevin McCarthy of Capsule Reviews of Original Work, or CROW, and artist Donna Tellam, have designed a Web site to put you in touch with book publishers and agents. It also tells you how to get your book reviewed so those publishers will accept it. As "a conduit for interaction, it shows you how make the manuscript selection process less subjective, and thus offers new hope for unknown talent." These pages, replete with interesting graphics and well-written, gimmick-free copy, offer tidbits and advice for first-time authors to efficiently improve their work. You can also sign up for CROW's newsletter, which includes example reviews and quarterly publishing news, and read what authors and publishers have said about the service. A novel approach to promoting a better understanding between writers, editors, agents, and producers. —(H.L.)

URL ▶ http://www.boms.com/crow/crow.html

Peter McWilliams

Peter McWilliams' Books Site

Prelude Press Jump 5907

Peter McWilliams is not only the author and self-publisher of one of the first and most successful computer books ever written (*The Personal Computer Book*), but he must surely be one of the first to offer full-text—and free—versions of his latest books on his Web site. You may be wondering why any sane publisher would offer their books for free. Well, as he explains here, perhaps if you read one of his books and enjoy it, maybe you'll consider buying one of his other books. Not a bad idea, and it's made even more appealing by the full range of subjects available. His titles include *Hypericum & Depression*, *Ain't Nobody's Business If You Do* (*The Absurdity of Consensual Crimes in Our Free Country*), and *How to Survive the Loss of a Love*. Each title here is also fully searchable, and you can find out how to order the books, through bookstores or through McWilliams' own publishing company, Prelude Press. —(J.P.)

URL ▸ http://www.mcwilliams.com/

Browse & Buy Bookstore

Dial-A-Book Chapter One Jump 2256

COMMERCE

Visit this site to read the tables of contents, first chapters, and other excerpts of selected special-interest books, with a few reviews thrown in for good measure. The emphasis is on Internet-related general-interest computer titles, and children's books, but new areas—and books—are added regularly. If you like what you see, you can even order online, although the service is free. —(L.S.)

KEY NEWSGROUP **alt.books.reviews** URL ▸ http://www.psi.net:80/ChapterOne/

Book Stop

Bookport Jump 4505

COMMERCE

If you like books at all, this is a great starting point. Not only does it feature books you can preview online, but also those you can order and download completely online, at significant discount, saving paper—both on the shelf and in your wallet. This site also includes links out to lots of other book-related and publishing sites on the Net. Like a well-thumbed book, this site is one you'll want to return to. —(T.W.)

URL ▸ http://www.bookport.com/welcome/aba

Comics & Graphic Novels

An Interesting Philosophy of Life

Mister Boffo Home Page

Jump 2740

If you've never seen Joe Martin's Mr. Boffo comic strips, you're in for a real treat. Provided, of course, you appreciate a skewed and slightly off-center perspective on life. From the pithy sayings on the Boffo's T-shirts that open the Sunday strips to the daily strips that are something akin to The Far Side meets The Honeymooners, there's nothing quite like Mr. Boffo—unless you count Willy 'n Ethel, another Martin strip that is promised to appear on this page, too. In the meantime, check in for a daily strip, or browse the growing archive of Mr. Boffos, dating back to 1988. —(L.S.)

KEY NEWSGROUP **rec.arts.comic.strips** URL ▸ http://www.wise-net.com/users/boffo/boffo.htm

30th Century Superheroes

The Legion of Super Heroes Jump 2588

If you're a fan of the Legion of Super Heroes or the 30th century version of DC Comics' Justice League of America, you must at least visit this site, if not make it your home on the Web. Vernon Harmon will give you the FAQs, give you a separate Legion Who's Who and events timeline, and link you to Omnicom, an online discussion list for fans, and its archives. Oddly, there aren't any images available here, but there is a link to a Legion-dedicated MUSH, where you can connect and act out your fantasies. —(L.S.)

KEY NEWSGROUP rec.arts.comics URL▶ http://www.cs.cmu.edu/afs/cs/user/vernon/www/lsh.html

Comics, Comics, Comics!

United Media Jump 7481

CONTENT

Admit it, you just love the Sunday comics. Well, here at United Media every day is Sunday. This site bills itself as "the Web's largest collection of comic strips and editorial cartoons." You can read our favorite, Dilbert, or check out Peanuts or Nancy, or enjoy the biting satire of the editorial cartoonists also featured here. A great way to start or end the work day! —(E.v.B.)

KEY NEWSGROUP rec.arts.comics.strips URL▶ http://www.unitedmedia.com/UM_home.html

The One, the Only... Migraine Boy!

MIGRAINE BOY Jump 7275

Migraine Boy is quite the animated fellow, who finds himself in many strange and amusing situations. You can see, read, and hear Greg Fiering's sometimes-whimsical, but sorta bizarre comic strip creations at this site. Listen to the characters speak by using the RealAudio Player program that Fiering so handily provides the link to. You can also read Fiering's "entertainment weekly" and hear music and other sound files he has selected for his visitors. Worth a visit just to see Migraine Boy's arms flap up and down. —(E.v.B.)

KEY NEWSGROUP rec.art.comics.strips URL▶ http://www.visualradio.com/migraineboy/

Krazy Kat Revisited

Coconino County Index Jump 7392

For Peter Wadsworth, the Krazy Kat comic strip, drawn by George Herriman, was one of the most imaginative works ever produced in comicdom. Set in Coconino County, the strip, to Peter, is "a wondrous poetic landscape, only somewhatsurreal. . . a twisted utopia, where love is bittersweet and often misunderstood." Come to these pages and share Peter's delight. You can browse in the Krazy Kat art gallery, read all about Herriman, and about the comic strip. You can also surf to other comic strip sites that Peter has collected for you. —(E.v.B.)

KEY NEWSGROUP rec.arts.comics.strips URL▶ http://www.krazy.com/start.htm

Political Satire, Hong Kong Style

The World of Lily Wong Jump 7393

The World of Lily Wong is a satirical comic strip created by an American cartoonist, Larry Feign, who lives in Hong Kong. It revolves around Lily Wong, a secretary. However, its focus is romance, culture clashes, and Hong Kong politics—especially involving the strip's political swipes against Hong Kong's impending takeover by the communist Chinese government. You can read the daily strip and access past strips. You can also read excerpts from the book, Quotations from Lily Wong, and other Feign creations. And don't worry if you don't understand the Hong Kong references—Feign has provided a glossary.—(E.v.B.)

KEY NEWSGROUP soc.culture.hongkong URL▶ http://www.asiaonline.net/lilywong.html

Comics Galore

WebComics Daily Jump 7201

The Who's Who of Net-published comic strips have been brought together by David de Vitry on this site. You can amuse yourself with the daily strips, such as Plato's Public, Kev's World, Strange Matter, and, of course, Dilbert, one of the first strips published on the Net. David also maintains a page for comics that only appear weekly. Aspiring Net comic strip artists can apply to have their comic art displayed here as well. Be warned—these pages take quite a while to download, because David has mounted the comics on one continuous Web page. —(E.v.B.)

KEY NEWSGROUP **rec.arts.comics.info** URL▶ http://www.eg.bucknell.edu/~devitry/comics.html

Cyber Espionage Thriller!

Cracks in the Web Jump 7439

Cracks in the Web, created by Jack Teetor and Guy Morris, is a weekly espionage thriller featuring Flap Jack and his band of hardy helpers. NASA, the White House, the Internet, the Pentagon—hey, we could go on and on—are all twisted and woven into the plot. Why not just surf over and follow the thrills and chills that accompany each new illustrated episode. Not for the faint of heart. —(E.v.B.)

KEY NEWSGROUP **misc.writing** URL▶ http://www.directnet.com./~gmorris/

Everybody's Favorite Geek: Dilbert

The Dilbert Zone Jump 2384

Anyone forced to deal with corporate (mis)managers, incompetent coworkers, or pets smarter than they are, will see something of their lives in the daily saga of Dilbert. Scott Adams maintains this page himself, and it features the same sense of humor, heavily laced with the same sense of irony, as that found in his strip. In addition to a daily dose of Dilbert, Dogbert, and Company, you'll also be able to learn more about the strip's characters, read the Dilbert Newsletter, join Dogbert's New Ruling Class, and dip into the archives and other aspects of Dilbertmania and Adams' life which are as entertaining as the comic itself. —(L.S.)

KEY NEWSGROUP **rec.arts.comics.strips** URL▶ http://www.unitedmedia.com/comics/dilbert/

(Image copyright by Peter Bagge)

The Sunday Funnies, All Day, Every Day

The Comic Book and Comic-Strip Page Jump 7088

Martin Ward obviously is a connoisseur of the comic book. His Web page is chock full of the best offerings of contemporary electronically published comic books and strips. Love Superguy, Tank Girl, and Dilbert? You'll find them here, keeping company with other comic characters such as Hong Kong Annie, and Poison Elves. Need more? Then check out Ward's information on the latest conventions, newsgroups, and the best offerings from European artists. —(E.v.B.)

KEY NEWSGROUP **rec.arts.comics.misc** URL▶ http://dragon.acadiau.ca/~860099w/comics/comics.html

Cartoons & Kids' Stuff

The Cyber Disney World

Disney.com Jump 7497

Can't get enough of Mickey and Minney? Disney's monster commercial site presents, in tabloid form, all you want to know about the latest events at Disney theme parks, new movie and music releases, and home video releases of classic Disney films. As well, you can dive into a sea of news and information on records, software, Disney television schedules, what's new at the Disney store, and access this site's most useful feature, an extensive overview of nearly everything you'd need to know before visiting any Disney theme park —(E.v.B.)

KEY NEWSGROUP **rec.arts.disney** URL▶ http://www2.disney.com/static/News/docs/HM_T/home.html

Internet Fun—Family-Style

SPECTRUM: The Family Internet Magazine Jump 8008

Here's an engaging, well-designed, lively e-zine for the whole family. Take your pick—do your children enjoy comics, puzzles, or

clip art? Or, would they prefer poetry, interactive stories, illustrated capsule biographies of famous people who've made a difference, and fun printout activities? They're all here—and so visually inviting! Parents will enjoy the resources posted by Spectrum: video and book reviews, links to educational resources, music online, humor and essays on the trials and joys of daily living. —(E.v.B.)

KEY NEWSGROUP misc.kids

URL▸ http://www.autobaun.com/~kbshaw/Spectrum.html

Learning Can Be a Blast

Knowledge Adventure Jump 5807 CONTENT

KnowledgeLand is an exciting world created just for kids, the sort of place on the Web where you can let them explore on their own without worry that they might encounter something you'd rather they hadn't. Created to promote Knowledge Adventure's line of JumpStart educational software titles, there's plenty here that's fun for kids beyond the promotional aspect of this site. Kids taking part can pick a fun, imaginary character to represent them, and have them walk through either the JumpStart Grad School campus or this site's online amusement park. They can even talk to other kids using a synthetic voice, while collecting "Knowledge Cards" along the way. The entire site integrates the core components of elementary education, allowing kids to learn while they have fun. And the best part of all is they'll be learning while they play! —(J.P.)

URL▸ http://www.adventure.com/

▲ *Big cow hot air balloon, from* **Cyberspace World Railroad Home Page** *at* Jump **2119**.

Kid'n Around

Kid'n Around: An E-Zine for Kids

Kid'n Around Jump 5821 

They say they aren't just kidding around, but Kid'n Around is a great place for kids to enjoy themselves—and learn a little, too. The Web version of the print publication by the same name, this site is easy to navigate and quick to load. And the content is great, too, with short editorial features like "Big Ideas," to projects that kids can do at home, book reviews and more. A site that's easy for kids to digest, but that never speaks down to them. —(J.P.)

URL▸ http://www.kidnaround.com/

KidsNet Kids' Spot

KidsNet Jump 5645 

Warning: If you let your children visit this site it might be weeks before you can pry them away from it! This is truly a Kids Net on its own, a wonderfully organized site where fun is the only game in town. For starters, kids can click on a Rastakan character, or the mushroom, and be transported to a surprise spot. Or they can join in Super's Studio, home of art by and for kids. Next up...Bamboozle's "must-read" booklist, and the software loft. Paradox's Puzzle has games and puzzles, and there's even a place where kids can send or read mail from other kids. —(J.P.)

URL▸ http://www.ponyshow.com/kidsnet/website.htm

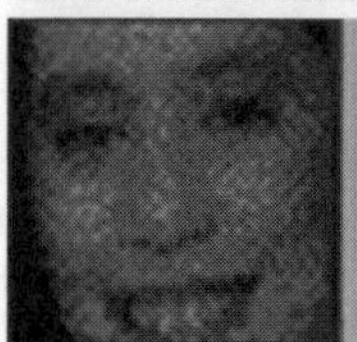

Go Susan!

Susan's World Wide Web Page Jump 3742 

Susan Kraft, at the age of 11, is quite possibly one of the youngest publishers on the Web. Her Web page is filled with charming and well-written stories, essays, and poems, as well as "The Image Times," her own Web publication. Filled with interesting anecdotes, facts, stories, and jokes ("What kind of meal do Barbies like to have? A Barbie-que!"), Susan has done a terrific job here—have your kids stop by and show their support! —(N.F.)

URL▸ http://www.newc.com/susan/

Frogs on the Web

Froggy Page Jump 6012

Sandra "Froggy" Loosemore knows an awful lot about frogs. So much so, in fact, that if you stop by her Froggy Page, you'll be surrounded by everything from froggy pictures to Songs of the Frog, and everything in between. Our favorite—Frogs on Ice, a compilation of pictures showing these froggy friends doing some intricate moves on skates. There's also a big collection of sounds, stories, and a great list of links to other sites. It's ALL here—make this your first stop for all your frog-related needs! —(N.F.)

URL▸ http://www.cs.yale.edu/homes/sjl/froggy.html

Virtual Sandbox

Jackson's Page For Five Year Olds! Jump 7374 

What a great Internet playground for five-year-olds has been created here! And who should know better what sites will appeal to that age group than Jackson himself—a five-year-old! Lots of fun pictures of the solar system and other neat stuff, a Goofy movie, an interactive story, lots of Lego information, and—a real crowd-pleaser for anyone in the single-digit age set—a visit to a dinosaur museum, complete with pictures, sounds and movies! Despite its creator's age, this site demonstrates what anyone likes to see on the Web: great graphics, appealing page layouts, and solid content. Way to go, Jackson! —(E.v.B.)

KEY NEWSGROUP misc.kids URL▸ http://www2.islandnet.com/~bedford/jackson.html

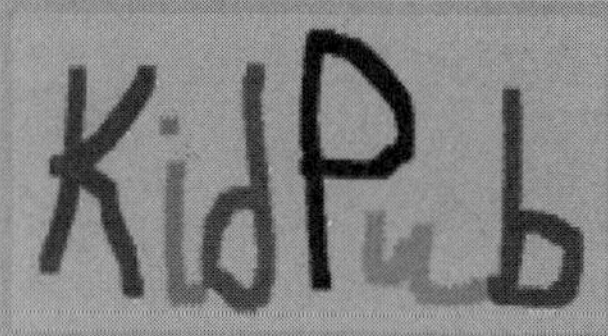

Stories by and for Children

KidPub WWW Publishing Jump 2230 

Budding young writers now have their own place to publish—provided they are very young writers. If your children have written any stories, fiction or non-fiction, just e-mail them to KidPub. They'll format and put them on this Web page, and you can watch your children's eyes light up when they see their names and their words in print. For non-writers, just reading the stories here can be a lot of fun, since children don't very often have the opportunity to read stories written by their peers. —(L.S.)

KEY NEWSGROUP k12.lang.art URL▸ http://www.en-garde.com/kidpub/

 Carlos' Coloring Book Home

Coloring Book Web Site for Kids

Carlos' Coloring Book Home Jump 2239 

This online coloring book is great fun for kids, and grownups, too. Carlos Pero has adapted pictures from Jim Allison's Coloring Book 2.0 for the Macintosh, and lets you choose colors and apply them with a simple point-and-click. There are two versions of the coloring book, and one of them lets you apply colors to multiple areas and process them as a batch, making it ideal for those with slower connections. When you're finished, you can download your picture as a GIF or Postscript file, print it out, and tape it to the refrigerator door. —(L.S.)

KEY NEWSGROUP misc.kids URL▸ http://robot0.ge.uiuc.edu/~carlosp/color/

▲ *A monoclonius yearling, undoubtedly the cutest dinosaur that ever lived, from* **Dinosaur Society** *at* Jump **5878**.

Fun Port

Theodore Tugboat Jump **2254**

CONTENT

Welcome to the home page of Theodore Tugboat, the Canadian TV series about a "cheerful tugboat who likes to be friends with everyone." And this site is about as cheerful as you are likely to find. There is something here for everyone—parents, teachers and kids alike. The kids will love the coloring book and the interactive story, where they can help Theodore decide what to do next. Or they can get their parents to fill out a form to receive a real postcard from Theodore. And for the parents, details of some of the shows, and descriptions of the characters (there are 30 of them!) as well some behind-the-scenes news. And don't forget to check out the links to over 400 kids sites! —(J.P.)

KEY NEWSGROUP **rec.misc** URL▶ http://www.cochran.com/tt.html

Rainy-Day Site for Kids

early childhood.com
Jump **6881**

CONTENT

Jump here and browse timely advice and tips from childhood experts with Earlychildhood.com's insightful articles covering such topics as the bilingual classroom, and whether computers really belong in early childhood settings. A visit to the site also lets you expand your family's collection of rainy-day projects. You'll find complete kid-readable instructions on how-to make grocery sack backpacks, "udder art," and handprint paperweights. —(L.T.)

KEY NEWSGROUP **misc.kids** URL▶ http://www.earlychildhood.com

CyberCrayons

Crayola * Crayola * Crayola * Crayola Jump 7373

COMMERCE

Did you know that paraffin wax, the basic ingredient of Crayola crayons, has to be heated to 240 degrees Fahrenheit to start the process? No? Well, you'll be an expert on crayon-making once you've surfed through this delightful kid's site. You discover facts about crayons you never knew and learn some crayon history. Kids will enjoy exploring the fun links provided here, as well as reading the online version of *Crayola Magazine*, and competing in contests. Although the site is designed for kids, grownups will also enjoy the colorful graphics, the stain removal tips, and—just for the kid in all of us—a contest for adults. You can enter a drawing, using crayons of course, of a memorable childhood moment and win large money prizes. Something for the whole family here. —(E.v.B.)

KEY NEWSGROUP **misc.creativity** URL▸ http://www.crayola.com/crayola/home.html

Kidland Kid's Activity Site

Kidland: The Webbie Web! Jump 6607

CONTENT

Here are some of the safest and most entertaining sites children can explore for their after-school or rainy-day enjoyment. Leap around with Webbie the Frog from site to site at Kidland, a comprehensive collection of kids' sites full of cartoons, games and software. Webbie will guide your children to the latest kid's music events in your area of the country, or to TeenNet Magazine, a computer and music publication written by teens. If your children are up for a challenge, they can play their favorite board games online, and access a special resource section for parents. You'll also find publications like Children with Diabetes, an e-zine for kids, parents and families living with juvenile diabetes. —(L.T.)

KEY NEWSGROUP **misc.kids** URL▸ http://www.kidland.com/

Kid's Activity Area on the Web

KidsCom Jump 2436

This virtual playground and Internet exploration area is designed specifically for children ages eight to twelve. Children can find penpals, play a fun and educational geography game, or just "talk" with other kids about their favorite (or unfavorite) things. There's a Graffiti Wall, where kids can exercise their creativity through one-line messages of any sort, and it's also monitored to ensure that nothing inappropriate for children appears. There also are links to other children's pages on the Web, and a question-and-answer section where kids can learn more about the Internet from net legend Scott Yanoff. It's all good, clean fun for kids, and an excellent blend of entertainment, education, and interaction. —(L.S.)

KEY NEWSGROUP **misc.kids.computer** URL▸ http://www.spectracom.com:80/kidscom/

Animaniacs: Everything You Ever Wanted to Know!

The Animaniacs Page Jump 3504

CONTENT

If you're a fan of Steven Spielberg's wild and wonderful Animaniacs, here's a Web site for you! It's loaded with lyrics, sound files, reviews, character lists, and the ultimate "Pinky, are you pondering what I'm pondering" list—not to mention pointers to additional pages that specialize in Animaniacs graphics and ASCII images, the FAQ, and related mailing lists, as well as to the related newsgroup, **alt.tv.animaniacs**. Compiled by Stewart Clamen, a Ph.D. candidate at Carnegie Mellon University, is just the thing for the rapidly-growing group of adults who can't pry themselves away from these cartoons. —(C.P.)

KEY NEWSGROUP **alt.tv.animaniacs**

URL▸ http://www.cs.cmu.edu:8001/afs/cs.cmu.edu/user/clamen/misc/tv/Animaniacs/Animaniacs.html

Fun & Games for Kids Online

Radio Aahs Online Jump 7351

Radio Aahs Online is just for kids—and what fun it is! Great graphics, jazzy colors and designs that appeal to the younger set. Kids can read interviews with popular personalities, check out lists of fun events for children in different U.S. cities, participate in an interactive story, figure out puzzles, and browse through fun facts. Radio Aahs is part of the huge Time Warner Pathfinder site, which houses one of the largest collections of news and entertainment publications and Web sites related to them. —(E.v.B.)

KEY NEWSGROUP misc.kids.computer URL▸ http://pathfinder.com/

Teen Girls' Web Zine

Foxy! Jump 7401

Foxy is the Web magazine for teenaged girls who think that print teen magazines like *Sassy* just aren't cool enough. Read about what boys really like, read interviews with movie stars, rock singers and models, skateboarders and snowboarders, and enjoy the really neat graphics. Fashion tips, daily horoscopes, and hot links to other Web pages of interest to the teen girl are also provided here. —(E.v.B.)

KEY NEWSGROUP alt.kids-talk URL▸ http://tumyeto.com/tydu/foxy/foxy.htm

Web Hangout for Teens

YaZone Home Page Jump 2437

Teenagers can find their voices at this site, produced by the same people who bring KidsCom to the Web for eight-to-twelve-year-olds. The YaZone is similar in concept, but concentrates on helping younger people connect and share with their peer group. Teens can find Net-pals, learn about the latest music and entertainment, and keep up on other news that affects their lives. There's also a section that lets teens speak out on whatever issues are on their minds, as well as a list of links to other Web sites of interest to this age group. —(L.S.)

KEY NEWSGROUP misc.computer.kids URL▸ http://www.spectracom.com:80/yazone/

Games: General & Video

Video Gamer's Web Spot

Video GameSpot Jump 5875

Some sites sneak up on you quietly and others come screaming around the corner and hit you smack in the face. Video GameSpot is a face-smacking kind of place. It's like a pinball game gone mad. Or the Las Vegas of the video game world. Which is the whole idea, of course. Bright lights and lots of things to do with your hands. But we digress; the bright lights threw us off. Playstation, Nintendo 64, and Saturn news. Game patches, new releases, upcoming software, tips, cheats and more. Everything for hard-core video gamers. You'll find it all here. —(J.P.)

KEY NEWSGROUP rec.games.video.arcade URL▸ http://www.videogamespot.com/

video games games (video)

Computers and Video Games News & Chat

Next Generation Online Jump 5908

Here's a great online version of a great print magazine dedicated to the world of computer and video games. The information here is updated daily, so you're sure to find the latest information on all the hot titles, including all they hype and glory from Nintendo 64 and PlayStation. Fans will enjoy the multitude of tips and reviews of the latest hardware and software, and everyone is welcome to take part in the many contests. There's also a new demo every day, as well as chat forums and dozens of great links. —(J.P.)

KEY NEWSGROUP rec.games.video.arcade URL▸ http://www.next-generation.com/

The Baseball Challenge

Bullpen Ace - The Baseball Trivia Game
Jump 6017 CONTENT

Think you know baseball? Test your knowledge by trying this addictive site. The score is tied in the last inning, and you must come in as the closer to pitch the last inning to save the game. You'll answer some tough trivia questions, and each correct answer gets the batter out. If you give up just one run, you've lost the game. To make it even more exciting, there are real prizes for those who can win the most consecutive games. But beware—you're up against some real heavyweight competition here, and you'll find you can't stay away! —(N.F.)

KEY NEWSGROUP **alt.sports.baseball** URL▶ http://www.dtd.com/ace/

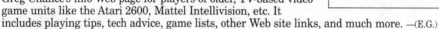

▲ *Argon Zark comic adventure, from* **Cracks in the Web** *at* Jump **7439**.

Classic Video Game Players' Page

Classic Video Games Home Page Jump **0094** CONTENT

Greg Chance's info Web page for players of older, TV-based video game units like the Atari 2600, Mattel Intellivision, etc. It includes playing tips, tech advice, game lists, other Web site links, and much more. —(E.G.)

KEY NEWSGROUP **rec.games.video.classic** URL▶ http://www2.ecst.csuchico.edu/~gchance/

Seeing Double?

The Official Magic Eye Home Page
Jump **7248** 

This is a pretty slick site devoted to the production of 3-D images popularized by the Magic Eye book fad. Many of the images featured on this site are stereograms—two images that magically (given the health of your optic nerve) meld into one in the back of the brain. Magic Eye hosts the creations of a number of 3-D artists around the world who can compete for monthly prizes. As well, you can read all about custom 3-D programs, buy reference works on the techniques, and access a host of other graphic information devoted to 3-D graphic production. —(E.v.B.)

KEY NEWSGROUP **alt.3d** URL▶ http://www.tiac.net/magiceye/

Football Trivia

Two Minute Warning, the NFL Trivia Game
Jump **7321** CONTENT

So, you think you know a lot of stats and facts connected with the National Football League? Well, link over here. Billed as the "NFL trivia challenge," this site lets you answer trivia questions to gain yards, score points, and compete for prizes such as autographed player photos. As well, you might even win a ride in the Goodyear Blimp if you win the Goodyear Scavenger Hunt. Check in every month and play a new game. —(E.v.B.)

KEY NEWSGROUP **rec.sport.football.pro** URL▶ http://www.dtd.com/tmw/

Win, Win, Win!!!

Wintertime WebStakes Jump **5845** CONTENT

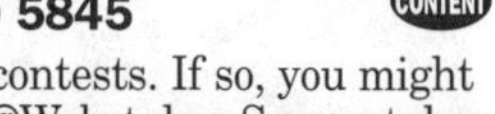

Feeling lucky? No, we mean with contests. If so, you might want to drop into the WinterTime@Webstakes Sweepstakes (what a mouthful!) and register to win, win, win. So how do you do it? Simple. There are a half-dozen prize categories each day, including BizStakes, LeisureStakes, SportStakes, and TravelStakes. If you want to try for the big prize, all you have to do is visit any of the qualifying sites, pick out the prize you want, and click on the "I-was-here" button. Sound easy? It *is* easy, and lots of fun too. And the best part is that you only have to register once and then you can try your luck every day. —(J.P.)

KEY NEWSGROUP **rec.gambling.lottery** URL▶ http://www.webstakes.com/

Internet Games! Cash Prizes!

Riddler Jump 7340 

Riddler, a Net-based entertainment network, has set up a series of online games you can play to win cash and prizes while exploring the Web. You play to build your "networth," on which the cash awards and prizes are based. So, pump up your competitive spirit and choose a game: TORTOISE and the HARE—150 trivia questions every week; MARLOW'S CRISPY CHALLENGE—Three new puzzles every day; QUIBBLER—If you don't know the answer, you're sent out on a journey through the Web searching for clues; RIDDLER'S CHOICE 10K—A race involving some of the most exciting sites on the Web. —(E.v.B.)

KEY NEWSGROUP **alt.cyberspace** URL▶ http://www.riddler.com/gameboard.html

Click and Win

Prizes.com Jump 5888 

Want to win up to $1 million? Instantly? Well, we can't guarantee you'll win, of course (we'd be the first in line if we could), but you might want to take your chances here at prizes. com. Newbies can click choose among the games offered. There's the $1 million game, another called "Incognito" (be the first to answer a question using clues), and "Click and Win," where you win a prize if you're the first to click on a particular pixel in a picture. There's also "Blackjack," a TV trivia contest, and much more. —(J.P.)

KEY NEWSGROUP **rec.gambling.lottery** URL▶ http://prizes.com/

Deal the Cards!

Blackjack Jump 7387 

Gamblers and other high rollers enter the Blackjack Emporium and play blackjack as you've never played before. Enjoy a virtual drink while you gloat over the virtual money you win. You will be accompanied by a cast of characters including Vinnie the Dealer, Rocco the Pit Boss, and Lenny the Loser. Don't worry if you don't know the jargon, because creators George Hockley and Matt Judson also provide a blackjack FAQ where you can look up all those inside blackjack terms, like "burn card." After you play blackjack here, using the neat program developed by Hockley and Judson, you can link to other venues such as the Virtual Vegas site. Go on, take a flyer! —(E.v.B.)

KEY NEWSGROUP **rec.gambling** URL▶ http://engr.sfsu.edu/cgi-bin/bjp

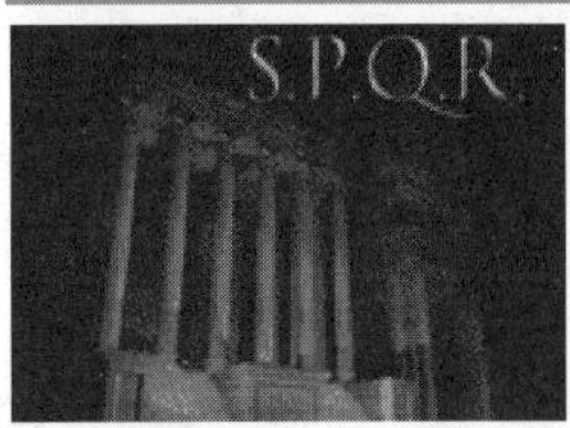

Virtual Rome

S. P. Q. R. The Quest Begins Jump 7413 

Ave! Fellow Romans—or you will be when you play the interactive quest game, S.P.Q.R, located in classical Rome and produced by CyberSites, Inc. Play a few rounds accompanied by characters Lucius, Verania, Calamitus, Sibyl, and Gordian and see if you don't get hooked! And keep coming back, because CyberSites plans to create an online community around S.P.Q.R., offering "citizenship" of Virtual Rome and special events, chat forums, and a gift shop. —(E.v.B.)

KEY NEWSGROUP **rec.arts.int-fiction** URL▶ http://pathfinder.com/

Cardiff's Video Game Database Browser

Video Game Info: Cardiff's Video Game Database

n/a Jump 0093 

An enormous video game information center created by the same folks who developed the equally enormous Cardiff's Movie Database, this site is a "must" first stop for video gamers of every stripe. It is full of keyword-searchable tips, tricks, and strategies for all TV and PC-based video games, FAQ files, and many links to other popular video gamer's Web sites. —(E.G.)

KEY NEWSGROUP **rec.games.video.misc** URL▶ http://www.cm.cf.ac.uk:/Games/

Follow the Leader

Oh No! The Lemmings Games Web Page Jump 1529

These are not your typical lemmings, but cute, imp-like, green-haired, featureless animated characters in the very popular Lemmings computer game, aimed at young children through college age adults. Your goal? Save as many lemmings as you can by helping them on their journey. Site creator Austrian Thomas Linder believes this 10-level game is highly addictive, "and once one starts to play it, it can be very difficult to stop." These pages detail the passwords, hidden levels, and strategies that will make you an expert. From these pages, you can download one of many versions of the game, demos, solutions, and "cheats." If you're still not satisfied, there are hundreds of Lemmings resources, links to other Lemming games and domains, newsletters, and even stories. Don't miss the collection of Lemming photos: at the beach, conducting traffic, with a haircut, and even Grandpa Lemming. If you get hooked, well, there's always the Lemming newsgroup, where you can discuss your progress with fellow Lemmingites. —(H.L.)

KEY NEWSGROUP **alt.lemmings** URL▶ http://stud1.tuwien.ac.at/~e8826423/Lemmings.html

Game Hints, Cheats, Patches, & More

Happy Puppy Software Games Onramp Cheats Page Jump 2338

The folks at Happy Puppy Software turn gaming frustration to gaming fun with this page of hints, tips, and outright cheats for the more popular computer and video games. Strategy games like Civilization and SimCity, role-playing games like Ultima, shoot-em-ups like Doom and TIE Fighter, plus video extravaganzas like Mortal Kombat and NASCAR Racer are just a few of the games covered here, with more being added every few days. You'll also find links to hints and cheats pages of other gamers, links to game FAQs and patches from the gamemakers, and even links to games you can play on the Web. All together, it makes an essential bookmark for both the serious gamer and the novice. —(L.S.)

KEY NEWSGROUP **rec.games.misc** URL▶ http://www.misha.net/~pup/

The Riddler Home Page

Win Cash at the Riddler Page Jump 3616

Riddler is the first interactive game on the Internet to offer cash prizes to players. Really! The game combines elements of trivia, scavenger hunts, and an online road rally through the Web. It's great fun, and offers great prizes! —(C.P.)

KEY NEWSGROUP **bit.listserv.games-l** URL▶ http://www.riddler.com/

Play an Interactive Web Game

Hunt the Wumpus Jump 4036

Brought to you by Glenn Bresnahan, this site offers one of the most exciting uses of the Web. You take part in an interactive game in which the goal is to "hunt the Wumpus monster...shoot the Wumpus before it eats you." This is done by clicking on graphics to "move" through the caves. You have arrows to shoot, but be careful, because you must also watch out for pits, bats, and other players who can also shoot you. A truly great and innovative application of Web technology. —(R.B.)

URL▶ http://www.bu.edu/htbin/wcl

Gamers' Help & Resources

Games Domain Jump 9500

This is the quintessential reference point to games-related information and resources available on the Internet. Dave Stanworth has done an outstanding job of organizing and maintaining this site, especially with the work he's done in creating this site's archive for easier downloading of games and demos than the FTP sites he also provides links to. There are general and game-specific FAQs, instructional walkthroughs and playing tips, links to gaming magazines, commercial and noncommercial games pages, and general information on computers and computer gaming. You can help Dave maintain this excellent site by converting FAQs and walkthroughs, improving link descriptions, or just making suggestions for improving the pages. —(L.S.)

KEY NEWSGROUP **rec.games.misc** URL▸ http://www.cs.umd.edu/~regli/ski.html

The Doom Information Web Page

DoomGate Jump 4043

DoomGate is the World Wide Web gateway to all things related to the popular PC game Doom. Brought to you by Piotr Kapiszewski and Steve Young, this site offers information on Doom (and Doom II), answering any question you might have and offering a remarkably comprehensive set of resources. There are links to FTP sites to download Doom-related software, and to the DoomWeb project, a collection of Doom-related World Wide Web nodes all around the Internet. —(R.B.)

KEY NEWSGROUP **rec.games.computer.doom** URL▸ http://doomgate.cs.buffalo.edu/index-html.html

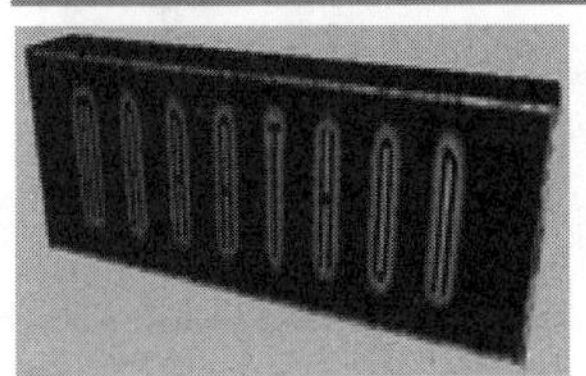

Marathon Gaming Home Page Site

The Complete Marathon Collection Jump 4044

The Macintosh answer to Doom is the new game Marathon, and this is the Web site to visit if you play the game. When Bungie Software decided it wasn't feasible to keep up a site for their game, the fans took over and created this awesome site. Very well-done graphics and resources including file archives, information on related software, and links to other marathon pages make this a site a must for Macintosh gamers. —(R.B.)

KEY NEWSGROUP **alt.mac.games.marathon** URL▸ http://www.amug.org/~marathon/index.html

Home Page for the Nintendo GameBoy System

Nintendo GameBoy Homepage Jump 4058

This is truly a "home page," as everything you could possibly want to know about the handheld video game system, the Nintendo GameBoy, is here. Marat Fayzullin has created one of the most subject-comprehensive sites we've ever seen. From GameBoy FAQ's to game cheat codes, to mail archives, even technical information and schematics, if you're into GameBoys, this site is your encyclopedia! —(R.B.)

KEY NEWSGROUP **rec.games.video.nintendo** URL▸ http://www.cs.umd.edu/users/fms/GameBoy/

Conquer the World: Civilization

Microprose Civilization FAQ Jump 5043

This is an invaluable resource for people addicted to Microprose's popular computer game, Civilization, a game about conquering the world. After a brief intro, there are links to extensive info on cities, strategies, tips, the future of Civilization, and, best of all cheats! There is also an overview of other strategy games, too. —(S.B.)

URL▸ http://wcl-rs.bham.ac.uk/~djh/civfaq1.html

The Sega Web

n/a Jump 4507

Total global domination is a dream for sports teams and deranged despots, but part of the day-to-day reality of SEGA, the computer game company that has done the best job of anyone of keeping an entire generation glued, rapturous, to their TV screens. If it's about SEGA, you'll find it here in graphicically-intense, well-designed pages that point you to tips and tricks, product information, and gaming-related non-commercial Web sites. —(T.W.)

URL▸ http://www.segaoa.com/

Games: Board & Strategy

A Rich Collection of Chess Players' Resources

Internet Chess Library Jump 0015

CONTENT

A comprehensive, interesting, and well-done collection of chess information for players at all levels, compiled by Chris Petroff and Karl Schwamb. This Web chess archive contains tons of game problems, match summaries, tournament ratings news and information, and computer chess game software programs. We especially like the sample chess problem presented as a chess board at the top of their Web page! A must-see site on the Web for "wood pushers" of all skill levels. —(E.G.)

KEY NEWSGROUP **rec.games.chess** URL▶ http://caissa.onenet.net/chess/

Chess Problems

Chess Problem Server Jump 0085

Sharpen your chess skills by practicing numerous chess problems from Karl Schwamb's Web site, featuring chess problems excerpted from fourteen well-known chess publications. —(E.G.)

KEY NEWSGROUP **rec.games.chess** URL▶ http://www.traveller.com/scripts/chess_problems

Two-Player Chess Games on the Web

The Chess Server Jump 0086

Tyler Jones' innovative, experimental chess server lets you play chess with another opponent, in real time, on the Web and lets spectators watch your game too! —(E.G.)

KEY NEWSGROUP **rec.games.chess** URL▶ http://www.willamette.edu/~tjones/chessmain.html

Chinese Chess Information Site

Xiangqi (Chinese-Chess) Home page Jump 4068

Peter Sung maintains this page containing everything you need or want to know about Chinese Chess. You can access the newsgroup, browse the FAQ, connect to the Internet Chinese-Chess server, read the rules of the game, and more. A wealth of information for folks who play, or are interested in playing, this game. —(R.B.)

KEY NEWSGROUP **rec.games.chinese-chess** URL▶ http://www.io.org/~sung/xq/xq.html

CyberCheckers

Chinook Jump 7185

Think you're a pretty hot checkers player? Then match your skills with Chinook—a world-class checkers program developed by researchers at the University of Alberta, Department of Computing Science. You can play at novice, amateur, or intermediate level. Be warned—Chinook's endgame database has been programmed with 400 billion resolved positions, so there's a good chance it'll smoke ya. As a warm-up, why not read about how the program was created, about its creators, and about past world championship matches. As well, the authors provide links to other checkers sites such as the International Checker Hall of Fame. —(E.v.B.)

KEY NEWSGROUP **rec.games.board** URL▶ http://web.cs.ualberta.ca:80/~chinook/

Games: Multi-Player

Clearly MUD

The MUD Connection Jump 2602

The Internet needed a comprehensive, searchable database of multi-user online games, so Andrew Cowan created this site, much to the joy of MUDders everywhere. You can scroll through the more than 100 MUDs listed, read their descriptions, and link to their home pages or jack into the game, if you want. Or you can use the search engine, which takes your keywords and returns the listings that match. Either way, it's easy to use, and with additional links to pages of player's resources, this is a great bookmark for any enthusiast. —(L.S.)

KEY NEWSGROUP **rec.games.muds.misc** URL▶ http://www.magicnet.net/~cowana/mud.html

Games: Fantasy

Tips for Role-Playing Gamers

Role-Playing Games Jump 2383

What began as an interesting concept called Dungeons & Dragons quickly became an obsession among thousands, if not millions, of people. It spawned numerous variations and competitors, resulting in a neverending series of board, computer and networked fantasy role playing games. For everyone from beginner to master, warrior to wizard, elf to human, Michael P. Duff, Jr. maintains a page with links that will improve and enhance game play. There are game tools, scenarios, FTP sites, and links to other fantasy role playing games and gamer's pages. Even if you don't play these games, it's an interesting starting point to browse and—just maybe—get hooked! —(L.S.)

KEY NEWSGROUP **rec.games.frp.misc** URL▶ http://www.acm.uiuc.edu/adnd/

A Home Site for Role-Playing Games

Fantasy Role-Playing Games Jump 4030

Michael Duff is the maintainer of this page that's all about fantasy role-playing games. The main focus of information at this site concerns the popular game Dungeons and Dragons. You'll find specific information, newsgroups, images, and the like concerning D & D, and you'll also have access to numerous Web links taking you out to all sorts of role-playing game resources. Also accessible from here is general role-playing information, as well as other specific game sites such as Robotech, Shadowrun, Magic, and more. —(R.B.)

KEY NEWSGROUP **rec.games.frp.misc** URL▶ http://www.acm.uiuc.edu:/adnd/

Humor & Jokes

The New Times York

All the News That's Fit to Sell Toyotas

Daily *New York Times* Satire

Daily New Times York Jump 5913

But the name sounds so . . . familiar. Don't be fooled by imitations. This is the real thing. "All the news that's fit to sell Toyotas." What we have here is not a failure to communicate, but a very funny and very cutting and irreverent look at the news of the day and a satire of that newspaper of record—*The New York Times*. No one is sacred, no topic off-limits. The end result—we are pleased to report—is very, very funny. We're talking laugh out loud funny here. But a word of warning: satire at this level is bound to offend, and there is in particular a word of warning for children. But the rest of us can enjoy our daily fix, produced by C3F. —(J.P.)

KEY NEWSGROUP **rec.humor.d** URL▶ http://c3f.com/ntytoday.html

Candy Hearts and Sweet Words on the Web

The Internet Candy Dish Jump 4033

This page offers a simple but sweet bit of web weirdness. Brought to you by Mike Miller and the Rainbow Confusion Boys, the Internet Candy Dish offers you a new handful of those candy hearts with slogans like "you send me" and "kiss me again" every time you reload the page. —(R.B.)

URL▶ http://204.220.40.200/ToyBox/ICD/ICD.exe

Uncle Al Views the World

The Outrageous On-Line Uncle Al Jump 7363

Uncle Al is a pretty funny guy. Read his take on carpenter's glue and skin, medflies, the environment, the politically correct American, recycled glass, and his essay on two ways to install a roll of toilet paper. Uncle Al doesn't stop there. He also provides links to some bizarre (Vancouver car dealerships lists), some yummy (chocolate!), and some helpful pages (lost friends' search pages). Stop by when your spirits need lifting. —(E.v.B.)

KEY NEWSGROUP misc.writing URL▶ http://vv.com/adsint/freehand/uncleal/

Your Starting Point for Laughter on the Net

The Jollitorium Jump 3634

"The silvery mist of colours reassembles itself into a picture of great fun and merriment as you find yourself at the centre of The Jollitorium. The air is filled with giggling, laughter, and bubbles... You take one..." So opens the home page of Jollitorium. A place with link after link to humor resources on the Net that's certain to bring a smile to even the meanest meanie. Whether you're after cartoons or jokes, you'll find them right here at the Jollitorium. —(C.P.)

URL▶ http://www.glasswings.com.au/GlassWings/jolly.html

The Joke's on Us

idiot wind magazine Jump 1567

idiot wind magazine, the only little humor magazine to come out of the former herring capital of the east coast in Occoquan, Virginia, is the brainchild of publisher Douglas Carroll. Mainly a vehicle for soliciting contributions, this site is mainly devoted to making you laugh. Between the Infrequently Asked Questions, parodies such as "95 Ways Windows '95 Will Change your Life," "Channelling Ken," and "Barney Finally Meets His Maker," you'll be filling out the free subscription form in short order. Do you want to review other zines? Send in your votes. Do you know what a crawlspace editor is? Find out here. Or maybe you just want to know what makes these zine writers and editors tick—that's here, too. —(H.L.)

URL▶ http://www.io.com/~mtbandit/iw/iwind2.htm

Lovelorn, Take Heed

Advice From Sir Charles Grandiose Jump 1542

There's no need to face life's mysteries alone when Sir Charles Grandiose is around. Designed to bring his wit and wisdom, "cleverly masquerading in the advice to the lovelorn and senseless, to the Net," Sir Charles answers all of your petty concerns with style. Find out the daring question Heartwarmer in Hampshire asked to get this in return, "One does not understand. Why should one bring one's nightshirt and cap? And why should I not inform the Lady Felicia?" Updated weekly by Vance Briceland, Sir Charles will tackle anything you ask—just look through archives of past humorous and oddball questions. This site also leads you through doors to other locations: links to a library of serious literary works by Jane Austin, Shakespeare, and others; MUD games; and a temple of Macintosh technology and FAQs. So, don't spend hair-splitting weeks worrying about troubling situations when you can get advice today, on the Web. —(H.L.)

URL▶ http://gopher.orsps.wayne.edu/charles/advice.html

Web Jokes Database

LaughWEB Jump 2116 

Do you collect jokes? Did you forget that lawyer joke you wanted to tell the gang? Just need a laugh after (or during) a hard day on the Net? Well, bunky, just fire up the browser and jump over here. If you're sensitive, you may be offended, particularly if you're one of the targets, or delve into the sexual/gender humor, insults, or gross jokes sections. But there's much good, clean fun: business, computer, educational, and political humor, parodies, current events, and Barney the Dinosaur jokes (a Net favorite!). Whatever you do, don't miss the "Canonical Lists" section covering lightbulb jokes, bumper stickers, the biggest lies, fulldeckisms (as in not playing with a), and the list of Bart Simpson's blackboard quotations. —(L.S.)

KEY NEWSGROUP **rec.humor** URL▸ http://www.misty.com/laughweb/lweb.html

Hope He Gets Respect on the Web!

Rodney Dangerfield Jump 1583 

There's a certain irony to a low-tech comedian like Rodney Dangerfield having a home page, and who knows if it will help him gain any respect. This site is an overview of familiar Dangerfield territory, with a few chuckles sprinkled in and plenty of his familiar jokes for you to download as WAV files. Rodney's Hot Links include (you guessed it) Kevin Renzulli's Howard Stern site. Plus there's a form to send e-mail to Rodney, who's reputed to be a big-time Web surfer in his own right. —(H.L.)

URL▸ http://www.rodney.com/

Laughs Online

Ratan Nalumasu's Humor Page Jump 2421 

When you need a break from the serious business of surfing the Web, Ratan Nalumasu gives you what you need. There are no fancy graphics here, so the page loads almost instantly, offering you a range of choices to suit any mood and any sense of humor. There are the standard doctor, lawyer, and answering machine jokes, but there's also an archive of the surreal humor of comedian Steven Wright, and choice quotes of bar regular Norm Peterson from the long-running TV series Cheers. If you can spend a little more time, there are longer stories, and the best of the **rec.humor** newsgroup, too. —(L.S.)

KEY NEWSGROUP **rec.humor** URL▸ http://www.cs.utah.edu:80/~ratan/humor/

Jokes, Jokes, Jokes

The Mother of all Humor Archives Jump 2618 

Humor lovers have many places on the Web to find jokes, but Christopher Kline's site certainly ranks among the most comprehensive and is tops on our own personal laugh-o-meter! It's categorical, but not alphabetical, and quite long. So if you're looking for something specific, you'll have to hunt around, using the find button and the scroll bar. Still, the effort is laugh-out-loud worthwhile, whether you want deep humor, stuff to pass around the office, knee slappers, quizzes, top 10 lists, or downright tasteless stuff. —(L.S.)

KEY NEWSGROUP **rec.humor** URL▸ http://www.tc.cornell.edu/~ckline/humor/maillist.html

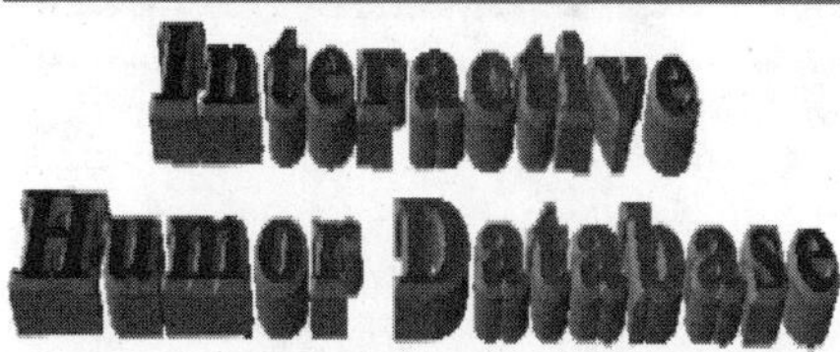

Ha Ha Ha! Hee Hee Hee!

Interactive Humor Database Jump 6676 

Having a down day? Need a good practical joke? This Web jokes archive is guaranteed to make you laugh. Whether you're interested in humorous riddles, jokes, limericks, lyrics, folklore or comedy routines, the entire contents of this site are searchable by author or keyword, so you can find the joke that fits the occasion. You can, if you like, just browse around this site's top 10 jokes for this month, or its top 20 of all-time, based on votes by other visitors to this site. You can also submit your own favorite jokes for all Web to see (Parents will want to note that we did find a some adult-oriented humor in a few spots.) —(L.T.)

KEY NEWSGROUP **rec.humor.funny** URL▸ http://humor.ncy.com/

One Big Humor Archive

Wrecked Humor Page Jump 4019

The disclaimer on this page states in part, "We are an equal opportunity offender," and that statement is definitely true. Maintained by Derek Cashman, this site is an archive for all things humorous. From canonical lists like light bulb jokes, to top ten lists, to song parodies (including several off-color versions of the Barney "I Love You" song), this page is a front-end to the world of laughter. —(R.B.)

KEY NEWSGROUP **rec.humor.d** URL▶ http://www.cs.odu.edu/~cashman/humor.html

A Standup Comedy Show on the Net

UN-CABARET Jump 4022

The folks at underground.net bring you what is billed as "The First (and Only) Comedy Show on the Internet!!!" This site offers video clips of stand up comedians, such as Bob Goldthwait, Janeane Garofalo, and Rick Overton, doing their bits. You can choose from the latest clips, or access the clip library archives. It's a video comedy show brought to you on the Internet! —(R.B.)

KEY NEWSGROUP **alt.comedy.standup** URL▶ http://bazaar.com/Uncabaret/uncab.html

Carrottop's Web Comedy Spot

Carrottop Jump 6533

If you've ever seen him, there's no way you could ever forget him. That hysterical (and hysterically funny) guy who haphazardly pulls out all those props from a toy chest, accompanied by an astounding headful of red curly hair. Carrottop now has his own equally laughable Web site, weaving his unique brand of humor with the usual self-promotion, such as his performance schedule. Revel in various audible splashes of his comedy clips and get answers to those nagging questions: Is that his real hair color, how tall he stands in heels, and what he eats each morning that furnishes him with so much manic energy. —(L.T.)

KEY NEWSGROUP **alt.comedy.standup** URL▶ http://www.carrottop.com/

Deep Thoughts by Jack Handey

Random Deep Thoughts by Jack Handey

Random Deep Thoughts
Jump 6685

You've seen Jack Handey's twisted little pearls of wisdom on Saturday Night Live. Now you can see them as many times as you like on this entertaining page. Tap the reload button frequently and a new quote will pop up on your screen. Here are a couple to get you started..."The face of a child can say it all, especially the mouth part of the face," or "Do you know what happens when you slice a golf ball in half? Someone gets mad at you. I found this out the hard way." —(L.T.)

KEY NEWSGROUP **rec.humor.d** URL▶ http://www.novia.net/~geewhiz/cgi-bin/deep.cgi

Music: Rock/Pop Talk

New Sounds from New Bands

RockWeb Interactive Jump 5780

Fans of new rock will want to load up on Netscape browser plug-ins and take a tour of the RockWeb site, intended to expose new alternative sounds to a wider audience, via the Internet. You'll find samples from virtually every music genre here, from the acoustic groove of Calobo, the new-world sounds of Jose Manuel Figueroa and Sergio Arau, and the rock of Zero, Apricot Jam, and Zoo People. There's even more, including a chat forum and zines section, on this nicely designed and executed site. —(J.P.)

KEY NEWSGROUP **alt.music.progressive** URL▶ http://www.rockweb.com/

Music on the Web

TheDJ Jump 5842 

How would you like to listen to 40 commercial-free music channels on your Web browser? Who wouldn't. And you can do it at The DJ. And it's all free. You'll need the RealAudio Player, which is free and available from links here, but once you've downloaded it you're all set. You'll find an amazing array of music here, with new selections being added all the time—everthing from Blues and Motown, to Ska, Gothic, and African music's available here. If you have any problems at all downloading or playing the music, a complete and easy-to-follow FAQ (Frequently Asked Question) file is available from this site's creators. —(J.P.)

KEY NEWSGROUP **rec.music.info** URL ▶ http://www.thedj.com/

Billboard Online

We're Moving... Click Here for More Info www.billboard.com

The PAY ZONE Searchable Archives

DAILY MUSIC UPDATE January 9, 1997

ROCK MEETS SALT: "We wanted to make a big rock record," says Veruca Salt's Louise Post of the act's forthcoming album. "We always saw ourselves sounding big -- we wanted our drums to sound huge." To that end, the act enlisted the production talents of Bob Rock, known for his work with metalists such as Metallica. The Rock-produced album is due Feb. 11 from Geffen-distributed Outpost Records. The album's title, "Eight Arms To Hold You," is taken from the Beatles' working title for "Help!" The album will be the last with the band for drummer Jim Shapiro, who left the act after completing the sessions for the new release. He's been replaced by former Letters To Cleo drummer Stacy Jones.

Veruca Salt

• More Daily Music News

Events Calendar

Billboard Newsstand

Internet Gallery

E-Mail@

President's Greeting

Hints for AOL users

Web Site Credits

Features Updated Weekly

New! This Day in Music — View daily music news from years past.

• Hot Product — Get a first look at the big releases for early 1997.

• Billboard Sneak Peek — Silverchair's youth movement continues; folk labels keep growing.

• Spotlight Reviews — Glen Velez unveils an exciting new release.

• Fred's Trivia Corner — Answer this week's question correctly and win a free CD! Plus: Chart Beat Chat and Chart Beat Bonus.

Charts Now with Music Samples

WEEK ENDING JAN. 18, 1997

• The Billboard 200 — No Doubt sits on top of the chart for a fourth week but the Soundtrack to Romeo + Juliet creeps up to the No. 2 postion.

• The Hot 100 Singles — Toni Braxton hangs onto No. 1 for another week but En Vogue is not far behind at the No. 2 position.

• Top R&B Albums — MAKAVELLI pulls into the No. 1 postion.

• Top Country Albums

▲ *Billboard's homepage, from* **BillboardOnline** *at* Jump 5813.

Rock Goes Establishment

Rock & Roll Hall of Fame + Museum Jump 2687 CONTENT

A Hall of Fame. A museum. Annual orgies of self-congratulation featuring aging rockers and youthful wannabes with questionable talent. Oh, well—so much for rock-and-roll as the voice of rebellion. And while this site has its good points, it has some problems. For example, one entry in the Today in Rock blurb told us it was Sophia Loren's birthday (what album did she put out), and the Rock News section doesn't have any news. So there's work to be done, but the site is still worth a visit. The section covering the Hall's inductees has short, sometimes interesting profiles, with sound files taken from the Museum. And the exterior photos of I. M. Pei's remarkable building are worth a look, too. —(L.S.)

KEY NEWSGROUP **alt.rock-n-roll** URL ▶ http://www.rockhall.com/index.html

The All-Digital Music Magazine Like No Other . . .

POP-i Music Magazine Jump 5809 CONTENT

Too often Web music magazines spend so much effort trying to be hip they forget the real reason they exist: To cover the music scene. POP-i calls itself a "music magazine like no other," and for a change they claim it's true. These folks know their stuff, to be sure, but they use this knowledge to good use. The interviews are intelligent and comprehensive, replete with downloadable great video and audio clips interspersed. The reviews section includes coverage of bands from across the alternative musical spectrum, including the likes of Dale Watson, Bela Fleck, the Pretenders, Big Sandy, the Fly-Rite Boys, and Rickie Lee Jones. —(J.P.)

KEY NEWSGROUP **alt.music.alternative** URL ▶ http://www.popi.com/

Peter Gabriel Fan Pages

And Through The Wire - Peter Gabriel Jump 1005 

There's very little you won't find on this multi-talented musician at this site. Everything from classifieds, to reviews and listings of stores are served up in this beefy Web site provided by John Underwood and fellow fans. —(J.V.O.)

KEY NEWSGROUP **alt.music.alternative** URL ▶ http://www.cs.clemson.edu/~junderw/pg.html

Rock 'n Roll Photographs

Rock Shots Jump 7422 

Photographer Niels Van Iperen has created an interactive gallery of rock 'n roll photographs. As he notes: "onstage, backstage, audience rage . . . it's all here!" Rock Shots features one-of-a-kind photographs that can be viewed in thumbnail format, can be searched by artist name, or the gallery can be entered as a whole. So, whether you want to view AC/DC, ZZ Top, the Breeders or Smashing Pumpkins in concert, and in action, this is the site to visit.—(E.v.B.)

KEY NEWSGROUP **alt.rock-n-roll.hard** URL▶ http://www.metaverse.com/vibe/rockshots/

Hootie!

Hootie and the Blowfish Jump 1577 

Follow one of today's hottest bands on their "official" Web page from Atlantic records. With 85 weeks on the record charts their first time out, Atlantic could have given Hootie and the Blowfish a more interesting home page, but surely fans are planning a more exciting venue soon. Although the site isn't interactive, it has the inside scoops on the group, their tour itinerary, how they spent their summer vacation, lots of their quotes, and what's up next for this folk-rock jangle, bluesy band. If you're in the mood, you can jump to Atlantic's own home page and look up other artists on their label. —(H.L.)

URL▶ http://www.atlantic-records.com/festival/hootie/trivia.html

Kraftwerk Fan Pages

Kraftwerk-INFOBAHR Jump 1024 

These grandfathers of electronic music would be happy to see their computer-assisted music represented on the Web. Anders Wilhelm has provided all you could want to know about the band, including excerpts from books on them, a band history, and reviews. —(J.V.O.)

KEY NEWSGROUP **alt.music.alternative** URL▶ http://wwwtdb.cs.umu.se/~dvlawm/kraftwerk.html

Rock and Roll on the Net and around the World

Rock Around the World Jump 3696 

If you're over 30 you'll remember "Rock Around The World"—that fabulous radio program from the 1970s that aired in every top market on over 160 radio stations. RATW introduced such artists as Eric Clapton, Elton John, and The Who to American radio audiences. Well, RATW is back, with the full arsenal of 232 broadcasts to keep Internet visitors hopping until sometime in the next century. You'll find feature articles, radio broadcasts, rock history, and much, much, much, much more. For anyone with an interest in rock (the way it used to be!) —(C.P.)

KEY NEWSGROUP **alt.rock-n-roll** URL▶ http://www.ratw.com/

Old Blue Eyes Online

The Frank Sinatra WWW Page Jump 2635 

Perhaps the greatest interpreter of popular music in this century, Frank Sinatra gets a Web page worthy of his talent, thanks to William Denton. You'll find news of Sinatra and his appearances and recordings, interviews, reviews, and a filmography and discography. There's a rather detailed Sinatra FAQ, information on Sinatra fan clubs and societies, and some interesting odds and ends, including Frank's spaghetti sauce recipe. A good selection of images includes album covers and performance photos. All together, it's a worthy homage to the "Chairman of the Board," and a must bookmark for any fan. —(L.S.)

KEY NEWSGROUP **rec.music** URL▶ http://www.io.org/~buff/sinatra.html

All about John Lennon

Sam Choukri's John Lennon Web Page Jump 3674 

Do you know where Abkhazia is? Well.... neither did we. Well, it turns out that it's one of the dozens of former Soviet republics—and its claim to fame has to be its special issue of a Lenin/Marx stamp, that's really a Lennon(John)/Marx(Groucho) commemorative! That kind of trivia and scads more awaits the die-hard John Lennon afficionado here at Sam Choukri's John

Lennon Page. This site is stuffed full of exciting Lennon memorabilia and information, from discographies to sound files—from downloadable picture files of Lennon's original drawings, to links to what must be every other Beatles site on the Web—this page is a winner, and a must for your bookmarks list. —(C.P.)

KEY NEWSGROUP **rec.music.beatles** URL▶ http://www.missouri.edu/~c588349/john-page.html

Madonna on the Web

The Madonna Homepage Jump 4054

The Material Girl comes to the Web, on this site maintained by Joe Barco. Along with news bulletins and chart positions of the rock star's current songs, you'll find FAQs, discographies, images, and links to other Madonna-related Net resources, including the Madonna lyric server and Madonna newsgroup. A must for any Net-connected Madonna fan. —(R.B.)

KEY NEWSGROUP **alt.fan.madonna** URL▶ http://www.mit.edu:8001/people/jwb/Madonna.html

For Led-Heads Only

Led Zeppelin Home Page Jump 5029

A really cool collage graphic introduces this Web page devoted to Led Zeppelin. Included are links to the FAQ list, guitar tablatures, lyrics to all songs, including the recent Page and Plant project, a discography complete with album covers, photos, digitized songs, other fan contacts, and more, including a French-language version of this page. —(S.B.)

KEY NEWSGROUP **alt.music.Led-Zeppelin**
URL▶http://uvacs.cs.virginia.edu/~jsw2y/zeppelin/zeppelin.html

Nez on the Web

Michael Nesmith Home Page Jump 1521

Hey hey, remember the Monkees? What ever happened to those impish, made-for-TV musical teen heartthrobs? You won't have to wonder any longer. Hardcore fan Brad Waddell and former Monkee Michael Nesmith, "the Nez," provide not only a plethora of Monkee trivia, including a link to the Monkee Web site, but reveal the Nez' eclectic talents. From his New Age electronic book, The Long Sandy Hair of Neftoon Zamora, to a spoof on favorite movies, complete with sound, to his latest musical score, he draws you in more than you'd expect. He answers fan's questions, such as "were the Monkees a hoax?" to how he feels about the Grammy Awards. Will the Monkees reunite? Find out here. Who's his favorite Monkee? Stay tuned. The most impressive section is a collection of all of Nesmith's song lyrics. These Web pages are like an interactive, constantly changing book in progress. —(H.L.)

KEY NEWSGROUP **alt.music.monkees** URL▶ http://www.primenet.com/~flex/nesmith.html

Australian Rock Music Talk & News

Australian Music World Wide Web Site Jump 7068

This "tribute to Australian music," lists nearly 850 Australian rock musicians—their discographies, song lyrics, and latest news. What's new, what's the gossip, where the gigs are—all are detailed, and some are accompanied by graphics. —(E.v.B.)

KEY NEWSGROUP **aus.music** URL▶ http://www.st.nepean.uws.edu.au/~ezsigri/ausmusic/

Rush Here

The Rush/NMS Home Page Jump 5030

This page is for fans of the Canadian band Rush. Included here are bios of Geddy Lee, Alex Lifeson, and Neil Peart, in addition to a downloadable album collage, access to The National Midnight Star (NMS) fan club mailing list, FAQ, articles and interviews with Rush, and the treasured unofficial tour dates listing.—(S.B.)

KEY NEWSGROUP **alt.music.rush** URL▶ http://www.cerf.net/rush/

Elvis Lives on the Web

Elvis Home Page Jump 4032 

This is the end-all be-all for the Elvis fan on the Net. Although the site has run into a few copyright problems with Elvis Presley Enterprises, Inc., Andrea Berman still has compiled the ultimate collection of Elvis resources. You can take an online tour of Graceland, look at Elvis memorabilia, and, of course, access links to all sorts of other Elvis sites. The King lives on through this page! —(R.B.)

KEY NEWSGROUP **alt.elvis.sighting**

URL▶ http://sunsite.unc.edu/elvis/elvishom.html

▲ *Elvis, on the day he visited President Nixon, from* **Elvis Home Page** *at* Jump 4032.

The Grateful Dead

Grateful Dead Fan Page

The Grateful Dead Jump 5502 

The place where Deadheads can find tour dates, set lists for every concert the boys played from 1972 to the present, and lyrics for most Dead tunes. Also includes practical information on what to look for in a cassette deck for taping Dead concerts, as well as the finer points of the etiquette of tape trading. Last, but not least, you can download the famous "Dancing Bear" screen saver. —(F.R.)

KEY NEWSGROUP **rec.music.gdead**

URL▶ http://www.cs.cmu.edu/~mleone/dead.html

JIMI HENDRIX

Jimi Hendrix Fan Page

Jimi Hendrix Server Jump 5503 

A good place to find information about one of the most flamboyant, original, and innovative musicians of the 1960s. Includes the lyrics to most of Jimi's songs, set lists for most of his concerts, plus a complete discography. You'll also find reviews of Hendrix performances available on video, as well as some nice photos you can download for personal use. —(F.R.)

KEY NEWSGROUP **alt.fan.jimi-hendrix** URL▶ http://147.109.8.1/jimi/jimi.html

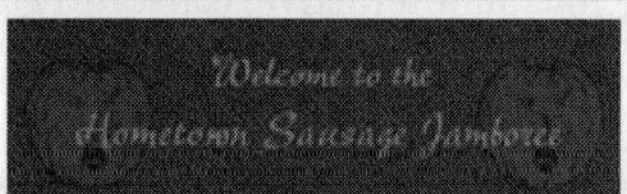

Zappa's Hidden Messages

Hometown Sausage Jamboree Jump 2642 CONTENT

The credibility of accusations of rock music containing satanic messages when played backwards notwithstanding, Frank Zappa did, indeed, hide jokes, asides, and references to other pieces, in his album tracks. If you're looking for prurience, though, you'll have to go elsewhere. What ol' Frank did was take lyrics from his other songs, solos, and other bits and pieces and integrated them into various other tracks. They are sometimes humorous, but mostly show that Zappa's genius went beyond composition to include a mastery of recording technologies. Jeremy Fox has collected some great examples, explains what and how it was done, and offers .wav files for your enjoyment. If you're a Zappa fan, don't miss this page. —(L.S.)

KEY NEWSGROUP **alt.fan.frank.zappa** URL▶ http://www.netaxs.com/~yirm/sausage/sausage.html

Motor City Madman

Stranglehold—Ted Nugent Homepage Jump 2661 

Hunting television program host, the newest member of the National Rifle Association board, and the NRA's current Poster Boy, Ted Nugent is first and foremost a rocker. Some of his fans, organized by Joshua Nelson, maintain this page honoring the man and his music. In addition to the Nugent discography and various images, you'll find lyrics to his songs, fans' reviews of his concerts, a concert schedule, and a collection of articles and interviews. There's even a section covering Spirit of the Wild, Nugent's TV show. —(L.S.)

KEY NEWSGROUP **alt.music.rock-n-roll** URL▶ http://thunder.indstate.edu/h5/jngonzo/.nuge.html

Zappa's Gone, but Not Forgotten

St. Alphonzo's Pancake Home Page Jump 2643

Frank Zappa offended many, mostly people who didn't understand that most of his popular work was satirical, while his more serious efforts put him atop the list of contemporary composers. A dedicated iconoclast who never missed an opportunity to challenge either social or musical convention, he was, in fact, a classically trained composer and a bona fide genius. If you're a fan, you'll find all you'd ever want to know about Zappa at this site maintained by Robbert Heederik. There are a variety of FAQs, a complete discography, regularly updated news and information about Zappa's legacy, plus miscellaneous audio, image, and video files. —(L.S.)

KEY NEWSGROUP alt.fan.frank.zappa URL ▶ http://www.fwi.uva.nl/~heederik/zappa/

Music: Urban, Blues & Jazz

Playing the Blues

Blues Access Jump 1555

This testament to the blues, created by the Roosterman, aka Cary Wolfson, shows the historical perspective of the blues direct from old blues hounds and younger advocates alike. Stories, articles, editorials, photos, information about hard-to-find record labels and easy-to-find clubs round out this online publication. Rooster's picks of the best blues artists today, along with running commentary, make this site interesting and educational. Wolfson invites you into discussions about the selling of "packaged blues" for a pop audience ("blues is NOT Hootie and the Blowfish or Sheryl Crow") and whether blues greats should appear on postage stamps. If you're a blues fan, this site is well worth your time. —(H.L.)

URL ▶ http://www.interactive.line.com/blues/bluesaccess/

Soul Blues

The Blue Highway Jump 7266

Curtis Hewston is singin' the blues online. His pages are a wonderful tribute to those African Americans who transformed their pain and sorrow into evocative, soul-stirring songs. Experience the blues from the Mississippi Delta to the inner cities. Robert Johnson, Leadbelly, Howlin-Wolf, Buddy Guy are only a few of the greats you'll see as you travel the Blue Highway. You can also read essays on blues topics, read bios, and browse the blues mall for merchandise. —(E.v.B.)

KEY NEWSGROUP bit.listserv.blues-l URL ▶ http://www.vivanet.com/~blues/

Jazz & Blues Photo Archive

NJIT Jazz/Blues/R 'n R Images Anonymous FTP Server

Jump 0194

This Web site at the New Jersey Institute of Technology features many interesting and hard-to-find photos of jazz legends like Charley Parker, Billie Holliday, Theolonious Monk, etc. for jazz fans. —(E.G.)

KEY NEWSGROUP rec.music.bluenote URL ▶ ftp://ftp.njit.edu/pub/images/

HipHop Home Page

The Hitlist Jump 2209

This is a site for fans of hiphop or urban, music. There are lots of pictures, including an urban art gallery, sections covering new releases, fashion, gossip, and an area for fans to contact each other for trading CDs and collectibles. There's also information on movies, links to home pages of performers and others involved in the scene, and information on specific labels. —(L.S.)

KEY NEWSGROUP rec.music URL ▶ http://www.cldc.howard.edu/%7Eaja/hitlist/htmls/index.html

Who's Blue?

BluesNet Home Page Jump 2265 

If you want to learn more about a specific blues artist, or even about blues music in general, Rob Hutton makes it easy. Here you'll find biographies of major and minor blues artists, written by their fans. That's the only caveat, since fans tend to be very biased, but it's also a plus since fans also tend to be the most detailed and comprehensive in their knowledge. There's also a "mentor" database of Internet-connected fans who have extensive or other special knowledge about an artist or blues style. For those who also want more general information about this musical style, Rob has included a list of documents to browse, as well as a nice set of links to other blues-related sites on the Web. —(L.S.)

KEY NEWSGROUP **bit.listserv.blues-l** URL▸ http://dragon.acadiau.ca/~rob/blues/blues.html

Jazz on the Web

WNUR-FM JazzWeb Jump 2371 

Whether it's swing or be-bop, artists or venues, essays or links, this site supplies the backbeat for your particular taste in jazz. Maintained by Joe Germuska of student-run WNUR-FM at Northwestern University, you'll find all the content and links you'd expect, plus charts of original jazz compositions supplied by fellow Net jazz fans and maintained by Sam Hoken. Like the music itself, this site is based on energy and creativity, and that attitude is reflected in its Cool New Stuff section. It changes periodically, but at any given time it gives you a hotlist to the the best, brightest, and most intriguing jazz-related information and links on the Web. —(L.S.)

KEY NEWSGROUP **rec.music.bluenote** URL▸ http://www.acns.nwu.edu/jazz/

Jazzy Trombones

Trombone-L Home Page Jump 7032 

Jazz trombonists take heed—Eric Nicklas has created a page to delight amateur and professional musicians alike. Browse biographies of greats like J.J. Johnson, study mouthpiece charts, learn from master class notes, and much, much more. It also might be worth your while to swing to this site's "Jobs, Jobs, Jobs" menu option where gigs are listed. —(E.v.B.)

KEY NEWSGROUP **rec.music.bluenote** URL▸ http://www.missouri.edu/~cceric/index.html

Music: Classical & Opera

JOHN PHILIP SOUSA AMERICAN COMPOSER & PATRIOT

John Philip Sousa: The March King

John Philip Sousa Home Page Jump 5817 CONTENT

They called him the March King and now he has his own home page, created by David Lovrien. And what a home page it is! Sousa, who lived from 1854-1932, is known as an American composer and patriot, two hats he wore proudly. This site is a celebration of the man and his music, which is—especially in today's politically-correct culture—refreshingly, unashamedly, upliftingly, patriotic. You'll find plenty of downloadable audio files of his most popular works, as well as special features like the "March of the Month." Reference sources include a great biography, list of related books and links, pictures of Sousa and his band and, of course, even more information on the music. —(J.P.)

URL▸ http://www.dws.org/sousa/

The Divine J.S. Bach

J.S. BACH Jump 7466 

What a treat to access so much information on that great classical composer, J.S. Bach. These pages, many of which were created by Jan Hanford, include the Bach archive and the J.S. Bach bibliography (900 titles!). As well, you can read an illustrated biography of the man, explore the musical world of the Cantatas, and gaze upon a few uploaded Bach portraits. Another site, the J.S. Bach Tourist pages are linked to and can be read in combination with the biography. —(E.v.B.)

KEY NEWSGROUP **rec.music.classical** URL▶ http://www.let.rug.nl/Linguistics/diversen/bach/intro.html

Wired to the Classics

Main Menu Jump **7307**

Ah, the sweet strains of Mozart, the heroic compositions of Beethoven, or the operatic highs of Puccini—classical music at its best. Enjoy a virtual tour of the classical music world at this site. You can read short bios of famous composers and favorite artists and browse the CD catalog looking for that last Bach piece to round out your collection. If this isn't enough, why not join other enthusiasts in the discussion rooms and chat about general classical music, opera, or early music. —(E.v.B.)

KEY NEWSGROUP **rec.music.classical** URL▶ http://classicalmus.com/main.html

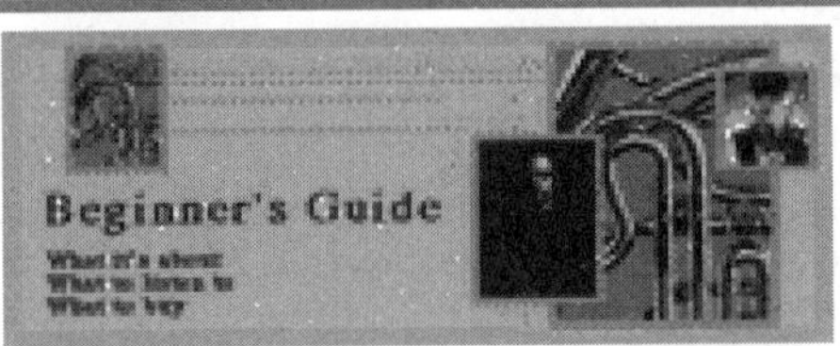

All about Classical Music

FutureNet: Classic CD—Beginners

Jump **2126**

This is not for scholars, or even would-be scholars. This is for the person who is new to classical music, enjoys it, and wants to learn more about it and how to build a collection. These days, most people are introduced to this music through TV commercials, and TV show and movie themes, so the first items on the page are lists of classical works used in these popular entertainments, hyperlinked to descriptions of the full pieces they're taken from. There's also a history of key classical periods, composers, and works, but don't worry—it's very brief, and designed to give you a broad brush to help your understanding and appreciation, not get you a master's degree. Most helpful to new listeners will be the Top 100 CDs, descriptions of the best pieces for creating your own classical library. —(L.S.)

KEY NEWSGROUP **rec.music.classical** URL▶ http://www.futurenet.co.uk/music/classiccd/Beginners/Beginners.html

Where the Fat Lady's Singing

The Opera Schedule Server Jump **2127**

Find out who's playing where around the world with this opera database maintained by Tamas Maray, that's searchable by city, artist, title, or composer. There also are descriptions of opera houses worldwide that include brief histories of the buildings and companies they house, as well as ticket prices and ticket office hours. Rounding out the page are a few links to other opera-related sites. But the value here is in the schedule database, and visitors are encouraged to help keep it as current as possible, by adding to it, and correcting mistakes they may find. —(L.S.)

KEY NEWSGROUP **rec.music.classical** URL▶ http://www.fsz.bme.hu/opera/main.html

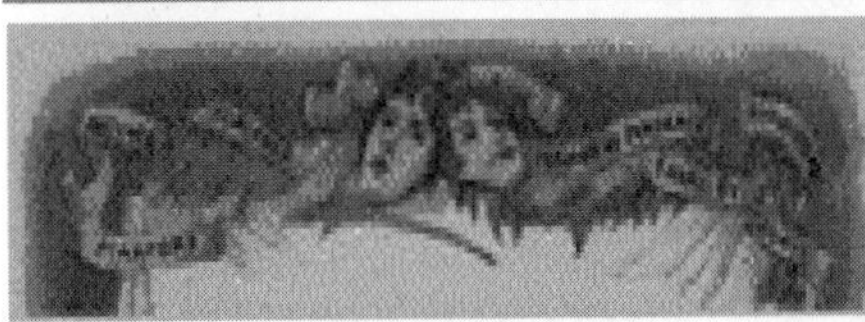

Nanki-Poo Meets Yum-Yum

Gilbert and Sullivan Archive HomePage

Jump **7157**

Gather around, all you fans of Gilbert and Sullivan, raise your glasses in a rousing toast to the keepers of this list. Nearly everything the dedicated fan needs and wants has been posted here by Jim Farron and Alex Feldman. For example, you can read the latest news on performances of these wonderful operas, download librettos and song scores, and even scan plot summaries for a quick fix. The page authors also provide links to the opera schedule server so you can search out performances, festival information, links to other G&S web sites, to photo collections, and even to art pages of related interest. Making a poster for a local performance? Well, feel free to download the G&S clip art that's here, too. —(E.v.B.)

URL▶ http://math.idbsu.edu/gas/GaS.html

Music: Folk, Ethnic & Country

The Steve Goodman Folk Legacy

Eight Ball Blues Jump 2467

If you're not a Chicagoan, you may not recognize the name Steve Goodman. The point man for the Chicago Folk movement of the 1960s and 1970s, he wrote "City of New Orleans," a major hit for Arlo Guthrie and what many believe is the best train song ever written. His songs were at turns touching and humorous, his enthusiasm always contagious, his guitar picking skills among the best in the business. The major regret of his many fans is that he died of leukemia at 36 before he achieved the widespread popularity he deserved. Toby Gibson does both fans and all lovers of good music a great service with this site detailing Goodman's songbook and collaborations with other artists, including Jimmy Buffett. If you're like the legion of fans who miss Steve Goodman, or just a lover of wonderful songs, stop by and learn about one of the best in the business. —(L.S.)

KEY NEWSGROUP **rec.music.folk** URL▶ http://tigger.cc.uic.edu/~toby-g/sg/good.html

The New Country Music Capital of the World

Branson Online Jump 1540

COMMERCE

If you like that old-time, foot-stomping music, then head on out to the Web site of Branson, Missouri, the "music show capital of the world." Hear sound clips of your favorite entertainers—there are theaters dedicated to the likes of the Osmonds, Wayne Newton, Lawrence Welk, Charley Pride, Glen Campbell, Mel Tillis, and more. If you're in the chatting mood, send Mickey Gilley an e-mail and he'll really answer! Then there's the beautiful scenery—take a pictorial tour of the Tri-Lakes area and its attractions, or get the scoop on real estate, lodging, and shopping. If you're a history buff, ride the Trivia Trail, a game to help you learn Ozark history, such as when Silver Dollar City opened its gates—answers are on the bountiful entertainment and attraction pages. With links to the Chamber of Commerce and other music sites, this is an example of good, clever local city promotion on the Web. —(H.L.)

URL▶ http://usa.net:80/branson/

Music: Miscellaneous

Jane's Addiction Web Pages

Jane's Addiction and Porno for Pyros Jump 1006

The funky, hyper sounds of Jane's Addiction fuel these fan pages created by Justin Hall. Drop in to hear some sound bites of main man Perry Farrell talking about all sorts of inspiring topics. —(J.V.O.)

KEY NEWSGROUP **alt.music.alternative** URL▶ http://raptor.swarthmore.edu/jahall/dox/JA.html

Breeders Web Page

The official Breeders Web Page Jump 1007

This is the official Web page for this melodic and noisy group. Check out tour info, discography, and news, direct from the source, as well as preview new material. —(J.V.O.)

KEY NEWSGROUP **alt.music.alternative** URL▶ http://www.nando.net/music/gm/Breeders/

Bjork's Pages

Björk's - Web sense Jump 1002

A beautiful set of pages created, as one fan puts it, "by the goddess herself." Includes everything from sound snippets to interviews to whole videos online. Expect the best, since this enchanted, quirky singer has her hand in its development. —(J.V.O.)

KEY NEWSGROUP **alt.music.bjork** URL▶ http://www.centrum.is/bjork/

Fan Pages for Dead Can Dance

Dead Can Dance Jump 1003

Touted as the official pages by its creator, Raven Zachary, no Dead Can Dance fan should miss this stop. Info on this melodic music ensemble includes notes, film scores and film showdates, and news updates, on top of the typical band tidbits. —(J.V.O.)

URL ▶ http://www.nets.com/dcd

▲ *Devo publicity photo, from* **MuteWeb** *at* Jump 1004.

Devo Fan Pages

MuteWeb Jump 1004

Fellow spudboy Per Henrik Johansen offers up this tribute to the unusual and unstoppable music of Devo. Find all your latest rumors and links to other Devo-sites from this one handy location. Visit the gallery to help relive some special moments of the Devolution. —(J.V.O.)

KEY NEWSGROUP **alt.fan.devo** URL ▶ http://www.nvg.unit.no/~optimus/devo/

Fan Pages for PJ Harvey

PJ Harvey - WWW Home Page Jump 1009

Jason A. Dour provides fans of this strange and forceful songstress with a home on the Web. Here you can find lyrics, bootleg info, and the usual stuff for you obsessed fans. —(J.V.O.)

KEY NEWSGROUP **alt.music.alternative** URL ▶ http://www.louisville.edu/public/jadour01/pjh/

Nine Inch Nails Home Page

The UnOfficial NINE INCH NAILS Home Page Jump 1011

Jason Patterson provides a Web home for all sorts of detail on this deep, dark, and ferocious crossover musical power. Get everything from images, to tour info and articles on the band from this hearty Web site. —(J.V.O.)

KEY NEWSGROUP **alt.music.nin** URL ▶ http://www.scri.fsu.edu/~patters/nin.html

New Order Pages

New Order Jump 1012

Here's a collection of information gathered from the net and the New Order mail list. This site will surely provide fans with the answers they need about these founders of the electronic music movement. —(J.V.O.)

KEY NEWSGROUP **alt.music.alternative** URL ▶ http://slashmc.rice.edu/www/html/ceremony/neworder.html

Home Page for Negativland

Negativworldwidewebland Jump 1013

Despite their legal problems, this band thrives on and off the Net. This site provides a great wealth of information on the band, including texts outlining their legal battles. Also, hear some of the heavy-sampling tracks that helped get these musicians into copyright hot water. —(J.V.O.)

KEY NEWSGROUP **alt.music.alternative** URL ▶ http://sunsite.unc.edu/id/negativland/

Boingo Fan Pages

The Boingo Page Jump 1014

This often spooky, often silly band that peaked in the 1980s is still going strong on the Web in the 1990s. Besides the scoop on their albums and related works, find interviews with lead man Danny Elfman. —(J.V.O.)

KEY NEWSGROUP **alt.fan.oingo-boingo** URL ▶ http://rhino.harvard.edu/dan/boingo/boingo.html

Pixies Pages

Pixies WWW page Jump 1015

A complete discography, as well as a selection of pictures and interviews await Pixies fans at this site. A fine tribute to the twisted and convoluted mix of sounds that were created by this now-defunct band. —(J.V.O.)

KEY NEWSGROUP alt.music.alternative

URL▶ http://www.stack.urc.tue.nl/~patrick/pixies/

Siouxsie and the Banshees Fan Pages

Siouxsie And The Banshees Home Page Jump 1016

CONTENT

Ryan Watkins provides fellows Siouxsie fans with this collection of texts, images, lyrics, and the like on the broody, dark, sensual sound of this long-lived musical group. —(J.V.O.)

KEY NEWSGROUP alt.gothic

URL▶ http://gothic.acs.csulb.edu:8080/Siouxsie/index.html

▲ *Siouxsie and the Banshees, from* **Siouxsie And The Banshees Home Page** *at* Jump **1016**.

Lords of Acid Official Pages

Lords of Acid Jump 1017

This band's label has built them a nice set of pages to celebrate their acquisition. Even though it is concerned mostly with recent works of Lords of Acid, you can still find out plenty of gory details on this infectuous, hardcore dance ensemble from Belgium. —(J.V.O.)

KEY NEWSGROUP alt.music.alternative

URL▶ http://american.recordings.com/American_Artists/Lords_Of_Acid/lords_home.html

Tangerine Dream Pages

Tangerine Dream Home Page Jump 1018

Over the span of 20 years and dozens and dozens of albums, Tangerine Dream has provided sounds ranging from new age to minimalist soundtracks. Scott A. Miller does an excellent job of helping fans walk through this mass of information with this Web site and even throws in back issues of their mailing list and some overview info for good luck. —(J.V.O.)

KEY NEWSGROUP alt.music.alternative URL▶ http://www.public.iastate.edu/~hunter/TD/tngdrm.html

Throwing Muses Fan Pages

Throwing Muses Jump 1019

Sleeve scans, pointer pages, and interviews punctuate the standard details on this site for Throwing Muses fans. Get the whole scoop on this ethereal, angst-ridden ensemble. —(J.V.O.)

KEY NEWSGROUP alt.music.alternative URL▶ http://debra.rau.ac.za:80/Music/Throwing_Muses/

Violent Femmes Pages

The unofficial Violent Femmes Home Page Jump 1020

This long-lived, angst-filled band has been providing college kids with theme songs for years, and now Mike Merryman provides a home for them on the Web. Get the usual mix of info here, as well as bonuses like a puzzle and list of letters and requests concerning the Femmes. —(J.V.O.)

KEY NEWSGROUP alt.music.alternative URL▶ http://umbc8.umbc.edu/~mmerry2/femmes.html

Fan Pages for Tom Waits

Tom Waits Digest Jump 1021

Seth Nielsen pools together film appearances, influences, and a whole pile of tidbits for Tom Waits fans in his site. No fan of this strange, rough-voiced guitar strummer will want to miss these pages. —(J.V.O.)

KEY NEWSGROUP **alt.music.alternative** URL▸ http://www.nwu.edu/music/waits/

Beastie Boys Home Page

Beastie Boys Home Page Jump 1023

The official pages for these uncategorizable crossover crazies. These pages are almost as wacky as they are, with lots of photos and merchandise galore. Also, fans can check out the Beasties' record label, Grand Royale. —(J.V.O.)

KEY NEWSGROUP **alt.music.alternative** URL▸ http://www.nando.net/music/gm/BeastieBoys/

Leningrad Cowboys Home Page

Finland: Leningrad Cowboys Home page Jump 1025

Is this band serious? Is it a spoof? You decide, with the help of these well-stocked Web pages. Find out how these underground cult heros made it to the movies and the bigtime. —(J.V.O.)

KEY NEWSGROUP **alt.music.alternative** URL▸ http://www.mofile.fi/biz/lc/lc.htm

Seattle Alternative Music Mecca

U/Jam Home Page Jump 2258

Seattle is the birthplace of the alternative rock scene, and if you plan a pilgrimage to this mecca of music and angst, visit these pages first for information about the bands, the labels, and the clubs. The club listings include performance schedules and, when appropriate, menus. The band listings include biographies, and record release information. If you just want to keep up with news of the Seattle music scene, that's here, too, updated almost every day. —(L.S.)

KEY NEWSGROUP **alt.music.alternative** URL▸ http://useattle.uspan.com/u-jam.html#bands

Need Some R.E.M.

R.E.M. Home Page Jump 5058

Simone Jarzabek pulled together loads of info for the R.E.M. home page, including the band's latest news, an index to lyrics, a FAQ, discography, articles on R.E.M., other R.E.M. Web resources, and a photo archive. There are also links to a tour FAQ and R.E.M. fan club info and updates. —(S.B.)

KEY NEWSGROUP **rec.music.rem** URL▸ http://www.halcyon.com/rem/index.html

Alternative Music—and Rabbits!

Bunnyhop Magazine Jump 5127

This is the home page for *Bunnyhop Magazine*, a publication that explores pop culture and alternative music. You can access excerpts from current and out-of-print back issues, reader surveys, information on future projects, fluffy pink rabbits, and more. You can also learn about the Bunnyhop staff...they all have a great sense of humor, too! Note, however, that there are no plans to create a full online version of the magazine. —(S.B.)

URL▸ http://slip-2.slip.net/~bunnyhop/

News, Info on Alternative Music & Clubs

Gspot Magazine Jump 5129

Alternative/underground music club reviews from London, New York, and Amsterdam, plus online Web shopping links, fashion links through "Lush and Livid" and "Suburban Electric," feature stories on a spotlighted bands are all here. You'll also find links to interviews, reviews, essays on music and fashion, commentary on clubs, art, technology and film, plus book reviews. The cartoonish graphics make this page very fun to view and read!—(S.B.)

URL▸ http://www.hardnet.co.uk/gspot

Music Talk & Reviews

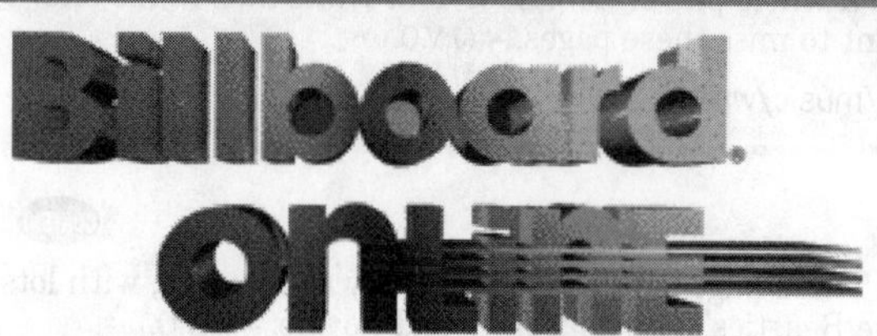

Billboard's Music Site

Billboard Online Jump 5813 CONTENT

When *Billboard*, the bible of the music world arrives on the Internet, it's big news in the music business. And they've done so with such style! Some of the services here are reserved for fee-paying customers, but no need to fret if you don't want to pay to sign on. You'll still have access to most that is the heart and soul of *Billboard*, including the complete charts for the Top 200, Hot 100 Singles, Top R&B, and Country charts and sound samples from many of these. The events calendar is a great addition, as is the Internet Gallery, a list of links to other sites. And of course, there are the lively feature articles to help you keep up on the latest music news. —(J.P.)

URL ▶ http://www.billboard-online.com/

The Sixties!

The Sixties! Jump 6561 

The essence of the 60's is alive and well on the Web, thanks to Don Fass. Don was an editor and broadcaster who came of age in that decade and now gathers its sounds, history and images on his fine personal Web site. Visit here and see echoes of the Kennedys, the Space Program, and pop music icons such as Peter, Paul & Mary, Bob Dylan, Led Zeppelin, the Grateful Dead, The Beatles and the Rolling Stones. You'll also find Don's references to such 60's people and places as Carnaby Street, psychedelia, Martin Luther King, Malcolm X, Elvis, Vietnam War Images, and a library of 60's TV Themes. —(L.T.)

KEY NEWSGROUP alt.rock-n-roll.oldies URL ▶ http://www.slip.net/~scmetro/sixties.htm

Web Intelligent Agent Tracks Your Musical Tastes

The Similarities Engine Jump 3739 

Now this is a neat stop on the Web. The Similarities Engine is a method of recommending new music based on your current musical tastes. Simply click your way to a favorite artist or band, then on to one of their albums and recordings, and The Instant Similarities Engine will recommend some other selections you might enjoy, based on your selection. There's also the Original Similarities Engine, which will do a more detailed analysis based upon five of your favorite recordings—you'll receive your analysis via e-mail in a few days. An early implementation of "intelligent agent" information gathering software, and it's lots of fun—give it a try! —(N.F.)

URL ▶ http://www.webcom.com/~se/

Vote on Your Favorite Songs & Albums

The LEO Archive WWW Charts Jump 2213 

Record charts like *Billboard Magazine*'s only track sales. They don't reflect enduring favorites or album tracks that aren't released as singles. Thanks to Christoph Lorenz and Thomas Eisenbock, you now have a place to vote for your favorite songs, regardless of when or how they were released. Just Web to this page and use the form. The charts are updated hourly, so you can track each day's voting. Or just review the weekly chart update, based on the current and previous three weeks' voting. It's not scientific, but it's fun. —(L.S.)

KEY NEWSGROUP rec.music.info URL ▶ http://www.leo.org/archiv/music/music_charts.html

Readin' & Rockin' Online

POP-i, v.01 — Table of Contents Jump 6009 CONTENT

Plan on spending several hours at this enormous site—truly a Web feast for music fans. View photos, hear the latest sound samples, catch up on an interview of your favorite band, even watch video segments. Great graphics make this site easy and fun to use. And just like you'd expect from a printed magazine, you get letters to the editor, great gossip columns, and, as POP-i's creators say: ". . . tons of absolutely fascinating stuff we can't mention here." —(N.F.)

KEY NEWSGROUP **alt.rock-n-roll** URL▶ http://www.webbiz.com/POPI/

Music News & Info Center

Welcome to Music World III Jump 7472

Here's a comprehensive music resource where you can find information about instruments, music books, music software, latest Net music news, and music companies. Here's a hint of what you'll see here: home pages and zines about your favorite bands and music, and resources available for music industry professionals, info from instrument manufacturers, and current news about the international music scene. —(E.v.B.)

KEY NEWSGROUP **rec.music.info** URL▶ http://www.mw3.com/

Find That Tune

CD Database Search Jump 2270

Use this search engine to find out if your favorite artists' recordings are available on CD, look for a disc with that obscure track you can't seem to find, or just settle a bet. With more than 110,000 CDs available, Craig Knudsen has created one of the more useful sites for music lovers of any stripe. There are actually two databases here, the comprehensive catalog of the Compact Disc Connection, and a smaller database created as part of the Xmcd CD player computer utility. —(L.S.)

KEY NEWSGROUP **rec.music.cd** URL▶ http://www.btg.com/~cknudsen/xmcd/query.html

One Man's Musical Opinion

Al's Review Archive Jump 2379

Al Crawford has written and posted more than 200 record album reviews to the **rec.music.reviews** newsgroup. He archives them here, and they make a very good resource for anyone interested in filling out a record collection with back titles. It's just as good for learning about new releases, since Al keeps writing reviews and has a separate section for the most recent 20. There's good use of Web hyperlinks, too, especially if you want to trace a specific artist's collaborations, participation in other groups, or solo career. And if you get bored reading reviews, but haven't had enough about music, Al thoughtfully includes a list of links to other music-related sites. —(L.S.)

KEY NEWSGROUP **rec.music.reviews** URL▶ http://www.access.digex.net/~awrc/review/

Finding New Music

HOMR—Helpful On-Line Music Recommendation Service Jump 2494

Some people follow the music scene so closely they don't need any help. But there are many others who like music, but for one reason or another don't keep up. For that group, there's HOMR, an interesting database designed to help you find new music that suits your tastes. HOMR asks you what artists you like, then searches its database and returns a list of artists it thinks may interest you. Click on a name and you get a list of albums that, in turn, link to descriptions and other details to help you decide if HOMR was on the mark or not. If nothing else, it's fun, but be careful: If the artists you type in are too diverse in style, HOMR will think you're too weird to be helped! —(L.S.)

KEY NEWSGROUP **rec.music.info** URL▶ http://jeeves.media.mit.edu/ringo/

Voyager CD Store Web Site

The Voyager Jump 3622

If you're into collecting CDs or laser discs, or if you're interested in music of any kind, visit the Voyager. Whether or not the artists they represent are of particular interest to you, this site will perk up your sensibilities. You can

count on finding something new each and every time you visit Voyager. It's an example of a very well-done, and very well-maintained site. —(C.P.)

URL ▶ http://www.voyagerco.com/

UK Music Scene

The Blue Planet Home Page Jump 5056

The Blue Planet Pages provide a complete guide to music entertainment in the United Kingdom. You can find reviews, news, and interviews. Top DJs compile record charts here, and of particular interest is the list of clubs in the UK. It's divided by region and lists clubs by their addresses, phone numbers, and schedules. This is a very nice looking page and is a great connection to the UK music scene. —(S.B.)

URL ▶ http://www.demon.co.uk/blueplanet/index.html

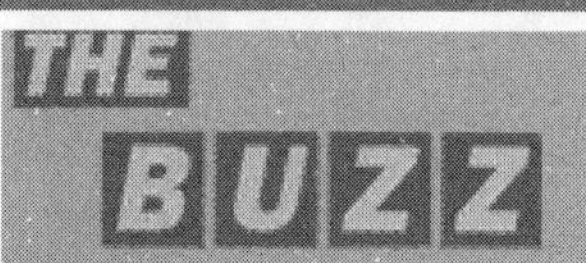

The Buzz (Melbourne's Music)

Buzz Front Page Jump 5095

An online version of the street rock music newspaper for Melbourne's southern suburbs and southeastern country regions, this page features interviews, reviews, and stories about local, national, and international bands touring Australia's southern city. If you want to be up on the Australian rock music scene, this is the place to get your info. —(S.B.)

URL ▶ http://www.ozonline.com.au/TotalNode/AIMC/TheBuzz/Index.html

Tips for Indie Bands

Indie Front by Malibu Stacey Jump 7171

Malibu Stacey, an independent band, maintains this online newsletter to provide information on the making and breaking of indie bands through its articles on business, music, distribution, personnel and networking issues. As well, you can see GIFs of other indie bands including Malibu Stacey, explore links to other indie sites, read reviews of bands and CDs, and read back issues of the Indie Front. —(E.v.B.)

KEY NEWSGROUP **rec.music.misc** URL ▶ http://charlemagne.uwaterloo.ca/home.html

Listen before You Buy

GeZi's Record Outlet Jump 2351

Of course, you can buy CDs through this page, but the real reason to visit is to learn about some worthy musicians who do not get the publicity afforded to major label artists. The offerings are limited, but growing, and the information about the bands and CDs is deep. You'll find a description of the CD, a complete list of tracks, including playing time, and background on the band and its music. Much effort goes into creating these pages, and if you're looking for good music that hasn't yet hit the mainstream, it's definitely worth the visit. —(L.S.)

KEY NEWSGROUP **rec.music.cd** URL ▶ http://www.gezi.com/gzworld/rec_out.html

Music Makers' Pages

Playing Your Guitar like a Violin

Granger's Fiddle Tunes for Guitar Jump 2184

Good fiddle music is real toe-tapping fun, and these pages will show guitar players how to simulate fiddle music on their instruments. The technique is called flatpicking, and Adam Granger has put the instructional guide to flatpicking from his book, *Granger's Fiddle Tunes for Guitar*, on the Web. If you don't yet know how to play, there's a tutorial on the basics of rhythm guitar, too. There are a few fiddle-to-guitar transcriptions included here, but if you want all 500 transcriptions, you'll have to buy the book. —(L.S.)

KEY NEWSGROUP **rec.music.makers.guitar** URL ▶ http://www.musicman.com/ag/gft.html

Guitar Player's Archive

Guitar Jump 2305

Guitarists looking for the chords of particular song likely will not need to look further than Paul Newton's page. A link to the University of Nevada music archive is here, with tablature for more than 6,000 songs. If it doesn't have what you want, or you need lyrics, discographies, or even lessons, you'll find links to most of the other guitar-related archives here, as well. There are also FAQs for classical and flamenco guitar, links to other guitar- and music-related Web pages, and an overview of the Usenet tablature newsgroups. —(L.S.)

KEY NEWSGROUP **rec.music.makers.guitar.tablature** URL▶ http://www.realtime.net/~bleonard/music_urls.html

All about Guitar Playing & Building

You're Plugged into Guitar Net
Jump 2741

An outgrowth of Gawain Reifsnyder's popular Chord-Of-The-Week site, GUITAR.NET is an online community of players, guitar makers, teachers, and resources. The result is one of the better music resources of any kind on the Web, excellent for professionals as well as enthusiasts. There is, of course, the Chord-of-the-Week. There's also Abe Wechter's Ask the Guitar Maker, where he offers tips on guitar making and care, plus an online archive with more than 10,000 transcriptions, chord charts, and tablature files for guitar and bass. —(L.S.)

KEY NEWSGROUP **rec.music.makers.guitar** URL▶ http://www.guitar.net/

Musical Plaid

The Bagpipe Web Jump 7378

CONTENT

Hoot, mon! John Wash has created a real tartan of a home page featuring some of the world's top bagpipe makers. John also chronicles the changes in Scottish music. The Great Highland Bagpipe page is a real squeeze and wheeze, as well are the smaller "clans"—pages for pipe bands from around the world. Real enthusiasts can also find pointers to and information on piping-related organizations, schedules for workshops, gatherings, festivals, etc., addresses of bagpipe music sources and bagpipe shops, as well as a full list of Internet piping resources. John also kindly allows you to post ads for selling or buying bagpipes. And once you have your pipes in tune, don't hesitate to download some of the GIFs picture files with piping tunes. —(E.v.B.)

KEY NEWSGROUP **soc.culture.celtic** URL▶ http://pipes.tico.com/pipes/pipes.html

Web Stop for MIDI Mavens

Yamaha XG Jump 3697

Yamaha (you know that name—you've seen it on products that range from grand pianos to (grand) Motorcycles—has arrived on the Web with a way-cool site promoting its new XG Standard, the latest and greatest thing to hit the world of electronic music. If you're a game developer, this site also offers detailed technical specifications, informational files and fabulous images of Yamaha's electronic music products. Great links to Internet MIDI and e-music sites, including every newsgroup of interest to electronic composers! —(C.P.)

KEY NEWSGROUP **comp.music** URL▶ http://www.ysba.com

MIDI Musicians' Resources

MIDI Home Page
Jump 0198

A MIDI player's treasure trove compiled by Heini Withagen. Features plenty of valuable articles and tech tips for novice through advanced MIDI players, links to many MIDI sequence and sample archives, MIDI software utilities, MIDI keyboard special-interest group links and much more. If you're into MIDI, this site is your best first stop! —(E.G.)

KEY NEWSGROUP **alt.binaries.sound.midi** URL▶ http://www.eeb.ele.tue.nl/midi/index.html

Musicians' Clearinghouse

The Buddy Project Jump 2401

Got a song you just can't finish? Need words for your music, or music for your words? Looking for collaborators in general? Want feedback on something you've written? Then come to The Buddy Project, where you can upload your compositions, connect with potential collaborators, or just download some new music from other composers. For those who aren't well-versed in creating computer-playable sound files, there's a good tutorial, as well as a downloadable software archive with helpful tools. And if you don't want to deal with digitizing your sounds, you can mail a cassette tape and The Buddy Project will upload it for you. —(L.S.)

KEY NEWSGROUP **rec.music.makers** URL▶ http://www.buddy.org/

Movies & Moviemaking

Actors Online

Actors Online Jump 5650

You don't have to be an actor to use Actors Online, the site devoted to promoting the talents of professional actors. There is something here for everyone, but if you are an actor, this has got to be one of "the" places to be. They offer free listings to actors who want to place an ad (including headshot) online, in the hopes that it might be seen by entertainment professionals in search of serious actors. A terrific idea, to be sure, and there is also a trivia section, news bytes, hotlinks to related sites, and a special Actor of the Week section. —(J.P.)

URL▶ http://www.actorsonline.com/

Microsoft Cinemania

Microsoft Cinemania Jump 5647

If you like movies you'll love Cinemania. It's the who's who and what's what of the film world. You can start off with the Film Appreciation 101, a somewhat controversial list (aren't they all!) of films you "must see before you die." Sounds rather drastic to us. But there's more, including up-to-the-minute film reviews, the latest video releases, and entertainment news. There is really and truly something here for every movie buff. —(J.P.)

URL▶ http://www.msn.com/cinemania/

Film Maker's Resource

The Independent Film and Video Makers Internet Resource Guide Jump 2251

This page is rich with links that will lead the independent film maker to virtually any resource on the Net. Financing, film festivals, and general resources are here, but Mike Vidal does a more important job in tracking resources for keeping current with the development and impact of new technologies, such as interactive television, multimedia, and movies on demand. For those just coming to the Internet, he also provides detailed descriptions of available e-mail discussion lists, which are the best places on the Net for independent film makers to learn from and share experiences with peers. —(L.S.)

KEY NEWSGROUP **rec.arts.movies.production** URL▶ http://www.echonyc.com/~mvidal/Indi-Film+Video.html

Hollywood In-Depth

THE HOLLYWOOD REPORTER Jump 7500

The Hollywood Reporter gives you the low-down on the business of Tinseltown. Solid news items give you the latest news on film studio mergers, news flashes on which star is signed for what film, or the titles of the newest music video releases. Stop by daily to sample constantly updated news briefs from the entertainment and media worlds. If you need more in-depth coverage, you can also subscribe to expanded newsstand versions of what's found online here. —(E.v.B.)

KEY NEWSGROUP **clari.living.entertainment** URL▶ http://www.hollywoodreporter.com/m.shtml

Hollywood Live!

Hollywood Live! Jump 6513

Grab some glitzy glamour and meet the Stars behind the Stars. Hollywood Live! delivers interviews with screenwriters Joe Eszterhas and Naomi Foner, and producers Henry Jaglom, David Permut, Bud Yorkin, and Wes Craven. While you're there, check out the Talking Book Directory, an extensive AudioBook Library, with recordings from Deepak Chopra, Jack Canfield, Barbara DeAngelis, and many other bestselling authors. Live Chat Lounges and events also provide a constant source of interaction for talk of the Big Screen.—(L.T.)

KEY NEWSGROUP **alt.celebrities** URL ▶ http://www.hollywoodnetwork.com/

Film Fest Jumplist

Film Festival Directory Jump 2673

Film buffs and even casual movie fans will find this listing of the world's film festival Web pages a handy bookmark. Maintained by the Chicago Film Festival, it's just a list of links, but it's very comprehensive and up to date. Of course, you can easily jump to the Chicago Film Festival's page, particularly if you want to see this year's very hot Victor Skrebneski poster. And if you're interested, the eyes on the Chicago festival's logo belong to silent film actress Clara Bow. —(L.S.)

KEY NEWSGROUP **rec.arts.cinema** URL ▶ http://www.ddbn.com/filmfest/filmfestdirectory.html

Special Effects from The Character Shop

The Character Shop Jump 6738

Amazed by Hollywood's special effects? Want some tips for breaking into the special effects field yourself? The Character Shop's site will show you the ropes. The creators of this site should know what they're talking about, since they were the ones responsible for creating the frog puppets you've seen in those entertaining Budweiser commercials. This site offers an inside look at the processes involved in creating special effects, interesting feature articles on the art and craft of Hollywood special effects, and even a glossary of FX terms.—(L.T.)

KEY NEWSGROUP **rec.arts.cinema** URL ▶ http://www.character-shop.com

Film Buff's Jumplist

Cinema Sites Jump 2279

If you're looking for film-related Web sites, don't miss this spot. David Augsburger has created a massive page of links covering every aspect of the movies, or at least every aspect with a Web page. Theatrical and TV movies, live action and animation, credits, news, and technology resources are all covered here. If the links to specific movies, guides, festivals, phonebooks, or commercial and other resources don't include what you want, the link to the Net's massive Cardiff movie database search sites (at Jump **0097**) likely will. —(L.S.)

KEY NEWSGROUP **rec.arts.movies** URL ▶ http://www.vir.com/VideoFilm/davidaug/Movie_Sites.html

Amateur Filmmaking

Fine Cut Jump 2734

Amateur moviemakers, whether experienced of just beginning, can hone their craft with the information at this site. Although it's heavily oriented toward video, Terry Mendoza's collection of articles and tips can be helpful for traditional film, too. Learn how to plan, edit, and enhance your movie to grab and keep your audience involved, discover the ins and outs of camcorders, and use the practical guides to moviemaking as a regular reference as you create. You can even find out where to show your films, with links to film and video festivals around the world. —(L.S.)

KEY NEWSGROUP **rec.arts.cinema** URL ▶ http://www.rmplc.co.uk./eduweb/sites/terrymen/movie1.html

For Fans of Quentin Tarantino

Quentin Tarantino Jump 2473

He burst onto the scene with "Reservoir Dogs" and earned his place as one of the cinema greats with "Pulp Fiction." He's violent, humorous, and always intriguing, melding the sensibilities of film noir with a personal vision that is purely contemporary. There's no one quite like Quentin Tarantino, which is why his fans are so dedicated to his art. One of them is Mike V., who offers this site of links to Tarantino's two major films, general Tarantino sites maintained by fans, and FTP sites for downloading other tidbits of Quentin-mania. If you haven't experienced Tarantino, and don't mind blood and gore, this is the best place to start your exploration. If you're already a fan, this is the place to go to keep up with the latest and the greatest. —(L.S.)

KEY NEWSGROUP **alt.fan.tarantino** URL▶ http://www.smartdocs.com/~migre.v/APXIB/tarantino.html

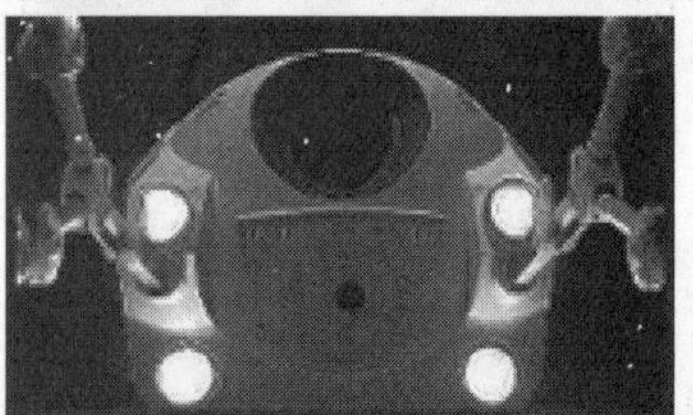

The Films of Stanley Kubrick

Kubrick on the Web Jump 1568

If you like Stanley Kubrick, you'll love Barry Krusch's self-proclaimed "high-level index to anything and everything of quality on the Web that pertains to Stanley Kubrick and his films." Read the "2001" screenplay online. Leap over to like-minded Patrick Larkin's Kubrick Multimedia Film Guide. If that's not enough, Krusch provides plenty of spots to link to Kubrick films on the Internet Movie Database. —(H.L.)

KEY NEWSGROUP **alt.movies.kubrick** URL▶ http://www.automatrix.com/~bak/kubrick/kubrick.html

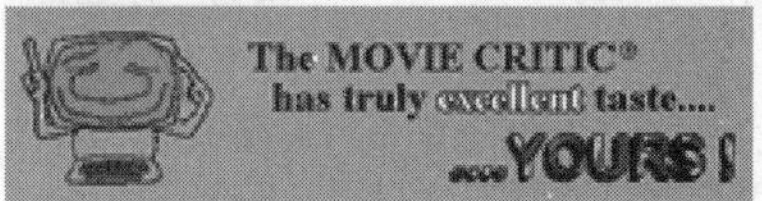

Will You Like That Movie?

The Movie Critic Jump 2732

This is one of the niftiest places on the Web for movie fans. The site takes information about how much you enjoyed, or didn't enjoy, movies you've seen, and uses that information to let you know how you'll probably feel about movies you haven't seen yet. Using artificial intelligence (which already puts it way ahead of most professional reviewers), it takes your ratings, compares them with the ratings others have given the same movies, and predicts how you'll rate new flicks. Even if it didn't work, it would be fun to play with. But it does work, although you have to take the time to rate a good number of movies before it can get a good handle on your tastes. —(L.S.)

KEY NEWSGROUP **rec.arts.movies.reviews** URL▶ http://www.moviecritic.com/

First-Run Movies & Sports

COMMERCE

Welcome To Viewer's Choice Jump 7386

Viewer's Choice television brings sweat, blood, and muscle-popping tension—through movies, of course—to your home television screen. Online, it's called VC InterActive—a one-stop source for film, wrestling, boxing, etc., and when it's all coming up on Pay-Per-View. You can browse through photos from the selection of pay-per-view films, and plot information. Check out the schedules for all six channels. Don't forget to participate in the monthly contests . . . you might win a prize! —(E.v.B.)

KEY NEWSGROUP **rec.video.cable-tv** URL▶ http://www.ppv.com/

The Movies—and More!

The Film Zone Jump 2746

There aren't too many Web sites as good as Film Zone, an all-encompassing site that covers film both as fine art and as pure entertainment. A must-see site for anyone with any interest in the movies, it starts with reviews and news about new films and new releases on laserdisc and video. But it offers criticism and analysis, too, with sections covering the art and artists that create the overall look and feel for a film, the music that enhances emotional impact, and interviews with leading filmmakers. There are sections covering foreign films and independent releases, animation, even rock videos. There's even a series of online film festivals that discuss films of similar theme, genre, or other shared attribute. And it's all accented with great graphics, sound, and links. —(L.S.)

KEY NEWSGROUP **rec.arts.cinema** URL ▶ http://www.filmzone.com/

The Internet Movie Database

Internet Movie Database Jump **0097**

A mind-blowingly massive Web database covering over 37,000 films, the Internet Movie Database is a volunteer effort put together by devoted Net movie fans around the world and rivals the quality of any commercially published movie guide. What's special about the Internet Movie Database (also known around the Net as Cardiff's Movie Database) is that you can be a part of it too, by submitting your ratings on the movies you've seen. This reader-contributed aspect of the Movie Database is what's made it so exciting, special, comprehensive and huge. Features extensive information on individual films—cast members, credits, plot summaries, technical filmmaker's information and trivia. Movies can also be searched in this database by genre, locations, soundtracks, actors, and plot summaries, so if you're a movie lover you can spend much time browsing here. Highly recommended! —(E.G.)

KEY NEWSGROUP **rec.arts.movies** URL ▶ http://www.msstate.edu/Movies/welcome.html

The Ultimate Film Site

Virtual Film Festival Jump **2757**

If you've ever wondered what it's like to be at a film festival, this site is as close as you can get without actually jetting off to Cannes or wherever. It's not just a series of pages, it's a true MOO, a multiuser object-oriented environment, that puts you in the thick of the hustle and bustle of a real film festival. Nor is it a fantasy. This is a real film festival that just happens to be online. You'll likely spend most of your time in the Screening Room with its film clips, sound clips, still photographs, and documentation on international films in a variety of genre. But don't miss stopping by the Café for bright and witty conversation, or the Press Conferences for information about new movies and the film industry in general. You'll want to check MagNet, too, the Virtual Film Festival's online magazine with news, features, and reviews. And if you're in the film industry, there's a Deal Makers Room with bulletins, jobs wanted and sought, and even real-time pitch sessions. This isn't a site to hit and run, or even spend just a few hours with. It's a site that will take several sessions over days to even begin to explore everything that's here, and one any film buff or professional will want to come back to regularly. —(L.S.)

KEY NEWSGROUP **rec.arts.cinema** URL ▶ http://www.virtualfilm.com/

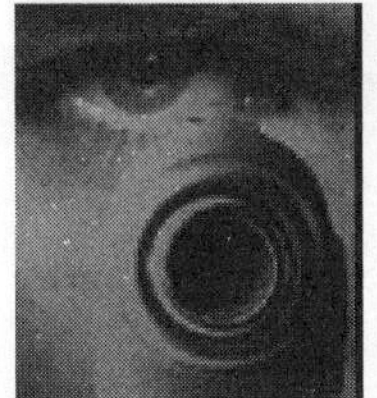

Bond, James Bond . . .

Commanders Club/San Francisco: James Bond 007 Home Page Jump **3709**

James Bond, 007, is more than just a character from a book or a movie. He's become a cultural icon. Stop by the Commanders Club, which "seeks to preserve the elegant lifestyle and sense of intrigue that was born of Fleming's writings and James Bond in the Cinema." They have quite a collection of Bond memorabilia, including British first editions, cinema art, photos, and original sountracks and recordings. And of course, plenty of details on the actors, the films, and the books. Lots of links, too, to other Bond Web pages to visit. —(N.F.)

KEY NEWSGROUP **alt.fan.james-bond** URL ▶ http://www.commanders.com/~bond/

Film Buff's Paradise

Welcome to Film.com Jump **7282**

Movies, movies, movies—classics and new releases are reviewed here in detail. If want to know what you can expect three months from now in movie theaters, you should read the Sneak Peeks section. CD versions of movie soundtracks are also reviewed, links to movie archives on the Net are posted, future film festivals are noted, and past ones are reviewed. Serious film buffs will find much to feed their obsession. —(E.v.B.)

KEY NEWSGROUP **bit.listserv.cinema-l** URL ▶ http://www.film.com/

Movie News & Previews

Hollywood Online Jump 7444 CONTENT

Movie buffs hang onto your hats. Has Hollywood Online Inc. got a load of entertainment information for you! Whether it's movies, television, music, or home videos you're interested in, Hollywood Online delivers. You can download one of its proprietary "Interactive Multimedia Kits," or view neat film-related photographs, electronic magazines, movie production notes, celebrity information, user libraries, promotional contests, games, interactive conferencing, including chat rooms and forums, topical message boards catering to both industry professionals as well as movie and TV fans. Enough? Well, if not, you can also explore links to other entertainment sites, sneak peeks of upcoming films, tour luxury homes, and watch some movie trailers. —(E.v.B.)

KEY NEWSGROUP rec.arts.cinema

URL ▶ http://www.hollywood.com/

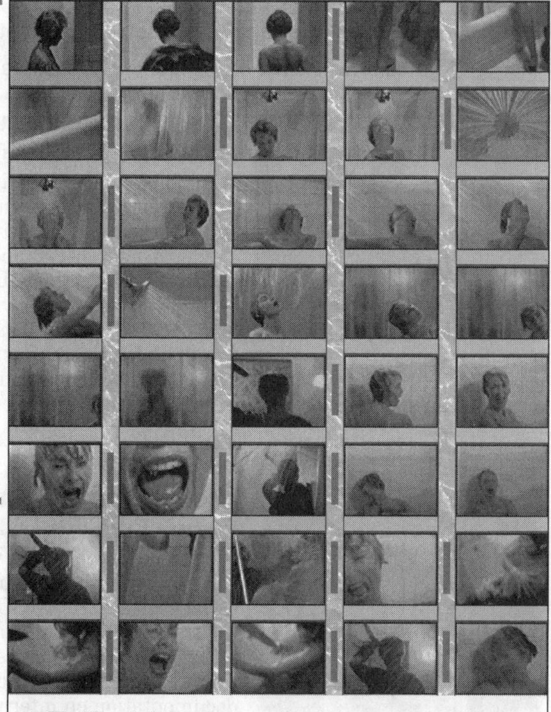

▲ *The "Psycho" shower scene, from* **The Hitchcock Page** *at* Jump 3725.

The Master of Suspense

The Hitchcock Page Jump 3725 CONTENT

Alfred Hitchcock, in his 80 years, was one of the greatest directors in the history of cinema. Original Cinema Productions, in this outstanding Web tribute, covers Hitchcock's life and times, along with a complete history of his works. The Filmography section, complete unto itself, will take you directly into The Internet Movie Database for even more details on over 70 Hitchcock films. The Hitch on Television section covers 20 episodes of the famous 1960s TV series. Hitchcock loved to appear in his works—track each and every appearance in the Cameos section. Pure Cinema is a neat concept that takes us, frame by frame, through the shower scene in *Psycho*. Stop by the Feedback section to ask any questions you may have, and while you're at it, take a shot at answering some tough trivia questions stumping this site's creators. A great place to visit! —(N.F.)

URL ▶ http://www.primenet.com/~mwc/

Alternative Cinema

Flicker Home Page Jump 7456

Scott Stark has developed a set of pages that define "the alternative cinematic experience." Here you'll find films and videos that "transgress the boundaries of the traditional viewing experience, challenge notions of physical perception and provide cutting-edge alternatives to the media information technocracy." That is, you will be able to access film and video artists' home pages and sample some of their works, find out where and when alternative film and video exhibitions are taking place, access a resource list for media artists, and enjoy a sampling of images from Flicker's collection of films and videos. As well, you can read about the hottest and freshest new films and videos, and find a listing of alternative cinematic sites. —(E.v.B.)

KEY NEWSGROUP rec.arts.cinema URL ▶ http://www.sirius.com/~sstark/

Doug Thomas' Cinemaven Online Movie Reviews

Cinemaven On-Line Home Page Jump 0154 CONTENT

Syndicated Seattle movie reviewer Doug Thomas' nicely-done Web site featuring Doug's latest reviews, his movie pick of the week, an online gallery of movie promotional pictures for downloading, top video rental picks, top ten movies selected by year, and an archive of his past movie reviews. A polished and professional Web site featuring top-notch writing! —(E.G.)

URL▶ http://www.uspan.com:80/mavin.html/

▲ *Harrison Ford and Sean Young, in "Blade Runner," from* **Off-World (Blade Runner Page)** *at* Jump **4042**.

Queen of the Toons

The Betty Boop Archive
Jump **2247**

The object of adolescent fantasies for several generations, and quite likely for at least several more, Betty Boop now graces the Web with this page of pictures and animations. You'll also find a complete list of Betty's film credits, a fantasized biography of the two-dimensional sex symbol, and comments from fans on the impact of Betty on their lives. Boopsters are encouraged to send their contributions to keep the page growing. Just e-mail your contribution to **voidmstr@phantom.com**. —(L.S.)

KEY NEWSGROUP **rec.arts.animation** URL▶ http://www.phantom.com/~voidmstr/BettyBoopArchive.html

Blade Runner Fans' Site

Off-World (Blade Runner Page)
Jump **4042**

This is the best and most popular site for information on the sci-fi cyberpunk classic film *Blade Runner*. "Off World" offers all sorts of resources dealing with the Phillip K. Dick-inspired movie, including the Blade Runner FAQ, compilations of discussions about Blade Runner issues, and links to lots of goodies like images, sounds, and clips from the movie. The perfect place for interested fans! —(R.B.)

KEY NEWSGROUP **alt.fan.blade-runner** URL▶ http://kzsu.stanford.edu/uwi/br/off-world.html

BLADE RUNNER

More *Blade Runner* Action

The Official BLADE RUNNER On-Line Magazine
Jump **7302**

CONTENT

If you're a *Blade Runner* fan, you're going to love this site. It's chock full of great pictures and a chronological rundown of each scene in the movie. If you have a favorite segment from the movie, such as searching for clues in the Animoid Mart, or watching super replicant Roy Batty seeking out Dr. Tyrell, you can view them on their own. A value-added feature is the last interview with the author, Phillip K. Dick. Audio files, links to other Blade Runner Web sites, and merchandise information are also available. —(E.v.B.)

KEY NEWSGROUP **alt.cult-movies** URL▶ http://www.wit.com/~xtian/blade_runner.html

Cult Film Home Base

The Cult Shop Jump **2546**

CONTENT

Cult movie fans don't always share the same tastes, but Adam Bormann nonetheless will appeal to most cultists with this site covering the more well-known cult movie figures. The two main sections feature directors and writers, such as the Coen Brothers, John Carpenter and Sam Raimi, and actors, including Bruce Campbell and Ted Raimi. With each, there are filmographies, images, and critical essays. New movies and movies in production featuring cult figures are here, too, and there's links to other cult movie sites on the Web. —(L.S.)

KEY NEWSGROUP **alt.cult-movies** URL▶ http://www.public.iastate.edu/~abormann/

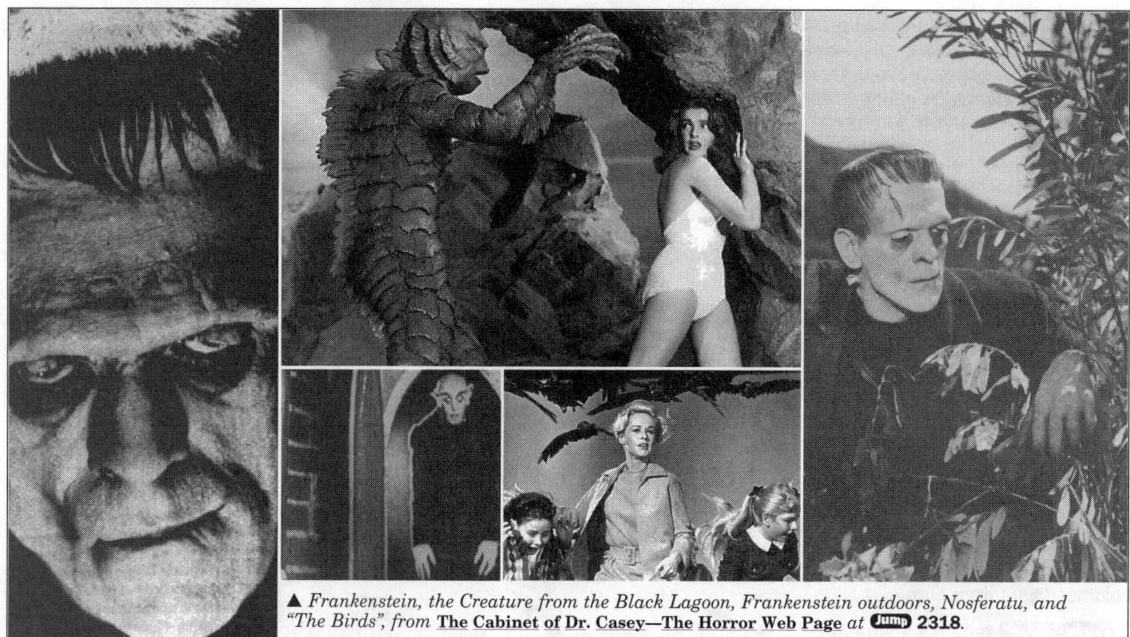

▲ *Frankenstein, the Creature from the Black Lagoon, Frankenstein outdoors, Nosferatu, and "The Birds", from* **The Cabinet of Dr. Casey—The Horror Web Page** *at* Jump 2318.

Fright Web

The Cabinet of Dr. Casey—The Horror Web Page Jump 2318 CONTENT

Horror fans will delight at Casey Hopkins's page covering the dark side of art and entertainment. There are pictures, video and sound clips, a Best Horror Movies list with biographies and filmographies of actors and directors, and a horror time line from the 13th century to the present. For readers, there's an author's list with bibliographies, online horror novels, and stories written by horror fans. The site is expanding, and if you have something you think fits, send it to Casey. —(L.S.)

KEY NEWSGROUP **alt.horror** URL▶ http://www.ee.pdx.edu/~caseyh/horror/horror.html

Asian Movie Cults

Hong Kong Movies Home Page Jump 2548 CONTENT

There are no doubt many fine Asian films and filmmakers, but that's not the point of this site. Rather, it's for those who love the dumb and cheap, but always exciting and often humorous, Hong Kong action film genre. For the newcomer, page maintainer Lars Erik Holmquist provides an excellent introduction, including a list of films that offer a good cross section of the genre. There are filmographies, faqs, information on how to find hard-to-get videos, and extended information on the leading Hong Kong actors and actresses, including action king Jackie Chan. There's even a searchable database of the site's contents, including a database of alternate movie names, a helpful feature considering that many movies have different titles depending on the country of release. —(L.S.)

KEY NEWSGROUP **alt.cult-movies** URL▶ http://www.mdstud.chalmers.se/hkmovie/

Godzilla Stomps the Web!

Mel's Godzilla Page Jump 2549 

The epitome of the cheap production values, stupid plots, and rabid loyalty that mark the best cult films, nothing compares to the *Godzilla* series. Mark Meloon does the King of the Monsters the justice he deserves with this page of Godzilla facts, fancies, images, sound files, and memorabilia. You'll be able to find out about all the movies, from the 1954 original to the 22nd and latest epic due out in December, 1995, as well as news about movie showings on television. You'll also learn details on all of Godzilla's enemies—from Mothra to King Kong, complete with scorecards rating their battles. There's even extensive information about Godzilla models and toys, with instructions on where to get them and how to care for them. —(L.S.)

KEY NEWSGROUP **alt.monster.movies** URL▶ http://www.ama.caltech.edu/~mrm/godzilla.html

---

Adventures with Indiana Jones on the Web

The Indiana Jones WWW Page Jump 4046

CONTENT

Micah Johnson maintains this site devoted to the popular adventurer and main character from the series of movies and books. You can access images and sounds from the movies, look up all sorts of information on them, read theories on the Lost Ark of the Covenant, and even look at some Indiana Jones spoofs! Great page if you enjoy this adventure series. —(R.B.)

KEY NEWSGROUP **rec.arts.movies** URL▶ http://astrowww.astro.indiana.edu/personnel/msjohnso/

Images of Marilyn

The Marilyn Pages Jump 7336

J. Ellen Cotton has created some beautifully-designed pages devoted to Marilyn Monroe. You can surf links to other Marilyn pages, find online sources of memorabilia such as movie posters and signed photographs, read a short biography, download a list of movies Marilyn appeared in, and browse through a gallery of images devoted to the beautiful Marilyn. —(E.v.B.)

KEY NEWSGROUP **alt.celebrities** URL▶ http://www.ionet.net/~jellenc/marilyn.html

---

Disney's Aladdin Site

Disney's Aladdin Jump 5634

You have to hand it to Disney when it comes to creating a franchise. Nobody does it better. And few can match the skill and dedication they have put into their Web sites, either. Children of all ages will enjoy taking part in this site's Aladdin trivia challenge, and seeing the wonderful colorful photos that are the hallmark of Disney animation. —(J.P.)

URL▶ http://www.disney.com/DisneyTelevision/Aladdin/AladdinG.html

---

Disney's *The Lion King*

The Lion King Jump 5013

Disney brought the "Circle of Life" to the silver screen with the release of *The Lion King*. Now you can bring it to your own home computer! Download and view QuickTime clips (they're rather large) from the film. While you're here, make sure to check out the links to press kit material and promotional stills (color as well as black-and-white images). This page includes the size of each file and the file type, so you know what you're getting into, before you start downloading. —(S.B.)

URL▶ http://bvp.wdp.com/BVPM/PressRoom/LionKing/LionKing.html

---

Coming Attractions from MGM/UA

The Lion's Den Jump 5042

The Lion's Den is MGM/UA's Web page, featuring info on their latest movies and previews of upcoming films releases. There are also links to upcoming projects, info on classic MGM/UA movies, The General Store for purchasing merchandise, and The Lab, where you can share your opinions on movie projects. There are also movie icons you can select to get an in-depth preview of an upcoming feature, complete with QuickTime movie clips and pictures. —(S.B.)

URL▶ http://www.digiplanet.com/MGM/

Screenwriters Alert

The Movie Cliches List Jump 7197

Giancarlo Cairella obviously watches a lot of movies, from which he has extracted an immense number of cliches. Screenwriters and movie buffs alike can educate themselves on plot twists and events that have been used once too often. You can search from A to Z—from airplanes to locks to traffic to women—and read the cliches associated with each subject. Humbling for the writer, but hilarious for the movie lover! —(E.v.B.)

KEY NEWSGROUP **rec.arts.cinema** URL▶ http://www.well.com/user/vertigo/cliches.html

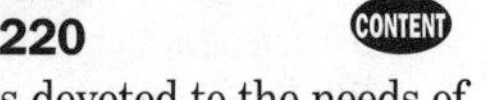

Independent Movie Makers

FilmMaker Magazine Jump 7220

CONTENT

This e-zine, *FilmMaker Magazine*, is devoted to the needs of and resources of independent film makers. The issues are packed full of news, profiles, and reviews. The site also supports a number of extremely useful links—such as to the Internet Movie Database, MCA/Universal Cyberwalk for their latest movie releases, Rogue Cinema, where filmmakers can meet and (maybe) find a distributor. Need more? The site also connects you to film festival resources, screenwriters, professional associations, and a host of relevant newsgroups. —(E.v.B.)

KEY NEWSGROUP **rec.arts.movies** URL▶ http://found.cs.nyu.edu/CAT/affiliates/filmmaker/filmmaker.html

I'm Ready for My Closeup!

Earthlink's Hollywood Jump 1569

COMMERCE

As every Web-wanderer knows, entertainment makes the Net go 'round. Earthlink is hoping to cash in big with the movie biz at this Web site. They say "our goal is to make these pages the most comprehensive resource for information about the Hollywood Entertainment Industry." You'll say: "Golly, yet another place to download Jim Carrey gifs." The site provides movie reviews, Hollywood events, and, it should go without saying, merchandise. There are links to other entertainment-related sites including Hollywood Online and Hollyweb. Maybe some big Hollywood producer will discover you as you hunch over mouse in some nondescript e-café perusing these pages. —(H.L.)

URL▶ http://www.earthlink.net/hollywood/

Film & Television Producers' Resources

HollyNet Newsgroup Jump 0150

COMMERCE

A project of the University of Southern California, HollyNet is an interesting Web site which provides all types of informational resources to anyone currently involved with, or wanting to be involved with, the film and television industry. Features comprehensive listings of producers, writers, talent, equipment and service suppliers for TV, and film plus listings of film, TV, and multimedia consultants. An interesting, fun place to browse, even if you're only just mildly interested in the film or TV business. HollyNet, a project of the Entertainment Technology Center at USC, is sponosered jointly by Paramount, Pacific Bell, Warner Brothers, Viacom, Radius, and Apple Computer. —(E.G.)

KEY NEWSGROUP **rec.video.production** URL▶ http://cwis.usc.edu/dept/etc/hollynet/

Theatre Arts

Smell the Greasepaint, Hear the Crowd

Theatre Central
Jump 2374

From 42nd Street to off-off-off Broadway, from high drama to low comedy, if it's theater and on the Web, it's here. Unlike similar sites, this page covers amateur and scholastic, as well as professional theater resources. There's a "What's New" list and general table of contents covering theater contacts, writing and literature, companies and calendars, academic programs, theater groups, and magazines and newsgroups. Aside from being excellently organized in general, maintainer Andrew Q. Kraft makes browsing the list easier, too, with icons to highlight new or recently reworked links, indexes, and links to theater-related services. —(L.S.)

KEY NEWSGROUP **rec.arts.theatre** URL▶ http://www.mit.edu:8001/people/quijote/theatre-central.html

The Shakespeare Home Page

Entrance to the Shakespeare Web Jump 0160

A fascinating Web resource that truly lives up to its claim as "a one-stop shopping center for all your Bard-related needs and desires!" Judging from the looks of this Web jump site, there's lots of Shakespeare stuff to do—try your hand at their quotation contest, participate in an online Shakespearean play on the Net, and even search the complete works of Shakespeare online. Also a nice stop for interesting Shakespeare FAQ files for many of us embarrassed Websters who would like to learn more about the Bard and his works. —(E.G.)

KEY NEWSGROUP **bit.listserv.literary** URL▶ http://sashimi.wwa.com/~culturew/Shakesweb/shakesweb.html

Wired Dancers

Troika Ranch Home Page Jump 7100

Troika Ranch, a performance group created by the innovative Mark Coniglio and Dawn Stoppiello, makes extensive use of interactive media in their live performances. The dancers wear sensors that transmit their movement to computers running synthesizers, and lighting, audio and video programs. Pretty neat. Interested in wiring yourself up? Check out the group's "geek page" for detailed instructions. Before you begin interacting with your computer, check out the photos of their performances, biographies, and reviews of their work. —(E.v.B.)

KEY NEWSGROUP **rec.arts.dance** URL▶ http://www.art.net/Studios/Performance/Dance/Troika_Ranch/TroikaHome.html

Wired Broadway

Broadway World-Wide Jump 7190

Are you an aspiring, New York-bound actor? Or just a theater lover? Well, this extensive site has offerings for both groups. Actors can scan the "help wanted" ads, or read the latest news about on- and off-Broadway shows—coming, going, or the ones which are just a gleam in a producer's eye. Theater lovers can download details—from seat cost to cast names to plot summaries—of plays that they can then choose from. Books and records are also listed. Playbill also recognizes that plays are happening in other areas of the world, so regional and London listings can be seen here, too. —(E.v.B.)

KEY NEWSGROUP **rec.arts.theater** URL▶ http://www.webcom.com/~broadway/

Radio Pages

Garrison Keillor Online

A Prairie Home Companion® Jump 7443

Is one of your favorite radio shows the *Prairie Home Companion*? If so, you're going to love this site. You can find the schedules and guests lined up for the next few months for the two-hour show, hosted by the one and only Garrison Keillor. Touring and ticket information, a bio of Keillor, and more information on Minnesota Public Radio is also available. As well, you can access the readings from Keillor's *The Writer's Almanac®*, a daily program of poetry and history, and then surf the links to some of the topics and people he discusses. —(E.v.B.)

KEY NEWSGROUP **rec.arts.wobegon** URL▶ http://www.mnonline.org/mpr/html/aphchome.htm

TV Pages

Warner Brothers Animation Site

Warner Bros. Animation Jump **6882**

Sheer online fun for all ages! Warner Bros. Online supplies a healthy dose of online games, including Dr. Scratchansniff's Identity Game, and Connect the Dots. You'll find all of your favorite animated characters here...Bugs Bunny, Daffy Duck and many more. But the real secret of this site lies within its Animation 101 section. Offering a virtual study of the entire animation process, it educates visitors on how wacky situations are created in the writer's brain and how this vision ends up on screen. —(L.T.)

KEY NEWSGROUP **rec.arts.animation** URL▶ http://www.wbanimation.com/

3rd Rock From The Sun

3rd Rock From The Sun Jump **6837**

This is NBC's site, all about those wacky alien scouts who've taken human, humorous, form. While presently you won't find a stockpile of multimedia features like video clips and cast photographs, you will find text-based information on stars John Lithgow, and Jane Curtin, and the rest of the cast. Additional offerings include full transcripts of online chat sessions recently conducted by cast members, and fresh, behind-the-scenes news. —(L.T.)

URL▶ http://www.nbc.com/entertainment/shows/rock/index.html

As the World Turns

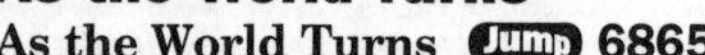

As the World Turns Jump **6865**

CBS' official network site for ATWT fans delivers page after page of scoops and data on this daytime drama. From star biographies to still shots taken from the set, you can also browse ATWT's family trees and express your opinion directly to the network via their latest online poll. Will you find any plot scoops for the coming days ahead? You bet! Additionally, there are daily Oakdale recaps, and regularly-scheduled cyberchats with ATWT stars Ashley Williams, Eileen Fulton, and Jordana Brewster. —(L.T.)

KEY NEWSGROUP **rec.arts.tv.soaps.misc** URL▶ http://www.cbs.com/daytime/atwt

The Official Baywatch Web Site

The Official Baywatch Website Jump **5638**

Surf's up at the Official Baywatch Web site. And we do mean "official." You can almost feel the sand between your toes as you travel about this site, taking in the wonderful cast photos, or reading the detailed episode guide. You can find out what will be happening on both Baywatch and its spin-off, Baywatch Nights, and take a peek at some behind-the-scenes snaps. There's also a chat area, where you can sign on and chat with fans from all over the world—and with one billion people watching the show weekly, you're bound to find someone else to chat with here! —(J.P.)

URL▶ http://baywatch.compuserve.com/

Beverly Hills, 90210

Beverly Hills, 90210 Jump **6838**

Photos, photos, and more vivid photos! All placed on the show's official site in fine Beverly Hills fashion. You'll find up-close-and-personal shots of Brandon, Dylan, and Kelly, but—of course, no snapshots of Brenda. While there aren't many details on the show's history, there is an informative "update" letter which Brandon wrote to his parents, Jim and Cindy. It will fill all of you 90210 fans in on what the gang's been up to while passing along a clue or two as to what's coming up for the new season. —(L.T.)

KEY NEWSGROUP **rec.arts.tv.soaps.misc** URL▶ http://www.foxworld.com/bh9indx.htm

The Bold and the Beautiful

The Bold and the Beautiful
Jump 6866

For this Web site of some of daytime TV's most glittery and glamorous, CBS offers B&B fans the very latest at its official page. From star biographies to still shots of the set, you can also browse B&B's family tree and let your opinion be heard through the show's latest poll. There's plenty of daily recaps and sneak peeks. Plus, you'll find the data you need to join individual fan clubs, like Kimberlin Brown's, Ian Buchanan's and Hunter Tylo's. —(L.T.)

KEY NEWSGROUP rec.arts.tv.soaps.cbs
URL▶ http://www.cbs.com/daytime/bb

Boston Common

Boston Common
Jump 6839

NBC's official network page provides biographies of cast members of this new sitcom about the lives and loves of a group of Boston college students. You'll also find transcripts of online chat sessions recently conducted by cast members, behind-the-scenes show data, and a miniature gallery of cast photos. —(L.T.)

KEY NEWSGROUP rec.arts.tv URL▶http://www.nbc.com/entertainment/shows/boston/index.html

Burden of Proof

Burden of Proof
Jump 6870

Burden of Proof's official Web site offers gavel-to-gavel coverage of the major legal cases featured in this show. Hosted by Greta Van Susteren and Roger Cossack, CNN's site for this legal talk show supplies a week's worth of full-text transcripts in case you miss an airing. To help you with legalese, you'll also find a comprehensive legal dictionary offering thorough definitions of legal terms. —(L.T.)

KEY NEWSGROUP misc.legal URL▶ http://cnn.com/CNN/Programs/burden_of_proof/index.html

▲ *Heather Thom and Eric Braeden from "The Young and the Restless," from* Washington University Archives *at* Jump 1569.

Caroline in the City

Caroline in the City Jump 6841

There's a bit of mystery to be unearthed at Caroline in the City's official network site. Read the details behind this quirky comedy and you'll uncover the real cartoonist who creates the illustrations used on the show. Cast biographies here, peeking into the careers of stars like Lea Thompson and Eric Lutes, who plays Del. There's also a collection of the most recent online chat transcripts as well as a complete listing of behind-the-scenes players. —(L.T.)

KEY NEWSGROUP rec.arts.tv URL▶ http://www.nbc.com/entertainment/shows/caroline/index.html

◀ *Frasier Crane and Eddie in the T.V. show "Frasier," from* **Hype! International** *at* Jump **2183**.
▲ *Images from TV favorites "I Love Lucy," "The Tonight Show," "Howdy Doody," and "Dallas," from* **Ad Age - It's All About Marketing** *at* Jump **7311**.

Chicago Hope

Chicago Hope Jump **6842**

If you're a dedicated fan of CBS' hit medical drama, you'll enjoy viewing Chicago Hope's gallery of large still photos found on this site. Included are close-up views of cast members Christine Lahti, Adam Arkin, Hector Elizondo, and Roxanne Hart. —(L.T.)

KEY NEWSGROUP **rec.arts.tv** URL▶ http://www.cbs.com/eyeware/mm_hope.html

Days of Our Lives

Days of our Lives Jump **6867**

Despite the fact this long standing soap is celebrating its 30th anniversary, its Web page pales in comparison to other network-produced daytime TV sites. Nevertheless, it does provide a somewhat useful historical launching ground, and some worthwhile reasons to visit as well, such as its daily recaps, a collection of classic "Days," episodes, and cast biographies of your favorites like Diedre Hall, the always re-appearing Joseph Mascolo (Stephano), and the bewitching Louise Sorel. —(L.T.)

KEY NEWSGROUP **rec.arts.tv.soaps.misc** URL▶ http://www.nbc.com/entertainment/shows/days/index.html

The Disney Channel

The Disney Channel Jump **5656**

Disney strikes gold again with the Channel's official Web page. A study in understated simplicity, the site is of course nevertheless filled to overflowing with timely and exclusive information. The weekly program listing includes not only programs for the week, but an A-Z listing and a Pick of the Day. You'll find first-hand information on movies and TV shows, even a few cool games. And it's worth a visit just to see the icons! —(J.P.)

URL▶ http://www.disney.com/DisneyChannel/

Frasier

Frasier Jump **6840**

NBC keeps this site on hand for those who'd like the rundown on Frasier's characters and their individual idiosyncrasies. There's a complete cast biography section on stars Kelsey Grammer, Peri Gilpin, even "Moose," who plays Eddie, TV's most beloved pooch. Cyberchat transcripts are also browsable here, with humorous comments from stars David Hyde Pierce and Jane Leeves. —(L.T.)

KEY NEWSGROUP **rec.arts.tv** URL▶ http://www.nbc.com/entertainment/shows/frasier/index.html

Friends

Friends Jump 6843 

Given the fact that Generation X-ers are big Net users, we would've expected a few more features than those offered at NBC's hangout for this Gen-X show. What this site does furnish are cast biographies for Courteney Cox, Jennifer Aniston, and David Schwimmer, and plenty of pictures. You'll also find a brief explanation about the show's history, and its Emmys. —(L.T.)

KEY NEWSGROUP **alt.tv.friends**

URL▶ http://www.nbc.com/entertainment/shows/friends/index.html

Frontline

Frontline Jump 5612 

Like most prime-time news documentary shows, PBS' Frontline generates a fair share of viewer comment, both positive and negative. Much of this can be freely exchanged and seen here, for instant feedback on the latest featured Frontline show. You can also link here for archives of viewer response to previous shows —(J.P.)

URL▶ http://www.pbs.org/wgbh/pages/frontline/

Homicide: Life on The Street

Homicide: Life on The Street Jump 6851 

NBC's official site furnishes a quick overview of the history behind this hour-long police drama. While currently there aren't any interactive features on this site, you will find full text-biographies on all the cast members, including Richard Belzer and Kyle Secor. Additional site features include full transcripts of cyberchat sessions recently conducted by cast member Andre Braugher, plus a directory of the show's crew members. —(L.T.)

KEY NEWSGROUP **rec.arts.tv** URL▶ http://www.nbc.com/entertainment/shows/homicide/index.html

▲ *Alex Trebek and the set from "Jeopardy!," via* **Washington University Archives** *at* Jump **1569**.

JEOPARDY! Home Page

JEOPARDY! Home Page Jump 5632 

Anyone who has ever watched Jeopardy is pretty much certain that they could do as well as any of the contestants on the show. If you're one of those people you'd better check out the official Jeopardy Home Page. Here you'll not only find out how to qualify for the show, you can take part in this site's online trivia challenge. You know, so you can sharpen up your skills for the big test. And you'll also find photos from the show (including Alex, of course) as well as exclusive information not found anywhere else. And long-time fans will also be pleased to know that Jeopardy has been renewed. Until 1999! —(J.P.)

URL▶ http://www.spe.sony.com/Pictures/tv/jeopardy/jeopardy.html

Late Show with David Letterman

Late Show with David Letterman Jump 5631 

Well, you know what to expect from the official David Letterman home page. You get plenty. The Top Ten is here, both past and present. You get a nice FAQ and guest list and information on how to obtain tickets for the show. And of course you get jokes. Lots of jokes. What do you expect from the King of Quips. "I think people living in New York City don't care much about astronomy. People living in New York City think that the planet Mars is a theme restaurant on 57th Street." Dave knows. —(J.P.)

URL▶ http://www.cbs.com/lateshow/

Law & Order

Law & Order Jump 6852 CONTENT

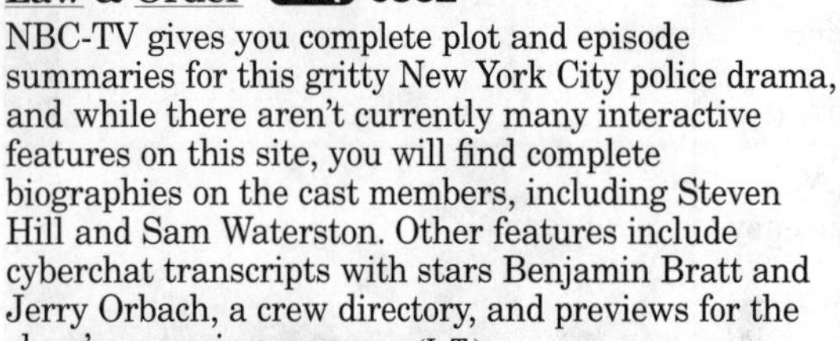

NBC-TV gives you complete plot and episode summaries for this gritty New York City police drama, and while there aren't currently many interactive features on this site, you will find complete biographies on the cast members, including Steven Hill and Sam Waterston. Other features include cyberchat transcripts with stars Benjamin Bratt and Jerry Orbach, a crew directory, and previews for the show's upcoming season. —(L.T.)

KEY NEWSGROUP **rec.arts.tv** URL▶ http://www.nbc.com/entertainment/shows/law/index.html

▲ *The only on-air tribute to Philo T. Farnsworth, the inventor of television, in a 1957 episode of "I've Got a Secret," from* **Museum of Television** *at* Jump **0220**.

Mad About You

Mad About You Jump 6854 

Recently voted by viewers as television's cutest couple, Paul and Jamie Buchman are standing by on the Web to tell you their story. While this show's official site won't answer the great "baby" question, it will fill you in on the couple's trials and tribulations. Cast biographies are readable on all the characters, including Ira, Murray the mouse-chaser, and the Buchman's dysfunctional sister, Lisa. —(L.T.)

KEY NEWSGROUP **rec.arts.tv** URL▶ http://www.nbc.com/entertainment/shows/mad/index.html

Married...With Children

Married ... With Children Jump 6855 CONTENT

Sony Pictures Entertainment provides an informational and entertaining site about this long-standing family series. You'll find all of the latest show happenings, including the shocking news about pet dog Buck Bundy, who sadly met his fate on May 25, 1996. You'll find creative use of still photos of the Married...With Children Cast, including a fun section vividly portraying how the kids, Bud and Kelly have literally grown up before our eyes. Planning on being in Los Angeles soon? Request tickets to attend a taping of show from its Web site. Brimming with exclusive from-the-set news, this site is a frequent must-visit if you've missed one or several episodes and need to catch up. Or view the latest episode as it airs, Sundays at 9:00 p.m. (ET) on FOX. —(L.T.)

KEY NEWSGROUP **rec.arts.tv** URL▶ http://www.spe.sony.com/Pictures/tv/married/married.html

4616 Melrose Place

Melrose Place Jump 6856 

Melrose's hip and creative official site contains as much dirt and dish as the show itself. Swing by and ring a character's doorbell for a personal, spoken message, or cast your votes for favorite or least-favorite episodes, or—if you just need a quick update—catch the latest news through this site's "Melrose in a Minute" feature. Episode guides, Melrose fact sheets, and photos taken of and by the cast members are abundant. This site's exclusive chat room hosts heated talkfests 24 hours a day—though they're especially heated after each show is broadcast! —(L.T.)

KEY NEWSGROUP **rec.arts.tv.soaps.misc** URL▶ http://melroseplace.com/

Mister Rogers' Neighborhood

Mister Rogers' Neighborhood Jump 5616 CONTENT

The King of Morning television comes to the Web in typical Mr. Rogers fashion, understated and simple—like a spring morning in the country. Here young fans will find personal greetings from Mr. R. himself and King Friday XIII, news about the series, play activities, and lyrics to the show's most popular songs. Now you can all sing along together! —(J.P.)

URL▶ http://www.pbs.org:80/rogers/mrr_home.html

I Want My MTV!

Welcome to MTV Jump 5044 

MTV's Web page contains info on their programs, including *The Real World*, *Oddities*, and *Beavis & Butt-head*. When you access a feature, you also get access to a pictures, on the show. Also here are previews of upcoming programs on MTV, including new *Oddities*, *Liquid Television*, and *The Brothers Grunt*. —(S.B.)

URL▶ http://mtv.com/

Motorweek

Motorweek Jump 5613 

Motorweek has been at the forefront of the car world for 15 years, providing news and reviews about the ever-changing world of the automobile. Here you will find everything else you need to know, about the show and about the cars. You can consult the show schedule, read the bios on those involved, and best of all, read some pretty special online road test reviews.—(J.P.)

URL▶ http://www.mpt.org/mpt/motorwk/home.html

▲ *Old NBC color TV logo, from* **Washington University Archives** *at* Jump **1569**.

The Nanny

The Nanny Jump 6859 

Sony Pictures Entertainment produces The Nanny's vivid Web page, which highlights the show and its star, Fran Drescher. You'll find the latest news as well as Nanny-related events taking place off the set and near your hometown. Planning on visiting the Los Angeles area? Request tickets to attend a taping of the show from this site. Loaded with high-resolution images of all the stars and their biographies, this site is a must-see if you're a devoted Nanny fan. (L.T.)

KEY NEWSGROUP **rec.arts.tv** URL▶ http://www.spe.sony.com/Pictures/tv/nanny/nanny.html

Party of Five Home Page

Party of Five Jump 6861 

Sony Pictures Entertainment dedicates this page to this once-cancelled show, which was resurrected after network execs were hit with some very heavy fan pressure. This drama can, thanks to all those calls and letters, be seen yet again on Fox. When you visit Party's site you'll find a library of still cast photos, exclusive news published as it happens from the set, and background on the series, which follows the lives of the five youthful Salingers. —(L.T.)

KEY NEWSGROUP **rec.arts.tv** URL▶ http://www.spe.sony.com/Pictures/tv/party/party.html

The Rosie O'Donnell Show

The Rosie O'Donnell Show Jump 6869 

Someone in the network boardroom listened to TV audiences about creating a quality daytime talk show, and Rosie's high ratings are responding accordingly. The show's official site offers a look back at her most recent memorable show highlights, plus a schedule of next week's guests. Browse comedic archives and you'll find Rosie talking about (among other things) her dogs, her adopted son, and Madonna's impending motherhood. A fine collection of photographs portray guests who've appeared recently, including a rare and humorous shot of George Clooney's initial acting days. —(L.T.)

KEY NEWSGROUP **rec.arts.tv** URL▶ http://www.rosieo.com/

Seinfeld

Seinfeld Jump 6857 CONTENT

NBC's official site for the #1 rated show in the U.S. brings Kramer, Elaine, George and, of course, Jerry together. As you're most likely aware, the show is "about nothing"—and, either intentionally or unintentionally, its Web site is about the same, though you will find some recent cyberchat transcripts, including one in which the show was discussed with Estelle Harris, who plays George's mom on the show. Also included are biographies on the major cast players, a crew member listing, and a run-down of awards this hit comedy series has received. —(L.T.)

KEY NEWSGROUP alt.tv.seinfeld

URL ▸ http://www.nbc.com/entertainment/shows/seinfeld/

Tonight Show Fans' Site

The Tonight Show with Jay Leno Jump 4024 COMMERCE

This is the official site for NBC's *Tonight Show*, starring Jay Leno. The well laid-out page offers you the chance to view daily video clips from the show itself, plus lists of upcoming guests, funny headlines, and a backstage peek at the workings of this ever-popular late-night TV show. —(R.B.)

KEY NEWSGROUP alt.fan.jay-leno

URL ▸ http://www.nbctonightshow.com/#Main

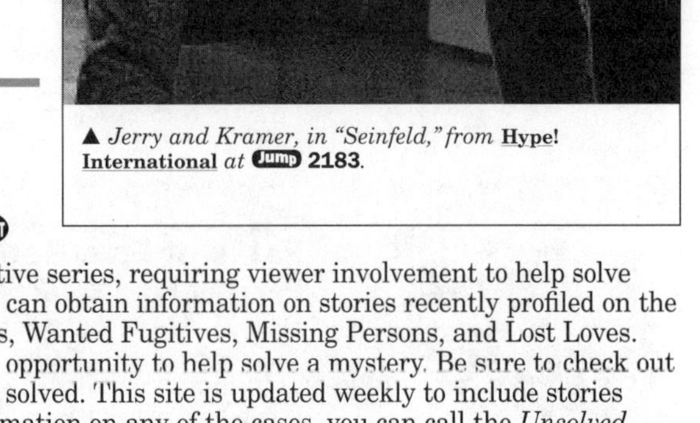

▲ *Jerry and Kramer, in "Seinfeld," from* Hype! International *at* Jump 2183.

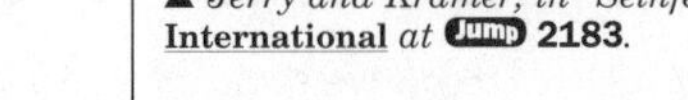

Help Solve a TV Real-Life Mystery

Unsolved Mysteries - Television Show Jump 3743 CONTENT

Unsolved Mysteries became one of television's first interactive series, requiring viewer involvement to help solve cases. Now it's expanded its reach to include the Web. You can obtain information on stories recently profiled on the long-running series in categories, such as Special Bulletins, Wanted Fugitives, Missing Persons, and Lost Loves. Lots of photos and details on all the cases will give you an opportunity to help solve a mystery. Be sure to check out this site's Update section to see what mysteries have been solved. This site is updated weekly to include stories from the most recent broadcast, and, if you have any information on any of the cases, you can call the *Unsolved Mysteries* phone center at 1-800-876-5353. —(N.F.)

URL ▸ http://www.unsolved.com/

Total TV Listings Online

Total TV On-Line Jump 5658

What do you get when you combine a comprehensive source of TV listings with terrific feature articles? You get Total TV. Weekly programming schedules are here, with the top daily picks sorted by time zone. And the columns, The Critical Eye, Wired, Plugged In, and The Soap Box cover all the bases. And the features? Well, with the new season just around corner, you can use this site to start planning your schedule. Bowling on Thursday nights? Better check here before committing yourself! —(J.P.)

URL ▸ http://www.tottv.com/

TV Guide Online

TV Guide Online Jump 6871

Here's an excellent and nicely executed on-screen program guide to tell you what's on TV tonight, from the venerable *TV Guide*. Just a few clicks gives you tonight's program grid, but this excellent site doesn't just stop there. You also get much of the editorial content of TV Guide's print version, including full pictorial layouts of stars featured on their most recent covers, including Lois & Clark star Teri Hatcher. You can also join in on a number of ongoing interactive chats taking place on many varied TV topics. —(L.T.)

KEY NEWSGROUP **rec.arts.tv** URL▶ http://www.tvguide.com/

TV/Film Links the Entire Web

TV Links Film and Television Website Archive Jump 6515

Here's a central Web spot that'll guide you to anything you can imagine (and then some) in film and television. This massive Web archive directs you to most every TV or film-related Web site. From a couch potato point-of-view you'll find the World TV schedules, Sports television, Behind-The Scenes photographs, Film and TV Archives, TV networks and Usenet newsgroups, and links to television shows like Wheel of Fortune, Bill Nye the Science Guy, Nova and Babylon 5, plus many more priceless resources to feed your remote. From a professional's standpoint, this archive is tops, with links to motion picture production companies, Screen and Video professional organizations such as The Directors Guild of America, Society of Motion Picture and Television Engineers, Society of Operating Cameramen and all current film festivals and Awards. —(L.T.)

KEY NEWSGROUP **alt.binaries.pictures.celebrities** URL▶ http://neog.com/timelaps/tvlink.html

Everything You Want to Know about TV Shows

Ultimate TV List Jump 2219

On this well-executed site, maintained by David Cronshaw of TVNet, not only will you find everything about television shows here, you'll find it quickly and easily. The "What's New" section lets you see what's been changed since your last visit. Otherwise, you can find what you want either through alphabetical, genre, or resource-type listings. However you do it, each show's listings include sections for episode guides, newsgroups, mailing lists, FAQs, Web pages (with descriptions), and miscellaneous links. Rounding things out is the series of simple, yet comprehensive, fill-in forms that lets any visitor add or update a listing. —(L.S.)

KEY NEWSGROUP **rec.arts.tv** URL▶ http://www.tvnet.com/UTVL/utvl.html

TV & Movie Gossip

Transient Images Home Page Jump 1517

As a weekly electronic 'zine devoted to television and film, Jol Padgett and Alex Agostini have created an interesting mix of eye-catching graphics and industry information. Their 'zine is written in a gossip-column format, complete with musings about celebrities and what they're up to—rumor or truth? Find out the scoop on your favorite TV sitcom, from soaps to talk shows, and even participate in rating the shows you watch, on this site. Although not scientific, it gives a picture of what Net cruisers view when they're not online. The site also links to movie and television resources, and offers opinionated reviews of the latest movies. If you feel just as opinionated, feel free to give the authors feedback, or write reviews and articles of your own. —(H.L.)

KEY NEWSGROUP **rec.arts.tv** URL▶ http://www.cais.com/jpadgett/www/home.html

A TV Guide for the Times

What's On Tonite! Jump 3685

Throw away that dogeared 5x7 magazine with the smiling TV stars on the front cover! Put the newspapers out in the recycling bin! And stop watching the cable TV channel's scrolling program guide. Everything you want to know about what's on can be found here! TV listings for the Internet Age! Organized by time zone, and available for display in grid format, time block, program category or channel lineup, all for your part of the country—you'll never look up a TV listing any other way again! —(C.P.)

URL▸ http://tv1.com/

Fox Network Fans' Web Site

Fox Broadcasting Jump 4028 CONTENT

While not an "official" page for the network, Aaron Greenhouse has put together a very complete site for those interested in Fox programming. Information includes a listing of all Fox programs with a description of each, and links to sites for some of the more popular shows such as *Animaniacs*, *The Simpsons*, *X Files*, and, of course, a link to "Spelling Land," a page that offers more links to info on *Beverly Hills 90210*, *Melrose Place* and several other Aaron Spelling-produced Fox vehicles. This site looks great and is of commercial quality. —(R.B.)

KEY NEWSGROUP rec.video

URL▸ http://www.eden.com/users/my-html/fox.html

▲ *The Philco Princess television set, from* **Museum of Television** *at* Jump 0220.

Public Broadcasting System Information Site

Welcome to PBS Jump 4029 CONTENT

This new site is the home of PBS, the Public Broadcasting System. Laid out in a clean and graphically pleasing style, this page offers all sorts of resources concerning public broadcasting. National programming schedules, local station lists, and available learning services are just a few of the broad topics you can access here. —(R.B.)

KEY NEWSGROUP rec.video URL▸ http://www.pbs.org/

PBS Programs Direct

PBS Program Pages Jump 3684 CONTENT

Gathered together in one location, the PBS Program Pages offers quick and easy access to Home Pages for several popular programs and series. You'll find *An Evening at the Pops*, *Frontline*, *The Great Indian Railway*, *Masterpiece Theatre*, *Nova*, and others for the adults in your household, and *Mr. Rogers' Neighborhood*, *Newton's Apple*, *Reading Rainbow*, and much more for the kiddie-crowd. Nicely done—and you'll also find historical information, feature articles, programming info, related links (especially to Net resources for kids), and lots of other terrific stuff. —(C.P.)

URL▸ http://www.pbs.org/programs/navigator/program_navigator.html

CBS Network's Web Home

CBS Television Home Page Jump 4025 COMMERCE

Billed as CBS's "Eye on the Net," this site serves as the gateway to this network's programming information. Information and images are available for all the shows, and links to several of the program's home pages, including *The Late Show with David Letterman*, *CBS News* and *CBS Sports* are also provided. Daily programming schedules are also available on this Web site. —(R.B.)

KEY NEWSGROUP rec.video URL▸ http://www.cbs.com/

TV Fan Pages

AMCPages.com: For All My Children Fans

All My Children Jump 6863 CONTENT

Looking for the lowdown on the past, present and future of All My Children? You've just found the Web's online authority, proudly produced by mega-fan Dan Kroll. A peek into the soap's past offers such meaty content as a Who's Who directory, an AMC family tree, and a special archive listing the biographies of just about every cast member who's ever graced this soap's set. What about the present? There are daily recaps, fun trivia contests, a real-time cyberchat area for impassioned AMC viewers, and backstage news. —(L.T.)

KEY NEWSGROUP rec.arts.tv.soaps.abc URL▶ http://www.amcpages.com

The Another World Home Page

Another World Jump 6864 CONTENT

This site takes you away to Another World, albeit unofficially. It offers a complete AW library that begins with major and minor character guides and ends with links to individual cast member Web pages. You'll also find all of the fun stuff—actors' birthdays, where auditions for new cast members are being held, new child characters born on the show, plus a special section containing ever-so-important couples data. Interested in still photos of memorable scenes dating as far back as 1986? You'll find these here, too. An outstanding Web page, composed by a group of devoted and talented AW fans. —(L.T.)

KEY NEWSGROUP rec.arts.tv.soaps.misc URL▶ http://worldlink.ca/~awhp/awhp.html

The Unofficial Brady Bunch Home Page

The Unofficial Brady Bunch Home Page Jump 5635 CONTENT

Did you know that the "real" Brady Bunch house was built in 1959? Or that the Bunch have hit the theaters with another motion picture? Well, hang on to your hats, because you've been invited to take a wild trip back to the 70s. Here you'll find a complete BB episode guide, blueprints of the house, sample scripts from the show, and a link to the official Brady Bunch movie site. Amazing, isn't it? Who would have thought that a show that lasted a mere three seasons would not only survive into the 90s, but would attract an entire new generation of followers? —(J.P.)

URL▶ http://www.teleport.com/~btucker/bradys.htm

The Chicago Hope Fans' Home Page

The Chicago Hope Homepage Jump 5639 CONTENT

You come near me with your bloated psyco-babble and I will take your head off, alright?" The line above, and many many more, are to be found in the Chicago Hope "Best Lines" section of this fan's site (and as fans know, this quote is on the mild side). There's much more here, too, including an episode guide, information on the cast and crew, and a few photos of your favorite stars. And, of course, what would CH be without the CH Drinking Game (Game disclaimer: "If you are drinking alcoholic beverages, do not drive, wash dishes, or perform experimental surgery").—(J.P.)

URL▶ http://www.cbs.com/eyeware/mm_hope.html

Late Night on the Web

Conan Jump 2640 CONTENT

Well, he's not Letterman, but Conan O'Brien has nonetheless developed a coterie of fans that love him anyway. It took Herbert Gambill, who maintains this page, awhile to reach that point, but reach it he did, and this page is for everyone who has seen a similar light, no matter how long it's taken. It's not too bad, either, for those who scratch their heads wondering what the attraction is. The best part of the page is its comprehensive archive of abstracts of Late Nightcum-Conan's 400-plus shows, created and maintained by a group of dedicated fans. There's also a companion listing of the guests on each of those shows. Fans are invited to supply annotations for the abstracts, either for past shows, or for the ongoing project to abstract current programs. —(L.S.)

KEY NEWSGROUP alt.fan.conan-obrien

URL▶ http://www.rbdc.com/~hgambill/conan.htm

▲ *Devo performing on the Merv Griffin Show, from* **MuteWeb** *at* Jump **1004**.

A New Breed of Sidekick

Andy Richter's Virtual Couch

Jump **2721** CONTENT

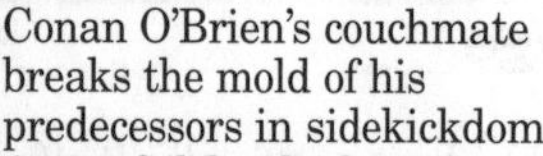

Conan O'Brien's couchmate breaks the mold of his predecessors in sidekickdom by refusing to be just a foil for the host. In fact, many of his fans think Andy Richter is more important to *Late Night* than Conan himself. However you feel, if you're a fan of *Late Night*, you'll want to learn more about Andy, and here you'll find his bio, an interview, and various factoids of his earlier career. And if you're indeed a fan, you'll also want to check out the images and sound files here, too. —(L.S.)

KEY NEWSGROUP alt.fan.conan-obrien URL▶ http://www.well.com/user/xkot/andy.htm

Deron's Muppet Page!!!

Deron's Muppet Page!!! Jump **5644**

One of Jim Henson's most endearing creations was the wonderful Muppets cast. Though he's no longer with us, Henson's characters have found a new life on terrific sites like Deron's Muppet Page. Here you'll find dozens of pictures of the entire Muppet crew, including one entitled "Pigs in Space," "Kermit with Banjo" and one with Henson himself, entitled "Operating Kermit". And you'll also find a number of other terrific Muppet links, including one to the always-hilarious Muppets Tonight show. —(J.P.)

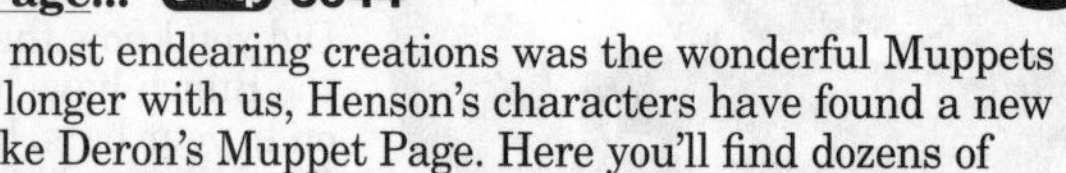

URL▶ http://www-leland.stanford.edu/~dsedy/muppets.html

John's Unofficial ER Homepage

John's Unofficial ER Homepage Jump **5619** CONTENT

It may well be billed as the Unofficial site, but John Callaghan deserves full credit for putting together the next best thing. Not only will you find the latest news about this hot show and its stars, but there's a wonderful picture gallery along with what John calls the "most complete listing of ER sites online." And he may just be right! —(J.P.)

URL▶ http://www.geocities.com/Paris/2079/index.html

George Clooney Fan's Site

George Clooney on the Web Jump **5688** CONTENT

Talk about a star on the rise! Not only is Mr. Clooney the heart-throbbing star of every female viewer's dreams, but he's the star of one of the top-rated TV shows and the new Batman! Yes, he has more than a few fans. And one of them, Courtney Patubo, has put together a wonderful tribute to the actor. Here you'll find links to the movie sites, plenty of pictures, a biography, filmography, and a list of George Clooney's greatest pranks! That George. All that fame, and a sense of humor too! —(J.P.)

URL▶ http://www.hooked.net/users/cpatubo/clooney.html

The ER FAQ

ER FAQ Jump 5620

Much like the operating room it documents, Donald Chow & Victor Chan have compiled a clean and complete list of frequently-asked questions for all ER fans. Here you'll find wonderful details on the cast, extensive episode synopses, and much more. If you don't find the answer here, maybe you'd best ask another question. —(J.P.)

URL▸ http://gpu.srv.ualberta.ca/~vichan/www/er.html

MEDIC ER Website

MEDIC ER Website Jump 5686

The first thing you'll want to do at the MEDIC ER Web site is register. Not the sort of thing you usually do at a "fan site," but in this case you might want to make an exception. Once you register (it's easy and free), you'll be a member of what organizer William Hughes calls "the world's fastest growing online fan club." As a member you'll be entitled to newsletters, a chat area, password for special online club events, and more. And you'll find more here too, including a wonderful history of the show and the stars. A professional site in every respect. —(J.P.)

URL▸ http://www.albany.net/~williamh/welcome.html

Roger's ER Page

Roger's ER Page Jump 5684

Saying this site is complete is like saying that the Mississippi River is wet. Roger Tsang has a way with the Web, and he puts it to good advantage here. The graphics are sharp and clean and the content is top-of-the-line—no filler for Roger. You'll find cast info, an episode guide and lots of great photos. But you can also read a glossary of medical terms—handy for those "ER medical moments," and you can take part in a neat survey. Vote for your favorite star of "ER", or pick the best episode yet! —(J.P.)

KEY NEWSGROUP alt.tv.er URL▸ http://www.ualberta.ca/~wtsang/er/er.html

Scott Hollifield's ER Page

Scott Hollifield's ER Page Jump 5685

If you are a fan of "ER" and happen to miss an episode, you know how frustrating a "water-cooler" review can be the next day. Who can remember all the twists and turns, all the plots and subplots and threads that hang on from week-to-week? Scott Hollifield can remember. And you can read all about it in Scott's wonderfully detailed "ER" review/synopsis site. We're talking frame-by-frame recounting here. And you'll also find a great FAQ, an episode list, and much more. Why, with this attention to detail, you'll be left wondering if Scott hasn't missed his calling! —(J.P.)

KEY NEWSGROUP alt.tv.er URL▸ http://www.cris.com/~scotth/erdex.html

Frasier Fans' Site

Frasier Jump 5629

Frasier has been wowing TV viewers since it first went on the air in 1993. Not only is it a finely crafted comedy, but it has rejuvenated the ensemble cast feel of the old days of Mary Tyler Moore. This site, maintained by Dean Adams, is a wonderful tribute to the show and its stars. The complete episode guide, written by Adams, is marvelous, and there are links to the official NBC biographies of all cast members. Including Eddie the dog, who, we are told "divides his time between Florida and California with his wife, Molly, and their three pups." If only we were so lucky. —(J.P.)

URL▸ http://www.nyx.net/~dnadams/frasier.html

A Shrine to Friends

Dan's Shrine to Friends Jump 6888

Dan Silverstein's site is a popular favorite amongst a large group of online "Friends fans." It's easy to see why! Dan's shrine immediately makes you feel like you're a member of the "must-see" sitcom. Amongst the many entertaining features located inside include a special section called 'The Friends Edited Lines Vault," FAQs that really do answer all of your most burning questions, episode guides, drinking games, a script library, and an insider's preview on which hot celebrities will be soon walking across "Friends'" lofty floors. This also happens to be the online spot to cast your vote for this site's annual "Crystal Duck" awards!. —(L.T.)

KEY NEWSGROUP **alt.tv.friends** URL▶ http://www-scf.usc.edu/~dsilvers/friends1.htm

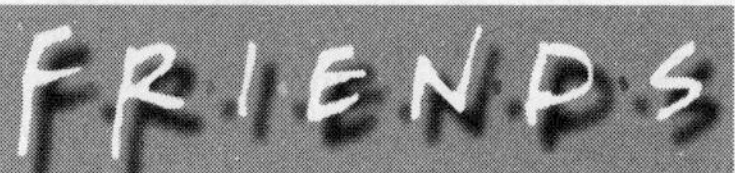

The Perfect Friends Page

The Perfect Friends Page Jump 5622

The Perfect Friends Page is—as you might have guessed—perfect. Not only will you find over 150(!) photos of the cast, but you'll also marvel at the sound and video clips, trivia contest and more. And you can read the newest of the new, a feature called "A Day in the Life of Rachel Green." We can only imagine what such a day would be like! —(J.P.)

URL▶ http://www.geocities.com/Hollywood/8526/

You Gotta Have *Friends*

Friends Jump 1536

From the popular, Generation-X television show comes this fanzine dedicated to those who can't get enough of the 30-minute sitcom about 20-something-aged friends who live in New York City. Andy Williams, a self-proclaimed "Frienatic," compiled an exhaustive FAQ all about the cast, characters, set, dialog, and plot, to answer burning questions as: "Can Chandler get a Brain?" or "Will Ross and Rachel ever get together?" Learn to play the theme song from the published guitar chords, or find out how to submit a script. What does the *Friends* cast think about fans discussing them on the Net? It's here. How long does it take to put together a typical show? You'll see. Join the "Friends Zone" on mailing lists, newsgroups, and in other sites also linked here. —(H.L.)

KEY NEWSGROUP **alt.tv.friends** URL▶ http://geminga.dartmouth.edu/~andyjw/friends/

Port Charles Online: General Hospital Fan Site

General Hospital Jump 6862

Fan Jeff Jungblut has composed what can only be described as one of the best soap sites on the Web today. A click here broadcasts more dish from Port Charles than you could gather by watching the latest installment of GH on ABC. Jeff's put together a virtual file cabinet of information, from on and off-screen photos of sudsy stars like Maurice Benard and Vanessa Marcil, to the latest "spoilers," in case you'll be missing the week ahead. Not ending there, he also furnishes daily updates, cast news and gossip, a history of GH, plus an interactive chat room so you can exchange your real-time thoughts with other passionate GH fans. —(L.T.)

KEY NEWSGROUP **rec.arts.tv.soaps.abc** URL▶ http://www.port-charles.com/

Gilligan's Island Discovered on the Web!

Gilligan's Island Home Page Jump 3677

Gilligan and his pals really haven't been lost for all these years at all! They're right here on the Web. If you're a Gilligan fan, you'll love this site. Whether you're looking for photos, sound clips, or trivia (did you know there are three versions of the *Gilligan's Island* Theme?), you'll find it all here, along with full filmographies of the Gilligan cast, and even this week's TV listings—all the way down to the name of the episode that will air next Thursday (8:05 AM EST daily on WTBS). This site is updated frequently, and well worth a visit! —(C.P.)

URL▶ http://www.epix.net/~jabcpudr/

Home Improvement Archive

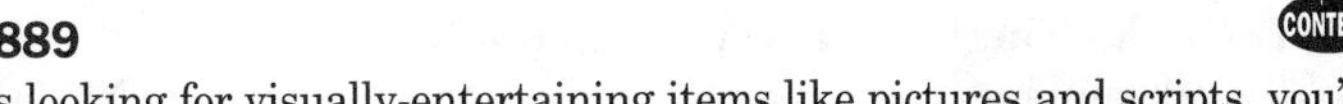

Home Improvement Archive Jump 6889

CONTENT

If you're a big Home Improvement fan who's looking for visually-entertaining items like pictures and scripts, you've found the right place. Created by mega-fan Jan Nielsen, this site features cast biographies, links, e-mail lists, and press materials. If you go for only one reason, make sure it's to check out the library of articles with all of "Home Improvement's" stars! On the shelves you'll find a hysterical interview with Tim Taylor, courtesy of the Laugh Factory, Patricia Richardson's recent interview with *TV Guide*, and Jonathan Taylor Thomas' life story, from *Teen Beat*. —(L.T.)

KEY NEWSGROUP **alt.tv.home-improvment** URL▶ http://www.diku.dk/students/normann/hi/

Home Improvement Cyberfan

New Home of Home Improvement Cyberfan Jump 5627

CONTENT

So, you can go home again after all. And when you get there (or here, for that matter) you'll find more information on Al, Tim, and the gang than you ever knew existed. You'll also find a season overview, ratings info, cast appearances, and info on the HI Cyberfan mailing list. So drop on in—and don't worry if you break anything; no one will ever notice! —(J.P.)

URL▶ http://www.morepower.com/homeimpr.html

Homicide, Life on the Web Fans' Site

Homicide, Life on the Web Jump 5630

CONTENT

It's Tuesday January 19th, 12:15 in the morning. The lieutenant looks over and yells in your face. So begins another day in the Homicide department. And so begins this site, Life on the Web. But at least you've got a choice. You can either continue on with the story (the first chapter of the book *Homicide, A Year on the Killing Streets* by Homicide writer David Simon, featured here) or you can head straight in to the guts of the precinct. Here you will find all Homicide fan Jason Lempka has been able to find on the show, from a fine FAQ, an episode list, filmographies of all the cast members, and much more. And then you can head back over to the lieutenant. He'll be waiting for you. You just know he will. —(J.P.)

URL▶ http://www.gl.umbc.edu/~jlempk1/homicide.html

Kevin Nagle's "Late Show with David Letterman"

Kevin Nagle's "Late Show with David Letterman" Web Site Jump 5640

CONTENT

Have you ever wondered what really happens when you manage to get tickets to Late Night with David Letterman? Well, if so, wonder no more. Not only has Kevin Nagle been to the show, but he has kindly documented his trip on his wonderful tribute page. And he's also compiled some personal tips, guaranteed to make your visit to the show all the more enjoyable. But that's not all you'll find here. Look for information on various Letterman discussion newsgroups, the Image of the Week, and reports from Dave's own trip to San Francisco. And don't forget to check out Kevin's Favorite Comedy Bits ("Can a guy in a bear suit hail a cab?"). —(J.P.)

URL▶ http://ibsys.com/~knagl/letterma.htm

Late Show News

Late Show with David Letterman Jump 0035

Jason Lindquist's Web site features Aaron Barnhart's wonderful weekly e-mail newsletter feature on the Letterman show, as well as other late night TV shows. Features plenty of "industry insider" info, personal observations, and more, from one of Dave's most devoted fans. Also featured are links to other Letterman show schedules, anecdotes, jokes, bits, etc. —(E.G.)

KEY NEWSGROUP **alt.fan.letterman** URL▶ http://www.cen.uiuc.edu/~jl8287/late.news.html

Lois & Clark—The Fan's Web Server

Lois & Clark - The Web Server Jump 6853

Lois & Clark fans are a highly devoted and extremely passionate Net group, and this fact is self-evident when you visit this big fan site. Home to the Lois & Clark FAQ (which stands for "Frequently Asked Questions"), this site is brimming with more than 1,000 still photos, fun show facts and complete episode guides. The FAQ answers such trivia as what the "K" in K Callan's name stands for, what happened to Cat Grant, and whether or not the show actually reads your fan letters. You can join the newsgroup that's linked to this site, or take part in fan Tyler Nally's Lois & Clark WWW Chat Room, which hosts show discussions around the clock. —(L.T.)

KEY NEWSGROUP alt.tv.lois-n-clark URL http://www.webcom.com/~lnc/index.html

Mad About You Fans' Site

Mad About You Jump 5636

You have to love them like you do. And you'll love this Mad About You page, too. We're talking details here, like a wonderful guide to every episode aired (keep this handy—the show has gone into strip syndication) and a terrific Frequently Asked Question file, and a link to a notable guest file that includes John Astin (in a hilarious turn as...John Astin), Cyndi Lauper, and Lyle Lovett. And don't miss the complete bios of Paul Reiser and Helen Hunt—you'll be amazed at how often you might have seen both stars before they became stars in this show. —(J.P.)

KEY NEWSGROUP rec.arts.tv URL http://www.alumni.caltech.edu/~witelski/may.html

Max Headroom Redux

Network 23—Main Menu Jump 7225

Nick Jarecki, who heads Network 23, a Internet access provider, has a serious interest in *Max Headroom*—remember that stuttering, computer-generated talking head from the popular cult TV show of the 1980s? You can view video clips, read stories, download images, and enjoy many other *Max Headroom* memorabilia. And don't leave without reading his "quote of the day." —(E.v.B.)

URL http://net23.com/

Melrose Place TV Fans' Site

Melrose Place TV Jump 5625

If Melrose Place if your kinda place then this is the place for you. You'll want to check out the MP Drinking Game (using fruit juices, no doubt!) a picture gallery, sound bites (more like shrieks) from cast members (updated every Thursday), and upcoming cast changes. You can even submit your favorite MP quote. And don't forget to register for the weekly synopsis, e-mailed to you free of charge. —(J.P.)

URL http://members.aol.com/MelroseTV/index.html

Melrose Space

Melrose Space Jump 5626

This site is billed as the "Home of the weekly 'Blow-By-Blow' Synopsis" for Melrose Place fanatics. Well, there is more, much more indeed, such as the MP Top 10 List (you can add your own here, too), the Weasel Boy Weekly Update (perhaps that means something to you?), a listing of the "Five Stages of MP Addiction" and even a FAQ. A fun place to be—in an odd sort of way. —(J.P.)

URL http://www.intergate.net/uhtml/sam/Melrose/index.html

Melrose Comes Alive

All Things Melrose Jump 5877

The folks on Melrose never tire, never run out of money, and they never have any regrets. Ah, such is life in TVLand. If you're a fan of "Melrose Place" you'll also be a fan of All Things Melrose (ATM). This really is a fan's

site, filled not only with information on the show, but with lots of group participation stuff as well. Our favorite: "Just Who Has Jake Slept With?" It would appear that it would be more apt to ask who he hasn't slept with, but never mind. The gossip runs thick and fast and there are also plenty of other MR links here. Not that you'll need much else once you've checked out this site for your weekly Melrose fix. —(J.P.)

KEY NEWSGROUP **rec.arts.tv.soaps.trivia** URL▶ http://members.aol.com/ALizbth/atm.htm

Mystery Science Theater 3000 Home Page

Mystery Science Theater 3000: Deus Ex Machina Jump **4039**

David Levine brings you this collection of resources and links of everything having to do with the popular Comedy Central cable television show *Mystery Science Theater 3000.* From FAQ's, to episode guides, to Usenet groups, to weekly schedules, the information here is enough to keep the show's fans busy for a while. There's also links to picture, sound and software archives, as well as numerous other MST3K sites along the Web. —(R.B.)

KEY NEWSGROUP **rec.arts.tv.mst3k** URL▶ http://sunsite.unc.edu/lunar/mst3k/mst3k.html

NYPD Blue

NYPD Blue Jump **6860**

NYPD Blue doesn't furnish an official Web page, but thankfully, one of its most devoted fans, Alan Sepinwall, went to great lengths to offer Blue fans a nice Web fan spot. Alan guides you around every nook and cranny of the show, through a display of vivid cast photographs, or a quick read through the pages of the NYPD Blue FAQ. This police drama's complete history is covered here, including a special section for ex-Detective John Kelly. There's even a biography of Blue creator Steven Bochco and an intriguing comparison Alan wrote himself, pitting the series against NBC's Homicide. Missed an episode? Summaries for all the shows are available here. —(L.T.)

KEY NEWSGROUP **alt.tv.nypd-blue** URL▶ http://force.stwing.upenn.edu:8001/~sepinwal/nypd.html

One Life to Live: The History Page

One Life to Live Jump **6868**

Need to know more about Marty's past? Need to know what all the hoopla is behind Todd's recent reappearance? Whether you need a complete rundown of this soap's history, or you'd like a sneak peek at OLTL's upcoming episodes, you'll find everything you need here, thanks to super-fan Sandy Weeks. Full of family trees, a unique index that lets you look up a specific storyline dating as far back as 1968, and the latest ratings rundown, catch up on Llanview's latest at this easy-to-use site. —(L.T.)

KEY NEWSGROUP **rec.arts.tv.soaps.abc** URL▶ http://www.bowdoin.edu/~sbodurt2/oltl.html

Phoebe's Songbook

Phoebe's Songbook Jump **5621**

You can try to deny it, but who hasn't found themselves sitting around late at night, cuppaJoe in hand, trying to remember the words to one of Phoebe's songs. Oh, it has never happened to you. Sure. And you never voted for Nixon, either. Still, if the urge strikes, this is the place to strike back. Sherri Lynn Slotman has compiled the best of the best, with words, music and audio clips for many of the songs. You'll find The Shower Song, Terry's A Jerk, Blackout, and, of course, Smelly Cat. Now how does that go again? —(J.P.)

URL▶ http://www-personal.umich.edu/~geena/friends/phoebesong.html

Seinfeld on the Web

Seinfeld On The Web Jump **5617**

Dan Kennedy is a fan of Seinfeld. You can tell he's a fan because not only has he sat down and transcribed the scripts to many of his favorite episodes, but he's also included them on this nice fan's Web site. You'll find a few of your favorites here: "Junior Mints," "The Airport," "The

Smelly Car," and more. And, of course, lots of quotes, trivia, and photos. Thanks Dan! —(J.P.)

KEY NEWSGROUP alt.tv.seinfeld

URL ▶ http://mypage.direct.ca/p/pakenned/main.html

The Seinfeldiest Fan Site on the Web!

The Seinfeldiest Site on the Web! Jump 5618

We haven't seen mention of the word "Seinfeldiest" in the dictionary yet, but you know how slow those dictionary people are to pick up on a trend. Thankfully, not everyone is so behind-the-times. Not only has Brendan compiled a wonderful selection of audio files, but he's also put together an interactive Seinfeld trivia contest. The answers will be mailed to anyone who plays, and the winner's name will be posted on the site. The height of Seinfeldism, if you ask us! —(J.P.)

KEY NEWSGROUP alt.tv.seinfeld

URL ▶ http://www.mosquito.com/~uofmich/seinfeld.html

▲ *Philco television advertisement, from* The TV Museum *at* Jump 0219.

Seinfeld Fans' Page

The Seinfeld Index Page Jump 0034

Ruben Sogaard's clever Web stop for *Seinfeld* fans! Contains neat pictures of Jerry, George, Kramer, Elaine and the gang, scripts, and story lines plus links to other *Seinfeld* Web sites on the Net. A must for *Seinfeld* fans! —(E.G.)

KEY NEWSGROUP alt.tv.seinfeld URL ▶ http://www.ifi.uio.no/~rubens/seinfeld/

Club de Seinfeld

Club de Seinfeld Jump 5682

This is some club, this Club de Seinfeld. If the TV show is about nothing, then this site is about everything—because that's what you'll find here. You might want to begin with this site's sound clips section; this is where you'll find dozens of clips from the show, divided up by character, and including, of course, the "Seinfeld" theme song. There's also a video clip library, and a section called "The Cast : Who They Really Are," a rundown of the real-life people the characters George, Kramer, and Elaine were based on. And you won't want to miss the scripts of a few of the best episodes, including "The Airport" and "The Old Man." There's even a section on Newman too! —(J.P.)

KEY NEWSGROUP alt.tv.seinfeld URL ▶ http://www.geocities.com/Hollywood/8883/seinfeld.html

Hello, Newman

Hello, Newman Jump 5683

Meet Wayne Knight, better known to TV viewers as the Postman of the Year on "Seinfeld." Yes, that Newman. The curl of the lip Newman. The won't go out in the rain Newman. Turns out that Mr. Knight has been around for quite some time, appearing in both TV and motion pictures. Here you'll find information on his career, as well as details on how the "Seinfeld" character came to be, and much more, written by Daniel Howard Cerone. —(J.P.)

KEY NEWSGROUP alt.tv.seinfeld URL ▶ http://www.iguide.com/tv/magazine/960701/ftr5a.sml

The Simpsons

The Simpsons Archive Jump 0033

Gary Goldberg and Howard Jones have done a wonderful job linking together tons of fun *Simpsons* picture and icon files, downloadable audio and video clips, FAQs and detailed episode information for devoted fans of Fox TV's *The Simpsons* (O.K., we confess—we downloaded Barney's burp into our Mac sound control panel—what can we say?). A fun stop for all *Simpsons* fans! —(E.G.)

KEY NEWSGROUP **alt.tv.simpsons** URL▸ http://www.digimark.net/TheSimpsons/index.html

Wings, The Fan's Home Page

Wings, The Home Page Jump 5637

In the age-old role of brothers-opposite, few have brought such charm to the small screen as Joe and Brian Hackett as they stumble about Nantucket Island. Aaron Moy, an obvious fan, has put together a wonderful tribute to the Hacketts and all their pals. Here you will find a detailed episode guide to the series, an odds-and-ends trivia area and even details on how to find out when the series airs in your local area. There's plenty of photos and information on the rest of the cast, including Fay, Roy, Helen and Antonio. And while there—don't forget to vote for your favorite character. —(J.P.)

URL▸ http://www.students.uiuc.edu/~a-moy/wings.html

Good Stuff for X Files Fans

The X-Files Jump 0102

Nicely executed Web links page for fans of FOX-TV's spooky cult hit show, *The X Files*. Plenty of links to story episode text files, photo and audio files, fan creative writing, downloadable graphic images, and plenty of background material will pull in those of you who are not yet
X Fans of this modern day heir to the *Twilight Zone* tradition. —(E.G.)

KEY NEWSGROUP **alt.tv.x-files** URL▸ http://www.rutgers.edu:80/x-files.html

X-Files Resources

X-Files Resource Jump 5696

If you're looking for an "X-Files" site that leaps out and grabs you by the lapels, the X-Files Resource Page could be the place for you. This is a site that not only has great style but detailed information on the show, the awards the show has received, a section on good guys (you know who they are) and bad guys (you know who they are, too!), a section on the paranormal, trading cards, magazines, and much more. Webmaster Martin Fularski has done a splendid job here. —(J.P.)

KEY NEWSGROUP **alt.tv.x-files** URL▸ http://upanet.uleth.ca/~FULARSKI/xf000.html

Make Your Own X-Files Episode

Make Your Own X-Files Episode Jump 5698

If you every wanted to write your own script for the "X-Files", but didn't think you would have enough skill or time, you should make an appointment at this site. The creators have offered what they call "practical advice" in doing so. You might call it cheating, but as long as it gets the job done, who cares! All you have to do is follow their step-by-step instructions, taking a piece from each of the three categories (Plot and Script, Cast and Equipment). And if renting the equipment sounds like too much trouble, you can do the job with a camcorder. —(J.P.)

KEY NEWSGROUP **alt.tv.x-files** URL▸ http://www.bizniz.com/xfile/

The X-Files Episode Guide

The X-Files Episode Guide Jump 5624

It is difficult to think of a show in recent television history that has so captured the hearts of its viewers. If you missed the beginning, or just want a nice refresher, check out Cliff Chen's wonderful Episode Guide. The FAQ is

▲ ▶ FBI Agents Dana Scully and Fox Mulder, in scenes from "The X-Files," from **Hype! International** at Jump 2183.

great for newcomers, and everyone will enjoy the information on the show and, of course its cast. And this being a world-wide (or is it universe-wide?) phenomenon, there is a guide to the show's UK's viewing history, and a Finnish one as well. —(J.P.)

URL ▶ http://bird.taponline.com/~cliff/

Netpicker's Guide to the X-Files

Netpicker's Guide to X-Files Jump 5695 

Used to be that fans of a TV show would sit back, put their feet up and do whatever they could to get lost in the plot. But no more! With the advent of VCRs it suddenly became possible to watch and re-watch just about anything. That in turn gave birth to the School of Slipups, those inevitable (or are they?) miscues and mistakes that have plagued moving pictures from the very inception. The Netpicker's Guide to X-files follows in that noble tradition as it invites fans to contribute 'mistakes' they have seen on the show. A clock that loses an hour in one scene? A band aid that moves around the face? Sounds like a Netpicker's analysis of an episode of the "X-Files!" —(J.P.)

KEY NEWSGROUP alt.tv.x-files URL ▶ http://aea16.k12.ia.us/ricke/netpickhome.html

The X Files Fans' Page

The Truth is Out There Jump 2419 

This is a great-looking Web site, with content to match. Whether you're a long-time watcher of this cult favorite that's turned into a hit television show, or just stumbled upon the program one lonely Friday night, Stephen R. Banks has enough here to keep you busily interested for quite a while. If you're new, begin with the *X Files* FAQ, a comprehensive document written in the style of one of Scully's reports. When you're through, you can browse the images of Scully and Mulder. If you've had an *X Files*-type experience, you can leave your story here for others to read, and then move on to fictional stories written by other *X Files* fans. There's also a general *X Files* image and art gallery, an episode guide, links to other sites, and more being added all the time, so you'll keep coming back! —(L.S.)

KEY NEWSGROUP alt.tv.x-files URL ▶ http://www.neosoft.com/sbanks/xfiles/xfiles.html

Science Fiction

Science Fiction Zine

Science Fiction Weekly Jump 7249 

This is a modest zine that presents the news, reviews, and stories from the always fascinating world of science fiction. In one issue you can read reviews of CD-ROM sci-fi releases, new hard-copy novels, or computer games.

Editor Craig Engler promises to deliver the most up-to-date information and news, so surf on over for some futuristic fun. —(E.v.B.)

KEY NEWSGROUP rec.arts.sf.misc

URL▶ http://www.scifiweekly.com/sfw/index.html

All about *Star Wars*

Star Wars Home Page At UPENN

Jump 4034

All sorts of information about the *Star Wars* movie trilogy is maintained on this page by Jason Ruspini. From multimedia files, to information on the movies, to collectibles and a whole lot more, you'll find everything you want or need to know about the *Star Wars* saga here. A must for fans of this all-time science fiction favorite! —(R.B.)

▲ *The Nightbreed "Mexico" from* Washington University Image Archives *at* Jump 0192 ▲ *Spock and Kirk, from an episode of "Star Trek," via* Virtual Image Archive *at* Jump 7315.

KEY NEWSGROUP rec.arts.sf.starwars

URL▶ http://force.stwing.upenn.edu:8001/~jruspini/starwars.html

The Sci-Fi Channel Home Page

Sci-Fi Channel: The Dominion Jump 4023

The Dominion is the official site set up by cable television's Sci-Fi Channel. The site is loaded with nice graphics and lots of information on the channel's programming. Split up into eight "zones," the resources here include information about original programming and upcoming special features, articles about science fiction, links to other SF Web sites, image, audio and video clips, and much more. —(R.B.)

KEY NEWSGROUP rec.arts.sf.tv URL▶ http://www.scifi.com/cgi-bin/rbox/incgif.prl

Star Trek

Trekker's Jumplist

(The Spider's Web) Star Trek Sites

Jump 2259

This is a hypertext version of Luca Sambucci's list of *Star Trek* sites on the Web, and it should be home port for any Trekker. There are general links to sites covering the original television show, *Star Trek: The Next Generation*, and the two currently running series *DS9* and *Voyager*, including air schedules. Then there are pages devoted to the movies, links for fans of characters or actors, information about the United Federation of Planets and its members, Starfleet, the Klingon language and various other bits and pieces of useful information. This page is maintained by Bob Allison of Spider's Web fame, and if you haven't checked out the Spider's Web, make sure you do so after taking your fill of Trekdom here. —(L.S.)

KEY NEWSGROUP rec.arts.startrek URL▶ http://gagme.wwa.com/~boba/trek.html

Science, Education, & Technology

Thanks to the Internet's origins in academia and scientific research, the Web features a rich collection of educational resources for all ages, with science-related sites to make science both colorful and accessible to all.

Students can take a virtual-reality trip through ancient Pompeii or the gardens of Versailles through CD-ROMs on computer drives, read books from faraway libraries through Internet connections, download up-to-the-minute flight data on a space shuttle, and find the exact research references they need through "hypertext links."

For those of us who went to school when slide rules dangled from students' belts and simple pocket calculators were so valuable they had to be bolted down to lab tables, the new high-tech classroom can be a culture shock.

But we'd better get with the program. As technology breaks down the barriers among academic disciplines and universities, "Knowledge is collapsing on itself," UC [University of Cincinnati] President Joseph A. Steger said.

"High Tech U. College of the Future Is Here Now," ***The Cincinnati Enquirer***

Web Resources for Education

A host of Web site authors, both teachers, experts, and talented amateurs alike, have created Web sites where children, their parents, and people of all ages can access a wide variety of educational topics. From how-to sites for teachers, for parents who choose to home-school their own children, and for academics, to hands-on Web sites that give students direct involvement in learning and make use of the Web multimedia capabilities, there's a rich variety here.

Another fascinating use of the Web are that give your children the opportunity to create their own Web pages, or publish their stories and drawings on the Web. Additionally, there are many fascinating educational Web sites covering an immense range of subjects, many of which can be a learning experience for anyone; not just students.

Accessible Science, Space, and Technology Resources on the Web

While the Internet was known first as the virtual gathering place and information repository for advanced scientific researchers and academics, there are many science-related Web sites that make all kinds of science easy to understand for all of us—and enjoyable, too. On the Web, you can access many sites which have been created by educational institutions, teachers, and enthusiastic amateurs alike, to help introduce you to many fascinating science and technology-related subjects.

For the astronaut in all of us, there are also Web sites created and maintained by NASA and other organizations, which are vast Net storehouses of the latest space news, earth and interplanetary satellite photos, and historic NASA images you can view on your PC.

Academia

Surviving Your MBA

The MBA Page Jump 2165

It's only two years, but since the goal of many graduate business programs is to flunk you out, it's a long two years! The Fisher College of Business at Ohio State University, taking a slightly more supportive view of things, has created this page of links to help the MBA student. Of most aid are the survival guides created by other grad students, with tips on how to juggle classwork, a social life, and the day-to-day minutiae of life without going completely bonkers. There also are links to various business research sites, case studies, MBA journals and news publications, good books for the aspiring business person, job search assistance, and, for a change of pace, links to fun stuff on the Web. —(L.S.)

KEY NEWSGROUP **soc.college.grad** URL▶ http://www.cob.ohio-state.edu/dept/fin/mba.htm

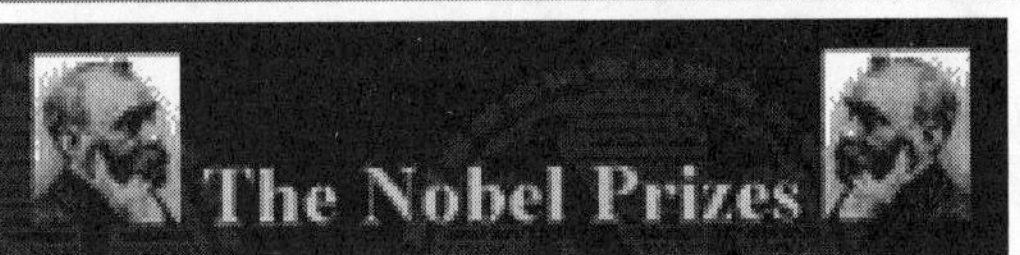

The Prize of Prizes

The Nobel Prizes Jump 2718

Ah, the rites of autumn. The World Series, football and . . . the Nobel prizes. Each October the Nobel Foundation in Sweden begins the announcement of winners of the world's most prestigious honors in literature, medicine, economics, physics, chemistry, and peace. And although some of the selections over the years have been questionable, there's no doubt the prizes are important, especially with the cash, now in the seven figures, that accompanies the medal. Maintained by Ona Wu and Boris Pevzner, this page lists the winners, along with links to background information on each. If you're curious about the past, there's also information available here on previous honorees and their backgrounds. —(L.S.)

URL▶ http://mgm.mit.edu:8080/pevzner/Nobel.html

Anthropological Futurists

Seeker1's CyberAnthropology Page Jump 2200

At first blush, this could be an elaborate joke. It's not. Steve Misrach is organizing a serious anthropological study of cyberspace via what could be the thoughtful Web user's ultimate home page. He offers a series of essays on the topic, from an explanation of cyberanthropology and modern primitives to the places of the old guard and cyberpunks in the evolving culture. It's interesting, if sometimes baffling, reading. Steve also gives you links to other texts and resources on the topic, a list of links to Web pages that typify the cyberculture, and rather long lists of newsgroups, and mailing lists that discuss or represent examples of virtual culture. —(L.S.)

KEY NEWSGROUP **alt.culture.internet** URL▶ http://www.clas.ufl.edu/anthro/Seeker1_s_CyberAnthro_Page.html

Information from the National Institutes of Health

NIH Home Page Jump 3518

The goal of the National Institutes of Health is to acquire new knowledge to help prevent, detect, diagnose, and treat disease and disability, from the rarest genetic disorder to the common cold. One of eight health agencies of the Public Health Service, NIH has 70 buildings on more than 300 acres in Bethesda, MD, and had an operating budget of more than $10 billion in 1994. Visit this site to see what they're doing with your tax dollars! Information includes offerings on research opportunities, topics on molecular biology, a calendar of events, library services, and much more. —(C.P.)

URL▶ http://www.nih.gov/

MBAs on Parade

Harvard Business School Jump 7181

You will not find the bread and circuses of the Net at this site. Befitting the sober image of the Harvard Business School, these Web pages are strictly no-nonsense, very businesslike—but certainly get the job done. You can read the fine details on the different academic programs offered by the School, as well as acquaint yourself with the various faculties, the research done at the School, and then branch out with links to Harvard's other Web resources. —(E.v.B.)

KEY NEWSGROUP alt.business.misc URL▶ http://www.hbs.harvard.edu/index.html

Educational Resources

Children's Reading Resource

Children's Literature Web Guide Jump 2262

This site is for everyone involved with children and reading, be they parents, teachers, or children themselves. David Brown has done an excellent job organizing and maintaining this site, especially in his descriptions of the links. There are links to news, newsgroups, and discussion lists, academic information, and the like, but the best features are those that will help parents encourage and excite their children to read. There are links to Web pages about fictional characters, links covering movie tie-ins (to take advantage of an interest sparked by a movie), links to children's books online, and links to Web pages written by and about young readers. There's much more to be found here, and browsing with your children will do much to keep their interest in books, as well as your own, growing. —(L.S.)

KEY NEWSGROUP rec.arts.book.childrens URL▶ http://www.ucalgary.ca/~dkbrown/index.html

Link Your Child's Project to the Web

Global Show-n-Tell Home Page Jump 2273

If you want to share the world of art or other projects your children have worked so hard on, this site will connect to your Web page or file holding the project, using a graphic from the work as the link. You and your children can also browse the site and find interesting things being done by children around the world. Or, if you're a teacher, you can have a link added for individual or class projects. It's free and easy, and a great way to give children extra encouragement and rewards for their work. —(L.S.)

KEY NEWSGROUP misc.kids URL▶ http://www.manymedia.com/show-n-tell/

Lions and Tigers and Bears—and More!

The Electronic Zoo Jump 2298

Veterinarian and self-proclaimed computer nut Ken Boschert has linked every animal-related Internet resource he could find, or has been told about, to this site. The colorful, easy-to-navigate pages are part of his NetVet server, and there are excellent links to animal health resources. But with a large section covering animals in general, as well as separate pages of links to publications, newsgroups, mailing lists, and Telnet, FTP, Gopher and Web sites, there's something for everyone here. The What's New section makes it easier to keep up after your first visit, and the search engine lets you easily find any resource anytime. —(L.S.)

KEY NEWSGROUP sci.bio URL▶ http://netvet.wustl.edu/e-zoo.htm

Learning the Web, Kid Style

Kidding Around Jump 2482

Learning to navigate and explore the Web isn't necessarily difficult, but it's rarely as much fun for middle school kids and teenagers as it is with this page by Heather McCammond-Watts. There are links to learn how to use the Web, and sections describing links to museums, science pages, and other educational stuff. But there are some really fun pointers, such as Fantastic Lands, Spooky Spots, Go on Safari, Amusement Parks, Puzzling Places, and other categories that emphasize fun as well as learning. There's also a rather large section devoted to links just for teenagers. Once the links here are exhausted, there's a good list of other sites for young people, including links to sites that teach kids how they can publish their own Web pages. —(L.S.)

KEY NEWSGROUP k12.ed.comp.literacy URL▶ http://alexia.lis.uiuc.edu/~watts/kiddin.html

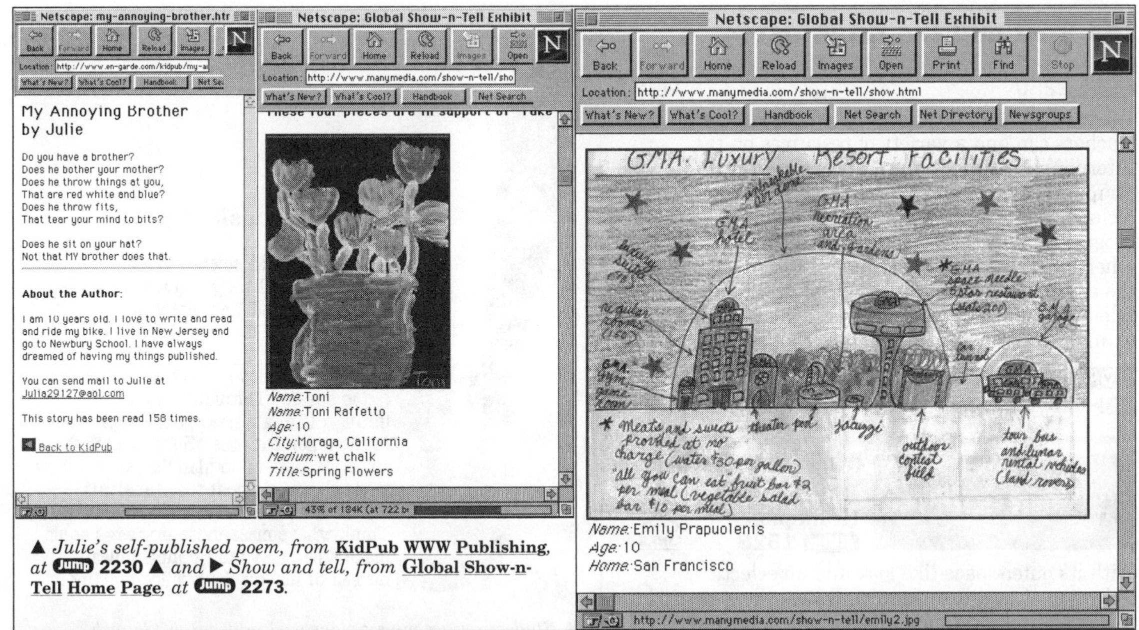

▲ *Julie's self-published poem, from* **KidPub WWW Publishing**, *at* **Jump 2230** ▲ *and* ▶ *Show and tell, from* **Global Show-n-Tell Home Page**, *at* **Jump 2273**.

Back to School Help For Parents

Family Planet Back to School Gateway
Jump 5802

The folks at Family Planet strike gold once again with this great primer on the trials and tribulations of sending the kids back to school. Features cover topics such as helping your kids make the transition from summer to school, and how to deal with schools that might emphasize sports over academics. This site's "Keeping Healthy" section helps with news on everything from immunization to sex education, while this site's forum section covers topics like dealing with bullies, and prayer in school. —(J.P.)

KEY NEWSGROUP misc.kids.info URL ▶ http://family.starwave.com/seasonal/school/index.html

Virtual Field Trips for Kids

KID List Jump 2498

KID stands for *Kid's Internet Delight,* and that is just what you'll find here, in a wonderful list of links compiled by Internet trainer John Makulowich. He originally started it for a demonstration of the Internet for children, but like so much on the Web, it will appeal to any curious soul. Catch a cold virus, see a comet crash into Jupiter, learn about dinosaurs, find a pen pal, play games, or tinker with examples of future electronics products. Whatever your age, wherever you go from here, you'll land at some of the best sites on the Web for kids! —(L.S.)

KEY NEWSGROUP misc.kids URL ▶ http://www.clark.net/pub/journalism/kid.html

Super Science Fair Projects and Experiments

Super Science
Jump 6643

This dynamic site encourages kids, teachers, and parents to design and perform entertaining and unique science experiments. Super Science provides all the tools you'll need to create science fair projects, along with many interactive projects and online experiments. Other goodies include a monthly science contest for kids, while science teachers can use this site to find the latest grant information. —(L.T.)

KEY NEWSGROUP sci.materials URL ▶ http://www.superscience.com/

The Best and the Brightest

Gifted and Talented (TAG) Resources 
Jump 2250

Talented and gifted children, their parents, and their teachers can find a variety of resources on the Internet and in the real world through this compilation maintained by Bruce User. Areas covered include special summer programs, distance learning programs, colleges offering early acceptance, and other educational and enrichment resources. While the emphasis here is on the notably gifted and talented, many of these resources will be of interest to any good students and their parents. —(L.S.)

KEY NEWSGROUP **k12.ed.tag**

URL ▶ http://www.eskimo.com/~user/kids.html

School Launch

Remember those science-class experiments where you put an egg in a foam holder and then threw the contraption off the school roof? Well, the Student Experimental Payload program takes that physics test to a higher level (so to speak). Through September, 4th- through 12th-graders choose payloads for a rocket that goes 15,000 feet in the air. Kids team up to plan the ride for their payload, and do post-flight analysis reports after the rocket's recovered. Think what a mess those raw eggs could make when they fall a couple miles instead of just off the science building.

▲ *Student science project plans payload for rocket launch, from* **Hot Wired: Net Surf Central**, *at* Jump **5751**.

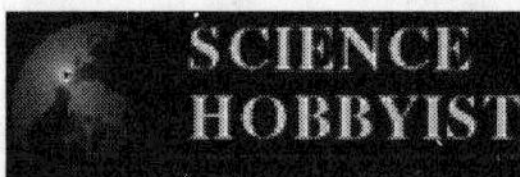

Mystery Science

Bill Beaty's Homepage
Jump 1528 LINKS

With its outer-space-like look and an eclectic collection of "weird science," Bill Beaty has created a huge resource for amateur scientists, kids, and education specialists alike. Although this site consists mostly of links to related information, his compilation does include original hobby projects, such as dangerous experiments (warning: possible consequences are not listed here) and strange inventions. Download demos of physics projects, see photos of alternative, crazy inventions—creating something from nothing is a classic—and discuss, with fellow science buffs, the misconceptions in standard science texts or the state of science education today. You can even submit your own experiments and thoughts and you, too, could become famous (or infamous) in the Web scientific community! —(H.L.)

KEY NEWSGROUP **alt.sci.physics.new-theories, alt.paranet.science** URL ▶ http://www.eskimo.com/~billb/

The Parents' and Teachers' Guide to Software
SuperKids™
Educational Software Review

Parent's and Teacher's Guide to Software

SuperKids Jump **5781** 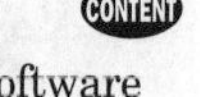

So you've got your heart set on picking up software for the kids, but you have no idea what to buy. Anything too violent is unacceptable, and anything too tame will be unplayable. At SuperKids, parents, teachers, and kids contribute unbiased reviews of children's software. And the reviews are among the most extensive we've seen online. If you're in the market for an CD encyclopedia, for example, you'll marvel at the review that includes a checklist of what you'll get with each, what's lacking, how to install the software, and more. And you'll also want to check their "What's New" section, and tips on where the find the lowest-priced software. —(J.P.)

KEY NEWSGROUP **misc.kids.computer** URL ▶ http://www.superkids.com/

Cool School Tools!

Neat-O K-12 Resource Page

Cool School Tools! Jump **2477** 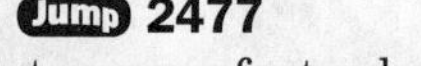 

This page is an excellent resource for teachers, but it's really designed as a fun-to-use interface for students themselves. With its open design, fun graphics, and "let's enjoy this" attitude, it's hard not to have fun learning while surfing. The subject index is split into sections covering general resources, philosophy and psychology, social science, religion, natural science and math, language, technology, the arts, literature, and geography. There's also a separate section of searchable dictionaries and other reference works. The links are collected by the CST Surf

Team—Shannon Brett, Lara Christian, Daryl Fletcher, Rachel Hoormann and Cissy McClenny—and anyone is invited to contact them with ideas for additions to this site. —(L.S.)

KEY NEWSGROUP **k12.ed.comp.literacy** URL▶ http://www.peop.tdsnet.com/ls590/group3/

Web Links for Social Studies Teachers

Index.html Jump **2366**

Don't be deceived by the simple, graphics-free page you'll find when you visit here. Its simplicity belies the amount of work done by Dennis Boals in compiling this comprehensive list of resources, but mirrors the ease with which users can find items of interest. The categories include archaeology, diversity sources, genealogy, geography/economics, government/politics, non-western, European and American history, humanities/art, and leisure/fun/health. Each link carries a description, some of which are very detailed, with sample menu items from the site. It's one of the best sites for teachers, and students, too, in finding general, specific, and obscure resources for social studies classes. —(L.S.)

KEY NEWSGROUP **k12.ed.soc-studies** URL▶ http://execpc.com/~dboals/boals.html

ELECTRIC LIBRARY

Online News Research

Welcome to The Electric Library Jump **8022**

A researcher's delight, the Electric Library gives you a free trial to its easily searchable database containing more than 150 full-text newspapers, 900 full-text magazines, national and international newswires, 2,000 literary works, over 18,000 photos, images and maps, television and radio transcripts, movie and software reviews, an encyclopedia, dictionary, thesaurus, almanac, and factbooks. It's an affordable (around $10 per month) news research service that's great for personal, small business, or family use. —(E.v.B.)

KEY NEWSGROUP **alt.journalism** URL▶ http://www.elibrary.com/

Research-It!

Research Reference Online

Research-It! Jump **6625**

Students and information junkies will find Research-It! a valuable online research tool. Research-It! puts all kinds of available Net resources in one spot, giving you an all-in-one stop for free access to worthwhile reference material online—dictionaries, thesaurus, language translators, acronym dictionaries, quotation databases, maps, phone numbers, postal information, and the latest financial data in one searchable, online visit. —(L.T.)

KEY NEWSGROUP **bit.listserv.libref-l** URL▶ http://www.iTools.com/research-it/research-it.html

Librarian's Best Picks for Web Research Links

Where The Wild Things Are Jump **6006**

Billed as "Librarian's Guide to the Best Information on the Net," this comprehensive index helps librarians—and the rest of us—utilize the vast amounts of information available on the Web. After all, who should know about research better than a librarian Web surfer? Developed originally for the St. Ambrose University Library in Davenport, Iowa, this site is a tremendous starting point for many Internet resources. Although designed for librarians, it's also a great source for the rest of us—students, historians, consumers, businesspeople, job hunters, etc. So be sure to bookmark this one. —(N.F.)

URL▶ http://web.sau.edu/index/

The Past That Is Our Prologue...

The Ancient World Web Jump **2377**

If you're curious about the roots of civilization and want to explore on your own, Julia Hayden provides the links. Most of sites she links to are databases, exhibits and museums, and she describes each one to help you narrow or otherwise guide your search. There also are what she calls "Handy Links" to archaeology and anthropology indexes, and paleontology and mythology resources. And if you want to participate in Usenet discussions on any of these topics, Julia includes reviews along with links to those newsgroups. —(L.S.)

KEY NEWSGROUP **sci.archaeology** URL▶ http://atlantic.evsc.virginia.edu/julia/AncientWorld.html

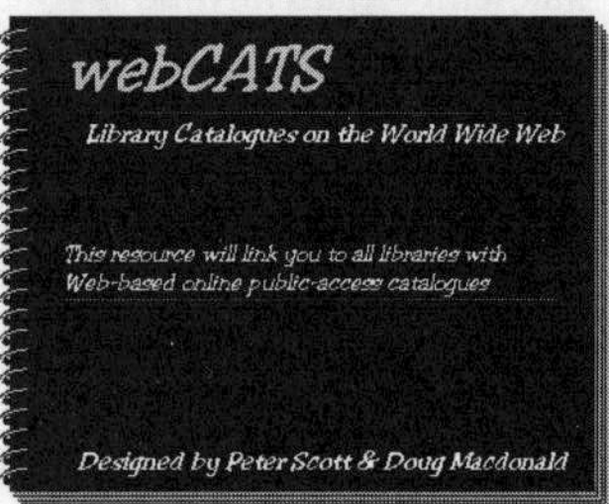

Library Catalogues on the World Wide Web

webCATS: Library Catalogues on the World Wide Web Jump 6876 

WebCATS will guide you to every online public-access library catalogue available on the Internet—fast! Use this site to access many libraries' online "card catalogues," for access to publications lists on most any subject imaginable. You can pick and choose from geographically-located libraries, from Canada to the Philippines, or by specialty, including medical, government, and religious collections. Virtually every educational institution's reference shelves can now be accessed, thanks to webCATS. —(L.T.)

KEY NEWSGROUP **bit.listserv.libref-l** URL ▶ http://library.usask.ca/hywebcat/

Learning about Your Personality

The Personality Pages Jump 2492 

As much as psychology these days promotes the growth of and respect for the individual, it can't resist the urge to pigeonhole people into neat little categories. Still, learning your tendencies and general traits can be helpful, especially when dealing with other people, and these pages, maintained by M.D.A. Varley, point you to resources to aid in this endeavor. An offshoot of the **alt.psychology.personality** newsgroup, you'll of course find the newsgroup's FAQ here, and it's a good source of information on personality typing, its uses and its implications. You can link to the Keirsey Temperament Sorter and take that test online, or go to a page describing each of 16 different personality profiles. If you get totally confused, or nearly educated, you also can link to the newsgroup itself and start talking about personality-related topics with others. —(L.S.)

KEY NEWSGROUP **alt.psychology.personality** URL ▶ http://www.brad.ac.uk/~mdavarle/personality.html

Medieval Studies and a Modern Day Labyrinth

Labyrinth Home Page 

Jump 3629

The Labyrinth is a global information network providing free, organized access to electronic resources in medieval studies through a World Wide Web server at Georgetown University. Unlike the fabled labyrinth of old, the user will be able to find an Ariadne's thread in order to navigate through the menus and hypertext links to databases, services and electronic texts that live on servers around the world. A fascinating and very well-done journey—well worth a visit. —(C.P.)

URL ▶ http://www.georgetown.edu/labyrinth/labyrinth-home.html

Historic Building Preservation Resources

Preserve/Net Jump 7020 

The National Council for Preservation Education has compiled a wide-ranging, worldwide list of links that will make every historian, preservationist and restorer's heart beat a little faster. You can explore art history resources, international heritage conventions, search specialized libraries, visit museums, and read the latest heritage legislation. In no time, you could be leading a campaign to save your town's historical sites and artifacts. —(E.v.B.)

URL ▶ http://www.crp.cornell.edu/preserve.html

Electronic Romper Room

Kid's Space Jump 7143 

Sachiko Oba, a Ph.D. student in education, has created a Net-based play area for children. Through colorful, clickable, whimsical graphics, children can explore this amusing playroom, and they're encouraged to download their musical performances, artistic creations, and stories and poems. So tell the little ones that now is the time to dust off the piano and record their version of "Twinkle, Twinkle, Little Star" for posterity. All actions are guided in easy-to-understand steps. If a child has a problem, he or she can check into the Doctor's Help Office to receive further instructions on navigating through various procedures on this site. It's multilingual, too: so far, Kid's Space is available in English, Dutch, and Japanese. —(E.v.B.)

KEY NEWSGROUP **csn.ml.kids**

URL▶ http://www.interport.net/~sachi/

▲ *Smiling dolphin, from* **Aquanaut**, *at* Jump **2565**.

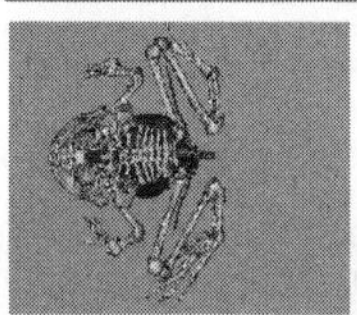

More Than One Way to Skin a Frog

Virtual Frog Dissection Kit

Jump **8045** 

Those smart folks at the Lawrence Berkeley National Laboratory sure know how to skin a frog, and this is how we would have liked to have dissected a frog in high school biology class—no mess, no fuss, no yucky smell. The frog here isn't very life-like, thank goodness, but all its essential parts are accurately rendered. You can take the skin off, look at various organs, resize the frog, rotate the frog for different views, and watch a video of what you've prompted the software dissector to do. Online references present all kinds of background information on organs and systems. Give your dissection flair by choosing from eight different languages to perform your operation in. —(E.v.B.)

KEY NEWSGROUP **sci.bio** URL▶ http://george.lbl.gov/ITG.hm.pg.docs/dissect/dissect.html

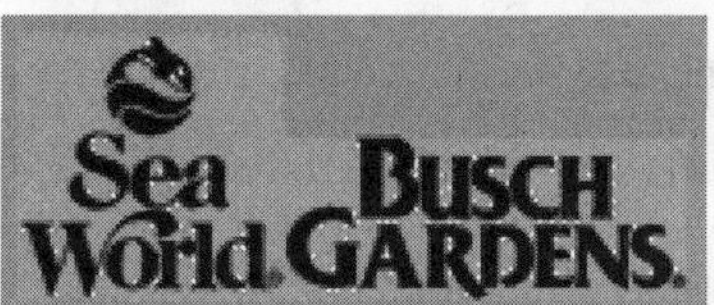

Wildlife Education for Children

Sea World/-Busch Gardens Information Database

Jump **2267** 

Many theme parks and attractions try to combine education and entertainment, but the people who run Sea World and Busch Gardens have taken it another step further with this Web site. Designed for children, but fun and informative for all ages, there's an animal database that describes various animals with interesting, as well as standard, facts and figures, pictures, and video clips. There are also special sections on coral reefs and endangered species. The Ask Shamu section lets students pose questions to the Sea World/Busch Gardens experts, and the online teacher's guides will help educators use these pages as the starting point for further discussion and study. —(L.S.)

KEY NEWSGROUP **k12.ed.science** URL▶ http://www.bev.net/education/SeaWorld/homepage.html

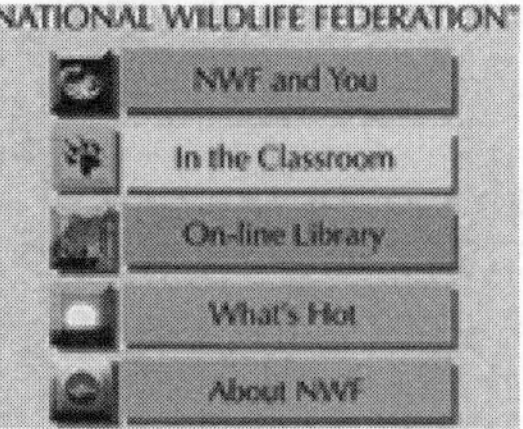

National Wildlife Foundation

NWF Home Page Jump **1553** CONTENT

This attractive, icon-oriented and easy-to-use site covers everything about the National Wildlife Foundation. From issues and action, education, and international activities to kids, news media, politics, and catalogs, this site is one of the best organized on the Web. You can click on a map of your region to find local NWF information, hit the action page for enviro-hotline numbers and legislative scores, and even find "How-Tos" for activists, including tips on raising money, organizing phone banks, running petition drives, and writing press releases. Download publications and reports from their online library, or read about NWF's plans for the 90s. Kids can learn from Animal Tracks, where they click on the blue paw icon for "gee-whiz" facts (did you know lobsters come in red, blue, white, and green?), or on the green paw for Ranger Rick's riddles. Guaranteed to keep you and your kids interested for hours. —(H.L.)

URL▶ http://www.igc.apc.org/nwf/

All about Penguins

The Penguin Page Jump 6020 

Kevin Welch, a graduate of the University of Pennsylvania with a Bachelor of Arts in Biology, did an independent study on penguins after participating in a project at the Philadelphia Zoo. He then put it all on the Web, and the results are truly extraordinary. This tremendous site, filled with first-rate graphics, will give you detailed information on 17 species of modern-day penguins, along with notes on their behavior. Find out about the penguin's relatives and predators. Stop into the Penguin Showcase, with a monthly feature on islands inhabited by penguins. Teachers and students can jump to the Blue Ice site, to find out how to participate in a classroom project on Antarctica. A beautiful, must-see site. —(N.F.)

URL▸ http://www.vni.net/~kwelch/penguin.html

Marine Turtles Online

Turtle Trax - A Marine Turtle Page Jump 7332 

Canadians Peter Bennett and Ursula Keuper-Bennett have created a fascinating set of pages devoted to "the wonder and beauty of the marine turtle." With mounting dismay, you read the reasons why all species of marine turtles are either threatened or endangered. The Bennetts' photographs are wonderful and the biographies they've written about the turtles they've studied over many summers are not only informative, but fun to read. As well, you can learn even more about turtles in their Turtle Library and read other interesting bits of great sea turtle lore. —(E.v.B.)

KEY NEWSGROUP **sci.environment** URL▸ http://www.io.org/~bunrab/

Fun with Science

Family Explorer Sample Activities Jump 2709 

Science can be fun, and it's easy for families to learn about the world around them with this page of activities. Taken from the Family Explorer monthly newsletter, it concentrates on entertaining activities that don't require any special knowledge, just natural curiosity. Each article offers clearly written instructions that explain the project or activity, what's involved, and what you can expect from it. New articles are added every month, so this can be a regular bookmark for fun, interesting, and educational things to do. —(L.S.)

KEY NEWSGROUP **k12.ed.science** URL▸ http://www.parentsplace.com/readroom/explorer/activity.html

Be Part of a Student Magazine

Press Return Home Page Jump 2185 

Budding journalists now have the opportunity to contribute to a real online multimedia magazine and work with professional editors through the Scholastic Network's "Press Return" program. Each quarterly issue covers a specific theme, with the contents selected from student submissions. Your school needs to be a member of the Scholastic Network, but for the nominal fee, your school gets access to the other programs of this interactive learning network. —(L.S.)

KEY NEWSGROUP **k12.ed.tech** URL▸ http://scholastic.com:2005/public/PressReturn/Press-Return.html

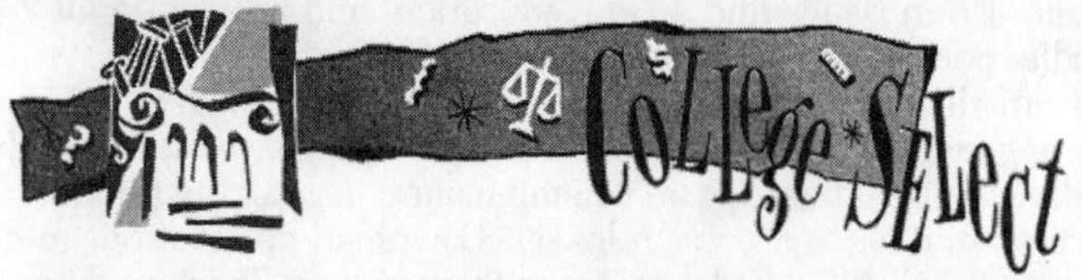

Choosing a College

College Select Jump 5786 

If you—or your child—are having trouble finding straightforward information on picking a four-year college, you're going to be spending a lot of time at this site. In the College Search database, you'll find a listing of colleges, as well as some great search tools, and a guide to the application process. Confused about financial aid? Check out their "Paying For College" section. There's also an online chat area and a wonderful feature called SelectFolder, a place where you can store all your search information. —(J.P.)

KEY NEWSGROUP **clari.news.education.higher** URL▸ http://www.collegeselect.com/cs/index.cfm

Advice for the College-Bound

Peterson's Educational Center Jump 2255

The aim of this site is to be the Net's most comprehensive resource for private education information, and they've made a good start. Use it to learn about undergraduate and graduate schools, their programs and their faculties, then download applications for the ones that interest you. That alone makes this a valuable site, but there also are links to summer jobs and educational opportunities for kids and teenagers, and plans to add even more educational resources. Keep coming back and you'll soon find information on primary and secondary schools, vocational schools, distance learning, and career planning resources. —(L.S.)

KEY NEWSGROUP **soc.college** URL▶ http://www.petersons.com:8080/

Info for the College-Bound

CollegeNET(tm) Home Page Jump 5104

Pretty much the best Net guide to colleges and universities, CollegeNET allows you to search for the school that's right for you. You can search for different colleges and universities by geography, tuition, and enrollment. Each record includes such useful info as location, enrollment, tuition rates, academic calendar, name and phone number to contact for a campus tour, list of degrees offered, main degree programs, academic requirements, information on student life, and much more. There is also financial aid and scholarship information. —(S.B.)

URL▶ http://www.unival.com/cn/collegenet.html

Free College Money & Advice

fastWEB Jump 6671

The Internet's first and only free scholarship search service offers students a tailored search of over 180,000 scholarships, grants, and loans. To start, you'll need to register your name and user ID. This sets up a special electronic mailbox which continuously stores your search results, no strings attached. If you're not ready to begin your search, you'll still have access to a college financial aid information page that's one of the best collections of free information available online. Protect yourself from the latest scams by taking a run through this site's Scam Alert, a service which uncovers suspicious scholarship opportunities. Additionally, you'll find numerous financial aid calculators, including a college cost projector, savings plan designer, student loan advisor, and a loan payment calculator. —(L.T.)

KEY NEWSGROUP **clari.news.education.higher** URL▶ http://www.studentservices.com/fastweb/

Scholarships for You

Student Services, Incorporated Jump 5134

With a database of 180,000 plus scholarships, fellowships, grants, and loans, Student Services, developer of this site, has the information resources to help college students find money for college. This Web page helps you find that scholarship out there waiting for you. On this site's main page, enter your major and click Go! You'll then receive a list of colleges that meet your search and scholarship needs. —(S.B.)

URL▶ http://www.studentservices.com/search/

Ben's Many Talents

The World of Benjamin Franklin Jump 7127

Benjamin Franklin was a complex man. He is honored as one of our founding fathers, but in addition to being a statesman, he was also a scientist, an inventor, a printer, a philosopher, a musician, and an economist. The Franklin Institute in Philadelphia has created a virtual exhibit on his life. It is an exemplary Web model of a museum-without-walls. We can see pictures of Franklin's inventions, trace his family tree, read about his life, even listen to a re-creation of him playing "Yankee Doodle" on one of his musical inventions. Although designed for schoolchildren, adults will also enjoy exploring this exhibit. —(E.v.B.)

KEY NEWSGROUP **soc.history** URL▶ http://sln.fi.edu/franklin/rotten.html

Sparking Kids' Creativity

SMARTKiD Magazine Jump 6786

Glancing at its title may lead you to believe that SMARTKID is just another Web e-zine for kids. In fact, it's for parents who can use its enlightening tools to help spark their children's creativity. Would you like to find the best places for family adventures, or a parents' primer to middle-school music? You'll find these and much more browsing these pages, such as what educators are saying about bilingual education. With this site's unique ideas for family-oriented art, technology and fun, you'll always discover new projects for the whole family to enjoy. —(L.T.)

KEY NEWSGROUP **misc.kids** URL▶ http://www.smartkid.com

Home Schooling Reference & Support

Home Education Resources Center Jump 2389

If your children learn at home, or you're planning to start them on a home school program, this site will be an important resource for you. Beginning with the online copies of state education regulations and home school support groups, and continuing through science and recreational activities for children, you'll have access to specific material and general ideas to make the home school experience a good one. There's even a section of reviews of educational materials, by parents who've used them. If you want to add a review, just upload it. Oh, yes, the site sponsor sells home schooling materials, but there's no selling on any of these pages...it's kept considerately separate. —(L.S.)

KEY NEWSGROUP **misc.education.home-school.misc** URL▶ http://www.cts.com/~netsales/herc/

▲ *Squirrel eating bread, from* **JumpCity**.

A Magazine by and for Kids

CyberKids Home Jump 2634

Cyberkids is a quarterly, online magazine featuring nonfiction and fiction articles, product reviews, artwork, games, puzzles, and other fun and educational things to do—all written by children. Material can be submitted by e-mail, and Mountain Lake Software, which produces the site, also accepts phone calls and faxes from interested people. Even if your children don't submit an article for the magazine, they still can participate through the CyberKids Interactive section. This is where readers can write about anything, from their likes and dislikes about the magazine, to suggestions, to asking for pen pals. —(L.S.)

KEY NEWSGROUP **misc.kids.computer** URL▶ http://www.mtlake.com/cyberkids/

Homeschooling Made Easy

Home's Cool Homeschool and Family Site Jump 5857

You don't have to be involved with homeschooling to enjoy this site, created by Net2Go, Inc., because there's really something here for any parent of school-age children. But the main scope here is to help those who have chosen to educate their children at home. Those folks will find plenty of information on the subject, ranging from subject-specific Web curriculum sites, on-line magazines, and other important Net sites for homeschoolers. There's a classified section where you can arrange to buy used curriculum books (and other items), and you can also purchase new books through a special arrangement with AMAZON.COM, the big Web bookseller site. There's a small membership fee for some of the services, but otherwise everything here is free. —(J.P.)

KEY NEWSGROUP **misc.education** URL▶ http://www.homes-cool.com/

Home Schooling Resources Page

The Homeschooling Zone

Jump **5858**

This site should be compulsory viewing for anyone interested in homeschooling. In fact, if you don't find what you're looking for here, it probably just doesn't exist on the Web. This site's main page provides a detailed, worldwide listing of organizations and people involved in home schooling. But it's the second page where you'll find the bulk of the information. And what a source it is! The list of links here will take you to newsletters, online shopping locations, chat areas and mailing lists, support, resources, and more. —(J.P.)

KEY NEWSGROUP **sci.edu** URL▶ http://www.caro.net/~joespa/

Homestyle Education

Homespun Web of Home Educational Resources

Jump **8046**

Trying to decide whether your child would be better educated at home, but not sure how to proceed? Well, this is the site for you. At the Homespun Web, you can read the many helpful materials in this site's getting started section. This site also lists organizations, curriculum suppliers, political hints and tips, Internet and other useful resources. The resource list, which contains good hot links, is extensive and spans everything from the arts to museums, to math, to religion and beyond. The Homespun Web also offers you easy and informative contact with other parents who have decided to educate their children at home. —(E.v.B.)

KEY NEWSGROUP **misc.education** URL▶ http://www.ictheweb.com/hs-web/index.html

Montessori Method Online

Montessori for Moms Jump **8018**

Need a different way of looking at your child's early education needs? Millions have been following Maria Montessori's methods, developed in the early 1900s, to help their children learn to learn. Now the method is emerging online. Montessori for Moms is a collection of many of Montessori author Sibyl Carroll's training guides for home schooling for children ages two to five years old. The site presents detailed lesson plans in outline format, and detailed instructions for making many of the simple Montessori teaching materials yourself. If you are new to this educational theory (which emphasizes development of a child's initiative, sense perception, and creativity), Carroll takes you through the method, and the philosophy, slowly and clearly. —(E.v.B.)

KEY NEWSGROUP **misc.kids** URL▶ http://www.primenet.com/~gojess/mfm/mfmhome.htm

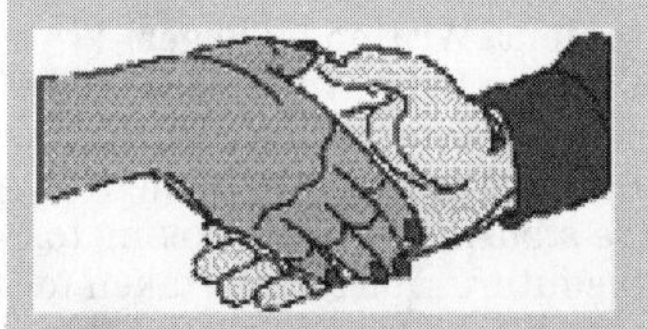

Better Teaching through Sharing

Teachers Helping Teachers Jump **2682**

CONTENT

This site is intended to offer ideas that inexperienced teachers can use immediately in their classes, as well as provide a forum for experienced teachers to share their experiences and tips. Well organized and updated weekly by Dr. Scott Mandel of Pacoima Middle School in Los Angeles, there are separate sections on classroom management, language arts, math, science, social studies, the arts, and special education. There's also a Topic of the Week, where an area of interest to teachers is discussed in depth. The success of the site depends on the participation of teachers, and all are invited to contribute, as well as submit questions or topic ideas. —(L.S.)

KEY NEWSGROUP **misc.education** URL▶ http://north.pacificnet.net/~mandel/

Educational Connections

Classroom Connect on the Net!

Jump 7261

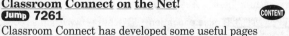

Classroom Connect has developed some useful pages containing interesting educational information available on the Net for K-12 teachers and administrators. You can surf links to other education-related Web sites, download Internet software, find education newsgroups, and access a number of special online educational conferences. Classroom Connect also offers online Internet seminars designed for educators. If you're a teacher, why not check out the funding seminar?—you might get some good ideas for upgrading your school's computer room. —(E.v.B.)

KEY NEWSGROUP **misc.education** URL ▶ http://www.wentworth.com/

Special Education Network

Special Needs Education Network

Jump 6593

Designed for parents, teachers, schools, and anyone else involved in the education of students with special needs, The Special Needs Education Network provides deep resources, all of which are easily searchable here. Browse around hundreds of reference features covering Attention Deficit Disorder, Autism, Blindness/Sight Impairments, Deaf/Hearing Impairments, Developmental Disabilities, Down Syndrome, Dyslexia, Family Support, Fetal Alcohol and Fragile X Syndromes, Multiple Sclerosis, and issues concerning technology and special needs. If you're seeking support for a special needs individual who is looking for a new friend, there's no better place to find one than through the Member Directory, where you can communicate with others via e-mail. —(L.T.)

KEY NEWSGROUP **misc.handicap** URL ▶ http://schoolnet2.carleton.ca/~kwellar

Web and Computer Educational Reform Resources

EdWeb Home Page Jump 7463

EdWeb, written and maintained by Andy Carvin, explores the worlds of educational reform and information technology. From these pages, check out "educational resources around the world, learn about trends in education policy and information infrastructure development, examine success stories of computers in the classroom, and much, much more." Andy, among many other interesting topics, also takes a look at the potential role the Web can play in the classroom. He also mounts information on WWWEDU—his Net mailing list discussion group, which explores the role of the Web in education. After you've finished with Andy's contributions, you can surf over to other Web resources on related education and information pages. —(E.v.B.)

KEY NEWSGROUP **sci.ed** URL ▶ http://k12.cnidr.org:90/

The Future of Technology in Education

Engines for Educaton

Jump 2176

This site is as interesting for its innovative organization as it is for its eye-opening content. Written by Roger Schank and Chip Cleary, the site itself discusses what's wrong with our educational system today, what needs to be done, and how technology in general, and computers and software specifically, can help to change things. The opening page, though, doesn't browbeat you. It lets you begin reading based on your level of interest—whether you're just curious, or you're someone interested in technological innovation, or you're a businessperson looking to see how education relates to business and industry, or an educator with a stake in the future. You're then taken to a page that summarizes the relevant issues and gives you a hyperlinked outline that will take you to areas of the book that reflect your interests. The authors are critical of our educational system, and you may not agree with their basic premises, but there's still a good deal of interesting and thought-provoking information here. —(L.S.)

KEY NEWSGROUP **sci.edu** URL ▶ http://www.ils.nwu.edu/~e_for_e/nodes/I-M-INTRO-ZOOMER-pg.html

Building the Virtual Schoolhouse

NetSchool Welcome Page Jump 2210

Lots of schools have Internet access, and there are numerous resource sites on the Web for educators and students. But this is the first project designed to create a true K-12 schoolhouse on the Net, and one of the true examples of what the Net can do for education. Being developed on the Web by Wilton Jones of the National Institute For Technology In Education, this schoolhouse lets everyone participate in its development. The working concept is that teachers and students—and anyone else who wants to participate—can design programs, teach, learn, or publish here. It's an exciting project that anyone interested in new educational technologies should visit. —(L.S.)

KEY NEWSGROUP **sci.edu** URL▶ http://netschool.edu/

Internet Starters for Educators

The Internet Educational Resources Guide Jump 2291

Teachers wanting to learn how to use the resources of the Internet will find these pages by John Woodbury very helpful. Here you'll find essential information on the Internet and its services, specific reference material on how to integrate Internet services into the classroom, a list of people and organizations who can help you implement online programs, and the usual links to other Web, Gopher, and Telnet sites related to education. Especially helpful are John's detailed descriptions and evaluations of available newsgroups, mailing lists, and magazines for educators that make deciding which to explore much easier. The entire site also is indexed on a WAIS database, to make finding what you want a simple matter. —(L.S.)

KEY NEWSGROUP **misc.education** URL▶ http://www.dcs.aber.ac.uk/~jjw0/index_ht.html

Calculators for Every Purpose

Calculators On-Line Jump 6749

This indispensable Web site provides over 100 different special-purpose calculators online. Go here and add up your taxes, predict sunrises, or compute travel distances. Students will find tools to help them estimate college expenses, or super homework helpers like statistical, physics, and medical calculators. Most importantly, these calculators can't be lost, and their batteries never need replacing. —(L.T.)

KEY NEWSGROUP **sci.math.stat** URL▶ http://www-sci.lib.uci.edu/HSG/RefCalculators.html

Net Center for Math Education Resources

The Math Forum Jump 6626

Searching for a virtual center on the Net for mathematics resources? It all adds up at this generous resource for teachers, students, parents, and mathematicians alike. The Math Forum selects each annotated resource based on their value and on how well each takes advantage of new technologies. You can opt for a quick search through its entire contents, or simply browse through categorized grade levels and math subjects from K-12 to advanced math. —(L.T.)

KEY NEWSGROUP **k12.ed.math** URL▶ http://forum.swarthmore.edu

Math Contests for Schools

MathMagic! Jump 2311

MathMagic! is an e-mail math contest that motivates students to use and sharpen their math skills while learning how to use computer technology and to work better with others. Challenges are presented in four school grade categories—K-3, 4-6, 7-9, and 10-12. Contestants are assigned a "Net partner," and together they work on a solution to the problem. While the contests are handled via e-mail, this page has the information needed to get involved. Also posted here are the current and past challenges, so teachers whose schools do not have student Internet access can use the challenges and team concept on their own. —(L.S.)

KEY NEWSGROUP **k12.ed.math** URL▶ http://forum.swarthmore.edu/mathmagic/

High-School Chemistry Resources

Resources for Chemistry Teachers Jump 2301

High-school chemistry teachers looking for new ideas, textbook reviews, and other information or suggestions for planning classes will find this site maintained by James Aldridge very helpful. The two main sections, one for regular and one for advance placement classes, hold essays and notes on course planning and equipment, as well as suggested labs and demonstrations. Another section contains suggested assignments for regular, honors and AP students, and there is a comprehensive list of links to other chemistry-related Web sites. Any teacher with ideas, labs, demonstrations or textbook reviews is also invited to submit material. —(L.S.)

KEY NEWSGROUP k12.ed.science URL ▶ http://rampages.onramp.net:80/~jaldr/

Periodic Table of the Elements

WebElements

Jump 3734

Calling all science students! WebElements brings the Periodic Table of the Elements to the Web. It's a colorful and fast way to present the Table, and details on any particular element are just a mouse click away. There are links to other data available on the elements, as well as a way to calculate isotope patterns and element percentages. Developed by the Department of Chemistry at the University of Sheffield in England, this is a great site for students of almost any age. —(N.F.)

URL ▶ http://www.shef.ac.uk:80/~chem/web-elements/

English As a Second Language

The Virtual English Language Center Jump 2404

Students and teachers involved in learning to speak English can use this site as a resource for books, software, and general links to pages that support language study. But the main feature is the Weekly Idiom, with definitions and sample usages of oft-used English phrases. Each idiom is demonstrated with sound files of the idiom itself and its use in conversation. And to help visitors practice their English skills, as well as to encourage learning about other cultures, there's an E-mail Pen-Pal Connection where you can register and establish e-mail relationships with people around the world. —(L.S.)

KEY NEWSGROUP alt.usage.english URL ▶ http://www.interport.net:80/~comenius/

Get a Free French Lesson Online

French Lesson Home Page Jump 6618

So you'd like to learn French? Here's a free, practical, learn-at-your-own pace way to accomplish that goal. Jacques L'eon has offered a remarkable service to the Web with his teachings and lesson plans. Accompanying sound files are an added bonus, covering pronouns, verbs, adjectives, plurals, sentence structures and French expressions, all contained in nine full sections. —(L.T.)

KEY NEWSGROUP soc.culture.french URL ▶ http://teleglobe.ca/~leo/french.html

Learn Hindi

Hindi Program at Penn Jump 7014

Namaste! That's Hindi for "hello." You can learn even more of this north Indian language, spoken by millions of Indians, by following the audio lessons provided by the University of Pennsylvania Hindi program. What's more, you can download a video demonstrating how to write the beautiful Devanagari script. —(E.v.B.)

KEY NEWSGROUP alt.hindu URL ▶ http://philae.sas.upenn.edu/Hindi/hindi.html

Study Abroad and Learn the Language

National Registration Center for Study Abroad Jump 2312

This site helps you identify and evaluate language immersion programs—foreign study programs where you take classes in the language of the specific country. The National Registration Center for Study Abroad maintains a database of the top programs in 30 countries, making it easy to compare them. If you're unfamiliar with these programs, online fact sheets tell you how to find the ones that are best for you. When you do, you can download pre-registration forms to begin the application process. —(L.S.)

KEY NEWSGROUP sci.edu URL▶ http://www.execpc.com:80/~nrcsa/

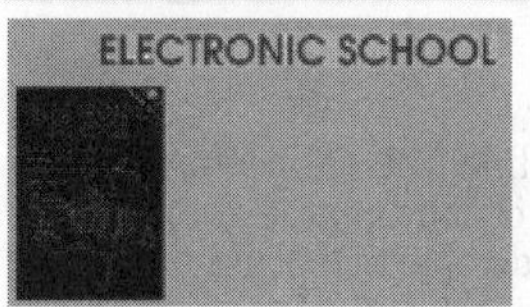

Integrating Technology into the Classroom

The Electronic School Jump 2455

Published by the National School Boards Association, *The Electronic School* is a monthly magazine devoted to helping teachers and administrators integrate electronic technologies into the K-12 classroom. The Web version takes all the articles from past issues and puts them online, adding hyperlinks where appropriate. Articles cover topics as diverse as determining the real cost of "donated" equipment, understanding fiber optic technology, specific classroom projects, and new Internet-related resources for educators and students. —(L.S.)

KEY NEWSGROUP k12.ed.tech URL▶ http://www.access.digex.net/~nsbamags/e-school.html

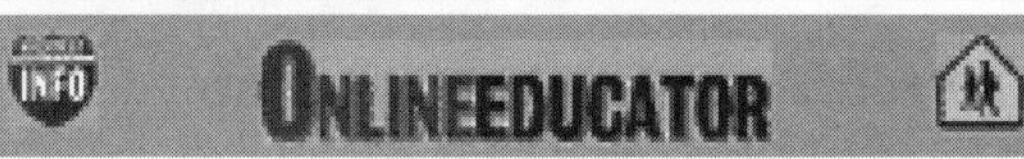

Online Lesson Plans & Activities for Teachers

The Online Educator Jump 2486

Teachers who use no other Internet education resource should at least use this one. Maintained by the staff of The Online Educator newsletter, this site offers specific activities and lesson ideas. And it's updated weekly, so you'll have a regular, ongoing resource for Internet-based classroom activities. The Newspapers in Education Lesson Plan takes a major news story, summarizes the issues, offers links to online news and story-related resources, and even offers sample discussion questions. The One-A-Day Teacher's Hot List gives you a week's worth of educational, interesting, or just plain fun sites, along with ideas for how to introduce them to the class. Past links are archived, along with sample articles from *The Online Educator*. —(L.S.)

KEY NEWSGROUP k12.ed.comp.literacy URL▶ http://www.cris.com/~felixg/OE/OEWELCOME.html

Distance Learning on the Internet

Your CASO Guide: The Internet University Jump 8036

Want to improve your mind, but don't want to leave the comfort of your living room? Sign on to the Internet University site, which contains a comprehensive listing of online college courses available—at last count over 700. You can also read profiles of over 30 accredited online course providers. And don't worry about going to the library—Cape Software, publisher of this site, also thoughtfully provides links to more than 2,000 Internet study resource sites. Come on, why not take an arts course, or one in business, or public administration, French, sociology or math? How about a little Haitian history, or a survey of modern Russian history for starters? They're all here! —(E.v.B.)

KEY NEWSGROUP misc.education URL▶ http://www.caso.com/

Internet Education Resources for Teachers

The Teacher Education Internet Server Jump 4008

Curator Bernard Robin, in collaboration with The Society for Information Technology and Teacher Education, The University of Virginia, and The University of Houston, has put together this site chock-full of resources exploring the ways in which the Internet can benefit teacher education. The site provides access to self-instructional modules on various subjects, Internet resources, electronic journals such as *Ed-Tech Review,* and much more. —(R.B.)

KEY NEWSGROUP comp.edu URL▶ http://curry.edschool.Virginia.EDU:80/teis/

Electronic Textbooks

Kids Web—A World Wide Web Digital Library for Schoolkids Jump 7114

New York State has funded the creation of a virtual library for students in K-12. The compilers have brought together an amazing amount of information that students can easily navigate, and that is targeted at school kids. The information and links are divided into main subject areas: the arts, the sciences, social studies. The science collection alone is impressively further divided into astronomy, biology, chemistry, computers, environment, math, physics, and weather. Knowing kids, the authors have also wisely added a fun and games section which contains humor, reference material, and sports sites. —(E.v.B.)

KEY NEWSGROUP **csn.ml.kids** URL▶ http://www.npac.syr.edu/textbook/kidsweb/

Knowledge On Screen

Welcome to Britannica Online Jump **7495**

The publishers of the venerable Encyclopedia Britannica have introduced Britannica Online, the online version of the massive hardcopy Encyclopædia Britannica. Britannica Online presents a mountain of solid material to sift through—more than 65,000 articles from the hardcopy publication, and includes hundreds of articles and other features not appearing in the print edition. You can sign up for a free trial or an annual subscription to the online publication, or try some of the free features that allow you to sample Britannica's wares. The search engine is powerful and flexible—you can search on words, a phrase, or even use it to ask questions, such as: "who was Julius Caesar's mom?" You can also access the site daily to read short bios of famous people born on that day. —(E.v.B.)

KEY NEWSGROUP **alt.education.research** URL▶ http://www.eb.com/

The Etext Archives

ETEXT Archives: The Web's Online Library

The ETEXT Archives Jump **6538**

The ETEXT Archives is home to a massive amount and variety of electronic texts, from the sacred to the profane, the political to the personal. ETEXT contains the full text of hundreds of publications grouped by subject, such as its Political text area, where you'll find full-text files covering subjects such as cable regulation, conspiracy, history, trade news, women's studies, and more. Their E-Books section features Project Gutenberg, where books whose copyrights have expired have been converted into electronic text on the Internet, making them freely available to the public, and Project Libellus, providing online texts of classical works which are left in their original form. The Magazines category offers regularly updated editions of electronic publications, ranging from titles such as "International Teletimes," an international culture magazine, to "Unit Circle", covering politics, art, music and literature for the 90's. —(L.T.)

KEY NEWSGROUP **alt.usage.english** URL▶ http://www.etext.org/

Educational Quest of American Literature

American Literature Survey Site Jump **6019**

This site was developed as part of an American literature class held at the University of Texas at Austin, by the instructor Daniel Larson and members of his class, and what a terrific job they've done! Works of American literature are analyzed and discussed here by the class, and you can follow along. You'll find class assignments, online texts, transcripts of discussions, student papers, and much more. You can read passages and text, and even make your own comments, which will then be shared with other visitors to this site. A fascinating and accessible approach to the classic works of American literature. —(N.F.)

KEY NEWSGROUP **misc.education** URL▶ http://www.en.utexas.edu/~daniel/amlit/amlit.html

America's Cultural History

American Memory Jump **2700**

CONTENT

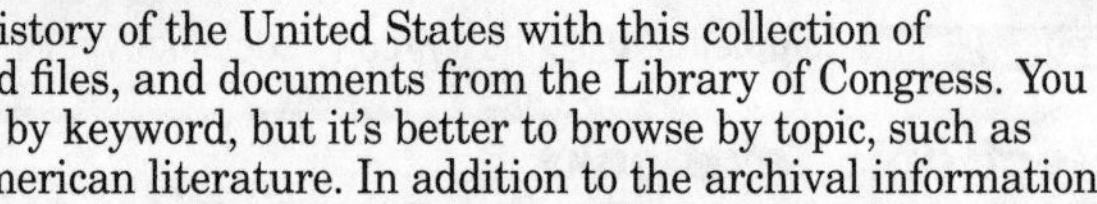

Delve into the cultural history of the United States with this collection of photographs, films, sound files, and documents from the Library of Congress. You can search the collection by keyword, but it's better to browse by topic, such as early filmmaking and American literature. In addition to the archival information, each topic area includes background information about the collection and a bibliography of pointers for more information. In some cases, interpretive material is also included. —(L.S.)

KEY NEWSGROUP **soc.history** URL▶ http://rs6.loc.gov/amhome.html

Making Sense of Life

Serendip Home Page Jump 2752

If you've ever thought that there were more than a few blank pages in life's little instruction book, you're not alone. Among the others who feel the same way are a group of scientists, businesspersons, and educators who founded this page, as a forum for and a set of resources to support intellectual and social change in education, and in how to make sense of life. The serendipity from which they take their name is that they open the page to whatever seems to fit, resulting in a wide-ranging collection of articles and resources. Most of them relate to behavior and intellectual development, but they're not all as esoteric as they may seem. In addition to the deep thoughts, you'll find a game or two to play, and always the opportunity to add your thoughts on any of the subjects covered. —(L.S.)

KEY NEWSGROUP **alt.society.paradigms** URL▶ http://serendip.brynmawr.edu/

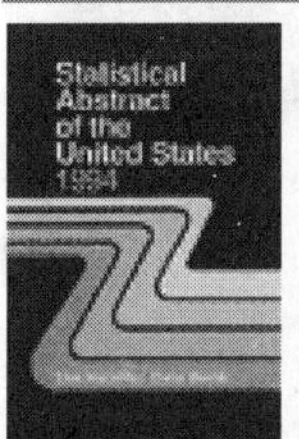

Stats Online

Statistical Abstract Jump 7306

What a great reference to have in your Web library! The Statistical Abstract of the United States contains a collection of statistics (over 1,400 tables and graphs) on social, economic, and international subjects. In addition, you can access data sources from the Census Bureau, federal agencies, and private organizations. The entire reference work is not online, but a good smattering of statistical information can be had at this site. —(E.v.B.)

KEY NEWSGROUP **misc.misc** URL▶ http://www.census.gov/stat_abstract/

Pages of Stones

Stone Pages Jump 5776

Here is an interesting site that's all about Stonehenge and those many other, mysterious, 10,000 year-old sites scattered around England. And believe us, there are many more sites like this than you'd think! The first thing you might want to do at this site is drop into the glossary. It is there, for example, you will learn that a cairn is a round or long mound of stones, often covering a chamber or burial area. The sense of history captured on this pages is quite captivating. The centerpiece is the Stones of England, Scotland and Ireland. Enter Scotland, for example, and you'll be given a guided tour of the many rock formations found there. Each stop includes a photo of the site, a map, a description of the meaning of the site, and more. And there's also photo and travel tips to make a real trip all that much more enjoyable and educational. —(J.P.)

KEY NEWSGROUP **sci.archaeology** URL▶ http://joshua.micronet.it/utenti/dmeozzi/homeng.html

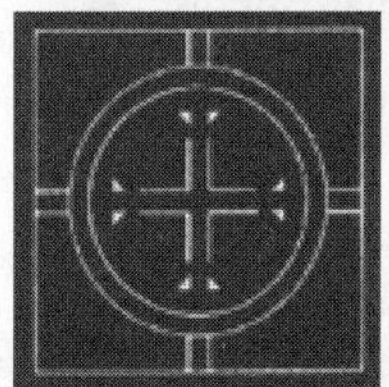

Architect of the Century

The Frank Lloyd Wright Page Jump 7324

T. Giesler has created quite the collection of information about one of the 20th Century's most famous architects, Frank Lloyd Wright. You can browse through photographs of his buildings—from his well-known residential and commercial projects, to university buildings, and more. Giesler also provides a wealth of links to Web pages around the world featuring this creative genius. He is also in the process of creating a comprehensive guide to Wright buildings that are open to the public. If this whets your appetite for more generalized architectural information, you can explore those links he also provides here. —(E.v.B.)

KEY NEWSGROUP **alt.architecture** URL▶ http://www.mcs.com/~tgiesler/flw_home.htm#pictures

One Potato, Two Potato

A SWEETPOTATO SAMPLER Jump 7368

Arthur Q. Villordon sure likes sweet potatoes! Quirky but informative, fun but scientifically based, these pages are sure to interest foodies and horticulturists alike. You can trace the cultivation history of the sweet potato, gain some insights into its adaptability, and read recent research concerning its nutritional properties. Good, solid botanical and horticultural information is found here. As well, Villordon provides links to related subjects found on the Web. We especially enjoyed learning that, in fact, the sweet potato is NOT a yam. —(E.v.B.)

KEY NEWSGROUP **rec.gardens**
URL▶ http://www.linknet.net/s_potato/

▲ *Ives, claimed as the first man to fly the stars and stripes in color on a television, from* **Museum of Television** *at* Jump **0220**.

What's the Big Deal about Today's Date?

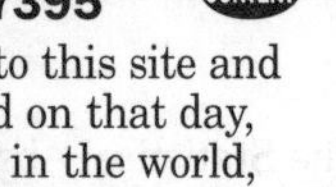

Today in History Jump **7395**

Every day you can surf over to this site and find out who was born or died on that day, what major events happened in the world, what famous books were published, even what television shows aired for the first time. It's really fun! For a treat, use page creator Warren Gill's neat search program to find out what great events took place on your birthday over the last hundreds of years. —(E.v.B.)

KEY NEWSGROUP **soc.history** URL▶ http://www.unison.com/wantinfo/today

The Story of the Father of Television

The Farnsworth Chronicles Jump **7434**

On these pages, Paul Schatzkin pays homage to Philo T. Farnsworth, a Mormon farmboy from Rigby, Idaho, who basically invented television in 1922. Schatzkin is in the process of recreating Farnsworth's story, based on archival research and interviews with the inventor's widow and son, in episodic, illustrated installments here at this superbly designed site. It's historic, educational, and, above all, a great story. You can also subscribe and receive the installments by e-mail. —(E.v.B.)

KEY NEWSGROUP **sci.philosophy.tech** URL▶ http://songs.com./noma/philo/

Television Museum and Picture Gallery

Museum of Television Jump **0220**

There are larger sites dealing with the history of broadcast television, but few are as well-designed as this one, created by Canada's MZTV Museum and its chairman, Moses Znaimer. This well-designed site contains some fascinating photographs and illustrations from the earliest days of television, including efforts at "mechanical television," during the 1920's. We especially liked this site's interesting gallery of photos of the way-futuristic Philco Predicta televisions, which were manufactured during the 1950s. MZTV also includes downloadable video archives of historical—and mundane—events as portrayed by television. While this site's focus is on preserving the hardware legacy of televisions produced over the past 70 years, its presented in an easy-to-understand format, which is enthusiastically collected and described here. —(E.G.)

URL▶ http://www2.mztv.com/mztv/mztvhome.html

New Technologies Televised

CONTENT

Hi-Tech Culture Jump **7319**

Hi-Tech Culture is a popular series on the Discovery Canada cable network. Always thought-provoking, hot topics range from indie bands on the Net to helping people with disabilities connect online to how computer technology is aiding the medical profession. You can access program synopses and also read previews of coming shows. The Webmasters also provide links and e-mail addresses to Web and Internet resources connected to each topic covered on every show. —(E.v.B.)

KEY NEWSGROUP **alt.society.futures** URL▸ http://giant.mindlink.net/htc/

The Media History Project

The History of Media

The Media History Project Jump 7430 CONTENT

Kristina Ross, creator of the Media History Project, has developed some amazing pages. Done as a collaborative effort between professional and lay media historians, the pages provide "a comprehensive guide to all online materials relevant to the study, appreciation, and understanding of media history." You can surf media history-related archives, syllabi, lectures, essays, and other relevant Web sites. Kristina would like us to consider the site as "an evolving, hypermedia, distributed textbook, a map to buried treasure, and a gateway to a laboratory for media historians and scholars." We think she's succeeded in her goal! —(E.v.B.)

KEY NEWSGROUP **soc.history** URL▸ http://spot.colorado.edu/~rossk/history/histhome.html

---

Thoughtful Television

Socratic Philosophy Television Jump 5154 LINKS

No Dogs or Philosophers Allowed is a PBS television show covering the world of philosophy and philosophers. This site's home page features the usual Web-type promotional info on the show, show times, reviews, souvenirs, etc., but the prime draw is its list of links to other philosophy-related Web sites all over the Net. Ken Knisely, the host of the program, has put together this site with a sense of humor and a good mix of photos, illustrations, and text. —(S.B.)

KEY NEWSGROUP **alt.consciousness** URL▸ http://www.access.digex.net/~kknisely/philosophy.tv.html

---

Smithsonian Online

The Smithsonian Institution Home Page  Jump 7432 CONTENT

The Smithsonian Institution bills itself as the "nation's treasure house for learning." This is also a very apt description of its home pages, where you can explore its many museums, galleries, research centers, and offices. Check out the Drylands-Bright Edges of the World online exhibit, or look at one of our favorites—the dinosaur pages. Or perhaps you'd enjoy the tips from Smithsonian photographers on how to photograph fireworks. This is just a sample of the wonders to be found here. In addition, you can read the schedule of new and temporary exhibitions and events for each museum and gallery, and check out information and links to a wide variety of social, cultural, political, or organizational subjects such as African American culture, computers, mammals, or oceans. And don't leave without browsing through the electronic Shopping Mall. —(E.v.B.)

URL▸ http://www.si.edu/start.htm

Smithsonian Perspectives

Smithsonian Magazine Jump 5827  CONTENT

Smithsonian Magazine is one of the best publications in the world for capturing the very essence of art, science, and history. So of course one would expect their Web site to be exemplary, and you won't be disappointed here. The pages have a sheen to them, just like the paper version, and the photographs—a startling collection of day-to-day life from some of the best photographers in the country—capture the very heart and soul of America. (Be sure to check out some of this site's Shockwave offerings from some of the photographers!) And of course, what would Smithsonian be without wonderful articles ranging from the wonders of space to the world of ice fishing? Back issues from 1990-1994 are also available for searching. —(J.P.)

URL▸ http://www.smithsonianmag.si.edu/

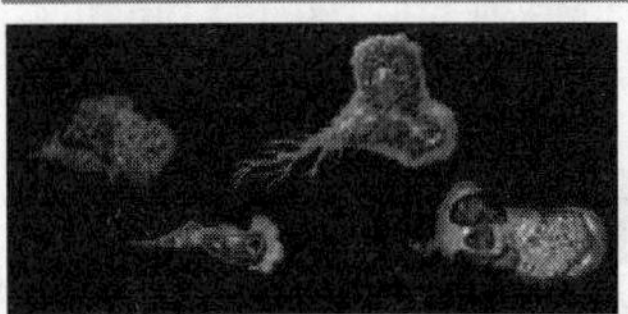

Multimedia Microbiology on the Web

CELLS alive!

Jump 7470 

Step right up ladies and gentlemen! See the white blood cell eat a Strep virus! Thrills and chills in the world of microbiology! Jim Sullivan, creator of these fascinating pages, has collected a host of animations and videos of such delights as white blood cells killing microbes, penicillin killing bacteria, or a cell committing suicide. Can't get enough of this violent microbial madness? Don't worry, Jim has amassed some other great Web links to virus, pathogenic microorganisms, and other microbiology sites. —(E.v.B.)

KEY NEWSGROUP **sci.bio**

URL ▸ http://www.whitlock.com/kcj/quill/

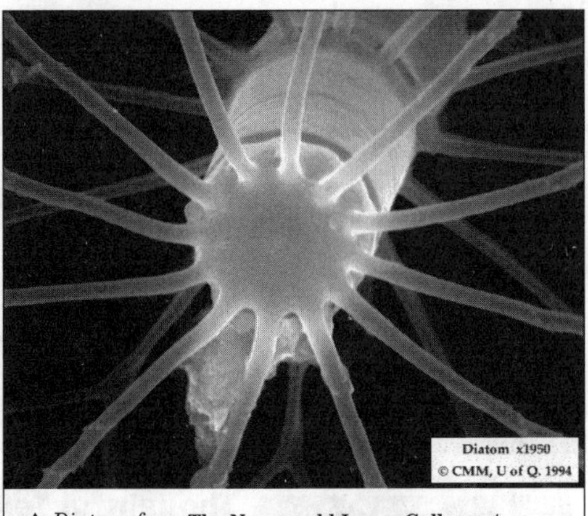

▲ *Diatom, from* **The Nanoworld Image Gallery** *at* Jump 7272.

Close-Ups of the Microscopic World

The Nanoworld Image Gallery Jump 7272 CONTENT

The Australian Centre for Microscopy and Microanalysis sponsors these pages crammed full of small delights—microscopic views of pollen, insect legs, even—if you find this delightful—the tubules of a bandicoot kidney. Be warned, these galleries contain very large graphic files despite the small nature of the subject. Flowers, rats, moulds, plankton—you name it, they've pointed their electron microscope at it. —(E.v.B.)

KEY NEWSGROUP **sci.misc** URL ▸ http://www.uq.oz.au/nanoworld/images_1.html

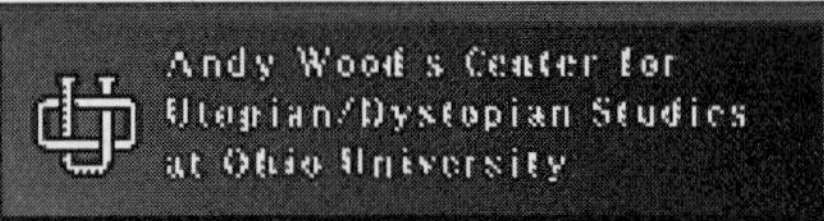

Utopian Discussions Online

Center for Utopian/Dystopian Studies Jump 7464 

Andy Wood has designed some very attractive pages that explore the yin and yang of Utopia and dystopia. As he notes, the material ranges "from bliss to despair." The theme he weaves through these intellectually stimulating pages is "the Utopian/dystopian dichotomy of the garden and the machine . . . it appears that utopias exist in a state of dialectical tension with hidden dystopian counterparts." See what you think as you explore his pages on Utopian literature, art, and architecture, and an array of other resources. —(E.v.B.)

URL ▸ http://oak.cats.ohiou.edu/~aw148888/

Environmental Bonding

The EnviroWeb— A Project of the EnviroLink Network Jump 7473 

EnviroLink, a nonprofit organization, claims to be the largest online environmental information service in the world, reaching over 1.5 million people in over 100 countries. The members of EnviroLink promote "an alternative sustainable society through the use of new communication technologies, in an effort to connect individuals and organizations." Their site is a great collection of online information, and their library is a clearinghouse of all environmental information available on the Internet—from resources on environmental activism to environmentally responsible businesses and products. And it's easy to find what you're looking for—whether it's information on old-growth forests or the threat to whales—just use their easy-to-navigate search program. —(E.v.B.)

KEY NEWSGROUP **talk.environment** URL ▸ http://www.envirolink.org/

Before You Get Your M.D....

The Medical Education Page Jump 8532

Before there were doctors, there were medical students. And pre-medical students. This site is for all of them. Here you'll find links to all medical schools and all hospitals on the Web. You can use its extensive list of "medical indexes" to link you to medical libraries and other online research places. Ever wonder what people get asked in medical school interviews? You'll find completed questionnaires from recent med school applicants about the process, and advice on how to prepare for it. But if you're already in med school, you'll especially like the extensive list of links that can supplement some medical courses, including some interactive ones with photographs and sound. Our only question about this site: How does the second-year medical student who maintains it find the time? —(R.B.)

URL ▶ http://www.scomm.net/~greg/med-ed/

The Interactive Doctor Simulator

The Interactive Patient Jump 8516

We have seen the future of medical education, and it is this Web site. If you're a doctor, medical student, or just have a fascination with medicine, you're in for a compelling experience. YOU are the doctor! A patient comes to your office, and you have the opportunity to ask questions in a conversational format, and get specific answers. You examine the patient by pointing and clicking on parts of the body you want to inspect, feel or listen to. Order laboratory tests and see their results. Evaluate the X-rays. Finally, select your diagnosis and e-mail it in; you'll get a reply from the authors, who are medical professionals at Marshall University School of Medicine. Although the cases are limited in number, this site demonstrates the immense power of interactive learning in general, and the Web in particular. —(R.B.)

URL ▶ http://medicus.marshall.edu/medicus.htm

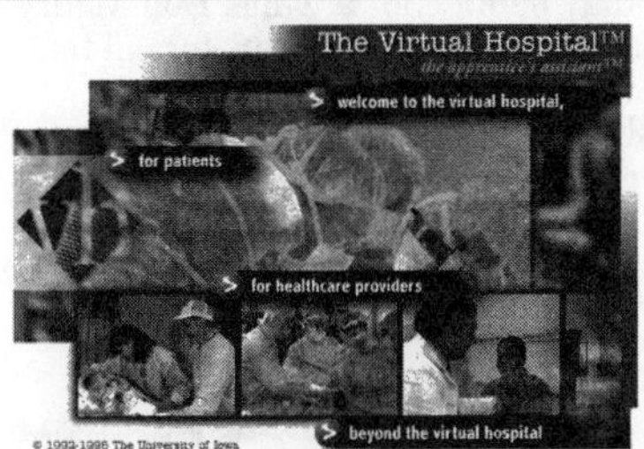

Everything but the Cafeteria food

The Virtual Hospital Jump 8545

This site has now become a premier medical site for both consumers and professionals. It's maintained by the Department of Radiology at the University of Iowa. But don't let that fool you; you'll find much more than X-rays (although some of these images are pretty cool, too!). If you happen to live in Iowa, you'll find lots of information about the medical center. But even if you live in the Rust Belt, and not the Corn Belt, you'll find a great depth of medical information. For physicians, this site provides a rich selection of multimedia textbooks, teaching files, case studies, and links to other clinical material. You can even find a full text version of the University's Family Practice Textbook. For consumers, there's a growing selection of educational materials on diseases and fields of medicine like surgery and ob-gyn. So click on over; this hospital has everything but bad food. —(R.B.)

URL ▶ http://vh.radiology.uiowa.edu/

What's in That Pill?

Pharmaceutical Information Network Home Page Jump 2523

Short of having your own, personal copy of the Physician's Desk Reference (which can be somewhat incomprehensible anyway), this is the best place to learn about specific prescription drugs. Just skip past the sections designed for professional pharmacists and go to the Drug Database. There you'll be able to find information on drugs, organized alphabetically by brand name. When available, you'll also be able to link to relevant threads from the **sci.med.pharmacy** newsgroup and articles from the Medical Sciences Bulletin. Or, if you want to learn about various drugs to treat specific conditions, you can go straight to the Medical Sciences Bulletin archives. —(L.S.)

KEY NEWSGROUP **sci.med.pharmacy** URL ▶ http://pharminfo.com/pin_hp.html

Doctors' Resources

Web Doctor Jump 8530

You go to college. You go to med school. You go to residency. Then, you should probably go here. There are lots of things to interest doctors, doctors-to-be, and other medical professionals here. The continuing education area gives lots of example cases to test your diagnostic accuracy. There are links to Clinical Practice Guidelines and online medical journals. But unless you're familiar with terms like "bronchiolitis obliterans organizing pneumonia," don't spend too much time trying to pick up medical tips here. —(R.B.)

URL ▶ http://www.gretmar.com/WebDoctorHome.html

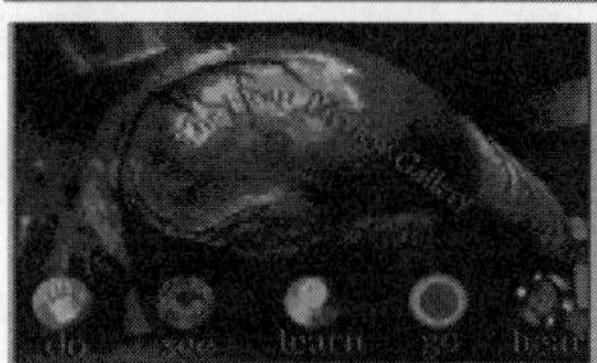

The Most Important Muscle

Preview the Heart Jump 2529

Only about the size of your fist, the heart is nonetheless one of the strongest and most important muscles in the human body. This interactive tour, combining downloadable movies, sound and text, will show you how the heart works and how you can keep it healthy. Look at x-ray images of the heart, get a surgeon's-eye view of heart surgery, or see how the heart beats. That's just some of what's in the first section. Move on, and you'll learn about how the heart is depicted in popular culture, how to take your own pulse properly, create a personal exercise program to strengthen your heart, and create heart-healthy meals. It's an informative, educational and highly entertaining tour, a must-see on the Web. —(L.S.)

KEY NEWSGROUP sci.med URL ▶ http://sln.fi.edu/tfi/preview/heartpreview.html

Historical Text Archives on the Net

Historical Text Archive Jump 6731

Get your reading glasses out—you may be here for a while. Don Mabry presents this massive archive, featuring just about every historical text available online. Leaf through famous letters written by historical figures, personal diaries, and official documents spanning many generations. A wide variety of material is available here, from The Mayflower Compact, The First Thanksgiving Proclamation, to Ronald Reagan's first inaugural address. Likewise, if you select the European, Asian, or Latin American sections, you'll find comparable historical text resources. It's a nice service for every history buff and academic researcher. —(L.T.)

KEY NEWSGROUP bit.listserv.history URL ▶ http://www.msstate.edu/Archives/History/

NOTABLE CITIZENS OF PLANET EARTH

Historical Biographical Dictionary

Notable Citizens of Planet Earth Biographical Dictionary Jump 6774

Access this keyword-searchable database and you'll find complete biographies of over 18,000 famous people. This resource features nearly every historical figure of note, from those who shaped ancient times to those headlining today's news. Find out when your favorite VIP was born, their profession, positions held, major acheivements, or any awards they may have received. Those studying specific eras can conduct a keyword search, for instance, of those born in the 1700's, or people who were influential in certain fields of interest. —(L.T.)

KEY NEWSGROUP bit.listserv.history URL ▶ http://www.tiac.net/users/parallax/

Biographies by Date

Britannica's Lives Jump 2613

The Encyclopedia Britannica is a restricted service, but they've opened this little gem to everyone with Web access. A combination of history resource and party game, you can pick a date (like your own birthday) and see who was born on that day, along with a short biography. Enter a year and an age group, and you'll be able to create your own "who else was born on your birthday" cards. For serious students, each mini-biography includes a link to a search engine that lets you tap into Lycos or Yahoo for more resources. There's also a link to search the encyclopedia, but you can't access it unless you're properly registered with Britannica. —(L.S.)

KEY NEWSGROUP **soc.history** URL▶ http://www.eb.com/calendar/calendar.html

National Science Foundation— Programs,Publications & More

National Science Foundation World Wide Web Server Jump 3513

This site offers loads of interesting information about programs, grant proposals, funding sources, publications, awards programs, and much more. There's something here for everyone with more than a passing interest in the progress of science, engineering, and mathematics and education programs in this country. Beyond the basics, the NSF server offers links to a selection of servers that host NSF-funded projects. —(C.P.)

KEY NEWSGROUP **info.nsf.grants** URL▶ http://www.nsf.gov/

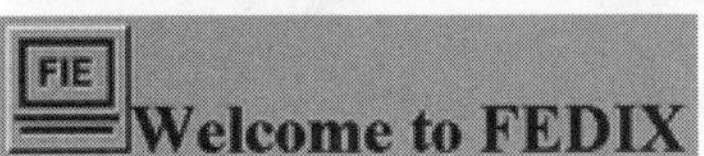

The Federal Information Exchange

FEDIX Jump 3537

The Federal Information Exchange, also known as FEDIX, offers comprehensive information about all opportunities and activities within federal agencies, including minority opportunities and activities. There is an amazing array of services described on this Web site, ranging from information about specialized internships to summer programs for students, special training opportunities and equipment leasing plans for minority schools. See how your federal dollars are being allocated in this area. —(C.P.)

URL▶ http://web.fie.com/web/fed/

Self-Help to Go Online

Mindmedia Jump 3653

If you haven't already had an opportunity to figure out who you really are, the folks at Mindmedia have something to offer. Take a Myers-Briggs Personality test online, or download a free copy of their personality inventory software. And when you're done with all that introspection, and if you have any energy left, you might want to wander down the psychological self-help links they've put on their pages for you. —(C.P.)

KEY NEWSGROUP **alt.self.improve** URL▶ http://mindmedia.com/

The Complete Virtual Bookshelf

Virtual Reference Desk Jump 3662

You'll never need another reference book as long as you have the Virtual Reference Desk on your bookmark window. Can't spell? See the dictionary. Need a synonym? See the thesaurus. Need to know where Sault Ste. Marie is?? That's right—see the U.S. atlas. Sure beats a trip to the library, doesn't it? Also find a ZIP Code directory, international country codes, and for those of you who are really lost in cyberspace—even the time and date! —(C.P.)

URL▶ http://thorplus.lib.purdue.edu/reference/index.html

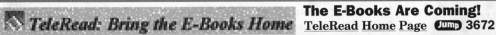

The E-Books Are Coming!

TeleRead Home Page Jump 3672

"Electronic Federalism" is the theme of this interesting site—predicated on the belief that the information systems we have today do more to get in the way of real progress than to encourage and/or nourish it. David Rothman presents a well-thought out and passionate argument for consolidated databases that would provide global access to a wide range of electronic texts—offering far more relevant content than the *Alice in Wonderland* and *Moby Dick* classics-genre that you're likely to find today. Great links to neat supporting Net resources—a bit early for the times, perhaps, but a great idea just the same. Pay a visit—see what you think! —(C.P.)

KEY NEWSGROUP **alt.zines** URL▶ http://www.clark.net/pub/rothman/telhome.html

Insect Studies for Kids

Gordons Entomological Home Page

Jump 2462 

Don't let the fancy name scare you. Gordon Ramel's page is engaging and interesting. And while it's designed for the benefit of K-12 students, anyone with an interest in small creatures will have a ball here. Gordon provides the type of information you'd expect from an educational page: an introduction to insects, an overview of evolution, and pages covering specific types of bugs. But he also talks about insect collecting and insects as pets. It's an excellent introduction to entomolgy, covering most everything you'd want to know—but if you still want more, there are links to related Web sites, too. —(L.S.)

KEY NEWSGROUP sci.bio

URL ▸ http://www.ex.ac.uk/~gjlramel/welcome.html

▲ *Beetle, from* Don't Panic Eat Organic, *at* Jump 1513.

The World of Insects—and Cockroaches!

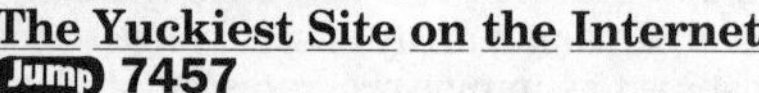

The Yuckiest Site on the Internet

Jump 7457 

What can we say—we love the yuckiest site on the Internet! Co-developed with the Liberty Science Center of New Jersey, it focuses, for now, on cockroaches. This site has been developed to introduce the fascinating world of insects to kids and adults. The current exhibition will help you learn "where cockroaches live, how their bodies look and work, what their habits are, and how to get rid of them." We really enjoyed clicking on a body part and seeing how it worked. You will also see where cockroaches live throughout the world (yea, we know—you really wanted to know this). For fun, read "Day in the Life" of a cockroach named Rodney. There's even a forum where you can swap cockroach stories. —(E.v.B.)

URL ▸ http://www.nj.com/yucky/

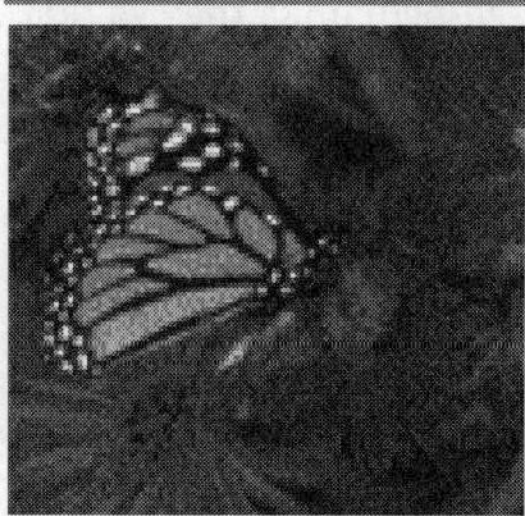

Butterflies for Your Virtual Garden!

Project Monarch Butterly

Jump 3687 

A collaborative project by the Nebraska Game and Parks Commission and the students of Fredstrom Elementary School in Lincoln, Nebraska, Project Monarch Butterfly comes to the Net! A local educational extension of the University of Kansas' four-year-old "Monarch Watch" butterfly migration sightings project, this site offers links to other educational programs involving the spring migration of butterflies and other wildlife, called "Journey North." A great site for teachers and students—and anyone who loves pretty flutter-bies. Post your own sightings of the Monarch to their interactive hypertext form! —(C.P.)

URL ▸ http://ngp.ngpc.state.ne.us/monarch/monarch.html

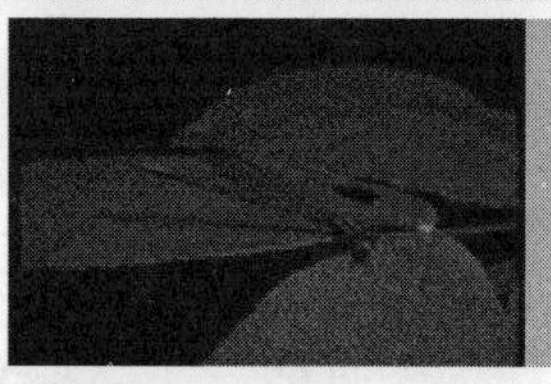

Insects Galore!

UD Entomology Home Page

Jump 7047 

The University of Delaware's Insect Database is a useful tool if, for example, you ever need to know how many types of dragonflies and damselflies there are in the world (4,900). As well, you can learn what the Latin name of each order means, how to pronounce it, plus the common names and distinguishing characteristics of all 18 insect orders. —(E.v.B.)

KEY NEWSGROUP sci.bio URL ▸ gopher://bluehen.ags.udel.edu:71/hh/.insects/.descriptions/entohome.html

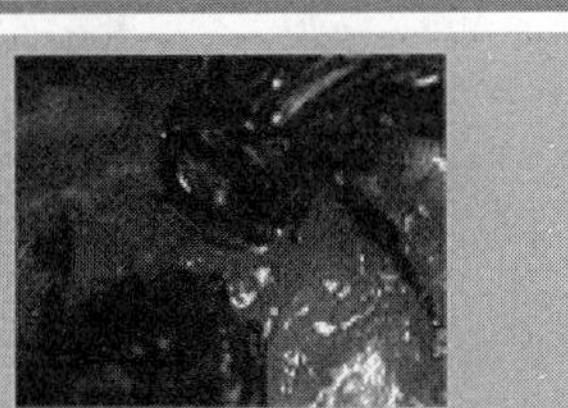

The World of Bees

Welcome to Carl Hayden Bee ResearchCenter!
Jump 7073

Vulture bees, honey bees, cactus bees—the whole bee world buzzes around your fingertips as you explore this site. See photographs of bees at work, and read the latest research on beekeeping. Bring a bit of nature safely inside—listen to these highly social insects communicating, or watch videos of bees at work. Software can also be downloaded. Can't get enough creepy-crawlies? Then, explore the Center's list of links to other insect-related sites. —(E.v.B.)

KEY NEWSGROUP **sci.bio** URL▶ http://gears.tucson.ars.ag.gov/

What a Bee Can See...

B-EYE: The World Through the Eyes of a Bee
Jump 7072

Ever wonder what a bee actually sees when it's confronting an ant? Curious about the workings of a bee's optics? Well, your curiosity can be put to rest when you visit B-EYE, the home page of neuroscientist and bee trainer, Andrew Giger. He has designed a computer program—read all the details about it here—that generates images as seen by a bee. The results, which you can download, are strange indeed. Oh, yes, Giger also tells us all about how bees can even be trained—bee-lieve it! —(E.v.B.)

KEY NEWSGROUP **sci.bio** URL▶ http://cvs.anu.edu.au/andy/beye/beyehome.html

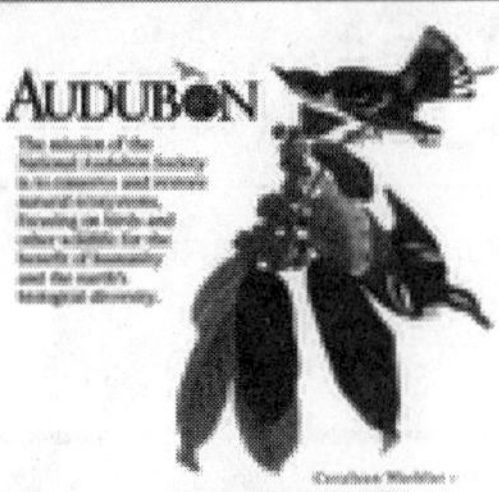

The National Audubon Society

AUDUBON Jump 5139

In addition to the usual links to news, upcoming events, and info on the National Audubon Society, this site also serves as an overall guide to the NAS—from its historical roots to current political and educational activities in the field of wildlife conservation. To get involved, or for more information, you can also link to the address and phone number of your local chapter. An interesting and educational feature of this site is its "virtual walk" in the Corkscrew Swamp Sanctuary, filled with interesting color photos and informative text relating to this subtropical forest near Naples, Florida. —(S.B.)

URL▶ http://www.audubon.org/audubon/

Dinosaur Club

Dinosaur Society Jump 5878

The Dinosaur Society is an organization dedicated to providing grants for research in the dinosaur sciences. Founded in 1991, it has become a home away from home for dinosaur scientists, authors, and the public. Here at their web site, you can learn about various digs, learn about the traveling exhibit entitled "The Dinosaurs of Jurassic Park," and even visit the Gift Shop. This is a great site for Dinosaur fans young and old. —(J.P.)

URL▶ http://www.dinosociety.org/

Hadrosaurus Park

Hadrosaurus Jump 3738

In 1995, Haddonfield, New Jersey, held a ceremony to declare a new National Historic Landmark. Why? Haddonfield is the site of the first discovery of a dinosaur skeleton in 1858. This skeleton of the creature, appropriately named "Hadrosaurus," became the world's first dinosaur skeleton to be mounted and put on exhibit at the Philadelphia Academy of Natural Sciences. Find out all

▲ *Tyrannosaurus rex, with and without skin, from* Dinosaur Hall, *at* Jump 2583.

about this historic discovery by stopping by this site, where you can read about the history of the discoveries, view great color photos, maps, and drawings, and link to other sites. —(N.F.)

URL▶ http://www.levins.com/hadrosaurus.html

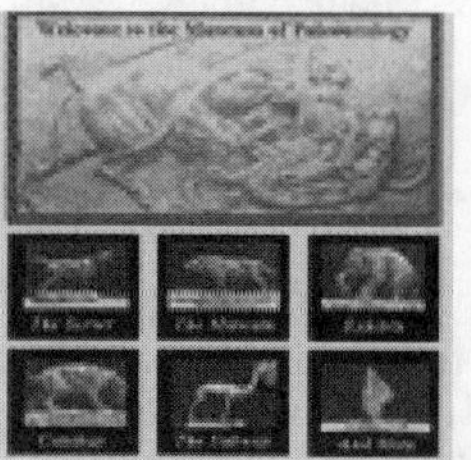

When Dinosaurs Roamed the Earth

Dinosaur Hall Jump 2583

Actually, most dinosaurs weren't as terrible, or as large, as popular literature depicts them. They came in all shapes and sizes, and they may not have completely died out, either. Many paleontologists believe that today's birds are direct descendants of dinosaurs. At the University of California's Virtual Museum of Paleontology, you can learn the facts behind the myths, see what's known about several of the more popular beasts, and visit dinosaur digs in North America. And if what you want isn't on this page, a handy search engine gives you access to all the museum's holdings. —(L.S.)

KEY NEWSGROUP **sci.anthropology.paleo** URL▶ http://ucmp1.berkeley.edu/exhibittext/dinosaur.html

The Dinosaur Lover's Dream Come True

Museum of Paleontology Jump 3690

CONTENT

Here's one of the best educational sites you'll ever find on the Web. Fabulous graphics (derived from a series of sculptures created for the Golden Gate International Exposition that was held on Treasure Island in the San Francisco Bay in 1939 and 1940), combined with the administration's attempt to present a fun and interactive visit to a virtual natural history museum, results in a winner. It's busy, too—150,000 accesses in one week alone! Presented by the California Museum of Paleontology, this site offers a virtual tour through the museum, and way-cool interactive online exhibits (try the Web Geological Time Machine for the ride of your life!). —(C.P.)

URL▶ http://ucmp1.berkeley.edu/

Prehistoric Whale Found in Vermont!

Charlotte, the Vermont Whale Jump 7006

A whale in Vermont? Surely you've been glued to the computer screen too long! But no, this skeleton of a Beluga whale was alive and well 12,500 years ago, swimming contentedly in the Champlain Sea after the glaciers had retreated. Wesley Alan Wright, of the University of Vermont, has designed an entertaining exploration, he calls it an "electronic museum for students," of the issues and facts surrounding this whale. How, why, what and where are answered in this interactive exhibit where you will discover much interesting information on prehistoric whales, glaciers, and paleontology. —(E.v.B.)

KEY NEWSGROUP sci.archeology URL▸ http://www.uvm.edu/whale/whalehome.html

The Discovery Channel

Discovery Channel Online Jump 3694

COMMERCE

Excellent information, interactive stories with film, music, photography and illustration, and superb graphic presentation are offered in this very content-rich, award-winning site. You could spend hours here in the Discovery Channel's excellent Web resources. This site changes constantly—and a full TV program schedule is available for you here, along with a nice selection of tools to help you navigate around the Web, and the obligatory Web shopping section. —(C.P.)

URL▸ http://www.discovery.com/

Eighteenth-Century History & Literature on the Web

Eighteenth-Century Resources Jump 5115

If the 1700s is your cup of tea, be sure to check out this page, a collection of 18th-Century-related Net resources, including literature, art, history, the history of science, and more. This site also includes a complete catalog of electronic texts from the 18th Century, from Milton to Keats. The comprehensive page is maintained, with a sense of humor, by Jack Lynch of the University of Pennsylvania English Department. —(S.B.)

URL▸ http://www.english.upenn.edu/~jlynch/18th.html

Alphabet Soup, Anyone?

The World Wide Web Acronym Server Jump 7015

CIDA, NAFTA, WTO—what do they mean? Stumped? Well, you wouldn't be for long if you had entered these acronyms into the easy-to-use World Wide Web Acronym Server. In a flash, you'd discover that those incomprehensible letters stand for: Canadian International Development Agency, North American Free Trade Agreement, and the World Trade Organization. —(E.v.B.)

URL▸ http://curia.ucc.ie/info/net/acronyms/acro.html

Cliff Life

Welcome to the Cliff Ecology Research Group Jump 7046

Ever wonder how trees manage to survive on bare, rocky cliffs? Visit the University of Guelph's Cliff Ecology Research Group to learn more about how trees and plants grow and thrive in these supposedly barren, but actually quite complex, ecosystems. —(E.v.B.)

KEY NEWSGROUP sci.environment URL▸ http://www.uoguelph.ca/CBS/Botany/index.htm

The Agricultural Alligator

The UF/IFAS AgriGator Jump 7071

The Web server of the Institute of Food and Agricultural Sciences at the University of Florida provides a fun romp through some serious subjects—environmental protection, biotechnology, and the future of agriculture. Be sure to visit this Web site's Funny Farm before you leave—first stop is the digital priest in the "confession booth." —(E.v.B.)

KEY NEWSGROUP alt.agriculture.misc URL▸ http://GNV.IFAS.UFL.EDU/WWW/AGATOR_HOME.HTM

I Think, Therefore I Surf

The Ultimate Philosophy Page Jump 7131

Feeling reflective? Enjoy a little Bertrand Russell over breakfast? Well, Sean Cearley of the Rensselaer Polytechnic Institute has pulled together some major resources in the pursuit of philosophy. You can read about the American Philosophical Association and other philosophy departments around the world, access a comprehensive list of journals, sample bibliographies of important texts, and even read about real-life philosophers. Major Gopher sites and other links are also included. —(E.v.B.)

KEY NEWSGROUP **talk.philosophy.misc** URL▶ http://www.rpi.edu/~cearls/phil.html

Science & Technology

Building with Atoms

Brad Hein's Nanotechnology Page Jump 7337

Brad Hein has gathered together an amazing number of links to all types of resources, from the academic to the popular, on nanotechnology, the construction of materials on an atom-by-atom basis. Many of these sources are linked to university departments, but surprisingly there are also a number of corporations who seem to be manufacturing on the atomic scale. If you want to know more about this hot new technology, come and browse the wealth of information here—Web sites, articles in popular magazines such as *Wired* and academic journals, links to newsletters, information on university research, and so much more. —(E.v.B.)

KEY NEWSGROUP **sci.chem** URL▶ http://www.public.iastate.edu/~bhein/nanotechnology.html

Wacky Patent of the Month™

Speaking of Better Mousetraps . . .

Wacky Patent of the Month Jump 2691

The inventor's mind knows no limitations, and M.J. Colitz shows you just how unlimited this thinking can be, by highlighting some of the more offbeat patents that have been awarded over the years. One month's selections, for example, are the Combined Grocer's Package, Grater, Slicer and Mouse and Fly Trap, and the Tapeworm Trap. Each featured product includes the patent application, plus illustrations—and some of these things look more like Rube Goldberg than Thomas Edison. But they're real, and fun to peruse, even if most of them never made it to market. —(L.S.)

KEY NEWSGROUP **alt.inventors** URL▶ http://colitz.com/site/wacky.htm

Women in Science Getting Their Due

4000 Years of Women in Science Jump 2710

You won't need to look far for evidence of the important role women have played in scientific and technical disciplines. But you can anyway, some 4,000 years back, if you visit this site. Based on talks given by Dr. Sethanne Howard of NASA, this site includes inventors, scholars, and writers in areas as diverse as physics and philosophy. The maintainers need the help of people who share their interests, so new contributions and additional information on any of those already included is wanted. —(L.S.)

KEY NEWSGROUP **soc.women** URL▶ http://www.astr.ua.edu/4000WS/4000WS.html

For Those Bad Technology Days

Technotripe Gazette Jump 2754

If you've got a love-hate relationship with your computer, or technology in general, you'll find a kindred spirit here, one not afraid to point out the limitations of the march of progress. Steve Magruder is a systems programmer who no longer buys into the belief that technology is, in and of itself, a good thing, and uses satire and a bit of straight reporting to critique and expose the negative effects that often are ignored or glossed over by today's technocrats. Whether you rail against the dehumanizing effects of technology, or are merely befuddled by the new toys and tools that seem to appear each day, this is the place for a fun, yet critical, look at what's happening. And if you've got some opinions on the broad range of topics covered here, Steve willingly accepts contributions. —(L.S.)

KEY NEWSGROUP **sci.philosophy.tech**
URL▶ http://www.iglou.com/candy/ttg/ttg.html

▲ *Old technology photo, from* On-Line Images from the History of Medicine*, at* Jump **0186**.

Virtual Reality Jumplist

Lara's VR Page Jump **2299**

Even more than the Internet, virtual reality (VR) has become the darling of technoculture, with VR being the subject or focal point of a growing number of movies and TV shows, with more and more computer games using 3-D virtual environments for play spaces. To help you learn more about and keep current with advancements in VR, Lara Ashmore maintains this list of links. There is general information, including links to online VR magazines, hardware and software resources, as well as links to research sites, newsgroups, and other VR-oriented pages. For fun, there are links to online VR implementations on the Web, too. If you want to skip to the really gee-whiz stuff, look for the "WOW" links. —(L.S.)

KEY NEWSGROUP **sci.virtual-worlds** URL▶ http://curry.edschool.virginia.edu/~lha5w/vr/

All about Volcanoes

VolcanoWorld Home Page Jump **2224**

Although the University of North Dakota designed this site primarily for K-12 students and teachers, anyone will find interesting and fun information about volcanos here. There are volcano tours, information about current and recent eruptions, plenty of pictures, and a growing database of information about how volcanos were formed, why they erupt, and more. If you have a question about volcanos, you can ask a volcanologist, and even learn how to become a volcanologist yourself. Interaction is key to good education, so in addition to offering your comments and suggestions for these pages, you also can send in your own articles about volcanos and volcano resources. —(L.S.)

KEY NEWSGROUP **k12.ed.science** URL▶ http://volcano.und.nodak.edu/vw.html

Did the Earth Move for You?

Earthquake Info from the USGS Jump **2398**

If you feel the Earth move, you can jump here and check the Current and Hot News sections of this site for up-to-the-minute earthquake information. If you just like learning about tremblers and seismology, this site, maintained by Andy Michael and the U.S. Geological Survey, is even better. You'll be able to track recent events, view and download maps, plots, and pictures, even listen to an earthquake. If that's not enough, the Seismosurfing section gives you links to other earthquake-related sites and Internet services, including links to daily earthquake catalogs worldwide. —(L.S.)

KEY NEWSGROUP **sci.geo.geology** URL▶ http://quake.wr.usgs.gov/

Seismo-Surfing the Net

Seismo-surfing the Internet Jump 6897

This seismic reference tool created by Steve Malone quickly leads you to earthquake research and data online without wasting a minute of your time. Steve's text-only site links you to seismology materials like earthquake catalogs, maps, and up-to-the-minute info on where the latest earthquakes are occurring. You'll also see informational resources such as fault maps, earthquake research activities, and graphics showing how earthquakes affect groundwater structures. —(L.T.)

KEY NEWSGROUP **sci.geo.earthquakes** URL▶ http://www.geophys.washington.edu/seismosurfing.html

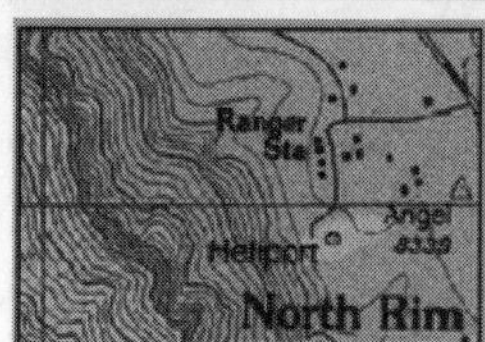

Information from the U.S. Geological Survey

US Geological Survey Jump 3542

These are the map people. And have they got maps for you...and plenty more, too! The USGS is the principal source of scientific and technical expertise in the earth sciences within the federal government. This site is stocked with information about many USGS projects, including the water resource program and the National Mapping program, as well as info about teaching packets and other educational programs for schools. Digital data is available from USGS in the areas of Agriculture, Foreign Trade, Census Data, etc. —(C.P.)

URL▶ http://info.er.usgs.gov/fgdc-catalog/main/census.html

Rocks & Minerals

Anethyst Galleries' Mineral Gallery Jump 2345

This database lets you learn about the Earth's various minerological riches, through searches by mineral class or by name. For browsers, there are also listings by gem type, such as gemstones and birthstones. Each entry features a description, including unusual characteristics and terrain indicators to look for to help determine if a specific area holds the mineral. The descriptions also are linked to related entries in the database. The images with each description are thumbnails, so loading is fast, and you can download larger, more detailed images if you wish. Since Amethyst Galleries is a commercial enterprise, you can buy mineral specimens from them online, but you don't need to be a customer to use the database. —(L.S.)

KEY NEWSGROUP **sci.geo.geology** URL▶ http://mineral.galleries.com/

Science the Easy Way

The Armchair Scientist Jump 7298

Loris Crudeli believes that one way of doing science is to be "comfortably seated in your own armchair, keeping up with the most advanced researches, sharing your work with scientists everywhere in the world, exchanging ideas, theories, challenges." In this Web magazine (which appears in both English and Italian), Crudeli presents news, astonishing images, and "curiosities that surpass fantasy and even science fiction." Some sections are for the interested layperson, others cater to the professional who enjoys obscure theories, mathematics, formulas, diagrams, esoteric terms, and acronyms. A fantastic collection by a dedicated science buff. —(E.v.B.)

KEY NEWSGROUP **sci.misc** URL▶ http://www.areacom.it/html/ita/loris/armchair.html

NASA Langley Research Center

NASA Access Jump 3554

This is a terrific jumping-off point to a huge number of government laboratories and information services, including ARPA, Navy OnLine, the U.S. Air Force, the Clearinghouse for Networked Information Discovery and Retrieval (CNIDR), the national laboratories at Argonne, the Idaho National Engineering Labs, Oak Ridge National Labs, the Superconducting Super Collider, and many more. Other federal links include the Census Bureau, Patent and Trademark Office, and the SBA. This is a useful and interesting site—worth keeping in your bookmark file. —(C.P.)

URL▶ http://mosaic.larc.nasa.gov/nasaonline/gov.html

The World of Science

Planet Science Jump 7425

Planet Science is the online version of *New Scientist*, a weekly magazine of popular science. Planet Science also publishes weekly and contains news, features, reviews and comments drawn from the newsstand edition. There's also material created just for the online version. You can also surf to related links and tour the publication's art gallery. —(E.v.B.)

KEY NEWSGROUP **sci.misc** URL▶ http://www.newscientist.com/

Saskwatch!

The Bigfoot Research Project Jump 2468

Not much is known about Bigfoot, the hairy, bipedal hominid that supposedly roams the forested mountain ranges of the Pacific Northwest. But what is known is here, in a page maintained by Henry Franzoni. The project itself, conducted in association with Boston's Academy of Applied Science, is the only serious, scientific examination of Bigfoot, so don't expect ghost stories or wild suppositions. Instead, you'll be able to learn what is known of this creature's history and habits, and see whatever actual evidence there is of its existence. The information is updated as it's found, and if you have something to share, or want to participate in some other way, you're help is needed. —(L.S.)

KEY NEWSGROUP **alt.bigfoot.research** URL▶ http://www.teleport.com/~tbrp/

All about Physicist Richard Feynman

Feynman Online Jump 7445

Richard Feynman, who died in 1988, was, according to many and including this site's creator, Scott Carter, an extraordinary man who played many interesting roles—from teacher to musician, to physicist. You can read a mountain of information here about Feynman's work on the atomic bomb and quantum electrodynamics, and learn more from his lectures on the nature of physics. You can also read reviews of his books, surf to other Feynman sites on the Web, and go further in-depth by exploring the many related sites that Scott has provided links to. —(E.v.B.)

KEY NEWSGROUP **sci.physics** URL▶ http://users.aol.com/plank137/feyn.htm#web

Science News

ION Science: Science and nature news and information Jump 7474

Science junkies can really feed their habit here. ION Science is a monthly zine "devoted to keeping an eye on and making sense of the latest news and trends in science and nature." Its articles, covering such subjects as global warming, measuring exhaust from the Concorde, new techniques that "foster faster flowering," or the upsurge in hurricanes, are written for the layperson interested in the latest scientific research. As well, the editors archive all past issues and provide hotlinks to other science sites that will help you further explore the issues raised here. —(E.v.B.)

KEY NEWSGROUP **sci.misc** URL▶ http://www.injersey.com/Media/IonSci/

The Tornado Project Online

The Tornado Project Online Jump 6896

Here's where you can study up on all those myths you've heard about tornadoes. For instance, conventional wisdom has told us that the southwest corner of a building, both above and below ground, offers the best protection. Not so, according to The Tornado Project Online, whose goal is to debunk such myths, but also offers safety tips, tornado facts, and personal stories. Other features of this site include a rundown of the top 10 twisters of all time, and tornado oddities, such as what really happens to a chicken's feathers when they're caught in the eye of a twister. —(L.T.)

URL▶ http://www.tornadoproject.com

Students Studying Salmon

The Salmon Page Jump 2465

Whether your interest in salmon relates to ecology or sport, you'll find something here, and don't let the fact that the page is maintained by K-12 students keep you away. The students of Riverdale School in Portland, Oregon, give you everything there is to know about salmon, and they do as good a job, if not better, than any grown-ups, too. You can link to news about salmon runs, connect to resources that discuss the endangerment of salmon species, learn about the life cycle of salmon, and find tips on salmon fishing. If you want more, Riverside School hosts the salmon e-mail discussion list, and you can learn how to subscribe here, too. —(L.S.)

KEY NEWSGROUP **sci.bio** URL▶ http://www.riverdale.k12.or.us/salmon.htm

The Smithsonian's Oceanographic Exhibit

Ocean Planet Home Page Jump 2544

All life came from the oceans, and humans depend heavily on the resources they provide. You'll find most everything there is to know about oceans and their importance to everyday life here, at the Smithsonian Institution's first online exhibit. It may take several visits to work your way through all the sections, but it's definitely worth the effort. If you don't want to browse and explore for yourself, there's a special tour, designed by the curator, that will take you through the highlights, as well as to an index of specific topics that you can search to find areas of interest to you. Among the major topics are oceanography, how people earn their livings from the sea, the everyday products we take for granted that we would never have without the bounty offered by marine life, and the ecological perils they face. There also are essays written by authors such as Peter Benchley, images, some fun, interactive things to do while you learn about oceans, and resources especially for educators to help them integrate the exhibit into their lesson plans. —(L.S.)

KEY NEWSGROUP **sci.bio.ecology** URL▶ http://seawifs.gsfc.nasa.gov/ocean_planet.html

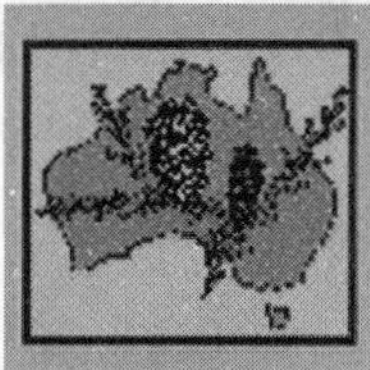

Plants Down Under

Australian National Botanic GardensBiodiversity Server Jump 7040

The Australian National Botanic Gardens (ANBG) offers a world of resources: illustrations, virtual tours, scientific papers, botanical glossaries, and much, much more. Interested in frogs or birds of the region, or in Aboriginal lore? Visit the ANBG—you'll learn a lot about the gardens and even more about Australian biodiversity issues. —(E.v.B.)

KEY NEWSGROUP **bionet.biology.tropical** URL▶ http://155.187.10.12/anbg/anbg.html

Not All Plants Are Vegetarian

Carnivorous Plant Archive Page Jump 2584

The most famous carnivorous plant is the Venus Fly Trap, but that's just one of many plants that have evolved into meat eaters. This page, with information compiled and maintained by several carnivorous plant enthusiasts, will lead you to everything there is to know about these always deceptive, and sometimes dangerous, life forms. There are lists of books and articles, links to carnivorous plant societies, information on care and feeding, sources of plants and plant supplies, and an extensive database of information about known carnivorous plants. —(L.S.)

KEY NEWSGROUP **sci.bio** URL▶ http://randomaccess.unm.edu/www/cp/cparchive.html

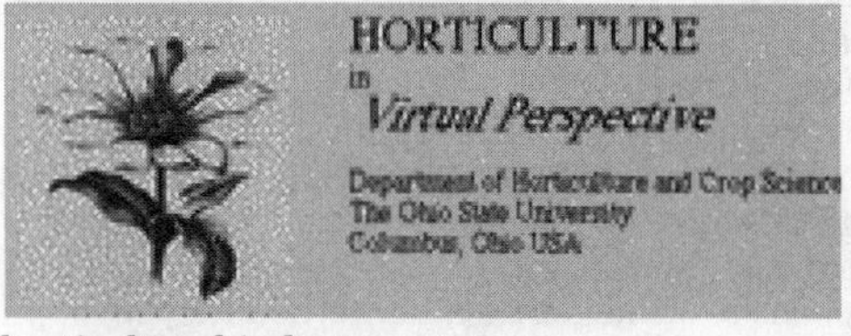

Cyber-Horticulture

Horticulture in Virtual Perspective Jump 7057

The Department of Horticulture and Crop Science at Ohio State University offers several horticultural courses over the Internet—one of which is computers in horticultural management. Explore course reading lists, consult the illustrated dictionary of plants and trees, and research economic and management issues in the horticultural industry. —(E.v.B.)

KEY NEWSGROUP **rec.gardens** URL▶ http://hortwww-2.ag.ohio-state.edu/hvp/HVP1.html

Fractals in Nature

CPS: The Dance of Chance Jump 2585

If you know of fractals, it's probably in the context of computerized images. But the idea for these artificial fractals came from nature, when scientists began to recognize that these random branching patterns sometimes behave in predictable ways. This virtual exhibit, from the Center for Polymer Studies at Boston University, helps you understand how fractals form. Using still images and movies, you'll see how fractals develop in nature—through soil erosion or by termite activity, for example—as well as learn how the experiments themselves were developed. Even if you don't want to learn about fractals, the movies and images are among the more entertaining and interesting you'll find on the Web, and this site is worth a visit for them alone. —(L.S.)

KEY NEWSGROUP **sci.fractals** URL▶ http://cps-www.bu.edu/~mkm/museum_project/Main.ian.html

Information about the Wilderness Society

The Wilderness Society Jump 3546

This Web site was produced for the Wilderness Society by the Internet Multicasting Service, and they have done a wonderful job. There are beautiful digital images of wilderness scenes, including Yellowstone and Yosemite National Parks and the Grand Canyon, detailed articles about forest fires and their impact on forest health, the protection of the wetlands, mining regulations, and much more. This site is an important stop for those who love nature, and who want to preserve the beauty of the wilderness. —(C.P.)

URL▶ http://town.hall.org/environment/wild_soc/wilderness.html

All about Canada's Wilderness Preservation Efforts

Western Canada Wilderness Committee Jump 3582

Western Canada Wilderness Committee (WCWC) is a nonprofit environmental society working for the preservation of Canadian and international wilderness through research and education. This Web site offers information about this group's mission and charter, as well as its current projects, complete with photographs. —(C.P.)

KEY NEWSGROUP **sci.environment** URL▶ http://www.web.apc.org/wcwild/Welcome.html

Science That Makes Sense

LANL Science at Home Jump 2556

The problem with science is that scientists tend to make it more complicated than it needs to be. Well, there's plenty of science going on right inside your own home, and this page from the Los Alamos National Laboratory offers more than two dozen "experiments" you can conduct using common household items. You'll develop a better understanding of the physical sciences as you discover what holds mayonnaise together, learn why boats float, make your own slime (three kinds!), or build an air car to manipulate Newton's Laws. The instructions and explanations are engaging, the diagrams and drawings often humorous, and the experiments themselves are a lot of fun, making them perfect for whole-family projects, especially on rainy days! —(L.S.)

KEY NEWSGROUP **sci.misc** URL▶ http://education.lanl.gov/SE/RESOURCES/Science.at.home/Contents.html

Birds of Prey

The Raptor Center at the University of Minnesota
Jump 7027

Raptors—fierce hunters of the bird world—are displayed and described on the Raptor Center's home page. The Center cares for injured and sick raptors, such as golden eagle, osprey, screech owl and many more, and then releases them back into the wild. You can also read the Center's newsletter, listen to bird calls and explore links to other raptor-related sites. —(E.v.B.)

KEY NEWSGROUP **rec.birds** URL▶ http://www.raptor.cvm.umn.edu/raptor/raptor.html

Desert Views

Boyce Thompson Southwestern Arboretum Jump 7041

Take a walk on the semi-wild side. Meander along the virtual tour of the Boyce Thompson Southwestern Arboretum located just outside Phoenix, Arizona. Established in the 1920s, this garden contains a fascinating collection of cacti and other desert plants. —(E.v.B.)

KEY NEWSGROUP **bionet.plants** URL▶ http://ag.arizona.edu/BTA/btsa.html

Responsible Tourism

Eco Travel in Latin America Jump 7042

Some travelers want to "walk lightly" wherever they visit. Eco Travel in Latin America home page presents information on the latest environmental issues, the most recent Latin American environmental projects, and descriptions of interesting Latin American sites to visit. —(E.v.B.)

KEY NEWSGROUP **rec.travel** URL▶ http://www.txinfinet.com/mader/ecotravel/ecotravel.html

Environmental Protection Resources

Information Center for the Environment Jump 2264

Based at the University of California, Davis, the content here naturally concentrates on California-related environmental projects. That information is good, but the best feature of these pages is the extensive list of links to the Internet's other environmental protection resources. Organized by topic, including current events and news items, each listing features detailed information about the site, as well as another set of pointers to related links, making searching for specific types of information quite easy. —(L.S.)

KEY NEWSGROUP **sci.environment** URL▶ http://ice.ucdavis.edu/#top of list

Ecological Solutions

EcoNet Home Page Jump 2497

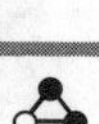

This site forms one of the best resources for current information on environmental activities and ecology references you'll find on the Web. The page starts out with a list of links either new or relevant to current ecological events, such as conferences, an organization's newly launched initiative, or an emergency situation. Each carries a description that informs and guides, as do all the general links that follow. Those are organized by category, including acid rain, energy, forests, population, toxic waste, wildlife, and more. Finally, a list of links describing the individual groups that make up EcoNet lets you see if there's one that matches your area of interest. —(L.S.)

KEY NEWSGROUP **alt.save.the.earth** URL▶ http://www.peacenet.apc.org/econet/

Environmental Education Resource

Welcome to EE-Link Jump 2461

A project of the National Consortium for Environmental Education and Training, this site serves as a complete K-12 teacher's resource. There are classroom resources, including ideas and links to support specific activities, bibliographies, audiovisual and software recommendations, fact sheets, and other support materials. For teachers involved in developing environment-related curricula, there are links to organizations and discussion groups that aid and support the process, plus news and grant resources. In addition, there's a separate section of links for exploration, suitable for the teachers developing class projects, as well as for students completing them. —(L.S.)

KEY NEWSGROUP **k12.ed.science** URL▶ http://www.nceet.snre.umich.edu/

Great Lakes Ecology

Great Lakes Information ManagementResource Jump 7064 CONTENT

Need to know the latest developments on the Great Lakes? Supported by Environment Canada, this Great Lakes resource indexes programs, publications, and databases relating to these large bodies of water. As well, you can read about the condition of the five lakes in both English and French. —(E.v.B.)

KEY NEWSGROUP alt.great.lakes URL▶ http://www.cciw.ca/glimr/intro.html

Environmental Clearinghouse

IIISDnet Home Page Jump 7034

The International Institute for Sustainable Development (IISD) is a nonprofit organization which promotes sustainable development in government, business, and everyday life. Based in Winnipeg, Manitoba, the IISD offers information on conferences, books, articles and worldwide programs and activities, all relating to sustainable development. —(E.v.B.)

KEY NEWSGROUP sci.environment URL▶ http://iisd1.iisd.ca/

Development on a Small Scale

The Microstate Network Jump 7192

The Microstate Network was created to help very small countries and territories overcome problems of scale, isolation or dependence to develop in a balanced manner. The Network contains a number of electronic resources—many of which you can explore—to help these underdeveloped nations create their own information-based economies and societies. Of interest is the Network's online newsletter, Microstate Communications, which tackles the main issues of telecommunications in this special area. —(E.v.B.)

KEY NEWSGROUP bit.listserv.devel-l URL▶ http://www.microstate.com/pub/micros/index.html

Skeptics' Home on the Web

Skeptics Society Jump 2280

Contrary to popular perception, skeptics are not naysayers. Rather, they are investigators examining and analyzing claims of all sorts to see how they stand up to scientific scrutiny. This Web page is the home of the Skeptics Society, which applies the disciplines of science to investigations of various theories and conjectures covering, among other things, conspiracy theories, life after death, creationism, Holocaust denial, witchcraft, and urban myths. There's an online version of the Society's magazine, information on current issues under investigation, and links to other skeptic's pages. If you wonder about the unknowable, and want to base your opinions on something more than someone else's, this is the place to start. —(L.S.)

KEY NEWSGROUP sci.skeptic URL▶ http://www.skeptic.com/

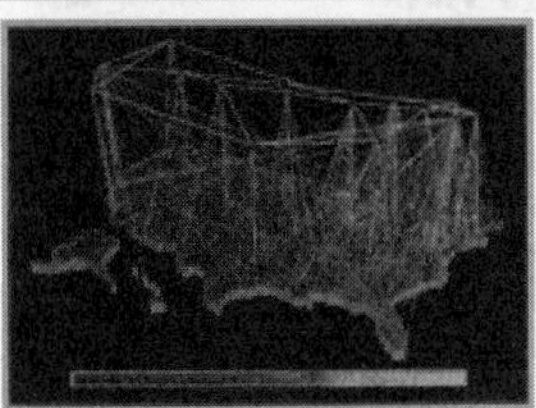

Information Infrastructure News

The Information Infrastructure Task Force Web Server Jump 3517

The IITF is a committee appointed by The White House, which is charged with articulating and implementing the Administration's vision for the National Information Infrastructure (NII). The task force consists of high-level representatives of the federal agencies that play a major role in the development and application of information and telecommunications technologies. Although this site might seem, at first glance, to be somewhat dull, there's a wealth of information to be found here, from the text of proposed legislation to a calendar of meetings that are open to the public—a site worth the time of anyone interested in the ongoing construction of the "Information Superhighway." —(C.P.)

KEY NEWSGROUP alt.politics.datahighway URL▶ http://iitf.doc.gov/

Remote Sensing Satellite Imagery

RSL World Wide Web (WWW)... Jump 7189

If you're interested in remote sensing—the detailed images transferred from special cameras in satellites to computers here on Earth—then the University of Minnesota's Remote Sensing Laboratory has a lot to offer you. Imagine images, taken from space, that are so detailed that you could see the flies on a cow's back. The lab has collected a comprehensive group of helpful documents, Web sites, online publications, and user guides of one sort or another. The site also supports a job directory for remote sensing specialists as well as their cousins, geographic information systems (GIS) experts. —(E.v.B.)

KEY NEWSGROUP **sci.image.processing** URL▶ http://wwwrsl.forestry.umn.edu:10000/

Declassified American Spy Photographs

Declassified Satellite Photographs Jump **5504** CONTENT

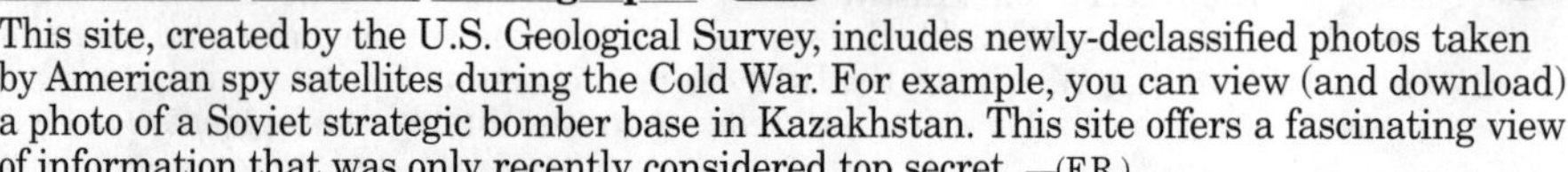

This site, created by the U.S. Geological Survey, includes newly-declassified photos taken by American spy satellites during the Cold War. For example, you can view (and download) a photo of a Soviet strategic bomber base in Kazakhstan. This site offers a fascinating view of information that was only recently considered top secret. —(F.R.)

KEY NEWSGROUP **alt.sci.planetary** URL▶ http://edcwww.cr.usgs.gov/dclass/dclass.html

Man Bites Snake

Poisons Information Database Jump **7011** CONTENT

You never know, a visit to Singapore may be in your future. To prepare, why not visit the Poisons Information Database supported by the National University of Singapore? Here you can explore an illustrated guide to the area's plant, snake, and animal toxins, as well as a directory of antivenoms, toxinologists and poison control centers around the world. —(E.v.B.)

KEY NEWSGROUP **sci.med** URL▶ http://biomed.nus.sg/PID/PID.html

News from the Centers for Disease Control

Morbidity & Mortality Weekly Report Jump **7155** CONTENT

You really want to know which terrible virus is headed your way this week? How many people have contracted it? How many people have died in the past seven days, and from what? All these statistics can be yours when you explore this weekly report prepared by the Centers for Disease Control and Prevention. As well, the maintainers of this page also provide links to state health departments and other health resources on the Net. To access the materials, however, you need to use Adobe's Acrobat Reader software, which can be freely downloaded from all over the Web. —(E.v.B.)

KEY NEWSGROUP **bit.listserv.mednews** URL▶ http://www.crawford.com/cdc/mmwr/mmwr.html#aboutMMWR

Bill Nye the Science Guy

Bill Nye the Science Guy's NYE LABS ONLINE Jump **7178**

They call this a children's show, and while it's true that kids will learn much from watching it, we're convinced that this is really a show for adults. We like to pretend we've just forgotten all the things Bill Nye the Science Guy talks about, but face it—we just never knew! But you'll know now. Check out the Demo of the Day, the wonderful Sounds of Silence and a preview of today's episode. Yes, Science Rules, and Bill is our leader! —(J.P.)

KEY NEWSGROUP **sci.edu** URL▶ http://nyelabs.kcts.org/

Space Exploration

Choice Space Sites

Cool NASA Site of the Week Jump **2170**

Daniel McCoy curates this site of quick links to the latest cool sites, as well as longtime faves that may have been lost in the Web links shuffle. The link could be to a general NASA project, such as the K-12 Internet Initiative that in itself is a list of cool links and activities, or related to a specific, newsworthy activity, such as International Space Station Alpha. Previous cool sites are archived, so you can drop by whenever just to browse. Best of all, you can

◀ *The historic Space Shuttle / Mir mission,* ◀ *Solar eclipse, and* ▲ *Space walk, image files via* **Images, Icons and Flags,** *at* Jump **2047** *and* ◀ *Commemorative stamps, from* **Joseph Luft's Philatelic Resources on the Web,** *at* Jump **2144**.

nominate cool links from this site. Just use the form on the page, provide the URL, and a reason why you think the site is cool, and you may just see your contribution the next time you visit. —(L.S.)

KEY NEWSGROUP **sci.space** URL▶ http://www.jsc.nasa.gov/nasa/Cool.html

SPACE NEWS

Space News Online

Space News Online Jump **6745**

Track the latest events happening in space, read fascinating interviews of people shaping space technology, and policy, and view hundreds of exciting space images here on this weekly space news site. You'll also find interactive space discusssion forums, and many links to cool space resources like NASA. Registration, although free, is required to access the this site. —(L.T.)

KEY NEWSGROUP **clari.tw.space** URL▶ http://www.spacenews.com/

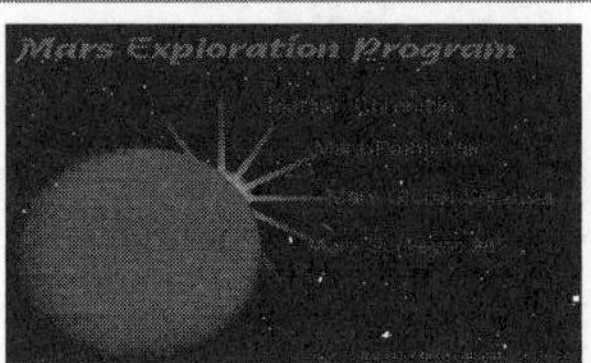

NASA's Mars Exploration Program

Mars Exploration Program Jump **6761**

Now that scientists believe they may have discovered life on Mars, there's been a resurgence in efforts to learn more about the Red Planet. Now, direct from NASA, this site provides updated information on upcoming missions to Mars. You'll find a fact sheet on the planet, live video shots of spacecraft testing, and a browsable atlas of Mars, complete with color maps. This site also features links to live shots of Space Shuttle astronauts, and information on the Pathfinder spacecraft program. —(L.T.)

KEY NEWSGROUP **clari.tw.space** URL▶ http://www.jpl.nasa.gov/mars/

Skywatcher's Guidebook

Visual Satellite Observer's Home Page Jump **2728**

Neil Clifford and Bart De Pontieu maintain this page for anyone interested in the satellites and other man-made objects that circle the sky these days. Here, you can learn what's up there, what they do, how to locate them yourself, and where to go for more information about them, although there's more than enough right here for most people. You can start with a basic introduction to observing satellites and the tools you'll need to see them, or go straight to specifics, such as where the Space Shuttle or Russian Mir space station will be. You can even learn how to make your own predictions, with the various software and tools available here, or just use the very good set of links here to learn more about the satellites themselves. —(L.S.)

KEY NEWSGROUP **alt.sci.planetary** URL▶ http://www.ipp-garching.mpg.de/~bdp/vsohp/satintro.html

Seeing Stars

The Astronomer Magazine Jump 7264 

Comets, asteroids, planets. Come to the *Astronomer Magazine* and let the solar system swirl around you in all its glory swirl. This Web magazine is designed for the "advanced" amateur. Here, you will find timely news of astronomical interest as soon as possible after sightings occur. The magazine has been published monthly since 1964, and is now proudly online, so polish up your telescope and join people from all over the world who enjoy sharing their photographs of auroras, and sightings such as the recently discovered new nova in the constellation Cassiopeia. —(E.v.B.)

KEY NEWSGROUP **sci.astro** URL http://www.demon.co.uk/astronomer/

Voyager News & Images

Voyager Project Home Page Jump 5654 

Having accomplished their primary objectives (the fly-bys of Jupiter, Saturn, Uranus and Neptune) the two unmanned Voyager spacecraft are entering a new—and potentially even more exciting—phase. Called the Voyager Interstellar Mission (VIM), the mission will take measurements to be made of interstellar fields, particles, and waves unaffected by the solar plasma. Sounds complicated, to be sure, but don't let the fancy words scare you off. The information found at this site is quite extraordinary, from dozens photos from the original missions, to weekly updates of the spacecraft themselves, as they continue the exploration of our solar system. —(J.P.)

URL http://vraptor.jpl.nasa.gov/voyager/voyager.html

▲ *Experimental DC-X, from* **Amdahl's WWW Hot Topics**, *at* Jump 2587
▲ *Radio telescopes, via* **Virtual Image Archive**, *at* Jump 7315.

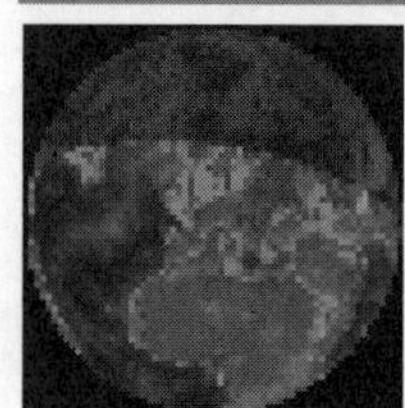

Take a Look at the Earth from Every Angle

Earth Viewer Jump 6694 

John Walker wants to make sure you can see every possible side, slant and angle of the earth. That's why he developed Earth Viewer. A single click generates fascinating views of our planet, all in real-time. View the globe from a satellite that's currently in earth's orbit, or study the latest topographical map. Way cool! Need global weather satellite imagery? It's here to, complete with cloud cover. Once you've learned how to use the viewer, click on the "esteemed expert mode," which lets you control the generation of any given image. You can even customize an image request, save it on your hotlist and come back as often as you like for real-time updates. —(L.T.)

KEY NEWSGROUP **comp.infosystems.gis** URL http://www.fourmilab.ch/earthview/vplanet.html

Look Up!

SKY Online - Home Page Jump 7318 

Here's a great site for all amateur astronomers. You can read newsletters, find out what's in the sky each week, get some great stargazing tips especially designed for the "backyard astronomer." Want to upgrade your telescope? Read reviews of the latest models and accessories. Computer software is described, lists of astronomy clubs and planetariums are also listed. You can even make a virtual visit to the Russian space station, or fly on the American space shuttle. Need more space travel? Then soar out into the Internet on links to other Web sites presented here. —(E.v.B.)

KEY NEWSGROUP **sci.astro** URL http://www.skypub.com/index.html

◀ *Images of Buzz Aldrin's moonwalk, from the Apollo 11 mission and* ▲ *Hubble Space Telescope image of Saturn, via* **Images, Icons and Flags**, *at* Jump **2047**.

Flying Telescope

NASA K-12 Internet: LFS Online-Registration Desk

Jump **7301** CONTENT

Wow, read all the latest on NASA's flying observatory, the Gerard P. Kuiper Airborne Observatory (KAO), dedicated to research on infrared astronomy. The observatory is housed in a C-141A jet, with a range of 6,000 nautical miles. It is capable of conducting research operations to 45,000 feet with the help of one heck of a telescope. This site contains everything you'd ever want to know about the specifications of the observatory's instrumentation, its missions, and support crews. This isn't just another science page for the professional. It's designed for teachers to use in K-12 classroom activities. Teachers can download guides, great photos, and lesson plans based on the KAO's experiments. As well, there's lots of live links that capture data as it's being transmitted from the KAO, and information on interactive, live programs that students can participate in. —(E.v.B.)

KEY NEWSGROUP **sci.astro** URL ▶ http://quest.arc.nasa.gov/cgi-bin/lfs.html

Adventures in Astronomy

Henrietta Leavitt Flat Screen Space Theater Jump **7471**

Wow! An online virtual planetarium, created by Carolyn Collins Petersen, for your viewing pleasure! Carolyn named her space theater after Henrietta Leavitt, who was an American astronomer working at the Harvard Observatory in the early 1900s. The planetarium show is well written and accompanied by some fantastic photographs. In the space gallery, check out a host of other photographs: black holes, supernovae, planets, and cataclysmic variables. Then, to learn more, read the site's suggestions and reviews, and surf the hotlinks to other astronomy sites. —(E.v.B.)

KEY NEWSGROUP **sci.astro** URL ▶ http://ucsu.colorado.edu/~peterscc/Home.html

Astronomy & Comets

Comet Hale-Bopp Jump **2750** CONTENT

This extensive and attractive site gives skywatchers everything they'd want and need to know about Comet Hale-Bopp, a body some 250 times brighter than Halley's comet, and last seen in these parts about the time humans were learning to write. In addition to covering the specifics about Comet Hale-Bopp, its discovery and how and when to view it, the site is rich in general information, including an introduction to astronomy, the nature of comets, and a monthly online magazine with news and features to keep you up to date on the comet and other astronomical information. —(L.S.)

KEY NEWSGROUP **sci.astro** URL ▶ http://www.halebopp.com/

The Best of the Hubble Telescope

HST Greatest Hits Gallery 1990-1995 Jump 2484

You no longer have to wade through gobs of probably useful, but beside the point, stuff to see the best photographs of the cosmos on the Web. Thanks to the Space Telescope Science Institute, you can go right to the good stuff with this page of the best photos taken by the Hubble Space Telescope. Even the thumbnail images here are spectacular, with colors and detail that make you think you're out in space yourself. Click on the thumbnail to download and view the full image, and your socks will be knocked so far off you may never find them! There's a brief description of the image with each thumbnail, and if you want to know more about it, or the Hubble project in general, there are links to all the information and resources you'll need. —(L.S.)

KEY NEWSGROUP **sci.astro.hubble** URL ▶ http://www.stsci.edu/pubinfo/BestOfHST95.html

Homemade Telescope Tips

Welcome to Mark's Home Planet Jump 7407

Mark likes to build telescopes—in fact, he enjoys it so much he decided to share his enthusiasm with others of like mind via the Web. Naturally, you'll find lots of information on telescope-making here. But Mark doesn't stop there—he also provides information and Web links on amateur science, astronomy and outer space, CCD imaging, computer graphics, and other fun stuff. Mark also uploads some neat code on different computer applications that he says cross his desk from time to time. —(E.v.B.)

KEY NEWSGROUP **sci.astro** URL ▶ http://webspace.com/markv/

15,000+ Astronomical Images!

Astronomical Image Library Jump 6734

Astronomy buffs of all ages will see plenty of stars searching through this database of 15,000 astronomical images that's growing at warp speed. Try using keywords like "Jupiter," or "Comet Hyakutake" (if you can spell it right the first time!) and you'll be amazed by all sorts of on-screen views. Don't feel like rushing through the site? You can also view this site, photo album-style, at your own leisure. Photo sources on this site range from the Finnish State Computing Centre to the Lund Observatory. —(L.T.)

KEY NEWSGROUP **sci.astro** URL ▶ http://www.syz.com/images/

Space Images from the Jet Propulsion Laboratory

Comet Shoemaker-Levy Home Page (JPL) Jump 0112

This part of the California Jet Propulsion Laboratory's enormously popular Web site features wonderful color images of the July 1994 collision of the comet Shoemaker-Levy with Jupiter. This fine educational Web site also features a wealth of space, satellite and telescope images from JPL and NASA , space news flashes and links to tons of space information and images on the Web—one of our most highly recommended Web stops for all members of the family! —(E.G.)

KEY NEWSGROUP **sci.space** URL ▶ http://NewProducts.jpl.nasa.gov:80/sl9/

Space Activist's Information Center

Space Activism Home Page Jump 1560

John Lewis created The Space Activism Page as a starting point for space fans to get involved. With today's national priorities away from space exploration, this site covers the current projects that space activists deem most important. First, read the Frequently Asked Questions, then go to Alert!! for information about critical events needing immediate attention. Read the guidelines for effective activism to help you become more efficient. Follow Lewis's tips on writing to legislators and organizations about the latest bills in Congress. For even more information, check out the comprehensive related links to articles, newsletters, and press releases about space development . If you believe that our country should be actively involved in space exploration, this is a site worth exploring, too. —(H.L.)

KEY NEWSGROUP **sci.space.policy** URL ▶ http://muon.qrc.com/space/start.html

Dates with the Cosmos

Space Calendar Jump 2169

When are they celebrating the 20th anniversary of the Apollo-Soyuz mission? What's the next milestone for the Galileo probe? When's the next solar eclipse? Where can you see the Moon eclipse venus? If it's happening in, or about, the known universe, you'll find it on the Jet Propulsion Laboratory's Space Calendar. It's a 13-month calendar that's updated monthly, so you'll always have access to the coming year's events. And if there's an Web site that has more information about the event, the link is included here, too. —(L.S.)

KEY NEWSGROUP **sci.space** URL▶ http://newproducts.jpl.nasa.gov/calendar/

A Short Course in Space Flight

History of Space Exploration Jump 2300

Using a combination of content and links, Calvin J. Hamilton has crafted an entertaining introduction to the history of space exploration. The story begins with the discovery and use of gunpowder by the ancient Chinese, and continues through the Space Shuttle missions. There are links to NASA's detailed pages on its manned missions, beginning with the Mercury program, and chronologies of space exploration by date and by planetary body. This is an excellent resource for teachers, and two helpful educator's guides are also online. —(L.S.)

KEY NEWSGROUP **sci.space** URL▶ http://www.c3.lanl.gov/~cjhamil/SolarSystem/history.html

Forget NASA—Get Yourself to the Moon!

Lunar Resources Company Jump 2507

If you dream of traveling the cosmos, you don't have to wait for NASA to start selling tickets. The Lunar Resources Company sponsors the Artemis Project, a venture to commercialize spaceflight and establish a manned lunar base. It sounds a bit wild until you learn that only 5 percent of the project involves rocket science. Then it starts sounding feasible, if not exactly easy. The remaining 95 percent involves the same talents it takes to create any earthbound commercial venture. The list of things that need to be done is lengthy, but if you're interested, this challenging task means there most likely is a spot for you if you want to change your role in space travel from a passive spectator to an active participant. —(L.S.)

KEY NEWSGROUP **sci.space** URL▶ http://www.access.digex.net/~dcarson/Lrc.html

Tour the Solar System

The Nine Planets Jump 2573

Tour our solar system with this multimedia guide. Using text, images, sounds, and movies, Bill Arnett shares what is known about the planets and their moons, as well as smaller astronomical bodies, such as comets, asteroids and meteors. There's even coverage of the spacecraft and missions that collected the images and other data Bill used in creating this fascinating series of essays. —(L.S.)

KEY NEWSGROUP **sci.astro** URL▶ http://seds.lpl.arizona.edu/billa/tnp/nineplanets.html

NASA Information Services

NASA Information Services via World Wide Web Jump 3525

This site offers an all-in-one jumping-off point for NASA resources on the Net. There's information about NASA news and subjects of public interest, announcements from the Office of Public Affairs and NASA Educational Programs, including access to NASA Online Educational Resources. But the neatest thing about this site is a clickable image map of the U.S. that features the locations of various NASA centers—and if you click on any one of them, you'll be transported via the Web directly to the center site's home page. —(C.P.)

KEY NEWSGROUP **alt.sci.planetary** URL▶ http://www.gsfc.nasa.gov/NASA_homepage.html

Saturn Up Close in 1995/1996

Saturn Ring Plane Crossings of 1995-1996 (JPL)
Jump **3644**

The NASA Jet Propulsion Laboratory has opened a Web site that's full of fascinating info about the plane crossings of Saturn's rings that are expected during 1995 and 1996. It takes so long for Saturn to do a complete revolution around the Sun (29.5 years) that after 1996, the next occasion for this interesting phenomenon will be in the year 2038. As it circles the Sun, the angle of Saturn's rings relative to the Sun varies. Twice during the 29.5 years, the rings are edge-on to the Sun. Earth crosses the ring plane at about the same time. Because Saturn's rings are so thin, when they are edge-on to the earth, they seem to disappear. That makes it possible to see Saturn "without" rings with any small telescope. —(C.P.)

KEY NEWSGROUP **alt.sci.planetary** URL ▸ http://newproducts.jpl.nasa.gov/saturn/

Link to NASA's Space Shuttle

Astro-2 Live Jump **5011**

CONTENT

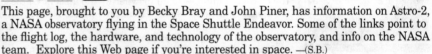

This page, brought to you by Becky Bray and John Piner, has information on Astro-2, a NASA observatory flying in the Space Shuttle Endeavor. Some of the links point to the flight log, the hardware, and technology of the observatory, and info on the NASA team. Explore this Web page if you're interested in space. —(S.B.)

KEY NEWSGROUP **sci.space.shuttle, alt.sci.planetary** URL ▸ http://indus.gsfc.nasa.gov:8080

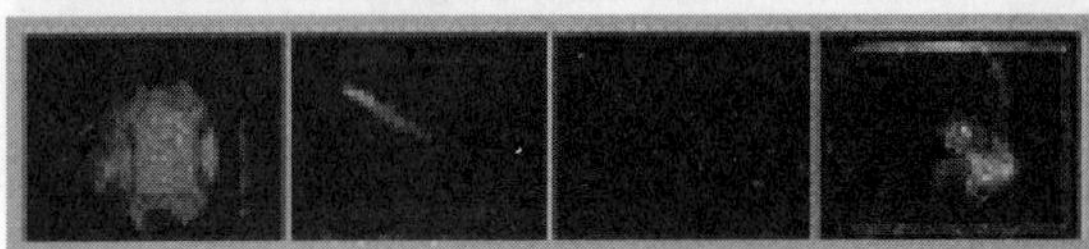

Stargazer's Site

Caltech Astronomy WWW Home Page
Jump **5096**

This is the home page of the Caltech Astronomy Department. Interesting graphics are the hallmark here. You can link to the Big Bear Solar Observatory, the Keck Observatory, and the Palomar Observatory. There's also a link to the Owens Valley Radio Observatory located near Big Pine, California. And you can get more info on the Caltech Astronomy Department via another link. If you're into stars, you'll find some interesting info here. This page is brought to you by Venky Ganesan. —(S.B.)

URL ▸ http://astro.caltech.edu/

Spacelab on the Web

Spacelab Home Page Jump **5124**

Take a tour of Spacelab, NASA's orbiting, Space Shuttle-based laboratory that's also a joint project with the European Space Agency (ESA). Access its archive of past mission histories, research projects, upcoming experiments schedule, and an extensive batch of downloadable Shuttle image files (the graphics are a bit large, though, so be patient). —(S.B.)

URL ▸ http://hvsun21.mdc.com:8000/~mosaic/

Space Junkies' Home Page

Shuttle Launch Countdown Page Jump **7183**

CONTENT

NASA has created a wonderful set of pages that allow you to track the progress of each Space Shuttle launch from liftoff to landing. You can read press releases and watch clips of the liftoff and the crew going about different tasks in space. You can read the biographies of each Shuttle crew, as well as a wealth of technical information on that mission's objective and the workings of the Shuttle while in orbit. In addition, a vast archive of downloadable photos, and other documentation of past missions can be accessed. —(E.v.B.)

KEY NEWSGROUP **sci.space.shuttle** URL ▸ http://www.ksc.nasa.gov/shuttle/countdown/

Personal Computing Resources

There have always been tremendous amounts of information, software, and other resources available on the Internet for personal computer users. Now the Web makes access to this wealth of productivity-boosting power easy, fast, and—best of all—free.

Bill Gates, the richest man in America and chairman of the world's largest PC software company, announces that his next business target is the Internet, the world's biggest—and most chaotic—computer network...But can Gates really control the Internet? For a variety of reasons—some structural, some cultural—that may not be as easy as it seems....the Internet is devoted to open—that is to say, nonproprietary—software systems. A week after the Internet community discovered that the GIF (Graphics Interchange Format) system used to exchange pictures over the network contained a patented compression scheme and that the patent holder was demanding royalty payments, somebody came up with an alternative: GEF, a graphics-exchange format that worked just like GIF but was patent-free.

[News item] Philip Elmer-Dewitt, reported by David S. Jackson, *Time*

Work-Enhancing, Skill-Boosting, Personal-Computing Resources on the Web, for All Skill Levels

Since the first Internet users were the computing-techie types, the Net has always been the world's largest repository of online computer information, documentation, vast quantities of downloadable personal computer software and image/multimedia archives, plus plenty of friendly, informal technical advice and referrals.

Unfortunately for non-technical computer folks, the process of finding, getting, and using all this material has been a nearly incomprehensible task, since doing so required the use of dreaded Unix commands and other equally cryptic Internet file access procedures.

But no longer: with its airy, graphical interface, the Web unlocks the Internet's vast personal computing resources, giving you instant, mouse-click access to downloadable shareware for almost any application imaginable, plus free, useful software utilities, problem-solving online documentation, tutorials, and FAQ (Frequently Asked Question) files for literally any personal computer type, commercial software application, and computer peripheral and programming language. And no matter where you are on the learning curve, whether novice or power user, you'd spend a lifetime trying to exhaust the personal computing resources available via the Web.

Computer Help

Your PC and Mac Tips of the Day

TipWorld Jump 6898

Want to be a pro at using your personal computer? Well, TipWorld, by computer publishing giant IDG, is home to over 100,000 such tips and more, including help for OS/2, the Internet, Lotus Notes, and Windows NT. While they aren't browsable on-site, each day TipWorld will deliver a tip to your desktop—for free. Simply visit the site, click on your topic choice and each day their team of experts will send you a free tip via e-mail. You can also grab sample online copies of some of IDG's most popular monthly newsletters, also free. —(L.T.)

URL▶ http://www.tipworld.com

Help Is Just a Click Away . . .

Trevin's Help for Ordinary Users Jump 2649

Here's the place to go when you want to know how to install that new hard drive, what to do when your new game returns "out of memory errors," or the printer doesn't print. Trevin's friends and family depend on him so much, that he's been able to create this page of helpful instructions and general advice covering the most common problems the ordinary user will encounter. It's neatly organized into sections covering hardware, software and peripherals, and is written in plain enough English so that most anyone can work through a problem just by reading through the pages. —(L.S.)

KEY NEWSGROUP comp.misc URL▶ http://www.xmission.com/~trevin/help/trevhelp.html

Computer Support Experts for Free

Tech Net Jump 2716

Just when you think the commercialization of the Internet might ruin everything, you find something like this: a group of people who enjoy helping others and thereby also help maintain the spirit of community and sharing, which made the Internet so attractive to so many. Brendan Brannan, Rick Leib, Jeffry Gray, Lise Quinn, and Rickey Baker all are computer and technical support professionals, from Microsoft and other companies, who have set up this page to offer free technical support to PC and Mac users. Just e-mail your question, and they'll e-mail back some help. Keep in mind that they do this on their own time, so they may not always answer immediately. But the caliber of talent represented here makes it worth the wait. —(L.S.)

KEY NEWSGROUP comp.misc URL▶ http://www.accessone.com:80/~gamegod/

Helpful Net & Personal Computing Information Resources

Steve Franklin - Net Help Pages Jump 0026

For those of you who are more technically-inclined Net and PC users, college student Steve Franklin has put together this useful Web jump page that's loaded with all kinds of helpful info on the Internet, PCs, Macs, UNIX, C, and PERL. A good source for starting your Net search of programming information, Internet power user resources and technical information for specific personal computer types. —(E.G.)

URL▶ http://www.hip.com/franklin/franklin.html

When Surfing Starts Hurting . . .

UN-L R.S.I. Page Jump 2003

Anyone who's hunched over a computer keyboard for any length of time knows it can get uncomfortable. But when it progresses from mere discomfort to long-term pain, you could be suffering from repetitive stress injuries. Paul Marxhausen suffers from RSI, and to prevent others from suffering needlessly he maintains this page. It explains what RSI is and how to prevent it, including MPEG videos demonstrating stretches and other exercises. There also are links to FAQs and other pages covering the topic. —(L.S.)

URL▶ http://engr-www.unl.edu/ee/eeshop/rsi.html

Virus Protection for Your Computer

ICARO Page Jump 2038 CONTENT

The Italian Computer Anti-virus Research Organization is an independent group that conducts research about this area of interest to anyone who uses a computer. While some of the text and other information is rather esoteric, this page provides the Web's best links to antivirus archives and software vendor pages. If you're interested in antivirus work, or have decided it's time to find out about protecting your computer against these destructive man-made menaces, ICARO is the place to start. —(L.S.)

▲ *Fifties-era data center, via* Virtual Image Archive *at* **Jump 7315**.

KEY NEWSGROUP **comp.virus**

URL▶ http://www-iwi.unisg.ch/~sambucci/icaro/index.html

Internet PC Service Station

PC Exit Ramp Jump 2067

Howard Gilbert wants you to know how your PC works, how it works with the Internet, and generally wants to give you more control as you cruise the Information Highway. So he created *PC Lube & Tune,* a self-service station where you get more than answers—you get knowledge. Howard's series of articles are clearly written, easily digested introductions to PC Internet protocols, operating systems, and PC hardware that inform and help you solve problems. There's also the Parts Catalog, a subject/definitions index that links you to the precise spot within the exact article you need to get your answer. —(L.S.)

KEY NEWSGROUP **comp.sys.ibm.pc** URL▶ http://pclt.cis.yale.edu/pclt/default.htm

Getting Browser Viewers to Work

WWW Viewer Test Page Jump 2136

If you've got a "raw" Internet connection, you don't just install a Web browser and surf the Net. You also need to install additional software to view the movies, pictures, and other files that make Web surfing so much fun. It's not always easy to find the viewers you need, though, and even then you'll never know if there's a problem with an installation until you crash while trying to view a file. Scott Nelson solves these problems with this page. At its most basic, it lets you test the viewers you use with your UNIX, Windows, or Mac browser. If you don't have a viewer for a particular file, you can jump to a page that tells you what's available, along with FTP links, and how to install it. —(L.S.)

KEY NEWSGROUP **comp.infosystems.www.misc** URL▶ http://www-dsed.llnl.gov/documents/WWWtest.html

Support Center Knowledge Base

The Computer Answer Robot

USC Knowledge Base Search Form Jump 2147

Indiana University's Computer Services Support Center gets a lot of questions. To make answering them as fast and easy as possible for everyone involved, they put close to 3,000 of the most commonly-asked questions and their answers on a searchable database. The beauty of the Knowledge Base, aside from its availability to the general Internet public, is that you don't have to ask a specific question to get a good answer. Just type in a phrase that generally describes what you need to know, and you'll get a list of possible questions and answers delivered in hyperlink format. And if that's not enough, there also are references to related topics that will give you even more information. —(L.S.)

KEY NEWSGROUP **comp.misc** URL▶ http://sckb.ucssc.indiana.edu/kb/expsearch.html

Computer Beeb Online

The Big Byte—BBC Radio Live—Home Page Jump 2234

You don't need a shortwave radio to get the latest and greatest on personal computing from the BBC. On these pages you will find the Beeb's Big Byte radio show online, with a review of the current week's program, hypertext links to the resources discussed on the show, and a preview of the next week's Big Byte. There's also an archive of program transcripts, so you can catch up if you've missed a week or two. —(L.S.)

KEY NEWSGROUP comp.misc URL▶ http://www.bbcnc.org.uk/bbctv/big_byte/

Learn the Internet Online

Roadmap Workshop Home Page Jump 2293

Patrick Crispen's Roadmap Workshop is one of the best, most fun, and easiest ways to learn how to use the myriad services offered on the Internet. The workshop usually is conducted via e-mail, and you can sign up for the e-mail version here, but Linda Sue Sohn has converted the lessons to HTML format, so now you can participate via the Web. The course covers everything, from e-mail to the Web, with clear explanations of the commands, exercises to test your knowledge and help you explore, and a light touch that makes the whole thing fun. Even if you don't take the course, you can bookmark or download the lessons for a handy how-to reference to Internet features. —(L.S.)

KEY NEWSGROUP alt.newbie URL▶ http://www.ll.mit.edu/Roadmap/

What's New with Web Browsers

BrowserWatch Jump 2363

Dave J. Garaffa makes it easy to learn about bug fixes, workarounds, and new releases, as well as general gossip about your favorite Web browser. It's all here in a page that puts the latest HTML specs to good use for an attractive, innovative format. There are lots of browser statistics, too, kept by browser version, as well as by site address. (You'd be surprised at how many obsolete browsers are still being used.) If you've got a not-generally known tidbit you'd like to share about the browser you use, send it to Dave, and he'll post it with the others. —(L.S.)

KEY NEWSGROUP comp.infosystems.www.misc URL▶ http://www.ski.mskcc.org/browserwatch/index.html

Corporate PC Help & Resources

The CIO Help Desk Jump 2412

Concentrating on resources for those responsible for PCs in a corporate setting, this site from Entex Information Services offers case studies, white papers and other reference material on PC acquisition, utilization, networking, purchasing strategies, and vendor relationships. There also are more general links to computing resources and FAQs, as well as sections of interest primarily to Entex customers. But that's toward the bottom of the links lists, and you don't need to be a customer to benefit from the information here. —(L.S.)

KEY NEWSGROUP comp.sys.ibm.pc.misc URL▶ http://www.entex-is.com/

Computing on the Go

Mobile Office Jump 9502

The companion to the hardcopy version of *Mobile Office Magazine,* this site gives the laptop and out-of-office computer user a wealth of information and resources for better computing and communications. Each week, there's news about the portable world, including product reviews, and an update of useful links and cool Web sites to browse. There's also an archive of product reviews representing Mobile Office's choice of the best systems, peripherals, phone and related products, as well as an extensive list of links to Web pages specifically geared to the mobile computer user. —(L.S.)

KEY NEWSGROUP comp.sys.laptops URL▶ http://www.mobileoffice.com/mobile.html

Computing for the Blind

Braille Translation with MegaDots from Raised-Dot Jump 2506

This page describes the MegaDots system of Braille computer translation, an advanced system to aid the blind in using computers. But there's much more here, enough to serve as an excellent primer for anyone interested in computing for the blind. There's an explanation of Braille and how to get computers to output this alphabet, and background on other input and output peripherals, such as optical character readers and voice recognition, and synthesis systems. And while MegaDots doesn't miss the opportunity to let you know how to get information on their products, they also provide pointers to information on the other products and systems discussed here. —(L.S.)

KEY NEWSGROUP **misc.handicap** URL▶ http://www.well.com/user/dnavy/

No-Forget Scheduling

e-minder Web Page Jump **5084**

By using a forms-based page, e-minder allows you to schedule reminders that are automatically sent to you via e-mail, to remind you of any important occasion. The service is free, anonymous (except for your e-mail address), and flexible; you may add, list, or selectively delete your scheduled reminders through a simple e-mail interface. A very useful service for the forgetful! —(S.B.)

URL▶ http://www.netmind.com/e-minder/e-minder.html

PC User Magazine

Monitor Magazine Jump **2415**

What began as a regional Canadian publication now is one of the better online magazines for personal computer users worldwide. Unlike many print magazines, which cover only one platform and offer limited selections of their content to Web surfers, *Monitor* is a fully online publication covering PC and Mac. Each issue contains in-depth features, industry and new product news, and product reviews, with columns on Windows, OS/2, Mac and MIDI applications. *Monitor* also covers user groups, BBSs and the Internet, offering readers an overall resource for keeping up with all aspects of computing and the online world. —(L.S.)

KEY NEWSGROUP **comp.sys.ibm.pc.misc** URL▶ http://www.globalx.net/monitor/

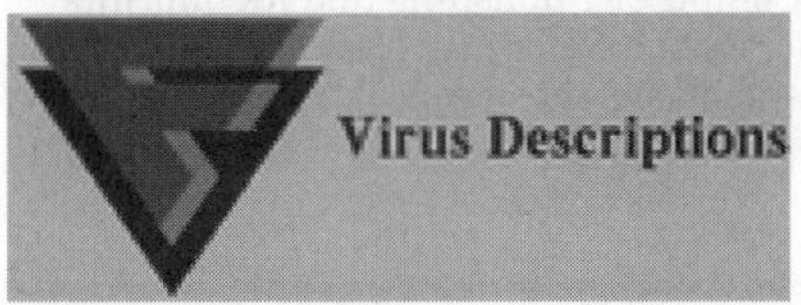

Computer Virus Database

Computer Virus Descriptions from F-PROT Professional Jump **1575**

COMMERCE

Don't be mislead into thinking you're just going to find one of the Web's best, most complete, highly organized, and continually updated database of computer virus descriptions at this site. What you'll also find are descriptions of various products offered by Data Fellows Ltd., a Finnish software development company. The products look good and useful, and have evidently won some prestigious awards. But don't bore yourself reading accolades and product hype. Click down until you get to the company photo. The staff is a fresh-scrubbed group of twentysomething soccer players with "who's gonna stop us?" looks in their eyes. With links to their own home pages (in Finnish, no less) available with just a click on every face, you're in for a treat. —(H.L.)

URL▶ http://www.datafellows.fi/vir-desc.htm

Computer Marketplace

Shopping Online for Personal Computer Products

PC Shopping Planet Jump **5779**

It is one of the givens of life; no sooner have you unpacked your brand new computer than you realize that you're in need of an upgrade. If you're like us and you're too busy to drag yourself back to the computer store, check out this site. In addition to their full-blown online computer shopping site, PC Shopping Planet offers many other special features, including a great PC upgrade chart, info on motherboard upgrade kits, and even an online service center. There's more, of course, so much in fact that you might want to stop in even if you aren't in need of more PC gear just yet. —(J.P.)

KEY NEWSGROUP **comp.misc** URL▶ http://www.shoppingplanet.com/

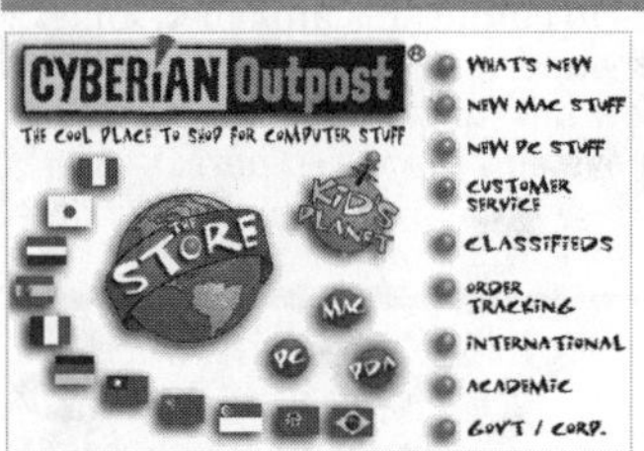

Buy Computer Stuff Online!

Cyberian Outpost Jump 5767 

Why is that some Web sites that sell computers and software look as though they've been created by artistically-deficient sleep-walkers? Well, rest assured that this is not such a site. Not only will you find great graphics and color, but the content is exceptional as well. The folks at the Cyberian Outpost sell computer stuff, lots of computer stuff as a matter of fact, and many happen to be things that we haven't seen as well presented at too many other Web locations. Their CD-ROM collection is to die for, in both PC and Mac formats, and ordering anything that catches your eye couldn't be easier. And there's plenty of hardware as well, and you can sign up for a newsletter if you want to keep up-to-date with the latest sales. —(J.P.)

KEY NEWSGROUP **comp.misc** URL http://www.cybout.com/cyberian.html

Commercial Software Directory

Internet Software Expo Jump 9501 

There's no selling going on at this site. It's just an excellent resource for locating all types of software. Organized by category, you'll find software for everything—from accounting to word processing. There's a brief description of each product, and a link to the software's home page for more information on features, system requirements, and pricing. This public service site from InfoTech Associates also is adding White Papers on software use and development, and is always looking for new URLs. If you have suggestions for either, you can let them know through this site's online e-mail links. —(L.S.)

KEY NEWSGROUP **comp.archives** URL http://www.sw-expo.com/

Shop for Computer Books on the Web

The Macmillan USA Information SuperLibrary(tm) Jump 5004 

Find and order computer-related books at a 20% discount from Macmillan Computer Publishing and its imprints (including Adobe Press, Hayden, Que, and Sams Publishing). In addition, access the Reference Desk for reports on books, the Software Library for shareware, freeware, and demo programs, and check out new book releases and coming attractions. This site also features sounds, graphics, and hyperlinks. —(S.B.)

URL http://www.mcp.com

Used Computer Classifieds

The Used Computer Mall Jump 2763 

The best use for most old computers is as a doorstop. But there are alternatives, including selling it. Stop by this page and you'll be able to check on the value of your used box, and perhaps even find a dealer willing to buy it, if you don't want to go the classified ad route to sell it yourself. If you're looking to buy used instead of new, you can search for dealers by the brand and type of computers they handle or, if you're not doing anything for awhile, browse dealers alphabetically. Either way, your first step should be to check the MicroPricer, which lists the asking prices for new and used computers available from thousands of dealers. —(L.S.)

KEY NEWSGROUP **misc.forsale.computers.other** URL http://www.usedcomputer.com/

Computer Hardware, Software, & Electronics Product Finder

U.Vision.Inc Home Page Jump 7281 

Need to find computer hardware or software? Well, the Computer ESP (Electronic Search Page) site is certainly worth a visit. The Webmaster has made it incredibly easy to find comprehensive, organized, up-to-date information on over 20,000 vendors, dealers, and their products. Software, hardware, memory chips, Internet providers, power bars, modems—the list goes on and on. And it's also easy to access, by using the simple search program provided. However, be warned, the pages are still under heavy construction, so not every product you may be looking for has been posted yet. —(E.v.B.)

KEY NEWSGROUP **biz.marketplace.computers.discussion** URL http://www.uvision.com/

Bargain Software on the Web

The Used Software Exchange Jump 2017

No longer play that shoot-'em-up game? Need a relational database, but don't want to pay hundreds of dollars? Try this page, a classified directory where you can buy or sell used software, thanks to Steven Grimm. Buyers can list their requests by software type, computer, and price. Sellers register their offerings with an input form that standardizes listings, but still allows room for comments for adding a little extra sell. Bookmark this page and you'll also have a quick interface to virtually every software archive of note on the Internet. It's a nice companion for readers of **comp.archives**, the newsgroup that announces additions to FTP sites. When you see a file you want, just load your Web browser, call this page, find the site, and go for it. It's not an archive browser, so if you want a specific file, you need to know it's in an archive, or find which archive has it with Archie. —(L.S.)

KEY NEWSGROUP **misc.forsale.computers** URL▶ http://www.hyperion.com/usx/

Computers: Other

Amiga Amigos

The Amiga Web Directory Jump 2042

Maintained by the Champaign-Urbana Commodore Users Group, this page links you to most, if not all, of the Net's Amiga computer resources. Software FTP sites, software and hardware support pages, magazines, and other general Amiga resources all are here. What makes this one of the better Web links pages is that each link has a brief description of what you can expect to find, making it a very descriptive index of resources. —(L.S.)

KEY NEWSGROUP **comp.sys.amiga** URL▶ http://www.prairienet.org/community/clubs/cucug/amiga.html

Amiga Users Worldwide

GAUHPIL Home Page Jump 2044

If you're looking for other Amiga users, you'll find them here. Dietmar Knoll has created an index of Amiga user's Web home pages organized by continent and country, so it's easy to locate other users nearby or far away. See what they do with their computers, and what links they've found that may be new to you. For statistics freaks, there's a graph of home page distribution (the U.S. and Germany run a close 1-2). You can also add your own home page to the list by sending e-mail to Dietmar. —(L.S.)

KEY NEWSGROUP **comp.sys.amiga** URL▶ http://www.omnipresence.com/Amiga/

Apple II Users' Resources

Apple II Resources Jump 2143

Forget the IBM PC. If it weren't for the Apple II, personal computing wouldn't be where it is today. They were great machines for their time, with a rabid following that continues to this day. Were it not for the Internet, the Apple II may have gone the way of the other consumer PC pioneer—the Radio Shack TRS-80—but the relatively few users that remain can keep in touch and keep their machines useful with this set of links maintained by Nathan Mates. There are links to newsgroups, FTP sites, and upgrade resources, each with a good description of what you can expect to find. Most of the links are for Apple IIGS, the last incarnation of the Apple II, but if you're a real Apple vet, there's also a link to Apple II Info-Web, one of the few, if not the only, Internet resources for the Apple II. —(L.S.)

KEY NEWSGROUP **comp.sys.apple2** URL▶ http://www.ugcs.caltech.edu/~nathan/apl2.resource.html

Pilot PDA Users' Site

Adam's USR Pilot Software Archive Jump 5757

Since its introduction last year, the Pilot personal digital assistant (PDA) from U.S. Robotics has received glowing reviews from computer users and the trade press. It packs a day planner, address book, notepad, and to-do list in an index card-sized package that also effortlessly transfers data to and from your desktop PC. If you're looking for all kinds of cool downloadable software and shareware to take advantage of your Pilot, this is the place to go. This is a regular archive, suppported by growing numbers of enthusiastic Pilot software developers who are writing all kinds of new and interesting software apps—you just pick out the software you're interested in and click to the link, or download it to your Pilot from here. And there's plenty of links to other related Pilot sites as well. —(J.P.)

URL ▸ http://www.inforamp.net/~adam/pilot/

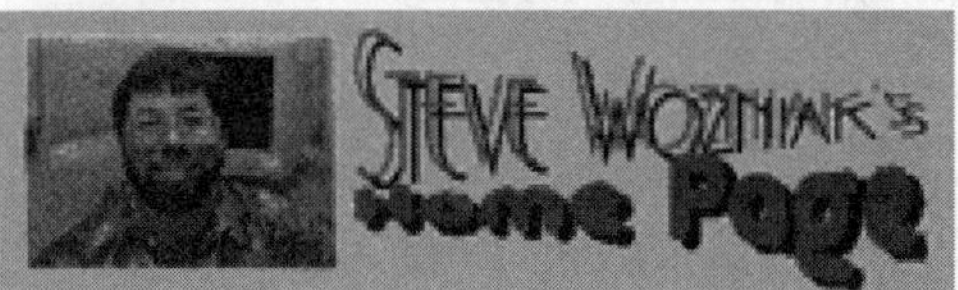

Page for "The Woz"

Steve Wozniak's Home Page Jump 2736 

While Steve Jobs was getting all the press, Steve Wozniak was in the back room sweating the details of getting the early Apple computers designed and working. The brains behind the original Apple and Apple II computers, he never got much credit outside of the small community of rabid Apple afficionados. No doubt, he liked it that way, and when he finally left Apple Computer, he didn't need any tag days. Still, you can gain some insights into this relatively unsung hero by visiting his home page and seeing what he's been up to since. —(L.S.)

KEY NEWSGROUP **comp.sys.apple2** URL ▸ http://www.woz.org/steve.html

Speech Recognition Info & News

Commercial Speech Recognition Jump 7244 

Whether you want to be able to talk to your computer because of a disability or injury, for dictation, or you just plain like to talk to your computer, this is the site to visit. Webmaster Russ Wilcox has assembled a comprehensive collection of the latest news on the wide range of speech recognition technology. As well, you can link to FAQ sites, mailing lists, FTP addresses, and newsgroups devoted to different aspects of this rapidly improving technology. We were impressed with Andrew's collection of vendor information, online demonstrations, and the latest findings from a number of research labs around the world. —(E.v.B.)

KEY NEWSGROUP **comp.speech** URL ▸ http://www.tiac.net/users/rwilcox/speech.html#NEW

Tech Talk and Trends for New PC Technologies

21st, The VXM Network Jump 5847 

With new ideas and products emerging so quickly, it seems that a new technology issued months ago might have already been pushed aside by a newer, better, brighter innovation. How do you keep up? One way is to read 21st, an online journal dedicated to giving users, vendors, system designers and others a place to talk about and discover new ideas. The magazine itself is divided up into several editorial features such as "convergence,"—the upcoming collision between TVs and PCs, the connection between human consciousness and new technologies, and more. This site may be a little more technical than your average *Popular Mechanics* article, but if you're in the business, you will find it interesting. —(J.P.)

URL ▸ http://www.vxm.com/

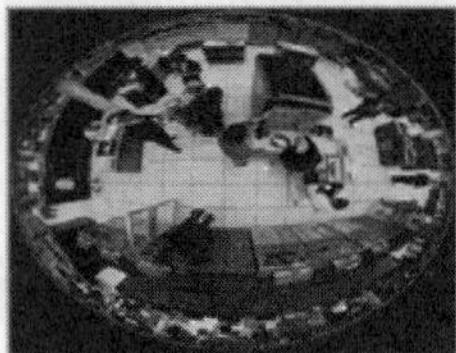

A Virtual Look at the History of Computing

Commercial Computing Museum Homepage Jump 3639 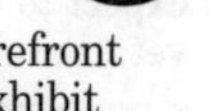

The Commercial Computing Museum has been busy exhibiting artifacts in a storefront window in downtown Waterloo, Canada since the summer of 1994, through an exhibit called "A Window to the Past." The museum's new Web site brings these fascinating displays to the Internet, so all can enjoy a peek through that window. Display changes monthly—so put it on your list of places to visit on the Web. —(C.P.)

KEY NEWSGROUP **comp.sys.misc** URL ▸ http://granite.sentex.net:80/~ccmuseum/

How to Say "Computer" in Russian

Russian-English Dictionary of Computer Terms Jump 4066 

This neat site can also be quite useful as well, especially if you need to discuss computer terminology in Russian. You can enter a word and it will return the translation, letting you set options for display depending on the type of personal computer you're using. Brought to you by Yury Avrutin, this page is a great example of how the Web assists global communication. —(R.B.)

KEY NEWSGROUP **soc.culture.russia** URL▶ http://solar.rtd.utk.edu/cgi-bin/slovar

Computer Abbreviations & Acronyms

BABEL: A Glossary of Computer Oriented Abbreviations and Acronyms Jump **5001**

Look it up in this hyperlinked glossary of obscure or frequently-used computer abbreviations and acronyms maintained by Irving Kind, who has been maintaining and updating this huge compilation of terms since 1989. Look for updates which are published in January, May, and September of each year. —(S.B.)

URL▶ http://www.access.digex.net/~ikind/babel95a.html

Zoomer: The Other PDA

Zoomer WWW Home Page Jump **2057**

This is the primary resource for Zoomer, the Casio/Tandy entry into the personal digital assistant (PDA) fray. There's a lot of good information and links here, from the Zoomer/Newton comparison chart to online help resources. In between, Brian Smithson gives you information on accessories, vendor contacts, and descriptions of available software with direct links, as well as links to FTP archives. —(L.S.)

KEY NEWSGROUP **comp.os.geos** URL▶ http://www.eit.com/mailinglists/zoomer/zoomer.html

BYTE's Web Magazine

BYTE Magazine Jump **1570**

BYTE Magazine is one of the longest-lived and most-revered print computer magazines around, and its Web site has the kind of quality and substance you'd expect from an industry elder. In addition to the requisite electronic versions of articles from the current month's issue and hot links to advertisers, the site has a very useful archive search form. And if you need to get your name into BYTE, you can submit a press release or product announcement at the Virtual Press Room. If you're a computer junkie, don't miss this one. —(H.L.)

URL▶ http://www.byte.com/

Macintosh Resources

Mac Tips, Tricks, and Shareware

The Mac Orchard Jump **5752**

The Mac Orchard is a terrific collection of software, links and reviews for Macintosh users. Drew D. Saur has set out to put together one of the best Mac sites on the Web and he has done a terrific job. It starts out with those tools most necessary to fully utilize your Mac for Internet Exploration. The contents are divided into categories (FTP, Gopher, etc.), with links to the review and download pages. The links section is also quite amazing, listing everything from Apple/Mac-related links, other software archives, online magazines and related newsgroups. And Drew has also included a writer's guideline if you'd like to submit a review of your favorite piece of shareware. —(J.P.)

KEY NEWSGROUP **alt.comp.shareware** URL▶ http://www.spectra.net/~dsaur/orchard.html

Ultimate Apple Search
www.ultimate-apple.com

The Ultimate Macintosh Search Site

Ultimate Apple Search Jump **5753**

The word "ultimate" is often overused when it comes to naming Web sites, but in this case it's right on the money. We've rarely seen such an all-encompassing site for Mac-related resources. Michael Bystrom is the main man at UAS, and he is obviously intent on finding virtually

everything there is to know about Macintosh-related resources on the Web, and he succeeds brilliantly! You'll find not only the latest software here (and we do mean the latest!) but also a news archive, other hardware sites, Mac news online, a list of Mac user groups, music software, links to all Apple sites, as well as all the latest news on Cyberdog, OpenDoc and Open Transport, Apple's latest net-related products. —(J.P.)

KEY NEWSGROUP **alt. comp.shareware** URL ▸ http://www.ultimate-apple.com/

One Stop Mac Resource

Internet Roadstop - The Complete Mac Resource Jump **5879**

If you own a Macintosh computer, or if you've ever wondered about all the fuss, you'll find plenty of information at the Internet Roadstop. They call themselves the Complete Mac Resource and it's pretty much true. The news section is updated at 5 PM EST and gives you a wonderful head start on what is happening. If a new software is announced, you can get to the download site before anyone even knows it's available! You'll also find great reviews, a section called MacTrack (which you can use to track Mac prices), reviews of Macs and software and some great monthly columns. And don't forget to check out the free e-zine. You can also have an HTML version e-mailed to you. —(J.P.)

KEY NEWSGROUP **comp.sys.mac.misc** URL ▸ http://www.digiserve.com/roadstop/

RISC Free

Power PC Resources and Information Jump **2008**

Here's the starting point for learning about the PowerPC RISC computer. You can keep up with current news, connect to Apple, IBM and Motorola PowerPC Web resources, and get the latest dirt on CPU development from the Berkeley campus of the University of California. But most valuable is the link to PowerPC shareware resources. After all, what good is leading-edge silicon if you can't take full advantage of it? —(L.S.)

KEY NEWSGROUP **comp.sys.powerpc** URL ▸ http://www.sci.sdsu.edu/ppc.html

---

Everything for Macintosh Fanatics

Robert Lentz's Macintosh Resources Jump **2010**

No matter what you're looking for, if it has to do with the Macintosh, Robert Lentz makes it easy to find, with these pages that combine links and content at a single site. Updated regularly, his What's New? section at the top of the main page lets you keep current with the state of the Mac. But you also get links to other Mac resources on the Web, FAQs, reviews of e-mail discussion lists with e-mail links to let you subscribe, software archives, hardware references, programming tips and documentation. There's also "Mind Candy"—QuickTime movies, games, and other purely recreational stuff. —(L.S.)

KEY NEWSGROUP **comp.sys.mac.applications** URL ▸ http://www.astro.nwu.edu/lentz/mac/home-mac.html

---

Newton PDA Resources

Rob Bruce's Home Page Jump **2056**

Don't let the extended biography of Rob Bruce that begins this page deter you from using it to explore online Newton resources (but if you use/struggle with this grasp-exceeding reach of a personal computer, you're used to working harder to get to things). There are links to software archives, news, product reviews, and system updates. Probably the most useful and interesting are the links to Newton user home pages. These are mostly programmer's home pages, and you can uncover some real software gold by browsing here. —(L.S.)

KEY NEWSGROUP **comp.sys.newton.misc** URL ▸ http://rainbow.rmii.com/~rbruce/

Newton Users' Page

Don's Newton Page Jump **2499**

Don Doherty has put together a list of essential links for Newton personal digital assistant users, one that will lead you to virtually anything you could want for your teeny-tiny Apple. In addition to general Newton links and FTP sites, there are links to medical

application-specific resources, Newton product reviews, and various Net-based newsletters. A separate section holds links to Newton software vendors, and a special link will let you add yourself to the Newton Folks page. —(L.S.)

KEY NEWSGROUP **comp.sys.newton.misc** URL ▸ http://opal.vcu.edu/html/medicine/rdoherty/newton.html

---

MACSENSE ONLINE

Mac Information Galore!

MacSense Home Page Jump **7366**

MacSense Online is a well-designed Web magazine offering Mac users up-to-the-minute news on Mac-related industry events, hardware and software, with embedded hotlinks to other resources covered in the articles. Don't worry if you miss an issue—you can browse through many months' worth of back issues. The site also offers great shareware and links to favorite Web sites. You can post messages on the bulletin board, or chat in the NetPub using Electric Magic's NetPhone software. Call right in to the server and converse with people—by voice!—hanging around in this virtual pub. —(E.v.B.)

KEY NEWSGROUP **comp.sys.mac.advocacy** URL ▸ http://www.macsense.com/MacSense/

Macintosh Resources on the Net

Rob's Mac Page Jump **0027**

Robert Porter has put together a really neat Web jump page that's another "must" for any Mac user! Features links to all the good stuff on the Net for Macs, like the best shareware, graphics and multimedia archives for free software, extensive vendor support links, and Mac product news. —(E.G.)

KEY NEWSGROUP **comp.sys.mac.advocacy** URL ▸ http://www.engr.scarolina.edu/engr/users/rob/robs_mac_home.html

---

The Big Macintosh Resources Site

The Well Connected Mac Jump **2039**

This is a list of links that improves on other Macintosh resource sites in both comprehensiveness and with additional content including descriptions of links, software reviews, information on Mac "celebrities," and more FAQs than you can shake a Newbie at. In some areas, it can seem a bit too comprehensive, the pages scrolling seemingly forever. But you get the feeling that if you need something that's nowhere else, it will be here, and there's much to be said for this. Elliotte Rusty Harold, the site's maintainer, encourages comments from users to help improve the site, as well as input on adding graphics and supplying product reviews. —(L.S.)

KEY NEWSGROUP **comp.sys.mac** URL ▸ http://rever.nmsu.edu/~elharo/faq/Macintosh.html

---

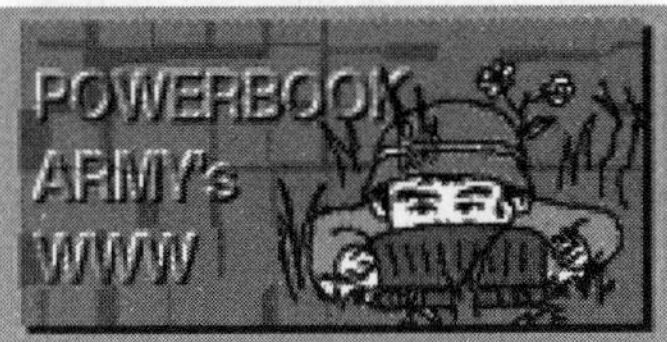

The Powerbook Army Wants You!

Powerbook Army's WWW Jump **2048**

Atsushi Iijima writes about Macintosh. He also rides Japanese trains five hours a day getting to and from work, so he has lots of time to use his Powerbook. The benefits of that experience can be yours. Link to this page and you can download Atsushi's picks of the best Powerbook utilities, get the latest Powerbook news, and even read articles he's written. If you like your Powerbook as much as Atsushi likes his, he wants to hear from you, both for suggestions, and to add your name to the rolls of the Powerbook Army! —(L.S.)

KEY NEWSGROUP **comp.sys.mac.portables** URL ▸ http://www.st.rim.or.jp/~papapa/

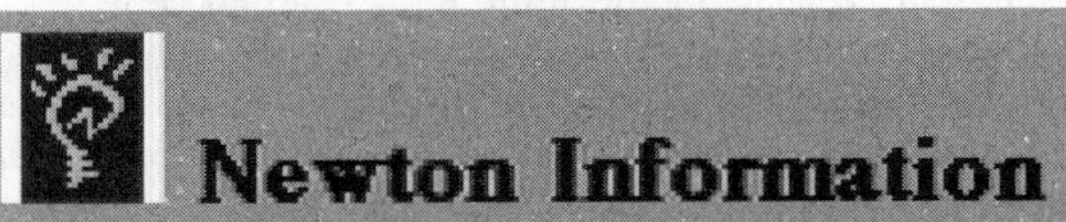

Newton: Free Software, Net News & Information

Newton Information Jump **0028**

Chuck Shotton's useful Web jump site with loads of links and good information for all you early adopters of Apple's quirky but promising Newton. The Newton has developed a devoted, almost cult-like following and an extensive range of home-grown software developed by its enthusiastic users, all of which is available from this useful site, which also features Newton news and product announcements. —(E.G.)

KEY NEWSGROUP comp.sys.newton.announce URL▶ http://www.uth.tmc.edu/newton_info/

Newton Info, News and Shareware: Stanford Newton User's Group

Index.HTML Jump 0178 

A comprehensive collection of Newton news, product announcements, rumors, discussions and links to extensive libraries of Newton freeware and shareware programs is maintained on this Web site by enthusiastic Newton owners of the Stanford (CA) Newton User's Group. —(E.G.)

KEY NEWSGROUP comp.sys.newton.announce URL▶ ftp://ftp.rahul.net/pub/flasheridn/snug/index.html

Multimedia Authoring Resources

ShockwaveCentral at macromedia.com

Shockwave: Movies on Your PC!

Macromedia: Shockwave Central 
Jump 5749

Here is the showcase for Macromedia, the industry's leading multimedia software publisher, and Shockwave, their latest Web creation, which brings full-blown audio-and-video multimedia to the Internet. Visit this site and download their Shockwave viewer (it's free), and check out their selection of Shockwave-enabled sites. Setting Shockwave up is not always easy, but Macromedia's FAQ and other guides, also accessible from this site, are quite helpful. —(J.P.)

URL▶ http://www.macromedia.com/shockwave/

Web Images Archive

Virtual Image Archive Jump 7315 

The Virtual Image Archive, compiled by Brian Casey, boasts that it contains links to thousands of digital images. Do you need a deep red tea rose, an animated mouse, or a multidimensional fractal? Well, don't look anywhere else but here. As well, you can access a number of photographer's pages, online art galleries, and individual pages for a wide range of artists. Not enough? How about a map, or an image from outer space? Or, maybe you want to talk to someone about digital images. If so, surf over to a related Usenet newsgroup on a link that Brian also provides. —(E.v.B.)

KEY NEWSGROUP comp.graphics URL▶ http://imagiware.com/via.cgi

Web Jump Site to Major Net Image Archives

My Hotlist of Jif FTP Site Jump 0191 

Net image file enthusiast Jonathan Salmon has compiled this short but useful Web page featuring links to all the major Internet image archive server sites, such as the University of Sweden, Stuttgart University, Washington University at St. Louis, and IDG Darmstadt. Click on any of Jonathan's links and connect directly to these massive photo, graphics and multimedia archives for hours of viewing fun! —(E.G.)

URL▶ http://www.dnai.com:80/~jsalmon/gif.html

Sounds, from "Get Smart" to "Get Shorty"

EARchives Jump 5810 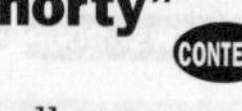

EARchives offers a great selection of sound bites from all your favorite shows. Most are taken from movies and television shows and all are in .WAV format (sound players can be dowloaded on-site) with the goal of providing the best quality and selection available on the Net. And have they? Well, a quick sampling of titles available reveals everything from "Ace Ventura," to "Blazing Saddles," "Get Smart," to Get Shorty, to "The Simpsons." New selections are added every week and sounds that might be inappropriate for young children are clearly marked, which is a help to parents as well. —(J.P.)

KEY NEWSGROUP URL▶ http://www.geocities.com/Hollywood/1158/earchive.html

Zounds! What Sounds!

Sites with Audio Clips Jump 2375

Want to make your computer talk? Or sing like a bird? Perhaps you'd like a nasty growl or blood-curdling scream to greet you when you start Windows, lest the fact that it hasn't crashed this week lull you into a false sense of security. Whatever, you'll probably find the audio clip you want through the links on Jennifer Myers's big Web metalist. The main categories are Sounds, Music, and Voice, and the links represent every conceivable type in each. Most of the links are self-explanatory, but when they're not, or there's something of particular note, Jennifer lets you know. —(L.S.)

KEY NEWSGROUP **alt.binaries.sounds.misc** URL▶ http://www.eecs.nwu.edu/~jmyers/other-sounds.html

Seybold's Site for Desktop Publishers

Seybold Seminars Online Jump 5898

Not only is Seybold one of the best-known names in the world of desktop publishing technology and industry analysis, but they've also put together a wonderful Web site featuring many handy resources for desktop publishing pros. It begins with links to the MacUsers Software Central Library, one of the best Mac-based software collections on the Web. This site's vendor directory also provides links to all of the companies involved with the Seybold Seminars covering everything from publicity to computers. In the publications section, you'll find detailed articles on DTP-related computer applications, editorial workflows, and more. —(J.P.)

URL▶ http://www.seyboldseminars.com/

Desktop Publishing and Web Design Tips from *Before and After*

Page Lab Jump 0237

As the very first beta-tester and pioneer commercial user of Aldus Pagemaker in the early 1980s, John McWade can truly say that he was the very first desktop publisher. But far from resting on his laurels, John McWade and his company, PageLab, publish *Before and After*, a wonderful print how-to magazine for desktop publishers and designers. We've enjoyed their magazine for years, and are now pleased to see them on the Web. The PageLab site carries over many of the truly ground-breaking and fresh design ideas promoted in *Before and After*, but with many significant modifications for Web publishing. Visit this fresh and graphically innovative site and discover some fascinating new ideas for Web design, peruse excerpts from back issues of *Before and After*, and get John's unique perspective on desktop—and Web—design. Highly recommended! —(E.G.)

URL▶ http://www.pagelab.com/

Desktop Publishers' Web Site

DTP Internet Jump List Jump 0157

A wealth of information for desktop publishers of all skill levels, maintained by Geof Peters. Contains extensive text articles on desktop publishing, DTP FAQ files, links to downloadable Internet font libraries, clip art and discussion groups plus files on related topics like writing and design. —(E.G.)

KEY NEWSGROUP **comp.text.desktop** URL▶ http://www.cs.purdue.edu/homes/gwp/dtp/dtp.html

Desktop Publishing Tips & Tricks

Get Info Jump 2150

CONTENT

This monthly online newsletter is chock-full of hints, tips, and tricks for the desktop publisher. It uses Mac implementations for its examples, but the software—Quark, Pagemaker, Illustrator, Photoshop, and the like—is available in other platforms, so the information is applicable for PC users. Jeffrey Glover also includes plenty of general design and composition tips, so anyone involved in DTP can benefit from visiting this site each month when a new issue comes out. —(L.S.)

KEY NEWSGROUP **comp.text.desktop** URL▶ http://www.winternet.com/~jmg/GetInfo.html

One Can Never Be Too Thin, Too Rich . . .

Phil's Fonts Jump 5803 

. . . Or have too many fonts. So goes the ancient desktop publisher's saying. We'll always have a soft spot in our hearts for Phil's Fonts. When we were breaking into the publishing business in Washington, D.C. back in the '70s, we knew Phil's (back then it was Phil's Photo) as one of the best old-style type houses around. With the advent of desktop publishing, which wiped out many of these old-fashioned typesetters, we're happy to see that Phil's has made the transition to full digital in grand style. And their site is a desktop designer's dream, offering a fascinating selection of original, new, and traditional fonts, all available for online purchase, in their wonderfully-designed commercial site. If you're looking for something a little bit different in a font, different but stylish and fashionable, you'll find it here, along with a super collection of clip art. You can order the fonts online, and you can even download a sample (Mac or PC) just by filling in the short survey. —(J.P.)

KEY NEWSGROUP comp.fonts URL▶ http://www.philsfonts.com/

Fonts on the Net

Internet Font Archive Jump 0167 

Norman Walsh's Web page features links to many of the Net's best font archives for Macs, PCs and UNIX machines, with links to public domain, shareware, and commercial font provider sites. —(E.G.)

KEY NEWSGROUP comp.text.desktop URL▶ http://jasper.ora.com/Internet-Font-Archive.html

Graphic Image Files Archive on the Web: DELFT Univeristy, The Netherlands

Digital Picture Archive on the Seventeenth Floor Jump 0123 

Patrick Groeneveld maintains this huge picture archive at the Netherland's DELFT University, with links to other equally big graphics archives around the world. On this site, you'll find all kinds of neat and interesting picture files—art, paintings, comics, faces, nature, technology and space, and much more. —(E.G.)

KEY NEWSGROUP alt.binaries.pictures.d URL▶ http://olt.et.tudelft.nl/fun/pictures/pictures.html

Library of Congress Web Site

Library of Congress World Wide Web Home Page Jump 0100 

A fascinating trek for Web information surfers! On the Library of Congress Web site, you can search their massive online card catalog and their college catalog network, access specially-created collections of graphics files, text, even video and sound files, Congressional legislative information, and more. Check their collections links for a rundown on the L of C's featured collection highlights. This site is often the first Web stop for professional researchers, but should also be on your list because there's something for everyone here! —(E.G.)

URL▶ http://lcweb.loc.gov/homepage/lchp.html

History of Medicine Image Library

On-Line Images from the History of Medicine Jump 0186 

An extensive collection of historical photographs, artwork and printed texts maintained by The National Library of Medicine. There are many interesting photographs here, many of which document the history of medical treatments for soldiers during World Wars I and II, portraits of noted doctors, historical photos of medical procedures, and much more, for those of you interested in the history of medicine. —(E.G.)

URL▶ http://www.nlm.nih.gov:8002/

Historic Computer Images Archive

Historical Computer Images Jump 0179 

An interesting, and (occasionally) unintentionally comical, collection of historic computer images scanned and compiled by Mike Muuss. Images include photos of old ENIAC computers, computers of the 1940s and '50s and many promotional/publicity photos of well-known mainframe and mini computers from the 1960s and '70s. A fascinating look at the visual history of the computer revolution! —(E.G.)

URL▶ http://ftp.arl.mil/ftp/historic-computers/

Space Images, Video & Sound Files

Astronomical Pictures - Images Astronomique Jump 0183 CONTENT

Another space multimedia archive, maintained by Frank Russel at Rennes' University of France. Features an extensive collection of space video and audio clips, supernova and comet pictures, earth solar system planet photos, and Space Shuttle shots. —(E.G.)

KEY NEWSGROUP sci.space

URL▶ http://www.univ-rennes1.fr/ASTRO/astro.html

▲ *Vintage computer photo, from* **Virtual Image Archive** *at* Jump 7315.

Big Graphics Clip Art Collection

Sandra's Clip Art Server Jump 0193 

Looking for interesting clip art to use in your desktop publishing and other PC graphics projects? Sandra Loosemore has done a nice job compiling and abstracting this extensive collection of PC clip art files. These files, which are mostly line drawings, cover a vast range of subject matter—people, vehicles, animals, etc.—including a good deal of public domain art from the Victorian Era. Sandra has also combined these clip art collections into massive single compressed files that you can download to use on your own personal computer. If you have plenty of hard disk space on your PC, you might want to download a bunch of these files to create your own personal images archive for future graphics projects. —(E.G.)

URL▶ http://www.cs.yale.edu/HTML/YALE/CS/HyPlans/loosemore-sandra/clipart.html

PSYCHED UP GRAPHICS

Henrik's Picture Archives

// Psyched Up Graphics // Jump 7338 

Henrik Gemal has collected over 1,800 graphic files for your viewing pleasure and use. Choose from a wide range of arrows, buttons, balls, bars, and icons that will put zing into your own Web pages. As well, Henrik has collected photographs of animals, butterflies, landscapes. Need more? Then dip into the outer space, numbers, letters, and symbols files. There's enough here to keep you downloading for hours! —(E.v.B.)

KEY NEWSGROUP comp.graphics URL▶ http://www.cbs.dk/people/nagemal/psyched/

Net Image Archive: Washington University

Index of /Multimedia/Images/ Jump 0192 

Web link to The Washington University at St. Louis' massive archive of photos and other illustrations covering a wide range of subjects. This is an extensive collection featuring many great images and one of our personal favorites! Features photos of famous celebrities, movie stars, historical photos, cult favorites, TV/movie shots, and much, much more! —(E.G.)

URL▶ http://wuarchive.wustl.edu:80/multimedia/images/

Silicon Graphics Web Site

The Gallery Jump 0173 

Silicon Graphic's Gallery Web site features a neat collection of images developed on Silicon Graphic's workstations, Silicon Graphic's contest winners, neat (but large) QuickTime video clips, and scientific graphic images. —(E.G.)

URL▶ http://www.sgi.com/free/gallery.html

Watching Movies on the Internet

Mpeg Movie Archive Jump 0013 

At the rate the technical capabilities of the Internet and the Web are growing, the experts say it won't be too much longer before we'll all be "watching television" on our personal computers over the Internet. Thanks to the Web, you, too, can be part of the interactive television revolution with the help of the MPEG Movie Archive. A fun way to kill time on the Web, this site contains MPEG movie files (MPEG stands for Motion Picture Experts Group, and a file format that compresses huge video files to smaller file sizes so they can be transmitted faster over the Net) on a variety of subjects like computer animations, movie and TV clips, space program clips, etc. Using your Web browser and a video viewing "helper application," you can download video clips and view them on your personal computer. A word of warning: Many of the video clips you'll download from the Net will be no larger than the size of a Saltine cracker, and the color quality sometimes looks like the bad reception you'll get from an East German television set, and at 9600 baud these files take many minutes to load, but, hey—the first television sets sold in the late 1930s weren't all that hot, either. Plus, you get to be a real pioneer, sitting there watching Internet video clips on your Compaq or Macintosh, while everyone else is just talking about the "500 Channel Universe." —(E.G.)

URL▶ http://www.eeb.ele.tue.nl/mpeg/index.html

National Archives Multimedia Footage Library

National Archives Jump 0171 

An interesting overview of the sound, film and video collections available from the National Archives in Washington, D.C., encompassing a massive collection of 35,000 sound recordings, 4.5 million photographic items, 150,000 reels of motion picture film, and over 20,000 video tapes in collections dating from 1894 to the present, and which cover almost any subject imaginable. Copies of these materials may be ordered from the National Archives for a modest fee (about $50) and are a fantastic resource if you're a video producer or multimedia developer. —(E.G.)

KEY NEWSGROUP **rec.video.production** URL▶ gopher://gopher.footage.net:2901/11/FOOTAGE.net/NationalArchives

Vanderbilt TV News Archive

Vanderbilt Newsgroup Jump 0172 

The Television News Archive at Vanderbilt University maintains this extensive archiving, indexing and abstracting service for national television newscasts dating as far back as 1968, and makes copyrighted news footage available to video/film/multimedia producers on a loan basis. You can find what you're looking for here, and get information on how to order the footage you need. —(E.G.)

KEY NEWSGROUP **rec.video.production**

URL▶ gopher://gopher.footage.net:2901/11/FOOTAGE.net/TvMovieLocator/Vanderbilt

TV & Film Images Library

Index of /pub/culture/TV Plus Film/pics/ Jump 0185

A nice image archive maintained by FUNET, an international scientific researcher's organization based in Finland. Features many interesting images from popular TV shows and movies, such as *Batman, 2001: A Space Odyssey, Bladerunner,* cartoons, etc. A good place to get those hard-to-find pictures from older TV shows or movies. —(E.G.)

URL▶ http://www.funet.fi/pub/culture/tv+film/pics/

Stock Movie & Video Footage on the Web

FOOTAGE.net Home Page Jump 0170

A valuable resource for video producers, multimedia developers and talented video amateurs, FOOTAGE.net's free service puts the film, movie and video news stock footage collections of scores of stock footage companies at your command. Companies that own these collections of film stock footage clips post descriptions of their libraries on FOOTAGE.net, which you can peruse through this Web site. There's a vast array of subject matter—old newsreel footage, TV news video, stock footage, sports films, military and historical films, and more. This Web site also features links to these stock film suppliers to request more information on clips available. —(E.G.)

KEY NEWSGROUP **rec.video.production** URL▶ http://www.footage.net:2900/

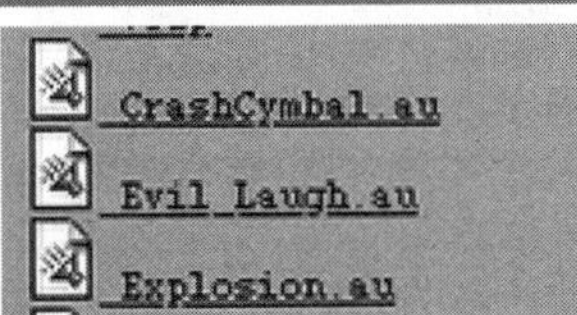

Celebrity, Historic, TV, Movie & Sound Effects Files

Celebrity, Historic, TV, Movie and Sound Effects Files Jump 0196

One of the biggest sound archives on the Net, maintained at the University of North Carolina, this Web site features tons of movie and TV sound clips, wild sound effects, famous Monty Python clips, soundtracks, commercials, and much more, all of which can be downloaded and saved to your own personal computer. —(E.G.)

URL▶ gopher://ftp.cs.ttu.edu/1ftp%3asunsite.unc.edu%40/pub/multimedia/sun-sounds/

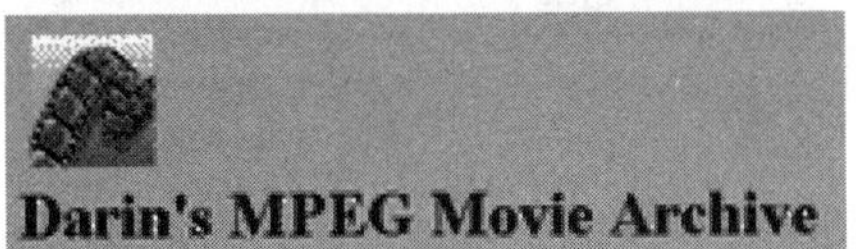

MPEG Movie Multiplex

Darin's MPEG Movie Archive Jump 2319

When you want to watch a movie on your computer, but don't know what you want to see, stop by Darin Hawley's page. You'll find an excellent selection of movie clips featuring supermodels, cartoons, action pictures, music videos, space and aviation, and auto races. To see examples of cutting-edge computer animation, there are fractals, Mandelbrots, and morphs. And for a complete change of pace, go to the miscellaneous section, for a varied selection of subjects, from "Ballet," to "Burning fingers." —(L.S.)

KEY NEWSGROUP **comp.archives** URL▶ http://www.ugcs.caltech.edu/~darinh/mpegs.html

Movie Sound Clips

n/a Jump 0200

This extensive sound archive at the University of North Carolina features many quirky, unusual and well-known sound dialogue clips and music themes from many popular past and current films. Where else on the Net could you find the sound clip of the southern jailer in *Cool Hand Luke*, who tells Paul Newman: "What we have heyeah, is failyah ta communicate," or that toothless hillbilly's tender entreaty to Ned Beatty to "squeal like a pig," in the movie *Deliverance*? If there's a well-known line in just about any movie you've seen, it's obvious that somone's spent a good deal of time capturing them to put up here. Highly recommended! —(E.G.)

KEY NEWSGROUP **rec.arts.movies** URL▶ http://sunsite.unc.edu:80/pub/multimedia/sun-sounds/movies/

Pictures! Movies! Music!

Rob's Multimedia Lab (RML) Jump 7138

Need a picture of a three-toed sloth? You'll probably find it here. Rob Malik must be one heck of a Net surfer. The collection of movie clips, photographs, sounds, fractals, stereograms, speeches, QuickTime clips, ASCII art—you name it—is seriously awesome. Take the TV music themes list, for example. Not only does Rob provide the music for a multitude of shows from *The Addams Family,* to *Murder She Wrote,* to *All My Children,* to *Rocky and Bullwinkle,* but he also augments the list with an explanation of the abbreviations for different operating system file extensions, provides links to free audio software, and lists of related newsgroups. —(E.v.B.)

KEY NEWSGROUP **comp.multimedia** URL▶ http://www.acm.uiuc.edu/rml/

HarperCollins Sound Files Site

Harper Audio Jump **0121**

Spoken excerpts of works by famous authors in modern and classic literature are available as sound files on this innovative Web site. Be warned, however, these files—whose listening times are typically ten minutes long—are three to five megabytes, so they'll take much longer than that just to download! Files include works by Charles Dickens, T. S. Eliot, William Faulkner, Ernest Hemingway, James Thurber, and others. —(E.G.)

URL▶ http://town.hall.org/Archives/radio/IMS/HarperAudio/

SOUNDPRINT Radio Sound Files

SOUNDPRINT Jump **0122**

Selected radio features available on the Web as sound files from NPR's *SOUNDPRINT* program. Since many of these sound files may take over four hours to download at 9600 baud (to listen to a feature that may be only fifteen minutes long!), the novelty wears off very quickly but, hey—you're a pioneer, so you can't expect the going to be easy! —(E.G.)

URL▶ http://www.town.hall.org:80/Archives/radio/IMS/Soundprint/

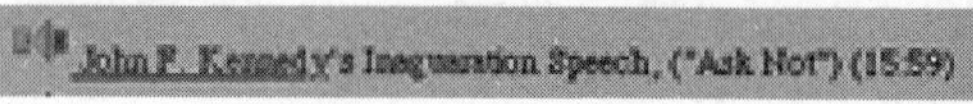

Historical Voice Clips Sound Library

MSU Vincent Voice Library
Jump **0151**

Sampling of speech and sound clip files of political leaders and other prominent figures from the G. Robert Vincent Voice Library at Michigan State University. Listen to John F. Kennedy's "Ask Not" inaugural speech, hear Babe Ruth talk about baseball, and Franklin D. Roosevelt accepting his party's nomination in 1936, in sound files that can be downloaded and saved to your personal computer. —(E.G.)

URL▶ http://web.msu.edu/vincent/index.html

Learn PostScript Writing Tips & Tricks

A First Guide to PostScript Jump **2031**

PostScript is the page description language for text and graphics. It's actually a programming language, and while most DTP and graphics software using PostScript does the thinking for you, sometimes, as P. J. Weingartner knows, you need to have at least some idea of how it works to get the most out of it. So P. J. created this online tutorial that will give you a basic understanding of PostScript. Once you've finished, there are pointers to reference books for further study. —(L.S.)

KEY NEWSGROUP **comp.lang.postscript**
URL▶ http://www.cs.indiana.edu/docproject/programming/postscript/postscript.html

Multimedia from Macromedia

Macromedia Jump **4503**

If you are at all interested in graphics or multimedia, this site is for you. Navigation is simple and intuitive through this well-designed Web site (as if that should be a surprise coming from the people who brought you the original, best-selling multimedia authoring program, Director). Plus, there's a free CD for taking a short survey, a free downloadable 3-D game, and mailing lists for technical information and special offers you can sign onto with just a few clicks of the old mouse. —(T.W.)

URL▶ http://www.macromedia.com/

Getting the Most from Acrobat

Acrobatics - The Journal for Acrobat Users Jump 2639 CONTENT

Acrobatics is a quarterly journal for users of Adobe Acrobat that will help you understand and make the most effective use of this software that allows documents, typefaces, and graphics to be viewed, universally, on previously incompatible computers. The journal is available in PDF format for the Acrobat Reader, of course, and it's a large file, so be prepared to wait. It's worth it, though, with news, developer's notes, information on using and embedding fonts, and other useful tidbits for understanding and getting the most out of this software. —(L.S.)

KEY NEWSGROUP **comp.lang.postscript** URL▶ http://www.ep.cs.nott.ac.uk/~dre/merlin/acrobatics.html

Toolbook Users' Web Site

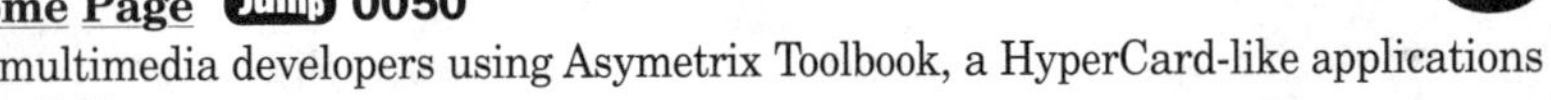

The Toolbook Users Web - Home Page Jump 0050 CONTENT

Text files, software, and advice for multimedia developers using Asymetrix Toolbook, a HyperCard-like applications development system for Windows. —(E.G.)

KEY NEWSGROUP **bit.listserv.toolb-l** URL▶ http://www.univ.trieste.it/tbkwww/tbkwww.html

Intelligent Computer Tricks

PC Demos Explained Jump 2045 CONTENT

We're not talking about sample software here. Demos are short, 3-D multimedia programs that show off your computer's capabilities, as well as those of the programmer, as they make your machine do tricks it isn't supposed to do. Jim Leonard considers them an art form. Whether or not you agree, they do make computers do tricks they otherwise could not. With this page, Jim gives you not just a clear description of what these programs are about, but also their history, information on how they are created, and links to FTP sites holding demos, including separate links to the best sites. —(L.S.)

KEY NEWSGROUP **comp.sys.ibmpc.demos** URL▶ http://www.mcs.net/~trixter/html/demos.html#whatisademo

Scanning Tips & Tricks from an Expert

Make Your Scanner a Great Design and Production Tool Jump 7316 CONTENT

Michael Sullivan, author of a print book of the same name as this promotional site, certainly knows his scanning techniques and, lucky for us, he wants to share them. You can read about scanning for output method, how to find your scanner's "sweet spot," how to scan 3-D objects, how to create great background effects with your scanner, and tons of other inside scanning tips. Michael also includes a scanning glossary, descriptions of all different types of scanners, and even advice on how to salvage a faded original. Check out his reference file for even more information. A must-visit for any desktop publisher! —(E.v.B.)

KEY NEWSGROUP **comp.graphics** URL▶ http://www.hsdesign.com/scanning/

Scanning Tips & Tricks for Desktop Publishers

The Scanning FAQ Jump 2124 CONTENT

This hypertext FAQ maintained by Jeff Bone is a must read for the would-be desktop publisher, and an excellent reference for the experienced. There are sections on scanning line art, halftones, gray scale, and color images, each with a combination introduction and hints and tips resource. The resources section covers image resolution, copyright issues, image formats, and flatbed scanners. There's also an excellent questions-and-answers section for the beginner. —(L.S.)

KEY NEWSGROUP **alt.graphics** URL▶ http://www.dopig.uab.edu/dopigpages/FAQ/The-Scan-FAQ.html

Guide to Memorable .Sig File Taglines

Taglines Galore! Jump 2199

Ever read those funny, wise, or otherwise memorable quotations people use in their newsgroup or e-mail signatures and wish you could be as pithy? Thanks to Neil Enns, you don't have to be. He's compiled close to 50,000 taglines you can choose from to reflect a point of view, a mood, add some humor to your posts, or even be compellingly cryptic. There are some subject categories, including aphorisms, fulldeck-isms, op codes, but all the good stuff is in the alphabetical listings. Browse them for grins, or use the search engine to help meet a specific need. And feel free to contribute to the lists. It may be huge, but there's always room for more! —(L.S.)

KEY NEWSGROUP alt.culture.usenet URL http://www.brandonu.ca/~ennsnr/Tags/

Photoshop Tips & Tricks

Photoshop Sites Jump 7349

Fans of Adobe's popular Photoshop software will find some interesting sites here related to image processing and digital photography. Commercial sites, pages full of Photoshop tips and tricks, and pages devoted to filters, plug-ins, and other additions can be found. As well, books are reviewed, and personal pages, portfolios and online galleries created with Photoshop can also be seen here. —(E.v.B.)

KEY NEWSGROUP rec.photo URL http://www.fns.net/~almateus/photos.htm

Making Photoshop Easy

Kai's Power Tips & Tricks for Adobe Photoshop Jump 1503

Learning complex software—especially Photoshop—isn't easy these days. Even the terminology is tough. But with Photoshop guru Kai Krause's entertaining and informative tips and tricks, you become more of an expert. Here you find that the use of channels are quite undervalued in Photoshop operations, and if you use them more frequently, you're ahead of the game. The Tech, MIT's student newspaper, and MIT's Edgerton Center for digital imaging, provide additional resources for this site, including a Photoshop newsletter, a background archive to help you add zip to your Web pages, and a MacArt zine, with even more Photoshop talk. If you don't know who Kai is, find out in the unforgetable Web interview here. Last but not least, this is a commercial page, so HSC Software makes its pitch, albeit only if you click on the option, to sell you the Photoshop power tools that Kai recommends. —(H.L.)

URL http://the-tech.mit.edu/KPT/KPT.html

Net & Web Tech Resources

One-Stop Announcements of Your Web Site

The PostMaster - Announce Your URL Everywhere! Jump 3729

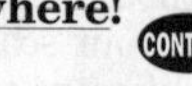

Just finished your own Web page and need to spread the word? The PostMaster by NetCreations is a great service you can use to announce your site all over the Web from a single point, by posting your announcement to Lycos, Yahoo, InfoSeek, Netscape, and over 100 other smaller directories and hotlists on the Web. For a fee, The PostMaster will spread the word on your behalf. Why use The PostMaster? You'll save time and get lots of exposure in key areas. Want to "try before you buy?" Use The PostMaster's guest list to get a message out to many popular sites and publications—no charge. This also gets your announcement prominently displayed in the PostMaster's own "What's New" listing. Stop wearing out your keyboard and check this one out—it may be just what you need. —(N.F.)

URL http://www.netcreations.com/postmaster/index.html

Finding Advertisers for Your Web Site

IPA Advertising Index Jump 3730

You've just developed a terrific Web site. You're envisioning mass appeal, and a constant throng of visitors. You're new, yet you need to find a way to draw traffic in and make the venture pay off. You need . . . yes! Advertisers! Here's a great

way to let THEM find YOU! The IPA Index allows advertisers to search a database of online publications in need of advertisers. Of course, if you're looking to advertise your own site, the IPA database can help you make the right choices. Rosalind Resnick, this site's developer and a noted Internet business book author in her own right, has created an invaluable service that will save both advertisers and Webmasters time and money. —(N.F.)

URL ▶ http://www.netcreations.com/ipa/adindex/index.html

Sound on the Web from RealAudio

RealAudio Download Page Jump 3736

Now you can have access to Internet sound programming and other sound streams with RealAudio products. The RealAudio player, available here as a free download, is a helper program for your browser that allows you to play RealAudio sequences with controls much like a VCR, with start, stop, and pause options. The player is available for both Windows and Macintosh. There's also the RealAudio Encoder, a software program that will allow all you programmers and developers to create and enhance RealAudio programming. The RealAudio Server software allows anyone producing and distributing large amounts of audio content to deliver RealAudio programming right through their server throughout the Internet. Progressive Networks provides a handy FAQ to get you around any technical difficulties, and even provides sound card drivers. You'll continue to see RealAudio data streams available all over the Web, so download your player today. —(N.F.)

URL ▶ http://www2.realaudio.com/release/download.html

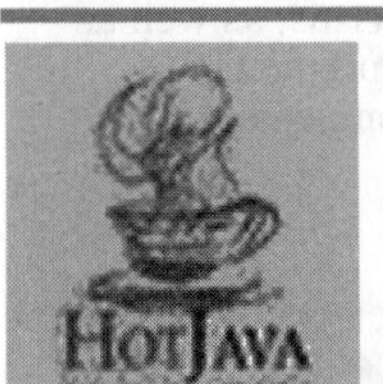

Java Information Center from Sun

Java(tm) Home Page Jump 6003

More than at any other time since the dawn of the computer, we have access to hordes of information—information that was created on many different platforms, and which needs to be accessible from many different platforms. To keep up with these increasing demands for information, Sun Microsystems Inc. needed a programming language that was simple, dynamic, reliable, and secure. Thus began the development of the Java language and environment, one of the Net's newest and most talked-about software technologies. Objectoriented, architecturally neutral, and highly portable, Java helps simplify the programmer's development task without the mundane tasks inherent in conventional software languages. The Hot Java Web Browser, described at this site, is a prime example of delivering information to the user transparently and automatically. Programmers can get started at Sun's Java site with the Java Development kit, Programmers Guide, and even sample Java applets. Expect to see Java evolve as one of the standards of application development for the Web, and for personal computing in general. —(N.F.)

KEY NEWSGROUP **comp.lang.java** URL ▶ http://java.sun.com/

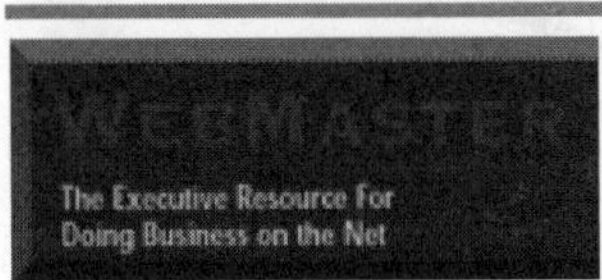

Support for Webmasters

WebMaster Magazine Jump 7262

Being a Webmaster can sometimes be a pretty challenging occupation. However, take heart, and surf over to the online version of the newsstand version of WebMaster. Here you can find newsletters with the latest news on trends, products, services, and resources that Webmasters need to know. As well, interviews with industry spokespersons, information on graphics, Internet surveys, and much more is available here. —(E.v.B.)

KEY NEWSGROUP **comp.infosystems.www.misc** URL ▶ http://www.cio.com/WebMaster

Leading-Edge Net Tech

net.tech Jump 7310

Kushal, a California high school student, has compiled a fascinating page of news, links, and descriptions about exciting new Internet and Web technologies. You can learn about Virtual Reality Modeling Language—a technology that allows you to navigate the Web in 3-D using a product called WebSpace. Or, how about reading about the new electronic cash payment programs, or the newest multimedia platforms? The links are all here. —(E.v.B.)

KEY NEWSGROUP **rec.answers** URL ▶ http://www.pulver.com/~krave/nettech.htm

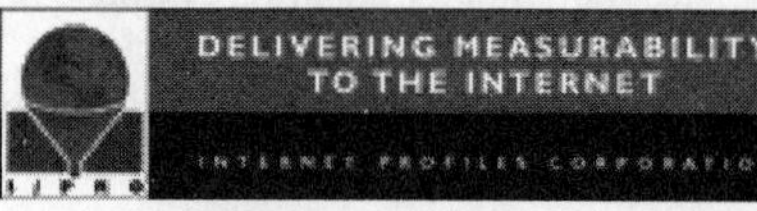

Tracking Usage on Your Web Site

I/PRO Internet Profiles Corporation
Jump 7479 CONTENT

Would you like to get more accurate, verifiable accounting of how many visitors are visiting to your home page? Well, I/PRO, a startup that has recently joined up with TV ratings giant Nielsen, and a self-described "provider of services and software for independent measurement and analysis of Web site usage," will help you find out. According to the company blurb, "the I/PRO System enables organizations that own or manage Web sites to understand how and by whom their sites are being used. Moreover, advertisers and media buyers can use the I/PRO System to determine the optimal sites for delivering their messages." The company provides demos for its count and audit programs at this site, to show you how such audits of your Web site could help you attract paid advertising sponsorship to your site, if you're so inclined. —(E.v.B.)

KEY NEWSGROUP **biz.misc** URL▸ http://www.ipro.com/

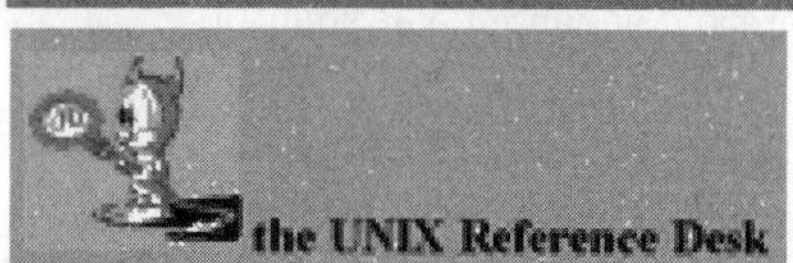

All about UNIX

UNIX Reference Desk **Jump 2016**

Whether you use a PC, Mac, Amiga or whatever, the Internet runs on UNIX. It's a great operating system for computer geeks, extremely cryptic to the uninitiated, but complex nonetheless for anyone. So Jennifer Myers put together this resource, a combination of search engines and links for everyone from beginner to expert looking for specific or general UNIX information. You can search for definitions of UNIX terms, as well as search databases covering programming, security, and networking. There are sections covering specific UNIX platforms, including PCs, and links to FAQs, articles, and general references. No matter what you need to know about UNIX and using it, it's here. —(L.S.)

KEY NEWSGROUP **comp.unix.questions** URL▸ http://www.eecs.nwu.edu/unix.html

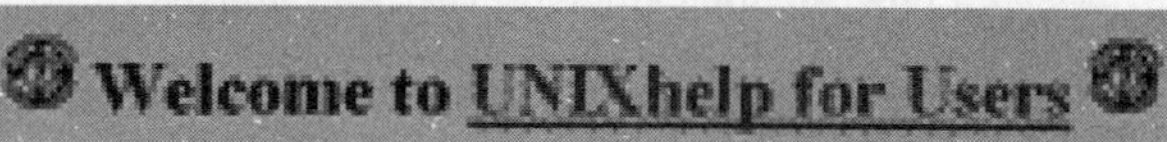

UNIX for Newbies

UNIXhelp for Users
Jump 2036

Organized into easy-to-digest bites of information, these pages serve both as tutorial and quick reference and are especially helpful if you have a UNIX shell account and can't figure out how to change directories, move files, or handle other housekeeping chores. Offered as part of the United Kingdom's Information Technology and Training Initiative and maintained by John Smith, the hypertext outline gives you a good grounding in UNIX capabilities and operations. But if you just want to know what a UNIX term means, there are also alphabetical glossary and index pages, so you can find the information you want quickly and easily. —(L.S.)

KEY NEWSGROUP **comp.unix.questions** URL▸ http://alpha.acast.nova.edu/UNIXhelp/TOP_.html

Help for Ailing Websters

Ask Dr. Web **Jump 2608**

There's help for the technically challenged, at least when it comes to using the Web. With Ask Dr. Web, you can ask technical questions about browsers, servers, CGI, or anything else related to using the Web. But before you ask, browse the excellent FAQ which answers the most common questions. If your answer isn't there, you can search the Web Developers Library by topic area and keyword. It's one of the best search engines available, a fitting companion to one of the best resources for Web information. —(L.S.)

KEY NEWSGROUP **comp.infosystems.www.misc** URL▸ http://WWW.Stars.com/Dr.Web/

Marimba: "Push" Media Comes to the Web

Marimba **Jump 0235** CONTENT

One of the biggest new developments to hit the Web has been the advent of new Web software and services that "broadcast" news and information to your desktop personal computer—instead of making you go out an link to the site you're looking for. PointCast is currently the largest provider of such "push" Web broadcasting, and another hot new company, Marimba, is attracting a lot of attention as well. Marimba, founded by the developers of Sun's Java programming language, is currently the best-known player in this new market for Internet broadcasting software tools. These are application builders that enable you to set up your Web site to broadcast information directly to a viewer's PC, at regular intervals. At Marimba's site, you can read the latest development notes on their products, and download the latest versions of their products. —(E.G.)

URL▶ http://www.marimba.com/

▲ *Historic computer photo image, from* **Historical Computer Images**, *at* Jump **0179**.

Modem Initialization Strings

Ask Mr. Modem Jump **2628**

The toughest part of getting online is setting the modem initialization string. That long line of near-indecipherable characters has crashed many a system. Now, thanks to the customer service department of Intellinet, you can take the guesswork out of setting up your modem. Ask Mr. Modem offers suggested initialization strings for hundreds of modems. Pick the brand name from the list, and you get another list of modem models to choose from. Pick again, and you get the basic string, plus advanced settings. It's that easy, and it's very fast. —(L.S.)

KEY NEWSGROUP **comp.dcom.modems** URL▶ http://www.intellinet.com/CustomerService/FAQ/AskMrModem/

UNIX Users Rejoice!

UnixWorld Online Jump **5090**

This page includes a technical, hands-on section from *Open Computing* (formerly *UnixWorld*) *Magazine.* It also supplies technical feature articles, practical how-to tutorial articles, and Wizard's Grabbag column. Reviews of various hardware, software, and other products can also be found here in addition to a column called Answers to Unix, and a media (largely book) review column. If you use UNIX, this page deserves a visit! —(S.B.)

URL▶ http://www.wcmh.com/uworld/

PC & Windows Resources

Windows 95 Help and Resources

Win95.com Jump **5824**

A popular Web spot for Windows 95 users, Win95.com is one of the best places we've seen to check out Windows 95 news, pointers, and downloadable software resources. This site is packed with everything, from 32-bit shareware to freeware, links to other sites and even help with Win95 tweaks. You might want to browse through the Win95 and NT FAQs available here, visit the online bookstore, or check out the separate sections on this site's online help disk, its rich directory of related sites, tips sheet, and more. —(J.P.)

KEY NEWSGROUP **comp.misc** URL▶ http://www.win95.com/

Software and More from PC World

PC World Software Library Jump **5836**

PC World, creators of this site (which is, itself, part of their massive Web site), calls it a software library, but it's actually much more than that. Which is not to say you won't find software; in fact you'll find a wonderfully complete shareware, game, and utilities library, complete with a state-of-the-art search engine. You'll also find tips on forthcoming new releases—either updates or brand new products—

and plenty of specs on the new stuff. And once you've done downloading you can take a few minutes to read the many online features all over this site. If you're a PC (and even a Mac) user, your stop here will not be brief. —(J.P.)

KEY NEWSGROUP comp.misc URL ▶ http://www.pcworld.com/software_lib/index.html

---

Windows Help and Software

PCWin Resource Center Jump **5837**

Here's a great site for Windows software. What we liked best about this site was the various files that they've included to help you with any Win-related problems you might have. Most notable of these are this site's "Tips & Tricks" area and its tips for installing files. And you won't want to miss their chat forum, "Win Talk." Got a question about networking, hardware or the Web? You're sure to find your answer here. Oh, and did we mention shareware? Yes, you can get plenty of shareware here, too. —(J.P.)

KEY NEWSGROUP comp.misc URL ▶ http://www.pcwin.com/index.shtml

---

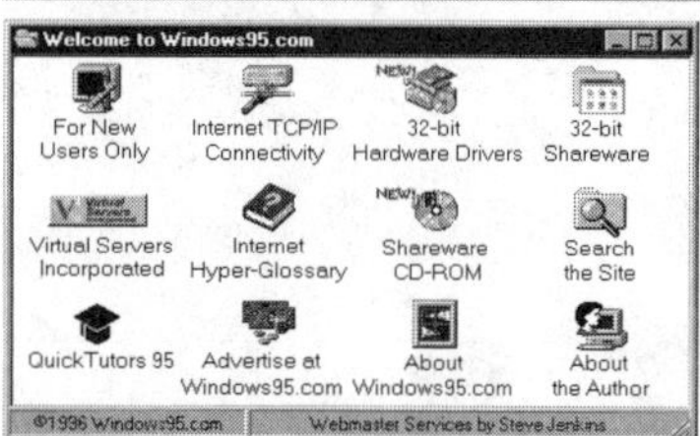

Windows 95 Tips, Info, and Resources

Windows95.com Jump **5916**

Still trying to cut through the maze of Windows95? Here's a great site for users new and old. The purpose here is to provide a complete information clearinghouse for Win95 information. Got a question? Read one of their great tutorials. They're complete, yet easy to understand, and can be downloaded for future reference. Once you're more familiar with Win95, you can start exploring the many other sections of this site, such as 32-bit hardware drivers, Internet tips, software, and more. Site creator Steve Jenkins has done a wonderful job of organizing and writing this information. And we wonder how he managed to cop that Windows95 URL from under Microsoft's nose! —(J.P.)

KEY NEWSGROUP comp.windows.misc URL ▶ http://www.windows95.com/

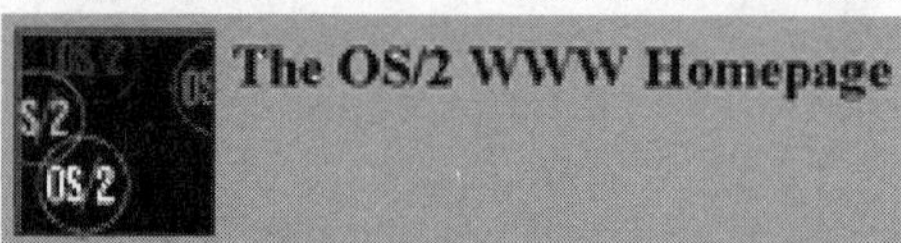

Warp the Web

The OS/2 WWW Homepage Jump **2076**

Here's an excellent list of OS/2 FAQs and links, maintained by Kent H. Lundberg and the MIT OS/2 Users Group. There are links to OS/2 home pages, FTP sites, and other resources to learn more about OS/2 or how to get more out of it if you're already running Warp. And there's an extensive list of user group home pages, often the best sources of information on using an operating system. —(L.S.)

KEY NEWSGROUP comp.os.os2 URL ▶ http://www.mit.edu:8001/activities/os2/os2world.html

---

Warp Home

Team OS/2 Online Jump **2261**

When IBM introduced its OS/2 operating system, it decided to recruit users to help spread the word. This is the Web home of those True Believers, otherwise known as Team OS/2. You can learn more about and join Team OS/2 at this site, but its real purpose is to help OS/2 users, and it does that well. From here you can link to the best OS/2 resources on the Web, download the latest versions of OS/2 Internet clients, and browse the resources available, whether you already use the operating system or are just considering it. —(L.S.)

KEY NEWSGROUP comp.os.os2.advocacy URL ▶ http://www.teamos2.org/

Software That Works

Linux Toys Jump **2742**

Linux is a great operating system, a free Unix for PCs. And there's plenty of good, free software to let you take advantage of it. But since it's free, and based on a standard being developed collaboratively, voluntarily and, some would say, haphazardly, what's available isn't always easy to use. John Fisk has spent a lot of time trying various pieces of software, and what's here are his favorites. Take advantage of this page and you'll find editors, utilities, and graphics, networking and telecommunications software that mostly works, along with some rather detailed descriptions and tips for installing and using each. —(L.S.)

KEY NEWSGROUP **comp.os.linux.misc** URL▶ http://www.tenn.com/fiskhtml/linux_toys.html

Visual Basic Programmer's Center

Visual Basic Online Jump **7279**

Visual Basic Online is an online magazine for Visual Basic programmers—beginners and advanced alike. In each monthly issue you'll find an assortment of articles covering every aspect of Visual Basic. If you're a Visual Basic power user, you'll also enjoy reading about advanced issues such as creating DLLs and VBXs to enhance Visual Basic programs. Not enough? Well, don't miss this site's Toolbox, which provides links to all the Visual Basic information available on the Internet. —(E.v.B.)

KEY NEWSGROUP **comp.lang.visual** URL▶ http://www.vb-online.com/

PC World Online

Welcome to PC World Online Jump **7345**

You'll find the same top-quality information here in the online version of the popular *PC World* magazine. Computers, printers, modems, monitors, software—you name it—are reviewed. You can also read weekly columns such as tips on running home offices, Net gossip, and lots more. If this isn't enough to feed your computer information needs, PC World also provides links to other, related online publications, such as InfoWorld, Digital Video, Reality Factory, and Multimedia World. —(E.v.B.)

KEY NEWSGROUP **comp.sys.misc** URL▶ http://www.pcworld.com/

Comprehensive Winsock Apps List

The Consummate Winsock Apps List Jump **2037**

Once you're familiar with Net access via Winsock, it's time to expand your horizons, either by trying new clients or by trying new Internet services. Either way, this is the source, and Forrest H. Stroud does a remarkable job in organizing and presenting what's available, including Web and Gopher helper applications, HTML editors, and TCP/IP stacks. Each product has a "star" rating giving Forrest's opinion, pricing (freeware or shareware/commercial price), and links to the software's home page, and downloading info. The pages are updated whenever new products or new versions are released, and Forrest makes it easy to check with a separate page of new clients. —(L.S.)

KEY NEWSGROUP **alt.winsock** URL▶ http://cws.wilmington.net/

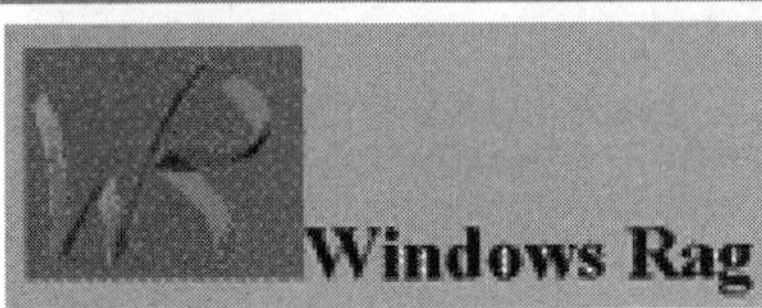

A Windows Magazine for Just Plain Folks

Windows Rag Jump **2075**

Most Web sites for print computer magazines are just recycled, condensed versions of the print editions. And they all suffer from the same problem—they concentrate on new (expensive) hardware, and the software reviews are based on tests done on those same machines. Ron Critchfield and his staff put out an alternative on the Web, a magazine for those of us who can't afford or don't want the latest and greatest hardware. The most powerful test platform is a 486SX-33, and products are tested on 386s, too. The articles are well written, pay attention to the needs of the user, cover the types of software most people need, and reader (real user!) submissions are also accepted. There's also a nice list of links to Windows software and hardware vendors, and other Windows resources. —(L.S.)

KEY NEWSGROUP **comp.os.ms-windows.misc** URL▶ http://www.eskimo.com/~scrufcat/wr.html

Help Installing OS/2

Frank McKenney's Warp Installation Notes Jump **2079**

Nothing's more difficult or intimidating than installing a new operating system. There's help here, provided you follow Frank McKenney's admonition to read the documentation first. It's a critical step that's too often skipped, and while you can get away with it with some application software, you can't with an operating system. Unless you read at least the "Getting Started" section of the Warp manual, you'll have trouble understanding the tips Frank offers, as clear as he makes them. —(L.S.)

KEY NEWSGROUP **comp.os.os2** URL ▶ http://www.zeta.org.au/~jon/McKenney/mckftips.html

OS/2 Tips & Tricks

Stupid OS/2 Tricks Jump **2077** 

These aren't really stupid tricks. Many of them, in fact, are rather clever, and all of them very useful. Melissa Woo of the Champaign-Urbana OS/2 Users Group has done an admirable job of compiling dozens of tips that will help anyone get the most out of OS/2. The list is always growing, thanks to submissions from readers. —(L.S.)

KEY NEWSGROUP **comp.os.os2** URL ▶ http://gopher.ag.uiuc.edu/WWW/OS2/tricks.html

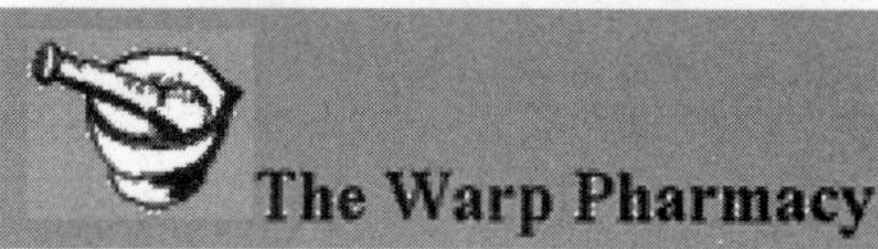

Troubleshooting OS/2

The Warp Pharmacy Jump **2078** 

Jon Seymour of Australia, aided by maintainers of mirror sites around the world, uses an aura of humor to mitigate the frustration of users having problems with Warp. "Tonics" are organized by hardware item and software, as well as by symptom, so finding the cure you need is relatively simple. While the organization may have a light touch, the information is presented clearly and in depth. If you've solved a problem yourself, submit it, and if you consider yourself something of an expert, watch the Wanted section to see if you can help the Pharmacists. When you first visit this site, go to the Mirrors section to find the site closest to you. You'll get faster connections and avoid overloading the main site. —(L.S.)

KEY NEWSGROUP **comp.os.os2** URL ▶ http://www.zeta.org.au/~jon/SwitchedWarpPharmacy.html

UNIX for Your PC

Welcome to the Linux Home Page Jump **2080** 

It's powerful. It's UNIX. It's free! Written by Linus Torvalds, Linux is a full UNIX operating system for 386 and 486 PCs. This is the home page for Linux worldwide, with documentation, FAQs and how-tos, FTP links, newsgroup pointers, and links to other Linux home pages. If you want UNIX on your PC, this is an excellent starting point. —(L.S.)

KEY NEWSGROUP **comp.os.linux** URL ▶ http://www.linux.org/

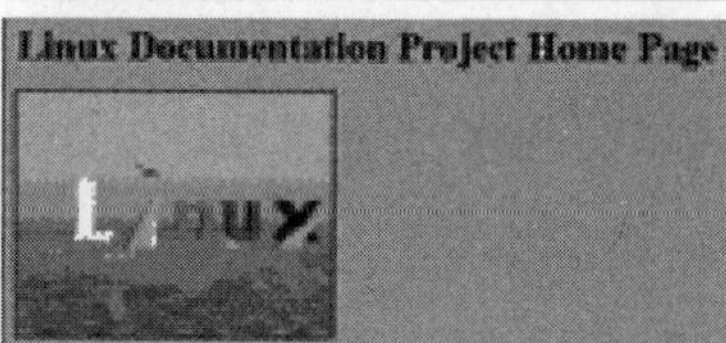

(Almost) All the Linux in the World

Linux Documentation Project Jump **2081** 

Matt Welsh and a band of loosely-organized Net volunteers are working to assemble the canonical archive of Linux documentation. While this goes on, this page of links and content lets you access what's been done so far, as well as other sources of Linux documentation and help. Whether it's how-tos, manuals, links to other pages, or FAQs, the information is here or there's a link. The What's New section makes it easy to keep up with changes, and a searchable archive of the Linux announcement newsgroup is planned. —(L.S.)

KEY NEWSGROUP **comp.os.linux** URL ▶ http://sunsite.unc.edu/mdw/linux.html#general

Linux Software Resource

Linux Software Map Jump **2082** 

This is a browsable database of Linux software that's also searchable by keyword and title. Converted to hypertext and maintained as a Web page by Thomas Boutell from data maintained by Lars Wirzenius, this listing of more than 1,800 titles is probably the most comprehensive database of Linux software on the Web. While there are no direct FTP links, each entry tells you where you can find the software, along with vital statistics about its function, author, and license terms. —(L.S.)

KEY NEWSGROUP **comp.os.linux.** URL ▶ http://siva.cshl.org/lsm/lsm.html

Help for Windows NT Users & Developers

The Windows NT Resource Center Jump 2241

This excellent resource is the Web home for consultants and developers, as well as users, of the Windows NT operating system. Dave Baker has created a consultant's database, compiled a list of links to NT FTP sites, including a section on new NT software. The best thing Dave did, though, was to put the NT error message database online as a searchable database. Especially for users who don't have a copy of the NT Resource Kit for developers, this feature can be invaluable in identifying and resolving errors. —(L.S.)

KEY NEWSGROUP **comp.os.mswindows.nt.misc** URL▶ http://www.bhs.com/winnt/resources.html

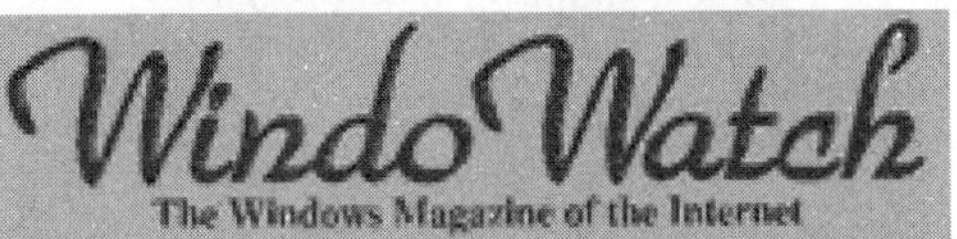

Windows User Magazine

WindoWatch Jump 2607

CONTENT

Here's a well-written, independent resource for Windows tutorials, news and product reviews. As it's an Internet-only publication, there's also an emphasis on Winsock applications and Windows-related surfing. Unlike many online magazines, the articles here are in-depth, often incisive, and always helpful. One feature from the current issue is available for viewing with a hyperlink, but to read the whole magazine, you need to download the ASCII, Readroom or Adobe PDF versions. An alternative is to use the links here to download the free Acrobat Reader and configure it as a helper application so you can read the magazine online. —(L.S.)

KEY NEWSGROUP **comp.os.ms-windows.misc** URL▶ http://www.channel1.com/users/winwatch/WindoWatch.html

The World of Windows (95)

Windows 95 Info Page Jump 2609

The 32-bit Windows 95 operating system is now available to the masses, offering terrific improvements over the old 16-bit Windows 3.1 and creating massive headaches as you try to upgrade, debug and generally get used to a totally new system. In anticipation of the great event, and to help those with the beta version, Mark Leary assembled this page. It begins with excellent FAQs on Windows 95 and continues with a lengthy list of links to virtually everything about the OS that can be found on the Web, including articles of hints and tips for getting up and running quickly. If you're planning to upgrade, get to this page as soon as possible—start reading! —(L.S.)

KEY NEWSGROUP **comp.os.ms-windows.misc** URL▶ http://www.tiac.net/users/snipe/win95home.html

Shareware Archives

Shareware.com's Big Shareware Site

SHAREWARE.COM Jump 5732

LINKS

It doesn't seem very long ago that the only way to find a particular shareware title on the Net was to fight your way through the obtuse world of FTP and Gopher sites. Sometimes you found what you wanted, and sometimes you found something else altogether. Those days are long gone for most of us, of course, but the problem still remains: How do you find—and find quickly—that piece of shareware you read about six months ago. You know, the one that allows you to read your Netscape cache files and lets you revisit the sites you visited last week? Easy. You sign onto SHAREWARE.COM, go to one of the search options (quick, simple, or power, depending on what you know and what you need), enter a few keywords and wait for the results. And the results are a list of up to a couple dozen choices, and from sites just about anywhere in the world where you can then link to find the software in question. These sites are even performance-rated, so you'll have a pretty good idea if you're likely to get through to the site in the first place. And that's not all. If you'd rather just browse, you can pick the Title of the Day or New Arrivals, and you're bound to stumble onto something you want but may not really need. But that's why we all go to shareware sites anyway, isn't it? —(J.P.)

URL▶ http://www.shareware.com/

ClNet's Demo Software Download Site

download.com Jump 5791 

The newest kid on the download block—specifically featuring downloadable demo, commercial, and vertical market applications—is also one of the best. C|NET, the big Web news operation, and owners of SHAREWARE.COM, has these things down to a fine art by now so we didn't expect any shortcomings in their handling of software downloads. In fact, you might not even notice one of their best innovations, the ability to determine, while downloading, what type of the system you're using. If it's a Mac you'll be taken directly to the Mac software pages, or to the PC section if you're using a PC. (You can of course switch to the other platform at any time). And once there, of course, you'll be able to take advantage of the great search menu—quick, simple or power—to find whatever you're looking for. And odds are if you're looking for it you'll find it here. In fact it's worth dropping in every few days just to check out their newest titles section. —(J.P.)

KEY NEWSGROUP comp.misc URL▸ http://www.download.com/

Dave Central's Shareware Archive

Dave Central Software Archive Jump 5773 

If you're looking for a well-organized collection of shareware software, look no further than Dave Franklin's Dave Central Software Archive. In addition to his nicely-organized main site, Dave has a list of 25 hot software titles and he updates the list daily. And the list is indeed hot; you'll find plenty here you've been looking for—and even more you may not have seen yet. And the archive itself is no slouch when it comes to software. Content areas include Home, Audio, Conferencing, Connectivity, E-mail, FTP, Java, VRML, Web Authoring, and much more. And you can sign up for e-mailed updates to keep up on Dave's latest additions —(J.P.)

URL▸ http://www.davecentral.com/index.html

Shareware Galore!

Jumbo! - ShareWare ShareWare ShareWare!!! Jump 7245 

When Jumbo says he's got the Web's biggest shareware site, Jumbo is right! By using the site's search program, you can select the program you need from the nearly 24,000 shareware titles featured here, divided into six main subject categories: business, games, home and personal, programming, utilities, and words/graphics. Jumbo has shareware for everyone: Mac, DOS, Windows, OS/2 and Unix owners. A nice feature is the shareware product description that you can read before deciding to download. As well, Jumbo presents information on how to install and run the programs you've downloaded. —(E.v.B.)

KEY NEWSGROUP alt.comp.shareware URL▸ http://www.jumbo.com/

Gamelan: The Web's Biggest Java Site

Gamelan Jump 5816 CONTENT

Gamelan is well-known as one of the Web's biggest hot spots for Java, a computer programming language that can be used to create small applications known as "applets," that appear on many Web pages, and allow these applications to run on any computer or operating system via the Internet. Their directory of programs looks a lot like any shareware directory, with plenty of games, specialized calculators, and vertical market applications to keep your browser hopping for hours. In addition to their large and growing collection of freely-available Java "apps," other links on the Gamelan site give you plenty of supplemental information and links on one of the Web's most fascinating and important new technological developments. —(J.P.)

URL▸ http://www-c.gamelan.com/index.shtml

TUCOWS: The "Udderly Incredible" Shareware Site

TUCOWS Jump **5750** 

Shareware authors better make sure their software titles are up to snuff before they submit them to TUCOWS, the Web's "udderly incredible shareware center." The fine folks at TUCOWS don't believe that reviews of bad software really help anyone at all. So they don't publish them at all. So if they review a new piece of shareware software and it receives a rating of under three cows, don't expect to find it here. But you will find just about everything else for just about every PC platform. The site is fully searchable, or you can browse by newest entries, or by platform. They also have a few dozen "mirror" sites, located in virtually every location in the world, which makes the downloading from this service more reliable than other shareware archives, most of the time. If you don't find it here, maybe it's not worth finding at all. —(J.P.)

KEY NEWSGROUP **alt.comp.shareware** URL▸ http://www.tucows.com/

THE SHAREWARE SHOP

The Shareware Internet Companion

The Shareware Shop Jump **5819** 

The Shareware Shop is another shareware archive, but with a few additional and interesting features. What makes it different from many other shareware sites both large and small is this site's "Shareware NewsWire." It's an interactive tool that brings you the latest shareware downloads and news while you surf the Internet. And it's updated every 10 minutes! Can you believe there'd be that much news? You can also search this site's database of over 40,000 programs from all over the Internet, plus their reviews on 1,000 specially-selected titles. —(J.P.)

KEY NEWSGROUP **comp.misc** URL▸ http://www.bsoftware.com/share.htm

Children's Software and More!

Software for Babies and Toddlers

Children's Software and More Jump **5761** 

While there are plenty of places to download shareware and demo software for kids, it wasn't until we saw this site, created by talented software author Grace Sylvan, that we realized that there are few sites that cater to the needs of not just kids, but toddlers as well. Toddlers are people, too, after all, and in this computer-driven world it stands to reason that the earlier they get their hands on a mouse the faster they'll learn all the rest. So if you're looking for such software, here is the place to start. The products (mostly shareware but some others as well), are divided into age-group categories: babies, beginners, ages 2-5, 4-8, and 8 and up. Each section contains software appropriate for that particular age group, some educational, others just for fun. And there's plenty more to explore, including a section for parents and teachers. And the site is mirrored in the U.S., U.K., and Russia! —(J.P.)

KEY NEWSGROUP **alt.comp.shareware** URL▸ http://www.gamesdomain.com/tigger/

Windows Freeware Magazine

Freeware Favorites Jump **3714** 

Kudos to the creator of this site for a great method of delivering freeware. What is freeware? Software programs available at no charge. The programs offered here are also thoroughly reviewed and described. Each issue of Freeware Favorites covers three or four Windows 3.x freeware programs, and includes graphics so you can see exactly what you're getting. Although you may not see a large quantity of offerings, you will get well-tested, quality freeware programs. —(N.F.)

KEY NEWSGROUP URL▸ http://www.execpc.com/~jeffo/webdes/frefavmn.html

Well-Indexed Windows Software Archives at Indiana University

The Indiana Archive Jump **0152** CONTENT

A massive, well-organized and cataloged shareware archive containing over 600 megabytes of public domain and shareware software for Windows-based personal computers, this very popular Net software archive should be your first stop when you're looking for good Windows software on the Net. Applications cover software for video, fonts, programming, demos, and templates—a wide range of useful and interesting software, all of it well organized and annotated. —(E.G.)

KEY NEWSGROUP **comp.os.ms-windows.advocacy** URL▶ http://emwac.ed.ac.uk/html/indiana/top.html

Windows NT Shareware

RMWNTUG Map Tour Jump **0132**

A well-done Windows NT shareware archive info and news Web site developed by the Rocky Mountain Windows NT Users Group. —(E.G.)

KEY NEWSGROUP **comp.windows.misc** URL▶ http://budman.cmdl.noaa.gov/RMWNTUG/RMWNTUG.HTM

Where's That Software?

Archie Request Form Jump **2019**

Archie is a searchable database of Net-based anonymous FTP sites and their contents. On this page, Guy Brooker and Martijn Koster offer a fill-in form to narrow the parameters and make the Archie search as quick and as efficient as possible. If you don't know the exact name of the file, you can search by partial filename. And if your browser doesn't support forms, you can still use Archie from this page. —(L.S.)

KEY NEWSGROUP **comp.archives** URL▶ http://hoohoo.ncsa.uiuc.edu/archie.html

All the Shareware in the World

Shase Virtual Shareware Library Jump **2020**

Updated regularly by Ziga Turk, this catalog of more than 60,000 shareware titles from the 15 largest archives will help you find and download software for most personal computers and operating systems. And you don't need to know the filename, either. If you're looking for a type of software and want to see what's available, this page will search file descriptions for you, so you can see what's available and download whatever looks good. If you just want to see what's new, you can see the latest additions to the archives automatically, or key in the date of your last visit and see the files added since that time. —(L.S.)

KEY NEWSGROUP **comp.archives** URL▶ http://www.fagg.uni-lj.si/SHASE/

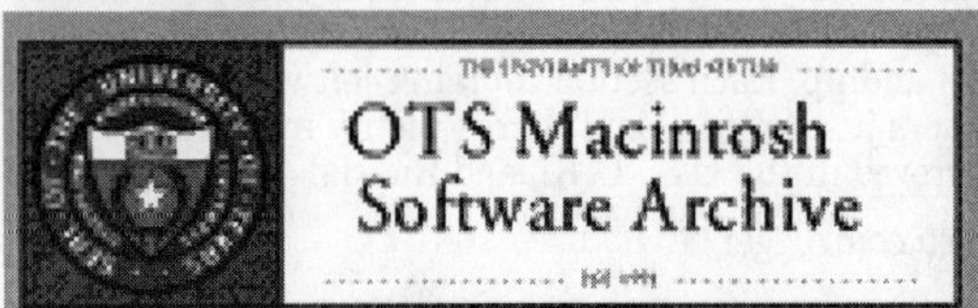

The Best Mac Software Archive

OTS/Mac Software Archive Jump **2023**

Chris Johnson has created one of the most attractive and easy-to-navigate set of pages on the World Wide Web, a demonstration of how it can—and should—be done. The archive is organized by software type, from antivirus programs to utilities. It also includes linked indices by author, date, and product linked. Much more than mere links, every file archived has the name and address of the author, cost and license terms, the master FTP site, file size, and a clear and concise description of its function. And, of course, you can also download the file. The archive is updated regularly, and there's a page listing all the recent additions. —(L.S.)

KEY NEWSGROUP **comp.archives** URL▶ http://wwwhost.ots.utexas.edu/mac/main.html

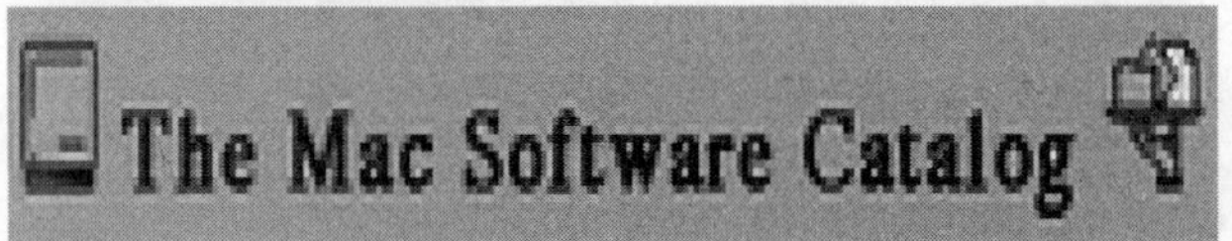

All The Macintosh Software that's Fit to Download

The Macintosh Software Catalog Jump **4077**

Brought to you by Nexor and maintained by Martin Koster, this site brings you a brilliant Web interface to the huge University of Michigan Macintosh software archive. You can browse through the directories or perform a

search for a specific piece of software, and then download it straight to your computer. A very user-friendly way for Mac users to find software on the Web. —(R.B.)

KEY NEWSGROUP **comp.sys.mac.** URL▶ http://pubweb.nexor.co.uk/public/mac/archive/welcome.html

Web Page Development

Web Developer's Massive Resource Library

Web Developer's Virtual Library Jump **5838**

If you've thought about creating your own home page, or if you're a skilled Web developer scouting for new utilities and tips, here's the spot for you. You could call this a do-it-yourself site, except that you don't have to do it all yourself because someone else has already done the legwork of gathering all the major Web development links, utilities, and online tutorials just for you. If you've got a question about authoring, what software to use, how to create a site map, or just about anything else, the answers are here. And it's all set up in easy-to-access, straightforward site presentation. —(J.P.)

KEY NEWSGROUP **comp.infosystems.www.developers** URL▶ http://www.stars.com/

Making Transparent & Interlaced GIF Images

Transparent/Interlaced GIF Resource Jump **2086**

If you're looking to learn how to create transparent or interlaced GIFs, Adam Bernstein has created the first, and so far only, comprehensive page of links covering these subjects. There are links to FAQs, tutorials, and software for PC, Macintosh, and UNIX machines. There are even links to services that will do some of the work for you. It's updated regularly, so if the subject interests you, but you don't want to read through the newsgroups looking for tips, keep this page on your bookmark list (there's also the world's ugliest transparent GIF at the top. One supposes it's a reflection of Adam's sense of humor. It certainly doesn't reflect the value of the page!). —(L.S.)

KEY NEWSGROUP **alt.graphics.pixutils** URL▶ http://dragon.jpl.nasa.gov/~adam/transparent.html#Disavowal

Getting Your Home Page Linked on the Web

Pointers to Pointers Jump **2117**

This list of links to pages that will link to your home page simplifies the process of letting the Web world know about your site. Just click on the ones you think are appropriate, and you'll be taken to the section of the page that lets you register yours. It's an easy way to be sure you don't miss any opportunity to tell the world, or just those parts of it you care about, that your page is up and ready. For good measure, there's also a list of newsgroups that take new Web site announcements. —(L.S.)

KEY NEWSGROUP **comp.infosystems.www.announce** URL▶ http://www.homecom.com/global/pointers.html

Transparent GIFs Made Easy

TransWeb Transparent GIF Service Jump **2085**

No matter how easy they make it sound, the mavens on the newsgroups can't make transparent GIFs for you. But TransWeb can—and will. This is a free service from the MIT Student Information Processing Board, and it makes creating a transparent GIF as easy as clicking on an image map. All you do is input the URL for the image, wait for the system to load it, and select the color you want made transparent by clicking on it. If your Web browser can't handle image maps, there's a forms-based page, too, but it's a bit more complicated. —(L.S.)

KEY NEWSGROUP **alt.graphics.pixutils** URL▶ http://www.mit.edu:8001/transweb.html

Creating Web Page Documents: HTML

Creating HTML Documents Jump **0133**

Want to create your own Web site? It's easier than you think! Using a coding scheme called Hypertext Markup Language (HTML) you can set up your written text files and include graphics to make your content available on the Web. "Coding" your documents with HTML involves not much more than inserting specific text specification commands within brackets to define headlines, links and other Web features in your text files—and it's much easier than it sounds! This site is a good starting point for learning more about creating your own Web site with its publications, "A Beginners Guide to HTML," "A Beginners Guide to URLs," and "HTML Editors and Converters." So, if you're hooked on the Web and you'd like to go the next step by creating your own Web site, here's the place to start. —(E.G.)

KEY NEWSGROUP comp.infosystems.www.providers

URL▶ http://www.ncsa.uiuc.edu:80/SDG/Software/Mosaic/Docs/d2-htmlinfo.html

Net Tech Products for Web Builders

Trel — Commercial Internet Product Finder

Jump 7239

Want to protect your server from unwanted guests, and need the latest information on firewalls? Come to Trel, where you can browse its database of hundreds of commercial Internet products, read product descriptions, and then link to the vendor's Web site for further information. This one-stop-shopping database contains information on news readers, VRML products, Gopher servers, censoring software, and many, many more subject areas. A value-added feature is a newsletter containing the latest news on a wide range of Internet tech topics. —(E.v.B.)

KEY NEWSGROUP biz.misc URL▶ http://www.lpac.ac.uk/Trel/

Web Page Hypertext Writer's Style Guide

Style Guide for On-line Hypertext Jump 0135

Tim Berners-Lee, the co-developer of HTML, produces this excellent guide, covering the new art and craft of Web page design. This well-written and accessible guide contains many helpful pointers for Web page designers and writers of all skill levels, covering such topics as how to include links within text for better readability, developing device-independent Web pages, informing your reader, Web etiquette, and links to useful background reading related to Web page creation. A thoughtful, interesting treatise on writing for the new Web media. —(E.G.)

KEY NEWSGROUP comp.infosystems.www. providers

URL▶ http://www11.w3.org/hypertext/WWW/Provider/Style/Overview.html

HTML HyperEdit: Windows Web Page Editor

HTML HyperEdit Jump 0141

Author Steve Hancock's home page for downloading his popular Windows-based Web page HTML editor. —(E.G.)

KEY NEWSGROUP comp.infosystems.www.providers

URL▶ http://www.curtin.edu.au/curtin/dept/cc/packages/htmledit/home.html

WYSIWYG HTML UNIX Editor

City University, HTML Editor Jump 0143

Home page for downloading Nick Williams' UNIX-based HTML Web page creation program, a freeware UNIX HTML editor. —(E.G.)

KEY NEWSGROUP comp.infosystems.www.providers URL▶ http://web.cs.city.ac.uk:80/homes/njw/htmltext/htmltext.html

HTML Writers of the World, Unite!

The HTML Writers Guild Homepage

Jump 5105

The HTML Writers Guild is a cooperative international organization of people involved in all aspects of creating, developing, and maintaining World-Wide Web pages and services. The Guild pages feature links to members' home pages, a selection of how-to and style guides, an FAQ, and info on how you can join the Guild. You can access their archives, which include documents, graphics, scripts and utilities of the Guild. There are member lists here, and of special interest, sources for Web page creation. Also, you can find a list of conferences and online journals. —(S.B.)

URL▶ http://www.mindspring.com/guild/

Web Page Creation Tips

Elements of HTML Style Jump 0134 

Web page creator Jonathan Cohen's interesting and informative article with advice for better design and organization of Web pages. Good technical tips for beginning Web page creators in this exciting new communications medium! —(E.G.)

URL▸ http://bookweb.cwis.uci.edu:8042/Staff/StyleGuide.html

HTML Writer: Web Page Creation Software for Windows

HTML Writer Home Page Jump 0138 

Author Kris Nosack's home page for his popular Windows-based Web page freeware editor, HTML Writer, with links for downloading this program also available here. —(E.G.)

KEY NEWSGROUP **comp.infosystems.www.providers**

URL▸ http://lal.cs.byu.edu:80/htmlwrit/htmlwrit.html

Macintosh Web Site Servers: MacHTTP Software

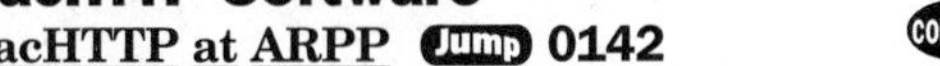

MacHTTP at ARPP Jump 0142 CONTENT

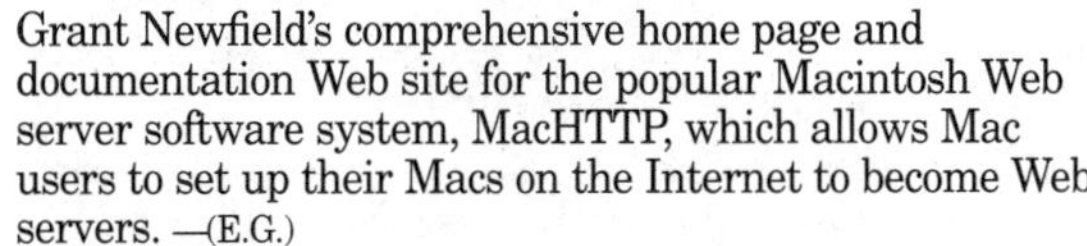

Grant Newfield's comprehensive home page and documentation Web site for the popular Macintosh Web server software system, MacHTTP, which allows Mac users to set up their Macs on the Internet to become Web servers. —(E.G.)

KEY NEWSGROUP **comp.infosystems.www.providers**

URL▸ http://arpp1.carleton.ca/machttp/

▲ *Vintage computer data center, from* **Virtual Image Archive**, *at* Jump **73115**.

Icon Searching on the Web

Image Finder Jump 2058 

Looking for a picture, but don't want to wade through archive file lists or hundreds of Web graphics pages? Robert Hartill has the answer. He's created a search engine that lets you search for images by filename, file description, and type. You can also narrow your search by using more than one of the criteria, or just browse everything by using one of the three. However you do it, it's one of the most painless ways to search for images on the Web. —(L.S.)

KEY NEWSGROUP **alt.graphics** URL▸ http://www.cm.cf.ac.uk/Misc/wustl.html

Browsable Icon Archives

Department of Computer Science: Icon Browser Jump 0188 

Another extensive collection of Web page icons, buttons and sample graphics, maintained by Gioacchino La Vecchia. You can view small "thumbnail" images of all icons contained in this archive; then select the ones you'd like to download for use in your own Web pages—a great way to see the wealth of icon images available for Web page creators! —(E.G.)

KEY NEWSGROUP **comp.infosystems.www.providers** URL▸ http://www.di.unipi.it/iconbrowser/icons.html

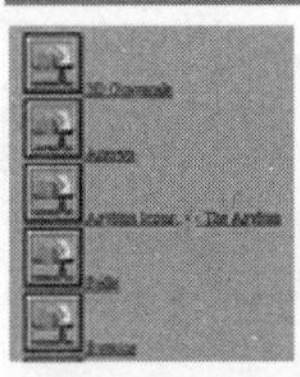

Icons Libraries for Web Page Creators

Daniel's Icon Archive  Jump 0184 CONTENT

If you're learning how to create your own Web pages, Daniel McCoy's Icon Archive is your one-stop Web link for all your Web icon needs! Dan's archive, widely acknowledged by top Web page creators to be the best, puts a mind-blowing collection of nearly 5,000 icons within easy reach. There are icons, buttons, lines, arrows, and more for just about any visual Web page application. You can even download the whole works and create your own personal icon library (better have plenty of hard disk, though—the entire collection takes up 12 megabytes). Dan's library includes many of those snappy icons, buttons, lines, and other doo-dads you'll see on all the Web sites you visit, so if you want to make your own Web site look first-rate, start with the icons you'll see here! —(E.G.)

KEY NEWSGROUP comp.infosystems.www.providers
URL ▶ http://www.jsc.nasa.gov/~mccoy/Icons/index.html

▲ *"The Time Tunnel," from* Hype! International, *at* Jump **2183**.

Hip Web Icons: Browsable Archive

Virtual Icon Collection Jump 0189 

A neat, browsable collection of Web icons, graphic files, lines and buttons, featuring many of those neat buttons and icons you've been seeing on some of the Web's best-designed pages, all of which can be viewed directly on-screen in this extensive icon archive at the University of Kansas. —(E.G.)

KEY NEWSGROUP comp.infosystems.www.providers URL ▶ http://inls.ucsd.edu/y/OhBoy/icons.html

Get Your Home Page on the Web

HomePage Publisher Jump 2059 

It's hard to put a home page on the Web if you don't have access to a Web server. Doug Stevenson, a student at Ohio State University and general Web altruist, gives the server-deprived the opportunity to publish a home page free of charge. The how-to instructions are, in typical Doug fashion, complete and easy to follow. You can create a home page online using his forms-based page creator, or create it on your machine and e-mail it. This free service is extremely popular, so expect to wait to have your page included. —(L.S.)

KEY NEWSGROUP comp.infosystems.www.users URL ▶ http://www-bprc.mps.ohio-state.edu/HomePage/

Web Page Development & Design Tips

Index to My Articles on Webspace Design Jump 2087 

Surf the Web for any length of time, and you'll start wanting to put up your own pages. While it's relatively simple to create a Web page, it's more difficult to create a Webspace that functions well. Jim Hurley shares his experience to give you tips, techniques, and ideas that will make your pages worth visiting. He goes beyond the usual "how to write" stuff and talks about how to read and use log files to make page viewing better, tips for naming links in your pages, and using templates to aid your design. —(L.S.)

KEY NEWSGROUP comp.infosystems.www.providers URL ▶ http://www.webcom.com/~hurleyj/article/index.html

Web Authoring Jump Start

Crash Course on Writing Documents for the Web Jump **2118**

HTML isn't simple, but it's not rocket science, either. Anyone can create a Web page quickly and easily, especially if they start with this article. Written by Eamonn Sullivan for the folks at PC Week Labs, it's a quick overview and how-to of the most important concepts: headings, body text, links, and images. Once you've mastered these, you can go on to more complex HTML tagging—or not, because the information here is all most people will need. —(L.S.)

KEY NEWSGROUP **alt.hypertext** URL▶ http://www.pcweek.ziff.com/~eamonn/crash_course.html

So, You Wanna Be a Webmaster?

Running a WWW Service Jump **2137**

This everything-you-need-to-know handbook by Brian Kelly is an excellent resource for the beginning Webmaster. In addition to answering all the hows of setting up a Web site, it also gives you information on Web browsers, HTML writing, graphics, and other Web-based services and capabilities. It's just as good a resource for the Web surfer, or the person that just wants to know how things work. And even if you don't care, the appendices, with links to Web topic mailing lists, newsgroups, and general resources, are valuable additions to anyone's bookmark list. There are several mirror sites, so once you link to this page, find the one that's closest to you for the fastest, most reliable connection for future visits. —(L.S.)

KEY NEWSGROUP **comp.infosystems.www.providers** URL▶ http://scholar2.lib.vt.edu/handbook/handbook.html

Replacing the GIF Standard

HA990.80 Jump **2181**

With the patent holder (Unisys) now demanding royalties for commercial use of GIF graphics compression, the future of GIF as an Internet graphics standard is in doubt. No one knows yet what will happen, but Jeremy Wohl has taken steps by offering information about FGF, the Free Graphics Format, as a replacement. If you want to get a head start, this page describes the format and its features, and includes links to download a GIF-to-FGF converter. —(L.S.)

KEY NEWSGROUP **comp.graphics** URL▶ http://twinbrook.cis.uab.edu:70/U/HA990.80

Designing Web Pages

Washington's Leading Internet Developers, Presence Providers, and Trainers. Jump **5149**

If you want to keep up on the latest developments in creating Web home pages, color design, and electronic publishing, jump to this site and get their free online newsletter, HTML & CGI News. In this Web site's index, there are also links to loads of info on CGI scripts, forms, HTML 3.0, HTML editors, and other information of interest if you're a more advanced Web page builder. —(S.B.)

URL▶ http://www.clark.net/pub/jrinker/rinker.html

"March Madness" is sweeping through cyberspace.

When they're not glued to the TV screen, increasing numbers of college basketball fans are following their favorite teams on the Internet computer network.

For college hoops junkies, it's like being wired directly into the tournament press office. Several free Internet-based services are now offering instant, around-the-clock access to NCAA Tournament scores and stories and statistics about games.

Some very big players in the sports media business—CBS and ESPN among them—are helping push the new online approach.

"We recognize that there's a world out there that not everybody knows about. We want to be on the leading edge of this as much as we can," said Jim Byrne, director of marketing communications for CBS.

John M. Moran, "For Fans, Internet Is Alternate Screen," ***The Hartford Courant***

Sports Talk & Recreation

Like you, many Web site authors have active lives beyond the Internet. On the Web, they share their information, experiences, and other resources on a wide variety of outdoor sports and recreational activities. For pro sports fans, the Web is also your instant source for news, scores and fan talk.

News, Scores, and Info for Sports Fans

There are also Web sites devoted to news, information, and rabid fan talk for every college and professional football, basketball, baseball, and hockey team, including up-to-the-minute sports scores and news, features, articles, photos, and other sports-minded attractions.

Sports and Outdoor Recreation for Active People

Many talented Web authors have provided the same rich information content and attention to detail to sports and recreation-minded Web pages as to those found on other Web sites on many other subjects. Whether you ride a bike, climb a mountain, walk along a wooded trail, or jump out of an airplane, there's a Web site for you, featuring large selections of original how-to information, articles, Q & A features, photos, and personal accounts. There's also plenty of good tips and advice on gear, equipment, supplies and related information, whatever the sporting activity.

In many cases, since individual Web authors do not yet have to moderate their editorial content to mollify editors and advertisers, the active sports and recreation-related advice you'll find on these Web sites can be refreshingly honest, unvarnished, and helpful, reflecting the real-world experiences of devoted adherents to any active sport.

Active Sports & Recreation

Women's Sports Pages

WWW Women's Sports Page Jump 2680

A fine example of simplicity and elegance of information design being more important than cool Web design alone, this page by Amy Smith takes on the job of collecting and organizing links to Web pages covering women and sports. The basic organization lists the links by sport, from baseball to waterskiing, and there are additional sections covering gender issues in sports and sports festivals. For the male chauvinists in the audience, the sheer number of links can be an education, as can visiting the pages that cover sports traditionally thought of as male-only—such as motor racing and boxing. —(L.S.)

KEY NEWSGROUP soc.women URL▶ http://fiat.gslis.utexas.edu/~lewisa/womsprt.html#issues

World Wide Web of Sports & Recreation Links Site

World Wide Web of Sports Jump 5606

It looks pretty odd at first. Not a picture in sight. No color. Just a few columns of words. And what words! Checkers, Boomerang, Curling, Darts, Footbag (?!?), and Rodeo. Turns out there is a reason why all these words have sprung up. Click on the word Walking (kid you not) and you'll be taken to another page that lists many other pages that talk about walking. And we'll warn you, there are many. Sounds hopeless, we know, but if you're ever out surfing the Web for a site dealing with shuffleboard (it could happen!) this is most certainly the place to start. —(J.P.)

URL▶ http://www.tns.lcs.mit.edu/cgi-bin/sports

Cyber Cycling Resources

Welcome to Specialized 2.0 Jump 7414

If you're into bicycles, link to the World Ride Web site created by Specialized Bicycle Components, Inc. Check their pages often for bike events, cycling news, new bike products, and online contests. As well, check their mountain bike trail directories, dealer directory home pages, and use their e-mail access to Specialized's engineers, pros, clubs and promotions. You can also explore the new bike trail preservation network that's forming in conjunction with the International Mountain Biking Association. Soon to come to this site are real-time chat, online riding demos, and a gallery of specialized prototypes and industrial design. —(E.v.B.)

KEY NEWSGROUP rec.bicycles.misc URL▶ http://www.specialized.com/bikes/

Bicycling & Bike Tips

The Reading Room Jump 0081

An interesting and informative collection of text and graphics files on bicycle commuting, physical training for cyclists, gear, sporting activities and touring, collected from Net newsgroups, mailing lists and material submitted by volunteer Netters. —(E.G.)

KEY NEWSGROUP rec.bicycles.misc URL▶ http://cycling.org:70/1/reading.room

Bicycle Racing Information

Racing Jump 0083

Bicycle racing tips, techniques and club events, compiled by George Theall. —(E.G.)

KEY NEWSGROUP rec.bicycles.racing URL▶ http://www.voicenet.com:80/1/leisure/sports/cycling/races

Competitive Cycling

VeloNews Jump 1520

VeloNews, a magazine devoted to all phases of biking, has combined all the competitive cycling information you'll ever want by way of links to this page. Created by Chris Rice, Tim Johnson, and Chas Chamberlain, and sponsored partly by Microsoft, this attractive site offers a calendar of upcoming races throughout the country, and reports the results as they come in. Want bike parts? Visit their

Images of the WOMBATS having tea ▲ outdoors and ▶ indoors ▶ and the seal of the WOMBATS, from **WOMBATS on the Web**, *at* Jump 7030.

classifieds. Want a free copy of their journal, books, videos, or just a simple racing T-shirt? You have your chance here. One of the more personable aspects of these pages is a report on the Microsoft Grand Prix, where you can see team profiles and interviews with the riders, and find out how you can join the race next year. The magazine is also looking for freelance writers, so if you're going to be racing, or enjoy the sport from any perspective, you, too, can be part of the fun. —(H.L.)

URL ▶ http://www.csn.net/VeloNews/

Mountain Biking in Style

WOMBATS on the Web Jump 7030

Live in California? Ride a mountain bike? Are you a woman? Well, if so, the Women's Mountain Bike and Tea Society—the WOMBATS—might fit you to a "T." Their home page leads you into the WOMBATS art gallery where you can see pictures of actual WOMBATS, where you can scan information on the club, read the latest issue of their well-written newsletter, or peddle into other interesting bike sites. —(E.v.B.)

URL ▶ http://www.wombats.org/

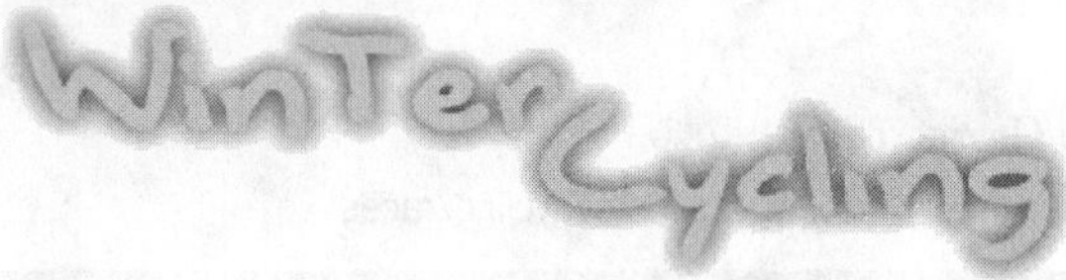

Winter Cycling Tips

Winter Cycling Jump 5692

It will probably come as no surprise to learn that Alaska "enjoys" about eight months of real winter every year. Eight months is a long time to hide indoors, and so perhaps it stands to reason that some folks in this region actively participate in winter sports. And one of the most popular ones, it turns out, is winter cycling. Now, needless to say, a day trip in the freezing cold of Alaska requires a certain attention to detail that might mean the difference between life and death. In the "Tech Tips" section of this site, created by All Weather Sports, we learn that drivers must pay attention to such various questions as what clothing to wear, differences in tires and lubricants, and much more. Good winter biking tips for those of us winter bikers in the "Lower 48," too. —(J.P.)

URL ▶ http://www.mosquitonet.com/~aws/

Wear a Helmet!

Bicycle Helmet Safety Institute
Jump 7029 CONTENT

Your mother always told you to wear a bicycle helmet—did you believe her? Well, here's official word on standards, models and other helmet-related information. Believe it. After reading this page, you will be convinced that just one head-related accident without the protection of a helmet could leave you permanently one brick short of a full load. —(E.v.B.)

KEY NEWSGROUP **rec.bicycles.misc**
URL ▶ http://www.bhsi.org/

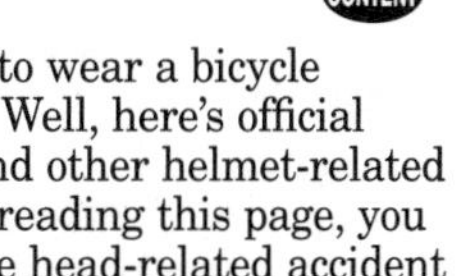

▲ *Airborne inline skater, from* **Skating the Infobahn**, *at* Jump **2567**.

Web Bicycling Resources

The WWW Bicycle Wain
Jump 0080 LINKS

A biker's information and news gold mine. Bryn Dole's excellent Web jump site features tons of bicycling-related links for news, how-to tips, racing events, pictures, club news and Net bicycling mailing lists, including extensive links to Net archives with all kinds of interesting articles on bicycling. —(E.G.)

KEY NEWSGROUP **rec.bicycles.misc** URL ▶ http://www.cs.purdue.edu/homes/dole/bike.html

Mountain Biking Links Page

n/a Jump 0082 LINKS

Web jump site with many interesting links to mountain biking trail information for many states, mountain biker news, and Net mountain biking text files. —(E.G.)

KEY NEWSGROUP **rec.bicycles.misc** URL ▶ http://xenon.stanford.edu/~rsf/mtn-bike.html

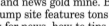

NBC Sports golf.com Golf Digest

Golf.com: The Golfer's Web Crossroads

golf.com
Jump 6776 CONTENT

From this polished, content-rich collaboration of NBC Sports and Golf Digest, you'll find results from virtually every golf tournament, including the PGA, LPGA and Nike challenges. Link to course maps and resorts, leaf through the pages of leading golf publications, or preview the new high-tech equipment golfers are using to shave their scores. This professionally-produced golfer's hub also features a live news ticker and a golfer's online chat area. —(L.T.)

KEY NEWSGROUP **rec.sport.golf** URL ▶ http://golf.com/

Everything for Golfers on the World Wide Web

GolfWeb Jump 3688 CONTENT

Who's the PGA Tour's all-time money leader? What are the latest Senior Tour standings? Need photos? Want a golf vacation? Interested in TV Listings? All of that and anything else golf you can think of is right here at GolfWeb. Once you've got this site on your hotlist, you won't need any other when it comes to golf. Regular columns, guest columns, directories of organizations, a library, courses, communities, resorts, and schools. Top flight! —(C.P.)

KEY NEWSGROUP **rec.sport.golf** URL ▶ http://www.golfweb.com/

The Golf Stop

iGolf - The Players' Exchange Jump 6008 CONTENT

A great Web stop for all things golf—standings, jokes, tips, course information, player facts. You name it, this site has it. From the leader boards to the library, you'll spend hours relaxing here. Created by InterZine Productions, iGolf is a prime example of a great interactive Web magazine—rich content, super graphics and multimedia—a great online read! This site is updated frequently, so plan on stopping in all the time. —(N.F.)

KEY NEWSGROUP **rec.sport.golf** URL▶ http://www.igolf.com/

Golfer's Information Center

The 19th Hole Jump 3689

Great information about current standings, links to various golf organizations (including the National Association of Left-Handed Golfers), a trading post and much more, including a great area with images for downloading, and some of the best golf graphics we've ever seen! Neat Web guestbook, too—you can leave your own message for every other golf fanatic who visits this site. —(C.P.)

KEY NEWSGROUP **rec.sport.golf** URL▶ http://www.tr-riscs.panam.edu/golf/19thhole.html

Foot-Launched Soaring

Hang Gliding WWW Server Jump 2326

There's so much information on this server, you could easily lose yourself here. It starts with a browsable image gallery, and a searchable archive of the hang glider's mailing list archive. It goes on to include every conceivable resource a hang glider or paraglider could wish for. Alec Proudfoot stores information for new pilots, including FAQs and lists of schools and clubs, offers QuickTime and MPEG movies, simulation software, glider design information, and includes a roster of hang gliding enthusiasts on the Internet that you can even add your name to. In the rare event that's not enough, come back when the monthly updates are posted, or use the links to hang glider club home pages, and servers for other air sports. —(L.S.)

KEY NEWSGROUP **rec.aviation.misc** URL▶ http://cougar.stanford.edu:7878/HGMPSHomePage.html

Climbing North America

Greg's Guide to the 50 Classics Jump 2723

Based on the book, *Fifty Classic Climbs of North America*, by Allen Steck and Steve Roper, this page by Greg Opland represents some of the greatest challenges climbers can find, the combination of adventure and character building that draws them to the sport. The material here is not intended to replace the guidebooks one should use before and during the climb, but the maps, tips, and other information here do, however, provide enough to help you decide which ones you may want to tackle. Greg is in the midst of climbing as many of the 50 as he can, and his reports of his experiences are also included. —(L.S.)

KEY NEWSGROUP **rec.climbing** URL▶ http://www.dtek.chalmers.se/Climbing/Guidebooks/NorthAmerica/FiftyClassics/

Walkabout

Volksmarch and Walking Index Jump 7039

Your boots made for walking? Well, then stroll over to the American Volkssport Association's home page on the Web for the latest information on conventions, literature, events and individual walking clubs. You can even download various walking-related images, too. —(E.v.B.)

KEY NEWSGROUP **misc.fitness** URL▶ http://www.teleport.com/~walking/

Climbing the Walls

The Climbing Archive! Jump 2211

Rock climbers of all stripes will find a home at this site maintained by Magnus Homann and Keith Amidon. Organized so it's easy to find what you want, there are guidebooks with climbing sites rated by difficulty, a directory for finding partners, and sections on climbing equipment and techniques. For more passive climbing entertainment, stories, songs, poems, and pictures are archived here, too. And if you don't feel like browsing, the contents are maintained on a WAIS database for fast searching by keyword. Submissions from other climbers on any related topic are encouraged; just see the submission guidelines to learn how to format your contributions. —(L.S.)

KEY NEWSGROUP **rec.climbing**

URL ▶ http://www.dtek.chalmers.se/Climbing/index.html

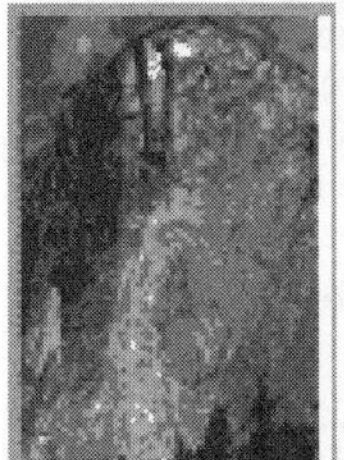

Climbing the Walls for Days

Big Wall Climbing Home Page Jump 2362 CONTENT

If you're looking for more challenges in your rock climbing, you're ready for the big walls. Big wall climbing takes on the challenge of huge rock faces, with the climbs taking multiple days and nights. John Middendorf gives you what you need to get started with information about equipment, difficulty, ratings, and specific climbing sites around the world. There also are pictures and stories of some of John's climbs, which communicate the sense of adventure, danger, and exhilaration of the sport. —(L.S.)

KEY NEWSGROUP **rec.climbing**

URL ▶ http://www.primenet.com/~midds/

▲ *Rock climber, via* **The Climbing Archive!**, *at* Jump 2211.

Hikers' and Walkers' Site

Hiking and Walking Home Page Jump 8550 LINKS

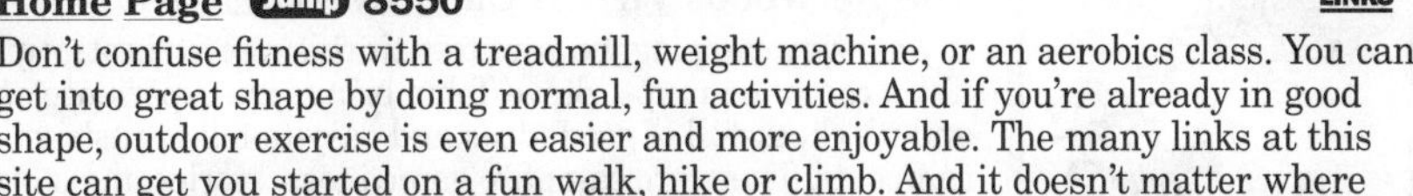

Don't confuse fitness with a treadmill, weight machine, or an aerobics class. You can get into great shape by doing normal, fun activities. And if you're already in good shape, outdoor exercise is even easier and more enjoyable. The many links at this site can get you started on a fun walk, hike or climb. And it doesn't matter where you live—the information is both national and local. The "Places to go hiking" page can get you to the National Park Service to find a new trail. "Walking resources" has links to events, publications, and tours. You will also find a very complete list of gear manufacturers who also have a page on the Web. —(R.B.)

URL ▶ http://www.teleport.com/~walking/hiking.html

Traveling with the Kitchen Sink

Campground OnLine Jump 7257 CONTENT

Ready to hit the open road, trailer bouncing behind you? Before you leave, why not check out these informative pages. You can browse through the campground directory, read newsletters for campers, find an RV rental store or a dealer near you, surf other RV and camping Web pages, and even find a schedule of RV trade shows. Not enough? Well, there's a great recipe for those sweet S'mores that will have you immediately loading the trailer and heading out to the nearest campfire. —(E.v.B.)

KEY NEWSGROUP **alt.rec.camping** URL ▶ http://www.channel1.com/users/brosius/

Information about our National Parks

Park Search Jump 2738 CONTENT

You can learn about almost 900 of our nation's parks and outdoor facilities, be they national, state, or local, with a simple search at this site created by the famous outdoors outfitters, L. L. Bean. Searchable by park name, activity, state or service, each listing gives you the facts you need to decide if it's a park you want to visit, along with photos and information to help you make your plans. —(L.S.)

KEY NEWSGROUP **rec.outdoors.national-parks** URL▶ http://www.llbean.com/parksearch/

As Big as All Outdoors

All Outdoors Jump **5882** 

Yes, it's as big as all outdoors and just as lively. And if you love the great outdoors, this is a great place to drop in and spend a couple of hours on a rainy day. It will take you that long to get through all the sites and links. There are eight monthly magazines here, three chat areas, hunting and fishing news updated daily, and an archive with hundreds of articles. You'll find other information on hunting and fishing, an extensive library, and 'of course' the links to fine magazines, including *The In-Fisherman*, *Sports Afield*, *Outdoor Daily*, and more. —(J.P.)

KEY NEWSGROUP **rec.outdoors. fishing** URL▶ http://www.alloutdoors.com/

The Great Outdoors from Outside Magazine

Outside Online Jump **7469** 

Outside Online presents the news of the outdoor life—from rock climbing, to the effect of federal budget problems on federal parks to skiing competitions. It also reviews equipment of all kinds from jeans to tents to map measuring devices. Its events section also covers a wide range of activities presented in article form. This Web version of the popular print magazine also features stories of hearty outdoor types—such as the family who sailed around the world or the two cyclists with the same goal. —(E.v.B.)

KEY NEWSGROUP **alt.rec.camping** URL▶ http://outside.starwave.com/outside/online/

Bring Your Own Marshmallows

The NetWoods Virtual Campsite Jump **2495** 

If you enjoy camping, be sure to visit this site for hints, tips, and activity ideas, especially if you camp in groups. Steve Tobin brings his experience as a scoutmaster to this page, and it's chock-full of good ideas and easy-to-follow instructions for making the most of your campouts. There are campfire game ideas, stories and storytelling tips, articles on choosing and using camping equipment, and recipes for campfire cooking. There also are suggestions for Scouting activities, but you don't need to be involved in Scouting to take advantage of what's here. Almost all of it is adaptable to any group or individual. —(L.S.)

KEY NEWSGROUP **rec.backcountry** URL▶ http://www.skypoint.com/members/srtobin/index.html

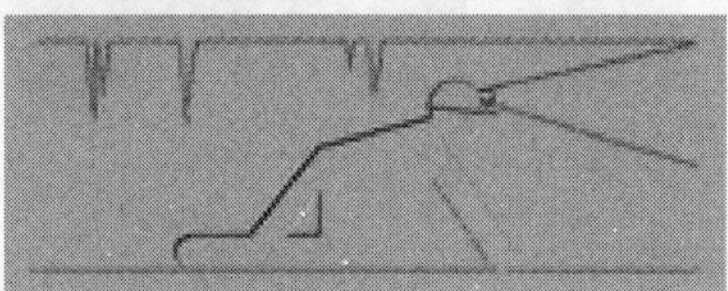

Caves & Caving

Speleology Server Home Page Jump **2545** 

Spelunking can be a very rugged sport, combining the physical challenges of climbing with the expertise of orienteering. It's also something of a science, since most of the excitement in caving is in exploring and discovering the myriad geological examples one finds only below the surface. For experienced cavers or tyros, this is the starting point for learning about caving and linking to caving resources on the Internet. There's information on caving equipment, cave surveys, archives of caving newsletters and periodicals, and links to the home pages of spelunkers worldwide. And if you just want to look (and not spelunk), there's an archive of excellent cave photos here, too. —(L.S.)

KEY NEWSGROUP **alt.caving** URL▶ http://speleology.cs.yale.edu/

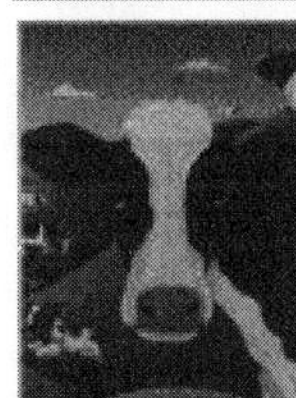

The Only Camping Guide You'll Ever Need

Skeeter's Camping Guide Jump 3673

A bit off the beaten trail, perhaps, but Skeeter's Camping Guide may well be the only backwoods survival guide you ever need. This site is stuffed full of good, common-sense information about how to survive in the deep dark forest—conveyed with sass and a chuckle. With pithy advice like: "Don't get lost, but if you are lost, remember that you're not lost, you've just misplaced the rest of the world..." Skeeter has also managed to hide some very useful, serious outdoors info among the jokes. —(C.P.)

KEY NEWSGROUP **rec.backcountry** URL ▸ http://www.cis.yale.edu:80/amstud/stibitch/stibma.html

The Great Outdoors

Sagi's Outdoor News, Arizona, Hunting, Fishing, Camping Jump 7156

This monthly newsletter brings the outdoors right into your computer. You can read fishing stories, learn the latest statistics on bear hunting, read about conservation activities, and download directions for building decoys. As well, you can search Sagi's helpful directories of skiing, camping, climbing, canoeing, and mountain biking destinations. Can't get enough fresh air? Stay outside a bit longer by exploring the links, also provided here, to other outdoor home pages. —(E.v.B.)

KEY NEWSGROUP **rec.backcountry** URL ▸ http://www.infop.com/outdoor/index.html

Help for Runner's Hurts

Dr. Pribut's Running Injuries Page Jump 2726

Runners have so many ways to injure themselves, it's a wonder they're ever healthy enough to pursue their sport. If you run, or are considering taking up the sport, use this page as a starting point and reference to prevent injuries and learn how to deal with them before they cut short your career. Maintained by podiatrist Dr. Stephen M. Pribut, who specializes in sports medicine and biomechanics, just about everything you would want or need to know is here. He covers the common runners' injuries and also discusses basic biomechanics so you can understand how to avoid them. Every other month he adds a new feature, such as shoe selection and cold-weather running or stretching, so runners should make his page a regular rest stop to keep apprised of how to be healthier in their sport. —(L.S.)

KEY NEWSGROUP **rec.running** URL ▸ http://www.clark.net/pub/pribut/spsport.html

The Runner's Column

Running With George Jump 7405

George Straznitskas likes to run and he likes to write about it too. Every Wednesday he uploads a column that covers important runner's info such as training tips, injury prevention, descriptions and evaluation of equipment, human interest stories about runners, or any other subject that touches the world of running. Don't worry if you miss a column, because George has archived all his past articles. —(E.v.B.)

KEY NEWSGROUP **rec.running** URL ▸ http://www.YBI.COM/run/index.html

Race You to the Corner!

The Running Page Jump 7035

Lace up those running shoes and speed over to Dennis Rears' page of running tips, clubs, upcoming races, publications, electronic newsgroups, and Rears' personal running statistics. Compare your running performance with that of other runners. Feeling a bit winded?—then be sure to read the Endurance Training Journal, also on this site. —(E.v.B.)

KEY NEWSGROUP **rec.running** URL ▸ http://polar.pica.army.mil/running.real/running.html

Inline Skating

Skating the Infobahn Jump 2567

Robert Schmunk calls his page the most comprehensive inline skating index on the Internet, and he's in no way immodest. You get an immediate idea of how well this site is organized by the links to Tony Chen's inline skating FAQ. You don't just get a link to the FAQ page, you get separate links for each section, so you can quickly get what you want without having to scan through one of the most extensive FAQs anywhere. You can also link directly to newsgroups, and find out about local and national clubs and organizations, speed skating, roller hockey, and extreme skating. Robert also compiles a list of images and sounds, events, safety and technical information, and links to other hotlists and directories. Each link is rated, from one to six starts, and new additions are highlighted, making navigation of this extensive site that much easier. —(L.S.)

KEY NEWSGROUP **rec.sport.skating.inline** URL http://www.panix.com/~rbs/Skate/

Figure Skaters' Web Resources

Figure Skating Home Page Jump 2569 CONTENT

While this page is designed primarily for competitors, there's a lot here for figure skating fans, too. Starting with the things of interests to skaters, Sandra Loosemore offers the figure skating FAQ, a link to Kevin Anderson's excellent page of movies and downloadable picture files to help people learn the difficult technical competition requirements, and assorted other links to help people develop and enhance their skills. For fans, there are links to pages covering the more famous figure skaters, a selection of interesting images, and an index of figure skating magazines. There's even a link to the Tonya Harding Fan Club page—for those looking for hints on how to get a little, er, "extra edge" in competitions! —(L.S.)

KEY NEWSGROUP **rec.sport.skating.ice.figure**

URL http://www.cs.yale.edu/HTML/YALE/CS/HyPlans/loosemore-sandra/skate.html

Scuba Diver's Web Resource

ScubaWorld Online Jump 5895

The background here is that lush green color of fresh warm water. You can almost feel the bubbles rising slowly to the surface. Dive in and discover a truly amazing array of information on scuba diving. You can begin your exploration with this site's bulletin board, where you can buy or sell gear, or chat with like-minded souls. Other site features include a links list of scuba clubs, followed by another for equipment and retailers. There are forums to visit and links to magazines, instructors and even news updates for sport divers. This a a great site, whether you are interested in scuba diving or not! —(J.P.)

KEY NEWSGROUP **rec.scuba** URL http://www.scubaworld.com/

SCUBA Web

Aquanaut Jump 2565

This Web page covers SCUBA diving, with reviews of diving equipment and dive destinations, a database of underwater wrecks, and listings of clubs and training organizations. You also can use this page as an easy entry point to the **rec.scuba** newsgroup, searching the group's archives by author or subject, as well as browsing recent postings. There's an image archive, tips on using video camcorders underwater, and a marketplace for buying and selling equipment, too. —(L.S.)

KEY NEWSGROUP **rec.scuba** URL http://www.terra.net/aquanaut/

Scuba Resources

Eric's SCUBA Page! Jump 7051 

Eric Lindquist obviously loves to explore the underwater world of Puget Sound, Washington. He has pulled together an interesting collection of scuba information: scuba gear is detailed, dive sites around the world are reviewed, organizations are listed, and major scuba Net sites are linked. You can even download pictures of Eric underwater. —(E.v.B.)

KEY NEWSGROUP **rec.scuba** URL ▸ http://diver.ocean.washington.edu/

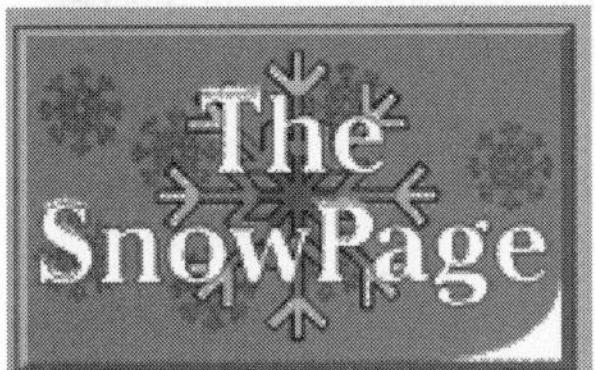

Hit the Slopes!

The Snow Page Jump 2005 

It's always winter somewhere for skiers, and Dan Homolka wants to be sure all you skiers have all the information you need to find that new powder. It's got everything you need to learn about and go skiing (Alpine and Nordic) or snowboarding. There are links to Net-based e-zines, resort reports, trail maps, stuff on snowboarding, commercial magazines, travel services and resorts, other Snow People, other Net resources, newsgroups and...well, it does seem to go on and on. If you're a snow sporter and you can't find a link here, it probably doesn't exist. Dan's even included a link to download the main graphic and buttons he uses to decorate his Web site. What a guy! —(L.S.)

KEY NEWSGROUP **rec.skiing** URL ▸ http://rmd-www.mr.ic.ac.uk/snow/snowpage.html

Plan That Ski Trip

Ski Maps! Jump 2006 

You've hoarded your vacation time, paid up the medical policy, and taken calcium supplements till your complexion is white as snow. You're ready to ski—but where? And what's the layout of the slopes when you get there? William C. Regli and the University of Maryland's Department of Computer Science can solve the dilemma with trail maps for U.S. and worldwide ski resorts. The maps are stored as JPEG files, so you can download and view or print them later on. Put them side-by-side to compare areas or plan your itinerary. Bring them with you so you don't have to depend on the kindness and print runs of the ski lodge. With the help of fellow skiers from around the world, this site is comprehensive. It also goes beyond serving maps to providing a very extensive list of links to commercial resorts, the **rec.skiing** FAQ, and pages maintained by other skiers. —(L.S.)

KEY NEWSGROUP **rec.skiiing** URL ▸ http://www.cs.umd.edu/~regli/ski.html

Big Tennis News & Resources Site

The Tennis Server Homepage Jump 6013 

The Tennis Server Homepage set a ratings record for the "Awesome Sports Site of the Month" recently, and for good reason. This is THE site for tennis fans and players alike. From regular monthly columns to tournament and player coverage, pictures and a great set of links to other stops on the Web, you'll find it all here. Put your name on the electronic mailing list and receive the monthly "Tennis Server INTERACTIVE" newsletter. Bookmark this one—you'll want to become a regular here. —(N.F.)

KEY NEWSGROUP **rec.sport.tennis** URL ▸ http://www.tennisserver.com/Tennis.html

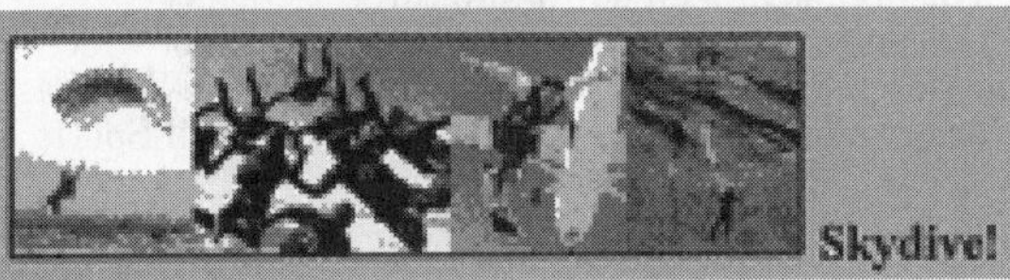

You Might as Well Jump!

Skydive Archive Jump 2113 

This must be the best Web site for skydiving information. After all, it was featured in the movie *Drop Zone*. Even without the endorsement of Hollywood moguls, it's clear that Bradley C. Spatz and Eric S. Johnson, with the help of many others, offer a comprehensive resource. There are online manuals to help you improve your skills, equipment information, FAA regulations, links to weather infomation and other skydiving pages, and the complete archives of **rec.skydiving**, going back to 1988. Of course, there also are movies and pictures, and a page of links to other jumpers charmingly titled "Geeks Who Skydive." —(L.S.)

KEY NEWSGROUP **rec.skydiving** URL▶ http://www.cis.ufl.edu/skydive/

Extreme Sports Center

HotWired: Adrenaline Jump **7304**

COMMERCE

Pump yourself up at *Wired Magazine*'s newest online site, Adrenaline. Never one for the mundane, *Wired* has created a multimedia extravaganza dedicated to alternative sports: surfing, river rafting, mountain biking, and rock climbing. News coverage, fantastic photos, and first-person accounts are sure to raise your blood pressure. Adrenaline also supports an interactive bulletin board where you can add your own sports experiences, like rocks to climb or mountains to conquer. —(E.v.B.)

KEY NEWSGROUP **rec.sport.misc** URL▶ http://www.hotwired.com/adrenaline/

Pigment Wars

Paintball Home Page (at warpig) Jump **2257**

Everything about paintball, with the possible exception of how to mix your own ammunition, can be found or accessed from these pages maintained by Steve Mitchell. There's a special section for novices, searchable newsgroup archives, articles on equipment, a technical reference, links to magazines, leagues and clubs, and a classifieds section for players looking for players in their area. You can even find out how to play paintball by e-mail. If that's not enough, use the links to other paintball pages, but there's so much here that it may take a while before you need to do that. —(L.S.)

KEY NEWSGROUP **rec.sport.paintball** URL▶ http://warpig.cati.csufresno.edu/paintball.html

---

Electronic Martial Arts

Judo Information Site Jump **7180**

Do you enjoy the thought of flinging yourself or others onto padded mats? Well, Neil Ohlenkamp has collected an amazing amount of information on the art, philosophy and technique of Judo to help you get started. You can study illustrated techniques, read up on the history of the sport, and learn tournament rules. Neil also posts local, national and international tournament results, profiles of current 10th-degree black belts, and a comprehensive list of links to other Judo resources. As well, he has a section devoted to training visually-impaired and blind athletes. —(E.v.B.)

KEY NEWSGROUP **rec.sport.misc** URL▶ http://www.rain.org/~ssa/judo.htm

Spectator Sports

America's Sports Center

America's Sports HQ Jump **5643**

If you've ever tried to search the Internet for information on a particular sport, you know that it can be a very frustrating business. But thanks to "the most comprehensive, user-friendly Sports Index on the WWW," your searching can now be done in one place. The area is broken down into three sections (Spectator Sports, Outdoor Adventure, and Recreational Sports), each of which contain literally dozens and dozens of links to the best sports sites the Web has to offer. Or if you'd rather browse, be sure to try out the "Web's only All-Sports Search Engine." —(J.P.)

URL▶ http://www.sport-hq.com/

NBC Sports

NBC Sports Jump 5609 

The Olympics may be over (for now, at least) but at NBC the sportsmeister never sleeps. Even as we speak, NBC is ready to take you on a tour of Golf, NBA, tennis and baseball. You can also check out NBC's TV schedule for the next few months (you got to plan those weekends, my man). And, speaking of weekends, there is also a link where you can check out the weather for just about anywhere. —(J.P.)

URL▶ http://www.nbc.com/sports/index.html

▲ *Kayaker, via* **Preston's Kayak Page**, *at* Jump 2559.

SportsLine USA: Chat With the Sports Superstars

SportsLine USA Jump 5603 

When it comes to publishing sports news on the Web, you gotta have a hook, and the hook better be good. Sure, it's nice to have all the scores and all the stats, but wouldn't it be nice to sit down and "chat" online with the superstars, one-on-one (or is that a few thousand on one!) Who could resist the chance to "chat" with Broadway Joe, or to read a letter from him, or hear him speak, or...well, you get the point. And there's more, from Arnold Palmer, Keyshawn Johnson and Monica Seles. And there's all that other stuff like news and stats, too! —(J.P.)

URL▶ http://www.sportsline.com/

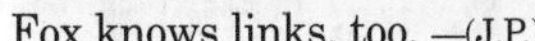

Fox Sports

Fox Sports Jump 5608 

The stadium in the logo is very fitting indeed. Fox knows TV sports and they've put all that talent to good use here, too. From the latest scores, the headlines that will make tonight's newscast, and even a contest or two. And don't forget to check out the other links. Fox knows links, too. —(J.P.)

URL▶ http://www.iguide.com/sports/

SportsNation

SportsNation Jump 5605 

If indeed there were a nation called Sports this would be its capitol city. Not only is there hockey and racing (NASCAR, IndyCar, and Formula One) but there's a live scoreboard that's truly live. Not hours ago—but by the seat of your pants, edge of your seat live. And headlines that have been posted just seconds ago. And a complete chart listing every sporting event taking place tonight, plus everything that happened while you were out washing the car. —(J.P.)

URL▶ http://www.sportnation.com/

The Sports Network

The Sports Network Jump 5604 

The key thing about The Sports Network is its sparseness—nothing flashy or splashy, just the facts. Clean and sweet. Click on the soccer ball and, well, you know what will happen. Same with the baseball and the hockey puck. And there's sports news, the latest and greatest, plus a whole lot more, but it doesn't slap you in the face. If there weren't so much to see it would almost be relaxing! —(J.P.)

URL▸ http://www.sportsnetwork.com:80/

Players INC

Players INC Jump **5705** 

If you need a fact on a football player, and you need it yesterday, this is the place to visit. Players INC is the official Web site of the NFL Players Association. And it shows! You can begin with a searchable index—type in the player's name and sit back. The stats will be right with you. Or if you'd prefer, you can check out the Hall of Fame list. They have every player listed here, from 1963 to the present. And that's a lot of players! There is also a special section of more player profiles, an appearance schedule, players of the week/month, and more. Add this to your Web sports must-see list. —(J.P.)

KEY NEWSGROUP **rec.sport.football.pro**

URL▸ http://www.sportsline.com/u/NFLPlayers/

It's Not College Football. It's Not the NFL. It's . . .

World League of American Football Jump **2381** 

The World League of American Football has been sniffed at by those in the States who consider anything that's not NFL unworthy, especially after WLAF play was suspended for two seasons. But that hasn't stopped the development of serious fandom for this strain of pro ball, either in Europe where it's played, or here in the States, and the fever has begun to pitch now that play has resumed. The most serious of the fans have created home pages honoring their favorite teams and players, and Bertram Lück brings you links as well as news, team schedules, and television outlets. Check it out, if for no other reason than to see pro players who, with top pay of $20,000 make less money than schoolteachers —(L.S.)

KEY NEWSGROUP **rec.sport.football.misc** URL▸ http://www.fb9-ti.uni-duisburg.de/wlaf/wlaf.html

▲ *Terry Allen of the Washington Redskins, from* NFL.COM, Jump **5704**.

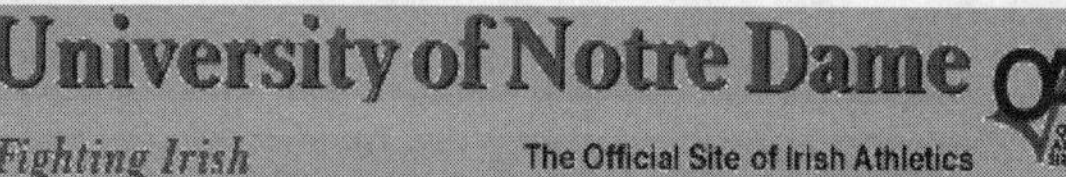

University of Notre Dame: Official Athletic Site

University of Notre Dame: Official Athletic Site Jump **5703** 

The University of Notre Dame began after a 28-year-old French priest, with $310 and three log buildings, had "the temerity to christen his enterprise the University of Notre Dame du Lac." Since then the home of the Fighting Irish has upheld its original mission to attain "the highest standards of excellence in teaching, scholarship" and, of course, sports. Although known primarily in some circles for its football, you'll also find plenty of links here to other sports, such as baseball, golf, soccer, volleyball, track and field, cross country, and tennis, to name but a few. You can also check out their sports calendar and read a history of the University. And along the way, you might run across a familiar, notable sports name or two. —(J.P.)

KEY NEWSGROUP **rec.sport.misc** URL▸ http://www.und.com/

NFL.COM: The Official NFL Site

NFL.COM Jump **5704** 

It is a sad fact of (Internet) life that most "official" Web sites leave much to be desired. The NFL.COM site, however, is an exception. This site brims to overflowing with stats, is easy to navigate, and easy on the eyes. Click on any of the team names and you're provided a wealth of information that includes the team stats, roster information, in-depth reports, information from the front office, team schedules, and even a link to the official team home page. Want more? There is more. How about an injury report, NFL standings and the day's highlights? And don't forget to check out the NFL FAQ. It's got loads of information telling you how to find what you want to find on the site. —(J.P.)

NEWSGROUP **rec.sport.football.pro**

URL http://www.nfl.com/index.html

Sports Information Jump Site

World Wide Web of Sports Jump 0014

"Spanning the globe to bring you a constant variety of sports information," this handy sports information page is brought to you by a research group headed by Professor David Tennenhouse at the MIT Laboratory for Computer Science, and contains links to many of the Web's best sports-related sites. Everything's covered here when it comes to links, from tennis to basketball, football, baseball, and the Olympics, to soccer, golf, rowing and even cricket. So sports fans take note—this site should be your first jumping-off point for sports info on the Web. —(E.G.)

URL http://tns-www.lcs.mit.edu/cgi-bin/sports

▲ *Steve Garvey of the Brooklyn Dodgers, from* **Total Baseball,** *at* Jump **5840**.

Bull Durham

Carolina League Jump 5068

The baseball teams of the Carolina League, including the famous Durham Bulls, have a Web site… and here it is! This Web page contains ticket prices, schedules, rosters, and more. Check out the "Weekly Notebook" for the latest info, including "Players of the Week." Play ball! —(S.B.)

URL http://carolinaleague.interpath.net/baseball/

Sports News & Chat from the Sports Server

The Sports Server Jump 5602

NandO—the *Raleigh News & Observer*'s Web site, was one of the first out of the starting gate to publish news on the Web, but they certainly hold their own in the sports department as well. Here you will find not only all the latest facts and figures, including stories and photos hot off the wire, but you can also enter their chat areas and talk about the really important things in life: baseball, basketball, football and hockey. Each has their own chat room. So sharpen up the barbs and head on in. —(J.P.)

URL http://www2.nando.net/SportsServer/

Off-Season Major-League Baseball

Fastball Jump 5806

Fastball is the complete off-season source for news about major-league baseball. They feature all the latest news about each team, complete with loads of stats, a chat area, and great feature articles. You can hear sports reports with RealAudio, and there are even links to every team's home page. And don't miss the video clips from the World Series, also linkable from here. —(J.P.)

NEWSGROUP **rec.sports.baseball** URL http://www.fastball.com/

The Baseball Server from NandO.net

The Baseball Server Jump 5607 CONTENT

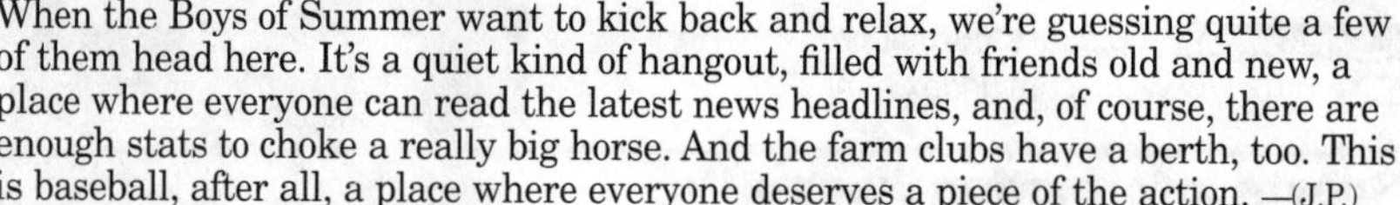

When the Boys of Summer want to kick back and relax, we're guessing quite a few of them head here. It's a quiet kind of hangout, filled with friends old and new, a place where everyone can read the latest news headlines, and, of course, there are enough stats to choke a really big horse. And the farm clubs have a berth, too. This is baseball, after all, a place where everyone deserves a piece of the action. —(J.P.)

URL▸ http://www1.nando.net/SportServer/baseball/

Minor League Baseball's Official Site

Minor League Baseball Jump 6893 CONTENT

The Minor Leagues were all baseball fans had to draw on when the Majors walked out on strike in 1995. While the Majors have now come back to play the game, let's not forget who never disappointed. And there's no better place than this, Minor League Baseball's official Web site to find news, stats and schedules of all your favorite league players and teams—from the Albuquerque Dukes to the Yakima Bears. Click on over to the news section, and you'll uncover such stories as how much money the leagues' logos produced in the current year (it's in the millions!), and what's behind the partnership with corporate America and the minor leagues. —(L.T.)

KEY NEWSGROUP **alt.sports.baseball.minor-leagues** URL▸ http://www.minorleaguebaseball.com/

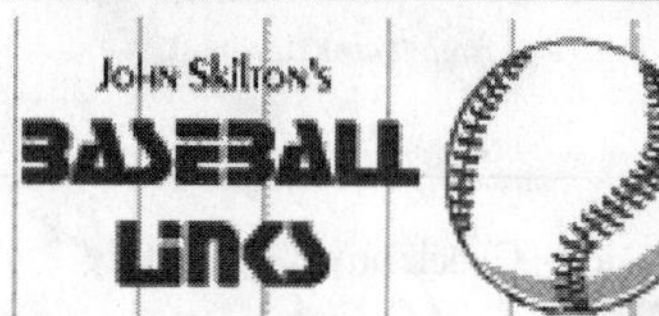

Ultimate Baseball Links Site

Skilton's Baseball Links Jump 6014 LINKS

John Skilton not only knows his baseball—he knows his way around the Web. As the author and creator of this site, John has created the ultimate set of links that should become your starting point when you're in the mood for a little baseball. Here you'll find links to current news, stats, scores, and schedules, as well as links to major and minor league team info and college, amateur and semipro ball sites. Find out where to go for cards and collectibles information, and jump right into Net baseball newsgroups and much more. —(N.F.)

KEY NEWSGROUP **alt.sports.baseball, us.sport.baseball, rec.sport.baseball** URL▸ http://ssnet.com/~skilton/baseball.html

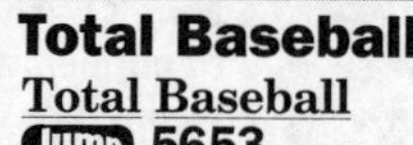

Total Baseball

Total Baseball Jump 5653 CONTENT

They call it Total Baseball, and that's exactly what they mean. Total. As in the *Official Encyclopedia of Major League Baseball*. Fans will find baseball history, biographies, and stats for "every player who every put on a professional uniform." And that's a lot of players. There's an interactive chat area, where fans from around the world can meet, as well four other sub-sites, Total Braves, Indians, Yankees, and Dodgers. And that, as you might have guessed, is just the start. —(J.P.)

URL▸ http://www.totalbaseball.com/

Bronx Bombers' Central

New York Yankees Home Plate Jump 6010 CONTENT

The Official Internet Web Site of the New York Yankees gives you great bios, stats, and other information on your favorite players, for starters. Need the schedule? It's here. Interested in the Yankee Minor League? It's here. The Archives section gives you terrific, photos, and text. You can also order official Yankee merchandise without leaving home (no surprise there!). Though you can't yet order tickets online, you can find how good your seat is by using the Yankee Stadium Seating Viewer—a useful feature.

Click on your section and you'll see the actual view of the stadium you'll have! Stop by for everything you'd ever want to know about the Yankees. —(N.F.)

URL ▶ http://www.yankees.com/

▲ *Steve Smith of the Hawks, from* NBA.COM, Jump 5706.

Grant Hill's Web Site

Grant Hill Jump 5709 

There are players who are in it for the hype and there are those who are in it for the game. One is left with the impression that Grant Hill is the player who wants nothing more than to play and play well. And that is what he does! If you want to learn more about the man and the player, you'll find plenty of information on both subjects here at the official Grant Hill Home Page. You can check out Grant's Hot Spots (a few links to Grant's favorite Net spots, including Duke University and a few sites in Detroit) and there's also a terrific photo album. But what we liked best was the section entitled "Stats & Facts." What you'll find here is an amazing collection of both, including highlights from his collegiate and high school years, a section on his school days, and even one on his Mom and Dad. —(J.P.)

URL ▶ http://www.granthill.com/

Two Fans' Basketball Site

On Hoops Jump 5710 

If you like your basketball news smart and sassy you'll love your stay at On Hoops. This is the place where site creators "Matt and Steve" decided—only half-jokingly—to try and predict the outcome of every single game to be played this year in the NBA. That is, until they realized that they would have to predict over 1,000 games! So they settled instead on commenting on the day-to-day stuff—and they do it very well. It's cocky and self-assured, but hey, if you can pull it off, why not? But this really is a terrific site and you'll want to visit it every couple of days during the season. —(J.P.)

KEY NEWSGROUP alt.sport.basketball.pro URL ▶ http://www.onhoops.com/

Basketball Down Under

The Unofficial National Basketball League (NBL) Page Jump 5091 

The most comprehensive NBL site on the Web is here. NBL is Australia's national basketball league. The NBL site features up-to-date news, results, statistics, and rosters. You can also link to info on all the NBL teams, the "Game of the Week," current standings, comments from others who access this Web page, and the history of the NBL. —(S.B.)

URL ▶ http://natsem.canberra.edu.au/private_web_home_pages/joshp/nbl/nbl.html

NBA.COM: The NBA's Official Basketball Site

NBA.COM Jump 5706 

The first thing you see when you sign on to this site is a list of 50 of the greatest players in NBA history. And what a history it is! You'll find all the great here, including Shaquille, Kareem, Julius and of course, Michael Jordan. The details here, as elsewhere on this site, are as factual as you could hope for. Stats and more stats, and biographies that read like a life story. And there's more here as well, including links to all of the teams, a scoreboard, a section called "NBA Basics," an NBA history, and the complete NBA schedule. —(J.P.)

KEY NEWSGROUP **alt.sport.basketball.pro** URL▶ http://www.nba.com/

ALLEYOOP.com

The Basketball Page for Thinking Fans

Alleyoop.com Jump **5711**

The folks at Alleyoop.com call this "The Basketball Page for Thinking Fans," and we're sure you will agree! But this really is an excellent page, filled with thoughtful articles and plenty of stats. You can begin your visit at the "Transaction Zone," where you'll find out all of the latest information on trades, free-agent signings, injuries, suspensions, and more. Then head over to this site's "College Top 20" and the "College Report." There is a NBA update, schedule, and players' ratings. Readers can speak their mind in the "Readers Speak" section, and they can also check out the feature articles. —(J.P.)

KEY NEWSGROUP **alt.sport.basketball.pro** URL▶ http://www.alleyoop.com/

HockeyNet

HockeyNet Jump **5642**

Hockey is one of the few sports that can be said to be truly international. Although it is sometimes difficult to find information on teams outside of North America, the task just became easier with HockeyNet's Journal of European Hockey. You'll also want to browse through the Amateur and Youth Hockey Center, and this site's fact-packed weekly magazine. And after you're done reading, you can head over to the chat area where you can discuss hockey issues with fans around the world. —(J.P.)

URL▶ http://www.hockeynet.com

National Hockey League Players' Association

National Hockey League Players' Association Jump **5610**

We don't know about you, but when we think union we don't think sparkling graphics and contests and players of the day. But of course the NHLPA is no ordinary union, and this is no ordinary site. Even during "off season" there is plenty to see here, from trivia contests to player playoff stats. And what would a players' association site be without a complete listing of player compensation. Here you will find out who makes what, in order, highest paid first, of course. But you gotta pity those poor boys taking all that money home in Canadian dollars. —(J.P.)

URL▶ http://www.nhlpa.com/

She Shoots, She Scores!

Information About Women's Hockey Jump **7044**

Women's hockey is quite an active sport in Canada, Sweden, Switzerland and a host of other countries. Andria Hunter, a Canadian hockey player herself, has assembled a comprehensive collection of book reviews, illustrations, FAQs, team news, and listings of international events and information. —(E.v.B.)

KEY NEWSGROUP **rec.sport.hockey** URL▶ http://www.cs.utoronto.ca/~andria/Womens_hockey_info.html

---

Racing Around the Web

r.a.s. Racer Archive Jump **4010**

The ultimate site for you auto-racing fans. Put together by Jay Corina, this site offers information on all types of auto racing, including Formula 1, IndyCar, and NASCAR. There are race results and details, team information, newsgroup links, and even a picture gallery of your favorite drivers. —(R.B.)

KEY NEWSGROUP **rec.autos.sports.info** URL▶ http://www.eng.hawaii.edu/Contribs/carina/ra.home.page.html

Sports, Sports, & More Sports

ESPNET SportsZone Jump 1508

COMMERCE

Hey sports fans—this is a site for you! Here you'll find the most up-to-the-minute, comprehensive Web coverage of all major sporting events. Presented by Starwave and ESPN, with sponsors such as Sun Microsystems and Gatorade, money talks—this is the best seat in the house right after a game. You can select the sport you're interested in, scroll through the hundreds of last-minute game scores and recaps, or read the top 10 stories of the day (reprinted from Knight-Ridder papers), including relevant sidebars, graphs, and charts representing the game's playing strategies. But that's not all. You can participate in sports talk live or through e-mail with a variety of sports personalities, including Cleveland Indians pitcher Orel Hershiser, ESPN anchor Craig Kilborn, and AFL commissioner Jim Drucker. Vote for your favorite all-star teams, read details about the players, search through archives to find out previous scores to settle old bets, and find out game schedules for the next day or the next week. Definitely a favorite place for any sports enthusiast! —(H.L.)

URL▶ http://web1.starwave.com:80/

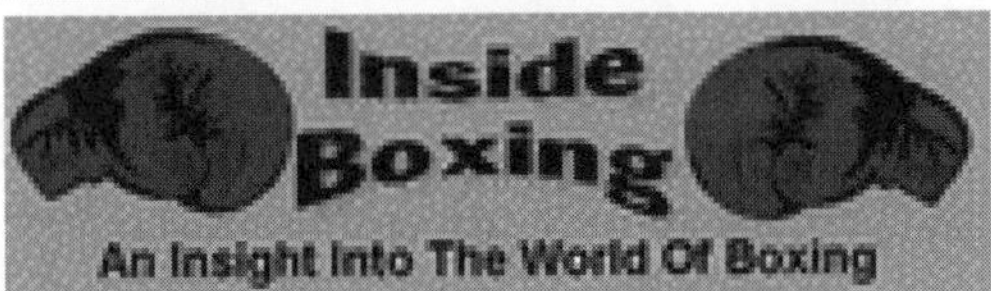

Understanding Boxing

Inside Boxing Jump 5026

Inside Boxing contains lots of great information, including short bios of boxing personalities. The page also answers your questions on how the scoring system works, the alphabet soup of boxing (info on the controlling organizations), training techniques, famous gyms, how to get tickets to big fights, and how to get autographs. There's also info on debate topics such as boxing vs. martial arts, and women in boxing. You are encouraged to share your comments and opinions with the maintainers of the page. —(S.B.)

KEY NEWSGROUP **rec.sport.boxing** URL▶ http://lemur.cit.cornell.edu/boxing/insite.html

Reebok's Planet on the Internet

Planet Reebok Jump 4026

COMMERCE

The headline on this athletic shoe giant's innovative Web site reads "Welcome To Planet Reebok...Stay as long as you like!," and you'll have plenty to do if you jump here on the Web! Resources available here include typical corporate PR Web fluff like company history, brand info, and research/human rights programs that Reebok is involved in, but the real fun is in the sports information provided. For example, in Planet Reebok's "Ask the Pros," you can read an interview with sports figures such as Notre Dame football coach Lou Holtz, and you can also find out which Reebok athletes will be doing live online interviews on this site, a regular feature (and a first for the Web) that's sponsored by Reebok. —(R.B.)

KEY NEWSGROUP **rec.sport.misc** URL▶ http://planetreebok.com/

Overheard at the Interactive Travel Marketing Conference...

NEW YORK—During the recent Interactive Travel Marketing conference, held here, speakers offered remarkably similar advice for travel providers interested in marketing their products online.

The recommendations follow:

- **Anything a business puts online needs to be informative, well thought out, unbiased and thoroughly researched.**
- **Net cruisers do not suffer sloppiness and incomplete information kindly, and they will let you and all their friends know of their displeasure...**
- **Use the soft-sell approach; the hard sell has been tried repeatedly and has failed repeatedly...**
- **Be willing to give out free advice. The people you treat well will come back...eventually.**

[News Item]
Travel Weekly

Local & International

Although most people think of the Web as a global network, there are many Web sites focusing on specific cities, towns, and countries, and which can be used as virtual travel and culture guides for many exciting locations around the world.

Metro U.S. & International Web Sites

Looking at the sheer volume of metro, international, and other geographically-related sites out there on the Web, it's clear that the Web has not escaped the eyes of many government travel and tourism office staffers in cities around the world. While many of these "official" travel and tourism Web sites are rather uninteresting, consisting of little more than online versions of color tourist brochures, there are quite a few of these sites, both official and unofficial, that can provide you with fascinating background history and full-color views of places to go and sites to see, both for any city in the U.S., and for many other European and Asian locations has well.

There are also many Web sites focusing on activities, sites, and places to go in various U.S. cities. Even if you're already living in the city covered by the Web site, these sites can provide you with useful pointers on good local attractions. In addition to providing you with a "sense of place" on the Web, these locally-oriented Web sites also contain hotlinks to the Internet's Usenet online discussion newsgroups for the specific cities they cover, and valuable Net connections to restaurants and local businesses, plus comments and feedback on good local attractions contributed by Net locals in that city.

Metro Area U.S. Sites

Greetings from Baltimore, Maryland!

Charm Net Baltimore Page Jump 3538 

Once you've been to Charm Net's Baltimore Page, you'll be ready to make a personal visit! This friendly old city has come into the Information Age in a big way with this Web site. You'll find everything from city highlights to subway info—from information about pubs (and which ones to visit) to alternative music and culture. This site boasts an interesting series of links to the historic old newspaper, the *Baltimore Afro American*, and subsequent links to other African-American resources on the Internet. —(C.P.)

KEY NEWSGROUP **balt.misc** URL▶ http://www.charm.net/baltimore.html

Boston's Web Central

Boston.com Jump 1582 

If you've ever been to Boston, you know it can be confusing to get around. But not anymore. Everything you wanted to know about the historic area, past and present, is right here. Read the *Boston Globe* online, find out WAAF-FM's latest playlist, and see who's who at WCVB TV. Check out the arts, entertainment, weather, sports, real estate, employment, maps, and even the latest technological advances out of this high-tech area. Let everyone know your views on the latest issues in Talk Live, or take a tour of Massachusetts's cities and towns and get to know the neighborhoods. Is your own home page relevant? Link it here. Can you guess the Farmer's Almanac prediction for winter? Take a vote and see the tallies. Splashy, interactive, fun—you get the feeling of living there, even if you don't. —(H.L.)

KEY NEWSGROUP **ne.general** URL▶ http://www.boston.com/

Cyber Boston Local Web Zine

the FIX Jump 7352 

The FIX is a hip, visually striking site that is part guide to Boston, part Web magazine. It blends information from multiple sources, including *Pit Report*, the *Boston Book Review*, the *Boston Globe*, the Massachusetts Film Office, college students, and other links. You can find something for every sense here: vision (read Dave's guide to Boston's used, discount, and vintage clothing stores); hearing (radio schedules, concert notes, and some sound files of local bands); taste (restaurant reviews and recipes); and mind (we really enjoyed visiting Cyber-Yenta: "the thinking person's matchmaker"). A very rich site for locals and visitors alike. —(E.v.B.)

KEY NEWSGROUP **ne.general** URL▶ http://www.boston.com/thefix/

Tour Colorado

State of Colorado Home Page Jump 1563 

Planning a visit to colorful Colorado? Do you already live there but don't know where your nearest voting precinct is? Then don't miss this Web page, chock full of visitor and citizen information. State history, facts, figures, arts, entertainment, sports teams and scores, government, auto registration, taxes, libraries, museums, retail, and more are all covered comprehensively. Known mainly for its outdoor splendor, the state's recreation pages are replete with skiing, mountain climbing, hiking, biking, and open space information, including wondrous scenes of Rocky Mountain National Park. Links to numerous regional communities and networks indicate that Colorado is one of the most Net savvy states. —(H.L.)

KEY NEWSGROUP **co.general** URL▶ http://www.state.co.us/colorado.html

MetroBeat's Guide to NYC

MetroBeat-NYC Jump 6759 

You could search for hours on the Web trying to find a comparable index that'll lead you to daily events in the Big Apple. Or, with a few clicks, you can hop on over to MetroBeat and locate New York City's finest art galleries, comedy clubs, lectures, restaurants, museums, or sporting events. Customize your event search to locate something just for the kids, or find free events in the city. Whether you're looking for something to do in Manhattan, Staten Island, or the Bronx, you'll always leave here with a few good ideas for the weekend. —(L.T.)

KEY NEWSGROUP **nyc.general**

URL ▸ http://www.metrobeat.com/nyc/index.html

▲ *The Brooklyn Bridge from the old ferry landing, from* **JumpCity**.

Traffic Conditions for L.A. Residents

Los Angeles Traffic Report

Jump **7033** CONTENT

California dreaming—or nightmare? Check the Los Angeles real-time traffic report for a view of life in the fast lane. Read up-to-the-hour information on road closures and weather, or access a road map of the L.A. area, showing how fast traffic is moving and exactly where problems are occurring—all in real time! —(E.v.B.)

KEY NEWSGROUP **rec.autos.driving** URL ▸ http://www.scubed.com:8001/caltrans/la/la_transnet.html

L.A.'s Unique Culture

Buzz Online: The Talk of Los Angeles

Jump **3746** CONTENT

L.A. is more than just a city in California—it's a state of mind. Visit Buzz Online to get a fascinating view of the City of Angels. You'll find What's New, with news, reports, essays, and photo features. What's the Buzz brings great gossip, news, reviews, and previews. Who are the 100 coolest people in the Buzz universe? You'll find it here! Chat with other buzzers, advertise, check out the archives, even contribute your own fiction. Hot Links gives you a great list of unusual, useful, and interesting L.A.-related sites. Brought to you by the publishers of *Buzz Magazine*. —(N.F.)

URL ▸ http://www.buzzmag.com/

Bay Area: Virtual Links

The PAN Islands Public Access Network

Jump **1581**

Internet culture-watcher Howard Rheingold is right—it's a small virtual world, after all. The Public Access Network is sponsored by the San Francisco Bay Area's Smart Valley, a consortium of companies with (among other things) the good of the community at heart. They've set up Net-wired kiosks in public places for Bay Area folks lacking access at home or work. And anybody can poke around their Web site. Don't be intimidated by the slow-loading GIFs; you'll be rewarded with a cute map with a dozen buttons leading to links ranging from local restaurants to probably every resource available on the Net. —(H.L.)

URL ▸ http://www.svi.org/pan.html

Have I Got a Deal for You!

Welcome to the Classified Flea Market's Online Edition

Jump **7122**

If you live in or plan to visit the San Francisco Bay area and you want to buy, sell or trade goods or services, this online forum will serve you well. There are over 90 categories to choose from—antiques, music, books, boats, pet supplies—you name it. Even if you don't live in the area, this virtual flea market publication is worth a visit just to read the great ads and check out a prime example of good Web publishing. —(E.v.B.)

KEY NEWSGROUP **misc.wanted** URL ▸ http://www.cfm.com/cfm/index.html

St. Louis, the Gateway to the West!

St. Louis Home Page
Jump 3543

The St. Louis Home Page is maintained by Washington University—and it does a fine job. If a you're on your way to this end of Missouri, be sure to check this site before you go. You can find information about the weather, interesting tourist sites, an event calendar, suggestions about which hot spots to visit, info about the Cardinals (baseball), and the Blues (hockey), shopping, local discussions, and other links for the Show-Me State. —(C.P.)

URL▶ http://www.st-louis.mo.us/

Explore Missouri

State of Missouri Home Page
Jump 3545

"Wake Up To Missouri!" That's the introductory message offered by this server, "the Show-Me state's official rest stop on the Information Highway!" You can browse through the home pages of cities, universities and government, read a couple of homegrown, Web-based publications that are really quite good, and visit other Missouri links as well. Be sure to check out the multimedia database offered by the Department of Economic Development—it will take you on a fascinating tour of Missouri communities, review the statutes of Missouri as they relate to business and economic development, and see online profiles of Missouri's available industrial properties. —(C.P.)

URL▶ http://www.ecodev.state.mo.us/

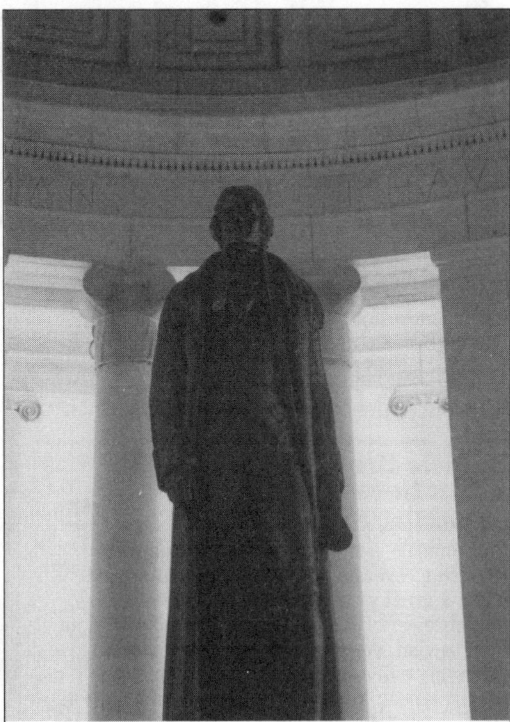

▲ *Statue of Thomas Jefferson at the Jefferson Memorial in Washington, D.C., from* **JumpCity**.

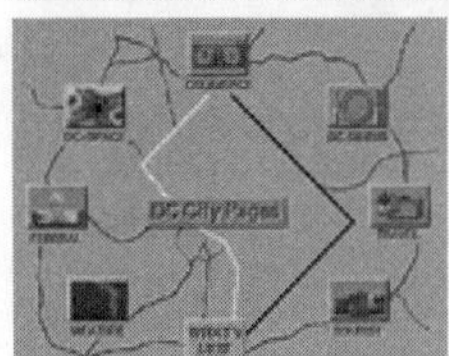

Washington, D.C., Information

The Washington DC City Pages Jump 3540

Talk about cool images: this site has one of the neatest clickable image maps we have seen. Select from options that range from Commerce to Dining, Weather to Tourism—it's all here, and it's done quite well. There's a frequently updated "What's New" page, a listing of restaurants and dining places in Washington, Maryland, and Northern Virginia, even a "site-seeing" tour for Web navigators and tourists. —(C.P.)

KEY NEWSGROUP **dc.general** URL▶ http://www2.ari.net:85/edc/

Visit Virtual Las Vegas

Vegas.Com Jump 3620

CONTENT

As honky-tonk online as it is in real life, Vegas.Com offers insight into what goes on in the daytime outside the casinos of Las Vegas. There's a culture page, pointers to businesses that operate online storefronts, links to boxing and other sports resources, and much more—even a guide to investing in gaming. Brash and garish, but worth a visit. —(C.P.)

KEY NEWSGROUP **rec.gambling** URL▶ http://www.vegas.com/

Daytona Beach Home Page

Daytona Beach, Florida
Jump 4011 CONTENT

This is the official site for "the world's most famous beach," Daytona Beach, on the east coast of Florida. You can find information on the surrounding communities as well as a calendar of events to make your trip-planning to this ever-popular location even easier. Among other things, you'll find details on accommodations and dining in the area and, of course, information on its two most famous events: Bike Week and Spring Break. —(R.B.)

KEY NEWSGROUP **alt.culture.beaches**

URL ▶ http://www.charm.net/~ibc/daytona/db2.html

Seattle Brew News & Local Attractions

Latona Pub News Jump 5152 CONTENT

Bob Sharble is the author of this Web page featuring coverage of Seattle's neighborhood pubs, a great place to sample Northwest microbrewery beers. If you're a Seattle local, or plan to visit, you can also link to the music calendar to find out about the live musical performances. You can also link to information on "Brewer Appreciation Night," a list of great beer finds, and brewery info from around the world. —(S.B.)

URL ▶ http://www.halcyon.com/rsharble/latona/welcome.html

▲ *Northwestern United States Indian mask, from* **NativeWeb**, *at* **Jump 7060**.

The Blacksburg Electronic Village—Big News in Cyberspace

BEV Home Page Jump 3572 CONTENT

The Blacksburg Electronic Village has been featured more often than you can imagine in the news as a model of the electronic village of the future. It's a small town in southern Virginia which was quick to become "wired," in that its local government and business community have developed an extensive Net presence. Anything you can think of that makes life in a small town pleasant can be found on BEV, from the Village Mall (a nice selection of local businesses and shops) to an active Community Center, and from an Education Center to a Computer Help Desk—even a Seniors Page! BEV is an excellent model of the perfect electronic community. —(C.P.)

URL ▶ http://crusher.bev.net/index.html

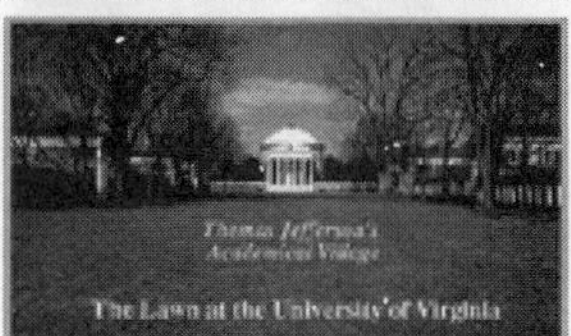

The University of Virginia—Thomas Jefferson's Gift

The Lawn Tour Jump 3571 

Charlottesville, Virginia—home to Thomas Jefferson some 200 years ago–is still home to the University of Virginia, whose architecture and grounds layout was designed by Jefferson himself. This prestigious university occupies land secured in 1819 by its founding father; its architecture and beauty are a tribute to that great man. Thomas Jefferson's Academical Village is a fascinating interactive tour of the University of Virginia's Great Lawn. This tour is full of photos, clickable image maps and history, and is not to be missed! —(C.P.)

URL ▶ http://teach.virginia.edu/~jet3h/Welcome.html

International Sites

Brazil's Web Hub

Meu Brazil Jump 5112

A solid Web starting point for any below-the-Equator information search, this Web page features screen views of different places in Brazil, along with maps, statistical information (economic, political, etc.), and links to other Brazilian servers, institutions, and news sources. You can link to sites that cover many different cities in this South American nation, including Rio, Brasília and São Paulo. There's also information on news and culture in Brazil. Very informative, with great graphics, too. —(S.B.)

URL ▶ http://darkwing.uoregon.edu/~sergiok/brasil.html

Information on Honduras & Central America

Honduras. ¡Tierra de Catrachos! Jump 5137

If you're studying up on Honduras, be sure to check this source. This site provides an extensive list of Honduran-related organizations in the U.S., universities and institutions, music and culture, recreational activities, and info on Latin American studies. A list of mailing lists related to Honduras and Central America are provided. There's also a list of contacts for more information about Honduras, as well as links to other interesting Latin American sites on the Web. Anuar René Pineda, a student at the University of Maryland, is developing this site, which provides some pages in Spanish and others in English. —(S.B.)

URL ▶ http://www.gl.umbc.edu/~apined1/

Exploring Canada

Canadian WWW Central Index Jump 2342

Cyberspace Research maintains this free listing of Canadian Web sites, giving surfers an excellent resource for exploring the Webspace of the Great White North. Organized by city, province, and server type, it's a simple matter to find whatever you may be looking for, and the What's New section is especially helpful for regular visitors. This site makes it easy to locate (or add your listing to) Canada-based commercial, government, university, or research servers and resources on the Net. —(L.S.)

KEY NEWSGROUP soc.culture.canada URL ▶ http://www.csr.ists.ca/w3can/Welcome.html

Try a Digital Tour of Ottawa

Ottawa Tourist Jump 3575

If you're ready for a trip to the Great White North, why not begin in Ottawa? Based in the capital city of Canada, Ottawa Tourist offers great information to the prospective traveler. Try its great hotel/motel accommodation finder, or check out its bed-and-breakfast listings for a truly great place to stay. Ottawa is a thriving, cultured city—pop on over for a visit! —(C.P.)

URL ▶ http://www.digimark.net/iatech/tour/

Canadian Forests

Model Forest Program/Programme de forêtsmodèles Jump 7004

Canadian forests account for 10 percent of the world's forests. Presently, the innovative Model Forest Program is exploring ways to manage 10 model forests across the country to ensure sustainable harvesting, protect biodiversity, and support environmental, social and recreational values. Enjoy an interactive slide presentation on the Model Forest Program. Listen to forest sounds. Learn about the newest techniques, for example, for conserving the pine marten bird habitat in the Western Newfoundland Model Forest. —(E.v.B.)

KEY NEWSGROUP bionet. agroforestry URL ▶ http://NCR157.NCR.Forestry.CA/MF.HTM

China News & Links: Free Internet News Sources

n/a Jump 0079

James Miles's excellent Web jump site with many well-organized links to a vast array of Net news and information resources for China, Hong Kong, Taiwan and Singapore, including links to Voice of America and Canadian Broadcasting Corporation radio broadcast audio files available on the Web. —(E.G.)

KEY NEWSGROUP soc.culture.china URL▶ http://www.umich.edu:80/~milesj/

The Best of British Web Sites

The Best of Britain's Corner of the Web

Jump 3625

The British put a characteristic spin on things—and this site does a terrific job of highlighting its "Best of the Web." Be it weather or entertainment, government or "just plain silly stuff" (their words, not ours) this Web site offers great material to be enjoyed by Anglophiles and just plain folks, alike. —(C.P.)

KEY NEWSGROUP soc.culture.british URL▶ http://www.demon.co.uk/pcw/bob.html

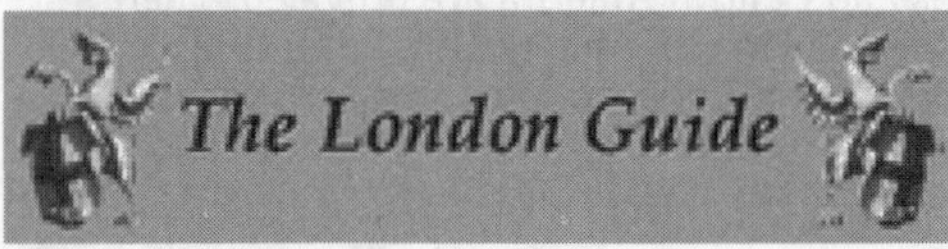

The Visitor's Guide to London

The London Guide Jump 3559

CONTENT

Going to London sometime soon? Stop by the London Guide for up-to-the-minute information about restaurants, hotels and entertainment, dancing, theaters and travel—all the way down to a cool Tube Journey Planner (what the Brits call their subway) that works like this: You put in a starting point and an ending point. Next, the Tube Journey Planner will come back with precise information about the location of the stations, the fare zone, the approximate travel time, other destinations from these stations and more. —(C.P.)

KEY NEWSGROUP soc.culture.british URL▶ http://www.cs.ucl.ac.uk/misc/uk/london.html

Dresden, Germany

City Information Jump 3578

Although much is still available only in the German language on this site, there's enough here in English to whet your appetite. Dresden has recovered from the terrible days of WWII that left it in ashes—and this lovely, ancient city along the banks of the Elbe River has lots to offer visitors. —(C.P.)

KEY NEWSGROUP soc.culture.german URL▶ http://www.tu-dresden.de/dresden/dresden.html

Information about Greece

NIR Resources Metamap Jump 3568

Read all about Macedonia, the land of Alexander the Great. Or, how about a visual tour of the frescoes, rocks and plateaus of Crete? Start at this page for a visit to Greece. You'll find home pages for Alexandria, Thessalonika and Heraclion, to name just a few—along with information about the geography, politics, tourist trade and much more. Also of interest to American tourists is the State Department Travel Advisory bulletin service. —(C.P.)

KEY NEWSGROUP soc.culture.greek URL▶ http://www.forthnet.gr/hellas/hellas.html

A Tour of Amsterdam

The Amsterdam Channel home page Jump 5143

This site is absolutely beautiful! The Amsterdam Channel is your guide to this lovely city. You can take a virtual guided tour or explore the city on your own, accompanied every "step" of the way by maps and pictures. You begin in front of the Central Station in Amsterdam, and choose to proceed on your own—via tram or foot—or take one of several tour variations, such as a cultural and historical tour, a shopping tour, a business tour, a fun tour, or a low-budget tour. You can also select the map of Amsterdam and zoom in on your area of interest. A very easy-to-use, great looking, and fun Web page! —(S.B.)

URL▶ http://www.xs4all.nl/~channels/tourist.html

Tour South India

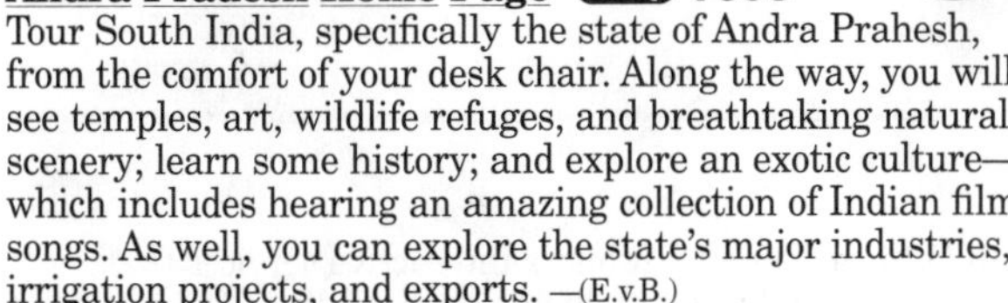

Andra Pradesh Home Page Jump 7005 CONTENT

Tour South India, specifically the state of Andra Prahesh, from the comfort of your desk chair. Along the way, you will see temples, art, wildlife refuges, and breathtaking natural scenery; learn some history; and explore an exotic culture—which includes hearing an amazing collection of Indian film songs. As well, you can explore the state's major industries, irrigation projects, and exports. —(E.v.B.)

KEY NEWSGROUP **soc.culture.indian.telegu**

URL ▶ http://www.site.gmu.edu/~sneelam/AP/ap.html

▲ *Wooden model of the H. M. S. Bounty, from* **Pitcairn Island Home Page** , *at* Jump **5867**.

A Glimpse of Irish Culture

The Gaelic Football Page Jump 3563 CONTENT

The Gaelic Football Home Page offers an interesting glimpse at life in Ireland. Goes to show you—football fans are as rabid in Europe as they are right here in the good old U.S. of A. Statistics are offered in a couple of different ways, sorted by division and by team, and there is year-by-year information about the All-Ireland championships for the past several years, complete with on-the-spot stringer reports! —(C.P.)

KEY NEWSGROUP **soc.culture.gaelic** URL ▶ http://jupiter.qub.ac.uk/michael/Gaelic.html

A Virtual Visit to Italy

Net'Tuno Jump 3561 CONTENT

"Molto bene" means (loosely) great stuff! This Web page offers a peek at Internet resources as they're offered to Italians—in Italian! The graphics are quite easy to understand in any language, though, so it's not difficult to navigate about, and there's lots of fascinating information (much of it in English) about Italian cities, environmental and educational programs, even familiar Internet resources, and much more. —(C.P.)

KEY NEWSGROUP **soc.culture.italian** URL ▶ http://www.nettuno.it/

New Zealand Revealed!

New Zealand Information Jump 3514 CONTENT

Although New Zealand may often take a back seat to the better-known (and much larger) Australia, it has plenty to offer! This site offers a large number of statistics on this island nation's climate, government, population, trade and similar topics—and an interesting analysis of how New Zealand stacks up against its worldwide neighbors in many of these areas. You'll also find the all-important FAQ for **soc.culture.new-zealand**, information about the capital city of Wellington, and a number of links to other New Zealand-related Internet sites. —(C.P.)

KEY NEWSGROUP **soc.culture.new-zealand** URL ▶ http://www.vuw.ac.nz/govt/nzinfo.html

The Island from Mutiny on the Bounty

Pitcairn Island Home Page Jump 5867 

Tiny South Seas Pitcairn Island is home to just 50 people, most of whom, it turns out, are descendants of mutineers—some of the crew from that famous British ship, The Bounty, immortalized in the book *The Mutiny on the Bounty,* and subsequent movies. You'll find plenty of interesting information here at this wonderful site that captures perfectly not only the historic importance of this island and the events that took place here, but also the special feeling of kinship shared by those who live here—many of whom are direct decendents of Fletcher

Christian and the crew of the Bounty. This is no more evident than in the section that includes photos of some of the inhabitants, as well as articles from the local paper, and the many maps that will bring to life this historical drama of long ago. —(J.P.)

URL▶ http://wavefront.wavefront.com/~pjlareau/pitc1.html

Welcome to Spain!

The Embassy of Spain in Canada Jump 3584

This neat Web site is supported by the Embassy of Spain in Ottawa, Canada. It offers interactive services that promote the exchange of information on Spanish current affairs, as well as on its history and culture. The site is presented in both English and Spanish, and covers a wide variety of topics–from geography to science, and from a Spanish tutorial to politics and foreign affairs. It even provides links to a huge number of Internet resources and Web sites based in Spain. —(C.P.)

KEY NEWSGROUP **soc.culture.spain** URL▶ http://www.civeng.carleton.ca/SiSpain/

A Gateway to Spain

Spain Internet Resources Jump 3567

Besides its way cool design, this Web site has links to every Internet site in mainland and offshore Spain. Whether they're Web sites, Gopher servers or FTP archives—if what you want is in the land of Don Quixote—you'll find it here. This page is also very nice to look at—the author has done a great job with the understated graphics. —(C.P.)

KEY NEWSGROUP **soc.culture.spain** URL▶ http://www.uji.es/spain_www.html

Visit Indonesia

Indonesian Home Page at Jakarta Jump 3535

Sponsored by the Indonesian government, this Web site is one of five—one each in Canada and Australia, and three in Indonesia, itself. Beyond this one, the other two Indonesian sites focus on different religious perspectives: the Muslim Network and the Christian Computer Network. You'll find information about travel and local customs–a cool clickable image map that lets you see information about a particular region—and even a peek into two Indonesian villages that run entirely on solar power! —(C.P.)

KEY NEWSGROUP **soc.culture.indonesia** URL▶ http://mawar.inn.bppt.go.id/

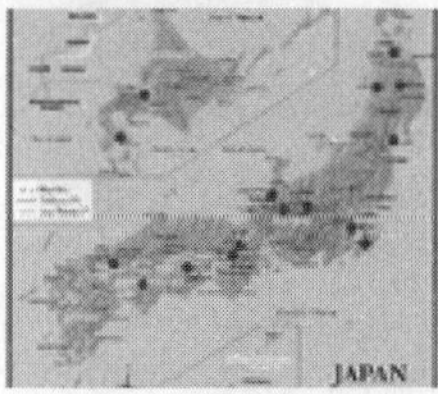

A Tourist's Guide to Japan

Japanese Information Jump 3539

This "Japanese Corner of the Web" is a must-see. Dazzling color images of traditional tourist sites in Kyoto, Nara, and Tokyo will have you itching to visit the mysterious Far East. A great deal of attention is paid to providing details about the geography, cultures and customs of Japan, and a clickable image map lets you browse through layers of nested information about any region you choose. Also on this site is information about sports, the government, law, communications and the Net in Japan, including pointers to all Japanese information servers, the FAQs for **soc.culture.japan**, **sci.lang.japan**, and the archives of **comp.research.japan**. —(C.P.)

KEY NEWSGROUP **soc.culture.japan** URL▶ http://www.ntt.jp/japan/index.html

Japanese Culturezine

Japan Infoweb Jump 5151

Here's a wonderful multimedia e-zine about Japanese culture, developed and maintained by Gordon Nash. From features on Zen Buddhism to delicious delectables from Japan, you can find it here. Its travel section includes features on visiting Buddhist temples, its cuisine section contains photos of Japanese foods with recipes to try at home, and there's even a food pronunciation glossary of audio clips you can download—so now you'll know how to say "I'd like more Wasabi" next time you're ordering sushi. There's also the marketplace, where you can find the finest Japanese natural food products, complete with order form. —(S.B.)

URL▶ http://electra.cortland.com:80/electrazine/japantour/

Hip Japan

Japan Edge (English)

Jump 7230

Japan Edge, a creation of Taishi Ichinose and Shuichi Kodama, brings together a mass of Japanese street/underground culture information. Divided into music, fashion, and links, the authors have made a graphically attractive site. You can explore the world of Japanese alternative music, check out what's hip in Japanese street fashion, and shop and visit a growing number of Japan-based record stores, clubs, and other links on this site. —(E.v.B.)

KEY NEWSGROUP **soc.culture.japan**

URL ▸ http://www.ces.kyutech.ac.jp/student/JapanEdge/e-index.html

Korea Online

KoreaLink

Jump 5905

KoreaLink is an effort to bring together the over 50 million Koreans who live around the world. And of course there is plenty here for anyone who is interested in world or current events, or has an interest in doing business in Korea. The database is extensive, and includes resources such as online yellow pages, a Korean FAX directory, as well as links to government, business, Web magazines and entertainment. You'll also find today's headlines, and daily Korean weather, stocks, movies, and TV show updates. And don't forget to check out this site's chat areas, and the special sections for pen-pals. —(J.P.)

URL ▸ http://www.korealink.com/home.htm

▲ *Bard Edlund graphic, from* SITO, *at* Jump 5728.

Great Pointers to Asian Studies

Asian Astrology

Jump 3669

You'll scratch your head as you try to resolve the various skills listed in W. L. R. Cassidy's (this Web site creator) resume. Heavy-duty intelligence experience (some pretty impressive credits there) combined with an affinity for tea leaves—well, alright, not tea leaves, maybe—but you get the idea, don't you? This site offers what claims to be the first attempt at consolidating English-language Asian Astrology and Divination Resources into a Bibliography—as well as some (fascinating) pointers to Chinese, Tibetan and Vietnamese resources on the Net. Chip below the surface for the best in this site—the front page is less than exciting. —(C.P.)

KEY NEWSGROUP **alt.chinese.fengshui** URL ▸ http://www.deltanet.com/users/wcassidy/astroindex.html

Southeast Asia Beckons

Welcome to Malaysia Jump 7056

Exotic scenes, interesting information on Malaysia, and intriguing links to other Asian sites will interest tourists and students alike. The more serious-minded can explore pages containing information devoted to agriculture, government, education, and research. Eventually, the site will be transformed into a hypertext encyclopaedia of all things Malaysian. —(E.v.B.)

KEY NEWSGROUP **soc.culture.malaysia** URL ▸ http://www.jaring.my/

Guide to Singapore

Singapore Online Guide Jump 7058 

Attractions, festivals, hotels, restaurants, sports, and shopping, shopping, shopping are all presented in this electronic version of the *Singapore Official Guide*. Everything the traveler needs to know about Singapore—from currency to weather to city maps—can be reached with a mouse click from this Web site. —(E.v.B.)

KEY NEWSGROUP **soc.culture.singapore** URL▸ http://www.ncb.gov.sg/sog/sog.html

South African Site Listings

Welcome to Marques Systems Jump 2491 

With the ending of apartheid, the advent of minority rule, and the subsequent lifting of trade restrictions, lots of good things are happening these days in the Republic of South Africa. If you want a Web-centric point of view of the changes, link to this site. South African access provider Marques Systems has a neatly organized site, divided into sections covering business, education, entertainment, news/magazines, organizations, science/technology, sports, and weather. —(L.S.)

KEY NEWSGROUP **za.misc** URL▸ http://minotaur.marques.co.za/index.htm

South African Wine

Rheboksklo of Estate Jump 3534 

When you think about taking a trip through wine country, we bet you never considered South Africa as a possibility, did you? This site is managed by the Rheboksklo of Estate winery, which dates back to 1692. The winery was named for the deer that used to roam the plains in this part of Africa centuries ago, and the site offers an interesting virtual tour of the winery and its three restaurants, and provides information about its history, the cultivation and viticulture methods that are used in their winemaking, and how to place an order as well. —(C.P.)

URL▸ http://www.os2.iaccess.za/rhebok/index.htm

The Complete Tibetan Reference

CERN/ANU - Tibetan Studies WWWVL Jump 7066 

Interested in Tibet? This page, maintained by Dr. T. Matthew Ciolek, is a major resource. Politics, history, language, literature, religion—even tourist—information is collected here within a wealth of archives, databases, contact organizations, and other resources. —(E.v.B.)

KEY NEWSGROUP **soc.culture.tibet** URL▸ http://coombs.anu.edu.au/WWWVL-TibetanStudies.html

Information about Venezuela

Venezuela Home Page Jump 3569 

Layers of clickable maps that offer information about tourism and science, as well as business and economic news, can be found here. You'll find weather, currency exchange rates, business practices and exports to the U.S., among other interesting things. This site is growing steadily, and you can also get to all other Internet-based Venezuelan Web sites from this site. —(C.P.)

KEY NEWSGROUP **soc.culture.venezuela** URL▸ http://venezuela.mit.edu/

Information about Yugoslavia

Yugoslavia Jump 3560 

From the looks of this Web page, you'd never know that this country is in the throes of a civil war. Since there is no hint of the dangers that might await tourists here—only a focus on the beauty that once was Yugoslavia—this page is an anachronism. You'll find info about each of the Yugoslav republics, suggested tourist spots, traditional food, statistics, profiles of famous Yugoslavs, international travel requirements, pointers to other European and Russian Web sites, and more. —(C.P.)

KEY NEWSGROUP **soc.culture.yugoslavia** URL▸ http://www.umiacs.umd.edu/research/lpv/YU/HTML/yu.html

Off the Wall

Here's where you'll find all of the odd, humorous, and downright strange uses of Web space: UFOs, Net religions, live camera feeds of ant farms, and other slices of real (and unreal) life.

Weird, Wacky, Useless, & Unique Jumping-Off Points Along the Web

Every new frontier has its own odd characters and colorful personalities, and the Web is no exception. Wherever you have a lot of clever, creative people, you're bound to have a few square pegs, and a lot of them have found their homes on the Web.

Mind you, we're not complaining—as with all of the Web's other topical subject areas, we think you'll especially enjoy the off-the-wall Web sites. The clearly satirical Web sites—such as clever 'zines and bizarre, whimsical commentaries on current events and media—are some of the very best humor and satirical writing you'd find anywhere, not just on the Web.

As for the rest...well, you'll just have to be the judge! We've collected these sites in our travels along the Web, just to show you what a strange, inventive place it can be.

Need to know the current temperature in Boulder, Colorado or Stockholm? Just point and click...Like to see how other people spend their days? There are live cameras, accessible through the Web, pointed at busy laboratories all over the world... What's truly bizarre is that people actually visit these places—not just in ones or twos but by the thousands. The hot spot this past holiday season was the Rome Lab Snowball Cam, which advertises itself as a robot arm, ice machine and camera setup that invites Internet visitors to heave snowballs at engineers working at an Air Force base in Rome, New York. Like so many other Pentagon projects, however, the Snowball Cam turned out to be less than it promised. The lab was real. So were the engineers. The snowballs, however, were "virtual"—which is to say, no fun at all. But that didn't prevent Internet users from stopping by the site before Christmas—at the rate of one every minute and a half.

Philip Elmer-Dewitt
"Snowballs in Cyberspace," *Time*

UFOs, Conspiracies & Paranormal

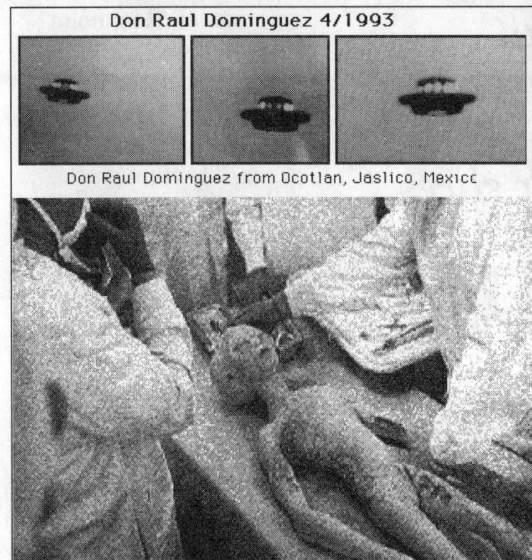

Don Raul Dominguez 4/1993
Don Raul Dominguez from Ocotlan, Jaslico, Mexicc

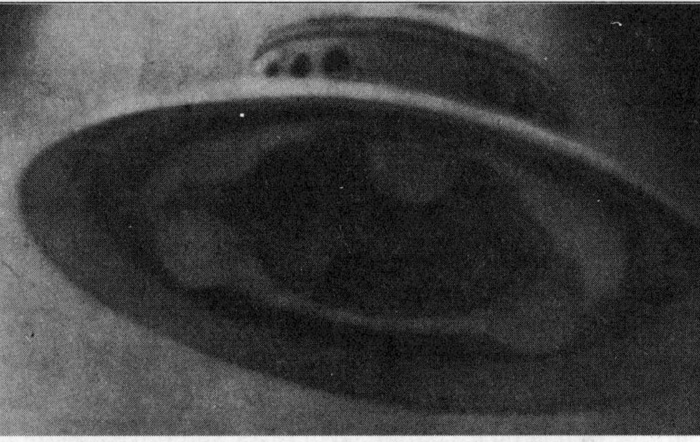

▲ *(Top left) UFO Photos and* ▲ *(Top right) alien spacecraft, from* **SPIRIT—WWW, Spiritual Consciousness on the WWW**, *at* Jump **2308**, *and* ◀ *(Bottom left) alleged alien autopsy photo, from* **Smitty's UFO Page**, *at* Jump **2285**.

Paranormal Parade

Alien Information Jump **1585**

Ron Bertino is an afficionado of the unexplainable. A mild-mannered Webmaster of Perth, Western Australia-based iiNet Technologies by day, he becomes king of the uncanny by night. This site provides links to every enigmatic incident Web site imaginable, from the Roswell UFO crash to the Crop Circle Connector. But bring a book to read while sitting in the waiting room—Bertino includes the most gif-heavy of any sites you've ever had the misfortune of twiddling your thumbs while waiting to download. —(H.L.)

URL▶ http://www.iinet.net.au/~bertino/alien.html

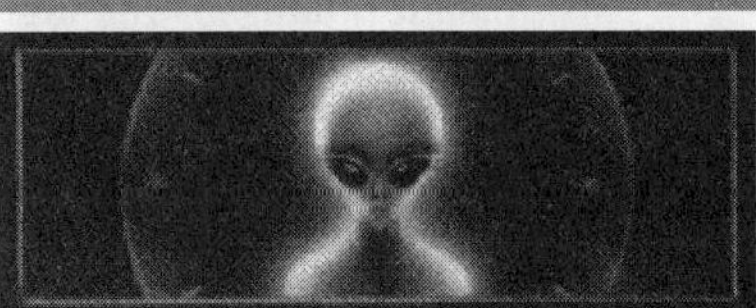

Alien Abductions

Intruders Foundation Online Jump **5694**

Anyone who has read anything at all about alien abductions has probably heard the name Budd Hopkins. So convinced was he that such abductions were real that he gave up just about every fragment of a "normal" life in order to try and assist those who were apparently suffering from the psychological scars brought on by such abductions. With this home page, maintained by John Velez on Hopkins' behalf, Hopkins and his followers make an attempt to reach even more people. Not only will you find pictures and articles pertaining to the subject of alien abductions, but victims are also invited to join in and share their experiences online. Fact or fiction? Who can say. —(J.P.)

KEY NEWSGROUP **alt.alien.visitors** URL▶ http://www.spacelab.net/~jvif/bhhp.html

UFO Reference Starting Point

alt.alien.visitors Frequently Asked Questions Jump **2284**

The **alt.alien.visitors** newsgroup was the first on Usenet for discussions of UFOs and related topics, so while the name of the group may sound specific, the discussion covers a broad range. The newsgroup's FAQ reflects this diversity, and it is one of the best starting points for the UFO newbie. Topics covered include terminology, alien races, abductions and theories about them, UFO projects, movies, documentaries and television programs, general theories and controversies, publications, and organizations. The information is well organized, linked to additional resources on a given topic, and presented objectively without sensationalism. —(L.S.)

KEY NEWSGROUP **alt.alien.visitors**

URL▶ http://zeta.cs.adfa.oz.au/Spirit/ufofaq.html#Abductions and Current Theories

United Nations Troops Fly UFOs In California

Reported December 4, 1996

California USA - "I was driving home from work last Thursday night about 8pm. I was in my Volvo wagon - it's the safest thing I can drive given the large number of UFO's that have crashed into cars recently.

Anyway...I was on Laird Road and saw a UFO coming straight for me in the Volvo. At the last minute it pulled up and landed in a field, and out came a bunch of UN soldiers - all wearing black. I shut the Volvo off, and walked quietly toward them. The strong smell of garlic and perspiration filled the air, leaving me with little doubt that these guys came from Europe. They smelled like a second class Paris metro car.

I didn't have my camera with me, but I did manage to get a baggie full of the odor that surrounded the troops. I'm keeping it in my freezer right beside the dinosaur eggs and my bigfoot scat."

▲ *Alien spacecraft sighting, from* **United Nations Invasion Tracking**, *at* Jump **5917**.

Everyone's Guide to UFOs

The UFO Guide Jump **2109** 

If you've been watching *The X Files* and scratching your head, you'll get straight answers to your questions about UFOs from this guide by Nick Humphries. It's the second edition, with expanded definitions, explanations of phenomena, overviews of important cases, and the answer to just about any UFO question. Well, most any question, anyway. There's a lot that just can't be answered, which is why many people can't think "UFO" without thinking "crackpot." But what can be answered is here, with an alphabetical list of references, clear writing, and links within each section to related information. —(L.S.)

KEY NEWSGROUP **alt.alien.visitors** URL▶ http://www.rahul.net/rogerd/ufo.guide.html

There's Something in the Wheat Field!

CROP CIRCLE CONNECTOR Jump **7256** 

Crop circles—those mysterious flattened areas that form regular designs—are often found in British farm fields and often cannot be traced to human or animal activity. Stuart Dike has created a set of interesting Web pages that record in word and picture the latest news on and evidence of crop circles found in the British Isles. As well, he offers links to crop-circle pages around the world, crop-circle artwork found on the Web, and related newsletters of interest. —(E.v.B.)

KEY NEWSGROUP **alt.alien.visitors** URL▶ http://www.hub.co.uk/intercafe/cropcircle/connector.html

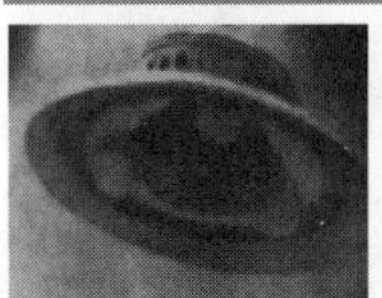

The Ultimate UFOlogists' Site

The Ultimate UFOLOGISTS WWW Page Jump **6565** 

This site offers all that's UFO-related, including complete descriptions of over 100 cases and sightings. Andy Page is the master of this central extraterrestrial resource, and provides more than you probably ever knew existed: UFO pictures, book reviews, theories, personal sightings' even a Who's Who in UFOlogy, mixed in with all the very latest UFO news. Andy's UFO Glossary is also a treat, defining such terms as FUFOR, MUFON, and BUFORA. —(L.T.)

KEY NEWSGROUP **alt.paranet.ufo** URL▶ http://ourworld.compuserve.com:80/homepages/AndyPage/

Tales of the Israeli Spy Agency

The Mossad Jump **2140** 

For Ludlum fans, conspiracy buffs, and those who, since the end of the Cold War, find no fun in kicking around the CIA anymore, Victor Ostrovsky can fill the void. A former case officer for the Israeli intelligence service, Ostrovsky gives you the skinny on the Mossad, albeit with a disgruntled attitude. You'll learn how the Mossad is organized, how it recruits the willing, unwilling and unknowing, and the technical and operational aspects of its spycraft. The author of two exposés about the activities of the Mossad, Ostrovsky also provides fodder for conspiracy discussions and righteous indignation with snippets from his latest book, which charges that the Mossad conducts industrial espionage within U.S. companies, works to sabotage the Arab-Israeli peace process, and undertakes other generally nasty operations. —(L.S.)

KEY NEWSGROUP **alt.conspiracy** URL▶ http://www.Phoenix.CA:80/mossad/index.html#vic

UFO Humor

Hastings UFO Society Jump 2314

The Hastings UFO Society lampoons the UFO scene, so stay away from this page if you take your extraterrestrials seriously. There are a few reports to read, but the main purpose of the site is to distribute the Society's Psicast radio programs. They're hilarious, a combination or Orson Welles's "War of the Worlds" and *Firesign Theater*. You can download and listen to reports of UFO sightings, alien abductions, and eyewitness accounts, along with similarly parodied radio commercials. New programs appear monthly, with an archive of previous programs also available. —(L.S.)

KEY NEWSGROUP **rec.humor** URL▸ http://www.santarosa.edu/hufos/

The Think-for-Yourself UFO Page

Smitty's UFO Page Jump 2285

Dave Schmitz approaches the UFO debate from a different angle. He doesn't question that, mathematically, there are more than enough planets in our galaxy that can support life. Dave's question is, if that is so, would these life forms possess the technology for interstellar travel? He doesn't try to answer the question for you, instead offers a site with articles and references on the subject to let you form your own opinions. He also archives general UFO information, and includes current news of sightings, theories, and a long list of links to other Web pages. There's more than enough here to let you draw your own conclusions, and begin questioning any you may have already made. —(L.S.)

KEY NEWSGROUP **alt.alien.research** URL▸ http://www.schmitzware.com/ufo.html

UFOs: The Project Blue Book Compilation

The Blue Book Jump 2286

The U.S. government's serious investigation of UFOs began in the 1950s, with the long-suppressed Project Blue Book. Under the auspices of the U.S. Air Force, Blue Book investigated reports of UFO sightings, interviewing witnesses, examining sites, and trying to come up with explanations for the phenomena. Here, Don Allen presents Don Berliner's compilation of Blue Book "unknowns" for your perusal. There is no commentary, other than some of the conclusions excerpted from Blue Book—but then the sheer numbers of reported unexplained sightings is commentary in itself. —(L.S.)

KEY NEWSGROUP **alt.alien.visitors** URL▸ http://www.cis.ksu.edu/~psiber/substand/bluebook.html#2

UFOs for the Rest of Us

UFO Directory and Forum Jump 2309

This is a page best suited for people interested in, but not passionate about, UFOs. It should be on everyone's UFO bookmark list, though, as the monthly articles presented here are informative, insightful, and interesting. Still, the objective is to provide an elementary resource, and it fulfills this promise with articles, a Web links list that offers a good cross section of Internet UFO resources, referrals to resources off the Internet, and interesting quotes from past and present UFO studies. —(L.S.)

KEY NEWSGROUP **alt.alien.visitors**

URL▸ http://galaxy.einet.net/galaxy/Community/Parascience/Unidentified-Flying-Objects/mark-hines/ufo-forum.html#book

Dream Weaving

dreamSources Jump 2272

If you're of a mind, there's much to be learned from your dreams. You can glean insights into your relationships, help pinpoint areas of strife and potential conflict, and generally develop an understanding of yourself by paying attention to your subconscious. These pages will help with this exploration and introduce you to new concepts, such as group dreaming and dream control, while you connect with others who share this interest. You can even share your dreams, via e-mail and an online data entry form, while you read about the dreams of others. This isn't a scientist's dreaming site, although there are links to academic dream resources. But it's for more than the curious—even if the term "serious dreamer" doesn't sound quite right. —(L.S.)

KEY NEWSGROUP **alt.dreams** URL▶ http://www.itp.tsoa.nyu.edu/~windeatr/dreamSources.html

Out-of-Body Experiences for Beginners

Out of Body Experience Jump **2296**

You not only can learn about out-of-body and lucid dreaming experiences here, you can also learn the techniques to do them. There is a good FAQ, several articles, and some general guides to give you the background you need to understand this phenomenon and develop your abilities. You'll also find personal stories of these experiences and links to books and institutes for further study, as well as sections on meditation and near-death experiences. —(L.S.)

KEY NEWSGROUP **alt.out-of-body** URL▶ http://www.protree.com/Spirit/obe.html

Exploding the Myth of the Bermuda Triangle

The Bermuda Triangle Jump **2323**

Kevin Quitt doesn't believe those stories about the Bermuda Triangle. He enjoys them, but he doesn't believe them. He explains why in this page, describing the dangers of the water currents in the area and discussing the scientific basis of how planes and ships can disappear without a trace. He also looks at some of the more popular Bermuda Triangle stories, including the sagas of Flight 19 and the Mary Celeste, and explains, point by point, why he believes they are nothing more than fanciful stories. —(L.S.)

KEY NEWSGROUP **alt.mythology** URL▶ http://tigger.cc.uic.edu/~toby-g/tri.html#o

Useless & Unique

Countdown to Eternity

The Death Clock Jump **5910**

We are forever haunted by death and taxes. We can't help you with the taxes, but we can help you with the death part. Well, we can't help you, but we do have connections. And you do, too. Welcome to The Death Clock, created by Raymond Camden. It is, quite simply, a clock that acturarially speaking foretells the day and date of your death, based on your birth date. Click on the death clock and you'll discover—whether you want to or not—the predicted date of your demise. And as a special bonus, you'll also find out how many seconds you have to live. It looks like a lot of seconds at first, but man,—they sure fly by quickly. —(J.P.)

URL▶ http://www.ucs.usl.edu/~rkc7747/death.html

Cyber Humor at its Best

Greg Bulmash's Humor Page Jump **5891**

Look out. You get a pretty good idea about what's around the next corner when the theme music on this site starts to play. We couldn't place it exactly, but it was something along the lines of a Laurel and Hardy-type thing. So we headed in, ready to be amused. And we were not disappointed. It starts with the site's main column, penned by this site's creator, Greg Bulmash. You can read the current one or search the archive. You'll want to do both. Next up is "The WASHED-UPdate™," where he hunts down celebrities whose stars no longer shine so brightly, and reports their latest doings. As he says, the idea is not to humiliate, and again he is true to his word. Another site feature, "Gong is G," is a cyber-church that exists only on the Internet. The head-honcho is . . . Mr. Bulmash again. This is off-the-wall humor at its best. We didn't see anything to offend, but you never know! —(J.P.)

KEY NEWSGROUP **rec.humor.d** URL▶ http://java.javabooks.net/~gbhp/

Net Urban Legends

Urban Legends Archive

Jump 5919

Perhaps you've heard of urban legends on the Internet. An urban legend is a story that, while it might sound plausible, is usually a work of fiction that takes on a life of its own after being passed from person to person. An example would be the one that states that increased pizza ordering in the Pentagon is indicative of a big news story, or the Good Times Virus that infects Internet e-mail (not true!), or deep-fried mice being found in buckets of fried chicken. You'll find dozens of other ones here, many of which you may have heard—and even believed! It's all in good fun, though, and a wonderful barometer of our society, produced and maintained by Jason Heimbaugh and Emily Harrison Kelly (NOTE: Some material on this site is not suitable for children). —(J.P.)

KEY NEWSGROUP alt.folklore.surburban URL▶ http://www.urbanlegends.com/

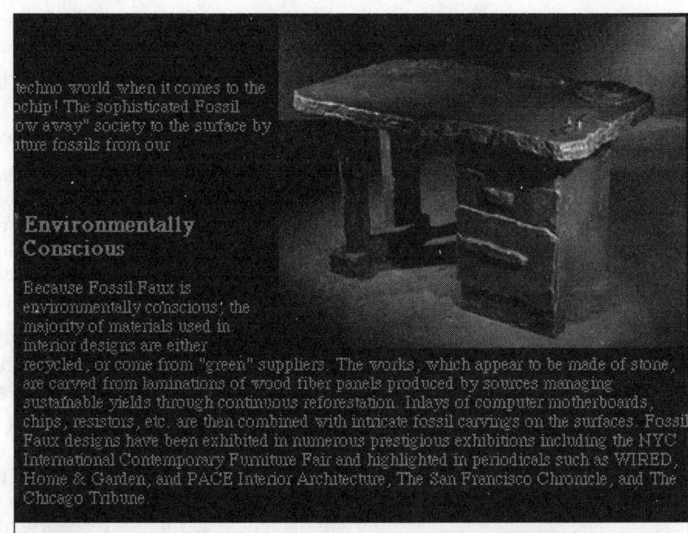

Environmentally Conscious
Because Fossil Faux is environmentally conscious; the majority of materials used in interior designs are either recycled, or come from "green" suppliers. The works, which appear to be made of stone, are carved from laminations of wood fiber panels produced by sources managing sustainable yields through continuous reforestation. Inlays of computer motherboards, chips, resistors, etc. are then combined with intricate fossil carvings on the surfaces. Fossil Faux designs have been exhibited in numerous prestigious exhibitions including the NYC International Contemporary Furniture Fair and highlighted in periodicals such as WIRED, Home & Garden, and PACE Interior Architecture, The San Francisco Chronicle, and The Chicago Tribune.

▲ *Flintstone-like decor, from* **Fossil Faux Furniture**, *at* **Jump 5894**.

Retro-Techno, Fake Fossil Furniture

Fossil Faux Furniture **Jump 5894**

Of course we all know what Fossil Faux Furniture is. Sure we do. If it doesn't have anything to do with fossil fuels, we're pretty much stumped. But it's our mission to dig up the dirt on such unknowns. So we are pleased to be able to inform you that Fossil Faux Furniture is . . . well, fake fossil furniture is . . . well, maybe not fake, really. It's furniture all right (well, sort of) but it's made to look like Fred and Barney left it at the curb one night and someone not only carted it off, but decided to make replicas. You got that? Anyway, drop in and take a look. You won't be disappointed. Confused, maybe—but not disappointed. Our job is done. —(J.P.)

URL▶ http://www.well.com/user/foslfaux/

furniture (fossil)

Wacky Headline Hunters

AM News Abuse **Jump 5893**

There is no word of explanation here at this site, so what you find is what you find. Our only tip is the subheading: "Your Daily Dose of Apparent Intelligence." Oh boy. Looks like trouble. Funny trouble, mind you. A sample headline is in order: "I Need Another Big One Over Here Dept: A Spokane, WA funeral home was fined $4,000 for cremating the wrong body and then filling that man's casket with the body of the man who wanted to be cremated." We warned you. Skip down to the bottom of the page and you'll find this site's Headline Hall of Fame, where you'll be amused (or infuriated by turn) with pun headlines, crime headlines, Hollywood headlines and much more. —(J.P.)

URL▶ http://www.texas.net/~kaz/

Watch those Blue Helmets!

United Nations Invasion Tracking

Jump 5917

You might think, by the heading of this site, that it might have something to do with a real function of the United Nations. You won't find any worldly happenings

▲ *A graphic demonstration of the combustible nature of strawberry Pop Tarts, from* Strawberry Pop-Tart Blow-Torches, *at* Jump 4055.

here, ladies and gentlemen. Oh, you'll see the very official-looking UN logo, and even some reports on UN sightings, but we're guessing the boys in light blue didn't have much to do with this site. And we don't know who did have anything to do with it, as a matter of fact, although on the day we visited there was a bright, color photo of Eddie Haskell. Yes, that Eddie. And we found some movie scripts as well, and they might well be the real thing, although we won't go on record as saying so. So if you've looking for a good laugh, drop in (just make sure you leave your guns at the door). —(J.P.)

KEY NEWSGROUP **rec.humor.d** URL▶ http://team2.teamnet.net/~kylek/menu.html

Don't Try This at Home!

Strawberry Pop-Tart Blow-Torches Jump **4055** CONTENT

This is one of the most ridiculous sites on the Web, and also one of the funniest. The page details author Patrick Michaud's attempt to test his hypothesis that "Strawberry Pop-Tarts may be a cheap and inexpensive source of incendiary devices." Apparently, by causing Pop-Tarts to become lodged within a toaster, it is possible to cause flames between 10 and 18 inches high. Michaud does just this, walking you through his experiment step by step—and yes, there are pictures too! —(R.B.)

KEY NEWSGROUP **talk.bizarre** URL▶ http://www.sci.tamucc.edu/%7Epmichaud/toast/

Change those Faces

Faces
Jump **5934**

Would Jennifer Aniston be the big star of TV's "Friends" if she had Jim Carrey's mouth and Bill Clinton's eyes? Would Bob Dole have fared better in the election if he had Demi Moore's head and Boy George's eyes? Well, we don't know, but you can check out all of the above, and many more combinations, at Cory R. Gilbert's Faces page. Using frames, Cory has developed a page that allows you to break a picture into three parts—head, eyes and mouth—and to choose from a list of various parts to construct your very own new face. It's great fun, but of course you do need a frames-capable browser. —(J.P.)

URL▶ http://www.web-usa.com/faces/

Don't Get Stuck Forever in the Black Hole of the Web

Black Hole of the Web Jump **4052** CONTENT

Brad Whitmore and Carlos Pero bring you this bit of Web weirdness. It seems as though they've put one of those cosmic distortions, a Black Hole, right on the Web! Heed the warnings: "Whatever you do, do not go near the Black

Hole! Stay Away!" There's a counter to show you how many others couldn't resist this fun little side trip on the Web (note: requires Netscape browser 1.1 for full effects). —(R.B.)

URL ▶ http://www.ravenna.com/blackhole.html

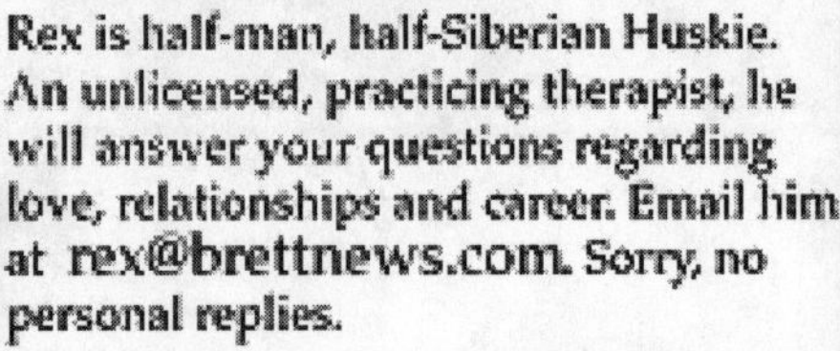

Ask Rex
Rex is half-man, half-Siberian Huskie. An unlicensed, practicing therapist, he will answer your questions regarding love, relationships and career. Email him at rex@brettnews.com. Sorry, no personal replies.
Rex, The Dog-Man

▲ *"Ask Rex the Dog Man" satirical feature, from* Brett News *at* Jump 1506.

Exactly Who's Laughing?

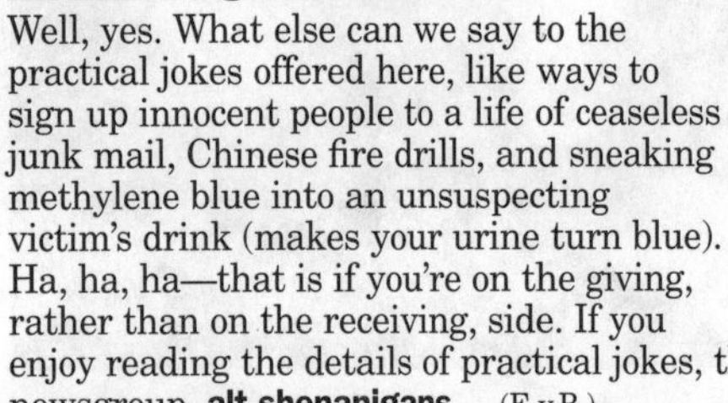

Practical Jokes from alt.shenanigans Jump 7394 CONTENT

Well, yes. What else can we say to the practical jokes offered here, like ways to sign up innocent people to a life of ceaseless junk mail, Chinese fire drills, and sneaking methylene blue into an unsuspecting victim's drink (makes your urine turn blue). Ha, ha, ha—that is if you're on the giving, rather than on the receiving, side. If you enjoy reading the details of practical jokes, then these are the best, culled from the popular and hilarious Net newsgroup, **alt.shenanigans**. —(E.v.B.)

KEY NEWSGROUP **alt.shenanigans** URL ▶ http://www.umd.umich.edu/~nhughes/htmldocs/pracjokes.html

On the Trail of the Missing Sock

THE BUREAU OF MISSING SOCKS Jump 8038 CONTENT

Every once in awhile a Web site appears that makes the Net worthwhile—a real public service for Internet citizens everywhere. One such service is the Bureau of Missing Socks. In the words of its creator: "The Bureau of Missing Socks is the first organization solely devoted to solving the question of what happens to missing single socks. It explores all aspects of the phenomena including the occult, conspiracy theories, and extraterrestrials. We offer support for the matching sock-deprived, and catalog, research, index, and document all extant material related to socks since the dawn of the shoe." We really enjoyed reading Great Sock Mysteries. Add your own tale of woe about your own Bermuda Triangle of missing socks. You might even find a missing sock using the easy interface of this site's search database: calf-length, plaid, dressy? —(E.v.B.)

KEY NEWSGROUP **rec.humor.d** URL ▶ http://www.jagat.com/joel/socks.html

World Nap Organization (WNO)

World Nap Organization (WNO) Jump 6684 CONTENT

Cherish your naps but feel guilty about taking them? Don't lose sleep over it...join the club! The World Nap Organization is a special interest group devoted to battling negative images of the blissful practice of nap taking. Read their napping FAQ, fill out a nap survey, or discover the difference between nap-time and night dreams. Apparently the reason so many are having difficulty napping these days is due to a lack of appropriate music, so the WNO is offering lots of MIDI files to help you out. Now you can feel a more comfortable about catching that next "power nap," knowing there are so many others out there just like you. —(L.T.)

KEY NEWSGROUP **alt.dreams** URL ▶ http://www.bluemarble.net/~amyloo/wno.html

ZUG: Humor and Pranks Online

ZUG Jump 7515 CONTENT

The unquestioned star of this humor zine is John Hargrave, whose deadpan responses to moronic junk e-mail alone make ZUG worth a visit. There's also a classic electronic exchange between an official at HotWired and Hargrave, who tells them he's launching an online venture called "HotWeird" (which falls through, he later claims, because of a lawsuit over a child who lost a leg playing a video game called "Space Winky"). "Techno-Shamans of Texas" parodies tragically hip Gen-X fiction, with hypertext links highlighting recurring themes such as "cactus" and "Garth Brooks." —(C.W.)

URL ▶ http://www.mediashower.com/zugmain/zugmain.html

Because everything in her home is waterproof, the housewife of 2000 can do her daily cleaning with a hose

▲ *A 1950s glimpse into the future of domestic chores in a waterproof home, from* Wall O' Shame *at* Jump 0111.

The (Ig)Nobel Prizes

Classical Gas Jump 2719 

Fans of dubious achievement awards should not miss this page. Not to be confused with the more prestigious awards from the Swedish Academy, the Ig Nobels seek out and honor those wastes of time and energy, which would be better ignored if they weren't so funny. As humorous or just plain silly as some of the recipients' achievements may be, they are real, and there's even an awards ceremony where some of them actually show up, with gratitude. Past prize winners include the psychologist cited for his 30-year study on the effects of punishing residents of Singapore for spitting, chewing gum, or feeding pigeons; the Alabama church that estimated, mathematically, how many state citizens will go to Hell if they don't repent; and the Japanese agency that undertook a seven-year study to determine if earthquakes are caused by catfish wiggling their tails. They're all true, which makes them even more hilarious. —(L.S.)

URL ▶ http://www.improb.com/projects/ig-home.html

SECTION 1: Education and Schooling

1. Have you ever taken a "higher" math course? (Trig, Calculus)
2. ...at the college level?
3. ...and received an A (3.7 grade point)?

Find Out If You're a Nerd

The (infamous) Nerdity Test! 

Jump 4080

This fun interactive site is brought to you by J. Bennet. You can take a 500-question interactive quiz, based on the "Nerdity Test" by Philip Kiser, and have your score calculated to see how you rank on the Nerd scale. This Web site is done in a tongue-in-cheek style, and it's worth the visit just to read the questions. —(R.B.)

URL ▶ http://gonzo.tamu.edu/nerd.html

Interactive Cindy Crawford Game Site

Cindy Crawford Concentration Jump 4071 

Here's a great site for you supermodel fans out there. You play the classic game "Concentration," trying to match pictures by clicking on choices from a 4x4 grid—but in this case, the pictures are all different shots of Cindy Crawford! A fun implementation of interactive Web capabilities. —(R.B.)

KEY NEWSGROUP alt.supermodels URL ▶ http://cad.ucla.edu:8001/concentration?begin

CAM

EarthCam's Live Shots from Around the Net

EarthCam - We Never Close Jump 5655 

You might have seen them before; someone might have placed a video camera in front of their fish tank or a coffee machine in Paris and, through the magic that is the Net, everyone in the world can see what is happening. Or not happening, as the case may be. They are loads of fun, of course, but how on earth do you ever find the cam you're looking for? EarthCam is a comprehensive directory to all the live video camera feeds, all over the Internet. Not only do they have links to all the sites by subject, but you can also do a keyword search. So, either way, searching or browsing, you can now find the camera that sits in front of the Hollywood sign (it's here, you know). —(J.P.)

URL ▶ http://www.earthcam.com/

Toasterlater Model #7, Serial #947:

One of the wackiest toasters made, this model has a sawtooth conveyor belt that jiggles the toast through its interior, passing it laterally by the heating elements. Has a porthole for viewing progress, and a darker/lighter control that adjusts toast travel speed in seven increments. Has an on/off switch. Is known to burn bread mercilessly.

▲ *A model #7 toaster, from* Toaster Museum *at* Jump 7446.

Toasters Online!

Toaster Museum Jump 7446

Berkeley Systems, creators of that famous flying toaster screen saver, have created a site honoring the humble kitchen appliance—the toaster. Although many of the sections seem to be under construction, they promise much. For example, you will soon be able to read tidbits from toaster history, send in a picture of your favorite toaster in order to "go down in kitchen appliance history," or tour the Howard Gelman collection (illustrated) of toasters from the Victorian Universal Flipper to modern-day electronic models. Great fun! Before you leave, explore some of Berkeley's other offerings, from free screen saver demos to Café Slack. —(E.v.B.)

URL ▶ http://www.berksys.com/www/funtour/toastmuseum.html

Take a Random Trip Along the Web

U Roulette Jump 0108

Funky Web jump site created by the University of Kansas jumps you to a random Web site at the click of a mouse key. The effect is somewhat akin to being driven, blindfolded, to a strange new location. Chances are, you'll be thrown to an interesting Web site you've never seen before. You can also contribute your favorite URLs so other users of this site can randomly jump to your favorite Web sites, too. All in all, yet another fun way to surf the Web! —(E.G.)

URL ▶ http://kuhttp.cc.ukans.edu/cwis/organizations/kucia/uroulette/uroulette.html

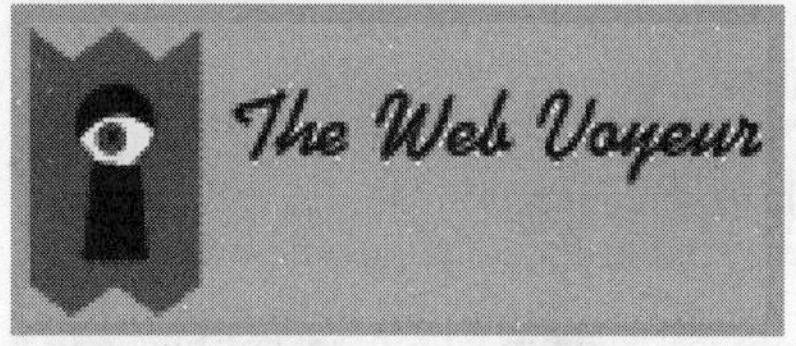

Peeping through the Web

The Web Voyeur—Live Images Jump 2321

Lots of Web sites have live or near-live video links, and many of them, while complete time killers, are nonetheless quite entertaining. For those of you with time on your hands, Larry Gilbert has assembled a page of links to let you browse and choose. He provides brief descriptions of each image, and, if those aren't enough, you can link to more information about the site before committing to a download. Among the links are live video feeds of landscapes, pets, robots, offices, and sanitation devices. The page is constantly updated, and if you have a contribution, e-mail the URL with a description to Larry. —(L.S.)

URL ▶ http://www.eskimo.com/%7Eirving/web-voyeur/

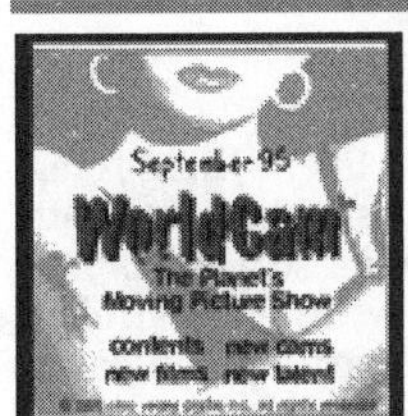

Be a Fly on the Web's Wall . . .

You're Watchin' WorldCam Jump 6002

Move over, America's Funniest Home Videos—now there's WorldCam! Submit your best videos—even your mediocre ones—to Ohio Valley Digital, Inc. for all the world to see. Do you have a great photo opportunity? Set up your camera and have your photos immediately posted to the Web, with updates every few minutes! Because this site is filled with user contributions, you never know what you may find, so take some extra care if you'll be here with the kids. —(N.F.)

URL ▸ http://worldcam.com/

The Meaning of Meaninglessness

Useless WWW Pages Jump 2605

Cyber-existentialists should stay away from this page, for while we all know that in a universe as vast as the Internet there will be many questionable exercises in Webcraftery, being confronted head-on with so much evidence of the pointlessness of virtual existence is likely to throw their angst meters permanently into the red zone. For the rest of us, Steve Berlin's collection of "Who cares?" pages will amuse, bemuse and fascinate. And if you think this page itself may be useless, think again. If you're looking for humor, the commentaries form one of the funniest satirical monologues you'll find—pointed, but not mean-spirited. If you're just killing time anyway, you'll know you're doing it right when you follow these links. If you just can't get enough, there's the Useless Hall of Fame, and the Home for Retired Useless Pages. And if you think your time here shouldn't be totally useless, read the essays on why particular page subjects are, indeed, useless. There are plenty of places that tell you what you should do with a Web page, but your education isn't complete until you read what you shouldn't do, by reading this one! —(L.S.)

KEY NEWSGROUP **alt.culture.www** URL ▸ http://www.primus.com/staff/paulp/useless.html

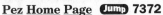

The World of Pez

Pez Home Page Jump 7372

Paul Telford uses his sugar high to good advantage—he has built some pretty fun pages dedicated to that sugary treat in the plastic dispenser—Pez. Got questions about Pez? Check the FAQ where anything to do with the candies will be found. As well, a whole page is dedicated to its history. Don't know what to do with the dispensers? Well, read Paul's suggestions and see what you think. You might also want to keep them around—they've become collectibles. You can also surf to other Pez-related pages from this site. Not enough? OK, stroll through Paul's Pez gallery and then subscribe to the Pez mailing list to get the latest news and views on the candy. —(E.v.B.)

KEY NEWSGROUP **alt.food.pez** URL ▸ http://wwwcsif.cs.ucdavis.edu/~telford/pez.html

The Web's Optical Illusion Center

Optical Illusions Jump 1571

Remember those optical illusion "experiments" you did in Psych 101? Are the lines in the picture parallel or bent? Are both lines the same length? Bob Ausbourne has collected some classic optical illusions in a Web site that has all the memory-firing potential of a Proustian madeleine. You jump from illusion to illusion, dredging up long-lost mental pictures of those dreaded 8 a.m. psych labs. Unlike your drab professor, Ausbourne provides historical background. For instance, W. E. Hill's drawing that moves back and forth between being a young girl and an old woman was originally published in *Puck* in 1915 as "My Wife and My Mother-in-Law." Optical Illusion isn't overloaded with gratuitous links. Since he's a professional artist, Ausbourne wants you to take a look at his resume and portfolio, both of which are also impressive. And he makes it easy to take a gander at other illusionary artists like M.C. Escher and Salvador Dali. —(H.L.)

URL ▸ http://lainet3.lainet.com/~ausbourn/

Worldwide Candid Camera

LEONARD'S CAM WORLD Jump 8033 

Snow falling in the Colorado mountains. Street life in Hong Kong. Watching traffic at the Finland-Russia border. Is it the next best thing to being there? Leonard sure seems to think so. He has mounted more than 130 links to live online cameras worldwide on his pages. You can check the weather, or stroll through various cities and towns of the world without having to get up to put your shoes on. Ah, virtual living at its best. —(E.v.B.)

KEY NEWSGROUP **rec.video** URL▸ http://jax.jaxnet.com/~len/camera.html#other

I've Got (Bio)Rhythm

Web-O-Rhythm Jump 1576 CONTENT

If you're feeling out of sorts today, chances are one or more of your cyclical biorhythms—Physical, Emotional, Intellectual, or Intuitional—is on the wane. Check it out at Web-O-Rhythm. All you do is type in your birth date and Brian Towles's remarkably fast program creates a personalized biorhythm chart based on the information you enter. You can also see into the future by requesting biorhythms for the next few months. So what if your mother-in-law is coming to visit next month—you know you'll be at the top of your emotional and intellectual cycles! If you need more details on weekly developments, Towles provides a link to your horoscope at Rob Brezsny's Real Astrology Web site, too. —(H.L.)

URL▸ http://www.qns.com/html/weborhythm

Isolate lily sir (Silly Solitaire)

Main Sanitary Nag (Anagram Insanity) Jump 1584 

Looking for a (another) fun Web time waster? This site will keep you occupied for hours as you effortlessly create your own anagrams. All you do is type in the words you want scrambled, press the send button, and out come the variations. Impress your friends with your anagramability! —(H.L.)

URL▸ http://infobahn.com:80/pages/anagram.html

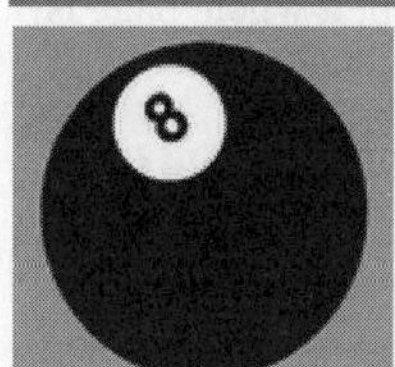

Magic Eight Ball Knows All

The Magic Eight Ball Jump 6016 

At last, a place to find the answers to life's most pressing questions. The Magic Eight Ball (yes, the same one we used as kids) is now on the Web, and will give sage advice on anything and everything you may be wondering about. And if the Eight Ball helped you on your quest for knowledge, you can share your story with others! Is this a fun spot? The Magic Eight Ball says "It is certain!" —(N.F.)

URL▸ http://www.elseware.com/eight/

Colorful Abuse at Your Fingertips

Abuse-A-Tron  7325 

Feeling masochistic today? Well, hurry on over to the Abuse-A-Tron page where, with just a click of the old mouse button, you will be told off in no uncertain terms, and in colorful, computer-generated boilerplate phrases. And you can hand it right back with another click of the mouse, and tell the creators of this page just what you think about them, the world, and the Internet. And, hey, don't be nice! —(E.v.B.)

KEY NEWSGROUP **rec.humor.d** URL▸ http://www.xe.com/loyalty/abuse.html

Denizens of Doom Motorcycle Club

DOD - Motorcycle Jump **0089** 

Rowdy Netters from the **rec.motorcycles** newsgroup have created a funky Web site for their satirical motorcycle club, the of Denizens of Doom. Tap into this Web site, become a member and read their funny stories, sing their songs, and join in on the activities of the Internet's first cyberspace motorcycle club whose motto says it all: "Live to Flame, Flame to Live!" —(E.G.)

URL▶ http://www.ssc.upenn.edu/~awhite/Interests/Motorcycle/DoD/DoD.html

▲ *Smallest mouth organ player, via* **Virtual Image Archive** *at* Jump **7315**.

Hackers' World & Culture

The Jargon File 3.1.0 Jump **0124** CONTENT

Pascal Courtois maintains this expansive, sometimes humorous guide to computer hacker jargon, writing and speech style, lexicon and folklore with a pseudoscientific style which reads as if it were written by Margaret Mead, the famous anthropologist. A fascinating look inside this strange and quirky subculture on the Net. —(E.G.)

KEY NEWSGROUP **alt.hackers** URL▶ http://web.cnam.fr/Jargon/?1

Jargon Watch

Get Out of My Mouth: 474 Top Jump **7341** 

A pretty funny site. The people behind Downtown Digital are dedicated to making a mockery of techno-speak. You are invited to create your own ridiculous acronyms and words. Both are collected in the Jargon Bargain Bin where you can add your own definitions. Then if you're really feeling mischievous, use the mock-lingo, as Downtown Digital says, "to send a vengeful missive to your favorite tech-head via e-mail!" —(E.v.B.)

KEY NEWSGROUP **comp.misc** URL▶ http://www.dtd.com/goomm/

So, What's Your Problem?

Auntie Lois Jump **7390** 

Oh, has Auntie Lois got advice for you! See how Jobless in Manhattan or Confused in Boston were counseled, and then send your own troubled question to Auntie Lois. But beware, she bites! And if you tire of Auntie Lois and her know-it-all attitude, well, then, why not surf over and visit with her good friend the Galactic Web Empress—it's quite a trip! —(E.v.B.)

KEY NEWSGROUP **rec.humor.d** URL▶ http://www.dfw.net/~soulmate/aunt.html

Boisterous, Almost Believable, Corporate Boilerplate!

AthenaNow - Technology Company Engine Jump **7396** 

Thinking of starting a company, but stuck on a name? And have you noticed that many new business names, especially for technology companies, sound nearly alike? Well, help is at hand. When you access the AthenaNow Technology Company Engine, it creates "a unique corporate profile of a fictitious, brand-new technology company that's ready for business." And, almost believable. What a hoot! You can even generate a hilarious company mission statement, a list of products, and even meet your company's fictitious top executives. Return often, because each page is generated randomly, so you'll never get the same page twice. —(E.v.B.)

KEY NEWSGROUP **alt.humor.d** URL▶ http://www.athenanow.com/engine.htm

The Spot: The Parody

Squat Intro Jump 7408

Here's a group of college students' Web parody of the slickly designed and popular episodic Web site, The Spot. Enter The Squat—a rather large trailer located in a Missouri trailer park—and follow the adventures of roommates Cleitus, Woody, Earl, and Larlene. The stories of their lives, work, loves, and hates are told in patented "Spot" style, except with a good-ole boy's (and girl's) twang. Very different, to say the least, and takes quite a few fine and richly deserved satiric swipes at The Spot. You are encouraged to write your own episodes, but first read past installments in order to put yourself into the narrative flow. —(E.v.B.)

URL ▶ http://theory.physics.missouri.edu/~georges/Josh/squat/

Great Site, Eh?

The Great Web Canadianizer Jump 7451

The Great Web Canadianizer, co-developed by Rob Stanley and Andrew Chak, is the ultimate Canadian revenge. This fearsome twosome got sick and tired of "American Hosers messin' around with our Canadian identity and stuff, eh?" They have taken on the Net and, ta-da!, Canadianized it, à la the McKenzie brothers, through one of the funniest, wickedest conversion programs we've seen lately. Enter a URL (which they call a hURL), and lo and behold, when you link, the page is Canadianized, eh, with burps, and back bacon, and beer and spelling conventions in honor of the original McKenzie brothers Hoser routines. So, don your toques, pop a Molsons, and enter the Great White North. Beauty, eh? —(E.v.B.)

KEY NEWSGROUP soc.culture.canada URL ▶ http://www.io.org/~themaxx/canada/can.html

Hackers in Suits

DigiCrime, Inc. Jump 7453

With tongue firmly in their cybercheek, the originators of this site look at information security issues, and note the many "vulnerabilities of information systems that can easily be exploited by a technologically advanced criminal element. We don't advocate doing this, but we often find it both amusing and alarming to ponder the possibilities." So what do they offer? Well, a fictional high-tech company's product line that's a real mixed bag of Net breakthroughs, so to speak: an airline rerouting service, phone rerouting service, password generation service, cryptographic key search service, and a favorite—a telephone wiretap service used to find out who your significant other really talks to on the cellular. If you want to join this satirical band, here's the qualifications for the job: "a healthy cynicism about information security, and a rapier wit." —(E.v.B.)

URL ▶ http://www.digicrime.com/

Tips for Living—Or Are They?

Terrapin presents the Top Tips Page Jump 7468

Bill Dossett has compiled an enormous list of what he called top tips (or perhaps they should be labeled guides for living) that many people have contributed to his pages. And you are encouraged to add more. But be warned, some of the tips are sexist, unfunny, and sometimes downright sophomoric. But, on the other hand, there are some funny contributions here and there. For example: "If your enemy wrongs you, buy each of his children a drum (Ancient Chinese Proverb)." —(E.v.B.)

KEY NEWSGROUP rec.humor.d URL ▶ http://www.emtex.com/toptips/

Antology of Ant Antics

Antics Page Jump 7475

Richard Davis is an ant lover, of sorts. He has compiled an "Antology featuring Anteractive cartoons of Antertaining Ants and Ant words." The gentle humor of this site won us over as we surfed through Richard's ant

cartoons. We especially liked the propel-ant—featuring a daredevil ant being shot out of a cannon. You can also follow Richard's links to other ant-related pages. A nicely designed and well-written site. —(E.v.B.)

KEY NEWSGROUP **rec.humor.d** URL▶ http://www.ionet.net/~rdavis/antics.shtml

Geekness Revealed

Geek Chic Jump **7477**

Geek Chic—it's the "in" thing these days! Very funny reading here, from the chapters in this site's "Geek Rhetorique" to the "Geek Mythologique," which chronicles the history of geeks in literature and cinema. Geek Idyllique was particularly amusing, with its digital photo album illustrating "typical geek lifestyles." We especially liked the pen protector in the tux pocket. And, well, we admit it, we even snuck a peek at the Nude Nerds pinup calendar. A great giggle of a site! —(E.v.B.)

KEY NEWSGROUP **alt.geek** URL▶ http://access.advr.com/~geekchic/

Calling All Jeffs!

Page of Jeff's Jump **7488**

Obsession—and specialization—knows no bounds on the Web. The creator of this site, Jeff, thinks all the world's a Jeff, and you can be one, too! Jeff has built this page—filled with links to other Jeff pages (those created by other guys named Jeff) on the Net—not only to honor all Jeffs, but also to induct anyone who wants to be a Jeff into the club. If you're a Jeff, just fill out the handy form and your page will be mounted in the growing list. Jeff wannabees can sign the guest book, too. —(E.v.B.)

KEY NEWSGROUP **rec.humor.d** URL▶ http://www.planettell.com/planett/PJeff/pageofjeff.html

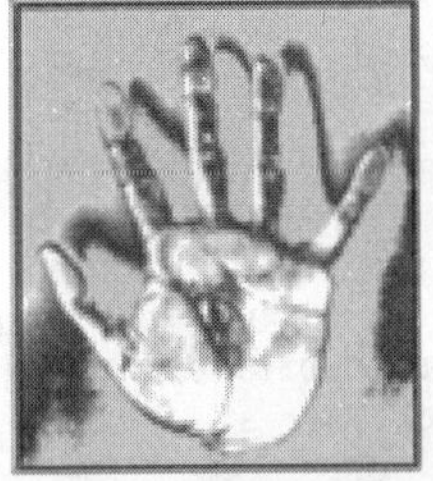

Annie's Healing Hand

Annie's Healing Page Jump **0058**

In a satirical homage to old-style TV Bible thumpers, Annie's Healing Hand offers miraculous restorative cures to all of us via the Web! Remember, though, that "screen savers might interfere with the session and should be disabled for optimal effects," and that, really, it's just all in good fun—Annie even lets you post your own personal testimonies to her page's miraculous effects. And while you're there, you can read comments posted by others as well. —(E.G.)

URL▶ http://www.NL.net/~jmathijs/

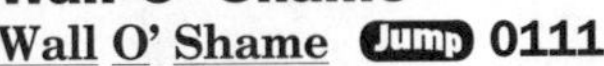

Wall O' Shame

Wall O' Shame Jump **0111**

Dan Bornstein's wild Web page is filled with hilarious newspaper excerpts, truly bizarre stories, weird personal experiences, and campy, kooky reprints of strange ads and other printed material. While you're here, check out Dan's well-done personal home page featuring his favorite Web links to many other funky sites along the Web. —(E.G.)

URL▶ http://web.kaleida.com/u/danfuzz/info/words/wall_o_shame/

Mr. Potato(e) Head

Mr. Edible Starchy Tuber Head Home Page Jump **1534**

Mr. Potato Head has been updated for the '90s—call him Mr. Edible Starchy Tuber Head, if you please. And he's adopted Dan Quayle's favorite spelling of his nickname; it's "Mr. Potatoe" now. But his disguise game is the same as it ever was. Here, you can build your own Mr. Edible Starchy Tuber Head by choosing from an array of facial and body features, and voilà—he's ready for another adventure. See what he's already done in the Hall of Fame, with memorable photos of Potatoe Without a Cause, Just Say No (any questions?), and The Amazing Flying Potatoe, among others. Learn Mr. Edible

Starchy Tuber Head's worst nightmare in 39 languages ("Oh my god! There's an axe in my head!") or venture "beyond the peel," where you'll find a repository of interesting sites of everything you wanted to know about those tubers, like growing and cooking them. You'll even see photos of the infamous former vice president chowing down on his favorite chips. A fun site for all ages. —(H.L.)

URL ▸ http://winnie.acsu.buffalo.edu/potatoe

Would you enjoy having the time to create crazy shit like this?
Learn the Secrets of Time Control . Quit your Job. Slack Off!
Send One Dollar to: SubGenius Foundation PO Box 140306 Dallas TX 75214

▲ *A message from the Church of the SubGenius, from* BOB (c) WEB!!!, *at* Jump 7219.

Legends of the Net

net.legends FAQ Jump 2343 CONTENT

Many newsgroup postings are peppered with references to people who qualify as **net.legends** and even **net.kooks** (the categories, by the way, are not mutually exclusive). If you want to trace these references, either to share the jokes or to study the variety of personality aberrations manifested on the Internet, check out Paul Roub's hypertext version of David DeLaney's FAQ. Browsing the articles is easy, since most of the entries on this site's contents page include a key phrase typical of the personality involved. You'll discover the well-, lesser- and almost totally unknown personalities, hoax perpetrators, and general miscreants of the Internet, along with many of the stories and links to home pages and more information about the subject. —(L.S.)

KEY NEWSGROUP **alt.net.personalities** URL ▸ http://www.shadow.net/~proub/net.legends/

BOB©WEB!!!

Bob's World

BOB (c) WEB!!! Jump 7219 

Net personality Andrew S. Damick is many things—a poet, a philosopher, a lover of the theater and the arts, and, not the least, he is Bob, and then again, many others are, too, if he's in a role-playing mood. Intrigued? Then visit this wacky Net cult site, and find out if you have "an inner cacti." While there, enjoy Club BOB(c), read some sonnets, poetry, and even a one-act play that Andrew has written, learn who the real Net personalities are, surf the cool links...and don't miss the BOB(c) FAQ. —(E.v.B.)

KEY NEWSGROUP **alt.fan.the-bob** URL ▸ http://www4.ncsu.edu/unity/users/a/asdamick/www/

Kibo Was Here?

Welcome To The Netly News Jump 8058 

Kibo, that zany, satiric Internet personality, still lives at Netly News. A recent issue focused on Kibo, complete with quotes from an exclusive interview. We also learn when he began his Net presence, how it grew, and what he did—complete with graphics and nice page layout design. —(E.v.B.)

KEY NEWSGROUP **alt.religion.kibology** URL ▸ http://pathfinder.com/

Aliens on Our Own Planet

NetCam: The link between cyberspace and "lightspace" Jump 1539 

By wearing a NetCam—a combination of a virtual reality helmet, an antenna, camera, and fanny pack of radio and recording devices—Steve Mann asserts that we can "send (photo or video) images captured immediately over the Internet with zero delay." This site is an unusual combination of photos taken from the NetCam through visual filters, explanations of what this all means to you and your safety on the planet, and where he thinks we're going with NetCam in the future. For example, one could send video postcards over the Internet from "wherever, whenever," with text and captions. Maybe you can wire up a radio-controlled car with a camera inside to take you on a tour of your office or hallway, or even go on a trek through the "highlights of your life." There may be other cameras, Mann says, "but this is the only wearable one." Seeing is believing here, so get ready and take this strange, humorous Web journey. —(H.L.)

URL▶ http://www-white.media.mit.edu/~steve/netcam.html

Sciences with an Attitude

Hot AIR: rare and well done tidbits from the Annals of Improbable Research Jump 2167

If you think scientists are a stodgy, boring lot who prefer the dark recesses of their research labs to the bright light of day, stop by this site and prepare to have your bubble burst. With observations, studies, and articles in the vein of "Feline Responses to Bearded Men," AIR is at turns sarcastic, irreverent, and hilarious, but at all times a parody of scientists for scientists and their followers. You can read some of the best of AIR at this site, and even contribute your own "research." Regardless, if you need a respite from those who take themselves too seriously, this is the place to go. —(L.S.)

KEY NEWSGROUP **rec.humor.funny** URL▶ http://web.mit.edu/afs/athena/org/i/improb/www/home.html

Help for the Romantically Tongue-Tied

The Cyrano Server Jump 2174

If you're shy and can't bring yourself to speak, or you're just no good with the lexicon of love, there's help for you here. Like the original Cyrano, this NandoNet service will translate your stuttering into eloquence. All you need to do is provide a few details, a couple of adjectives and adverbs, and an e-mail address. If you're looking for a good laugh, try some nontraditional words. Even if you remain traditional, the results sometimes can be amusing, if not downright confusing. However, you may want to have the results e-mailed back to you, lest you end up looking sillier than a lovestruck cybergeek already does. —(L.S.)

KEY NEWSGROUP **alt.romance** URL▶ http://www.nando.net/toys/cyrano.html

Rockets for Sale

Russia House Jump 5069

The Space Commerce Corporation is selling off the Russian Space Program—one piece at a time. View and purchase Russian space art, memorabilia, and actual Russian spacecraft. Prices range from $2 for a Soviet space postcard to astronomical sums for larger objects, such as pieces of rockets or a banner flown from the Mir Space Station. —(S.B.)

URL▶ http://www.NeoSoft.com:80/Russia_House/

The Hoax Host for the Internet

April Fool's on the Net Jump 2333

Internet hoaxes are something of an art form, and April Fool's Day is when the best and funniest appear. Thanks to David Barberi, you no longer have to wait for the annual onslaught from bit-headed comedians, wade through megabytes of unfunny attempts, or risk missing the best of the lot. Just go to this page, with archives of April Fool's newsgroup postings from years past. If you've saved any postings from this rite of Spring, send them to David so he can add them and make this archive as complete as it is funny. —(L.S.)

KEY NEWSGROUP **rec.humor** URL▶ http://sunsite.unc.edu/dbarberi/april-fools.html

Readin', Surfin', Wastin' Time

dimFLASH e-zine Jump 2216

Subtitled "the e-zine with too much time on its hands," *dimFLASH* looks at the Internet from more than a bit off-center. The result is a combination of humor, satire, social critique, and general good times.

It's edited and mostly written by David Futrelle, an honest-to-gosh journalist, so the editorial quality already is better than most e-zines. There are essays on the weird and silly, mystery links and connections to other Web diversions, excerpts from particularly stupid, silly, or otherwise notable Usenet postings, and contests. New material is added throughout the week, and you can even submit your own tidbit, to prove that you have too much time on your hands. —(L.S.)

KEY NEWSGROUP **alt.culture.internet**

URL ▶ http://turnpike.net/metro/futrelle/index.html

▲ *Dodohead on the move, from* **After the Taj Mahal: New Music by Christopher Penrose**, *at* Jump **0197**.

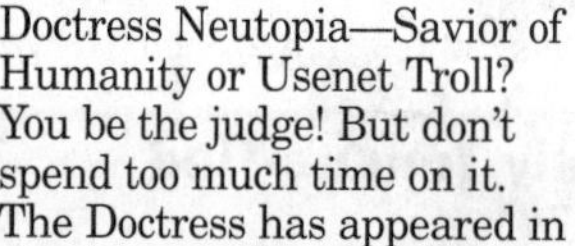

Gaia Messiah

Neutopia
Jump **2480** CONTENT

Doctress Neutopia—Savior of Humanity or Usenet Troll? You be the judge! But don't spend too much time on it. The Doctress has appeared in a Time magazine article about the Internet, but whether it was part of an elaborate scam, or if she's really serious about this, is likely to remain unanswered. The arguments on various newsgroups rise and recede like the tides, and none have come close. The Doctress herself tends to stay above the fray, save for a few posts which serve only to confuse the arguers even more. With this page, she outlines the tenets of Gaia, the religion she created for her alleged doctoral thesis at the University of Massachusetts, Amherst. True to her Net persona, however, there are no e-mail links, signatures, or anything else which would lend credence to her existence. Whether you take this seriously or not, it's interesting stuff, in a pulp fantasy sort of way, and a good guide if you want to start a **net.religion** of your own. —(L.S.)

KEY NEWSGROUP **alt.society.neutopia** URL ▶ http://twain.oit.umass.edu:80/~neutopia/

Penn and Teller Site for Fans

Penn and Teller Jump **4060** CONTENT

An "unofficial" site, but a good one nonetheless. Paul Nielsen has put together a really fun collection of resources related to the sometimes morbid, but most-of-the-time hilarious magician duo Penn and Teller. Along with a load of information on the two, you'll find images, links to other sites for Penn and Teller resources as well as magic in general, and some interesting little subsections which include "The Web's first card trick." —(R.B.)

KEY NEWSGROUP **alt.fan.penn-n-teller** URL ▶ http://ai.eecs.umich.edu/people/nielsen/penn-n-teller.html

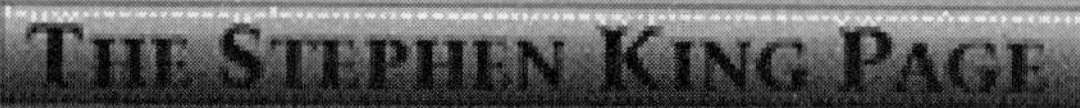

Not That Stephen King

The Other Ones
Jump **2604**

It sounds like the title for one of the horrormeister's sequels, but in fact the only thing this page has to do with the popular author is that the people represented here aren't him—they're all folks who have the misfortune of being named Stephen King. Considering some of the questions these people are asked, it's a wonder Stephen King (not that one, the one who maintains this site) has enough of a sense of humor left to create such an entertaining page. Here you'll learn some of the really stupid questions these people are asked, their best, wittiest answers, and you can even read their favorite stories about being "the other Stephen King." And to show just how nice these "Others" really are, there's even a set of links to "that Stephen King" for fans who stumbled across this page expecting images of paperback horror. —(L.S.)

URL ▶ http://www.isisw3.com/sking/

The Life of Brian

Brian Jump 7227

Brian, a satirical publication, begs you not to take it too seriously. This is hardly likely, as you'll be laughing too hard to even think the word "serious." Find out more about Brian, read a parody of L. Ron Hubbard's analysis of Brian's personality, and surf to some other fun links. Don't miss Sim-Brian's cautionary tale about Uncle Jeb. Oh, and don't turn your eyelids inside out–Brian warns that they'll stay that way. —(E.v.B.)

KEY NEWSGROUP **alt.zine**

URL ▶ http://streams.com/brian/index.html

Mirsky's Web's Worst

This is the Worst

Jump 7126

CONTENT

Andy Warhol once said we would all have 15 minutes of fame. Well, Mirsky, a self-styled Net critic—and, by now, truly a Web legend—has ensured that some of the worst home pages on the Net receive a moment of...well, surely not glory. Exploring this page is not for the faint-hearted. Mirsky has links to the gross, the stupid, the fraudulent and the unaesthetic sites all over the Web. Along the way, he makes fun of everyone and nearly everything he defines as "the Worst." And, you know, his taste is right on, too. —(E.v.B.)

▲ *A gathering of cute animals, via* **This is the Worst**, *at* Jump 7126.

KEY NEWSGROUP **alt.culture.internet** URL ▶ http://turnpike.net/metro/mirsky/Worst.html

Delicious Weirdness

Dr. Fellowbug's Laboratory of Fun & Horror

Jump 3666

Lots of fun stuff at this site—but the most amusing by far is the archive of the "Keeper of Lists." Useless (but utterly hilarious) lists along the lines of: "The Top 59 Good Deeds That Will Help You Get Into Heaven," or "The Top 66 New Techie Buzzwords," or "The Top 72 Things That Tell You You Ate Too Much At The Picnic..." Great graphics, sound files, and general silliness. Absolutely worth a visit. Try it on a bad day—you'll leave with a smile. —(C.P.)

KEY NEWSGROUP **alt.horror** URL ▶ http://www.dtd.com/bug/

Tell Time on the Web

Web Clock Jump 3649

If all else fails, you can find out what time it really is by taking a look at the World Wide Web clock. Interesting in that it automatically updates each minute, and offers a random quote (it changes each minute, too). Nominated for one of the Net's "Useless Pages"—jump to it and see if you agree! —(C.P.)

URL ▶ http://www.higgs.com/x.acgi$Time

A Page for PI

The PI Section Jump 4061

Christophe Pauliat brings you this slice of Web weirdness. Basically what this page shows is the

mathematical term PI (π) calculated out to its first 500,000 digits. We'll take his word on that, as we didn't take the time to count. As if this weren't enough, there's also a link to more information about PI. —(R.B.)

URL▶ http://www.enst.fr/~pauliat/pi_io.html

The Web's Live Ant Farm

See the Live Ants! Jump 7025

Ants galore—see them industriously digging tunnels, building bridges, creating cul-de-sacs in their effort to create the ultimate ant farm. This one resides in Steve Chambers' home, with a live video camera attached to his Web site. Snapshots are updated automatically every hour. This site also features ant lore and downloadable movie clips to delight the real ant lover. —(E.v.B.)

KEY NEWSGROUP **sci.bio** URL▶ http://sec.dgsys.com/AntFarm.html

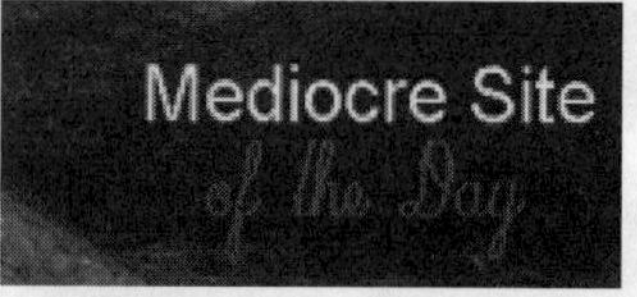

Virtual Vanilla

Mediocre Site of the Day Jump 7173

Jensen Harris is dedicated to helping us all "revel in mediocrity." He feels that the Web is overpopulated with best and worst sites, and that the other 98%—"the mediocre, the unremarkable, the so-so" sites—should also have some attention. Pages devoted to drawbridge racers, siblings, rejected magazine covers—all reveling in their vanilla pudding existence—can be easily accessed through Harris's links. And just think, this list is updated every day! —(E.v.B.)

KEY NEWSGROUP **alt.culture.internet** URL▶ http://minerva.cis.yale.edu/~jharris/mediocre.html

What SnOOz with You?

What SnOOz? Page Jump 7174

The author of this page has his tongue stuck firmly in his cheek. What looks like a multilinked page is really a series of chapters of a funny parody entitled Most F***ed-Up Person Alive Tells All. All roads, so to speak, lead to yet one more chapter of this "autobiography of being p***ed off." As well, the author promises: "Available online, absolutely free, complete with the actual digitized sounds of the author's pain and an optional "Bogus-Hypertext(tm) Front-End for Zero Attention-Span (tm)," nonlinear access to the text. —(E.v.B.)

KEY NEWSGROUP **rec.humor.funny** URL▶ http://www.digimark.net:80/mfu/whasn0Oz.html#topten

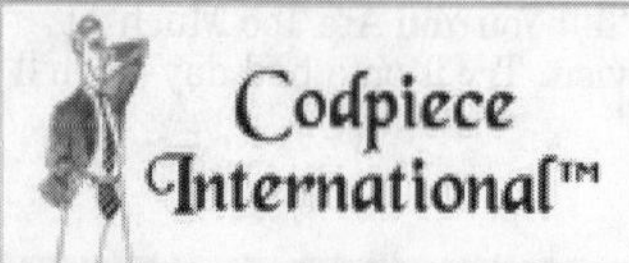

A Home for the Codpiece

Codpiece International Home Page Jump 4056

Believe it or not, this is the home site for Codpiece International, a company dealing with products related to the codpiece. You can order codpiece T-shirts, find information on their "Bring Back the Codpiece" campaign, or learn about the Codpiece Resurrection Society. Of course, there's a section explaining what exactly a codpiece is, for those of you who aren't quite sure (that is, if you really want to know, anyway). Done in a tongue-in-cheek style, it's a funny little place to visit. —(R.B.)

URL▶ http://www.teleport.com/~codpiece/

Beverly Hills Internet

n/a Jump 4513

There's a lot more going on at this good-looking commercial site, but we'll admit that what we really like is the live video feeds from Hollywood & Vine, updated several times a minute. Watch someone waiting for a bus. See them catch it. Wonder where they're heading. Ponder why they're squandering all this computing power on a camera aimed at a bus stop. Decide to not worry about it, and keep watching! —(T.W.)

URL▶ http://www.bhi90210.com/

Cult Candy Commercials

Mentos—The Freshmaker!

Jump 7175

Heath Doerr, who maintains this sugary site, has collected the most amazing information on this candy, and its strange, strange TV commercials which have attracted quite a cult following on the Net. A synopsis of every Mentos commercial, jingle lyrics, and manufacturer's data (did you know each candy is 3/4" in diameter and weighs 1.3 oz.?). Do you really want to know more? O.K., Heath reveals the mysteries of the packaging, ingredients (eeeeeuuu, gum arabic seems to play a leading role), and commercial history of this "fresh-making" candy. What, you want to know Mentos's nutritional benefits? Well, that you'll have to write away for to find out, but don't worry–Heath has provided the address. —(E.v.B.)

KEY NEWSGROUP rec.humor.d URL▸ http://www.best.com/~dijon/tv/mentos/

Slimy Slime

House of Slime Jump 7194

John Stone thinks that "slime is what has been missing from the clean, dry, electrical world of computers." To correct this deficiency, he has added as much information as he could find on slime in all its different forms of squishy glory: plain old slime, slime molds, mucus membranes (as in irritation of, allergies), and those animated bits of slime–slugs. He particularly sings the praises of various links on the Net that are devoted to slugs and then presents the links for you to explore. —(E.v.B.)

KEY NEWSGROUP sci.bio URL▸ http://www.teleport.com/~jleon/

Way, Way Weird

Twinkies Uncovered

The T.W.I.N.K.I.E.S. Project Jump 7334

Chris Gouge and Todd Stadler have applied their scientific curiosity to—Twinkies. T.W.I.N.K.I.E.S. stands for Tests With Inorganic Noxious Kakes In Extreme Situations. Chris and Todd were determined to discover the properties of that incredible cake-like food, the Twinkie. Thus inspired, they ran a rapid oxidation test, a solubility test, a maximum density test, a resistivity test , a gravitational response test, a radiation test, and last, but not least, a Turing test. After obtaining the results (go to the site to see what they were for yourself), they wrote them up in an epic-length series of poems they called haiku—although the pieces are a rather bizarre form of this type of poetry. —(E.v.B.)

URL▸ http://www.rice.edu/~gouge/twinkies.html

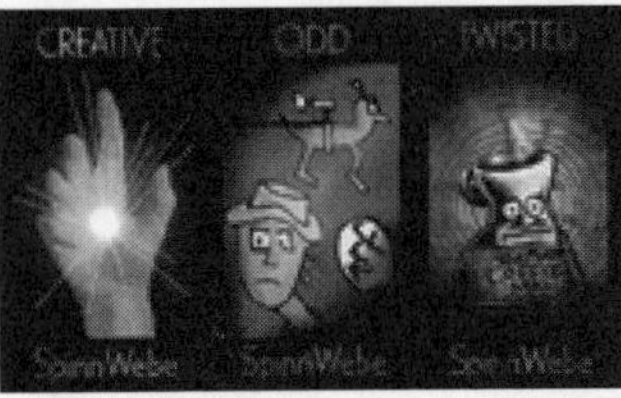

Twisted Sister

SpinnWebe Jump 1590

What the heck is a SpinnWebe? You may never find out, but Greg Calcik makes it fun for you to try. This electronic zine may be confusing at first, but try clicking on a few original links and you'll get the hang of it. View the Temple of Spinnwebe—a real-time photo of 3-D art that changes every 10 minutes, check out the unusual exhibits, or find out Calcik's personal pet peeves. The best part of the site is the contests—you can submit your home page for Creative, Twisted, or Odd awards. Past winners include the Slide Rule Home Page, Censored Deep Thoughts, and Find the Spam. Maybe you think your favorite picture would enhance the experience. Join the extravaganza. Geeks are sure to love it here! —(H.L.)

URL▸ http://www.thoughtport.com/spinnwebe

The Web's First Virtual Funeral Home

Carlos A. Howard Funeral Home Jump 2434 CONTENT

Visionaries who prophesy the benefits of the Information Superhighway touching everyone from cradle to grave can rest comfortably, knowing at least one end is now covered. The perfect place for compulsive planners or the morbidly fixated, the first funeral home on the Internet offers answers to the obvious and not-so-obvious questions, as well as a truly unique online shopping experience. The assortment of caskets is actually quite nice, and gives the Net's vampyres a good selection of pictures to swipe and use for their virtual daytime resting spots! —(L.S.)

KEY NEWSGROUP **alt.culture.www**

URL ▶ http://www.melanet.com/melanet/howard/

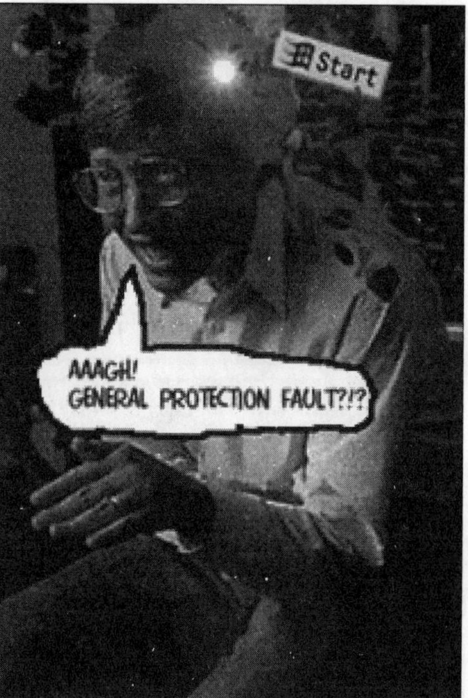

▲ *Watch Bill Gates's head explode, from* **The Exploding Head Page**, *at* Jump 7339.

Swelled, Swelled, SWELLED Heads

The Exploding Head Page Jump 7339 CONTENT

Exploding heads is just about the right description for this satirical set of pages. The creative folks at Virtual Visions take public figures—Rush Limbaugh, Bill Gates, Bob Dole—write captions to fit a series of their photos, and then, well, make their heads explode. Rather bizarre way of artistic expression, but hey, this is the Digital Age. You can enter the fun by submitting your own captions. —(E.v.B.)

KEY NEWSGROUP **rec.humor.d**

URL ▶ http://www.vv.com/~gilmore/head/heads.html

Drop Everything!

Drop Squad!!!
Jump 7411 CONTENT

The Rensselaer Drop Squad, a group of students at Rensselaer Polytechnic Institute in Troy, New York, like to, uh, drop things—from very high places—video the process, and then run away before being caught. These high-tech pranksters have brought their exploits to the Web. You can read about what they drop, watch the movie, check out the photographic evidence, or read documents (such as newspaper articles and university correspondence) that further substantiate their pranks and their aftermath. —(E.v.B.)

KEY NEWSGROUP **rec.humor.d** URL ▶ http://www.dropsquad.com/

Lies, All Lies!

Sex and Drugs and Sausage Rolls
Jump 7327 

Dave wants to protect us from the lies he says are prevalent on the Internet. You know those outdated facts, popular misconceptions, even mistruths presented as fact. However, we think Dave has his tongue firmly in self-professed truthful little cheek. His page presents lies of the day, guest liars, celebrity liars, and even a liar's database. He's sort of a one-man creator of urban legends. Very funny at times, and worth a visit. —(E.v.B.)

KEY NEWSGROUP **rec.humor.d** URL ▶ http://www.cs.man.ac.uk/~hancockd/lies.htm

We're All Crazy

The Asylum Jump 1502 CONTENT

If you're looking for some zany, eclectic fun and are prepared to hang out for a few hours, or even days, visit inmates Joe "Madman Loose in Disneyland" Cates and Aure "The Enforcer" Prochazka at the Asylum. You'll never tire of the amount of interesting things you can do here. Create your own masterpiece artwork and compare it to everyone else's. "Scream and shout your opinions to the world on pressing questions of the day," such as whether Barney should be killed off once and for all. If you need fiction therapy—well, write as much as you like on any topic, then publish it! Add your favorite list of URLs, and go on a whirlwind tour of random sites at rollercoaster speed. And if you're still not tired, listen to a variety of barnyard animals while you figure out what Ren and Stimpy are up to. This creative use of the Web is what makes the Web so fun to cruise. —(H.L.)

URL▶ http://www.galcit.caltech.edu/~ta/cgi-bin/asylhome-ta

He's Dead, Jim!

Dead People Server Jump 1578

It's virtual trivial pursuits time and your opponent keeps harping about which Kennedys are alive and which are dead. No need to argue. Enter the Dead People Server and scroll down till you get to the Kennedy clan. Then you can confidently tell your pal the Dead Kennedys have been dead since 1986 (that's the music group, not the political dynasty). This Web site is a list of celebrities who are, or might plausibly be, dead. If you have a question about someone who isn't included, there's an e-mail link to site manager Rick Holmes. He also provides a link to Lindsay Marshall's Obituary Page, where you and your bud can find out more about the recently deceased Gilles Deleuze (who?) than is really, truly necessary. —(H.L.)

URL▶ http://web.syr.edu/~rsholmes/dead/

A Cornucopia of Weirdness

Kooks Museum Lobby Jump 1531

Kooky is definitely the word here! According to creator Donna Kossy, a kook is "a person slightly stigmatized by virtue of outlandish, extreme, or socially unacceptable beliefs that underpin their entire existence." This well-designed and intriguing site sports a huge collection of kook paraphernalia of the vast cornucopia of forgotten, discredited and extreme ideas. Between the Schizophrenic Wing, full of book excerpts, letters, and audio tapes, and the Conspiracy Corridor, where you can browse through the library of questionable scholarship, you'll be amazed at the number of oddities that have been published as gospel. The site's best part is the Solution to World Problems section, whereby ideas from all over the world, such as the voluntary human extinction movement, are contrasted. Funny stuff! Search through the database of over 350 well-known kooks, or peruse the Archive of Useless Research for even more amazing works. You can also purchase Koss' book on the topic, postcards, and the infamous pamphlet "I am Insane." But best of all, if you know of any kooks, you can share your own finds with the public here. —(H.L.)

URL▶ http://www.teleport.com:80/~dkossy/

Strange & Dangerous Antics Site

AGD Antics and Mayhem Page Jump 4074

The best description of this Web site comes straight off of its own disclaimer: "This page is a documentary about some of the antics, mayhem, destruction and general fooling around that goes on in AGD (the Advanced Graphics Division at SGI)." You can read about and view video clips of the strange antics of this group, including carbon dioxide bombs, surgical tubing slingshots, and the destruction of SPAM cans with light focused from a Fresnel lens. Of course, they in no way endorse or encourage trying any of this at home! —(R.B.)

URL▶ http://reality.sgi.com/employees/dbg/antics/

Bloodsucking Creatures of the Night

Vampyres Only Jump 2227

Vlad III, who is, according to himself, the great-grandchild of Vlad the Impaler (the real Dracula) maintains this site for vampire fans and wannabes. There are pages and pages of frequently asked questions, electronic novels, lists of books, films and other vampire-related materials, and an image archive that includes art and film clips. For those concerned about their personal situations, there also are handy online tests to determine the probability that you are, indeed, a vampire, or to evaluate your vulnerability to the neck biters. And if there's not enough here to satisfy your bloodlust, there are links to other vampire resources on the neck (ur, Net!) too! —(L.S.)

KEY NEWSGROUP **alt.vampyres** URL▶ http://www.wimsey.com/~bmiddlet/vampyre/vampyre.html

Virtual Waste of Time

Virtual Kissing Booth Jump 3679

Love waiting for 100K graphics to load to your screen? Delighted when you discover that after the interminable wait, it wasn't worth waiting for at all? Then stop by this spot on the Web. It'll be sure to satisfy all your innermost cravings for a "good Web experience," as you're invited to kiss the young lady's kissing face which appears on your screen. Now complete with advertising to such wonders as "Peter Paul Nurseries where you can buy a carnivorous plant to brighten someone's day . . . " Delightful. A sure candidate for the Useless Pages—and almost good enough to inspire its own newsgroup—**alt.don't.bother**. Bleccch! —(C.P.)

URL http://cvp.onramp.net/smooch/smooch.html

How Much Is That Doggie on the Highway?

RNN Home Page Jump 4012

This is the site for the Roadkills-R-Us News Network, billing itself as "an Internet-based disinformation center...and a misapplication of the World Wide Web." You'll find information about the company along with (ack!) roadkill recipes and pricing ("All prices per carcass unless otherwise noted"). An entertaining but strange bit of Net humor that will make you laugh until you gag! —(R.B.)

KEY NEWSGROUP **talk.bizarre** URL http://www.pencom.com/rru.html

Fortean Times: Journal of Strange Phenomena on the Web

Fortean Times online Jump 4078

This site is home to the online version of the *Fortean Times,* "a bi-monthly magazine of news, reviews and research on all manner of strange phenomena and experiences." Maintained through the Applied Computer Studies Division of the University of Dundee, this page gives you access to information on the magazine, pictures and news stories straight from its pages, links to other sites with Fortean material, and much more. A great site to visit if you're interested in the truly bizarre. —(R.B.)

KEY NEWSGROUP **alt.misc.forteana** URL http://forteana.mic.dundee.ac.uk/ft/

Pagans on the Net

Welcome to Paganlink Jump 7031

To encourage the pagan in you, a group of dedicated folks have established Paganlink to "make pagan and magickal ways accessible to anyone who is seeking them." See pagan art, read pagan literature, learn pagan rituals, and link with European, Irish and British pagans. —(E.v.B.)

URL http://www.tardis.ed.ac.uk/~feorag/paganlink/plhome.html

Bizarre Talk Hits the Web

Page-O Bizarro Jump 7232

The title says it all—this is a bizarre collection of essays, opinions, rants and raves. If this is your type of fun, well, prepare yourself for a barrel and a half of bizarre laughs. John, who tries to remain semianonymous, has collected the FAQ that's connected to the **talk.bizarre** newsgroup, as well as an amazing collection of **talk.bizarre** postings. As well, we can dip in and out of John's collection of his own postings to this group which he characterizes as "sometimes loud, crass, cliquish, dense, childish, insulting, rude, and more wired than Wired will ever be." Don't say we didn't warn you—enter at your own risk. —(E.v.B.)

KEY NEWSGROUP **talk.bizarre** URL http://www.perry.com/bizarre/bizarro.html

Master Web Subject Index & Finder

While the Web makes it incredibly easy to access information, the sheer number of Web sites still makes it an overwhelming task to find Web sites containing the information of interest to you. Use our big 8,422-word Subject Index to find the Web site you're looking for.

Finding What You're Looking for Along the Web

While the Web may eliminate the mystery of *getting* to everything that's out there on the Internet, it doesn't do much to organize what's out there so you can *find* it. This need can become especially urgent, for example, when you must locate only those Web sites relating to a single, specific topic. In this case, merely scrolling through a list of 700 or so "business" Web sites on one of the big Web indexes can be especially frustrating when all you're trying to do is get to a couple of good Web sites relating to starting a new business, for example.

When you need to find it fast, our Subject Index helps you locate the Web Site(s) which best fits the subjects for which it has been indexed, and you can reach all of these sites instantly by entering its four-digit Jump Code on **JumpCity**. So now you can save the hours you'll spend just surfing the Web for when you actually have the time.

Web Index/Finder

Subject | Web Site Jump | Page

Subject **Web Site** Jump **Page**

Web Index/Finder

Subject Web Site Jump Page

Subject Web Site Jump Page

Web Index/Finder

Subject Web Site Jump Page

Subject Web Site Jump Page

Subject | Web Site Jump | Page

Subject | Web Site Jump | Page

Subject | Web Site Jump | Page

Subject | Web Site Jump | Page

Subject **Web Site Jump** **Page**

Subject	Web Site Jump	Page

Subject Web Site Jump Page

Web Index/Finder

Subject Web Site Jump Page

Subject Web Site Jump Page

Subject Web Site Jump Page

Web Index/Finder

Web Index/Finder

Subject | Web Site Jump | Page

About the Authors...

Eric Gagnon is the president of Internet Media, a publishing company specializing in print and electronic Internet books, magazines, and online content development. Gagnon has 17 years' experience as an entrepreneur in the online consumer database, software publishing, and new venture development fields, including new product and business development for The Source, the first-ever consumer online information service.

Edwinna von Baeyer is the author of five books and numerous articles, and editor of several newsletters. Through her company, New Century Communications, she pursues editing and writing assignments in the areas of the environment, forestry, heritage, cultural landscapes, and online issues. She lives with her husband and family in Ottawa, Ontario, Canada.

Lee Stral is president of Essential Presence, a World Wide Web site development and marketing firm, and a co-founder and member of the Steering Committee of the HTML Writers Guild. In addition to being a regularly published journalist and author, he has more than 20 years' experience in high technology industries, including work in advertising, public relations, and trade journalism.

Liz Tompkins is a professional Web reviewer, whose NBNSoft Content Awards can be seen on many of the Web's best sites. She lives with her husband and son in Massachusetts.

James Porteous is a freelance fiction and non-fiction writer in Ontario, Canada.

Norine Fullan is the owner of The PC Home Consultants, a computer and software training company in Croton-on-Hudson, New York.

Christine Klauberg Paustian has been published widely on technical topics, and does a daily radio feature called "WinTips" that is currently in syndication around the country. She is a regular columnist for *BookPage* "NewMedia," and National Computer Tectonics *Web Magazine*. She also offers expertise in Web page development and technical writing through her company, NetSurf Technologies. She lives in Westchester County, NY.

Hilary Lane is a freelance writer specializing in business, the Internet, health and environmental issues. She is an Internet columnist for *The Boulder County Business Report*, has reviewed books for publishers, and has written for several national publications, including *E Magazine* and *Utne Reader*. Ms. Lane also has several years experience as a technical writer for software, database and Web applications. She lives in the foothills of Boulder, Colorado.

Jon van Oast is a Web site designer and co-owner of The Scribble Company, a Web site development firm based in Portland, Oregon, and co-founder of the award-winning SITO collaborative Web art project.

Tim Windsor is the creative director of an advertising agency in Baltimore, Maryland.